ECONOMICS
of the
PUBLIC SECTOR

ECONOMICS of the PUBLIC SECTOR

JOSEPH E. STIGLITZ

Princeton University

W. W. NORTON & COMPANY · New York · London

FIRST EDITION

Cover photograph courtesy of Jeanne White, Audubon Collection/PR.

ISBN 0-393-01808-3

W. W. Norton & Company, Inc., 500 Fifth Avenue, New York, N.Y. 10110
W. W. Norton & Company Ltd., 37 Great Russell Street, London WC1B 3NU

1 2 3 4 5 6 7 8 9 0

To My First Teachers,
Nat and Charlotte

Contents

2   **The Public Sector in the United States**   22

8 Externalities 178

PART THREE
EXPENDITURE PROGRAMS

9 The Analysis of Expenditure Policy 201

10 Cost-Benefit Analysis 217

PART FIVE

TAXATION IN THE UNITED STATES

Preface

Had this text been written twenty-five years ago, it would have been entitled *Public Finance*, and its focus would have been on sources of revenues. The title *Economics of the Public Sector* and the broader coverage it implies is, however, no accident. In recent years, government spending has reached record levels, and it now accounts for more than a third of gross national product. The accompanying federal budget deficits have alarmed economists of all political and intellectual persuasions. It is no longer enough to know where the money comes from; one must give equal time to how it is spent.

Meanwhile, the economic theory of the public sector has burgeoned. Some of this recent literature is devoted to analyzing government expenditures. From cost-benefit analysis to public choice theory, economists now have much to say about how government spends its funds. Much of the recent literature reflects the development of new and more sophisticated models, such as the theory of optimal taxation. I have chosen to present the modern view of public-sector economics in a simple and intuitive way, to relate the most important contributions of this fast-growing literature to undergraduates taking a first course in public finance.

Public-sector issues include some of the most exciting in all of economics. Health, defense, education, social security, welfare programs, and tax reform all receive steady attention in the news media. Economic analysis brings special insights to the debates. Should education be publicly provided? What is the long-term outlook for our social security program? How do current proposals for tax reform match our knowledge of incidence, efficiency, and equity? These kinds of questions breathe life into the course, which is why I give them careful attention.

Examining specific tax and expenditure programs offers an additional benefit: it underscores the importance of design features. One of the lessons we have learned in the past decade is that good intentions are not enough. Urban renewal programs, intended to revitalize our cities, had the unintended consequence of reducing the supply of housing to the poor. Whether the broadened availability of Individual Retirement Accounts has succeeded in its goal of stimulating savings or has simply given a tax break to those who were saving already is, at best, an open question. I use examples like these, of unintended consequences, not only to enliven the course but also to instill in students the important habit of testing theory against the complex environment in which public-sector decisions are enacted and implemented.

In their analysis of public-sector problems, economists cannot pretend to have a unified viewpoint, and I have not tried to patch over the differences. Rather, I inquire into the reasons economists disagree, whether about reform of social security, our medical care delivery system, our welfare system, or our tax system; whether about the incidence of the corporation income tax or the consequences of IRAs. At the very least, a course in public-sector economics should help students develop intelligent perspectives on policy issues. To do so, they need to know why economists reach differing conclusions.

Economists, as teachers, also disagree about the sequence of topics in the public-sector economics course. The sequence I follow is, first, to introduce in Chapters 1 and 2 the fundamental questions and institutional details. Chapters 3 and 4 then review the microeconomic theory underlying the role of the public sector. Part Two develops the theory of public expenditures, including public goods, public choice, and bureaucracy, while Part Three applies the theory to the five largest areas of public expenditure in the United States: health, defense, education, social security, and welfare programs. Parts Four and Five repeat this pattern, presenting the theory of taxation and its analysis, respectively. Part Six takes up state and local issues in more detail. A perfectly workable alternative to this sequence would be to cover taxation before expenditures. Parts Four and Five have been carefully developed so that the teacher wishing to go straight to taxation after Part One can do so without loss of continuity.

Further tips on how courses can be organized, as well as lecture notes, test questions, and coverage of advanced topics that some teachers may wish to include in their lectures, are contained in the *Instructor's Manual*, which has been prepared with the assistance of Eleanor Brown of Princeton University and Pomona College.

The list of those to whom I am indebted is a long one. My teachers at Amherst College, James Nelson and Arnold Collery, not only stimulated my interest in economics, and in the particular subject of this course, but laid the foundations for my later studies. They also showed me, by example, what good teaching meant; I hope that some of what I learned from them is reflected in this book. At M.I.T. Dan Holland (currently editor of the *National Tax Journal*) and E. Cary Brown introduced me to the formal study of public economics. Again, I hope some of the blend of policy, theory, and institutional detail that marked their work is reflected here. The insights of my colleagues and collaborators at the institutions at which I have worked (M.I.T.,

Yale University, Stanford University, Princeton University, Oxford University, Cambridge University, and the National Bureau of Economic Research) and the government agencies (Treasury, Labor, Interior, Energy, Agency for International Development, State of Louisiana, State of Texas) and international organizations (World Bank, Interamerican Development Bank, Organization of Economic Cooperation and Development) for which I have consulted have also proved invaluable. I should mention Henry Aaron (Brookings Institution), Alan J. Auerbach (University of Pennsylvania), Greg Ballantine (former assistant secretary of the Treasury for Tax Policy), William J. Baumol (Princeton University), Charles T. Clotfelter (Duke University), Partha Dasgupta (Cambridge University), Peter A. Diamond (M.I.T.), Avinash Dixit (Princeton University), Martin Feldstein (Harvard University), Harvey Galper (Brookings Institution), Robert E. Hall (Stanford University), Arnold C. Harberger (University of Chicago and University of California, Los Angeles), Charles E. McClure (Hoover Institution; former deputy assistant secretary of the Treasury), James A. Mirrlees (Oxford University), Alvin Rabushka (Stanford University), Harvey Rosen (Princeton University), Michael Rothschild (University of California, San Diego), Agnar Sandmo (Bergen), Eytan Sheshinski (Hebrew University), Nick Stern (London School of Economics), Larry Summers (Harvard University), and in particular Anthony B. Atkinson (London School of Economics), Peter Mieskowski (Rice University), Raj Kumar Sah (Yale University), and Steven L. Slutsky (University of Florida). I am also especially indebted to those who provided comments on earlier drafts of the manuscript, including Michael Boskin (Stanford University), Lawrence Blume (University of Michigan), David Bradford (Princeton University), John Burbidge (McMaster University), Paul N. Courant (University of Michigan), Victor R. Fuchs (Stanford University), Don Fullerton (assistant deputy secretary of the Treasury for Tax Policy; University of Virginia), Roger Gordon (University of Michigan), Mervyn King (London School of Economics), Laurence J. Kotlikoff (Boston University), Robert J. Lampman (University of Wisconsin), Jerry Miner (Syracuse University), Joseph A. Pechman (Brookings Institution), Jim Poterba (M.I.T.), and John Shoven (Stanford University).

My indebtedness to Jane Hannaway is more than that customarily owed to a spouse, for her insights into the behavior of governments in general, and bureaucratic behavior in particular, have been instrumental in shaping my own views, although I am afraid I have had less influence on her than she has had on me.

Invaluable secretarial assistance was provided by Linda Siegal of the Hoover Institution, Stanford University, and Rosemary Handley and Amy Johnson of Princeton University. Jim Bergin (Northwestern University) served as both research assistant and critic.

PART ONE

INTRODUCTION

How does the government affect the economy? Why are some economic activities undertaken in the public sector, some in the private? How has the government grown over the past fifty years? These are some of the basic questions addressed in Part I of this book.

The first two chapters describe the scope of the book and of the public sector in the United States. The third chapter provides an introduction to welfare economics, which is concerned with how economists make judgments concerning the desirability of different government programs and policies.

The United States has a mixed economy, with some economic activities undertaken in the public sector, some in the private. Chapter 4 delineates those circumstances in which private markets may not work well, where some form of government action may be required.

1

The Public Sector in a Mixed Economy

From birth to death, our lives are affected in countless ways by the activities of government.

• We are born in hospitals that are publicly subsidized, if not publicly owned, and our delivery into this world is supervised by doctors who were trained in medical schools that were, at least partly, publicly supported. Our arrival is then publicly recorded (our birth certificate), entitling us to a set of privileges and obligations, as American citizens.

• Most of us (almost 90 percent) attend public schools.

• Though the government, through the Tenth Amendment, abolished slavery, or compulsory servitude, the government has frequently resorted to compulsion, to the military draft, to recruit young men to fight our country's wars.

• About 15 percent of us live in housing that is either directly subsidized by the federal government or whose mortgages are insured by the federal government; about 10 percent of us receive food from the government, and more than 40 percent of medical expenditures are paid by the government.

• Virtually all of us, at some time in our lives, receive money from the government, either as children—for instance, through the government's student loan program; as adults, when we are unemployed, disabled, or impoverished; or in retirement, through social security and medicare.

• All of us pay money to the government—in local and state sales taxes, in federal excise taxes on such commodities as gasoline, liquor, telephones, air travel, perfumes, and tires, in property taxes, in income taxes, and in social security (payroll) taxes.

• A fifth of the work force is employed by the government, and for the rest, the government has a significant impact on employment conditions. If we are injured on the job in spite of the safety precautions insisted upon by the government, we are protected by workmen's compensation. Unions, whose rights and responsibilities are defined by the government, negotiate work conditions including the hours and pay of a substantial fraction of the labor force. The government encourages pension plans through tax incentives and backs them with insurance in the event an employer goes bankrupt.

• The prices for wheat, corn, and dairy products are controlled or strongly influenced by the actions of the government. In many areas of production— steel or automobiles, shoes or shirts, television sets or computers—profits and employment opportunities are greatly affected by whether the government allows foreign competitors to sell goods in America without a tariff.

• As consumers, we are affected by the government: the prices we pay for cigarettes, alcohol, automobiles, and many other commodities are high because of the taxes, tariffs, quotas, and regulations government imposes; while the prices of other goods (utilities, telephones, water, gas and electricity, and housing) *may be* lower because of government regulation. What we eat and drink is regulated by the government. Where we can live and what kinds of houses we can live in are regulated by various public agencies.

• We are all the beneficiaries of public services: we travel on public roads and publicly subsidized railroads. Our garbage is collected and our sewage is disposed of (in most communities) by a public agency; the water we drink is provided by public water companies, and the cleanliness of the air is regulated by public agencies.

• Our legal structure provides a framework within which individuals and firms can engage in mutually beneficial interactions. Our laws specify the nature of the contracts that we can sign. When there is a dispute between two individuals, the two may turn to the courts to adjudicate the dispute.

THE MIXED ECONOMY

The United States has what is called a **mixed economy**. While many economic activities are undertaken by private firms, others are undertaken by the government. In addition, the government alters the behavior of the private sector, either intentionally or unintentionally, through a variety of regulations, taxes, and subsidies. By way of contrast, in the USSR and the Soviet bloc countries, most economic activities are undertaken by the government. In many Western European economies, the government is responsible for a much larger share of economic activity than in the United States. For instance, in Britain the government is responsible for the production of coal and steel. What the government is responsible for in the United States has also changed dramatically. One hundred years ago there were some private highways and all railroads were private; today there are no major private roads and most interstate railroad passengers travel Amtrak, a publicly established and subsidized enterprise. It is because mixed economies are constantly facing the problem of defining the appropriate boundaries between government and private activities that the study of public finance in these countries is both so important and so interesting.

Why does the government do some things and not others? Why has the scope of government activity changed over the past hundred years, and why does it do more in some countries than it does in the United States, while in other countries it does less? Does the government do too much? Does it do what it attempts to do well? Could it do it better? These are the central questions with which public finance is concerned. They have been at the center of political, philosophical, and economic debates for centuries. The debate continues, and even though economists cannot provide definitive answers, they still have much to say. Our understanding of economic activities in the private and public sectors has increased enormously in the past fifty years as we have become aware of the strengths and limitations of both.

AN IMPETUS FOR GOVERNMENT ACTION: MARKET FAILURES

In the period between the Great Depression (1930s) and the early 1960s, economists (and politicians) became aware of a large number of ways in which the free-market economy, even the richest free-market economy in the world, seemed to fail to meet certain basic social needs. The economy had suffered from periodic episodes of unemployment, some of them massive. In the Great Depression, the unemployment rate reached 25 percent and national output fell by about 30 percent from its peak in 1929. The depression brought to the fore problems that, in less severe form, had been there for a long time. Many individuals lost virtually all of their money when banks defaulted and the stock market crashed. Many elderly people did not have the resources on which to survive. Many farmers found that the prices they received for their products were so low that they could not make their mortgage payments, and defaults became commonplace.

In response to the depression, the federal government not only took a more active role in attempting to stabilize the level of economic activity but also passed legislation aimed at alleviating many of the specific problems: unemployment insurance, social security, federal insurance for depositors, federal programs aimed at supporting agricultural prices, and a host of other programs aimed at a variety of social and economic objectives, including improving working conditions and regulating the stock market. Together, these programs are referred to as the "New Deal."

After World War II the economy recovered, and the country experienced an unprecedented level of prosperity. But it became clear that the fruits of that prosperity were not being enjoyed by all. Many individuals seemed, by the condition of their birth, to be condemned to (or at least very likely to live) a life of squalor and poverty; they would receive inadequate education, and their prospects for obtaining good jobs were bleak.

These inequities provided the impetus for many of the government programs that were enacted in the 1960s, when President Lyndon B. Johnson declared his "War on Poverty." While some programs were aimed at providing a "safety net" for the needy—for instance, programs to provide food and medical care to the poor—others, such as job retraining programs, were directed at improving the economic opportunities of the disadvantaged.

Could government actions alleviate these problems? How was success to be gauged? The fact that some program did not live up to the hopes of its most enthusiastic supporters did not, of course, mean that it was a failure. Medicaid, which provides medical assistance to the indigent, was successful in eliminating some of the differences in access to medical care between the poor and the rich, but the difference in life expectancy between these two groups was not eliminated. Medicare, which provides medical care for the elderly, was successful in relieving the elderly and their families of much of the anxiety concerning the financing of their medical expenses but left in its place a national problem of rapidly increasing medical expenditures. While the social security program provided the aged with an unprecedented level of economic security, it ran into financial crises in the late 1970s and early 1980s that raised questions about whether future generations would be able to enjoy the same benefits.

Twenty years after the War on Poverty began, it is clear that poverty has not been eradicated from America. The question is, have the expenditures had a significant effect in reducing it? While there is no concensus on the answer to this question, both critics and supporters of the government's programs agree that it is not enough to have good intentions: many of the programs designed to alleviate the perceived inadequacies of the market economy had effects that differed markedly from those the proponents thought (or hoped) they would have. Urban renewal programs designed to improve the quality of life in inner cities have, in many instances, resulted in the replacement of low-quality housing with high-quality housing that poor people cannot afford, thus forcing them to live in even worse conditions. Though many programs designed to promote integration of public schools have succeeded, some have instead increased residential segregation or led some parents to enroll their children in private schools, weakening support for public education. A disproportionate share of the benefits of the farm program accrue to the large farmers; the government programs have not enabled the small farms to survive. There were allegations that many government welfare programs had contributed to the break-up of families and to the development of an attitude of dependency.

Supporters of continued government efforts claim that critics exaggerate the failures of government programs and argue that the lesson to be learned is not that the government should abandon its efforts to solve the major social and economic problems facing the nation but that greater care must be taken in the appropriate design of government programs.

GOVERNMENT FAILURES

While market failures led to the major government programs of the 1930s and 1960s, in the 1970s the shortcomings of the programs led economists and political scientists to investigate government failure. Under what conditions would government not work well? Were the failures of government programs mere accidents, or were they predictable results, following from the inherent nature of governmental activity? Are there lessons to be learned for the design of programs in the future? There are four major reasons for the systematic failures of the government to achieve its stated objectives.

First, the consequences of many actions are complicated and difficult to foresee. When New York City passed its rent control legislation, it did not anticipate (although perhaps it should have) that the legislation would lead to a decline in the supply of rental housing and that it would contribute to the wholesale abandonment of properties. When the federal government adopted its urban renewal programs, it did not anticipate that they might lead to a decline in the supply of housing available to the poor. Similarly, the government did not anticipate the precipitous increase in expenditures on medical care by the aged that followed the adoption of the medicare program.

Second, the government has only limited control over these consequences (particularly within a democracy such as ours). In the example above about rent control, many advocates overlooked the fact that apartments were supplied by individuals who would turn elsewhere for investment opportunities if the return to their investment declined. A consequence that was unanticipated by many advocates of rent control (though not by economists) was that the supply of rental housing decreased and that the quality of services provided by landlords deteriorated. Though the government attempted to control the deterioration of quality by imposing standards on landlords, these attempts were only partially successful and exacerbated the decline in the supply of rental housing. There was little the New York City government could do to stop this, short of repealing the rent control statutes.

Third, those who design legislation have only limited control over the implementation of the program. While Congress in passing legislation often tries to specify clearly what its intentions are, it delegates implementation to some government agency. This agency may spend considerable time writing detailed regulations; how these detailed regulations are drafted is critical in determining the effects of the legislation. The agency may also be responsible for ensuring that the regulations are enforced. For instance, when Congress passed the Environmental Protection Act its intent was clear—to ensure that firms did not pollute the environment. But the technical details—for instance, determining the admissible level of pollutants for different industries—were left to the Environmental Protection Agency (EPA). During the first two years of the Reagan administration, there were numerous controversies over whether the EPA had been lax in enforcing and promulgating regulations, thus subverting the intentions of Congress. In many cases, however, the failures to carry out the intent of Congress are not deliberate attempts to avoid the wishes of Congress but are a result of the ambiguities in Congress's intentions. And, there is a further problem of ensuring that administrators whose job it is to execute the law will do so fairly and efficiently. Just as one of the main subjects of inquiry in standard economics is the analysis of the incentives within the private sector, so one of the main subjects of study here is the analysis of incentives within the public sector; what causes various bureaucrats to take the actions they take?

Fourth, our political process is one in which those who are elected to serve the public sometimes have incentives to act for the benefit of special-interest groups. The failure of politicians to carry out what would seem to be in the public interest, then, is not just the consequence of the greed or

malevolence of a few wayward politicians but may be the inevitable consequence of the workings of political institutions in democratic societies.[1]

Critics of government intervention in the economy believe the four sources
of government failure are sufficiently important that the government should
be restrained from attempting to remedy alleged deficiencies in markets.
But even if one does not agree with this conclusion, recognition of the four
limitations on government action is a prerequisite for the design of successful
government policies.

EARLIER VIEWS CONCERNING THE ROLE OF GOVERNMENT

The vacillation in views concerning the role of the government that has
occurred during the past fifty years has occurred frequently before.[2] For
instance, in the eighteenth century a dominant view, particularly among
French economists, was that the government should take an active role in
promoting trade and industry. Those who advocated this view were called
mercantilists.

It was partly in reaction to this view that Adam Smith (who is often viewed
as the founder of modern economics) wrote his book *The Wealth of Nations*
(1776), in which he argued for a limited role to government. Smith attempted
to show how competition and the profit motive would lead individuals—in
pursuing their own private interests—to serve the public interest. The profit
motive would lead individuals to supply the goods other individuals wanted.
Competing against one another, only firms that produced what was wanted
and produced it at as low a price as possible would survive. Smith argued
that the economy was led, as if by an **invisible hand,** to produce what was
desired and in the best possible way.

Adam Smith's ideas had a powerful influence both on governments and on
economists. Many of the most important nineteenth-century economists, such
as the Englishmen John Stuart Mill and Nassau Senior, promulgated the
doctrine known as **laissez faire,** which argued that the government should
leave the private sector alone; it should not attempt to regulate or control
private enterprise. Unfettered competition would serve the best interests of
society.

Not all of the nineteenth-century social thinkers were persuaded by Smith's
reasoning. They were concerned with grave inequalities in income that they
saw around them, with the squalor in which much of the working classes
lived, and with the unemployment that workers frequently faced. While
nineteenth-century writers like Charles Dickens attempted to portray the
plight of the working classes in novels, social theorists, like Karl Marx, Sis-
mondi, and Robert Owen, attempted not only to develop theories explaining
what they saw but also to suggest ways in which society might be reorga-
nized. To many, the evils in society could be attributed to the private ownership of capital; what Adam Smith saw as a virtue they saw as a vice. Marx,

---

[1] This view has been particularly argued by George Stigler. See, for instance, his "Theory of Regulation,"
Bell Journal, Spring 1981, pp. 3–21.

[2] See A. O. Hirschman, *Shifting Involvements: Private Interest and Public Action* (Princeton, N.J.: Princeton University Press, 1982). Hirschman has put forth an interesting theory attempting to explain the constant
changes in views on the appropriate role of the government.

if not the deepest of the social thinkers, was certainly the most influential among those who advocated a greater role for the state in controlling the means of production. Still others saw the solution neither in the state nor in private enterprise but in smaller groups of individuals getting together and acting cooperatively for their mutual interest.

These continuing controversies have stimulated economists to attempt to ascertain the precise sense in which and the precise conditions under which the invisible hand guides the economy to efficiency. It is now known that the presumption of the efficiency of the market economy is valid only under fairly restrictive assumptions. The failures we noted above made it apparent that there were many problems with which the market did not deal adequately. Today, among American economists, the dominant view is that *limited* government intervention could alleviate (but not solve) the worst problems: the government should take an active role in maintaining full employment and alleviating the worst aspects of poverty, but private enterprise should play the central role in the economy. There is still considerable controversy about how limited or how active a role the government should take. Some economists, such as Harvard University Professor John Kenneth Galbraith, believe that the government should take a more active role, while others, such as Nobel laureates Milton Friedman of Stanford University's Hoover Institution and George Stigler of the University of Chicago, believe that the government should take a less active role. Views on this subject are affected by how serious one considers the failures of the market to be and by how effective one believes the government can be in remedying them.

WHAT OR WHO IS THE GOVERNMENT?

Throughout this chapter we have referred to "the government." But what precisely is the government? We all have some idea about what institutions are included: Congress, the President, the Supreme Court, and a host of alphabet agencies, such FHA, IRS, FAA, FTC, SEC, and NLRB. The United States has a *federal* governmental structure—that is, governmental activities take place at several levels: local, state, and federal. The federal government is responsible for national defense, the post office, the printing of money, and the regulation of interstate and international commerce. On the other hand, the states and localities have traditionally been responsible for education, welfare, police and fire protection, and the provision of other local services, such as libraries, sewage, and garbage collection. Though the Constitution asserts that all rights not explicitly delegated to the federal government reside with the states and the people, the Constitution has proven to be a sufficiently flexible document that the exact boundaries are ambiguous. While education is primarily a local responsibility, the federal government has become increasingly involved in its support. The constitutional provision giving the federal government the right to control interstate business has provided the basis for federal regulation of almost all businesses, since almost all businesses are involved, in one way or another, with interstate commerce.

At the local level, there are frequently several separate governmental structures, each of which has the power to levy taxes and the responsibility for administering certain programs. In addition to townships and counties, there are school districts, sewage districts, and library districts. A 1977 study estimated that there are 80,000 such governmental entities in the United States, down from 155,000 in 1942.

The boundaries between what are public institutions and what are not public institutions are often not clear. When the government sets up a corporation, a public enterprise, is that enterprise part of the "government"? For instance, Amtrak, which was set up by the federal government to run the nation's passenger railway services, has received subsidies from the federal government, but otherwise it is run like a private enterprise. Similarly, in Britain, the government nationalized the steel industry. But the British Steel Company is still run in most respects like companies in the United States. Should the British Steel Company be included in the government? Matters become even more complicated when the government is a major stockholder in a company but not the only shareholder.

What distinguishes those institutions that we have labeled as "government" from private institutions? There are two important differences. First, in a democracy the individuals who are responsible for running public institutions are elected, or are appointed by someone who is elected (or appointed by someone who is appointed by someone who is elected . . .). The "legitimacy" of the person holding the position is derived directly or indirectly from the electoral process. In contrast, those who are responsible for administering General Motors are chosen by the shareholders of General Motors; while those who are responsible for administering private foundations (such as the Rockefeller and Ford foundations) are chosen by a self-perpetuating board of trustees.

Secondly, the government is endowed with certain rights of compulsion that private institutions do not have. The government has the right to force you to pay taxes (and if you fail, it can confiscate your property and / or imprison you). The government has the right to "force" its young males to serve in the armed forces, at wages below those that would induce them to volunteer. The government has the right to seize your property for public use (this is called the right of eminent domain).

Not only do private institutions and individuals not have these rights, the government actually restricts the rights of individuals to give to others similar powers of compulsion. For instance, the government does not allow you to sell yourself into slavery.

In contrast, all private exchanges are voluntary. I may want you to work for me, but I cannot force you to do so. I may need your property to construct an office building, but I cannot force you to sell it. I may think that some deal is advantageous to both of us, but I cannot force you to engage in the deal.

This ability to use compulsion does mean that the government may be able to do some things that private institutions cannot do. And the differences in the processes by which those who administer public and private institutions are chosen may have important implications for the behavior of those institutions. It is important to keep these differences in mind as we discuss, in later chapters of this book, alternative views of the role of the government.

11
The Public
Sector and
the Funda-
mental Eco-
nomic
Questions

THE PUBLIC SECTOR AND THE FUNDAMENTAL ECONOMIC QUESTIONS

Economics is the study of *scarcity*, of how societies make choices concerning how to use their limited resources. Four questions are asked:

What is to be produced?

How is it to be produced?

For whom is it to be produced?

How are these decisions made?

Like any field of economics, the economics of the public sector is concerned with these fundamental questions of choice. But it focuses on the choices made within the public sector itself, on the role of the government, the extent to which these choices are made in the public sector, and the extent to which the government affects the decisions made in the private sector.

What Is to Be Produced? How much of our resources should be devoted to the production of public goods, which for now we can think of as any good or service provided by the government, such as education and defense, and how much of our resources should we devote to the production of private goods, or goods provided by the market, such as cars, TV sets, and video games? We often depict this choice in terms of the **production possibilities schedule,** which traces the various amounts of two goods that can be produced efficiently with a given technology and resources. In our case, the two goods are public goods and private goods. Figure 1.1 gives the various pos-

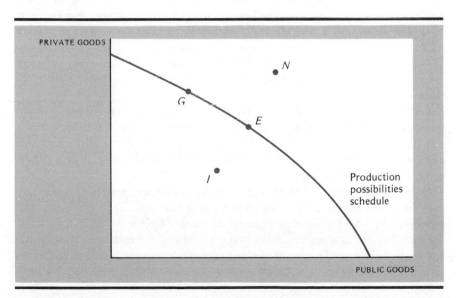

1.1 SOCIETY'S PRODUCTION POSSIBILITIES SCHEDULE This depicts the maximum level of private goods that society can enjoy for each level of public goods. If society wishes to enjoy more public goods, it has to give up some private goods.

sible combinations of public goods and private goods that the society may produce.

Society can spend more on public goods, such as national defense, but only by reducing what is available for private consumption. Thus, in moving from G to E along the production possibilities schedule, public goods are increased, but private goods are decreased. A point such as I, which is below the production possibilities schedule, is said to be *inefficient:* society could get more public goods and more private goods. A point such as N, which is above the production possibilities schedule, is said to be *infeasible:* it is not possible, given current resources and technology, to have at the same time that much expenditure on public goods and that much expenditure on private goods.

How Should It Be Produced? The second question, how what is produced should be produced, is as important as the first question. When should the government take direct responsibility for production of the goods that are publicly provided, and when should the government procure these goods from private firms? While most of the weapons used by the military are produced by private firms, only a small percentage of public educational expenditures goes to private schools. In many countries, government enterprises produce goods (such as telephone services, steel, and electricity) that are sold to individuals. While some individuals believe that, unless such commodities are directly produced by public enterprises, consumers will be exploited, other individuals believe that state enterprises are inevitably less efficient than private enterprises.

Other issues are subsumed under this second question. Government policy affects how firms produce the goods they produce; environmental protection legislation restricts pollution by firms; payroll taxes that firms must pay on the workers they employ make labor more expensive and thus discourage firms from using production techniques that require much labor; other provisions of the tax code may change the attractiveness of one machine relative to another. Though discussion of these questions seldom comes to the center of political debates, recent debates about the distorting effect of taxation and the desirability of nuclear reactors as energy sources are important exceptions.

For Whom? The Question of Distribution. Government decisions about taxation or welfare programs determine how much income different individuals have to spend. Similarly, the government must decide what public goods to produce. Some groups will benefit from the production of one public good, others from another.

How Are Collective Choices Made? There is one area that is of more concern to public-sector economics than to other branches of economics: the processes by which *collective* choices are made. Collective choices are the choices that we as a society must make together—for instance, concerning our legal structure, the size of our military establishment, our expenditures on other public goods, etc. Introductory economics texts focus on how individuals make their decisions concerning consumption, how firms make their decisions concerning production, and how the price system works to ensure that the goods demanded by consumers are produced by firms. Collective decision making is far more complicated: individuals often disagree about what is desirable. After all, just as some individuals like chocolate ice cream and some like vanilla ice cream, some individuals get greater enjoyment out of public parks than do others. But while with private goods, the individual who likes chocolate ice cream can simply buy chocolate ice cream, and the individual who likes vanilla ice cream can buy vanilla ice cream, with public goods we must make a decision together. Anyone who has lived in a family knows something about the difficulties of collective decision making (should we go to the movies or go bowling?). Public decision making is far more complex. One of the objectives of public-sector economics is to study how collective choices (or, as they are sometimes called, social choices) are made in democratic societies.

The recognition of this divergence of views is important in itself. It should make us wary of expressions such as "It is in the public interest" or "We are concerned with the good of society." Different policies may be good for different individuals. One should carefully specify who will benefit from and who will be harmed by each policy.

STUDYING THE ECONOMICS OF THE PUBLIC SECTOR

The study of the economics of the public sector can be divided into three categories.

1. *Knowing what activities the public sector engages in and how these are organized.* The complexity of the government's operations is so great that it is difficult to assess what its total expenditures are and what they go for. The budget of the federal government alone is a document that is more than 600 pages, and within the budget, activities are not easily compartmentalized. Some activities are undertaken in several different departments or agencies. Research, for instance, is funded through the Department of Defense, the National Science Foundation, the National Institutes of Health, and the National Air and Space Administration, among others. Also, a department such as the Department of Health and Welfare undertakes a myriad of activities some of which are only vaguely related to others.

Further, as we have noted, taxes and expenditures occur at several different levels: in some places, individuals pay not only federal and state taxes but a separate tax to the school district, another tax to the township, another tax to the county, still another tax to the jurisdictions that provide water and sewage, and still another tax to support the library.

2. *Understanding and anticipating, insofar as possible, the full consequences of these governmental activities.* When a tax is imposed on a corporation, who bears the tax? It is unlikely that the tax will do nothing more than reduce corporate profits. More likely, at least partly it will be passed on to consumers. Or, perhaps, onto employees, as wages fall. When the government passes a rent control law, what will be the long-run consequences? Will renters really be better off in the long run? What are the consequences of the government changing the age of retirement for social security? Of charging tuition in state universities? Of providing free medical care to the aged?

We have already noted that the consequences of government policies are often too complicated to predict accurately. There is often controversy about what the consequences will be. Indeed, even after a policy has been introduced, there is often controversy about what its effects are. In this book we shall attempt not only to present all sides of some of the major controversies but also to explain why such disagreements have persisted, and why it is difficult to resolve some of these important questions.

3. *Evaluating alternative policies.* To do this, we need not only to know the consequences of alternative policies but to develop criteria for evaluation. We need, in other words, to understand the objectives of government policy. We then must ascertain the extent to which the particular proposal meets (or is likely to meet) those criteria. But even that is not enough. Many proposals have effects other than the intended effects, and one must know how to predict these other consequences and to bring them into the evaluation.

NORMATIVE VERSUS POSITIVE ECONOMICS

The distinction we have just made, between analyzing the *consequences* of a government policy and making *judgments* concerning the desirability of particular government policies, is an important one. The former kind of analysis is often referred to as **positive economics,** the latter as **normative economics.** Positive economics is concerned not only with analyzing the consequences of particular government policies but with describing the activities of the public sector and the political and economic forces that brought these particular programs into existence. When economists step beyond the pure analysis of positive economics, they move into the realm of normative economics. Normative economics is concerned with making judgments concerning the desirability of various policies and with designing new policies that better meet certain objectives.

Normative economics makes statements like, "If the government wishes to restrict the importation of oil in a way that is least costly to the government and consumers, tariffs on the importation of oil are preferable to quotas." Or, "If the objective of the farm program is to assist the poorer farmers, a system of price supports is not as good as a system of appropriately designed income transfers." In other words, in normative economics, economists compare the extent to which various government programs meet certain desired objectives. In contrast, positive economics makes statements like, "The imposition of quotas on oil in the 1950s led to higher domestic prices and the more rapid depletion of our natural resources."

When economists make such statements, they try not to impose their own criteria, their own values. They often view themselves as providing "technical assistance" to policy makers, helping them to attain their objectives.

At the same time, economists often do try to say something about the objectives that politicians and policy makers put forth. They attempt to see, for instance, to what extent the various objectives may be in conflict with one another and, when they are in conflict, to suggest how these conflicts can be resolved. They try to clarify the full implications of alternative value systems. They attempt to see which values are basic and which values can be derived from other, more fundamental values. Economists' work on these questions often comes close to that of political philosophers.

The two approaches, the positive and the normative, are to some extent complementary; to make judgments about what activities the government *should* undertake, one must know the consequences of various government activities. One must be able to describe accurately what will happen if the government imposes some tax or another or attempts to subsidize some industry or another.

Some examples may help clarify the distinction. Assume Congress is considering increasing a tax on cigarettes or alcohol. Positive economics is concerned with questions such as:

a) How much will the prices of cigarettes or alcohol rise?

b) How will this affect the demand for cigarettes or alcohol?

c) Do lower-income individuals spend a larger proportion of their income on smoking (drinking) than do higher-income individuals?

d) What are the likely consequences of the tax on the profits of the cigarette industry or the liquor industry?

e) What will be the repercussions of a cigarette tax on the prices of tobacco and hence on the income of tobacco farmers? Of an alcohol tax on the price of alcohol and hence on the income of distilleries and breweries?

f) What will be the consequences of reduced smoking for the incidence of lung cancer and heart disease? What fraction of the associated medical expenditures are borne directly or indirectly by the government itself? What will be the consequences of reduced drinking on automobile accidents, and on the associated medical costs? What effect will the increased longevity from reduced smoking have on the social security system?

On the other hand, normative economics is concerned with *evaluating* the various consequences and coming to a judgment concerning the desirability of the tax changes:

a) If our primary concern in the choice of taxes is with their impact on the poor, which tax is preferable, the liquor tax or the tobacco tax?

b) If our primary concern in the choice of taxes is how the tax distorts behavior (from what it would be in the absence of the tax), which tax is preferable, the liquor tax or the tobacco tax?

c) If our concern is with reducing medical costs, which tax is preferable, the liquor tax or the tobacco tax?

d) Are there better taxes than either of these for attaining any particular objective of the government?

As a second example, assume the government is considering imposing a fine on steel firms generating pollution to discourage them from pollution, or a subsidy on pollution abatement equipment to encourage them to clean up their act. Positive economics is concerned with questions such as:

a) How much of a reduction in pollution will be caused by fines (or subsidies) of different magnitudes?

b) How much of an increase in the price of steel will be caused by the imposition of such fines?

c) How much of a decrease in the demand for steel produced in the United States will be induced by these price changes?

d) What will be the employment consequences of these reductions in demand? What will happen to the profits of the steel industry?

e) How much are those living in the vicinity of the steel mill willing to pay for the reduction in the level of pollution? That is, how much is it worth to them?

Again, normative economics is concerned with evaluating the different effects:

a) If our concern is primarily with the poor, which system, a tax or a subsidy, would be preferable? The poor are affected as consumers by the change in prices of all commodities using steel. Since they are more likely to be near the steel mill, pollution is more likely to affect them than the rich. But if a fine reduces the demand for steel and employment in the steel industry, the poorer, unskilled workers are the ones who would suffer the most. How do we add up all of these effects? And what is the level of tax or subsidy that maximizes the welfare of the poor?

b) If our concern is with maximizing the value of national income, which system, a tax or a subsidy, would be preferable? Or should we have neither? And again, if it is desirable to have one or the other, what is the level that maximizes national income?

This example is typical of many such situations that we face in economic policy analysis: there are some gainers (those who can now breathe the cleaner air) and there are some losers (consumers who pay higher prices, producers who have lower profits, workers who lose their jobs). Normative economics is concerned with developing systematic procedures by which we can compare the gains of those who are better off with the losses of those who are worse off, to arrive at some overall judgment concerning the desirability of the proposal.

The distinction between normative statements and positive statements arises not only in discussions of particular policy changes but also in discussions of political processes. For instance, economists are concerned with *describing* the consequences of majority voting. When there are differences in views concerning how much should be spent on national defense, how do the divergent viewpoints get reflected in the outcome of any particular political process? What will be the consequences of requiring a two-thirds majority for increments in public expenditures exceeding a certain amount? What will be the consequences of increasing politicians' pay? Of restricting private contributions to political campaigns? Of public support for political campaigns? But economists are also concerned with evaluating alternative political processes. Are some political processes better, in some sense, than others? Are they more likely to produce "consistent" choices? Are some political processes more likely than others to yield equitable or efficient outcomes?

DISAGREEMENTS AMONG ECONOMISTS

In the preceding paragraphs we have divided the analysis of policy into two steps: analyzing the consequences and evaluating them. Both steps are fraught with controversy.

Unanimity is rare in many of the central questions of policy debate. Some individuals think school busing is desirable, some do not. Some think that the income tax should be more progressive (i.e., that wealthy individuals should pay a higher percentage of their income in taxes, while poor individuals should pay a lower percentage); some believe the opposite. Some believe that the government should provide a tuition tax credit for private schools, some believe that it should not. Some believe that the government's loan program to college students should be cut back, others that it should be expanded. One of the central concerns of policy analysis is to identify the sources of disagreement.

There are three broad areas in which disagreements arise. The first two are disagreements that arise from the positive analysis of the consequences of the policy; the third has to do with the judgments that are the basis for normative analysis.

Failure to Trace the Full Consequences of a Government Policy

Many controversies arise because one side or the other (or both) fails to trace the full consequences of the government policy. We have already noted several examples of this: in rent control, where the proponents failed to take into account the consequences for the supply of rental housing.

An early example of the failure to think through the full consequences of a government policy was the window tax, which was enacted in England in 1696 (under the Act of Making Good the Deficiency of the Clipped Money). At the time, windows were a luxury, and wealthy individuals had houses with more windows than those of poor individuals. It would have been administratively difficult to have an income tax; the government did not have the capacity to ascertain what each individual's income was. Indeed, individuals did not keep the kinds of records that would enable them to ascertain what their own income was. Thus the window tax base may have been a good measure of ability to pay; windows were an expensive luxury. Those who could afford to have many windows were presumably in a better position to pay taxes; windows may have provided, in other words, an equitable basis of taxation. It was undoubtedly not the intention of those who levied the tax that the windows should be blocked up, but this was one of the major consequences of the tax. To avoid the tax individuals built houses with few windows. The tax led to dark houses.

In the following chapters we shall frequently point out that the consequences of government policies are markedly different from the intended result. In the *long run*, individuals and firms respond to changes in taxes and other government policies, and these long-run responses need to be taken into account. Moreover, as a result of these adjustments, a tax or subsidy on one good may have consequences for others. Any major tax change is likely to lead to repercussions for the whole economy. Although many of the individual effects may be small, in total, when all the effects are taken into account, these indirect repercussions may indeed be serious. In our subsequent discussion, we shall point out some dramatic examples of this—where, for instance, a tax on wages turns out to leave workers unaffected but to lower the price of land.

Differences in Views about How the Economy Behaves

Economists agree that in evaluating a policy one should take into account all consequences; in fact, they view the identification of these consequences as one of their primary roles in policy analysis. They often disagree, however, about how the economy behaves, and hence about what the consequences of a government policy will be. There are two broad sources of disagreement that we can identify. First, they often disagree about the extent to which the economy is competitive. In much of the analysis of this book we shall assume that the economy is very competitive; that there are many firms in each industry competing actively against each other. Each is so small relative to the market that it has no effect on the market price. There are no barriers to entry into the industry, so that if there are profitable opportunities in the industry, they will be quickly seized upon. Few economists believe that in all sectors of the economy these assumptions are valid, but many economists believe that the economy is sufficiently competitive that the insights that one obtains from analyzing a competitive economy are relevant to an under-standing of the effects of government policy in the American economy. Most economists also agree that there are some industries that are not well described by the competitive model, and that the analysis of the effects of taxation in those industries requires an analysis of how monopolies (industries with a single firm) or oligopolies (industries with a few firms) operate. But there are some economists, such as Harvard's John Kenneth Galbraith, who believe that the economy is basically not very competitive, and that one obtains little insight into the effects of a tax by assuming that it is. Still others believe that there is a great deal of competition in the long run but that in the short run competition is more limited. We cannot resolve these disagreements, but what we can do is to show how and when different views lead to different conclusions.

Economic Models. In analyzing the consequences of various policies, economists make use of what are called **models.** Just as a model airplane attempts to replicate the basic features of an airplane, so too a model of the economy attempts to depict the basic features of the economy. The actual economy is obviously extremely complex; to see what is going on, and to make predictions about what the consequences of some change in policy will be, one needs to separate out the essential from the inessential features. What features one decides to focus on in constructing a model depend on what questions one wishes to address. The fact that models make simplifying assumptions, that they leave out many details, is a virtue, not a vice. An analogy may be useful. In going on a long trip, one often uses several maps. One map, depicting the interstate highway system, provides an overview, enabling one to see how to get from the general area where you are to the general area where you wish to go. You then use detailed maps, to see how to get from your point of origin to the expressway and from the expressway to your final destination. If the interstate highway had every street and road in the country, the map would have to be so large as to limit its usefulness; the extra detail, though important for some purposes, would simply get in the way.

All analysis involves the use of models, of simple hypotheses concerning how individuals and firms will respond to various changes in government policy, and how these responses interact, to determine the total impact on the economy. Everybody—politicians as well as economists—uses models in discussing the effects of alternative policies. The difference is that economists attempt to be *explicit* about their assumptions, and to be sure that their assumptions are consistent with each other and with statistical evidence.

In our earlier discussion about the sources of disagreement in policy analysis, we noted that economists often disagree about the extent of competition in the economy. That is, some economists believe that a model of the economy in which firms are assumed to compete vigorously against each other provides a good basis for forming predictions about the consequences of, say, an increase in the tax on corporations. These economists may agree that there are a few instances in which firms do not compete vigorously. But, in their view, these are the exceptions rather than the rule. Other economists believe that most industries are dominated by three or four large firms; that though they may compete in some directions—for instance, in attempting to develop new products—in other areas, such as pricing policy, there is often tacit collusion. In their view, the traditional competitive model is likely to give misleading results. They contend that an appropriate model needs to take into account the limitations on the extent of competition.

Disagreements about Magnitudes. Even when economists agree about the kind of response that a particular policy will elicit, they may disagree about the magnitude of the response. That is, they may agree that decreases in taxes will induce individuals to work harder, but some may feel that the effect is very likely to be small, while others may believe that the effect is likely to be large. This was one of the sources of dispute about the consequences of President Reagan's 1981 tax cut. Proponents of the tax believed that the lower rates would provide such a spur to the economy that tax revenues would actually increase. Critics agreed that the tax cut might provide some spur to the economy but that the increase in national income was likely to be so small that tax revenues would decline. This decline would, in their view, lead to large deficits, which would, in turn, have a deleterious effect on the economy. As it turned out, in the short run the response of the economy was even smaller than some of Reagan's critics predicted.

Although a central concern of modern economics is ascertaining the magnitude of the response of, say, investment to an investment tax credit, of consumption to a change in the income tax rate, of savings to an increase in the interest rate, etc., it is an unfortunate fact that various studies, using different bodies of data and different statistical techniques, come up with different conclusions. As economists obtain more data and develop better techniques for analyzing the limited available data, some of these disagreements may be resolved.

Disagreement over Values

While the two previous sources of disagreement arise within positive economics, the final source of disagreement lies within normative economics. Even if there is agreement about the full consequences of some policy, there may be a disagreement about whether the policy is desirable. There are frequently *trade-offs:* a policy may increase national output but increase inequality; a policy may increase employment but also increase inflation; a policy may benefit one group but make another group worse off. There are, in other words, some desirable consequences of the policy and some undesirable consequences. Individuals may weigh these consequences in different ways, some attaching more importance to price stability than to unemployment, others attaching more importance to growth than to inequality.

On questions of values, there is no more unanimity among economists than there is among philosophers. What we shall do in this book is to present some of the major views and assess some of the criticisms that have been leveled against each.

SUMMARY

1. In mixed economies, such as the United States, economic activity is carried on by both private enterprise and the government.

2. Since the time of Adam Smith, economic theory has emphasized the role of private markets in the efficient supply of goods. Yet economists and others have come to recognize important limitations in the ability of the private sector to meet certain basic social needs. The attempt to correct these failures has led to the growth of government's role in the market economy.

3. The government, however, is not necessarily the solution to private-sector failures. The failure of many public programs can be attributed to three factors: a) The consequences of any action by the government are complicated and difficult to foresee. b) The government has only limited control over these consequences. c) Those who design legislation have only limited control over the actual implementation of the government programs.

4. The United States has a federal government structure, with certain activities being primarily the responsibility of states and localities (such as education) and other activities being primarily the responsibility of the federal government (such as defense).

5. Economics is the study of scarcity, of how resources are allocated among competing uses. Public-sector economics focuses on choices between the public and private sectors and choices within the public sector. It is concerned with four basic issues: what gets produced; how it gets produced; for whom it gets produced; and the processes by which these decisions are made.

6. In studying public finance, positive economics looks at the scope of government activity and the consequences of various government policies. Normative economics attempts to evaluate alternative policies that might be pursued.

7. Disagreements about the desirability of policies are based on: failures to trace out the full consequences of government policies; disagreements concerning the nature of the economy; and disagreements concerning values and objectives.

KEY CONCEPTS

Mixed economy	Public sector
Market failure	Production possibilities schedule
Invisible hand	Normative economics
Laissez faire	Positive economics
Private sector	Economic models

1. Consider the following discussion of our current program of support for farmers:

> A The objective of our farm program is to ensure that all farmers have a reasonable standard of living. The way it does this is to ensure that farmers receive fair prices for their commodities. It is no more right that farmers should produce for substandard prices than for workers to work for substandard wages.
>
> B Our farm program has been a failure. The benefits of the price subsidies accrue largely to large farmers (because they produce more). Many farmers still have incomes below the poverty line. The high prices have induced increased production, which has meant high costs for the government. Acreage restrictions have had only limited effect, since farmers have kept their best land in production. Direct grants to farmers would be preferable to our price-support program.

   a) Which of the statements in the discussion are normative, which are positive? (The fact that you disagree with a normative statement or that you think a particular "positive" statement is inaccurate does not change the nature of the statement.)

   b) Identify the sources of disagreement: Are they due to differences in values and objectives? Differences in perceptions about the nature of the economy? Or to a failure on one (or the other) side of the debate to take into account the full consequences of the government's action?

2. For each of the following programs, identify one (or more) "unintended" consequences:

   a) Rent control
   b) Minimum wages
   c) Medicare (free hospital care to the aged)
   d) Improved highways making suburbs more accessible to the city
   e) Forced integration of central city schools
   f) Agricultural price supports
   g) Lowering the speed limit to 55 miles an hour to save on gasoline

3. "In recent years there has been considerable concern over the viability of our social security (old-age and survivors' insurance) program. Some individuals believe that with current birth rates, death rates, etc., the current level of benefits can only be sustained with marked increases in taxes. Some believe that the appropriate response is to reduce the current level of benefits, others believe the appropriate response is to increase taxes in the future. Still others, worried about the effects of even higher tax rates but believing that it would be unfair to lower the benefits of those presently receiving social security, argue that benefits in the future should be cut."

   In this discussion, separate out the positive statements from the normative statements. To what extent are the disagreements attributable to differences in values? To what extent are the disagreements attributable to differences in views of the economy?

2

The Public Sector in the United States

Traditionally, taxes and expenditures have been the two main activities studied in public-sector economics, or public finance. In the United States, tax revenues were $1,133 billion in 1984, or 31 percent of total income. Public-sector expenditures were $1,258 billion, or 34 percent of total production. By contrast, in 1913, prior to World War I, taxes and expenditures were less than 10 percent of national income. How do we account for this dramatic change in the role of government? What does the government spend all of this money on?

We identify six different roles that the government performs. It provides the legal framework, within which all economic transactions occur, it regulates, and it produces. It also purchases goods and services (it acts as a "consumer"), it provides social insurance, and it redistributes income, taking money away from some individuals and giving it to others. Most of the government's expenditures are accounted for by these last three roles.

LEGAL SYSTEM

First, the government establishes a set of laws that provide a framework within which firms and individuals can engage in economic interactions. Economists and philosophers often try to imagine what life would be like in the complete absence of government. Without laws defining property rights, only the exercise of force would stop one individual from stealing from another. Without the ability to protect property, individuals would have little incentive to accumulate assets. Needless to say, economic activities would be severely restricted.

The United States legal system does much more than just protect property rights. It enforces contracts between individuals. It also imposes restrictions on the kinds of contracts that are legally enforceable. Our bankruptcy laws limit the liability of investors. Product-liability laws have an important effect on the quality of goods produced. Antitrust laws attempt to encourage competition among firms; they restrict mergers, acquisitions, and unfair business practices.

The effects of our legal system are pervasive, but expenditures on running the court system and maintaining law and order are relatively small: if police and prisons are included, expenditures are slightly higher than 4 percent. Less than 2 percent of total government expenditures are for general administration, legislative, and judicial activities.[1]

GOVERNMENT AS REGULATOR

In addition to providing the basic legal framework within which individuals and firms interact, the government has taken an increasingly active role in regulating business activity to protect workers, consumers, and the environment and to ensure equality of treatment.

The Occupational Safety and Health Administration attempts to ensure that workers' places of employment meet certain minimal standards. The National Labor Relations Board attempts to ensure that both management and unions deal fairly with each other. The Federal Trade Commission attempts, among other things, to protect consumers from misleading advertising. The Environmental Protection Agency attempts to protect certain vital parts of our environment by regulating, for instance, emissions from automobiles and toxic-waste disposal.

In addition to these broad categories, there are regulations that apply to specific industries. The banking industry is regulated both by the Federal Reserve Board and the Comptroller of the Currency; trucking and railroads are regulated by the Interstate Commerce Commission; the airlines are regulated by the Federal Aviation Administration; the telephone and telecommunications industry is regulated by the Federal Communications Commission; the securities industry is regulated by the Securities and Exchange Commission.

In recent years, there has been a concerted attempt to reduce the extent of federal regulation. The process of reducing or eliminating regulations is referred to as **deregulation.** There has been deregulation in the airline industry (with the elimination of the Civil Aeronautics Board in 1984), in natural gas (gas prices have been allowed to rise gradually to market levels), in trucking, and in banking (the range of services that banks are now allowed to provide has been greatly increased.)

Federal outlays for the regulatory agencies represent just 1 percent of the federal budget.[2] But these expenditures do not give an accurate view of the

[1] In 1983, the last year for which comparable data for federal, state, and local expenditures were available, expenditures were as follows: administrative, legislative, and judicial activities, $20 billion; law and order, $31 billion. (Total expenditures were 4.4 percent of total government expenditure.)

[2] Surprisingly, in spite of deregulation, this percentage was essentially unchanged from 1974 to 1981. See the *Economic Report of the President*, 1982, p. 136.

impact of the federal regulatory agencies. The extent to which they influence virtually every aspect of business practices goes well beyond the simple measure of government expenditures. A very indirect measure of the broader impact may be had by looking at the costs of reporting, of filling out forms, costs which are borne by firms.

During the Carter administration, an effort was made to reduce paperwork costs, and a Paperwork Commission was established with this as its objective. In its last detailed report, in 1979, the commission estimated that 786 *million* hours were spent by nongovernmental employees in completing government forms.[3] This corresponds to approximately 400,000 workers working full time for a year. Compared to the 2,823,000 employed by the federal government in 1979, these "indirect employees" equaled 14 percent of direct federal government employment.

GOVERNMENT AS PRODUCER

One of the major differences between the United States and many of the Western European countries is the limited role that the government takes in *production*. The Constitution of the United States gives the federal government responsibility for running the postal service and for printing money. The U.S. Postal Service has a monopoly on the delivery of first-class mail, but more than 50 percent of all parcels and an even higher percentage of express mail are now delivered by private firms.

At the local level, the government has taken a major responsibility for the production of education: approximately 90 percent of elementary and secondary-school students and 80 percent of college students are enrolled in public schools.[4]

Many of the production activities of the government are similar to corresponding activities carried out by private firms. Electricity is produced both by government enterprises (the most famous of which is perhaps the Tennessee Valley Authority) and by private firms. The government sells electricity just as private firms do.

Looking across countries, we see that some industries frequently fall within the public sector, while other industries seldom do. Agriculture appears to be one of the more difficult industries for public production. On the other hand, in most countries, telephones, railroads, and at least part of the radio and TV broadcasting industry are in the public sector. In some countries, such as Britain, the government produces steel and coal, though the government has considered selling off its steel plants and has already turned over its phone system to a newly created private firm (in which it retains half of the shares). The process of converting government enterprises to private enterprises is called **privatization.** In many countries the banking system is **nationalized**—that is, owned and operated by the government; in the United States it is closely regulated but privately owned.[5]

---

[3] *Paperwork and Red Tape: New Perspectives, New Directions,* Office of Management and Budget, 1979.

[4] Source: Projections of Education Statistics, 1990–91, Table 4, p. 32. National Center for Education Statistics.

[5] The Federal Reserve Banks, which are responsible for the management of the banking system, are, however, publicly owned. Their profits are turned over to the Treasury. In 1980 these amounted to $11.7 billion. There is, however, some controversy about how these profits are to be interpreted.

The distinction between government enterprises and private enterprises is often not a clear one. The government may own more than 50 percent of a firm but allow it to operate as if it were totally private. In the United States, the government has established several enterprises. These include Amtrak, which runs the nation's passenger railroad system, and Comstat, for the development of the commercial use of satellites. These firms, too, operate much like private firms.

Overall, public production by the federal, state, and local governments accounts for about 12 percent of national output.[6] This is up considerably from just over 8 percent in 1947, but down from the peacetime peak of 13.1 percent it reached in 1970. The colored line in Figure 2.1 traces the levels of government production since 1930.

Government production (like the production of any firm) is measured by the difference between the value of output and the value of goods and services purchased. This is called the **value added**. But while the value of output in private firms is measured by the price the goods and services are sold for, most publicly produced goods are not sold but used directly in the public sector or provided freely to customers. Since there is no market price to value such items, they must be valued at the cost of their inputs. Thus, while the value added of a private enterprise is equal to its wages, interest payments, and profits, the value of government production is just equal to wages plus interest. A firm that decided to pay its workers 5 percent more (without eliciting any increased productivity) would find its value added unchanged: wage payments would be up by 5 percent, but profits would be down by a corresponding amount. If the government pays it workers 5 percent more, since the value of output is measured by the value of input, it appears as a 5 percent increase in production.

Because of these problems, many economists believe that one obtains a better picture of the size of government as a producer by looking at its employment. This is shown by the black line in Figure 2.1. In 1984 there were 18.2 million public employees (including the armed forces), which represented 17 percent of total employment. This was triple the percentage in 1929 (when it was 6 percent of the labor force) but down slightly from 1980. Note that the expansion in the public sector appears to have proceeded at a fairly steady pace (apart from World War II). It increased as rapidly during Hoover's administration (1929–1933) as it did during Roosevelt's New Deal (1933–1945). Though there was a slight decrease in the pace of growth during the Eisenhower years, the size of the public sector did not begin to decline until the Nixon-Ford administration. These trends continued during both the Carter and Reagan administrations. It is also important to note the variations in the relative roles played by the federal, state, and local governments, as suggested by the bottom line in Figure 2.1. Comparing it to the top line, we see that total government employment and federal government employment do not always move together; while federal employment declined in the early 1970s, this decline was offset by the rise in employment at the state and local level.

---

[6] *Economic Report of the President,* 1984. Table 10, p. 232.

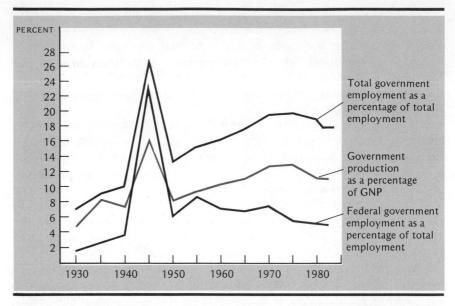

2.1 PUBLIC PRODUCTION AND EMPLOYMENT Government production as a percentage of GNP provides a first view of the government's role as producer. Because employment figures correct for wage inflation in government production, they provide a better estimate of the government's role as producer. SOURCE: *Tax Foundation Facts and Figures,* 1983; *Economic Report of the President,* 1984; *Handbook of Basic Economic Statistics,* 1983

The Government and Private Production

The government not only produces goods itself, but it affects private producers in a number of ways. We have already mentioned its role in regulating private firms, in enforcing contracts, and in ensuring that firms do not engage in anti-competitive practices. In addition, the government subsidizes many industries either directly or indirectly.

In the United States, the most important set of direct subsidies are for agriculture. These amounted to almost $12 billion in 1984, down from the record level of $20 billion the previous year, mainly for government purchases of agricultural crops to maintain the prices of these crops at a high level. While there are other direct subsidy programs, most of the subsidies are indirect and often hidden. The government provides, for instance, subsidized loans under a variety of special programs. When the Chrysler Corporation was on the verge of bankruptcy in 1979 the government guaranteed its loans; though it turned out that Chrysler was able to meet its debt obligations, the loan guarantee represented a large subsidy, enabling Chrysler to obtain funds from banks at a much lower rate than it otherwise could have.

Some of the subsidies do not show up directly in the statistics on government expenditure. For instance, when the government restricts the importation of some foreign good or imposes a tariff on its importation, this raises the prices of those goods in the United States; American producers of competing goods are helped. There is an effective subsidy to American producers paid not by the government but directly by consumers.

There are two areas in which the government has taken on a particularly large role: credit markets and insurance. Since there are no current budgetary costs, loan guarantees are a less painful (at least in the short term) method of subsidizing an industry. The costs only show up later if the government has to make good on the guarantee. Much of the government's activity in this area grew in response to a perceived failure of the private markets to provide credit at reasonable terms. For instance, loan programs are available for housing and for college education. Federal credit activity has grown immensely over the past decade, to the point where in 1984, 11.8 percent (down from the 20 percent level it had reached a couple of years previously) of the total funds advanced in United States credit markets[7] were advanced under federal auspices. If we take into account federal borrowing to finance the deficit, the role of the government appears even more striking; in 1984, 36.6 percent of funds raised in United States credit markets were raised under federal auspices.

These data reflect the large role of the government today in affecting the *flow* of funds. The data on the cumulative value of outstanding loans to the private sector are equally dramatic. The cumulative value of federal and federally assisted credit increased fivefold between 1972 and 1984; by 1985 it reached a trillion dollars; in real terms it increased by 50 percent in a decade.

Government as Insurer

In the period since the Great Depression, the government has taken an increasingly large role in providing insurance. There are two groups of government insurance programs. The first, called **social insurance,** includes social security (old-age retirement and survivors' insurance), medicare (medical insurance for the aged), unemployment insurance, disability insurance, and workmen's compensation (insurance for injuries on the job). These have grown to 26 percent of total government expenditures and 33 percent of federal government expenditures. As we shall see in later chapters, some of these so-called insurance programs are not just insurance programs: they provide a means by which income gets redistributed to some groups who are felt to be particularly needy. To the extent that they serve to redistribute income, they are more rightfully classified as **transfer** programs, which we discuss later in this chapter.

The second category of insurance programs is focused on commercial risks. Though these insurance programs are intended to be self-sustaining, in recent years several of the agencies that administer them have had losses exceeding their income. While the Federal Deposit Insurance Corporation (which insures deposits in commercial banks) has built up more than $10 billion of reserves, other programs have used up all of their reserves. This is the case for Pension Benefit Guaranty Corporation, which guarantees the workers of participating private firms against the possibility that their pension funds will be

---

[7] *Special Analysis: Budget of the United States Government,* 1985.

unable to meet their obligations. (When premiums exceed losses, the difference is added to reserves; when losses exceed premiums, the difference is taken out of reserves.) Many economists believe that the value of potential losses facing the Pension Benefit Guaranty Corporation are enormous. Other federal insurance programs include the Federal Savings and Loan Insurance Corporation (FSLIC) and the Federal Emergency Management Agency, which administers flood, crime, and riot insurance.

GOVERNMENT AS CONSUMER

Every year the government buys billions of dollars' worth of goods and services. It does this to provide for our national defense, to maintain a network of highways, to provide education, police protection, fire protection, and parks. These purchases of goods and services amount to one-fifth of the total production in the United States.

Though there is a close link between "government as consumer" and "government as producer," the two are conceptually and practically distinct. Though most goods produced by the government (such as education and defense), are "consumed" by it, the government buys much of what it consumes from private firms (including most military hardware) while it sells some of what it produces (most notably electricity) to private consumers and firms.

There are different ways that we can group the kinds of goods and services that the government purchases. Figure 2.2 shows the allocation of federal, state, and local and total government consumption expenditures in 1983. At the federal level, the single most important category of expenditures was national defense. This constituted more than three-fifths of federal consumption expenditures and a quarter of total government consumption expenditures.

There are two other kinds of expenditures that are closely related to defense: 1) Expenditures for veterans' programs can be thought of as payments for previous services in the armed forces. These amounted to a little more than 13 percent of federal consumption expenditures. 2) Much of the space research and technology program was originally motivated by defense considerations. If we add these categories together, then defense and related expenditures amounted to more than three-quarters of the federal consumption expenditures, or a third of total government consumption expenditures.

Of the nondefense expenditures, the single most important item is education, representing a quarter of the total government consumption expenditures. Though the role of the federal government has increased markedly in recent years, federal expenditures on education still represent only 8 percent of total education expenditures.[8] The second most important category of nondefense expenditures today is health and hospitals, which amount to over 7 percent of total consumption expenditures.

The third most important category is transportation—including roads, airports, and public mass transportation—which amounts to 6.2 percent of total

---

[8] Most of this is in the form either of aid to students or grants to states and localities (and hence is included under state and local expenditures). Of the $14.7 billion expenditure in 1983, $6.8 billion was distributed to state and local governments and $6.4 billion was given directly to individuals.

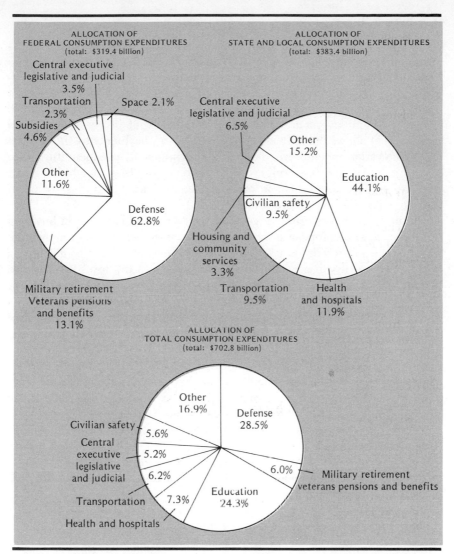

ALLOCATION OF
FEDERAL CONSUMPTION EXPENDITURES
(total: $319.4 billion)

Central executive legislative and judicial 3.5%
Transportation 2.3%
Space 2.1%
Subsidies 4.6%
Other 11.6%
Defense 62.8%
Military retirement Veterans pensions and benefits 13.1%

ALLOCATION OF
STATE AND LOCAL CONSUMPTION EXPENDITURES
(total: $383.4 billion)

Central executive legislative and judicial 6.5%
Other 15.2%
Education 44.1%
Civilian safety 9.5%
Housing and community services 3.3%
Transportation 9.5%
Health and hospitals 11.9%

ALLOCATION OF
TOTAL CONSUMPTION EXPENDITURES
(total: $702.8 billion)

Other 16.9%
Defense 28.5%
Civilian safety 5.6%
Central executive legislative and judicial 5.2%
6.2%
6.0%
Military retirement veterans pensions and benefits
Transportation 7.3%
Education 24.3%
Health and hospitals

2.2 ALLOCATION OF GOVERNMENT CONSUMPTION EXPENDITURES (EXCLUDING NET INTEREST PAID), 1983 Defense spending dominates federal consumption expenditures, while at the state and local levels, education is the major expenditure. When we look at expenditures of all levels of government as a whole, the two are nearly equal. SOURCE: *Survey of Current Business,* 1984

government expenditures. While almost half was *financed* by the federal government, the state and local governments administered 80 percent of the expenditures.[9]

There are other programs, aimed at, for instance, promoting and regulating commerce, providing housing and urban development, and maintaining our natural resources and the environment.

[9]These numbers are derived from the *Survey of Current Business,* July 1984.

Tax Expenditures

The expenditures described in the previous paragraphs represent direct government spending to purchase goods and services. There are, however, a number of indirect ways that the government can spend money—to subsidize, in effect, the private purchase of goods and services. If the government gives educational grants to students, these appear as an expenditure; but if the government gives a tax credit for educational expenditures (that is, if the government allows the individual to reduce his tax payments by the amount of the education expenditure) then it does not appear as an expenditure. The government could just as well tax the individual, and then give him a grant; the two are, for all intents and purposes, equivalent. Yet they show up in the statistics in a very different way.

Similarly, if the government gave a grant to a firm to assist it in buying a machine, it would appear as an expenditure; if the government allows the firm to take a tax credit on its expenditures on machines (that is, if it buys a $100 machine, it will get a $7 tax credit; it reduces the taxes it otherwise would have paid by $7), it does not appear as a government expenditure. But again, the two are, for all intents and purposes, equivalent.

We call these implicit grants **tax expenditures.** In recent years, they have become very large. We calculate their value in the following way. We first calculate how much each individual or firm would have paid in taxes if there were not special provisions allowing deductions and credits for a variety of categories of expenditures. The difference between the actual tax and what the tax would have been is the value of the tax expenditure. We can think of the government as taxing the individual without these special provisions, and then giving the individual a grant (to buy a machine, to go to school, to buy medical services). In fiscal 1984 it was estimated that these tax expenditures amounted to $388.4 billion or approximately 44 percent of federal government outlays. Table 2.1 lists the five budget areas enjoying the bulk of tax expenditures in 1983.

Important categories of tax expenditures included those for health ($33.9 billion or 6 percent of direct outlays), commerce and housing ($149.5 billion, which was more than 7,000 times direct outlays), income security (the tax expenditures associated with the nontaxability or partial taxability of disability payments, unemployment compensation, etc., which amounted to $121.7

Table 2.1   TAX EXPENDITURES: THE MAJOR RECIPIENTS (1984)

Budget Function	Current Services Outlays	Tax Expenditures (in billions of dollars)
Commerce and housing credit	2.1	149.5
Health	92.9	33.9
Income security	289.7	121.7
General purpose fiscal assistance to state and local government	7.2	33.0
Education, training, employment, and social services	27.1	26.0

Source: J. Pechman, ed., *Setting National Priorities: The 1984 Budget* (Washington, D.C.: Brookings Institution, 1983).

billion), education and training ($26.0 billion, 95.9 percent of direct outlays), and energy ($6.7 billion, more than 1½ times direct outlays).

GOVERNMENT AND REDISTRIBUTION

The government takes an active role in redistributing income, in taking money away from some individuals and giving it to others. There are two major categories of programs: public assistance and social insurance.

Public assistance programs take two forms. Some provide cash while others provide only specific services or commodities. The latter are referred to as **in-kind benefits.** The largest cash programs are Aid to Families with Dependent Children (AFDC) and supplemental security income (SSI). SSI provides supplemental income to the aged. The medicaid program, providing medical assistance to the indigent, though enacted only in 1965, is already by far the largest public-assistance program, amounting in 1983 to $32.4 billion, or 32 percent of public assistance.

Table 2.2 GOVERNMENT REDISTRIBUTION AND PUBLIC-ASSISTANCE PROGRAMS*

Program	Date Enacted	1972 Outlay	1983 Outlay
CASH BENEFITS			
AFDC	1935	$ 6.9 bn.	$ 14.2
SSI	1972	3.4	9.5
General Assistance	—	0.7	2.1
Special Unemployment Benefits		—	5.4
Other Assistance		1.7	6.2
IN-KIND BENEFITS			
Medicaid	1965	8.5	32.4
Food Stamps	1964	2.0	11.1
Housing Assistance	1937	1.5	8.6

Source: Survey of Current Business, July 1984, and Health Care Financing Review, Fall 1985.
*Not including social insurance programs

Table 2.2 provides a listing of the public-assistance programs, with the date they were enacted and the benefits. Approximately 55 percent of benefits were restricted to providing particular goods or services. In total, public-assistance programs in 1983 amounted to $102 billion, or 9 percent of total government expenditures, and 12½ percent of federal expenditures.

Social insurance, the second category, differs from public assistance in that an individual's entitlements are partly dependent on his contributions, which can be viewed as insurance premiums. But since what some receive back may be far in excess of what they contribute (even on an actuarial basis), there is a large element of redistribution involved.

The largest of these programs is the old-age, survivors', and disability insurance program (OASDI, the proper name for social security). Figure 2.3 gives the relative size of the various social insurance programs. The medicare program, providing medical services to the aged, has (like medicaid)

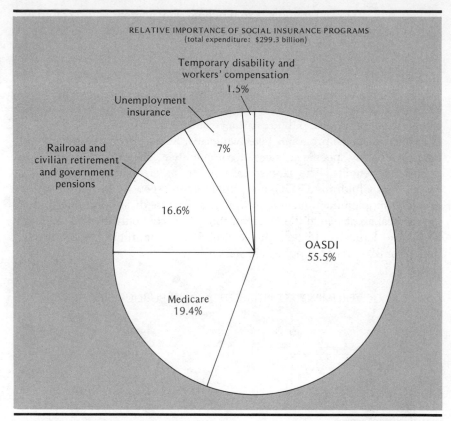

RELATIVE IMPORTANCE OF SOCIAL INSURANCE PROGRAMS
(total expenditure: $299.3 billion)

Temporary disability and
workers' compensation
1.5%

Unemployment
insurance

Railroad and
civilian retirement
and government
pensions

7%

16.6%

OASDI
55.5%

Medicare
19.4%

2.3 RELATIVE IMPORTANCE OF SOCIAL INSURANCE PROGRAMS Social security
(OASDI) is by far the largest social insurance expenditure. SOURCE: *Survey of Current Business,*
1984; *Health Care Financing Review,* Fall 1984.

grown rapidly since it was first introduced in 1965, and now is the second
largest program.

Government expenditures for social insurance and redistribution are
referred to as *transfer* payments.[10] These expenditures are qualitatively different from government expenditures, say, on roads or guns. Transfer payments are simply changes in who has the right to consume goods. When the
government builds a road, it reduces the amount of other goods (e.g., private consumption goods) that society can enjoy. When the government makes
a transfer payment, it affects who can enjoy certain goods but not the total
amount of goods that can be enjoyed.

All expenditure programs have distribution effects. The government may
build a road to an exclusive island on which only very rich individuals have
homes. Though all individuals may have the right to use the road, the benefits clearly accrue to a limited number of individuals. Assessing the distributional implications of expenditure programs is often a quite complicated
matter. In contrast, transfer programs are focused on redistribution.

---

[10] Standard expositions often treat interest as a transfer payment. Effectively, this entails treating purchases
of capital services differently from purchases of labor services (wages). There is one way in which they are
different: while we can identify labor services with the provision of certain goods and services, interest cannot
in general be so allocated.

The government affects the distribution of income not only through subsidies and grants but through the tax system. One could imagine the government taxing everyone at the same rate but then giving grants to those whose income fell below a certain level. This would have the same effect as taxing the lower-income individuals at a lower rate. Thus there is a certain arbitrariness in distinguishing between transfer payments through public assistance programs and the implicit transfers through the tax system.[11]

GOVERNMENT EXPENDITURES: AN OVERALL VIEW

Figure 2.4 depicts the role of the government as a consumer, as a provider of social insurance, and as a redistributor of income. As Panel A shows, consumption expenditures for nondefense purposes (education plus other consumption expenditures) are approximately 40 percent of all expenditures.

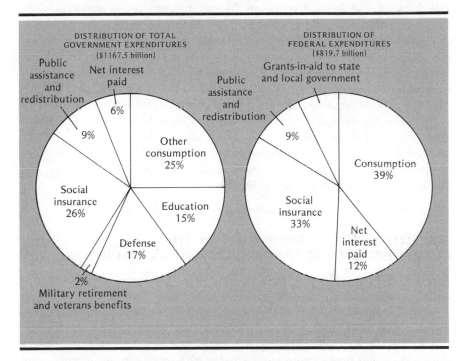

2.4 ALLOCATION OF TOTAL GOVERNMENT EXPENDITURES, 1983 Overall, Social insurance and redistributive expenditures exceed total nondefense consumption expenditures, while at the federal level, social insurance and redistributive expenditures exceed all consumption expenditures including defense. Total government expenditures are less than the sum of federal expenditures and state and local expenditures, because federal grants-in-aid to state and local governments are concluded within both federal expenditures and state and local expenditures. SOURCE: *Handbook of Basic Economic Statistics*, 1983; *Economic Report of the President*, 1984.

---

[11] Some of the tax expenditures can be viewed explicitly as forms of social insurance. The fact that unemployment insurance and social security are only partially taxed, and disability benefits not taxed at all, means that a dollar of expenditures for those purposes goes further than it would if subjected to taxation. There are other ambiguities in determining whether a particular expenditure is treated as a transfer, as part of the government's role in redistribution. We have treated veterans' payments as delayed compensation for services performed, rather than as a transfer. We have created direct grants to students as transfers, but expenditures on higher education, allowing state universities to charge lower tuitions, are not. The distinction is somewhat artificial.

Social insurance is 26 percent of all expenditures. Social insurance plus public assistance can be thought of as transfer payments, and together they constitute 35 percent of all public expenditures. Transfer payments are, however, far more important within the federal budget (Panel B), constituting roughly 42 percent of federal expenditures. Nondefense consumption expenditures represent only a quarter of federal expenditures. With a budget deficit of approximately $200 billion in 1984, it thus almost equaled total nondefense consumption expenditures. Balancing the budget without raising taxes or cutting defense or social insurance was a virtual impossibility.

DIFFERING RESPONSIBILITIES OF THE STATE, LOCAL, AND FEDERAL GOVERNMENTS

The discussion so far has focused on the general activities of government in the United States. But we saw in Chapter 1 that we have a *federal structure;* the federal government takes primary responsibility for the provision of certain goods and services, while state and local governments provide others. While the federal government accounted for 100 percent of the defense expenditures, it accounted for 8 percent of education expenditures, 70 percent of public assistance, and almost half of transportation expenditures.

In 1983 state and local expenditures amounted to $434 billion, somewhat more than half of the federal expenditures of $819 billion in that year. Of that, educational expenditures amounted to $172 billion (or almost two-fifths); public welfare amounted to $67 billion (or slightly more than an eighth); and transportation $39 billion (slightly less than a tenth).

THE SIZE OF THE PUBLIC SECTOR IN THE U.S.: COMPARISONS OVER TIME AND ACROSS COUNTRIES

A central question of debate in the United States, and in other mixed economies, is the appropriate size of the public sector. There are those who believe that the public sector is too large, while others have argued that the public sector is unduly deprived in our society, which is characterized by private affluence.[12] Some insight may be gained by comparing the size of the public sector in the United States today with its size in earlier years, and with its size in other countries. Our previous discussion should have made it clear that there are a number of roles that the government plays; no single number is thus going to provide an accurate indicator of the full impact of the public sector.

One number that economists have found particularly convenient to use is the size of public expenditures relative to the size of the total economy. A standard measure of the size of the total economy is Gross National Product (GNP), which is a measure of the value of all the goods and services produced in the economy during a given year.

During the past fifty years, public expenditures, as a share of GNP, have

---

[12] J. K. Galbraith, *The Affluent Society* (Boston: Houghton Mifflin, 1958).

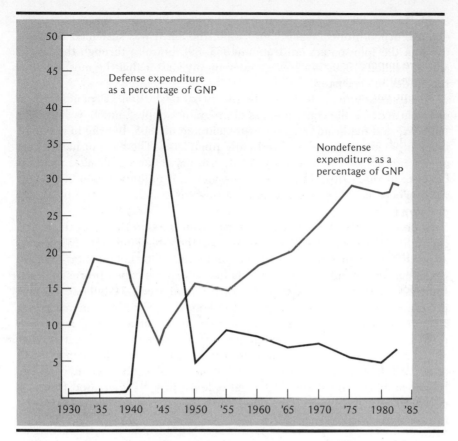

2.5 DEFENSE AND NONDEFENSE EXPENDITURES AS A PROPORTION OF GNP
Defense expenditures as a percentage of GNP declined slowly after the Korean War, with a
slight increase during the Vietnam War, and have grown somewhat in recent years under President Reagan. By contrast, the percentage of government expenditure on nondefense items has
grown markedly. SOURCE: *Social Security Bulletin Annual Statistical Supplement,* 1982; *Survey
of Current Business,* 1978, 1984; *Health Care Financing Review,* Fall 1983.

grown rapidly. In 1930 they were 11 percent of GNP. Today, they represent
a third of GNP, as we see in Figure 2.5.[13]

The changes in recent years in the relative composition of public expenditures have been even more dramatic than changes in the level of expenditures. From 1960 to 1983, while the share of defense expenditures in GNP
decreased from 8.8 percent to 6 percent, the share of nondefense expenditures in GNP increased from 18 percent to 28 percent (see Figure 2.5).

The data do not show a large increase in expenditures in the late 1960s,
as is commonly thought to have resulted from the War on Poverty. And they
do not show a decrease in expenditures in the early 1980s in spite of Reagan's

---

[13]This includes transfer payments. Government consumption is considerably less. Recall from our earlier
discussion the arbitrariness of this measure; for instance, if the government switches from providing aid to
education through direct grants to providing it through tax expenditures, these statistics would show a fall in
the share of public expenditures.

efforts to cut the size of government. The period of rapid increase in non-defense expenditures began before 1960, though it was sustained not only through the Johnson administration (1963–69), but also through the Nixon administration (1969–74). It was under Jimmy Carter that the most notable recent decline occurred.

These statistics may, however, be somewhat misleading. Expenditures in one year may be the consequences of programs adopted much earlier. The medicare and medicaid programs were adopted in 1965, but the full costs of these programs were not realized until much later. The current high levels of expenditure on social security are the results of certain changes made in benefits in the 1970s. The current expansion of military expenditure will have effects on budgets for years from now, as systems ordered today are delivered.

Not only did the share of defense shrink from 1960 to 1977, but the actual expenditures increased at a rate slower than the rate of inflation. In order to avoid the misleading impressions that can be caused by failing to take appropriate account of inflation, economists like to express expenditures in "constant dollars"; thus, if last year the government spent $1 billion on some program, and this year it spends $1.1 billion, but prices have increased by 10 percent, we say that the current expenditures (measured in last year's prices) are $1 billion; in constant dollars, expenditures have not increased at all. Thus, in constant dollars, defense expenditure *shrank* from an average of $77.3 billion in 1970–74 to $72.5 billion in 1980, but increased to $90 billion in 1984. The share of national defense in GNP increased from 4.9 percent in 1979 to 6 percent in 1984. Further increases are projected for the future.

Sources of Growth in Expenditures

The rapid growth since 1960 in nondefense expenditure was largely accounted for by increases in transfer payments. Figure 2.6 shows what accounts for the increased transfer payments. Social Security and other retirement programs have increased from 17 percent of the federal expenditures in 1960 to an estimated 33 percent of federal expenditures in 1983. By 1983, medicare payments had increased to an estimated 7 percent of federal expenditures. These sharp increases have caused a crisis in both areas and have motivated a reexamination of the role of the government in each.

These programs are sometimes referred to as **middle-class entitlement** programs, because the main beneficiaries are the middle class, and benefits are provided not on the basis of needs but because the beneficiary satisfies certain eligibility standards (e.g., age). As soon as they satisfy these criteria, they become **entitled** to receive the benefits.

Thus during the period 1960–1980 there was a marked increase in the overall size of the government (relative to GNP) and a marked change in the composition of the government expenditures, with socially oriented programs and redistributive programs increasing while defense and other civilian programs declined.

The period since 1980 has seen some reversal in these patterns. The Reagan administration accelerated the military build-up that began under Carter. It was not successful, however, in lowering transfer programs as a whole,

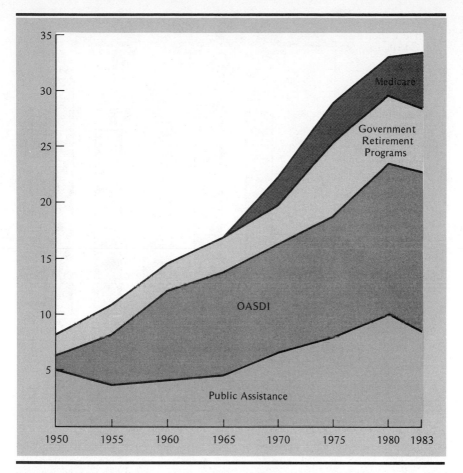

2.6 GOVERNMENT TRANSFER PROGRAMS AS A PERCENTAGE OF TOTAL GOVERNMENT EXPENDITURE Since 1950, government transfer programs have grown from less than 10 percent of total government expenditure to more than 30 percent, with the bulk of the increase accounted for by social security (OASDI). This figure includes as transfer programs some expenditures, such as government retirement programs, that might properly by thought of as deferred compensations. It does not include some of the redistributive programs we identified earlier. (Public assistance programs include all items listed in Table 2.2 except grants to nonprofit institutions and students.) It does show, however, the major sources of increase in transfer payments. SOURCE: *European Economic Community Reports,* 1983; *Survey of Current Business,* 1982.

but public assistance programs were decreased, while social security and medicare continued their growth, essentially unchanged. Nondefense purchases of goods and services decreased significantly, while interest payments increased, due both to the rising debt and to the high interest rates.

Comparison of Expenditures across Countries

Still, one needs to keep these figures in perspective. The share of government appears to be smaller in the United States than in most other Western countries (Figure 2.7), and its relative growth has been much smaller than

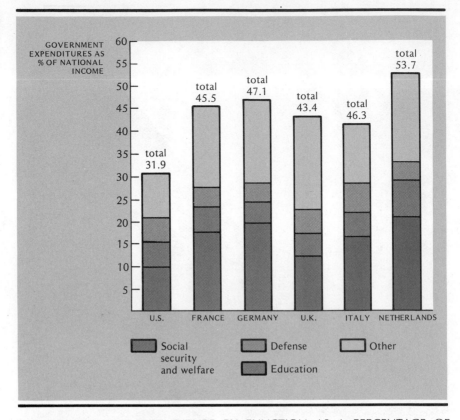

2.7 GOVERNMENT EXPENDITURE BY FUNCTION AS A PERCENTAGE OF NATIONAL INCOME, 1978 In spite of the growth in transfer payments expenditures in the United States, we see here that they represent the smallest percentage in comparison to five other industrial countries. SOURCE: *OECD Historical Statistics*, 1960–1980; *U.N. International Statistics*, 1980

in most other industrialized countries. The contrast is more dramatic if we take into account differences in national income. There appears to be a slight tendency for countries with higher per capita incomes to have a relatively large public sector, as Figure 2.8 illustrates. Among the countries with the ten highest per capita incomes, the share of public expenditures in the United States was lowest. Because defense expenditures play a larger role in the United States, the relative size of nondefense expenditures is particularly low, viewed from this international perspective.[14]

GOVERNMENT REVENUES

Now that we have examined what the government spends its money on, we turn to the methods by which government raises revenue to pay for these

---

[14]Comparisons across countries always need to be treated with caution. Particular problems are raised by the treatment of public enterprises. The fact that tax expenditures are relatively more important may result in an understatement of the "effective" relative size of the public sector in the United States.

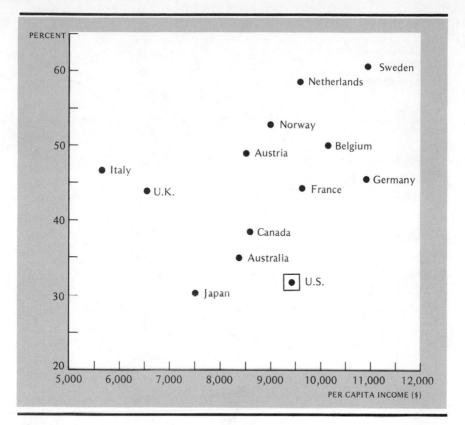

PERCENT

60 — ● Sweden
● Netherlands

● Norway

50 — ● Austria ● Belgium

● Italy ● Germany

● U.K. ● France

40 —

● Canada

● Australia

□ U.S.

30 — ● Japan

20 —

5,000   6,000   7,000   8,000   9,000   10,000   11,000   12,000

PER CAPITA INCOME ($)

2.8   GOVERNMENT OUTLAYS AS A PERCENTAGE OF NATIONAL INCOME Compared to other industrial countries with similar per capita incomes, U.S. government outlays rank rather low as a percentage of national income. In this and the next figure, national income is measured by gross domestic product, which equals gross national product minus income earned. SOURCE: *Council of Economic Advisors, Economic Indicators*, 1964, 1980.

expenditures. The government levies a variety of taxes. When the revenues that it receives from taxes are less than its planned expenditures, it must either cut back expenditures or borrow the difference.[15]

Federal Taxation

The federal government relies on five major forms of taxation: the individual income tax, payroll taxes (social security), corporate income taxes, excise taxes (taxes on specific commodities, such as gasoline, cigarettes, airline tickets, and alcohol), and customs taxes (taxes levied on selected imported goods).[16] The individual income tax is the single largest source of tax revenue for the federal government, accounting for almost half of government revenues in 1984. Social Security taxes accounted for another 36 percent, the corporation

[15] In many countries, when there is a gap between expenditures and revenues, the difference is financed by printing money. This is how the Continental Congress financed the revolutionary war. (The expression "not worth a continental" arose from the fact that the currency was not highly valued.)

[16] The estate and gift tax, while it may not raise much revenue, may have important effects on the economy.

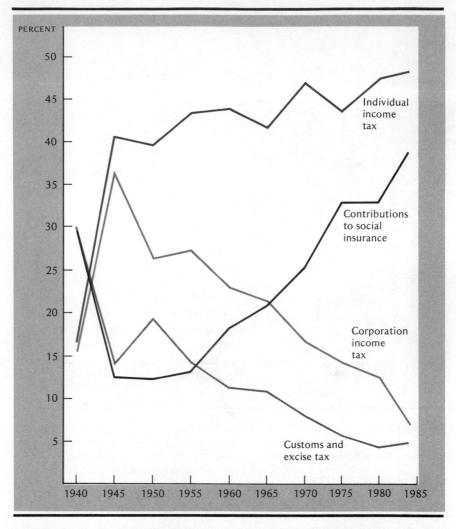

2.9 DISTRIBUTION OF FEDERAL BUDGET RECEIPTS BY SOURCE The two main sources of federal receipts are the individual income tax and the social security tax. The corporation income tax's role has dwindled to nearly nothing. SOURCE: *Economic Report of the President, 1984.*

tax 8 percent and customs and excise taxes accounting for approximately 6 percent of government revenue.

Just as there has been a marked shift in the composition of expenditures over the past fifty years, so too has there been a marked change in the source of government revenue, as Figure 2.9 shows. Prior to 1913, the federal government did not impose any income tax on individuals. Indeed, such taxes had been declared to be unconstitutional. By 1927 the individual income tax accounted for 25 percent of government tax revenue, and by 1960 it amounted to 44 percent; since then the percentage has increased only slightly. The corporation tax has played a decreasingly important role, from 36 percent in 1927, to 23 percent in 1960, and to 8 percent in 1984.

At one time excise taxes and customs were the major source of revenue

for the federal government, providing 95 percent of the revenues at the turn
of the century. Today they are relatively unimportant. On the other hand, the payroll tax has increased from 18 percent in 1960 to 36 percent in 1984.

State and Local Government

The sources of revenue for the states and localities are markedly different. The federal government supplies approximately one-fifth of state and local revenue. Much of this is directed at specific programs like road construction, bilingual education, vocational education, and libraries; during the late 1960s and 1970s the federal government provided substantial unrestricted funds, under a program referred to as General Revenue Sharing.

As Figure 2.10 shows, states and localities used to rely almost exclusively on property taxes, but they have come to rely increasingly on sales tax and

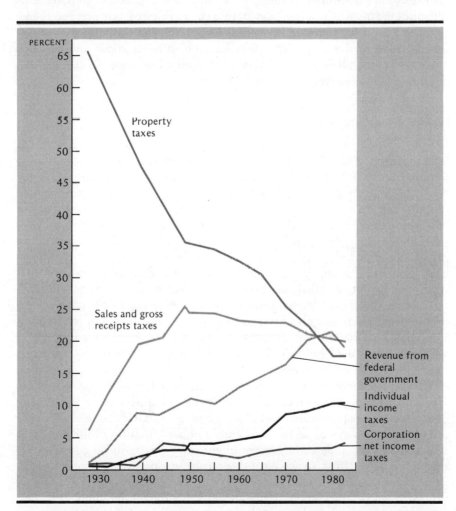

2.10 DISTRIBUTION OF STATE AND LOCAL GOVERNMENT RECEIPTS BY SOURCE We see the declining role played by property taxes in state and local receipts, and the increasing role played by income taxes and revenue grants from the federal government. SOURCE: *Economic Report of the President, 1984; Budget of the U.S. Government, 1975, 1984.*

income taxes, both on individuals and corporations, as a source of revenue. In 1983 the sales tax was the single largest source of revenue, amounting to just over 22 percent of the revenue; the property tax was the next most important tax, raising 19 percent of the revenue; while the individual income tax raised 12.3 percent and the corporate tax raised 3.3 percent of the revenue.

Comparison of Taxation across Countries

The patterns of taxation differ from country to country. Although social security taxes, for instance, have increased markedly in the United States, they are still lower than in many Western European countries. In France, for example, they account for 40 percent of revenues. While the individual income tax is less important in most European countries (it represents 40 percent of revenues in England and less than 20 percent in France), taxes on goods and services are more important. For most, the value-added tax (a tax imposed on the value of the output of a firm less the value of goods and services purchased from other firms) is a major source of revenue, in many cases accounting for a quarter of government revenue.

Deficit Financing

When expenditures exceed tax revenues there is a **deficit.** The size of the federal deficit, both in dollar terms (approximately $200 billion) and, more importantly, as a fraction of GNP (6.4 percent) and of the budget (17.7 percent), reached an all-time high (for peacetime) in 1984. The increasing size of these deficits in the 1980s caused great consternation both in and outside of Washington. Because of the federal government's ability to tax, these deficits do not cause the same kinds of problems that large debts incurred by private firms or individuals would. But there is a concern that the deficits contribute to inflation, that they lead to higher interest rates and lower levels of investment, and that they put an unfair burden on future generations.

The deficit is the *additional* value of the debt incurred by the government in any year. There has also been increasing concern about the total size of the debt. Because the government has had large deficits for a number of years, the total debt held by the public has increased markedly, reaching more than $1.3 trillion in 1984.

To assess the significance of the debt and deficit, we need to put them into some perspective. Figure 2.11 shows the deficit, both as a percentage of government expenditures and as a percentage of GNP. As always, there are alternative ways of seeing the same number. Because of inflation, the real value of the outstanding government debt was reduced considerably during the late 1970s. To see what this means, assume you promised to pay someone $100 next year. If the prices of all goods and services rose by 10 percent, that person could purchase next year with $99 the same goods that he could have purchased with $90 this year. The "real value" of what you have to pay him has declined. Figure 2.12 traces the real value of the government debt. During the period 1977–1980, when there were large deficits, the real value of the government debt held by the public fell by more

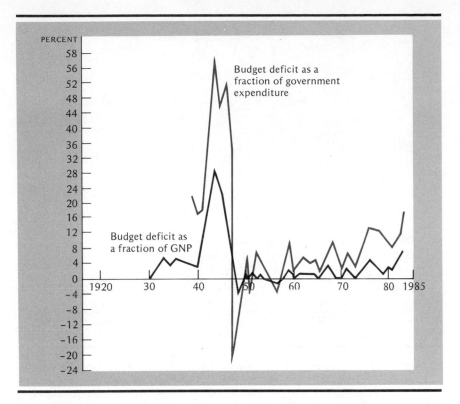

2.11 FEDERAL BUDGET DEFICIT AS A PERCENTAGE OF GNP AND GOVERN-MENT EXPENDITURES Both have increased markedly since 1980. SOURCE: *Budget of the U.S. Government,* 1985.

than $14 billion (in 1967 prices). Thus, from this perspective the increase in real deficits during the period 1980–1984 is more dramatic.

TAXES AND THE CONSTITUTION

The issue of taxation was very much in the mind of the founders of the Republic. Indeed, the Revolution began as a tax revolt, with the Boston Tea Party, a protest against the tax on tea (which was just one of the taxes to which they were objecting), and with the slogan "Taxation without representation is tyranny." The first article of the Constitution provides that "The Congress shall have power to levy and collect Taxes, Duties, Imposts, and Excises, to pay the Debts and provide for the Common Defense and General Welfare of the United States."

Three restrictions were imposed: the government could not levy export taxes, "all tax Duties, Imposts and Excises" had to be "uniform throughout the United States" (referred to as the uniformity clause), and "no capitation or other direct tax shall be levied unless in proportion to the Census of Enumeration herein directed to be taken" (referred to as the apportionment clause). (A capitation tax is a tax levied on each person. These taxes are also called head taxes or poll taxes.) The intent of these provisions was to ensure

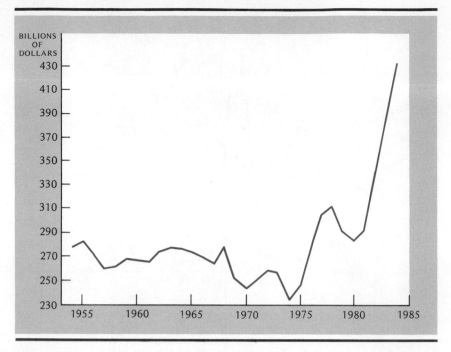

2.12   REAL DEBT HELD BY PUBLIC IN 1967 PRICES In real terms the debt held by the public has grown enormously since 1974. Debt held by government agencies, including the Federal Reserve Board and the social security trust funds, is excluded. SOURCE: *Economic Report of the President*, 1982.

that no group of states took advantage of the other states; the restriction on export duties, for instance, was enacted because the Southern states were worried lest the Northern states impose a duty on the export of cotton, the burden of which (though uniformly applied) would fall on Southern producers. Similarly, the richer states were worried that the poorer states might force them to pay a disproportionate—from their view—share of the taxes, and thus the only direct tax that was allowed was a head tax.

The writers of the Constitution rightly anticipated that issues of discriminatory taxation of one group of states might split the Union, but they did not fully anticipate the range of instruments by which such discrimination could be effected. Tariffs not only raise revenue, but they increase the prices received by domestic producers. The issue of tariffs on goods manufactured in the North—effectively, a subsidy to Northern producers paid for by the South— was one of the most divisive issues during the period preceding the Civil War.

Though the issues may not be so divisive, the conflicts are still present. Congress recently enacted a tax on oil (the so-called Windfall Profits tax), which exempted the oil produced on Alaska's Northern Slope. Texas and the other large oil-producing states viewed the tax to be discriminatory, to violate the uniformity clause of the Constitution. The U.S. District Court agreed with them, but upon appeal, the Supreme Court ruled in 1983 that the distinction between "North Slope" oil and other oil was not an arbitrary distinction and that, accordingly, Congress did not violate the uniformity provision.

The provision restricting direct taxes did, however, prove to be a problem. An income tax was first imposed during the Civil War. In the first court ruling in 1880, the income tax was considered an excise tax rather than a direct tax, and thus did not fall under the apportionment rule. But in 1895 the Court reversed itself, and in 1913 Congress, in anticipation of the need for funds for financing a war, passed the Sixteenth Amendment: "Congress shall have the power to levy and collect taxes on incomes, from whatever sources derived, without apportionment among the several states, and without regard to census or enumeration."

The apportionment provision still may restrict Congress's ability to impose taxes. Several countries impose national property taxes or wealth taxes. These are likely to be considered direct taxes, and thus precluded in the United States by the apportionment provision.

THE FEDERAL GOVERNMENT'S BUDGETARY PROCESS

The federal government, in its yearly budget, looks closely at planned expenditures and anticipated revenues. The Constitution provides only a bare outline for the budgetary process. Tax and appropriations bills must begin in the House of Representatives; as with all legislation, enactment requires a majority vote of both Houses and the signature of the president. The president may veto any bill, and Congress can override his veto by a two-thirds vote.

This description does not reflect adequately the process by which budgetary decisions get made and the central role of the president in formulating the budget. As we noted, federal expenditures in 1983 amounted to $819.7 billion. There are thousands of government agencies, most of which claim they need more money. There must be some systematic method of reviewing these needs and ensuring that the total amount allocated to the different agencies is roughly commensurate with the revenue raised through taxation. The government agency that is responsible for doing this is the Office of Management and Budget (OMB). The OMB formulates a budget, proposing how much to spend on each agency, how much it will raise through taxes, and what the deficit or surplus will be. The president sends the OMB proposal to Congress.

Congress's assessment of the nation's priorities often differs markedly from that of the president, particularly when the two are of different parties. The difficulty facing Congress is to come up with an alternative budget. In the past, it would take up appropriations for each area separately; that is, it might first pass a defense budget, then a road budget, then a foreign-aid budget, etc. It was difficult, in this process, to ensure that the total expenditures equaled the revenues and that priorities were assessed in any systematic way. Congress has attempted to remedy this by setting up a Congressional Budget Office and a procedure (with a specified timetable) for formulating a congressional budget. This begins with an initial congressional resolution, calling for an overall level of spending and tax, and a breakdown by major categories. This serves as a guide to the separate appropriations committees, considering bills in each of the separate areas. After these bills are passed, Congress then looks at the overall budget again, seeing whether the totals fit within the earlier targets and, if not, deciding whether to change the targets or scale back some programs.

The process is a cumbersome one, but there is no readily apparent alternative, short of delegating more authority to the president, something that Congress, quite rightly in the view of most observers, is reluctant to do.

The concern with the budgetary process is not only that it is cumbersome but that it fails to produce a balanced budget. Prior to the Great Depression it was thought that the president should present a balanced budget, except in times of war. The development of Keynesian economics led to the view that it might be desirable for the government to run a deficit in a recession, to stimulate the economy. But there remained a consensus that in a nonrecessionary, nonwar year, the president should propose a balanced budget. While President Reagan was successful in getting a major tax reduction enacted in 1981, he failed to obtain corresponding reductions in expenditures; as we already noted, this led to record deficits.

The Gramm-Rudman Act

In 1985, popular enthusiasm for balanced budgets led Congress to pass an act, which President Reagan signed into law, called the Gramm-Rudman Act, after its sponsors, Senator Phil Gramm of Texas and Senator Warren Rudman of New Hampshire. The bill calls for automatic reductions in expenditures when the deficit exceeds a certain critical level, aimed at achieving a balanced budget by 1991. The act relies on the threat of these automatic cuts as a disciplinary device. To avoid setting them in play, it is thought, the president and Congress will work harder on each year's budget to keep revenues and expenditures at the same level. If they should fail, the Gramm-Rudman Act sets in motion across-the-board cuts in most areas of expenditure, along with cancellation of some cost-of-living increases. Criticism of the act has come from many directions: those who question its constitutionality, on the grounds that it interferes with the separation of powers; those who worry that it deprives the government of needed flexibility; and those who feel that the incentive to find a way around the act's stern provisions will lead to loopholes, rendering its intent meaningless. We shall describe below, for instance, some methods by which government can easily change the apparent size of the deficit. The Gramm-Rudman Act may simply encourage the use of these tricks.

Impounding Funds

The failure of the president and Congress to come up with a budget that is in balance is perhaps the most important source of concern over the budgetary process. But it is not the only source of controversy. In recent years, there has been some controversy about the extent of presidential budgetary powers. Though it seems clear that the president has no right to spend funds that Congress does not authorize, there is some debate about whether he has the right not to spend funds Congress has authorized him to spend; that is, can the president impound funds at his own discretion? President Nixon attempted to impound funds from the Office of Economic Opportunity, which had the responsibility for running many of the poverty programs. Allowing the president to impound funds is equivalent to granting him a line veto (to veto a particular provision of a law, rather than the whole law), something that Congress has been loath to do. Moreover, by impounding funds, the president can override the wishes of Congress, even if Congress has overridden a presidential veto.

The Function of Budgets

The budget of the government measures the cash flow, the annual receipts and expenditures of the government, just as the income statement of a corporation describes its receipts (sales) and its expenditures. The budget gives a picture of what the government is doing, where its money is going, and where it is coming from.

But in assessing the state of a private corporation, far more important than the cash flow accounts are the capital accounts. These describe the assets of the firm, and its liabilities (what it owes to other individuals and firms). The difference between the two is the *net worth* of the firm. If the liabilities of a firm are increasing faster than the assets, its net worth is decreasing; an investor will be concerned about the future well-being of the firm. On the other hand, a firm with a large and increasing debt but with assets increasing at a rate more than matching these increases in liabilities is likely to be viewed as being in a strong financial position.

Unfortunately, the government does not publish a good set of capital accounts. Figure 2.13 shows that between 1967 and 1977, if we ignore social

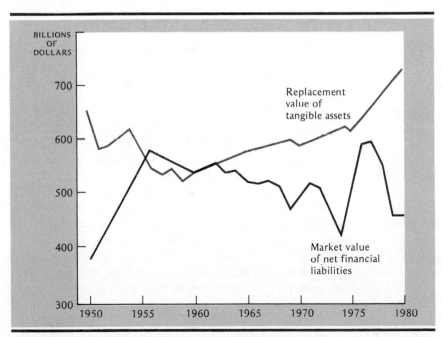

2.13 REPLACEMENT VALUE OF ASSETS AND MARKET VALUE OF NET FINANCIAL LIABILITIES OF THE FEDERAL GOVERNMENT source: *Economic Report of the President,* 1982.

security, there was a slight increase in the difference between the market value of net financial liabilities of the government and the replacement value of its tangible assets. It should be noted that the government's assets, representing the results of its past investments, were decreasing in value in real terms. The deterioration of the public capital stock—including our roads, highways, and bridges—has become a source of concern in recent years.

A complete accounting of the assets and liabilities should include, of course, the value not only of buildings, structures, and equipment ("tangible assets") but also "nontangible" assets, the most important of which consists of investments in the future productivity of Americans (what is called "human capital"), through public education and training programs, and of investments in research and development (R&D), which increase the productivity of the entire economy.

The absence of a capital account has some serious implications for economic policy. It creates a systematic bias, particularly in periods of recession where the government faces a large deficit, to cut back on investment expenditures, including investments in human capital and R&D, the consequences of which will not be felt for some time in the future. Similarly, when the government sells some of its land or leases some oil fields, it appears in the current budget as revenue; there appears to be no cost associated with raising revenue in this way. A capital account would make it clear that the assets of the United States government are thereby decreased.[17]

Playing Tricks with the Data on Government Activities

The federal budget sets out the current expenditures and receipts of the government. As we have seen, however, it provides only a partial view of the size of the government and the effect of the government on economic activity. As a result, one must treat with caution any comparisions of the size of the public sector either over time or across countries.

We have already discussed how tax expenditures may result in misleading conclusions concerning not only the size of the public sector but the composition of its expenditure. If the federal government wishes to hide the size of its subsidies to business, it provides tax credits to businesses; it hides the extent of its subsidies to states and localities by providing "tax expenditures" in the form of tax deductions on the personal income tax for state and local taxes and tax exemption for interest on state and local bonds.

We have also noted a second method by which the budget may be manipulated: by selling assets one obtains revenues, while the cost, the reduction in the assets of the government, is not recorded. The converse of this is to provide subsidies with no current financial outlay. Loan guarantees are one example. The outlays occur in the future if there is a default. Increasing social security benefits has some effect on current financial outlays, but the primary burden lies sometime in the future (in some later administration).

---

[17] There is some controversy concerning the construction of capital accounts. The question is, what should be included in the liabilities, what in the assets. The government has the ability to tax, and in this sense it is fundamentally different from a private corporation. In one view, all potential sources of revenues should be included in the asset side. Similarly, there are questions about which commitments of the government should be included as liabilities. Should one, for instance, include future social security obligations as a liability?

One can decrease the overall size of the public sector (but not the deficit) by setting up independent agencies and enterprises. It makes no real difference whether the post office is a department of the U.S. Government or a separate "corporation" receiving a subsidy from the federal treasury. But if it is a department, all of its income and all of its expenditures may be included in the government budget; if it is a separate enterprise, only the deficit (the difference between its expenditures and income) is recorded. Cross-country comparisons of the size of the public sector are difficult, partly because countries differ in the practices they follow, and partly because there are many enterprises that are neither purely public nor purely private. Should an enterprise in which the government owns 51 percent of the shares—a controlling interest—be classified as public or private?

Though these problems make it difficult to make precise comparisons—and provide considerable room for politicians to choose statistics to support their views—the changes in the level and structure of expenditures and taxation in the United States over the past twenty-five to fifty years have been sufficiently marked that there can be little question about the major observations that we have made:

1) There has been a marked increase in the size of the public sector.
2) There has been a marked increase in transfer payments.
3) There has been a marked increase in the role of the individual income tax as a source of revenue.

SUMMARY

1. The government performs many roles:
   a) It provides the basic legal framework within which we live.
   b) It regulates economic activities. It encourages some activities by subsidizing them and discourages others by taxing them.
   c) It produces goods and provides credit and loan guarantees and insurance.
   d) It consumes (uses) goods and services.
   e) It redistributes income, transferring income from some individuals to others.
   f) It provides social insurance, for retirement, unemployment, disabilities, and medical care for the aged.

2. The size of the government relative to GNP is much larger now than it was thirty years ago. Much of this is accounted for by increased transfer payments and social insurance.

3. The relative size of the public sector in the United States is smaller than in most other Western European countries.

4. The five major areas of government expenditures are defense, social insurance, income maintenance, education, and health. Together, these account for 70 percent of governmental expenditures in 1983.

5. The major source of revenue for the federal government is the individual income tax, followed by the payroll tax, corporation tax and customs and excise taxes.

6. The major sources of revenue for the states are the sales tax, the property tax and the income tax.

7. The Constitution provides the basic framework for the government of the United States. It provides some restrictions on the taxes that can be imposed but no effective restrictions on what the government can spend its money on.

8. The government attempts, through the budgetary process, to ensure that there is some balance between expenditures and receipts and that expenditures are allocated according to national priorities.

KEY CONCEPTS

Privatization

Nationalized

Value added

Income Tax

Social Insurance

Social Security (payroll) tax

Constant dollars

Real expenditures

Social insurance

Transfers

Tax expenditures

Excise taxes

Custom duties

Deficit

QUESTIONS AND PROBLEMS

1. To see what is going on, economists often "adjust" the data to reflect changes in the economy. For instance, in the text, we discussed the adjustments made for inflation. Another adjustment that is frequently made is to take into account the increase in population. What adjustments might you make in looking at education expenditures? At social security expenditures?

2. In each of the following areas, give one or more (where possible) examples in which the government is involved as a regulator; a producer; a consumer (purchaser of goods and services distributed directly to individuals):
   a) education
   b) utilities
   c) transportation
   d) credit markets
   e) insurance markets
   f) food
   g) housing

3. In each of the following areas, give an example of a tax expenditure and a conventional expenditure. Explain how the same results could be obtained by converting the tax expenditure into a conventional expenditure:
   a) medicine
   b) housing
   c) education

4. Assume you were president and your planned expenditures exceeded your receipts. Describe some of the tricks you might use to reduce the apparent budget deficit while maintaining current levels of services and transfers (subsidies).

   Assume, on the other hand, that you had run on a platform of keeping the growth in total governmental expenditures down to 3 percent. Once in office, you see, however, that you would like expenditures to rise by 5 percent. How might you do this while appearing to keep your election promises?

3

Welfare Economics

One of the central concerns of public-sector economics is evaluating alternative proposals for changes in public policy. To do this, we economists have to describe the consequences of each policy and, on the basis of this, make some judgments about which policy is most desirable. For instance, a few years ago the social security program faced a financial crisis: projected payouts exceeded tax revenues by $1 trillion, according to one calculation. One proposal was to raise social security taxes. Another was to reduce benefits. Still another entailed postponing the retirement age. A fourth involved paying for the deficit out of general revenues. Different individuals would have been affected differently by each of these alternatives. Reducing future benefits would hurt future recipients. Postponing the age for eligibility from sixty-five to sixty-seven would adversely affect those who would like to retire at 65. Tax increases would make those who are currently working worse off.

Economists focus on two attributes of any program under discussion: its effect on economic efficiency and its distributional consequences. Does the program promote (or at least not interfere with) economic efficiency, and is the program fair? What is meant by these terms? Is there a way of quantifying the efficiency effects or the distributional consequences?

Welfare economics is concerned with the formulation and application of criteria by which judgments about the desirability of alternative proposals may be made. This chapter is concerned with the basic conceptual issues; in Chapter 10 we shall show how economists have attempted to develop quantitative measures of these effects. In Chapter 4 we show how economists have used these basic concepts to discuss the efficiency of private markets and the role of government.

EFFICIENCY AND DISTRIBUTION TRADE-OFFS

Consider a simple economy with two individuals, whom we shall refer to as Robinson Crusoe and Friday. Assume initially that Robinson Crusoe has 10 oranges, while Friday has only 2. This seems inequitable. Assume, therefore, that we play the role of government and attempt to transfer 4 oranges from Robinson Crusoe to Friday, but in the process 1 orange gets lost. Hence Robinson Crusoe ends up with 6 oranges, and Friday with 5. We have eliminated most of the inequity, but in the process the total number of oranges available has been diminished. Thus we see a trade-off between efficiency—the total number of oranges available—and equity.

The trade-off between equity and efficiency is at the heart of many discussions of public policy. The trade-off is often represented as in Figure 3.1. To get more equity, some amount of efficiency must be sacrificed. Two questions are debated. First, there is disagreement about the nature of the trade-off. To reduce inequality, how much efficiency do we have to give up? Will 1 or 2 oranges be lost in the process of transferring oranges from Robinson to Friday? For instance, attempting to reduce inequality by progressive taxation is commonly regarded as giving rise to work disincentives, thereby reducing efficiency.

Second, there are disagreements on how much value should be assigned to a decrease in inequality, and how much value should be assigned to a decrease in efficiency. Some people claim that inequality is the central problem of society, and society should simply minimize the extent of inequality, regardless of the efficiency consequences. Others claim that efficiency is the central issue. Still others claim that in the long run, the best way to help the poor is not to worry about how the pie is to be divided but to "increase" the

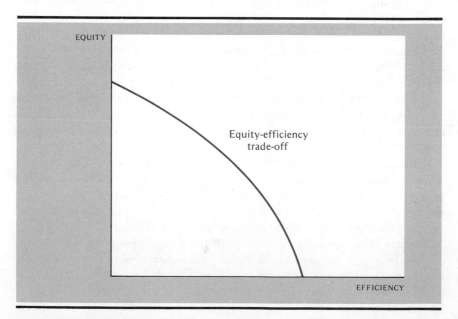

EQUITY

Equity-efficiency
trade-off

EFFICIENCY

3.1 EQUITY-EFFICIENCY TRADE OFF To get more equity, some amount of efficiency must, in general, be sacrificed.

size of the pie, to grow as rapidly as possible, so there are more goods for everyone.

Maximizing efficiency is frequently equated with maximizing the value of national income; a program is said to introduce an inefficiency if it reduces national income, say through discouraging work or investment. And a program is said to promote equality if it transfers resources from someone who is richer to someone who is poorer.

Although this provides a first approximation, economists have devoted considerable attention to assessing the circumstances in which using these measures may be misleading or inapplicable. For instance, one program may make the very poor and the very rich worse off and the middle-income group better off. Has inequality increased or decreased? Suppose the government increased taxes, and squandered the proceeds, but individuals, in order to maintain the same standard of living, worked harder and longer than they had previously. National income, as conventionally measured, would go up, but "efficiency"—as we normally think of it—has decreased.

The measures chosen often have an important impact on policy. A common measure of inequality that has been used during the past twenty-five years is the Poverty Index, which measures the fraction of the population whose income falls below some critical level (defined as the poverty level). Though there is considerable debate about how this poverty line should be defined, this does not concern us here.

What does concern us is the fact that government officials have often evaluated alternative programs in terms of their effect on the Poverty Index. Thus, assume the government was attempting to choose between two programs, one of which moved some individuals who were just below the poverty line to a level of income just above it, and the other of which increased the income of some very poor individuals, but not enough to move them over the poverty line. The government might be led to conclude that the first project was preferable, since it reduced "measured" poverty; while the second program left the number of individuals below the poverty line unchanged: it had no effect on "measured" poverty.

This example illustrates another feature of most indices: they contain implicit value judgments. Implicitly, the Poverty Index says that changes in the distribution of income among the very poor (those below the poverty line) and changes in the distribution of income among the very well off (those above the poverty line) are not as important as changes that move individuals from below the poverty line to above the poverty line. Although virtually any measure of inequality contains some implicit value judgments, in recent years economists have been concerned with bringing these value judgments out into the open.

Are there circumstances in which policy evaluations can be made without making value judgments? Economists have identified one important set of circumstances in which this may be done.

PARETO OPTIMALITY

Although, as we have noted, most policy changes involve some individuals becoming better off while others are made worse off, occasionally there are changes that make some better off without making anyone worse off. Such changes are referred to as **Pareto improvements,** after the great Italian economist-sociologist Vilfredo Pareto. When there are no further changes that make someone better off without at the same time making someone else worse off, we say that the resource allocation is **Pareto optimal,** or Pareto efficient.

Assume, for instance, that the government is contemplating building a bridge. Those who wish to use the bridge are willing to pay more than enough in tolls to cover the costs of construction and maintenance. The construction of this bridge is likely to be a Pareto improvement. We use the term "likely" because there are always others who might be adversely affected by the construction of the bridge. For example, if the bridge changes the traffic flow, some stores might find that their business is decreased, and they are worse off. Or an entire neighborhood may be affected by the noise of bridge traffic and the shadows cast by the bridge superstructure.

Frequently on summer days, or at rush hour, large backlogs develop at toll booths on toll roads and bridges. If tolls were raised at those times and the proceeds used to finance additional toll booths or more peak-time toll collectors, everyone might be better off. People would prefer to pay a slightly higher price in return for less waiting. But it is possible that even this change might not be a Pareto improvement: among those waiting in line may be some unemployed individuals who are relatively little concerned about the waste of time but who are concerned about spending more money on tolls.

Economists are always on the lookout for Pareto improvements. The belief that any such improvements should be instituted is referred to as the **Pareto principle.**

"Packages" of changes together may constitute a Pareto improvement, where each change alone might not. Thus, while reducing the tariff on steel would not be a Pareto improvement (since the producers of steel would be worse off), it might be possible to reduce the tariff on steel, increase income taxes slightly, and use the proceeds to finance a subsidy to the steel industry; such a combination of changes might make everyone in the country better off (and make those abroad, the foreign exporters of steel, also better off).

Pareto Optimality and Individualism

The criteron of Pareto optimality has an important property upon which we should comment. It is *individualistic,* in two senses. First, it is concerned only with each individual's welfare, not with the relative well-being of different individuals. It is not concerned explicitly with inequality. Thus, a change that led the rich to be much better off but left the poor unaffected would still be a Pareto improvement. Some people, however, think, that increasing the gap between the rich and the poor is undesirable. They believe that it gives rise, for instance, to undesirable social tensions. Many less-developed countries often go through periods of rapid growth during which all major segments of society become better off; but the income of the rich grows more rapidly than that of the poor. To assess these changes, is it enough simply to say that everyone is better off? There is no agreement on the answer to this question.

Second, it is each individual's perception of his own welfare that counts. This is consistent with the general principle of **consumer sovereignty,** which holds that each individual is the best judge of his needs and wants, of what is in his own best interests.

Consumer Sovereignty versus Paternalism

Most Americans believe strongly in consumer sovereignty; yet there are some important limitations that should be noted. Parents often believe they know what is in the best interests of their children. They believe—and there is some evidence for this—that children are not aware of and/or do not take into account fully all the consequences of their actions; that they are often myopic, paying excessive attention to the short-run pleasures relative to the long-run costs or benefits. They may decide to go to a movie rather than study for an important economics exam, or quit school to earn enough income to buy a car, thus jeopardizing their long-run life prospects. While governments can do little about the first problem, they do try to do something about the second: most states require children to remain at school until they are sixteen years old.

The belief that adults may be shortsighted and need guidance from the government is called **paternalism.** There are elements of paternalism in a number of government policies; for instance the attempt of the government to discourage smoking reflects the belief that many adults do not fully comprehend the consequences of their actions; Prohibition in the 1920s was similarly based on the belief that drinking was bad but that individuals would not do what was in their own best interest unless restrained by the government. Laws concerning the use of marijuana fall in the same category.

There are many who believe that it is inappropriate for the government to play a paternalistic role, that in evaluating public policies, only individuals' own perceptions of how those policies affect their welfare should be employed. Though there may occasionally be a case that merits a paternalistic role for the government, these economists argue that it is virtually impossible to distinguish such cases from those where it is not. And they worry that once the government assumes a paternalistic role, special-interest groups will attempt to use government to foster their own beliefs about how individuals should act or what they should consume.

Still, there are some important instances where there is widespread—but not universal—agreement that evaluations of government programs should not be based simply on individualistic assessments: the large number of laws restricting discriminatory practices—fair housing, equal opportunity in employment, etc.—are perhaps the most important illustrations of this.

PARETO OPTIMALITY AND DISTRIBUTION

The most severe limitation of the Pareto principle is that it provides no guidance concerning issues of income distribution. Most government programs (when their costs are taken into account) benefit some individuals at the expense of others. One way of seeing what guidance the Pareto principle can and cannot provide is in terms of the **utility possibilities curve.**

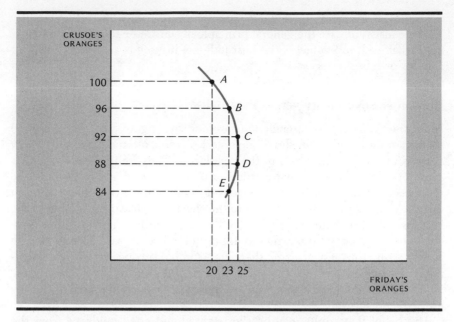

3.2   THE OPPORTUNITY SET The possible combinations of oranges enjoyed by Crusoe and Friday, if, as we attempt to transfer more oranges to Friday, more oranges get lost in the process. Point *D* is Pareto inefficient: Crusoe is better off at *C*, and Friday is no worse off.

The Utility Function and Marginal Utility

Returning to our example of Robinson Crusoe and his friend Friday, assume now that Crusoe has initially 100 oranges and Friday only 20, as shown by point *A* in Figure 3.2. Assume, further, that as we try to take more oranges away from Crusoe and give them to Friday, we lose more than a proportionate number of oranges. Thus, if we try to take away 4 oranges, Friday gets 3 (point *B*). But if we try to transfer 8 oranges, we lose 3 oranges, so Friday gets only 5 more (Point *C*). The set of possible combinations is called the **opportunity set.** Notice that beyond that point *C*, even if we try to take more away from Robinson, Friday gets no additional oranges (he can only carry a certain number of oranges). We say that a point such as *D* is Pareto inefficient: moving to *C* makes Robinson better off but Friday no worse off. It is even possible that in trying to carry more oranges, he succeeds in carrying fewer. Thus, if he tries to carry 16, he drops all but 3. At *E*, both Robinson Crusoe and Friday are worse off than at *C*.

Often changes engendered by a policy are complex. Assume the government increases taxes to supply some public amenity. The individual may work harder (his leisure decreases) and consume less, and from these changes he is worse off; at the same time he is better off, because of his access to the public amenity. We summarize these changes in terms of their effect on the individual's welfare, or *utility*. If these changes make the individual better off, meaning that he prefers the new situation to the old, we say that his utility has increased.

Thus, as we give Friday more and more oranges, his utility increases. The relationship between the number of oranges and his level of utility we call

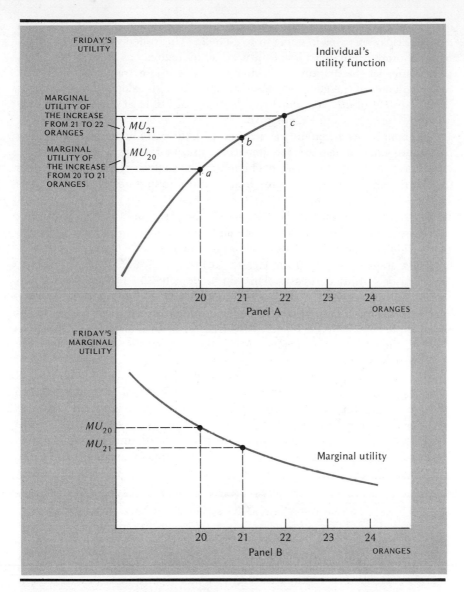

3.3 THE UTILITY FUNCTION AND MARGINAL UTILITY (A) *The utility function.* As we give Friday more oranges, his utility increases, but each additional orange gives him less extra utility. (B) *Marginal utility* decreases as the number of oranges given to Friday increases, corresponding to the decreasing slope of the utility function.

the **utility function;** it is depicted in Figure 3.3A. The extra utility he gets from an extra orange we call his **marginal utility.** Thus, we have denoted the marginal utility from increasing Friday's oranges from 20 to 21 by MU_{20}, and we have denoted the marginal utility from an increase from 21 to 22 oranges by MU_{21}. In each case, the marginal utility is the *slope* of the utility functions. The slope is the ratio of the change in value of utility to the change in the number of oranges; more generally the slope of a curve is calculated by dividing the change along the vertical axis by the change along the horizontal axis, when the size of the change along the horizontal axis is small.

Notice that the extra utility in going from 21 to 22 is less than the extra utility Friday receives in going from 20 to 21. This reflects the general principle of **diminishing marginal utility.** As an individual has more of anything, it becomes, at the margin, less valuable; that is, the extra gain from having one extra unit of the good becomes smaller. Thus, the slope of the line *bc* is less than that of *ab*. We plot Friday's marginal utility at each level of consumption of oranges in Figure 3.3B.

(Economists are frequently concerned with the extra benefits from shifting one more unit of a resource into one use or into another; they are concerned, in other words, with the marginal benefits. The analysis of the consequences of shifting one unit of a resource from one use to another is referred to as *marginal analysis.*)

By the same token, as we take away oranges from Crusoe, his utility decreases; and as we take away more and more oranges, the extra utility he loses from each additional loss of an orange is increased.

As we transfer oranges from Crusoe to Friday, Friday's utility increases, and Crusoe's utility decreases. This can be depicted by a *utility possibilities schedule,* which gives the utility that one individual (or group of individuals) in the economy can attain, given the levels of utility that the others have. In our simple case, with each successive transfer of an orange from Crusoe to Friday, the increment to Friday's utility becomes smaller, and the decrease in Crusoe's utility becomes larger. Thus, in moving from point *A* to *B* in Figure 3.4, and then from *B* to *C*, though we take away the same number of oranges from Crusoe in each instance, his loss in utility in moving from *B* to *C* is much greater; while Friday's gain in utility in moving from *B* to *C* is smaller than in moving from *A* to *B*, for two reasons. Even if only 1 orange were lost in going from *B* to *C* (as in going from *A* to *B*), diminishing marginal utility would imply that successive equal increments in consumption lead to

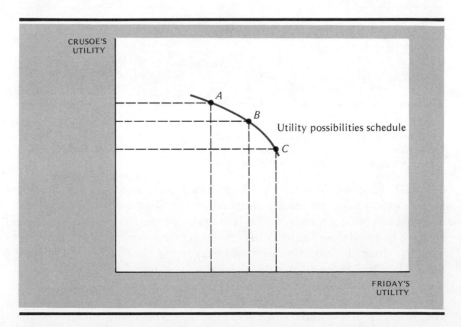

3.4   THE UTILITY POSSIBILITIES SCHEDULE FOR CRUSOE AND FRIDAY

successively smaller increments in utility. But in addition, we have hypothesized that as the government attempts to redistribute more and more income from Crusoe to Friday, a larger fraction of the oranges taken away from Crusoe is lost before Friday receives the oranges.

This is a simple case. Government policy usually affects the utility not just of two individuals but of whole groups of individuals. The government programs are more complicated than simply transferring some oranges from one individual to another. But the utility possibilities curve still provides a good conceptual framework for analyzing government policy.

The Utility Possibilities Schedule and Pareto Optimality

Consider the utility possibilities schedule shown in Figure 3.5. If resources are not efficiently allocated, the economy will be operating at a point such as I, below the utility possibilities schedule. Any change that leaves the economy at a point such as I' (above and to the right of I) is a Pareto improvement: both groups in society are better off. Any point along the utility possibilities schedule corresponds to a Pareto-optimal or Pareto-efficient resource

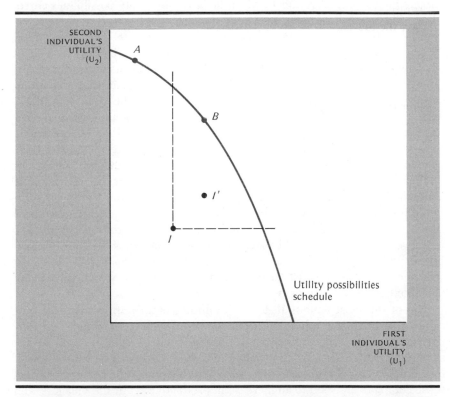

3.5 PARETO IMPROVEMENTS AND THE UTILITY POSSIBILITIES SCHEDULE The utility possibilities schedule gives the maximum utility that can be attained by the second individual, given the level of utility attained by the first. The movement from I to I' is a Pareto improvement. The movement from A to B is a movement along the utility possibilities schedule; both points are Pareto efficient. The movement from I to A is a movement from an inefficient point (I) to an efficient point (A), but it is not a Pareto improvement, since individual 1 is worse off.

allocation. No one can be made better off without someone else being made worse off.

Thus, the first question to ask in the evaluation of any public program is, does it represent a movement from an inefficient point, below the utility possibilities curve, to an efficient point, on (or at least closer to) the utility possibilities schedule? Or does it simply represent a movement along the utility possibilities schedule, entailing one individual (or group of individuals) being better off while another individual (or group of individuals) is worse off?

President Reagan seemed to believe that his 1981 tax cut would be a movement like the one from I to I'. Though higher-income individuals received proportionately larger reductions in their taxes, he believed that the stimulating effect of the tax cut would be so great that all individuals would benefit. On the other hand, the debate over whether current or future social security benefits should be decreased is largely a question of a movement along the utility possibilities schedule, such as the one from A to B; the trade-off is between the welfare of the current aged and the welfare of the future aged.

Unfortunately, the Pareto principle does not provide any criterion for ranking points, such as A and B, which lie along the utility possibilities curve. Thus it does not allow us to say whether A is preferable to B or B is preferable to A. It does not provide us with an answer to the question, Should current social security benefits be cut or future benefits be cut? Indeed, it does not even allow us to make statements concerning movements from points below the utility possibilities schedule, such as I, to points on the utility possibilities schedule, which do not lie above and to the right of I. Thus, though A is Pareto efficient and I is not, the Pareto principle does not allow us to say whether A is preferable to I or conversely, whether I is preferable to A. If a point is not Pareto efficient, we know that there must exist some change that will make everyone better off, but that is all that we know.

Many inefficiencies pose precisely this problem. Consider the example concerning increasing the tolls at a bridge during rush hour to pay for additional toll collectors, which would facilitate the flow of traffic. The value of time saved far exceeds what we would have to pay the toll collectors. The arrangement with fewer toll collectors appears to be below the utility possibilities schedule. But if we increase the number of toll collectors, financing the increase by an increase in the toll, an individual for whom time is not valuable but for whom money is will be worse off.

One of the most famous historical examples of an improvement in efficiency that led many individuals to be worse off occurred in England.[1] Earlier, each village had common land, on which any villager could graze his sheep and cattle. The fact that individuals were not charged for the use of the common land led to excessive utilization (overgrazing). The enclosure of these common lands led to an increase in productivity; but the villagers who lost the right to graze their cattle and sheep were worse off. The new equilibrium was on (or closer to) the utility possibilities schedule, but the change was not a Pareto improvement.

---

[1] See M. Weitzman and Jon S. Cohen, "A Mathematical Model of Enclosures," in J. Los and M. Los, *Mathematical Models in Economics* (London and Amsterdam: North Holland, 1974), pp. 419–31.

Pareto Optimality and the Compensation Principle

We saw earlier that it is frequently possible to design packages of changes that lead to a Pareto improvement. Steel prices in the United States are maintained by import tariffs on steel from other countries. If the government were considering lowering the tariff, it could ask consumers how much they would be willing to give up in return for a reduction in the price of steel. If the amount that they would be willing to give up exceeds the reduction in profits of the United States steel industry, then it would appear, in principle, that if we combined the lowering of the tariff with an appropriate tax on consumers, we could design a Pareto improvement. We could compensate the steel producers for the lowering of the tariff.

In practice, the required compensations are seldom made. When a new highway is built, businesses along the old highway frequently decline, but the owners of the businesses are never compensated. (Occasionally, some attempt at partial compensation is made; those who live in the vicinity of an airport that is about to be constructed, and who find that the value of their property has thereby been reduced, may receive some compensation.)

There are those who believe that, nonetheless, the appropriate criterion for evaluating policies is whether the dollar value of the policy change to those who benefit from it exceeds the dollar value of the loss to those who are worse off. In these circumstances, the gainers could, in principle, compensate the losers. This principle is referred to as the **compensation principle.** It makes the implicit assumption that a dollar's worth of gain to one individual should be weighed the same as a dollar's worth of loss to another.

Critics of the compensation principle point out that if a policy has distributional consequences, these should be explicitly dealt with. One should attempt to quantify the magnitude of the gains and losses to each group; but there is no justification to weighing the gains of the winners equally with the losses of the losers.[2] Society may be more concerned about a decrease of $100 in the income of a poor individual than about a $106 decrease in the income of a rich individual.

The compensation principle tells us that Robinson Crusoe and Friday should not be asked to swap oranges unless, in the process, more oranges become available. In the earlier example, no movement from the original allocation, where Robinson has 100 oranges and Friday 20 oranges, is desirable, since in the process of redistributing oranges some oranges are lost. On the other hand any project that increased the total number of oranges would be desirable regardless of its distributional consequences. Thus, a change which increased Robinson's oranges to 120 and decreased Friday's to 10 would be desirable according to the compensation principle. Since there are now more oranges, Robinson could, in principle, compensate Friday for the change.

The compensations that would enable some policy change to be a Pareto improvement frequently are not made because it is often difficult to identify either the gainers and losers or the magnitudes of their gains and losses.

---

[2]There are further objections to the compensation principle. There are circumstances in which, if some new policy is instituted, the gainers can more than compensate the losers; but once in the new situation, if the government contemplated a movement back to the original situation, those who gain in returning to the original situation can more than compensate the losers. Thus the compensation principle does not allow us to rank the two situations unambiguously.

Suppose, for instance, that we were considering building a new neighborhood park. The people in the neighborhood will be much better off as a result. Suppose further that you were the park commissioner, and, by supernatural insight, you knew the tastes of each individual. When you calculated how much better off each was as a result of the park, you found that the total dollar value of the park (what they would be willing to pay) was greater than the cost of the park. Some individuals, of course, value the park much more than others. If you imposed a charge on each individual in accordance with how he benefits from the park, the park would be a Pareto improvement. By way of comparison, suppose that you cannot distinguish those who benefit a lot from the park from those who benefit only slightly (though you still know how much they value the park in the aggregate). If you impose a uniform tax on all the houses in the neighborhood to finance the park, the construction of the park will not be a Pareto improvement: there are some households whose benefits will be less than the tax they have to pay. Limitations on the information that is available provide an important set of constraints on the kinds of redistribution and compensation schemes that are possible.

The Social Indifference Curve and Income Distribution

The Pareto principle does not, as we have said, allow us to make comparisons between situations where some individuals are better off while others are worse off. Such changes involve questions of income distribution. How do we weigh the gains of the winners against the losses of the losers?

The basic tool economists employ when analyzing trade-offs is the **indifference curve.** Consider an individual making choices between packages containing different combinations of apples and oranges. The individual prefers packages with both more apples and more oranges. He will be indifferent between two packages, one of which has fewer apples than the other, provided it has sufficiently more oranges. Those combinations of apples and oranges among which the individual is indifferent are plotted in Figure 3.6 and trace out his indifference curve. This can be put in a slightly different way. Indifference curves trace out the variety of packages that offer an individual equal levels of utility. The individual has a whole family of indifference curves relating to different levels of utility; in Figure 3.6, for instance, we see all those combinations of apples and oranges that give him the same level of utility as 100 apples and 100 oranges, the curve labeled U_1. We also see all those combinations of apples and oranges that make the individual indifferent to having 200 apples and 200 oranges, labeled U_2.

Clearly utility is higher on the second indifference curve than on the first. The more apples and oranges, the higher the level of utility.[3] Indifference curves free us from a precise measurement of utility. All that matters is that if an individual is on a higher indifference curve, his level of utility is higher.

---

[3] We represent the utility function mathematically by

$$U = U(c_1, c_2, \ldots),$$

where c_1 is his consumption of the first commodity, c_2 his consumption of the second commodity, etc.

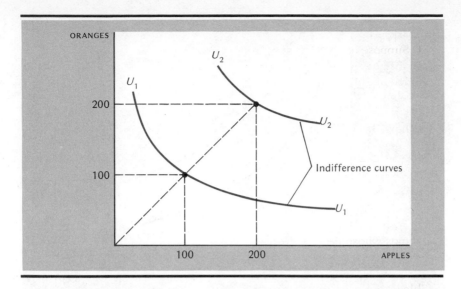

3.6 INDIVIDUAL INDIFFERENCE CURVE An indifference curve gives those combinations of goods among which an individual is indifferent. The individual prefers any point on the U_2 indifference curve to any point on U_1.

By analogy to the individual's utility function and the individual's indifference curve, we can define the **social welfare function** and the **social indifference curve.** Just as individuals derive utility from the goods they consume, so society derives its welfare from the utility received by its citizens. The social indifference curve gives those combinations of utilities of different individuals among which society is indifferent. Social indifference curves provide a convenient way of thinking about the kinds of trade-offs society often faces in which one group is better off and another worse off.

Obviously, society is better off if everyone is better off—this corresponds to the Pareto principle. Thus, in Figure 3.7, all combinations of the utility of Group 1 and Group 2 that are on the social indifference curve labeled W_2 yield a higher level of social welfare than do those combinations on the curve labeled W_1.

Just as there is a simple relationship between utility functions and indifference curves, there is a simple relationship between social indifference curves and social welfare functions. Recall that the individual indifference curve is defined as the set of combinations of goods that yield to the individual equal levels of utility—for which, in other words, the utility function has the same value. The social indifference curve is defined as the set of combinations of utility of different individuals or groups of individuals that yield to society equal levels of welfare—for which, in other words, the social welfare function has the same value.

The **social welfare function** provides a basis for ranking any allocation of resources, unlike the Pareto principle, in which we can only say that one situation is better than another if everyone is at least as well off, and someone is better off. The problem, as we shall see, is how to determine what the social welfare function should be.

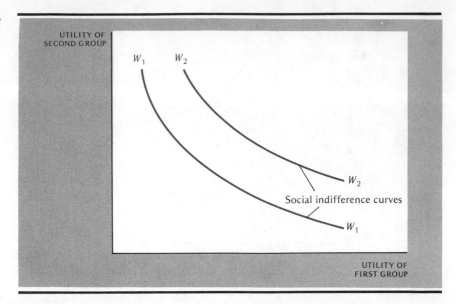

UTILITY OF
SECOND GROUP

W_1 W_2

W_2

Social indifference curves

W_1

UTILITY OF
FIRST GROUP

3.7 SOCIAL INDIFFERENCE CURVES A social indifference curve gives those combinations of utilities of group 1 and group 2 among which society is indifferent. Society is willing to trade off some decrease in one group's utility for an increase in another's. Points on the social indifference curve labeled W_2 yield a higher level of social welfare than do points on the social indifference curve labeled W_1.

SOCIAL CHOICES

We have now developed the basic tools with which we can describe conceptually how social choices can be made. First, we identify the opportunity set, the set of alternatives that are available to society. We characterize these by the levels of utility that will be obtained by different individuals under the various options that are available. Thus, in Figure 3.8, the initial situation is depicted as point A, and alternative projects may move us to points $B, C, D,$ or E. Each point describes the utility level of Robinson Crusoe and Friday. This way of characterizing the options makes clear the trade-offs. After first eliminating the Pareto-inefficient options (D and E), that is, the options for which there are alternatives in which at least one person is better off and no one is worse off, we then examine the trade-offs: as we move from A to B to C, Friday becomes better off, while Robinson Crusoe becomes worse off. The question, then, is how do we evaluate these trade-offs?

This is where we make use of social indifference curves. We wish to get to the highest social indifference curve among the options that are available. It is clear in Figure 3.8A that point B represents the best option. In moving from B to C, society's valuation of the losses to Robinson Crusoe exceeds that of the gains to Friday, and such a move is not desirable. On the other hand, the gain to Friday in moving from A to B is valued more by society than the loss to Robinson in that move, and hence B is preferred to A (or C).

Obviously, with different social indifference curves, a different option might be preferable. If society has a strong preference for equality, its social indif-

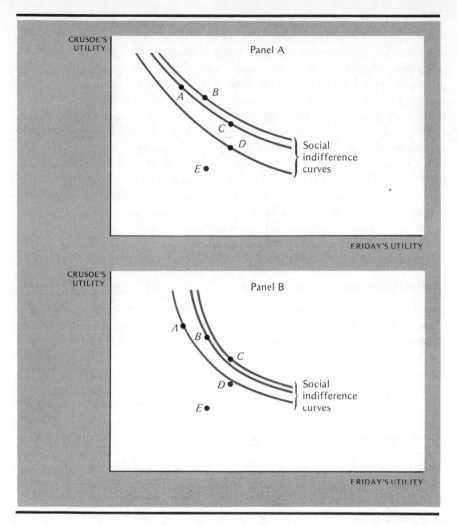

3.8 ALTERNATIVE ASSUMPTIONS ABOUT SOCIAL CHOICE With the social indifference curves shown in Panel A, point *B* is the best option. It lies on the highest social indifference curve. With the social indifference curves shown in Panel B, point *C* is the best option.

ference curves might look as Figure 3.8B, in which case option *C* may be preferable.

Social indifference curves thus provide us with a convenient way of conceptualizing social choices.

Social Choices in Practice

In practice, government officials do not derive utility possibilities schedules, nor do they write down social welfare functions. But they do attempt to identify the effects of government programs on different groups in the population. The impacts are often summarized in terms of their effects on efficiency and equality. The process may be characterized much as we have done it here: the opportunity set is identified, and the trade-offs between efficiency and equality are analyzed; some balancing of the two occurs, which might be reflected in a social indifference curve, now depicting society's attitudes toward equality and efficiency. In some cases, this social indifference curve may be derived from the more basic social indifference curves, representing society's attitudes toward the welfare of different individuals.

We shall encounter numerous examples where choices between equality and efficiency have to be made. For instance, in general, the more effective a tax system is in redistributing income, the greater the inefficiencies it introduces. There is a trade-off between equality and efficiency. There are, of course, important instances of poorly designed tax systems; in such cases, it may be possible to increase both equality and efficiency. Such tax systems put the economy below its utility possibilities schedule.

Utilitarianism versus Rawlsianism

Social indifference curves do nothing more than reflect society's attitudes. Thus, a society that was very concerned with equality might not care that Robinson has to give up 70 oranges for Friday to get 1 orange. So long as Friday was poorer than Robinson, any sacrifice on the part of Robinson that makes Friday better off is justified.

On the other hand, a society might care only about efficiency and not at all about equality. Then, of course, no redistribution of oranges from Robinson to Friday would be justified if, in the process, a single orange were lost. These views have been widely discussed among economists and philosophers.

One of the oldest views holds that society's welfare should be represented simply as the sum of the utilities of different individuals. This view is called *utilitarianism* and was set forth by Jeremy Bentham in the first half of the nineteenth century. Thus, in our simple economy with two individuals, the social welfare function is of the form

$$W = U_1 + U_2.$$

This criterion has the strong implication that society should be willing to give up a little utility of a poor individual for an equal gain in the utility of a rich individual. The trade-off that society is willing to make between the two individuals does not depend on the level of utility of either of the two individuals. That is why the social indifference curve is a straight line (with slope equal to minus one—that is, society is willing to give up one unit of Individual 1's utility for a gain of one unit of Individual 2's utility), as depicted in Figure 3.9A. (Moreover, the trade-offs between any two groups (individuals) does not depend on the incomes of other individuals in society.)

Many individuals argue that when one individual is worse off than another, society is not indifferent to a decrease in the utility of the poorer (Individual 2) matched by an equal increase in the utility of the richer (Individual 1). Society should be willing to accept a decrease in the utility of the poor only if there is a much larger increase in the utility of the rich. Social indifference

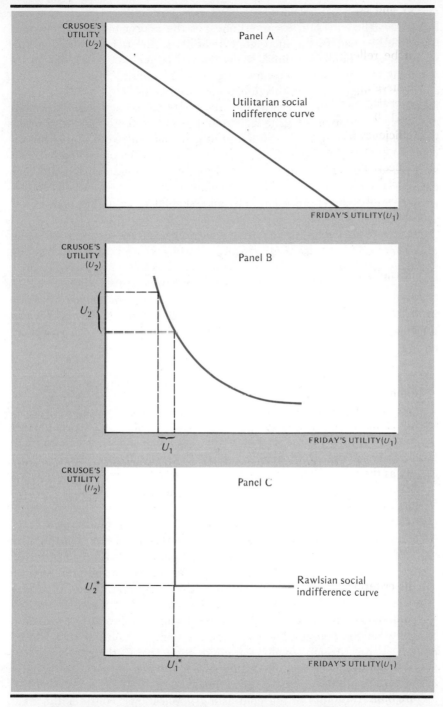

3.9 ALTERNATIVE SHAPES OF SOCIAL INDIFFERENCE CURVES (A) A utilitarian is willing to give up some utility for Crusoe so long as Friday gains at least an equal amount of utility. The social indifference curves are straight lines. (B) Some argue that society requires more than an equal increase in the utility (U_2) of a rich individual to compensate for a decrease in the utility (U_1) of a poor individual. (C) Rawls maintains that no amount of increase in the welfare of the rich can compensate for a decrease in the welfare of the poor. This implies that the social indifference curves are L-shaped.

curves reflecting those values are drawn in Figure 3.9B, where they appear not as straight lines but as curved ones; as the poorer individual becomes worse and worse off, the increment in utility of the richer individual that makes society indifferent must be larger and larger (i.e., the slope of the social indifference curve becomes steeper and steeper).

The extreme position of this debate has been taken by John Rawls, a professor of philosophy at Harvard University.[4] He has argued that the welfare of society only depends on the welfare of the worst-off individual; society is better off if you improve his welfare but gains nothing from improving the welfare of others. There is, in his view, no trade-off. To put it another way, no amount of increase in the welfare of the better off individual could compensate society for a decrease in the welfare of the worst-off individual. Diagrammatically, this is represented by an L-shaped social indifference curve, as in Figure 3.9C.

Consider a society in which Group 1 has utility U_1^* and Group 2 has utility U_2^*, where U_2^* is at least as great as U_1^*. If we increase U_2's utility, keeping U_1 unchanged, we remain on the same social indifference curve; that is, society is no better off. It is not willing to give up any utility of Group 1 for any increment in utility of Group 2. If both groups initially have the same utility level, society's welfare increases only when both groups 1 and 2 have their welfare increased; and the increase is only equal to the smallest increase on the part of any group.

A Comparison of Utilitarian and Rawlsian Social Welfare Functions

Utilitarian and Rawlsian social welfare functions have very different implications. Since under utilitarianism, an increase in utility by all individuals is valued the same, if we could costlessly transfer resources from one individual to another, we would wish to equate their marginal utility of income. That is, if the extra utility that a poor person gets from an extra dollar of income (his marginal utility) exceeds the loss in utility to the rich person of losing a dollar (his marginal utility), then total social welfare (the sum of the utilities) will increase by transfering the dollar. If it costs something to transfer resources from the rich to the poor, we stop short of this. On the other hand, with a Rawlsian social welfare function, we continue transferring resources from the rich to the poor so long as we can in the process make the poor better off; we pay no attention to the costs imposed on the rich.

In terms of our earlier example involving transferring oranges from Crusoe to Friday, a Rawlsian would continue to take away oranges so long as Friday gets more oranges. He would choose point C. A utilitarian would not go that far. An extreme equalitarian might argue that E, though Pareto inefficient, is preferable, since inequality (the difference between the number of Crusoe's oranges and Friday's) is reduced.

As another example of the contrasting implications, consider the treatment of an individual who has lost his leg. Assume that he can be fitted with an artificial leg, and that with the artificial leg he is able to do virtually anything a person with a normal leg can do. A utilitarian would say that

---

[4]John Rawls, *A Theory of Justice* (Cambridge, MA: Harvard University Press, 1971).

society should give the person who has lost his leg a new leg; but having done that, it should give him the same level of income as someone with a natural leg, so that the marginal utility of income is the same for individuals with and without legs. A Rawlsian would argue that we should give him enough extra income that the individual would be indifferent between keeping his natural leg and losing his leg, getting a new one, and receiving compensation. He is not concerned with equating marginal utilities but with maximizing the welfare of the worse-off individual (here, the individual who has lost his leg).

Another way of seeing the difference in the implications is the following. Suppose we could either give $1 to someone with an income of $10,000 or $1.05 to someone with an income of $20,000. Which should we do? Assume that all individuals have the same utility function. A Rawlsian has a simple answer: give it to the individual with the lower income—A utilitarian would ask, Is $1 to the person with an income of $10,000 worth more than $1.05 to the person with an income of $20,000? Because of diminishing marginal utility, it is likely he would give $1 to the individual with $10,000. But now assume we had a choice between $1 to the person with an income of $10,000 and $1 million to the person with $20,000. The Rawlsian answer remains unchanged. In other words, the Rawlsian criterion makes no trade-offs. The utilitarian criterion does. It says that if there is a sufficiently large offsetting gain to those who are already better off, it is worth making them still better off.

Rawls and Equalitarianism

Rawls's position is not, however, the most equalitarian position taken. There may be changes that make the worst-off person in society a little better off, the richer individuals much better off. By most measures, inequality has increased. Yet Rawls—like a utilitarian—would say such a change is desirable because the poorest individual—the only one he cares about—is better off, while some strong equalitarians would say that such a change is undesirable, since it increases inequality. Similarly, a change that makes the worst-off person worse off would be opposed by Rawls, regardless of what it does to measured inequality. Thus Rawls would oppose a tax increase in the rich if it results in their working less hard, reducing the government's revenue, and thus reducing what it could distribute to the poor, regardless of the effect of this tax increase on inequality.

SOCIAL WELFARE FUNCTIONS AND THE CONTRACT THEORY OF THE STATE

Recently, some philosophers and economists have attempted to use an extension of the contract theory of the state, or social contract theory, to support their view of the appropriate social welfare function. Social contract theory (originally developed more than 200 years ago by the French philosopher Jean Jacques Rousseau) says that one should view the state as if individuals voluntarily got together, for their mutual interest; they sign a "contract" assigning certain rights and powers to the state, in return for which the state provides certain services that, without the state, they could not obtain, or could obtain only at much greater cost. Thus in this view, an "acceptable" tax program must be such that the individual is better off than he would have been in the absence of government. When examined in detail, however, the theory provides little guidance to policy. If one imagines a society with no public roads, no public education, no laws, no police force—no governmentally provided goods of any kind—it is possible that even the individual with the highest income and a high tax rate might be worse off in the individualistic world with no taxes and no state.

Rawls makes a further assumption: he argues that to arrive at a set of principles for guiding how society should be organized, one must abstract oneself from the selfish interests that would predominate if one knew into what position one were to be born. The individual should arrive at a view of what is "fair" before he knows what his position in society will be. The individual should ask herself, "What would I view as fair behind a veil of ignorance where I didn't know whether I would be the daughter of Rockefeller or of a poor woman?"

The central point in imagining choices behind the **veil of ignorance** is that one is removing the effects of personal advantages from the analysis. Rawls claims that all individuals would, in that situation, wish society to follow the principle of maximizing the welfare of the worst-off individual. He claims, in other words, that individuals would not be willing to make any trade-offs—for example, a much higher income if they happen to be born in a reasonably comfortable circumstance versus a slightly lower income if they happen to be born into poverty.

A similar argument for utilitarianism has been put forward by John Harsanyi of the University of California. Behind the veil of ignorance individuals may be thought of as facing a risk, a chance of being a high-income individual and a chance of being a low-income individual. The question of how individuals behave when facing risky situations has been studied extensively; under quite plausible (but still not universally accepted) assumptions, individuals maximize their average utility. If individuals, in choosing among different income distributions (social programs), behave in the same way (behind the veil of ignorance) as they would in choosing among different risks, then it can be shown that social welfare can be evaluated using the utilitarian criterion. Utilitarianism can thus be derived from some more basic premises.

LIMITATIONS ON SOCIAL INDIFFERENCE CURVES

Social indifference curves provide a convenient way of thinking about the trade-offs facing society. Since many policy changes entail one group's being better off at the expense of some other group, we need to ask how much of a decrease in the welfare of one group we are willing to trade for an increase in the welfare of another group. This is precisely the kind of question that social indifference curves are concerned with.

It is possible, of course, for one person to announce what trade-offs he thinks are appropriate, and for another to announce that he thinks a different set of trade-offs is appropriate. We often talk, however, as if there is a social indifference curve for society or for the government. Does this simply refer to the preferences and attitudes of the person in the position of making the relevant decision, or can the social indifference curve be derived from the attitudes and preferences of the citizens making up our society? Unfortunately, whenever there is no unanimity—and there seldom is unanimity on questions of distribution—there is no acceptable way of "adding together" the preferences of the different individuals in society to arrive at a social welfare function.

Interpersonal Comparisons

Many economists object to the use of social welfare functions on a different basis. First, they argue that although we can make meaningful statements about an individual being happier (better off) in one situation than in another, we have no meaningful way of quantifying the extent of his increased happiness. Formally, we say that utility is an ordinal, not a cardinal, concept. That is, we can make rankings but not numerical comparisons. Secondly, they point out that one cannot compare the utilities of two individuals; one cannot say whether one individual is happier than another, or compare the increase in welfare (utility) of one individual with that of another. I may claim that although I have a much higher income than my brother, I am unhappier; not only that, I may claim that I know how to spend income so much better that the extra increase in my utility from a dollar given to me is much greater than the extra increase in utility that he would get from receiving an extra dollar. Though I might make such a claim, little credence would be given to it.

Since there is no "scientific" basis for making such welfare comparisons, many economists believe that economists should limit themselves to describing the consequences of different policies, pointing out who are the gainers and who are the losers; but that should be the end of their analysis. These economists believe that the only circumstances in which economists should make welfare judgments is when the policy change is a Pareto improvement. Unfortunately as we have said, few policy changes are Pareto improvements, and hence without making interpersonal comparisons of welfare, economists have little to say.

To make **interpersonal utility comparisons,** as a practical matter, one must not only assume that utility comparisons are possible but also hypothesize that all individuals have roughly the same utility function. That is, we postulate that the marginal utility of an extra dollar given to an individual depends only on his income, and that the marginal utility of a dollar given to a richer individual is lower than that given to a poorer individual.

This hypothesis has been attacked as meaningless (since interpersonal utility comparisons are not possible) and as wrong (even if they were possible, why should we believe that rich individuals get less utility out of an extra dollar than a poor individual?). In fact, some economists have argued that it is reasonable to assume that individuals who have the ability to earn higher incomes (that is, are more productive in translating their labor into wages) also have a higher ability to consume (are more productive in translating their goods into utility).

One can, however, view social welfare functions as providing a convenient way of summarizing the data concerning the effects of a policy change. A concern for equality implies valuing a dollar given to the poor more than a dollar given to the rich. Social welfare functions simply provide a systematic way of evaluating increments in income to individuals at different income levels.

SUMMARY

1. A change that makes at least one individual better off without making anyone worse off is a Pareto improvement.

2. The Pareto principle—that changes constituting Pareto improvements should be adopted—is based on individualistic values: such changes should be adopted regardless of what it does to any measure of inequality.

3. The principle of consumer sovereignty holds that individuals are the best judges of their own needs and pleasures.

4. The compensation principle provides one criterion for policy decisions in situations where policy changes make some individuals better off and others worse off, and hence are not Pareto improvements.

5. The social welfare function provides a framework within which the distributional consequences of a policy may be analyzed. It specifies the increase in utility of one individual that is required to compensate for a decrease in utility of another.

6. In the utilitarian social welfare function, social welfare is equal to the sum of the utilities of the individuals in society.

7. In the Rawlsian social welfare function, social welfare is equal to the utility of the worst-off individual in society.

8. As a practical matter, in evaluating alternative proposals we do not, in general, detail the impact each proposal has on each individual in society, but we summarize its effects by describing the impact of the proposal on some measure of inequality (or the impact on some well-identified groups) and describing the efficiency gains or losses. Alternative proposals often present trade-offs between efficiency and distribution; to get more equality one has to give up some efficiency. Differences in views arise concerning the nature of the trade-offs (how much efficiency one needs to give up to get some increase in equality), and in values (how much efficiency one should be willing to give up, at the margin, to get some increase in equality).

KEY CONCEPTS

Welfare economics	Diminishing marginal utility
Trade-offs	Compensation principle
Pareto principle	Indifference curves
Pareto optimality	Social welfare function
Consumer sovereignty	Social indifference curves
Paternalism	Utilitarianism
Utility possibilities curve	Interpersonal utility comparisons
Utility functions	Contract theory of the state
Opportunity set	Veil of ignorance
Marginal utility	Rawlsian social welfare function

1. Assume that Friday and Crusoe have identical utility functions described by the following table.

UTILITY FUNCTIONS FOR FRIDAY AND CRUSOE

Number of Oranges	Utility	Marginal Utility
1	11	
2	21	
3	30	
4	38	
5	45	
6	48	
7	50	
8	51	

Draw the utility function. Fill in the marginal utility data for Table 3.1 and draw the marginal utility function.

2. Assume that there are eight oranges to be divided between Friday and Crusoe. Take a utilitarian view—assume that social welfare is the sum of the utility of the two individuals. Using the data from Problem 1, what is the social welfare corresponding to each possible allocation of oranges? What allocation maximizes social welfare? Show that it has the property that the marginal utility of an extra orange given to each individual is the same.

3. Now take a Rawlsian view and assume that the social welfare function is the level of utility of the individual with the lowest utility level. Using the data from Problem 1, and again assuming there are eight oranges, what is the social welfare associated with each allocation of oranges? What allocation maximizes social welfare?

4. Draw the utility possibilities schedule based on the data from Problem 1. Mark the points that maximize social welfare under the two alternative criteria from Problems 2 and 3.

5. Assume that Crusoe's and Friday's utility functions are as described in Problem 1. But assume now that initially Crusoe has 6 oranges and Friday 2. Assume that for every 2 oranges taken away from Crusoe, Friday gets only 1, an orange being lost in the process. What does the utility possibilities schedule look like now? Which of the feasible allocations maximizes social welfare with a utilitarian social welfare function? With a Rawlsian social welfare function?

6. An individual is indifferent among the combinations of public and private goods shown in the following table.

Combination	Public Goods	Private Goods
A	1	16
B	2	11
C	3	7
D	4	4
E	5	3
F	6	2

Draw the individual's indifference curve. Assuming that the economy can produce 1 unit of public goods and 10 units of private goods, but that it can produce 1 more unit of public goods by reducing its production of private goods by 2 units, draw the production possibilities schedule. What is the maximum production of private goods? The maximum production of public goods? Can it produce 5 units of public goods and 1 unit of private goods? Which of the feasible combinations maximizes utility?

7. Consider an accident like the one cited in the chapter, where an individual loses his leg. Assume that it lowers his utility at each level of income but increases his marginal utility (at each level of income) though only slightly. Show diagrammatically the utility functions before and after the accident. Assume that whether the accident does or does not occur is beyond the control of the individual. Show that if you were a utilitarian, you would give more income to the individual with the accident, but that the level of utility of the individual with the accident would still be lower than that of the individual who did not have the accident. Show the compensation that a Rawlsian would provide.

Is it possible for a utilitarian to give more to the individual who had experienced the accident than a Rawlsian?

Under what circumstances would a utilitarian give nothing to an individual who had experienced an accident?

8. For each of the following policy changes, explain why the change is likely or not likely to be a Pareto improvement:
   a) Building a park, financed by an increase in the local property tax rate.
   b) Building a park, financed by the donation of a rich philanthropist; the city acquires the land by exercising the right of eminent domain.[5]
   c) Increasing medical facilities for lung cancer, financed out of general revenues.
   d) Increasing medical care facilities for lung cancer, financed out of an increase in the cigarette tax.
   e) Replacing the system of agricultural price supports with a system of income supplements for poor farmers.
   f) Protecting the automobile industry from cheap foreign imports by imposing quotas on the importation of foreign cars.
   g) Increasing social security benefits, financed by an increase in the payroll tax.
   h) Replacing the primary reliance at the local level on the property tax with state revenues obtained from an income tax.
   i) Eliminating rent control laws.
      In each case, state who the losers (if any) are likely to be. Which of these changes might be approved under the compensation principle? Which of these changes might be approved under a Rawlsian social welfare function?

9. Give some examples where the government seems to violate the principle of consumer sovereignty.

10. Assume you are shipwrecked. There are ten of you in a lifeboat; you know that it will take ten days to reach shore and that there are only rations for ten man-days. How would a utilitarian allocate the rations? How would a Rawlsian? Some people think that even Rawlsian criteria are not sufficiently equalitarian. What might an extreme equalitarian individual advocate? What does Pareto efficiency require?

[5]The right of eminent domain gives public authorities the right to take property, with compensation, for public uses.

4

The Role of the Public Sector

In the United States, as in most other Western economies, primary reliance for the production and distribution of goods lies in the private rather than the public sector. Those who believe in the private-enterprise system believe that this form of economic organization has certain desirable characteristics; in particular, that it leads to an efficient allocation of resources. This belief is, in fact, one of the oldest tenets of economics. If this is true, then why is government needed? To answer this question, we use the basic concepts of welfare economics developed in Chapter 3 to examine the successes and failures of private markets.

THE EFFICIENCY OF COMPETITIVE MARKETS: THE INVISIBLE HAND

In 1776, Adam Smith, often viewed to be the founder of modern economics, argued in his treatise *The Wealth of Nations* that competition would lead individuals in the pursuit of their private interests (profits) to pursue the public interest, as if by an *invisible hand:*

> . . . he intends only his own gain, and he is in this, as in many other cases, led by an invisible hand to promote an end which was no part of his intention. Nor is it always the worse for the society that it was no part of it. By pursuing his own interest he frequently promotes that of the society more effectually than when he really intends to promote it.[1]

---

[1] Adam Smith, *The Wealth of Nations* (New York: Modern Library, 1937). Originally published in 1776.

To understand the significance of Smith's insight, we should look at the commonly held views about the role of the government prior to Smith. There was a widespread belief that achieving the best interests of the public (however that might be defined) required an active government. This view was particularly associated with the mercantilist school of the seventeenth and eighteenth centuries; its leading proponents included Jean Baptiste Colbert in France and Thomas in England. These economists argued for strong government actions to promote industry and trade. Indeed, many European governments had taken an active role in promoting the establishment of colonies, and the mercantilists provided a rationale for this.

Some countries (or some citizens within those countries) had benefited greatly from the active role taken by the government, but other countries, in which the government had been much more passive, had also prospered. Some of those with strong, active governments had not prospered, as the resources of the country were squandered on wars or on a variety of unsuccessful public ventures.

In the face of these seemingly contradictory experiences Smith addressed himself to the question: can society ensure that those entrusted with governing society actually pursue the public interest? Experience had shown that while at times governments pursued policies that seemed consistent with the public good, at other times they pursued policies that could not by any reasonable stretch of the imagination be reconciled with it. Rather, those in the position of governing often seemed to pursue their private interests at the expense of the public interest. Moreover, even well-intentioned leaders often lead their countries astray. Smith argued that one did not need to rely on government or on any moral sentiments to do good. The public interest, he maintained, is served when each individual simply does what is in his own self-interest. Self-interest was a much more persistent characteristic of human nature than a concern to do good, and therefore provided a more reliable basis for the organization of the society. Moreover, individuals are more likely to ascertain with some accuracy what is in their own self-interest than they are to determine what is in the public interest.

The intuition behind Smith's insight is simple: if there is some commodity or service that individuals value but that is not currently being produced, then they will be willing to pay something for it. Entrepreneurs, in their search for profits, are always looking for such opportunities. If the value of a certain commodity to a consumer exceeds the cost of production, there is a potential profit for an entrepreneur, and he will produce the commodity. Similarly, if there is a cheaper way of producing a commodity than that which is presently employed, an entrepreneur who discovers this cheaper method will be able to undercut competing firms and make a profit. The search for profits on the part of firms is thus a search for more efficient ways of production and for new commodities that better serve the needs of consumers.

Notice that no government committee needs, in this view, to decide whether a commodity should or should not be produced. It will be produced if it meets the market test—i.e., if what individuals are willing to pay exceeds the costs of production. Nor does any government oversight committee need to check whether a particular firm is producing efficiently: competition will drive out inefficient producers.

There is a widespread (but not universal) consensus among economists that competitive forces do lead to a high degree of efficiency, and that competition does provide an important spur to innovation. However, during the past two hundred years economists have come to recognize that there are some important instances where the market does not work as perfectly as the more ardent supporters of the free market suggest. The economy has gone though periods in which there have been massive unemployment and idle resources; the Great Depression of the 1930s left many who wanted work unemployed, pollution has choked many of our larger cities, and urban decay has set in on others.

THE TWO FUNDAMENTAL THEOREMS OF WELFARE ECONOMICS

In what sense, then, and under what conditions, do competitive markets lead to economic efficiency? This is a question that has been at the center of much of the theoretical research in economics during the past few decades. The central results are summarized by what are referred to as the two **fundamental theorems of welfare economics.**

The first theorem says that competitive markets—in which there are so many buyers and sellers that no individual believes he can affect the market price—lead to a Pareto efficient allocation of resources. To put it another way, recall that we defined in the previous chapter the utility possibilities schedule, giving the maximum level of utility that could be attained by one individual, given the level of utility that was attained by other individuals. The first fundamental theorem of welfare economics states that a competitive economy will attain some point along the utility possibilities schedule (Figure 4.1).

The second theorem states that every point on the utility possibilities schedule can be attained by a competitive economy provided we begin with the correct distribution of resources. For instance, assume that initially we were at point E along the utility possibilities schedule depicted in Figure 4.1. By taking away some resources from Robinson (the second individual) and giving them to Friday (the first individual), we can move the economy form point E to point E'.

As we saw in the last chapter, to say that the economy is Pareto optimal says nothing about how "good" the income distribution is. In a competitive equilibrium Robinson Crusoe might be very well off, while Friday lives in dire poverty. All that the statement that the economy is Pareto optimal says is that no one can be made better off without making someone else worse off, that the economy is on its utility possibilities schedule. The second welfare theorem says, however, that if we don't like the income distribution generated by the competitive market, we need not abandon the use of the competitive market mechanism. All we need do is redistribute the initial wealth, and then leave the rest to the competitive market. Corresponding to E, E', or any final distribution of utilities that one would like to obtain, there is some initial distribution of resources.

The second fundamental theorem of welfare economics is a remarkable result. It says that every Pareto-efficient allocation can be attained by means of a **decentralized market mechanism.** It is not necessary to have a central

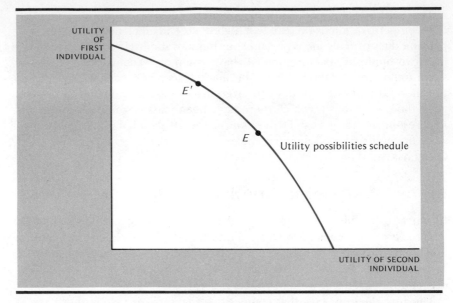

4.1 UTILITY POSSIBILITIES SCHEDULE The first fundamental theorem of welfare economics asserts that the competitive economy attains a point on the utility possibilities schedule (*E*). The second fundamental theorem of welfare economics asserts that every point on the utility possibilities schedule (such as point *E'*) can be attained simply by redistributing resources from one individual to another (but then allowing the market mechanism to work).

planner, with all the wisdom an economic theorist or a utopian socialist might attribute to him: competitive firms, attempting to maximize their profits, can do as well as the best of all possible social planners. This theorem thus provides a major justification for the reliance on the market mechanism. To put it another way, if the conditions assumed in the second welfare theorem were valid, the study of public finance could be limited to an analysis of the appropriate governmental redistributions of resources.

The reason that the competitive market leads to a Pareto-optimal allocation of resources is one of the primary subjects of study in standard courses in microeconomics. Since we will be concerned with understanding why under some circumstances competitive markets do not lead to efficiency, we first need to understand why competition under ideal conditions leads to efficiency.

THE PARETO EFFICIENCY OF THE COMPETITIVE ECONOMY

Basically, competition leads to efficiency because in deciding how much of a certain good to buy, individuals equate the marginal benefit they receive from consuming an extra unit with the marginal cost of purchasing an extra unit, which is just the price they have to pay; and firms, in deciding how much of a good to sell, equate the price they receive with the marginal cost of producing an extra unit.

In Figure 4.2 we have depicted the marginal benefit the individual receives from consuming some commodity, say ice cream cones. As the individual consumes more and more ice cream cones, the marginal (extra) benefit he

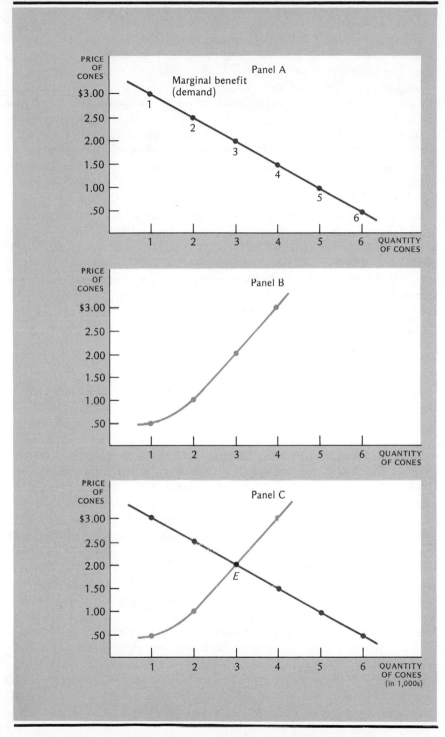

4.2   DEMAND AND SUPPLY OF ICE CREAM CONES Market equilibrium occurs at the point where the marginal benefit of consuming an extra ice cream cone is just equal to the marginal cost of producing an extra ice cream cone.

receives from consuming an additional ice cream cone decreases. The marginal benefit curve thus declines. Thus his marginal benefit from the first cone (in dollar terms) is $3; from the second, $2.50, from the third, $2.00; from the fourth, $1.50; from the fifth, $1.00; from the sixth, $0.50, at which point the individual becomes satiated. How many ice cream cones does an individual buy? He buys them up to the point where the marginal benefit of the last ice cream cone just equals its cost—i.e., the price he must pay for it.

If an ice cream cone cost $2.50, the individual would buy 2; if an ice cream cone cost $1.00, he would buy 5. The curve describing the individual's marginal benefits at each quantity of ice cream consumed thus also describes the quantity of the good the individual demands at each price. We thus refer to this curve as the individual's *demand curve*. We form the market demand curve simply by adding up the demand curves for each individual. In Panel C of Figure 4.2 we have drawn the market demand curve, assuming that there are 1,000 identical individuals. Thus at a price of $2 a cone, each individual demands 3 cones, and market demand is 3,000 cones.

In Panel B of Figure 4.2. we have depicted the marginal (extra) cost a firm incurs as a result of producing an extra unit of the good (making an extra ice cream cone.) We have depicted the curve as upward sloping. As the firm produces more and more of a commodity, the costs of producing one more unit increase.[2] In the diagram, the marginal cost to produce the first ice cream cone is $0.50; to produce the second, $1.00; the third, $2.00; the fourth, $3.00.

How many ice cream cones does a firm produce? It produces them up to the point where the marginal cost of the last ice cream cone just equals what the firm receives—i.e., the price of an ice cream cone. If the firm can get $1.00 for selling an ice cream cone, it produces just 2; if it can get $2.00, it produces 3. Thus the curve describing the firm's marginal costs at each quantity of ice cream cones produced also describes the quantity of the good the firm produces at each price. We refer to this curve as the firm's supply curve. We form the market supply curve simply by adding up the supply curves for each firm. We depict the market supply curve in Panel C. At a price of $2.00 each of the 1,000 identical firms supplies 3 units, so market supply is 3,000 units.

Efficiency requires that the marginal benefit associated with producing one more unit of any good (the extra benefit resulting from the production of one or more unit of the good) equals its marginal cost—that is, the extra cost associated with producing one more unit of the good. For if the marginal benefit exceeds the marginal cost, society would gain from producing more of the good; and if the marginal benefit was less than the marginal cost, society would gain from reducing production of the good.

Market equilibrium occurs at the point where demand equals supply, point *E* in panel C of Figure 4.2. At this point, the marginal benefit equals the price, and the marginal cost equals the price; both equal $2.00, hence the

---

[2]Although this is taken to be the normal case, in some instances the marginal costs may not increase. Industries for which costs neither increase nor decrease are said to have constant costs. There are a few industries where the marginal costs of production may actually decrease with an increase in production.

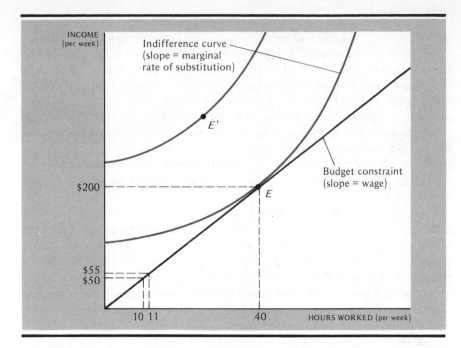

4.3 INDIVIDUAL'S DECISION ON NUMBER OF HOURS TO WORK The individual maximizes his utility at the point where his indifference curve is tangent to the budget constraint, point E. At E the slope of the budget constraint (the wage) is equal to the slope of the indifference curve, the individual's marginal rate of substitution.

marginal benefit equals the marginal cost, precisely the condition we identified earlier as that required for economic efficiency.

Indifference Curve Analysis. We can illustrate the general principle that a competitive economy leads to an efficient allocation of resources in a slightly different way, making use of indifference curves. Consider an individual who has to decide how many hours he wishes to work. His wage is $5.00 an hour. Thus if he works 10 hours he gets $50, and if he works 40 hours he gets $200. The relationship between the number of hours he works and his income we call the individual's *budget constraint.* We depict the budget constraint in Figure 4.3. Note that for each increment in hours worked, income increases by $5. As we saw in Chapter 3, the change in the value of the variable measured along the vertical (income) axis, as a result of a unit increase in the variable measured along the horizontal axis (hours worked), is called the slope of the curve. Thus, the slope of the budget constraint is equal to the individual's hourly wage.

In Figure 4.3 we have also depicted the individual's indifference curve through *E*, showing that he is indifferent to working more, provided his income is increased sufficiently. As the individual works more and more, the amount by which his income must be increased to compensate him for working an additional hour increases. The amount of extra income that can just compensate an individual for working an extra hour is called the individual's **marginal rate of substitution.** Diagrammatically, the slope of the indifference curve gives the individual's marginal rate of substitution.

Through any point, the individual has an indifference curve giving those combinations of income and work among which the individual is indifferent. We illustrate one such indifference curve, through Point E' in Figure 4.3. Clearly, since at any level of work the individual prefers more income to less, higher indifference curves represent higher levels of utility. Thus the indifference curve through E' represents a higher level of utility than that through E. The individual wishes to be on the highest possible indifference curve; this is just the point of *tangency* between the indifference curve and the budget constraint, point E.

At the point of tangency, the slopes of the two curves are the same—i.e. the marginal rate of substitution (the slope of the indifference curve) is equal to the wage.

Consider now a representative firm. The more labor input it hires the greater its output. The relationship between inputs and outputs is called the firm's **production function** and is depicted in Figure 4.4. In this simple example, labor is the only input. The slope of the production function is called the **marginal product** of labor; it gives the extra output that is produced by an extra hour of labor. Since the firm transforms labor services into goods, economists sometimes refer to the slope of the production function as the **marginal rate of transformation.**

The firm wishes to maximize its profits. In deciding how much labor to hire, it compares the extra benefit it receives, the value of the marginal product, with the extra cost, the wage. So long as the value of the marginal product of an extra hour of labor exceeds the wage, the firm continues to hire more labor. In equilibrium, then, the value of the marginal product of labor is just equal to the wage. The value of the marginal product is just what

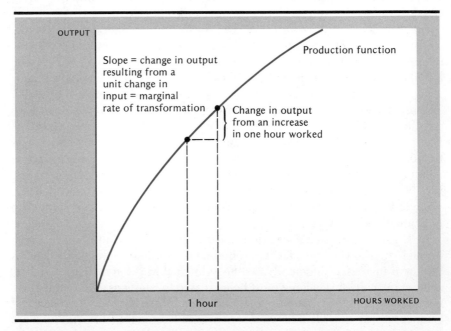

4.4 FIRM'S PRODUCTION FUNCTION The firm produces at the point where the value of the marginal product equals the wage.

the firm receives from selling each unit of output (the price) times the number of extra units that are produced with an extra unit of labor (the marginal product of labor, or the marginal rate of transformation). Assume, for simplicity, that what is being produced has a price of $1. Then we see that the firm will set the marginal rate of transformation (the marginal product of labor) equal to the wage. But recall that the laborer set his marginal rate of substitution equal to the wage. Thus, in equilibrium, *the marginal rate of substitution equals the marginal rate of transformation*. But this is precisely what efficiency requires. Assume that individuals were willing to give up 1 hour of leisure, provided they could have 4 ice cream cones. Assume that with 1 hour of work, 5 ice cream cones could be produced. Clearly, it would be desirable to have the individual work an hour more; he would produce 1 more ice cream cone than he requires to leave him just as well off. Conversely, assume in 1 hour of work, only 3 ice cream cones were produced. Then the individual should work an hour less. By working an hour less, output would be reduced, by 3 ice cream cones. The individual was willing, however, to give up 4 ice cream cones for an hour's reduction in work. Thus the equality of the marginal rate of substitution and the marginal rate of transformation is required for Pareto efficiency of the economy and is ensured by the competitive market.

Competition and Innovation

The analysis just presented to explain why competitive markets lead to efficiency is not quite the same as Adam Smith's argument. He was also concerned with the incentives for innovation, for taking advantage of new profitable opportunities. As firms compete, those who are most successful may establish temporary monopolies. The threat of competition will still force them to be efficient; they must continue to look for profitable opportunities, lest some other firms grab these opportunities and take their market away. Thus, while the fundamental theorems of welfare economics explain why an economy with no technological change, in which all firms are sufficiently small that they have no effect on prices, would be Pareto efficient, Adam Smith's argument was based on a much broader perspective. Many of the current discussions of the role of the government and the virtues of competition take on this broader perspective rather than the more narrow view reflected in the Fundamental Theorem of Welfare Economics.[3]

MARKET FAILURES: A RATIONALE FOR GOVERNMENT ACTIVITY

There are eight principal sources of market failures, each of which has been used to justify the possibility of government activity in the marketplace. The

---

[3]Sometimes the views come into conflict: to provide the incentives for firms to engage in research and development may require granting temporary monopoly rights—as through the patent system, where a person can obtain sole rights to an invention for a period of seventeen years. This alternative view was stressed by the great Harvard economist Joseph Schumpeter (1883–1950). It has more recently been revived in the work of Richard Nelson and Sidney Winter at Yale (see for instance, their book *An Evolutionary Theory of Economic Change* [Cambridge, Mass.: Harvard University Press, 1982]).

first six describe circumstances under which the market may not be Pareto efficient. The last two describe situations where government intervention may be justified even if the economy is Pareto efficient.

1. Failure of Competition

For the invisible hand to work, there must be competition. In some industries—automobiles, aluminum, photographic film—there are relatively few firms or one or two firms that have a large share of the market. (When there is only one firm in a market, we say it is a monopolist.) This suggests the absence of strong competition. However, the presence of only a few firms in itself does not necessarily imply the firms are not acting competitively. If there are a large number of *potential* entrants (either domestic or foreign firms), the existing firms may not be able to act monopolistically; as soon as existing firms attempt to reap any monopoly profits, a potential entrant might enter the market and drive down the price.

A second difficulty in ascertaining whether a market is competitive arises from the problem of defining the market. DuPont may have had a monopoly in cellophane or, more widely, in transparent wrapping materials. But there are other wrapping materials (brown paper). These may be sufficiently close substitutes to make DuPont act competitively.

When transportation costs are large, the relevant market may be limited geographically. Though there are many cement companies in the United States, cement customers in Dubuque, Iowa, cannot look to Ohio for a better price on mixed cement. If there is only one cement firm in a particular area, there may be no (or very limited) competition.

Some monopolies are created by the government. The British government gave the East India Company the exclusive right to trade with India. Also, the patent system grants inventors a monopoly over their inventions for a limited period of time.

In other instances, there are barriers to entry arising from what economists refer to as increasing **returns to scale.** These are cases where the costs of production (per unit output) decline with the scale of production. It is less expensive to have one large electrical generator serve a region than to put one in every neighborhood. It thus may be more efficient to have only one generator serving a particular local market. Similarly, it may be efficient to have only one telephone company serving a particular local market, or one water company (imagine the duplication in power lines, telephone lines, and water mains if every other house used a different water or electricity company).

When a firm has attained its monopoly position as a result of increasing returns to scale we say that it is a **natural monopoly.** Whether a particular market is characterized by a natural monopoly depends on circumstances. Thus, the development of new telecommunications technologies has led to the elimination of AT&T's natural monopoly over long-distance telephone services.

If entry into and exit from a market were costless, even natural monopolies might be forced to behave competitively by the threat of entry.[4] But governments have seldom relied on this. In the United States, some natural monopolies are regulated. Examples include telephone service and electricity. Other natural monopolies are run directly by the government. Water companies are frequently publicly owned, and there are a number of large, publicly owned electric utilities (including the Tennessee Valley Authority). In all countries, the post office is public (though there has been a rapid growth in the private provision of many postal services, such as overnight package delivery and parcel post). The United States is unusual, however, in having its telephone services supplied privately. In most countries telephone services are publicly provided.

Monopoly Pricing and the Welfare Loss from Monopoly. We have noted that under certain circumstances it may be more efficient to have only one firm producing than many. Why is it then that monopolies are generally viewed as bad? The reason is that, if unregulated, monopolies (whether natural or not) will restrict output to attain a higher price.

A monopolist produces to the point where the extra revenue he would receive from producing an extra unit is just equal to the extra cost of producing that extra unit (his marginal cost). The extra revenue he receives is referred to as his **marginal revenue.** In Figure 4.5 we have drawn the marginal revenue schedule and the demand curve. Notice that the marginal revenue schedule is everywhere below the demand curve: the extra revenue the monopolist receives from selling an extra unit is less than the price at which he sells it. As the monopolist increases sales, he knows that the price must be lowered. Thus the extra revenue from selling an extra unit is the price he receives for this additional unit less the loss in revenue from lowering the price on all other units that he sells. In the figure, for outputs below Q_o, the first effect is greater than the second: the marginal revenue is positive; for outputs in excess of Q_o, the monopolist's revenues are actually reduced by further sales.

Thus, in Figure 4.5, the monopolist operates at Q^*, where marginal revenue equals marginal cost; clearly output at Q^* is less than Q_1, where price equals marginal cost. Notice that at Q^*, price, which measures how much individuals value an *extra* unit of the good exceeds the marginal cost. This is why we say there is a welfare loss from the restriction in output arising from monopoly.

We can ask how much extra, in total, individuals would be willing to pay for an increase in output from Q^* to Q_1 beyond what it costs to increase output from Q^* to Q_1. This is the measure of the welfare loss resulting from the reduction in output from monopoly. Since at each level of output, the price measures the marginal evaluation of consumers, the total that individuals would be willing to pay for an increase in output is the area under the demand curve, area Q^*BCQ_1. The extra cost of producing an extra unit is the marginal cost; thus the extra cost of increasing output from Q^* to Q_1 is

---

[4]This is the view taken, for instance, by William J. Baumol of Princeton University and New York University in his presidential address before the American Economic Association. See W. J. Baumol, "Contestable Markets: An Uprising in the Theory of Industry Structure," *American Economic Review*, March 1982, pp. 1–15. This view has recently been criticized, on the grounds that even if there are very slight entry costs, firms may be able to exercise considerable monopoly power.

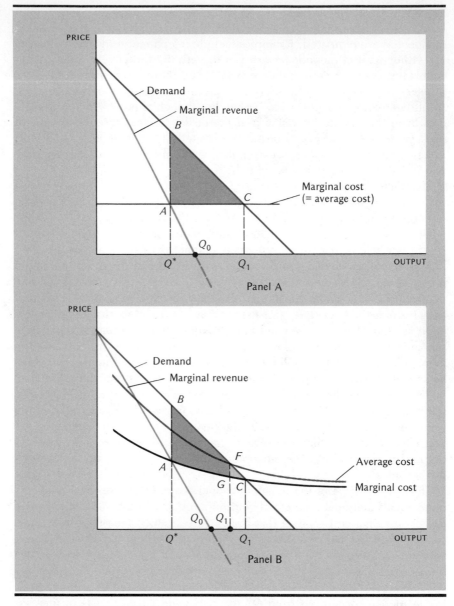

PRICE

Demand

Marginal revenue

B

Marginal cost
(= average cost)

C

A

Q_0

Q^* Q_1 OUTPUT

Panel A

PRICE

Demand

Marginal revenue

B

F

A   Average cost

G C

Marginal cost

Q_0 Q_1

Q^* Q_1 OUTPUT

Panel B

4.5   MONOPOLY PRICING Monopoly output is lower than competitive output, or the output at which profits are zero. There is a resulting welfare loss.

the area under the marginal cost schedule, Q^*ACQ_1. Thus the welfare loss is the difference between the area Q^*BCQ_1 and the area Q^*ACQ_1,—i.e., the triangle ABC. The area ABC is sometimes referred to as the *deadweight loss* from monopoly. (We shall return in Chapter 10 to an extended discussion of why the area ABC measures the welfare loss.)

In Figure 4.5B we depict the cost curves of a natural monopoly, where marginal cost is less than average cost. Clearly, if price were set equal to marginal cost, at Q_2, a loss would be incurred. Q_1 is the largest output at which the firm breaks even. At Q_1 price equals average cost. A monopolist would restrict output, to Q^*, with the associated welfare loss relative to Q_2 measured by the shaded area ABC, while the welfare loss relative to the zero profit output Q_1 is the area $BAFG$.

2. Public Goods

There are some goods that either will not be supplied by the market or, if supplied, will be supplied in an insufficient quantity. An example on a large scale is national defense; on a small scale, navigational aids (such as a light buoy). These are called pure public goods. They have two critical properties: first, it does not cost anything for an additional individual to enjoy the benefits of the public goods. Formally, there is a zero marginal cost for the additional individual enjoying the good. It costs no more to defend a country of one million and one individuals than to defend a country of one million. The costs of a light buoy do not depend at all on the number of ships that sail past it. Secondly, it is, in general, difficult or impossible to exclude individuals from the enjoyment of the public good. If I put a light buoy in some rocky channel, to enable my ships to navigate safely, it is difficult or impossible to exclude other ships entering the channel from the navigational benefits of my light buoy. If our national defense policy is successful in diverting an attack from abroad, we all benefit; there is no way we could exclude any single individual from these benefits.

The market either will not supply, or will not supply enough of, a pure public good. Consider the case of the light buoy. Since it would be difficult, if not impossible, to collect payments from ships that make use of the light buoy, no one who does not depend on the light buoy himself will have an incentive to provide one. A large ship owner, with many ships making use of the light buoy, might decide that the benefits he himself receives from the buoy exceed the costs; but in calculating whether or how many buoys to put in place, he will only look at the benefits he receives, not the benefits received by others. Thus there will be some buoys for which the total benefits (taking into account *all* of the ships that make use of the buoy) exceed the costs but for which the benefits of any single ship owner are less than the costs. Such buoys will not be put into place, resulting in too small a supply of light buoys. The fact that private markets will not supply, or will supply too little of, public goods provides a rationale for many government activities.

3. Externalities

There are many cases where the actions of one individual or one firm affect other individuals or firms, where one firm imposes a cost on other firms but does not compensate the other firms, or alternately, where one firm confers a benefit on other firms but does not reap a reward for providing that benefit. Perhaps the most discussed example in recent years has been air and water pollution. When I drive a car that is not equipped with a pollution control device, I lower the quality of the air. (Of course, the effect on air quality if only one person does this may be negligible, but when a large number of individuals do this, the effect is significant.) I thus impose a cost on others. Similarly, a chemical plant that discharges its chemicals into a nearby stream imposes costs on downstream users of the water. They may have to spend a considerable amount of money to clean up the water in order to use it.

Instances where one individual's actions impose a cost on others are referred to as **negative externalities.** Not all externalities are negative. There are some important instances of **positive externalities,** where one individual's actions confer a benefit upon others. If I plant a beautiful flower garden in the front of my house, my neighbors may benefit from being able to look at it. An apple orchard may confer a positive externality on a neighboring bee-keeper. An individual who rehabilitates his house in a neighborhood that is in decline may confer a positive externality on his neighbor.

There are a large number of other examples of externalities: an additional car on a crowded highway will add to road congestion, both reducing the speed at which other drivers can travel safely and increasing the probability of an accident. When an additional fisherman starts fishing in a given pond, he may reduce the amount of fish that others will be able to catch. If there are several oil wells drilled in the same oil pool, taking an excessive amount of oil from one of the wells may reduce the amount of oil available for extraction from the other wells.

Whenever there are such externalities, the resource allocation provided by the market may not be efficient. Since individuals do not bear the full cost of the negative externalities they generate, they will engage in an excessive amount of such activities; conversely, since individuals do not enjoy the full benefits of activities generating positive externalities, they will engage in too little of these. Thus there is a widespread belief that without government intervention of some kind, the level of pollution would be too high. To put it another way, pollution control provides a positive externality, so without government intervention there would be an underprovision of pollution control.

Governments respond to externalities in several different ways. In some cases (mainly involving negative externalities) they attempt to regulate the activity in question; thus the government imposes emission standards for automobiles and imposes regulations for air and water pollution by firms.

Alternatively, the government could attempt to use the price system by imposing penalities (fines) on negative externalities and rewards for positive externalities; individuals are made to realize the cost they impose and to recognize the benefits they confer upon others. Thus, rather than regulating the level of automobile emissions, the government could have imposed a charge, proportional to the level of emissions over some critical level. By charging for the use of roads, at least at peak times, the government would make road users aware of the congestion costs they impose on others.

4. Incomplete Markets

Pure public goods and services are not the only goods or services that private markets fail to provide adequately. Whenever private markets fail to provide a good or service, even though the cost of providing it is less than what individuals are willing to pay, there is a market failure that we refer to as **incomplete markets** (a complete market would provide all goods and services for which the cost of provision is less than what individuals are willing to pay). Some economists believe that private markets have done a particularly poor job in providing insurance and loans, and that this provides a rationale for government activities in these areas.

The private market does not provide insurance for many important risks that individuals face, though insurance markets are much better today than they were seventy-five years ago. The government has undertaken a number of insurance programs, motivated at least in part by this market failure: following the bank failures of the Great Depression, the government set up the Federal Deposit Insurance Corporation to insure depositors against a loss of savings arising from the insolvency of banks. The government has been active in providing flood insurance. Following urban riots in the summer of 1967, most private insurance companies refused to write fire insurance in certain inner-city areas, and again the government stepped in.

Although the absence of adequate private risk markets may provide the political justification for these insurance programs, some insurance programs are designed to transfer resources (perhaps in a disguised way) to the beneficiaries of the program. If their sole or major objective were to provide insurance, they would be designed and paid for in a substantially different manner. For instance, one justification for the government's farm program is that farmers face large risks from price fluctuations, risks against which they cannot obtain insurance.[5] Government-provided support programs reduce these risks. But our farm programs not only stabilize farm prices, they also substantially increase the average income of farmers. Only part of this "gift" to farmers is reflected in the government's budget. The rest is reflected in the higher prices consumers must pay for agricultural products. If the true objective of the price-support program were to stabilize the income of farmers, to reduce the risks that they face, there are ways of doing this more effectively and at less cost. The government might, for instance, simply provide price insurance, at a premium accurately reflecting the costs of providing such insurance.[6]

Capital Markets. In recent years, the government has taken an active role not only in remedying deficiencies in risk markets but in ameliorating the effects of imperfect capital markets. Until 1965 it had been difficult for individuals to obtain loans to finance their college education; in that year the government passed legislation providing for government guarantees on student loans. As the program expanded in the 1970's the initial objective, making loans available, became mixed with a second objective, subsidizing education: the interest rates charged were often substantially below market rates.

But this is only one of several government loan programs. The Federal National Mortgage Association provides funds for home mortgages (referred

---

[5] For the major crops, farmers can obtain some price insurance by trading in futures markets.

[6] For many (but not all) crops, this kind of insurance can actually be purchased in private markets.

For a more extended discussion of the distinction between programs aimed at stabilizing farmers' incomes and those aimed at redistributing income to farmers, see D. Newbery and J. E. Stiglitz, *The Theory of Commodity Price Stabilization* (New York: Oxford University Press, 1981).

to as Fanny Maes); the government provides loans to farmers; the Export-Import Bank provides loans to businesses engaged in international trade; the Small Business Administration provides loans for small business, and so forth. In each of these cases, there were allegations that access to the credit market was restricted.

Complementary Markets. Finally, we turn to the supply problems associated with the absence of certain complementary markets. Suppose that all individuals only enjoy coffee with sugar, that without sugar it tastes bitter and is unpalatable. Assume, moreover, that there was no market for sugar without coffee. Thus an entrepreneur considering whether to produce coffee would not do so, because he would realize that he would have no sales. And an entrepreneur considering whether to produce sugar, given that coffee was not produced, also would not do so, since he too would realize that he would have no sales. If, however, the two entrepreneurs could get together, there would be a good market for coffee and sugar. Each *acting alone* would not be able to pursue the public interest, but acting together they could.

This particular example is deliberately quite simple, and in this case the coordination (between the potential sugar producer and the potential coffee producer) required might easily be provided by the individuals themselves without government intervention. But there are many cases where large-scale coordination is required, particularly in less-developed countries, and this may require government planning. Similar arguments have been put forward as justification for public urban renewal programs. To redevelop a large section of a city requires extensive coordination among factories, retailers, landlords, and other businesses. One of the objectives of government development agencies is to provide that coordination (if markets were complete, the prices provided by the market would perform this "coordination" function.)

Great care is required in analyzing the appropriate response to this kind of market failure. There may be good reasons that private producers have failed to provide a particular good or service. There may be large transaction costs associated with providing it. Banks may not make certain categories of loan because the probability of default is so high that to earn the same return as on other loans the bank must charge such a high interest rate that there would be little demand for the loans.

5. Information Failures

A number of government activities are motivated by imperfect information on the part of consumers, and the belief that the market, by itself, will supply too little information. For instance, in 1968, the government passed a Truth-In-Lending bill requiring lenders to inform borrowers of the true rate of interest on their loans. The Federal Trade Commission and the Food and Drug Administration have both adopted a number of regulations concerning labeling, disclosure of contents, etc. Recently, the Federal Trade Commission proposed that used-car dealers be required to disclose whether they had tested various parts of the car, and if so, what the outcome of the test was. These regulations generated a considerable amount of controversy, and under pressure from Congress, the FTC was forced to back down.

Opponents of these regulations contend that they are unnecessary (the competitive market provides incentives for firms to disclose relevant information), irrelevant (consumers pay little attention to the information the law requires firms to disclose), and costly, both to government, which must administer them, and to the firms, which must comply with the regulations. Proponents of these regulations claim that, though difficult to administer effectively, they are still useful.

The government's role in remedying information failures, however, goes beyond these simple consumer protection measures. Information is, in many respects, a public good. Giving information to one more individual does not detract from the amount others have. Efficiency requires that information be freely disseminated, or more accurately, the only charge be for the actual cost of transmitting the information. The private market will often provide an inadequate supply of information, just as it supplies an inadequate amount of other public goods. The most notable example of government activity in this area is the U.S. Weather Bureau. Another example is the information provided to ships by the U.S. Coast guard.[7]

6. Unemployment, Inflation, and Disequilibrium

Perhaps the most widely recognized symptoms of "market failure" are the periodic episodes of high unemployment, both of workers and machines, that have plagued capitalist economies during the past two centuries. Though these recessions and depressions have been greatly moderated in the period since World War II, perhaps partly because of government policies, the unemployment rate still climbed over 10 percent in 1982; that is low, however, compared to the Great Depression, when unemployment reached 24 percent in the United States.

Most economists take these high levels of unemployment as *prima facie* evidence that *something* is not working well in the market. To some economists, high unemployment is the most dramatic and most convincing evidence of market failure.

The fact that markets have failed to produce full employment—that there is a serious market failure—does not in itself imply that there is a role for the government to play; one must be able to show, in addition, that there are policies through which the government can improve the functioning of the economy. This has long been a subject of controversy.

The issues raised by unemployment and inflation are sufficiently important, and sufficiently complicated, that they warrant a separate course in macroeconomics. But we shall touch on some aspects of these issues in Chapter 28, where we shall be concerned with the consequences of government deficits and attempt to survey some of the important ways that these macroeconomic considerations affect the design of tax policy.

Relationships among Market Failures. The market failures we have discussed are not mutually exclusive. Information problems often provide part

---

[7]The market failures associated with incomplete markets and imperfect information are, in fact, broader than our discussion has indicated. For instance, incomplete risk markets may lead to inefficient levels of investment; this may be true even when the costs of setting up new markets exceed the benefits. For an extended discussion, see B. Greenwald and J. E. Stiglitz, "Economies with Imperfect Information and Incomplete Markets," *Quarterly Journal of Economics*, forthcoming, 1986.

of the explanation of missing markets. In turn, externalities are often thought to arise from missing markets: if fishermen could be charged for using fishing grounds—if there were a market for fishing rights—then there would not be overfishing. Public goods are sometimes viewed as an extreme case of externalities, where others benefit from my purchase of the good as much as I do. Much of the recent research on unemployment has attempted to relate it to one of the other market failures.

Redistribution and Merit Goods

The preceding six sources of market failure resulted in the economy being inefficient in the absence of government intervention—that is, the market economy, if left to itself, would not be Pareto optimal. But, even if the economy were Pareto optimal, there are two further arguments for government intervention. The first is income distribution. The fact that the economy is Pareto efficient says nothing about the distribution of income; competitive markets may give rise to a very unequal distribution of income, which may leave some individuals with insufficient resources on which to live. One of the most important activities of the government is to redistribute income. This is the express purpose of welfare activities, such as Aid to Families with Dependent Children.

The second argument for government intervention in a Pareto-optimal economy arises from concern that the individual may not act in his own best interest. Many individuals believe that evaluating each individual's welfare by his own perceptions—as with the criterion of Pareto optimality—provides an inappropriate or inadequate criterion for making welfare judgments. Even if fully informed, consumers may make "bad" decisions. Individuals continue to smoke, even though it is bad for them, and even though they know it is bad for them. Individuals fail to wear seat belts, even though wearing seat belts increases the chances of survival from an accident, and even though individuals know the benefits of seat belts. Many individuals continue to buy sugar-laden breakfast cereals, even though they know that serious questions have been raised concerning the nutritional value of these cereals for their children. There are those who believe that the government should intervene in these cases, where individuals seemingly do not do what is in their own best interest; and the kind of intervention that is required must be stronger than a simple provision of information. Goods that the government compels individuals to consume, like seat belts and elementary education, are called **merit goods.**

The view that the government should intervene because it knows what is in the best interest of individuals better than they themselves do, is often referred to as paternalism, mentioned earlier, in Chapter 3. In contrast to the paternalistic view, many economists and social philosophers believe that the government should respect consumers' preferences. By what right, opponents of the paternalistic role of government ask, can one group of individuals impose their will and preferences over another group?

The paternalistic argument for government activities is quite distinct from the externalities argument we discussed above. One might argue that smoking causes cancer, and since individuals who get cancer are treated in public hospitals, smokers imposes a cost on nonsmokers. This, however, can be dealt with by making smokers pay their full costs—for instance, by imposing a tax on cigarettes. Alternatively, smoking in a crowded room does indeed impose a cost on nonsmokers in that room. But this, too, can be dealt with directly. Those who take a paternalistic view might argue that individuals should not be allowed to smoke, even in the privacy of their own homes, and even if a tax, which makes the smokers take account of the external costs imposed on others, is levied. Though few have taken such an extreme paternalistic position with respect to smoking, this paternalistic role undoubtedly has been important in a number of areas, such as government policies toward drugs (marijuana) and liquor (prohibition).

A ROLE FOR THE PUBLIC SECTOR

The fundamental theorems of welfare economics are useful because they delineate clearly a role for the government. In the absence of market failures and merit goods all the government needs to do is worry about the distribution of income (resources). The private enterprise system ensures that resources will be used efficiently.

If there are important market failures—imperfect competition (from, say, increasing returns), imperfect information, incomplete markets, externalities, public goods, and unemployment—there is a presumption that the market will not be Pareto efficient. This suggests a role for the government. But there are two important qualifications.

First, it has to be shown that there is, at least in principle, some way of intervening in the market to make everyone better off. Secondly, it has to be shown that in the attempt to remedy a market failure, the political processes and bureaucratic structures of a democratic society are not likely to interfere with the proposed Pareto improvement.

Thus when information is imperfect and costly, the analysis of whether the market is Pareto efficient must take into account these information costs; information is costly to the government, just as it is to private firms. Markets may be incomplete because of transaction costs, the costs of establishing an additional market; but the government would face costs of establishing markets—for instance, for insurance—and there would be administrative costs of running a public insurance program.

Recent research has established a variety of circumstances under which, assuming that the government has no advantage in information or transaction costs over the private market, the government could, in principle, bring about a Pareto improvement.

The fact that there may exist government policies that would be Pareto improvements does not, however, necessarily create a presumption that government intervention is desirable. We also have to consider the consequences of government intervention, in the form it is likely to take, given the nature of our political process. This distinction, between an ideal government and actual governments, did not play an important role in our discussion of the fundamental theorems of welfare economics. There, we showed that in the absence of market failures, not even an ideal government could improve the efficiency with which resources are allocated. Now, in the face of these market failures, we have to understand how governments function if we are to assess whether government action is likely to remedy these market failures.

In the 1960s, it was common to take a market failure, show a government program existed that could lead to a Pareto improvement (someone could be made better off without making anyone worse off), and conclude that therefore government intervention was called for. When programs were enacted and failed to achieve what they were supposed to, the blame was placed on petty bureaucrats or political tampering. But, as we shall see in Chapter 7, even if bureaucrats and politicians behave honorably, the nature of government itself still may help explain government's failures.

Public programs—even those allegedly directed at alleviating some market failure—are instituted in democracies not by ideal governments or benevolent despots but by complicated political processes.

A Positive Approach to the Role of the Public Sector

The market-failure approach to understanding the role of the public sector is largely a normative approach. The market-failure approach provides a basis for identifying situations where the government *ought* to do something, tempered by considerations of public failure.

Some economists believe that economists should focus their attention not on normative analysis but on positive analysis, on describing the consequences of government programs and the nature of the political processes.

The popularity of the market-failure approach has resulted in many programs being justified in terms of market failures. But this may simply be rhetoric. There is often a significant difference between the stated objective of a program (to remedy some market failure) and the design of the program. Political rhetoric may focus on the failure of markets to provide insurance against volatile prices and the consequences that this has on small farmers, but the programs may in practice transfer income to large farmers. One may gain more insight into the political forces at work and the true objectives of the program by looking at how the programs are designed and implemented than by looking at the stated objectives of the legislation.

A few economists take the extreme position that normative analysis is irrelevant. They ask, of what relevance are statements about what the government should do? Just as one can describe a market equilibrium without referring to how resources "should be" allocated, so too one can describe a political equilibrium without referring to what the government should do. The outcomes depend on the rules of the political process, the incentives facing various participants in the political process, etc. If one fully understands the nature of the government, one fully understands what it is that the government *will* do. There is little room left over to discuss what the government should do.

Although there is some truth to this view, it is extreme: discussions by economists (and others) of the role that government "should" play constitute an important part of the political process in modern democracies. Legislators recognize that much of the information with which they are supplied comes from those with vested interests; they thus frequently turn to economists for an alternative view of what the government should do. For instance, economists' arguments against tariffs, quotas, and other trade restrictions, though they have not always prevailed, have been important in limiting the scope of trade restrictions.

SUMMARY

1. Under certain conditions, the competitive market results in a Pareto-efficient resource allocation. When the conditions required for this are not satisfied, a rationale for government intervention in the market is provided.
2. Six reasons that the market mechanism may not result in a Pareto-efficient resource allocation were noted.
3. Even if the market is Pareto efficient, there may be two further grounds for government action. First, the competitive market may give rise to a socially undesirable distribution of income. And second, some believe that individuals, even when well informed, do not make good judgments concerning the goods they consume, thus providing a rationale for regulations restricting the consumption of some goods, and for the public provision of other goods, called merit goods.
4. Though the presence of market failures implies that there may be scope for government activity, it does not imply that a particular government program aimed at correcting the market failure is necessarily desirable. To evaluate government programs, one must take into account not only their objectives but also how they are implemented.

KEY CONCEPTS

Invisible hand	Marginal benefit
Fundamental theorems of welfare economics	Returns to scale
Pareto-efficient resource allocation	Natural monopoly
Decentralized market mechanism	Marginal revenue
Marginal rate of substitution	Public goods
Production function	Externalities
Marginal rate of transformation	Incomplete markets
Marginal cost	Merit goods

QUESTIONS AND PROBLEMS

1. For each of the programs listed below, discuss what market failures might be (or are) used as partial rationale:
    a) Automobile safety belt requirements
    b) Regulations on automobile pollution
    c) National defense
    d) Unemployment compensation
    e) Medicare (medical care for the aged)
    f) Medicaid (medical care for the indigent)
    g) Federal Deposit Insurance Corporation
    h) Federally insured mortgages
    i) Law requiring lenders to disclose the true rate of interest they are charging on loans
    j) National Weather Service
    k) Urban renewal
    l) Post office

m) Government prohibition of the use of narcotics

n) Rent control

2. If the primary objective of government programs in each of these areas were the alleviation of some market failure, how might they be better designed?

a) Farm price supports

b) Oil import quotas (in the 1950s)

c) Special tax provisions for energy industries

3. Many government programs both redistribute income and correct a market failure. What are the market failures associated with each of these programs, and how else might they be addressed if there were no distributional objectives?

a) Student loan programs

b) Public elementary education

c) Public supported universities

d) Social security

4. Try to define clearly arguments for the following programs based on merit goods, externalities, and redistribution. Contrast the ways in which considerations of consumer sovereignty would weigh in each of these instances.

a) Social security

b) Education

c) Control of pornography

d) Public provision of medical care

e) Public provision of medical care for children

5. In Chapter 3 we discussed social contract theory which focuses on the gains to be had from individuals joining together for their mutual interests. Would someone who believed in the social contract theory of government find the market-failure approach of any use? Explain.

PART TWO

PUBLIC EXPENDITURE THEORY

This part is concerned with the basic theory of public expenditures. Chapter 5 explains what public goods are and describes what it means to have an under- or oversupply of public goods. Chapter 6 describes how the level of expenditures on public goods is determined. We focus in particular on the consequences of majority voting.

Governments both provide and produce goods. Some of the goods they provide are privately produced; some of the goods they produce are sold, just like private goods. Chapter 8 is concerned with the government as a producer. It asks, for instance, whether there are reasons one might expect the government to be less efficient than private firms.

In recent years, governments have taken an increasingly active role in attempting to control the adverse effects of a number of important externalities, including air and water pollution. Chapter 9 explains why market "solutions" may not be effective and discusses the merits of alternative public remedies.

5

Public Goods and Publicly Provided Private Goods

Few question whether the government should be involved in supplying public goods. How much should be spent on public goods, however, is frequently a matter of heated debate. There are those, for instance, who believe that the public sector is too large, that it spends too much on public goods. Others find the nation unresponsive to public needs that exist in a society of private affluence.

In this chapter we examine in detail two sets of questions:

1. What are public goods and how do they differ from conventional private goods?

2. What do statements such as "There is an undersupply of a public good" or "There is an oversupply of a public good" mean? How can we characterize the efficient level of supply of public goods? To what extent does the efficient level depend on distributional considerations or the system of taxes used to finance the public goods?

DEFINITION OF PURE PUBLIC GOODS

Pure public goods have two critical properties. The first is that it is not *feasible* to ration their use. The second is that it is not *desirable* to ration their use.

100
Public Goods
and Publicly
Provided Pri-
vate Goods
(Ch. 5)

Goods for Which Rationing Is Infeasible

The clearest example of a good for which rationing is not possible is national defense. If, for instance, our national defense achieves its objective in deterring an attack from the Soviet Union, then there is no way that any individual could be excluded from the benefits. Also, it is essentially impossible to exclude an individual from the benefits of a national health program, such as polio vaccination, that reduces the incidence of certain epidemics. It would be very costly to exclude individuals from small local parks; to do so would require that a fence be constructed around the park, which might interfere with the visual enjoyment of the park, and there would have to be someone always on duty to check permits or to collect entrance fees.

The Free Rider Problem. The infeasibility of rationing by the price system implies that if the good is to be provided, it must be provided publicly. Assume that the government did not provide for the national defense. Could a private firm enter to fill this gap? To do so, it would have to charge for the services it provides. But since every individual believes that he would benefit from the services provided, regardless of whether he contributes to the service, he has no incentive to pay for the services *voluntarily*. That is why individuals must be forced to support these goods through taxation. The reluctance of individuals to contribute voluntarily to the support of public goods is referred to as the **free rider problem.**

Two other examples may help illustrate the nature of the free rider problem. One of the methods by which the incidence of some diseases is reduced is through vaccination. Those who are vaccinated incur some cost (discomfort, time, money, risk of getting the disease from a bad batch of the vaccine). They receive some private benefit, in reduced likelihood of getting the disease, but a major part of the benefit is a public good, the reduced incidence of the disease in the community, from which all benefit. In many cases, the private costs exceed the private benefits, but the social benefits— including the reduced incidence of the disease—far exceed the costs. Because of the free rider problem, governments frequently require individuals to become vaccinated.

In many communities, fire departments are supported voluntarily. Some individuals in the community refuse to contribute to the fire department. Yet, in an area where buildings are close together, the fire department will usually put out a fire in a noncontributor's building because of the threat it poses to adjacent contributors' structures. But there have been instances of fires at isolated noncontributors' buildings where fire departments refused to put out the fire. The fire departments were severely criticized. This is an example in which exclusion is feasible; the fire department can withhold its services from those who do not contribute to its support. The fire departments claim that in the absence of such sanctions, everyone will wish to be a free rider. Why should they pay, if they can obtain the service for nothing? Because of the outrage that occurs, however, whenever a fire department refuses to put out a fire, most communities prefer to provide the service to everyone; but to avoid the free rider problem, they usually require everyone to support it (through taxes).

It is in the interest of all to agree to be coerced to pay taxes to provide for public goods. In Figure 5.1 we have depicted two utility possibilities sched-

ules, one drawn under the assumption that the government does not provide
public goods and the other under the assumption that it does. Compare
point A to point E. At A, with the government providing public goods,
everyone is better off than at E, where it does not. (Recall the definition of
the utility-possibilities schedule: it gives—under a particular set of circumstances—the maximum level of utility of one group or individual consistent
with the level of utility attained by the others.) But once the power of coercion is granted, unless it is somehow circumscribed, it is clearly possible for
some group to take advantage of this power to extract resources from some
other group, a situation corresponding to Point B in Figure 5.1. Thus, granting the government the power to coerce has the potential of making all individuals better off; it also has the potential of making some individuals better
off at the expense of others.

Free rider problems arise, of course, in a variety of other contexts. There
are often members of a family who fail to pull their own weight; for example,
children who attempt to avoid doing the household errands that have to be
done. These children know that it is unlikely that the quantity of the services
they receive will be significantly affected by their actions. Somebody else
will pick up the slack and make sure everything gets done.

Most of the goods provided within the family are provided in much the
same manner that public goods are: individuals normally do not pay for the
food they eat at home in the way they would if they were buying it in a
restaurant, nor do they get paid for the services they perform. Exclusion is
costly, if not impossible, just as it is for public goods. The costs of adminis-

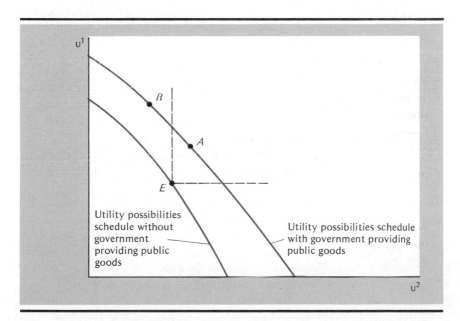

5.1 THE UTILITY POSSIBILITIES FRONTIER The utility possibilities frontier gives the
maximum utility attainable by one individual (one group) given the utility level of the second.
With government providing public goods (coercing both to contribute), both individuals can
be better off than without government provision, as at point A. But the power of coercion can
be used by one group to gain at the expense of another, as at point B.

102
Public Goods
and Publicly
Provided Pri-
vate Goods
(Ch. 5)

tering a price system within a family would be prohibitive—imagine charging a family member for each morsel of food he consumed, or each time he made use of a room. As a result, families often face the same kinds of free rider problems that communities do. But while social sanctions mitigate the effects of the free rider problem within the family, more explicit coercion is usually employed both at the local and national level.

Goods for Which Rationing Is Undesirable

The second property of a public good is that it is not desirable to exclude any individual: one individual's consumption does not detract from the amount that is available for others to consume. Equivalently, the marginal cost of supplying the good to an additional individual is zero. If the government creates a military establishment that protects us from attack, it protects all of us; national defense costs are essentially unaffected when an additional baby is born or an additional individual migrates to the United States. This is in sharp contrast to private goods. If I am sitting on a chair, I deprive others of being able to sit on that chair. If I eat an ice cream cone, you cannot eat the same ice cream cone. It is important to distinguish the marginal cost of supplying the good from the marginal cost of an additional individual enjoying the good. It costs more having more lighthouses, but it costs no more for an additional ship to make use of a lighthouse when sailing by.

Pure and Impure Public Goods

National defense is one of the few *pure* public goods, satisfying both conditions: the impossibility and undesirability of exclusion. Another example are lighthouses: it is difficult (but not impossible) to exclude those who do not contribute to the support of the lighthouse from enjoying its benefits. The lighthouse owner could, of course, turn off his light upon the approach of a noncontributing ship, provided that there was not, at the same time, a contributing ship in the vicinity. In nineteenth-century England there were, in fact, some private lighthouses. Moreover, the marginal cost of an extra ship receiving the benefits of the lighthouse is zero.

Many goods have one or the other property and have these properties in varying degrees. For instance, exclusion may be feasible but undesirable. This is the case of an uncrowded road, for which a toll can be levied. But the toll would restrict the use of the road, even though once the road is paid for there are no significant costs associated with its use. In other cases, exclusion may be feasible but costly, and it therefore saves to provide the good publicly. For instance, some communities provide water free of charge; though it is possible to install water meters, the costs exceed the benefits. In other cases, the marginal costs associated with supplying the good to another individual, though small, are still not zero.

Figure 5.2 shows the ease of exclusion along the horizontal axis, and the (marginal) cost of an additional individual using the commodity along the vertical axis. The lower lefthand corner represents a pure public good, where the cost of exclusion is prohibitive and the marginal cost of supplying the good to an additional individual is zero. The upper righthand corner is a

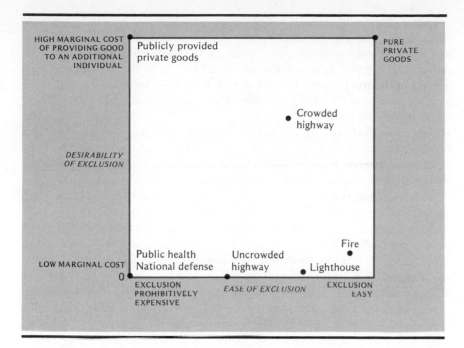

5.2 PURE AND IMPURE PUBLIC GOODS Goods differ in the ease and desirability of exclusion.

pure private good, where the cost of exclusion is low and the marginal cost of an additional individual using the commodity is high (equal to the average cost).

In the diagram are several "impure" cases. The marginal cost of usage of an uncongested road is close to zero, but there is a cost of exclusion (the toll collectors, and the loss in time to pay the toll). For a congested road, on the other hand, there may be a large social marginal cost associated with an additional individual using the road.

Most of the time, firemen are not engaged in fighting fires but are waiting for calls. Protecting an additional individual then has little extra cost. Only in that rare event when two fires break out simultaneously will there be a significant cost to extending the protection to an additional individual. On the other hand, the costs of excluding an individual from the services of the fire department are relatively low.[1]

Inefficiencies from the Private Provision of Public Goods

The kinds of goods we have called "public goods" may sometimes be provided privately. The argument for public provision is that it is more efficient to have them publicly provided.

---

[1]There may be disagreements about precisely where a particular program should lie. We have represented public health programs as being close to pure public goods. A program that results in the elimination of some disease (such as polio) from the population benefits everyone in society; it would not be feasible or desirable to exclude any individual from the benefits. On the other hand, the public health service provides other services that are like private goods—e.g., the provision of yellow fever vaccinations, which benefits primarily those who travel internationally.

104
**Public Goods
and Publicly
Provided Pri-
vate Goods
(Ch. 5)**

There are two sources of inefficiencies that may arise from the private provision of public goods. First, when there is no marginal cost to an additional individual using the good, then, as we have said, it should not be rationed. But if it is to be privately provided by a firm, the firm must charge for its use; and any charge for its use will discourage individuals from using it. Thus when public goods are privately provided, an *underutilization* of these goods will result.

This is illustrated in Figure 5.3 for the case of a bridge. We have drawn the demand curve for the bridge, describing the number of trips taken as a function of the toll charged. Lowering the toll results in increased demand for the bridge. The capacity of the bridge is Q_c; for any demand below Q_c, there is no congestion and no marginal cost associated with use of the bridge. Since the marginal cost of usage is zero, efficiency requires that the price for usage be zero. But clearly, the revenue raised by the bridge will then be zero.

Exclusion is, however, feasible: a private firm could construct the bridge and charge any toll it desired. It might, in particular, be possible for it to charge a toll that would more than cover the cost of construction. But whenever it charges a toll, the usage of the bridge will be reduced, and some trips, the benefits of which exceed the social cost (zero), will not be undertaken. We can measure the loss in welfare by the shaded triangle in Figure 5.3. This is referred to as the deadweight loss. To see this, we recall that the points on the demand curve measure the individual's marginal willingness

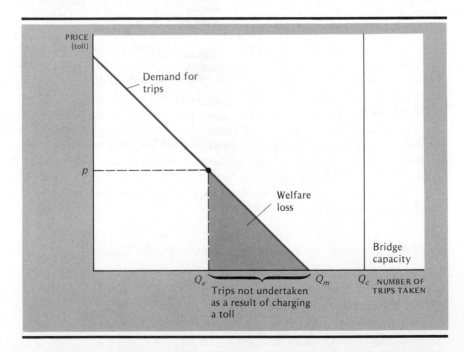

5.3 BRIDGES: GOODS WHERE EXCLUSION IS POSSIBLE BUT NOT NECESSARILY DESIRABLE It is feasible to charge a toll for crossing a bridge, but if the capacity of the bridge is large enough, it is not desirable to do so.

to pay for an extra trip at different quantities. Assume a price, p, was charged for the use of the bridge. The number of trips taken would then be Q_e. At Q_e, the individual's marginal willingness to pay (the price he is willing to pay) for an extra trip is just p. The cost of providing an extra trip is zero. The welfare loss from not taking the trip is the difference between what he is willing to pay (his marginal benefit) and the marginal cost; thus the welfare loss is just p. At slightly higher levels of output, the loss is still the marginal willingness to pay, but this is now smaller. The total welfare loss is the loss from not taking the $Q_e +$ first trip, $Q_e +$ second trip, etc.

This argument suggests that goods for which the marginal cost of provision is zero should be freely provided, regardless of whether it is feasible to charge for them. Occasionally, there may be a small marginal cost for using the public good, in which case the individual should be charged only the marginal cost. These **user charges** will not be sufficient to cover the total cost of the public good. The revenue required to pay for the public good must be raised in some other way. As we shall see in later chapters, most of the taxes used to raise revenue entail significant costs. The argument for the public provision of goods for which user charges could be levied is thus that the costs associated with charging for the use are *greater* than the costs associated with raising the revenue in some other way, such as through the income tax.

The second inefficiency that arises with the private provision of public goods is that, if they are supplied at all, they may be supplied in too small a quantity. This is seen most clearly in the case for which exclusion is impossible. Individuals' private enjoyment of the good may still be sufficient to induce them to purchase some of the public good. Thus, my neighbor across the street may enjoy the flowers I plant in front of my house as much as I do, and vice versa; the flowers are a public good; still, I plant them (even though he does not contribute to their support) because of the enjoyment I receive from them. There will, of course, be an undersupply of flowers. When I decide on how much effort to spend on my garden, I balance out the enjoyment I receive with the costs I have to pay. I do not include my neighbor's enjoyment.

Goods for Which Exclusion Is Feasible but Costly

There are, of course, costs associated with exclusion for private goods as well; that is, there are costs associated with running the price system. For example, the check-out clerks at grocery stores and the collectors of tolls along toll highways and at toll bridges are part of the administrative costs associated with operating a price mechanism. But while the costs of exclusion are relatively small for most private goods, they may be large (prohibitive) for some publicly provided goods.

Even when there is a marginal cost associated with each individual using a good, if the costs of running the price system are very high, it may be more efficient simply to provide the good publicly and finance the good—again, through general taxation.

We illustrate this in Figure 5.4, where we have depicted a good with constant marginal costs of production, c. It costs the firm $\$c$ to produce each

106
**Public Goods
and Publicly
Provided Pri-
vate Goods
(Ch. 5)**

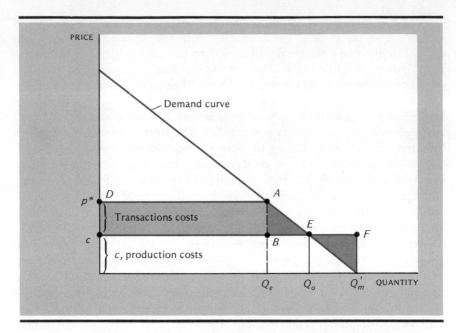

5.4 TRANSACTION COSTS When transaction costs are sufficiently high, it may be more efficient to supply the good publicly than to have the good supplied by private markets.

unit of the good.)[2] However, to sell the good requires certain *transaction costs;* these raise the price to p^*. Assume now the government supplied the good freely. This eliminates the transactions costs, and the entire heavily shaded area $ABCD$ is saved. There is a further gain as consumption increases from Q_e to Q_o, since individuals' marginal valuations exceed the marginal costs of production. The lightly shaded area ABE measures the gain. On the other hand, if individuals consume the good until the marginal value is zero, in expanding consumption from Q_o to Q_m, the marginal willingness to pay is less than the cost of production. This is obviously inefficient. To decide whether the good should be provided publicly, we must compare the savings in transactions costs and the gain from increasing consumption from Q_e to Q_o with a) the loss from the excessive consumption of the good (the shaded area EFQ_m in Figure 5.4), plus b) the loss from the distortions created by the taxes used to raise the revenue required to finance the provision of the good.

The high costs of private markets providing insurance has been used as one of the arguments for the public provision of insurance. Insurance does not satisfy the second property of public goods; the marginal cost of insuring one additional individual is, for instance, approximately equal to the average cost. For many kinds of insurance, the administrative costs (including the selling costs) associated with providing the insurance privately are more than 20 percent of the benefits paid out, in contrast with the administrative costs associated with public insurance, which (ignoring the distortions associated with the taxes required to finance the social insurance programs) are usually less than 10 percent of the value of the benefits.

---

[2] We assume, moreover, that the demand curve does not shift significantly as we raise taxes.

Publicly provided goods for which there is a large marginal cost associated with supplying additional individuals are referred to as **publicly provided private goods.** Though the costs of running a market provide one of the rationales for the public supply of some of these goods, it is not the only rationale. Education is a publicly provided private good. One of the usual explanations given for public provision is concerned with distributive considerations. For education, many feel that the opportunities of the young should not depend on the wealth of the parent.

If a private good is freely provided, there is likely to be overconsumption of the good. Since the individual does not have to pay for the good, he will demand it until the point where the marginal benefit he receives from the good is zero, in spite of the fact that there is a real marginal cost associated with providing it. In some cases, such as water, satiation may be quickly reached, so that the distortion may not be too large (Figure 5.5A). In other cases, such as the demand for certain types of medical services, the distortion may be very large (Figure 5.5B). Again, the welfare loss can be measured by the difference between what the individual is willing to pay for both the increase in output from Q_e (where price equals marginal cost) to Q_s (where price equals zero) and the costs of increasing production from Q_e to Q_s. This is the area of the shaded triangle in Figure 5.5B.

Rationing Devices for Publicly Provided Private Goods: Uniform Provision

It is likely, then, that some method for controlling consumption will have to be used. Any method restricting consumption of a good is called a **rationing system.** Prices provide one rationing system. We have already discussed how user charges may be used to limit demand. Another commonly employed way of rationing publicly provided goods is to supply the same quantity of the good to everyone. Thus, typically, we provide a uniform level of education to all individuals, even though some individuals would like to have more and some less. (Those who would like to purchase more may be able to purchase supplemental educational services on the private market, such as tutoring.) This, then, is the major disadvantage of the public provision of private goods: it does not allow for the adaptation to differences in individuals' needs and desires as does the private market.

This is illustrated in Figure 5.6, where we have drawn the demand curve for two different individuals. If the good was privately provided, individual 1, the high demander, would consume Q_1, while individual 2, the low demander, would consume the much smaller quantity Q_2. The government chooses a level of supply that is somewhere in between, Q^*. At this level of consumption, the high demander is consuming less than he would like; his marginal willingness to pay exceeds the marginal cost of production. On the other hand, the low demander is consuming more than the efficient level; his marginal willingness to pay is less than the marginal cost. (Since he does not have to pay anything for it, and still values the good positively, he, of course, consumes up to the point Q^*.)

108
**Public Goods
and Publicly
Provided Pri-
vate Goods
(Ch. 5)**

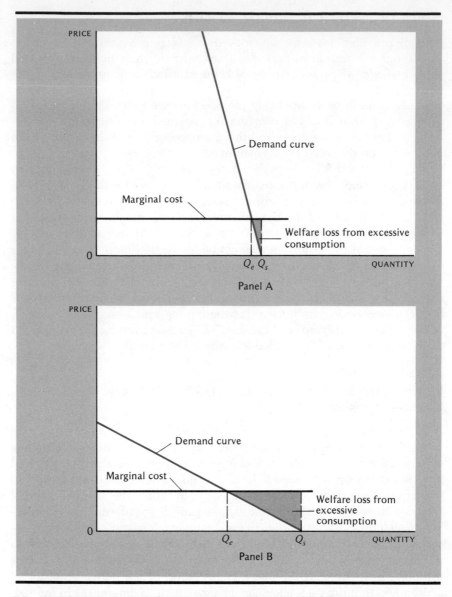

5.5   DISTORTIONS ASSOCIATED WITH SUPPLYING GOODS FREELY (A) For some goods, such as water, supplying the good freely rather than at marginal costs results in relatively little additional consumption. (B) For other goods, supplying the good freely rather than at marginal costs results in extensive overconsumption.

For certain types of insurance (say, social security for retirement), the government provides a basic, uniform level. Again, those who wish to purchase more can do so, but those who wish to purchase less cannot. The distortion here may not, however, be very great; if the uniform level provided is sufficiently low, then there will be relatively few individuals who are thereby induced to consume more than they otherwise would, and the

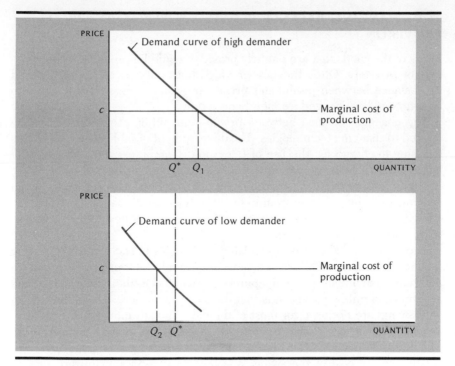

5.6 DISTORTIONS ASSOCIATED WITH UNIFORM PROVISION When the publicly provided private good is supplied in equal amounts to all individuals, some get more than the efficient level and some get less.

savings in administrative costs that we referred to earlier may more than offset the slight distortion associated with the uniform provision of the basic level of insurance.

Queuing as a Rationing Device

The second method of rationing that is commonly employed by the government is queuing: rather than charging individuals money for access to the publicly provided goods or services, the government requires that they pay a cost in waiting time. This enables some adaptability of the level of supply to the needs of the individual. Those who have a stronger demand for medical services are more willing to wait in the doctor's office. We have replaced one rationing mechanism with another. While it is claimed that money is an undesirable basis upon which to ration medical services—why should the wealthy have a greater right to good health than the poor?—it is not clear that willingness to wait in the doctor's office is any better a basis for rationing medical services; why should those for whom time is less costly have greater access to medical services than those for whom time is more costly? Using queuing as a rationing device has a cost (the use of time) for which there is no direct benefit. This is a cost that could be avoided if prices were used as a rationing device.

110
Public Goods
and Publicly
Provided Pri-
vate Goods
(Ch. 5)

THE CHANGING BALANCE BETWEEN PUBLIC AND PRIVATE PROVISION

Many of the goods that are publicly provided could be provided either publicly or privately. Often they are provided both publicly and privately; and the balance between public and private provision differs from country to country and has changed frequently over time.

The changing balance between private and public provision is partially related to changing technologies. The development of cable television makes it easier to charge for the use of television. Computers have lowered the administrative costs associated with many collection systems. For instance, it is now feasible to charge more for the use of subways at peak hours. Each car and each busy corner could conceivably be equipped with electronic devices to measure roadway use by individuals during peak hours, much as telephone use is now measured.

The changing balance is also related to changes in the standard of living (income per capita). Children's swings are provided in public parks, and, in addition, individuals privately purchase swings for their backyards. The advantage of public provision is that the swings are more fully utilized. Private swings are not used for most of the day. The advantage of private provision is that it saves on transportation costs. If the cost of transportation (including the value of the time it takes to go to the public park) increases relative to the cost of the swing, one might expect a shift toward private provision.

Albert Hirschman of the Institute for Advanced Study has recently suggested that these changing patterns are the consequences of changes in tastes.[3] He argues that there are periodic swings in the balance between private and public consumption. As individuals find disappointment or incomplete satisfaction in what they obtain in their private lives, they turn their attention to public service and to the public provision of goods and services. But their anticipations about the satisfaction that they can obtain in the public sphere are, in turn, unfulfilled, and in their disappointment they turn again to the private market.

EFFICIENCY CONDITIONS FOR PUBLIC GOODS

A central question of concern is how large the supply of public goods should be. What does it mean to say that the government is supplying too few or too many public goods? In Chapter 3 we provided a criterion that enables us to answer this question; a resource allocation is Pareto optimal if no one can be made better off without making someone else worse off. There we established that Pareto efficiency in private markets requires, among other criteria, that the individual's marginal rate of substitution equal his marginal rate of transformation.

In contrast, pure public goods are efficiently supplied when the sum of the marginal rates of substitution (over all individuals) is equal to the marginal rate of transformation. Assume when we increase our production of guns (national defense) by one, we must reduce our production of butter by

---

[3]A. O. Hirschman, *Shifting Involvements* (Princeton, NJ: Princeton University Press, 1981).

one pound (the marginal rate of transformation is unity). Guns used for national
defense are a public good. We consider a simple economy with three individuals: Robinson, Friday, and Fred. Robinson is willing to give up one-third of a pound of butter for an extra gun; that is, his marginal rate of substitution is one-third. Robinson would be happy to give up one-third of a pound of butter if the government were to buy one more gun for national defense. But his one-third pound alone does not buy the gun. We must consider the marginal rates of substitution of Friday and Fred. Friday is willing to give up one-half a pound of butter for an extra gun, and Fred is willing to give up one-sixth of a pound of butter. The total amount of butter that this small society would be willing to give up, were the government to buy one more gun, is

$$\tfrac{1}{3} + \tfrac{1}{2} + \tfrac{1}{6} = 1;$$

the total amount they would *have* to give up to get one more gun is also 1. Thus, the sum of the marginal rates of substitution equals the marginal rate of transformation; the government has provided an efficient level of public goods. If the sum of the marginal rates of substitution exceeded unity, then, collectively, individuals would be willing to give up more than they had to; we could ask each of them to give up an amount slightly less than the amount that would make them indifferent, and it would still be possible to increase the production of guns by one unit. Thus they could all be made better off by increasing the production of the public good (guns) by one.

This contrast between the condition for efficiency for private goods and for public goods can be seen most clearly in Figure 5.7. Panel A shows Robinson's indifference curve between guns (a public good representing the level of national defense) and butter, and in Panel B we have drawn Friday's indifference curve. (For simplicity, we omit Fred.) In Panel C we have drawn the production possibilities schedule, which describes the maximum amount of butter that can be produced for any given level of production of guns. If we produce more guns, we have less butter to consume. Initially, the level of production of guns is G^*; Robinson consumes B_R butter and Friday consumes B_F butter. The sum of the two adds up to aggregate production of butter, B^*. We wish to know whether this is an undersupply or an oversupply. Assume the government contemplates increasing the production of guns by one to G_1. Robinson is willing to give up the amount denoted by x, which is just his marginal rate of substitution, the amount of butter he is willing to give up to have one more gun publicly provided. Similarly, Friday is willing to give up the amount denoted by y. The total amount that they would be willing to give up is thus $x + y$, the sum of their marginal rates of substitution. From Panel C we see the amount that they have to give up; the output of butter must be reduced by z to produce the extra gun. z is the marginal rate of transformation. If the marginal rate of transformation is less than the sum of the marginal rates of substitution, production of guns should increase from G^* (since the individuals, in total, are willing to give up more butter than is necessary to obtain an extra gun). Similarly, if the marginal rate of transformation is less than the sum of the marginal rates of substitution, production of guns would be reduced. Only when the two are identical is there an efficient level of production.

112
**Public Goods
and Publicly
Provided Pri-
vate Goods
(Ch. 5)**

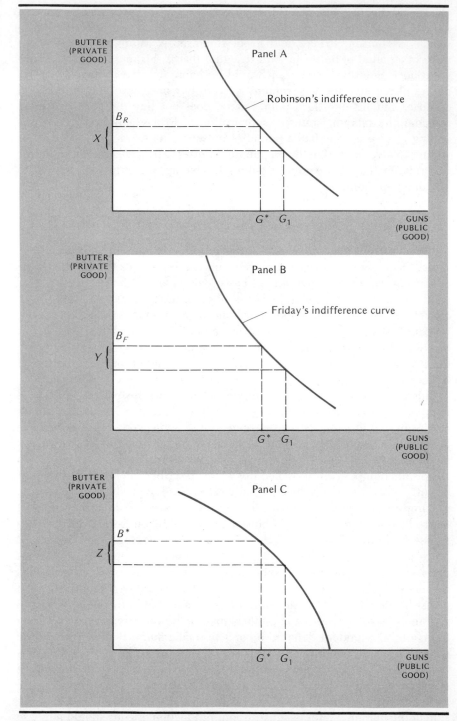

5.7 EFFICIENT LEVEL OF PRODUCTION OF PUBLIC GOODS (A) Robinson's indifference curve. (B) Friday's indifference curve. (C) Production possibilities schedule. At the efficient level of production, the sum of the marginal rates of substitution $(X + Y)$ equals the marginal rate of transformation.

Demand Curves for Public Goods

In Chapter 4 we described a market equilibrium as the intersection of a demand and a supply curve. We showed that at this point, the marginal benefit of producing an extra unit was equal to the marginal cost. That is why the market equilibrium is Pareto efficient.

We can use a similar apparatus to describe the efficient level of production of public goods. We can derive the individual's demand curve for public goods in the same way we can derive the individual's demand curve for private goods.

Assume we told Robinson that he had to pay 50¢ for each gun purchased by the government. We could then ask him how many guns he would like the government to purchase. Robinson would approach this problem in the same way that he would approach the problem of how to divide his income between apples and oranges. We first represent his budget constraint as in Panel A of Figure 5.8. Assume that initially the individual has 100 pounds of butter, and that butter costs $1 per pound. Then, for every gun the government purchases, he has to give up ½ pound of butter. The line *AA* gives his *budget constraint;* for each level of consumption of butter it gives the maximum level of guns he can ask for. The slope of the budget constraint, which says how many extra guns he can get for each pound of butter, is equal to the ratio of the prices, 2. He picks the point on the budget constraint where his indifference curve is highest; that is, point *E*, where his indifference curve is tangent to the budget constraint, so the marginal rate of substitution (the slope of the indifference curve) is equal to the price ratio, the slope of the budget constraint. Assume now that we require he pay 25¢ for every gun purchased. Then his budget constraint is the line *AA'* (if he spent all his income on guns, he could now get 400). He chooses the point *E'*. As we change the price ratio, we trace out the different points on the demand curve, shown in Panel B.

We can go through a similar analysis for Friday and add up the demand curves *vertically*. Since each point on the demand curve of an individual represents his marginal rate of substitution at that level of government expenditure, by adding the demand curves vertically we simply obtain the sum of the marginal rates of substitution (the total marginal benefit from producing an extra unit). The result is the aggregate demand curve shown in Figure 5.9.

We can draw a supply curve just as we did for private goods; for each level of output, the price represents how much of the other goods have to be foregone to produce one more unit of guns; this is the marginal cost, or the marginal rate of transformation. Thus at the point of intersection of the aggregate demand curve and the supply curve, the sum of the marginal rates of substitution equals the marginal rate of transformation, and the total marginal benefit equals the marginal cost as required by economic efficiency.

Though we constructed the demand curve for public goods in a manner exactly analogous to the manner in which we constructed the demand curve for private goods, there are some important distinctions between the two. In particular, while market *equilibrium* occurs at the intersection of the demand and supply curves, we have not provided any explanation for why

114
**Public Goods
and Publicly
Provided Pri-
vate Goods
(Ch. 5)**

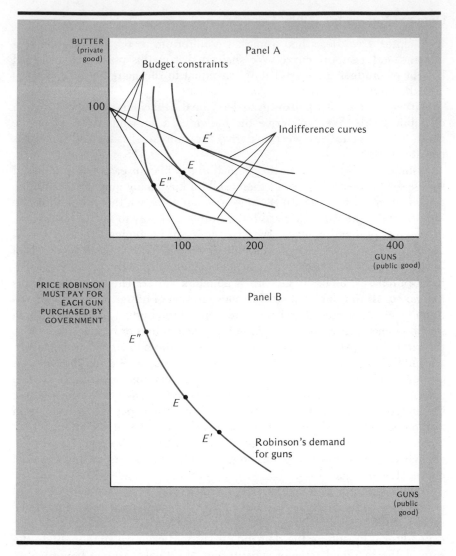

5.8 DERIVATION OF DEMAND CURVES FOR PUBLIC GOODS Robinson's demand
curve for guns may be derived by asking the individual how much of the public good he would
like, if he has to pay a given amount for each unit produced.

the equilibrium supply of public goods should occur at the intersection of
the demand curve we have constructed and the supply curve. We have only
established that if it did, the level of production of the public good would be
Pareto efficient. Decisions about the level of public goods are made publicly,
by governments, and not by individuals; hence, whether production occurs
at this point depends on the nature of the political process, a subject we
discuss at length in the next chapter.

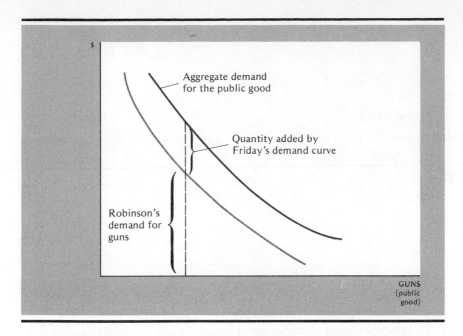

5.9 AGGREGATE DEMAND FOR PUBLIC GOODS Since at each point on the demand curve the price is equal to the marginal rate of substitution, by adding the demand curves vertically we obtain the sum of the marginal rates of substitution, the total amount of butter that the individuals in society are willing to give up to get one more gun. The vertical sum thus can be thought of as the aggregate demand curve for the public good.

Pareto Optimality and Income Distribution

There is not a unique Pareto-optimal supply of public goods. The intersection of the demand and supply curve in Figure 5.10 is one of these Pareto-efficient levels of supply, but there are others as well, with different distributional implications.

To see how the efficient level of public goods depends on the distribution of income, assume the government transferred a dollar of income from Robinson to Friday. This would normally shift Robinson's demand for public goods (at any price) down and Friday's up. In general, there is no reason why these changes should exactly offset each other, so that the aggregate level of demand will normally change. With this new distribution of income, there is a new efficient level of public goods. Efficiency is still characterized by the sum of the marginal rates of substitution equaling the marginal rate of transformation.

The fact that the efficient level of public goods depends, in general, on the distribution of income has one important implication: one cannot separate out efficiency considerations in the supply of public goods from distributional considerations. Any change in the distribution of income, say, brought about by a change in the income tax structure, will thus be accompanied by corresponding changes in the efficient levels of public-goods production.[4]

---

[4]Some economists have suggested that decisions concerning the efficient level of public-goods production and distribution of income can be separated; for instance, there is a view that concerns about the distribution

116
**Public Goods
and Publicly
Provided Pri-
vate Goods
(Ch. 5)**

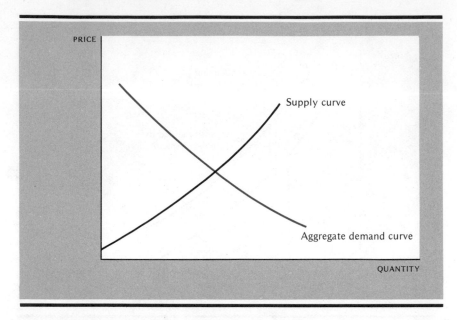

5.10   EFFICIENT PRODUCTION OF PUBLIC GOODS An efficient supply of public goods occurs at the point of intersection of the demand curve and the supply curve. The aggregate demand curve gives the sum of what all individuals are willing to give up, at the margin, to have one more unit of public goods (one more gun), while the supply curve gives the amount of other goods that have to be given up to obtain one more unit of the public good.

Limitations on Income Redistribution and Efficiency

Governments, in evaluating the benefits of a public program, often seem to be particularly concerned with the question of *who* benefits from the program. They seem to *weight* benefits that accrue to the poor more highly than benefits that accrue to the rich. Yet the previous analysis suggested that one should simply add up the marginal rates of substitution, the amounts that each individual is willing to pay at the margin for an increase in the public good, treating the rich and the poor equally. How can these approaches be reconciled?

In our previous discussion, we showed how we could trace out the utility possibilities schedule simply by taking away resources from one individual and giving them to another. The process was assumed to be a costless one, and nothing was lost along the way. But in practice, the process of transferring resources from Robinson to Friday may be very costly. Recall our parable from Chapter 3, where in the process of transferring oranges from Robinson to Friday some of the oranges were lost. In our economy, we use the tax system and welfare system to redistribute resources; not only are the administrative costs of running this system large, but the taxes may have

---

of income should be reflected in tax schedules and welfare programs, but that decisions concerning the supply of public goods can and should be made quite independently of such considerations. There are some cases where the decisions can be separated (see Atkinson and Stiglitz, *Lectures in Public Economics* [New York: McGraw-Hill, 1980]) or L. J. Lau, E. Sheshinski, and J. E. Stiglitz, "Efficiency in the Optimum Supply of Public Goods," *Econometrica* 46 [1978]: 269–84), but these are indeed special.

important incentive effects—for instance, on individuals' savings and work decisions. The fact that redistributing resources through the tax system is costly implies that the government may look for alternative ways to achieve its redistributive goals; one way is to incorporate redistributive considerations into its evaluation of public projects.

Distortionary Taxation and Efficiency

The fact that the revenue raised to finance public goods is raised through taxes, such as the income tax, which have important effects on incentives, has some important implications for the efficient supply of public goods. The amount of private goods that individuals must give up to get one more unit of public goods is greater than it would be if the government could raise revenue in a way that did not entail these incentive effects and that was not costly to administer.

We can define a *feasibility* curve, giving the maximum level of private-goods consumption consistent with each level of public goods, for our given tax system. The tax system introduces inefficiencies, so this feasibility locus lies inside the production possibilities schedule, as in Figure 5.11.

The amount of private goods we have to give up to obtain one more unit of public goods, taking into account these extra costs, is called the marginal **economic rate of transformation,** as opposed to the marginal **physical rate of transformation** we employed in our earlier analysis. The latter is completely determined by *technology,* while the marginal economic rate of transformation takes into account the costs associated with the taxes required

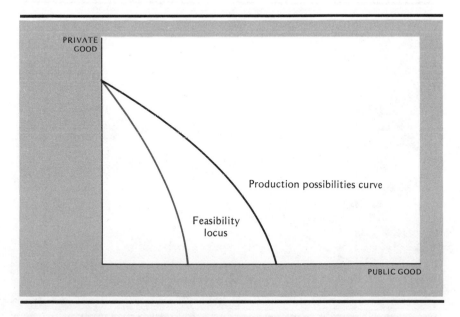

5.11 THE FEASIBILITY LOCUS The feasibility locus gives the maximum output (consumption) of private goods for any level of public goods, taking into account the inefficiencies that arise from the taxes that must be imposed to raise the requisite revenue. The feasibility locus lies below the production possibilities schedule.

118
**Public Goods
and Publicly
Provided Pri-
vate Goods
(Ch. 5)**

to finance increased public expenditure. Thus we replace the earlier condition that the marginal physical rate of transformation equal the sum of the marginal rates of substitution with the new condition, that the marginal economic rate of transformation equal the sum of the marginal rates of substitution.

Since it becomes more costly to obtain public goods when taxation imposes distortions, normally this will imply that the efficient level of public goods is smaller than it would have been with nondistortionary taxation.

Indeed, it appears that much of the debate in recent years about the desirable level of public goods provision has centered around this issue. There are those who believe that the distortions associated with the tax system are not very great, while there are others who contend that, with our present high tax rates, the cost of attempting to raise additional revenues for public goods is great. They *may* agree on the magnitude of the social benefits that may accrue from additional government expenditures, but disagree on the costs.

In Figure 5.12 we have drawn a *backward-bending feasibility locus.* There is a maximum level of public goods that can be provided; attempts by the government to raise more revenue, by imposing additional taxes, lead individuals to reduce their effort and induce firms to reduce investment, and thus lead to a lower level of private-goods consumption *and* a lower level of tax revenue (and hence government expenditure). This curve has been popularized in recent years as the Laffer curve, after Arthur Laffer of the University of Southern California, although the possibility of the effect the curve

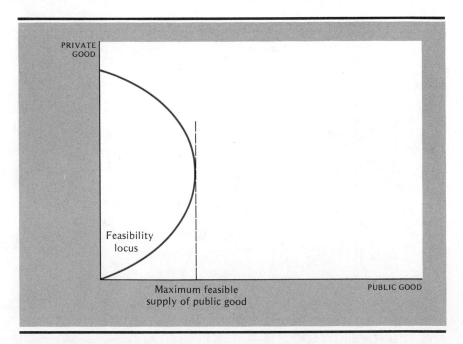

5.12 THE LAFFER CURVE Raising tax rates beyond some level may so decrease incentives that output, and tax revenues, are actually reduced. There is then a maximum feasible level of government expenditure.

describes has been noted by others earlier. It has provided one of the bases of what has come to be called *supply-side* economics, which claims that reducing tax rates would increase tax revenues. Although this is clearly theoretically possible, there is no evidence that this is a relevant concern at current tax rates.

EFFICIENT GOVERNMENT AS A PUBLIC GOOD

One of the most important public goods is the management of the government: we all benefit from a better, more efficient, more responsive government. Indeed, "good government" possesses both of the properties of public goods we noted earlier: it is difficult and undesirable to exclude any individual from the benefits of a better government.

If the government is able to become more efficient and reduce taxes without reducing the level of government services, we all benefit. The politician who succeeds in doing this may get some return, but this return is only a fraction of the benefits that accrue to others. In particular, those who voted against the politician who succeeds in doing this gain as much as those who worked for his election, and the individual who did not vote, who attempted to free-ride on the political activities of others, benefits as much as either.

SUMMARY

1. This chapter has defined an important class of goods, pure public goods. They have two critical properties:
   a) It is impossible to exclude individuals from enjoying the benefits of the goods, and
   b) It is undesirable to exclude individuals from enjoying the benefits of the goods, since their enjoyment of these goods does not detract from that of others.
2. While there are a few examples of pure public goods, such as national defense, for most publicly provided goods exclusion is possible, although frequently costly. Imposing user charges may result in the underutilization of public facilities.
3. Private markets either will not supply or will provide an inadequate supply of public goods.
4. The problem with voluntary arrangements for providing public goods arises from individuals trying to be *free riders*, of simply enjoying the benefits of the public goods paid for by others.
5. For publicly provided private goods, some method of rationing other than the price system may be used: sometimes queuing is used, while at other times the good is simply provided in fixed quantities to all individuals. Both of these entail inefficiencies.
6. Pareto efficiency requires that a public good be supplied up to the point where the sum of the marginal rates of substitution equals the marginal rate of transformation. Different Pareto-optimal levels of consumption of the public good will be associated with different distributions of income.
7. The basic rule for the efficient level of supply of public goods must be modified when there are costs (distortions) associated with raising revenue and redistributing income.
8. Efficient management in government is a public good itself.

120
**Public Goods
and Publicly
Provided Pri-
vate Goods
(Ch. 5)**

KEY CONCEPTS

Pure public goods   Publicly provided private goods
Exclusion   Uniform provision
Free rider problem   Rationing system
User charges   Marginal physical rate of transformation
                                 Marginal economic rate of transformation

QUESTIONS AND PROBLEMS

1. Where should each of the following goods lie in Figure 5.2? Explain why each is
   or is not a pure public good. Where applicable, note instances where the good is
   both publicly and privately provided:
   a) College education   h) Retirement insurance
   b) A local park   i) Medicine
   c) Yosemite Park   j) Police protection
   d) Sewage collection   k) TV
   e) Water   l) Basic research
   f) Electricity   m) Applied research
   g) Telephone service

2. What happens to the efficient allocation between public and private goods as an
   economy becomes wealthier? Can you think of examples of public goods, the consumption of which would increase more than proportionate to the increase in
   income? Less than proportionate to the increase in income?

3. The government rations a variety of publicly provided private goods or public-
   goods (in which there is congestion) in a variety of ways. Discuss how each of these
   are rationed, and consider the effect of alternative rationing systems:
   a) Public higher education
   b) Health services, in the U.K.
   c) Yellowstone National Park
      What happens to a publicly provided good in which congestion can occur
      (such as a highway or swimming pool on a hot, sunny day) but in which no
      direct rationing system is employed?

4. To what extent do you think differences in views between those who believe there
   should be less spending on public goods and those who believe there should be
   more spending can be attributed to differences in judgments concerning the marginal cost of public goods, including the increased distortions associated with the
   additional taxes required to finance public goods? What are other sources of disagreement?

5. What implications might the fact that efficient government is a public good have
   for the efficiency with which governments function?

APPENDIX: AN ALTERNATIVE EXPOSITION OF PUBLIC-GOODS
EFFICIENCY: THE LEFTOVER CURVE

In this chapter we developed public-goods efficiency through indifference curve
analysis. The conditions for Pareto efficiency can be shown in another way.

In Figure 5.13A we have superimposed Robinson's indifference curve on the production possibilities schedule. If the government provides a level of public goods G,
and wishes, at the same time, to ensure that Robinson attains the level of utility
associated with the indifference curve U_1 drawn in the figure, then the amount of
private good that is "leftover" for the second individual is the vertical distance between

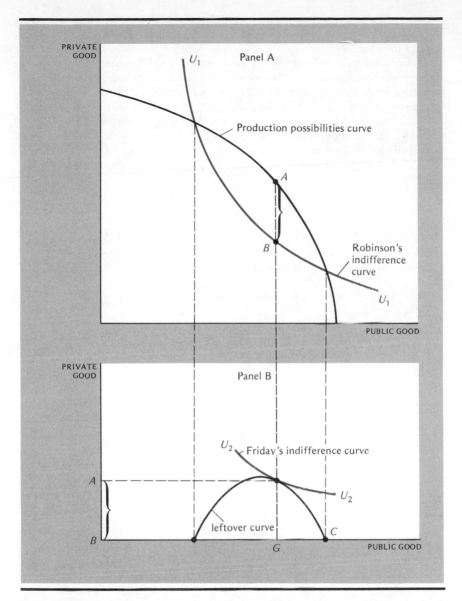

5.13 DETERMINATION OF THE EFFICIENT LEVEL OF PRODUCTION OF PUBLIC GOODS (A) If the level of public goods is G, and the first individual is to get level of utility U_1, then the distance AB represents the amount of private goods left over for the second individual. (B) The second individual's welfare is maximized at the point of tangency of his indifference curve and the "leftover" curve.

the production possibilities schedule and the indifference curve. Accordingly, we call the (vertical) difference between the two the leftover curve. This leftover curve is plotted in Figure 5.13B. We now superimpose on Figure 5.13B Friday's indifference curves. The highest level of utility he can attain, consistent with the production possibilities schedule, and consistent with the prespecified level of utility of the first individual, is at the point of tangency between his indifference curve and the leftover curve.

122
Public Goods
and Publicly
Provided Pri-
vate Goods
(Ch. 5)

Since the leftover curve represents the difference between the production possibilities schedule for the economy and the first individual's indifference curve, the slope of the "leftover" curve is the difference between the slope of the production possibilities schedule and the slope of the individual's indifference curve. The slope of the production possibilities schedule is, as we just saw, the marginal rate of transformation, while the slope of the indifference curve is the marginal rate of substitution. Since if G is the optimal level of public goods the leftover curve must be tangent to the second individual's indifference curve, the Pareto efficiency of the economy requires that the slope of the leftover curve be equal to the slope of the second individual's indifference curve—that is,

$$MRT - MRS^1 = MRS^2$$

or

$$MRT = MRS^1 + MRS^2,$$

where MRT stands for the marginal rate of transformation and MRS^i stands for the ith individual's marginal rate of substitution. The marginal rate of transformation must equal the sum of the marginal rates of substitution.

6

Public Choice

The supply of conventional goods is determined by market forces. Equilibrium occurs at the intersection of the demand and supply curves. As we saw in Chapter 3, these market forces ensure that what is produced reflects the tastes of consumers. In contrast, the supply of public goods is determined through a political process. This chapter is concerned with two sets of questions:

1. What can we say about how the level of public-goods expenditure is determined in a democratic society, such as the United States, where such decisions are made by majority voting (or by elected representatives who are chosen on the basis of a majority vote)? How accurately are the preferences of the citizens reflected? Is the supply Pareto efficient? If not, are expenditures on public goods too high or too low?

2. Are there better democratic procedures for determining the level of public goods? Are there procedures that better reflect the preferences of the individuals in society? It is often alleged that the government acts in an inconsistent manner, making a series of choices and decisions that appear to be incompatible. Is this a reflection of incompetence on the part of government officials, is it a consequence of particular aspects of the political process in the United States, or is this an *inevitable* consequence of democratic decision making?

These questions bring us to the border between political science and economics. Our concern is understanding economic aspects of the political process. Traditional political science has been particularly concerned with the role of special-interest groups and how various political institutions and groups in society exercise "political power." Our focus is somewhat more abstract. We say nothing about particular institutions, and little about interest groups. Nor do we discuss the influence of particular individuals, of a Ronald Reagan or a Franklin D. Roosevelt on the outcomes of the political process. We are concerned with questions such as: How can we explain the tendency in the United States for both political parties to move toward the center, with the consequence that voters are presented with relatively little choice? How successfully can we predict, on the basis of economic variables alone, the outcomes of elections and the voting patterns of the elected representatives?

We begin our discussion with an analysis of how the political process for determining the level of public goods differs from market mechanisms.

PRIVATE MECHANISMS FOR ALLOCATING RESOURCES

The market economy provides a simple and effective method for determining the level of production of *private* goods: the price system. It provides incentives for firms to produce goods that are valued and it provides a basis for allocating the goods that are produced among the various consumers. We often speak of the important role that prices play in conveying information: from consumers to producers, concerning the value they attach to different commodities, and from producers to consumers and from one producer to another, concerning the costs of production and the scarcity of these commodities.

Equilibrium in private markets is determined at the intersection of the demand curve and the supply curve; when, for one reason or another, the demand for some commodity increases, the demand curve shifts up, the price rises, and this induces firms to produce more. Thus, information about a change in individuals' taste is conveyed, through the price system, to firms. Similarly, when, for one reason or another, it becomes less costly to produce some commodity, the supply curve for that commodity will shift down, the price will fall, and individuals will be induced to shift their consumption toward the commodity that is now cheaper. Again, the price system has conveyed information about the change in technology from the firm to consumers. Indeed, one of the central results of modern welfare economics, as we pointed out in chapter 4, is that in a competitive economy, the resulting resource allocations are efficient.[1]

PUBLIC MECHANISMS FOR ALLOCATING RESOURCES

Decisions about resource allocations in the public sector are made in quite a different manner. Individuals vote for elected representatives, these elected representatives in turn vote for a public budget, and the money itself is spent by a variety of administrative agencies. There is thus a major difference between how an individual decides to spend his own money and how, say, Congress decides to spend the public's money. A congressman, when he votes, is supposed to reflect the views of constitutents, not just his own views. In deciding how to vote, he faces two problems: first he must ascer-

---

[1] It is important, however, to bear in mind the many caveats to this basic result that we discussed in Chapter 4. In particular, the simple heuristic argument concerning the informational role played by prices in efficient production needs to be treated with some caution. Traditional anaylsis makes very strong and unrealistic assumptions concerning the nature of the information that is available to the various agents in society. When more realistic informational assumptions are made, the welfare theorem needs to be qualified.

tain what the views of his constituents are; secondly, since these views are likely to differ, he must decide how much weight to assign to various positions.

125
**Public Mecha-
nisms for
Allocating
Resources**

The Problem of Preference Revelation

While individuals may express their views about the desirability of one private good versus another by a simple action—they decide either to buy the good or not—there is no comparably effective way that individuals can express their views about the desirability of one public good versus another.

Federal elections of senators and representatives convey only limited information about voters' attitudes toward specific public goods; at best, they convey a general notion that voters prefer more or less government spending. At the state and local levels, voters are sometimes asked to approve specific appropriations (often bond issues for provision of highways and mass transportation). But even then, the information obtained is limited; if an individual voted for what is in his own best interest, it would simply indicate that he believed that his gain from the public program exceeded its cost to him. If a majority votes for the program, it means that this is true for at least half the voters, but not that the sum of the benefits exceeded the costs.

Economists have also worried, in those circumstances where individuals are asked what their preferences are, whether they would *truthfully* reveal their preferences. Is there any way in which individuals could be induced to reveal truthfully their preferences concerning public goods?

The decision maker in private decisions knows his own preferences. The decision maker in public decisions has to ascertain the preferences of those on whose behalf he is making the decision. This is the first important difference between public and private resource allocations.

The Problem of Aggregating Preferences: Reconciling Differing Views

Even if all individuals correctly and honestly reveal their preferences, the politician must have some way of putting the information together to make a decision. In the private market, the firm does not have to balance the claims and interests of one group against those of another. If an individual is willing to pay a price for the commodity that exceeds the marginal cost of production, it pays the firm to sell the commodity to the individual. Decisions are made on an individual basis. In contrast, in the public sector, decisions are made collectively—when a politician votes to increase the expenditure on some public good, it is not as if he has to pay for the good himself. His vote is intended to represent the interest of his constituents, but their opinions are not likely to be unanimous. Some individuals would like more military spending, others less. Some individuals would like more expenditures on welfare, others less. How should the politician vote in the face of such conflicts?

One view is that he should read the previous chapter of this book. He will then realize that efficiency requires that the sum of the marginal rates of substitution equal the marginal rate of transformation. If his course of action is clear, he could obtain the requisite information.

There is another view, which sees the politician as an individual acting in his self-interest (just as consumers and producers act in their own self-interest). The politician is interested in staying in office. The "price" he pays (or receives) for voting one way or another on budgetary issues is a loss (or gain) in votes. (This assumes, of course, that there is some significant relationship between how the politican votes on particular budgetary matters and how citizens vote in the next election). What implications this hypothesis has for the voting behavior of politicians is a question we shall soon investigate.

But even when a particular representative decides about his position on a specific issue, other representatives are likely to have differing views. The problem of reconciling differences arises whenever there must be a collective decision. Popular political discussions often refer to what the "people" want. But since different people want different things, how, out of these divergent views, can a social decision be made? In a dictatorship, the answer is easy: it is the preferences of the dictator that dominate. But in a democracy, there is no such easy resolution. A number of different voting rules have been suggested, among them unanimity voting, simple majority voting, and two-thirds majority voting. Of these, perhaps the most widely employed rule for decision making in a democracy is majority voting.

MAJORITY VOTING

The majority voting rule says that, in the choice between two alternatives, the alternative that receives the majority of votes wins. The alternatives can be thought of as two different levels of expenditure on some public good, or the decision to undertake one project, say, building a new swimming pool, rather than another, say, building a new set of tennis courts.

How the Typical Taxpayer Casts His Vote

We first analyze the *preferences* of the voter. We shall assume that he casts his ballot on the narrow grounds of self-interest: he evaluates the benefits he receives from any new government program and compares it with the extra costs he has to bear. Thus, in Figure 6.1A, as the government increases its expenditures on public goods, the individual gets some extra benefit (the *marginal utility* of an additional expenditure on public goods). The *marginal costs* he has to bear depend on the tax structure. Assume, for instance, that the tax burden is shared equally among 100 individuals. Then, if the government spends $1,000 more on public goods, his extra tax is $10; his *marginal cost* (in utility terms) is the marginal utility of each dollar (which he would otherwise spend on the consumption of private goods) times his incremental tax ($10).[2]

If the government is spending very little on public goods, the marginal utility of the public good is very high; as the government spends more and more, the marginal utility of the public good diminishes. At the same time, as the government spends more on public goods, individuals have fewer

---

[2]Throughout this discussion, we assume that a unit of the public good costs the same as a unit of private goods. (There is no loss of generality in doing this.)

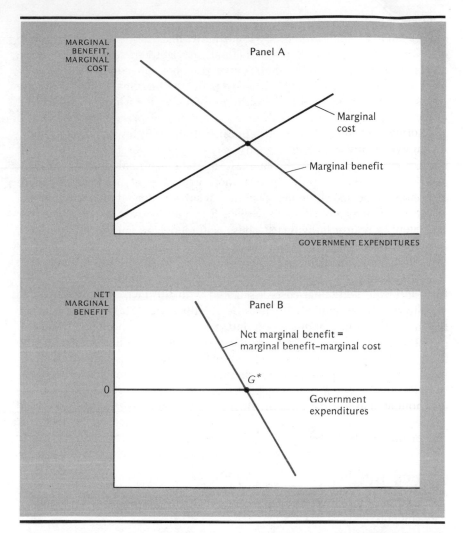

MARGINAL
BENEFIT,
MARGINAL
COST

Panel A

Marginal
cost

Marginal benefit

GOVERNMENT EXPENDITURES

NET
MARGINAL
BENEFIT

Panel B

Net marginal benefit =
marginal benefit–marginal cost

G^*

0

Government
expenditures

6.1 INDIVIDUAL'S EVALUATION OF THE DESIRABILITY OF INCREASED GOV-
ERNMENT EXPENDITURES As public expenditure increases, the marginal benefit of increased
expenditures decreases, and the marginal cost (of foregone private expenditures) increases. As
a result, the *net* marginal benefit of public expenditures eventually becomes negative. G^* is the
individual's most preferred level of expenditures.

private goods, and the marginal utility of private goods thus increases, so
the marginal cost (in utility terms) of the public good increases. Since the
marginal benefits from public goods are diminishing, and the marginal costs
are increasing, the *net marginal benefit*, while positive for low values of
government expenditures, is negative for high values of government expenditures, as we see in Figure 6.1B. To put this another way, the individual's
utility increases initially with increased government expenditures (there is a
positive net marginal benefit) but eventually decreases. The level of government expenditures most preferred by the individual is obviously that level
at which utility is maximized, or where the *net* marginal benefit—the marginal benefit minus the marginal cost—is zero.

There are three factors that determine an individual's attitudes toward public-goods expenditure. First, some individuals may simply like public goods more than others. Some individuals may get a great deal of pleasure out of public parks, while others never use them. Secondly, individuals' incomes differ. For individuals who are poor, the marginal utility of private goods will be higher than for wealthy individuals. Poor individuals will be less willing than the wealthy to give up a dollar of private goods to get a given increment in public goods. Because they have fewer private goods, the marginal utility of public goods may be higher for them as well, but under normal conditions, the increase in their marginal utility of private goods exceeds that for public goods; more generally, at any level of expenditure on public goods the marginal rate of substitution—how many units of private goods they are willing to sacrifice for a unit increase in public goods—is smaller for poorer individuals. These statements are not inconsistent with the observations that poor individuals may demand more public goods; this is because of the third determinant of individual's attitudes toward increased public expenditure—the nature of the tax system, which determines what fraction of the additional costs associated with the increased public-goods expenditures each individual has to bear. Thus, with a tax where everyone has to pay the same amount, a poor individual is likely to prefer a lower level of public-goods expenditure, since the marginal cost to him (in terms of the foregone utility from the private goods he has to give up) is higher, as shown in Figure 6.2. But if the poorer individuals have to pay less than the richer individuals, then poor individuals may prefer a higher level of public-goods expenditure. Obviously, an individual who does not have to pay taxes at all

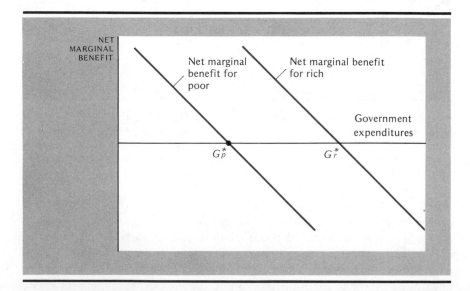

6.2 NET MARGINAL BENEFITS FOR DIFFERENT INDIVIDUALS With a uniform tax (where everyone has to pay the same amount), if all individuals have the same preference, the poorer the individual, the lower his most preferred level of expenditure of public goods. Although the marginal benefit is the same for all, the marginal cost (the marginal utility of private goods foregone) is higher for the poor. Thus G_p^*, the most preferred level of expenditure for the poor, is less than G_r^*, the most preferred level for the rich.

receives only benefits from increased public expenditures and will vote for
as high a level of expenditure on public goods as is feasible.

We call the extra payment that an individual has to make for each extra dollar of expenditure on the public good his **tax price**. Thus, with uniform taxation, in an economy with N individuals, the tax price facing each individual is $1/N$. With *proportional taxation* (where everyone pays the same percentage of his income), the tax price for an individual whose income is Y_i is

$$\frac{Y_i}{\overline{Y}} \cdot \frac{1}{N},$$

where $\overline{Y}$ is the average level of income in the population. That is, someone whose income is average pays exactly $1/N$th of the total taxes paid and faces exactly the same tax price as before. An individual with no income pays no taxes and thus has a tax price of zero.[3] Thus poorer individuals face a lower tax price, and this leads them to increase their demand for public goods; but at any given tax price, poorer individuals prefer a lower level of expenditure on public goods than wealthy individuals. These two effects offset each other, and it is thus possible with proportional taxation that poorer individuals prefer higher or lower levels of public expenditures than do richer individuals.

The individual's most preferred level of public expenditure, at any given tax price, can be analyzed in exactly the same way that we analyze demand for private goods. Assume that the individual's tax price is p, that is, for each dollar of government expenditure, he must pay p. Then, the total amount the individual can spend, his *budget constraint*,[4] is:

$$C + pG = Y,$$

where C is his consumption of private goods, G is the total amount of public goods provided, and Y is his income. We represent the budget constraint in Figure 6.3A by the line BB. Along the budget constraint, if government expenditures are lower, consumption of private goods is obviously higher. The individual wishes to obtain the highest level of utility he can, consistent with his budget constraint. In Figure 6.3A we have also drawn the individual's indifference curves between public and private goods. The individual is willing to give up some private goods if he gets more public goods. The quantity of private goods he is willing to give up to get one more unit of public goods is his marginal rate of substitution. As he gets more public goods (and has fewer private goods), the amount of private goods he is willing to give up to get an extra unit of public goods becomes smaller—that is,

---

[3]This formula for the tax price may easily be derived. Let t be the tax rate. Total government income is

$$t \cdot N \cdot \overline{Y},$$

since total national income is average income, $\overline{Y}$, times the number of individuals. This must equal government expenditure,

$$t \cdot N \cdot \overline{Y} = G.$$

If government expenditure increases by a unit, the *tax rate* must increase by $1/N\overline{Y}$. The tax paid by an individual with income Y_i is just tY_i, and so his incremental tax—his tax price—is just $Y_i/N\overline{Y}$.

[4]Recall from Chapter 4 the definition of budget constraint: the combinations of goods (here, public and private goods) that individuals can purchase.

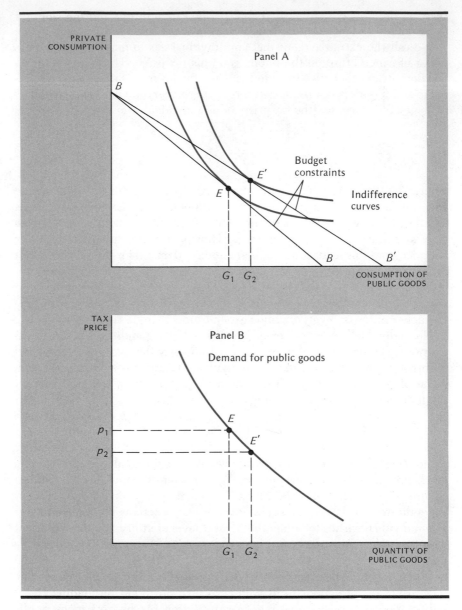

6.3   DEMAND CURVE FOR PUBLIC GOODS The individual's most preferred level of expenditure is the point of tangency between the indifference curve and the budget constraint. As the tax price increases (the budget constraint shifts from *BB* to *BB'*), the individual's most preferred level of public expenditure decreases, generating the demand curve of Panel B.

the individual has a diminishing marginal rate of substitution. Graphically, the marginal rate of substitution is the slope of the indifference curve. Thus as the individual consumes more public goods and fewer private goods, the indifference curve becomes flatter.

The individual's highest level of utility is attained at the point of tangency between the indifference curve and the budget constraint, point *E* in

Panel A. At this point, the slope of the budget constraint and the slope of the indifference curve are identical. The slope of the budget constraint tells us how much in private goods the individual has to give up to get one more unit of public goods; it is equal to the individual's tax price. The slope of the indifference curve tells us how many private goods the individual is willing to give up to get one more unit of public goods. Thus at the individual's most preferred point, the amount that the individual is willing to give up to get an additional unit of public goods is just equal to the amount he has to give up to get one more unit of the public good. As we lower the tax price, the budget constraint shifts out (from BB to BB') and the individual's most preferred point moves to point E'. The individual's demand for public goods will normally increase.

By raising and lowering the tax price, we can trace out a demand curve for public goods, in the same way that we trace out demand curves for private goods. In Figure 6.3B we have plotted the demand curve corresponding to Panel A. Points E and E', from Panel A, show the quantity of public goods demanded at tax prices p_1 and p_2. We could trace more points for Panel B by shifting the budget constraint further in Panel A.

We noted earlier that individuals with different incomes are likely to demand different levels of public goods. Figure 6.4 shows the effect of lower income on the demand for public goods. First, Panel A shows the lower budget constraint corresponding to the poorer individual. At the same tax price, he will clearly demand fewer public goods: points E_p and E_r represent the tangencies between the budget constraints and indifference curves. Thus the poorer individual's demand curve, illustrated in Panels B and C, will always be below that of the rich. But the poorer individual will normally face a lower tax price. In Panel B this effect outweighs the effect of having a lower demand, while in Panel C, just the opposite is true.

The Median Voter

We have now described how each voter decides on his most preferred level of expenditure. Individuals will differ on their most preferred level. What can we say about the equilibrium that results when these individuals vote?

To analyze the majority voting equilibrium, we first consider a simple example, where there are three individuals with different incomes. We assume that the wealthier the individual is, the more government spending he or she prefers. (This will generally be true, as we have noted, for uniform taxation, but not necessarily for proportional taxation.) In Figure 6.5, we have plotted the level of utility as a function of the level of public expenditure for the three income groups. In each case, utility at first increases and then decreases. The most preferred level of the poor, G_1, is lower than that of the middle income group, G_2, which, in turn, is lower than that of the rich, G_3.

First, consider a vote between G_1 and G_2. Both the middle- and upper-income individuals vote for G_2, so G_2 wins. Now consider a vote between G_2 and G_3; clearly both the middle- and low-income individuals prefer G_2 to G_3; so G_2 again gets 2 out of 3 votes. More generally, consider G_2 against any other level of expenditure lower than G_2. Both the high-income individ-

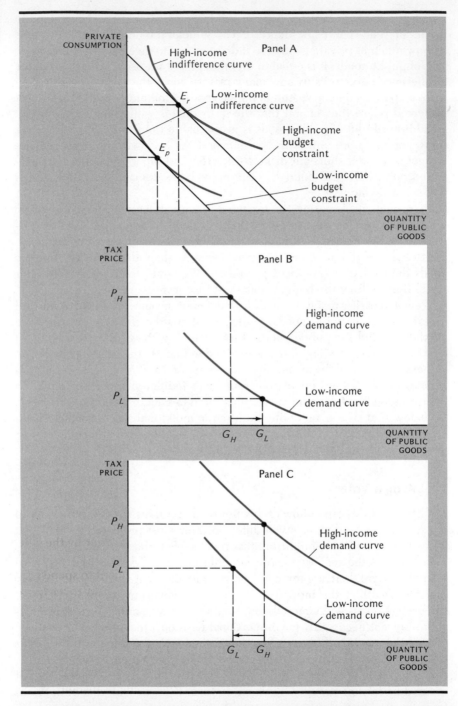

6.4 EFFECT OF DIFFERENCES IN INCOME ON DEMAND FOR PUBLIC GOODS
At any given tax price, individuals with a lower level of income will normally demand a lower
level of public goods. Because individuals with lower incomes have a lower tax price, their
demand for public goods may be higher (as in Panel B) or lower (as in Panel C).

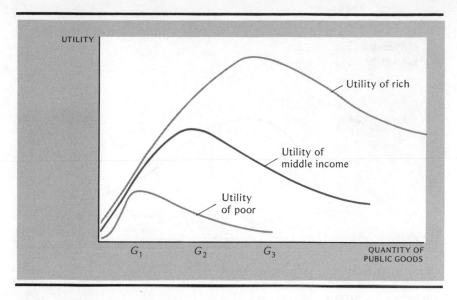

6.5 UTILITY LEVELS AS A FUNCTION OF GOVERNMENT EXPENDITURES The higher the income, the more government spending is preferred (with uniform taxation).

ual and the middle-income individual will prefer G_2. Conversely, for any level of expenditure slightly in excess of G_2 both the low-income and middle-income individuals prefer G_2. Thus, G_2 can win a majority vote over all other levels of expenditure. The **median voter** is the one for whom the number of individuals who prefer a higher level of expenditure (the number of individuals who have a higher income) is exactly equal to the number of individuals who prefer a lower level of expenditure (the number of individuals who have a lower income). The result we have just obtained is general: the *majority voting equilibrium level of expenditures is the level that is most preferred by the median voter.*[5]

To find out who the median voter is and therefore what the level of expenditures on public goods will be, we arrange individuals in order by the level of expenditures they most prefer. For each level of government expenditure we can ask what fraction of individuals prefer the government to spend less. The median voter is that voter for whom exactly half prefer the government to spend less (and correspondingly, exactly half prefer the government to spend more).

The median voter may have an income that is above or below average income. Assume that wealthier individuals demand more public goods. Then if all individuals vote, the median voter is the individual who has the median income. In Figure 6.6 we have depicted the distribution of income, which gives the percentage of the population at different income levels. As we have drawn it, the income distribution is not *symmetric*—that is, there are many more people who have very low incomes than have very high incomes. The few people with very high incomes raise the average level of income, so with

---

[5] Provided a majority voting equilibrium exists. We shall see such an equilibrium may not exist.

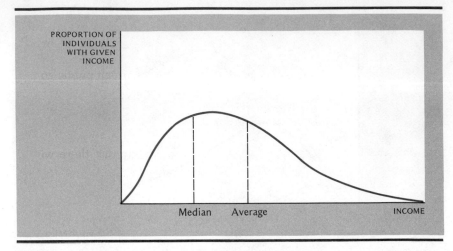

PROPORTION OF
INDIVIDUALS
WITH GIVEN
INCOME

Median   Average   INCOME

6.6 RELATIONSHIP BETWEEN AVERAGE AND MEDIAN INCOME With a skewed distribution of income, the median is much less than the average. The median income is the income such that 50 percent have incomes below that number, 50 percent have incomes above that number. In a skewed distribution, the very large incomes of the very rich increases the average, resulting in the average exceeding the median.

this kind of income distribution, the individual with a median income has a lower income than the average income.

The median voter theory implies that if there is a redistribution of income within a community, so that the income of the median voter increases, then the demand for public goods in the community will rise even though the average income remains the same.

The Inefficiency of the Majority Voting Equilibrium

Since the median voter determines the level of expenditure, to ascertain whether there is too much or too little expenditure on public goods we need only examine how he votes, and contrast that with the conditions for efficiency discussed in Chapter 5. The median individual is assumed to compare only the benefits he receives with the costs that he bears. His benefits are lower than total social benefits (which includes all the benefits that accrue to others), but so are his costs. Whether there is too much or too little expenditure on public goods depends thus on whether his share of total (marginal) costs is less than or greater than his share of total benefits.

Consider first the example where all individuals are identical, and there is uniform taxation. Then, if there are N individuals, the individual's private benefits are $1/N$ of the total benefits, and his costs are $1/N$ of the total costs. The majority voting equilibrium is efficient.

Now consider a case where all individuals obtain the same marginal benefit from the public good; the median individual's private assessment of benefits is $1/N$ of total marginal social benefits. Assume that there is proportional taxation, and that the distribution of income is very skewed (so that there are few very wealthy individuals, and many poor individuals, as in

Figure 6.6). Then the median income will be much lower than the average income, so the tax price of the individual is very low. He thus bears a small share of the total costs. Even if the marginal value of a dollar of private consumption is worth somewhat more to the median-income person than to the rich individual, there will be an excessive expenditure on public goods.

Our federal income tax structure is *progressive*—that is, the fraction of income paid in taxes increases with income. With progressive taxation, in which the percentage of income taxed increases at higher levels of income, the share of the costs borne by the median individual may be even smaller than with proportional taxation, so that it is more likely that there will be excessive expenditures on public goods with progressive taxation than with proportional taxation.

It should be clear that there may be certain other public goods that generate large benefits to the wealthy but relatively few to the poor, and which with uniform taxation would thus be in undersupply. With proportional or progressive taxation, such goods could be either in undersupply or oversupply.

The Voting Paradox

A more widely discussed limitation of majority voting is the possibility that there does not exist an equilibrium. This problem was noted as early as the eighteenth century by a famous French philosopher, Condorcet, and may be seen in the following simple example, where there are three voters and three alternatives, denoted A, B, and C.

Voter 1 prefers A to B to C
Voter 2 prefers C to A to B
Voter 3 prefers B to C to A

Assume we vote on A versus B. Voters 1 and 2 vote for A, so A wins. Now we vote on A versus C. Voters 2 and 3 prefer C to A, so C wins. It appears that C should be the social choice. C wins against A, which wins against B. But let us now have a direct confrontation between C and B. Both Voter 1 and Voter 3 prefer B to C. So B is preferred to C. This is referred to as the **voting paradox,** or the paradox of cyclical voting. There is no clear winner. B beats C and C beats A but A beats B.

If we employ majority voting, then it is clear that it may be very important to control the agenda. Assume we structure the election as first a contest between A and B, and then the winner of that contest against C. Clearly, C could win that election. But suppose instead we structured the election as first a contest between B and C, and then the winner of that contest against A. A would win that election. Finally, suppose we structured the election as first a contest between A and C, and the winner of that election against B. Then clearly B would win. Thus the winner of each of these elections is determined solely by the order in which the pair-wise comparisons were made.

Note, too, that if the individuals realize there is going to be a particular sequence of votes, they may wish to vote strategically. That is, in the first round of the vote, Voter 1 may not vote his true preferences on, say, A versus B, but think through the *consequences* of that for the eventual equilibrium. He may vote for B, even though he would prefer A, knowing that in a contest between C and B, B will win, while in a contest between A and C, C might win. Since he prefers B to C, he votes initially for B.

Single-Peaked Preferences and the Existence of a Majority Voting Equilibrium

The voting paradox does not always arise. Indeed, earlier, we showed that, in voting on the level of public goods, there was a well-defined majority voting equilibrium, which corresponded to the preferences of the median voter. What distinguishes those cases where an equilbrium exists from those where it does not?

In Figure 6.5, we plotted the level of utility as a function of the level of expenditure on public goods. There, each individual had a single peak to his preference profile. This property of **single-peakedness** is enough to guarantee the existence of a majority voting equilibrium. Note that the *peak need not be "interior"* but could lie on the "ends," so that preferences such as those in Figure 6.7A are also consistent with single-peakedness.

On the other hand, preferences such as those illustrated in Figure 6.7C are not consistent with single-peakedness. Both 0 and G_1 are (local) peaks. Unfortunately, such examples arise naturally in considering many public choice problems.

For instance, consider the problem of an individual's attitudes toward expenditures on public education. If the level of expenditure on public education is below a certain minimal level, a rich individual may prefer to send his children to private schools. If he does this, any increase in expenditure on public schools simply increases his taxes; he gets no direct benefits. Thus his utility decreases with government expenditures to a critical level at which he decides to send his children to public school. For increases beyond that level, he derives some benefit. Of course, beyond some point, the increases in taxes more than offset the benefits. For this individual, a high level of expenditure is preferred to no expenditure, but no expenditure is preferred to an intermediate level of expenditure. There may be no majority voting equilibrium in this case.

Although preferences for a *single* public good (with no private-good option, unlike education) are usually single-peaked, when we have to rank choices involving more than one public good, those rankings are seldom single-peaked.[6] To obtain single-peakedness, we have to restrict ourselves to voting on one issue at a time.[7]

Equally important, there will not be a majority voting equilibrium for most distribution issues.[8] This can be seen most clearly in considering the structure of income taxation. Suppose we are voting among three income tax

---

[6] See G. Kramer, "On a Class of Equilibrium Conditions for Majority Rule," *Econometrica* 41 (1973): 285–97.

[7] See S. Slutsky, "A Voting Model for the Allocation of Public Goods: Existence of An Equilibrium," *Journal of Economic Theory* 11 (1975): 292–304.

[8] See D. K. Foley, "Resource Allocation and the Public Sector," *Yale Economic Essays* 7 (1967): 45–98.

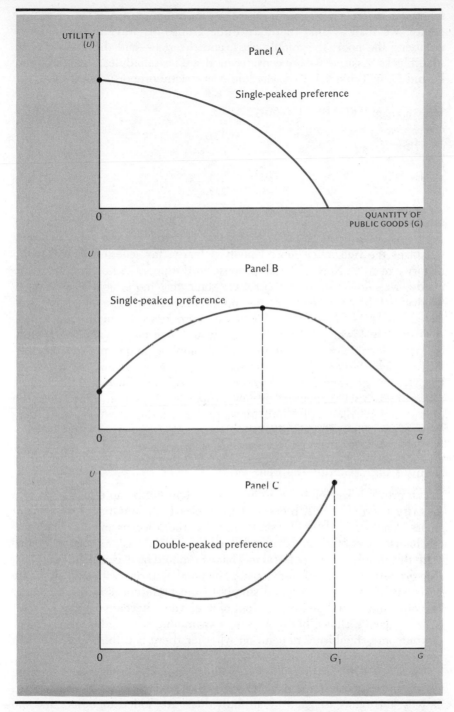

6.7 SINGLE-PEAKED AND DOUBLE-PEAKED PREFERENCES With single-peaked preferences (Panels A and B), there always exists a majority voting equilibrium. Without single-peakedness (Panel C), there may not exist a majority voting equilibrium.

schedules that are designed to raise the same amount of revenue. For simplicity, we shall assume there are three groups of individuals with equal numbers: the poor, the middle class, and the rich—and that they vote in solid blocks. Assume we are considering three tax schedules, denoted by A, B, and C, in Table 6.1. Tax schedule A is strictly proportional; it takes the

Table 6.1 ALTERNATIVE TAX SCHEDULES

Fraction of Income Paid in Taxes	A	B	C
Poor	20%	18%	17%
Middle	20%	18%	21%
Rich	20%	24%	22%

same fraction of income from each individual. The poor and the middle then get together and propose tax schedule B. This reduces the taxes they pay but taxes the rich much more heavily. Clearly, tax schedule B will win a majority over A. Now, the rich propose to the poor: "Since you are more needy, why don't we lower your taxes somewhat more; at the same time, we'll adjust the tax schedule at the upper end, to reduce the inequities associated with excessive taxation." Thus they propose tax schedule C, which, relative to B, lowers the taxes on the low and high income and raises them on the middle income, so that now both the middle- and upper-income individuals pay a larger proportion of their income in taxes than do the poor. Clearly, tax schedule C wins a majority over B. Now, however, the middle class proposes we go back to straight proportional taxation. Since both the upper- and middle-income individuals prefer schedule A, A defeats C. We again get a cyclical pattern of voting.[9]

Arrow's Impossibility Theorem

In the previous section we saw that there might not be an equilibrium to a majority voting political process. This is clearly an unsatisfactory state of affairs. A natural question to ask, then, is whether there is any other political mechanism, any other set of rules for making social decisions, that will eliminate this problem. The political mechanism should have certain other desirable properties: it should, for instance, be nondictatorial (with a dictator, the decisions of society correspond simply to the preferences of the dictator). The outcome should be independent of irrelevant alternatives; that is, if we have to make a choice between, say, a swimming pool and a tennis court, the outcome should not depend on whether there is a third alternative (a new library).

A number of alternative rules have been examined, for instance, requiring a two-thirds majority or rank-order voting (where individuals rank the alternatives, the ranks assigned by all individuals are added together, and the alternative with the lowest score wins). All of those examined fail to meet

[9]If we restrict the set of tax schedules over which voting occurs, for instance to tax schedules with an exemption level and a fixed marginal tax rate (these are called flat-rate tax schedules), there may be a majority voting equilibrium. See T. Romer, "Individual Welfare, Majority Voting, and the Properties of a Linear Income Tax," *Journal of Public Economics* 4 (1975): 163–85.

one or the other criterion. The quest for an ideal system came to an end with a result of Nobel Laureate Kenneth Arrow of Stanford. He showed that there was no rule that would satisfy all of the desired characteristics. This theorem is referred to as **Arrow's impossibility theorem.**[10]

Arrow's impossibility theorem has one further interesting and important implication. We often hear expressions such as: "The government should do such and such . . .," "It is the responsibility of the state to . . .," "The government seems to be acting in an inconsistent manner . . .," or "Why doesn't the government determine its priorities and then act upon them?" This language personifies the government, treats the government as if it were an individual. Language is important: although we all know that the government is not a single individual, speaking of it as if it were, we are frequently led to believe that it is. We come to expect that government should act consistently like a rational individual. But Arrow's impossibility theorem suggests that, short of granting some individual dictatorial powers, one should not expect the government to act with the same degree of consistency and rationality as an individual. In subsequent chapters, we shall often talk of the "government." But in doing so, we do not wish to personify it, to treat it as if it were a single individual, to ascribe to it more wisdom than the individuals who compose it have. The caveats that we have raised throughout this and the next chapter must be constantly borne in mind.

The Two-Party System and the Median Voter

We noted earlier that an elected representative bears a negligible fraction of the costs of, and receives a negligible fraction of the benefits from, an increase in government expenditure. What can economic theory say about how he should vote? A natural supposition is that the politician wishes to stay in office and that, accordingly, he wishes to maximize his votes, given the position taken by his rival. A vote-maximizing voting strategy can easily be defined as follows. Party 1 takes the position of Party 2 as given. Focusing on a single issue, the level of expenditure, denote by G_1 the "position" (that is, the level of public expenditure advocated by the party) of Party 1, and by G_2 the "position" of Party 2. For each value of G_2 there is an optimal (i.e., vote-maximizing) position for G_1.

Under the hypothesis that each party seeks to maximize its vote given the position of the rival, what will each party do? Let G_m be the preferred level of expenditure of the median voter. Suppose Party 2 chooses $G_2 > G_m$. Then if Party 1 takes a position between G_m and G_2, it will get all the voters who prefer an expenditure level less than or equal to G_m, and some who prefer slightly more. Thus Party 1 gets over 50 percent of the votes and wins. In response, Party 2 will choose a position between G_m and G_1—G_2—which wins against G_1. The process continues until both parties stand for the same position: that of the median voter (G_m). See Figure 6.8.

This result is consistent with the widely observed allegation that with our two-party system voters get no choice: both parties take a "middle-of-the-road" position. This is precisely what the theory predicts.

[10] See K. Arrow, *Social Choice and Individual Values* (New York: Wiley, 2nd ed., 1963).

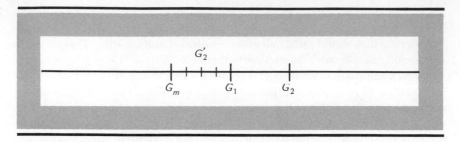

6.8 TWO-PARTY SYSTEM With the two-party system, in which both parties try to maximize their vote, taking the position of the rival as fixed, in equilibrium both parties will adopt the position of the median voter.

There are, however, some important limitations of the theory that need to be borne in mind. First, we noted earlier that, in general, there may not exist a majority voting equilibrium. There does if individuals have single-peaked preferences. In the present context, this requires that we should be able to arrange issues along a single dimension—for example, conservative-liberal. If, however, there are a variety of dimensions—some individuals are "liberal" on some issues and conservative on others—then the median voter is not well defined and there may be no equilibrium to the political process.

Secondly, we have ignored questions of participating in the political process. There are costs associated with being actively involved in it; as a voter, there are costs associated with becoming informed and voting. These costs are sufficiently great relative to the perceived benefits that slight changes in the weather, making it slightly less pleasant to go outside to vote, have significant effects on voter participation. In particular, voters whose preferences are near the median have little incentive to be active politically, particularly if they believe that the political process will reflect their preferences anyway. Thus, it may be in the interests of those who are more extreme to attempt to pull their party away from the center. This tendency for greater political activism at the extremes may partially offset the median-directed tendencies noted earlier.

POLITICS AND ECONOMICS

The discussion of the political process in the preceding section differs markedly from the kind of analysis one might typically find in a political science course. There, one might discuss the roles of special-interest groups and political institutions. A full discussion of the relationship between economic theories of the political process and other theories would take us beyond the scope of this book. In the following pages, we touch on some economic interpretations of certain political phenomena.

Why Do Individuals Vote?

In the previous section, we observed that in many elections voter participation rates are low, and that they are sensitive to such chance occurrences as changes in the weather. The reason for this, as we have noted, is that the benefits of voting are low—there is little chance of affecting the outcome. The alternatives may differ so little that the outcome is inconsequential, and, though the costs are relatively low, they are not low in relationship to the benefits. Indeed, in a fully rational calculation, no one would vote: the probability that an individual's vote would make a difference to the outcome (since in most cases the individual cares only about whether his candidate wins or loses, not the magnitude of the win or loss) is essentially zero. Yet individuals do vote.

This paradox is resolved, in a tautological manner, simply by assuming that individuals get utility out of voting or more generally out of participation in the political process. More to the point, individuals do give money to charity; they are brought up to believe that it is good to be considerate of others (and that more is entailed by this than simply the view that it is in the individual's self-interest to be considerate of others). So, too, considerable time and energy are devoted to inculcating into our children notions of civic responsibility, and among these civic responsibilities is the responsibility to be an informed voter.

The same considerations imply that when the individual votes, he may not act in the narrowly self-interested manner that we have assumed in our discussion so far. Individuals may vote for closing some loophole in the income tax system because it would result in a more equitable distribution of the tax burden, even though their personal tax liability might thereby be increased.

Elections, Interest Groups, and Corrupt Politicians

The models we have discussed in the preceding sections have assumed that all individuals are well informed about the consequences of all alternatives under consideration, all individuals vote, and they cast their votes on the basis of the implications that each alternative has for their own (private) welfare.

There are many who believe that this does not provide an adequate description of the political process. Although constitutionally each person has one vote, some votes seem more effective than others. The outcome of the political process, in this view, reflects the political power of special-interest groups.

Assessing the validity of these views is beyond the scope of this chapter. We limit our discussion here to a more narrow set of questions: What can economic theory say about the kinds of interest groups that are likely to be effective? And how can we reconcile the effectiveness of special-interest groups with the fact that each individual does, in the United States, have only one vote?

The answer to these questions is related to our earlier discussion in the previous chapter of the public interest as a public good. We saw there that the efficient management of the public sector was a public good. Similarly, choosing elected officials who are competent and who reflect values similar to our own is a public good.

At the same time, we should note that the free rider problem may not be as serious in small groups as it is in large. Thus it is easier to form an interest group of a small number of steel producers to attempt to persuade Congress to restrict steel imports than it is to form an interest group of the large number of steel users who would be adversely affected by such restrictions. *Each* of the producers has more to gain than each of the consumers has to lose, though the aggregate gains of producers may, in fact, be less than the aggregate losses to consumers.

Trade unions have long recognized the nature of the free rider problem, and that is why they have sought closed shops, forcing all workers to support the activities they believe to be in the collective interests of workers. But once they have this power, they can attempt to use it not only at the bargaining table but also in the political arena, where they act as a special-interest group.

The Power of Special-Interest Groups

How are interest groups able to exercise power? There appear to be at least three mechanisms. First, we noted before that individuals have little incentive to vote or to become informed concerning the issues. Interest groups can attempt to lower the costs of voting and information, particularly for those voters who are likely to support them. They do so by making information (obviously supporting their own views) readily available; and they often assist directly by providing transportation, child care, etc., on polling day.

Secondly, we noted the difficulty that politicians have in obtaining information about the preferences of their constituents. There is no simple demand revealing mechanism for public goods as there is for private goods. Interest groups attempt to provide such information. Politicians may lack the technical information required to make informed political decisions—for example, they may not know the consequences of continued imports of cheap foreign steel. Interest groups are a primary source of information, and it is through providing information that they often exercise influence.

The third mechanism is through direct and indirect bribery of the politician. Direct bribery does not occur often, at least in most jurisdictions in the United States. (Presumably, this may not be due to the purity of our politicians so much as the costs associated with being caught.) But indirect bribery is important: special-interest groups provide financial and other forms of support for politicians who support their interests. Again, this is important because voters must be informed of the positions taken by a candidate, and providing voters with information is costly. Voters must be persuaded that the benefits of voting warrant their going to the trouble of voting, and their private costs must be reduced through providing assistance in going to the polls. We earlier hypothesized that we could explain politicians' behavior by their wish to stay in office; they increase the probability of reelection by maximizing the number of people who are likely to vote for them. Politicians realize that what is of concern is how their stands on particular issues affect the number of individuals who will actually vote for them as opposed to their opponents. They must take into account all the effects, including the increased opportunity to get in touch with the voters that the additional support of a special-interest group provides.

The Altruistic Politician?

An alternative view says that many politicians do not behave in as self-interested a way as we have assumed throughout this chapter. Just as individuals behave altruistically as private citizens, and give to charity, so too do they behave as public citizens, in their capacity as elected officials. In our society considerable status and respect is accorded to public statespeople and public service. Effective government depends on the quality of these civil servants.

Although there is some grain of truth in this "noneconomic" view, three qualifications should be noted. First, while the majority voting theory provided clear predictions concerning the outcome of political processes, no such clear predictions emerge for a political process that depends on some political leader's views of the public interest. Indeed, it was precisely the seeming capriciousness of the actions taken by political leaders (whether or not allegedly in the public interest) that led Adam Smith to suggest that there was a better way that the public interest might be served: by each individual pursuing his private interest. Unfortunately, though Adam Smith's invisible hand may work well for most goods, it does not work well for public goods.

Secondly, there is the selection problem. So long as not all individuals running for office are disinterested, the voters must select between those who are and those who are not. If voters believe that it is better to be a "disinterested" public statesperson than a selfish politician, then self-interested politicians will all attempt to resemble a disinterested public statesperson. How is the voter to choose among them on the basis of the limited information he normally has available?

Thirdly, there are those who contend that there is no such thing as disinterested behavior in pursuit of the public interest, or at least it is such a rarity as not to be the basis of an adequate theory of the public sector. Even if individuals do not act in their own selfish interest, they act in their "class interest," in the interests of those with whom they have associated for life. They are often indeed not conscious of acting in this way.

Unfortunately, we cannot test the validity of these alternative views. There is, perhaps, some truth in all of them: many politicians do, undoubtedly, act in their self-interest, and the simple "voter" maximization model we have discussed here does provide some insights into their behavior. Not all politicians, however, act consciously in their self-interest; some, undoubtedly, believe that they are acting for the public good. But it is not clear what this means—that is, what interpretation is to be associated with "acting in the public good" when there are alternative views of what is in the public interest, and there is (by Arrow's impossibility theorem) no simple way of consistently resolving these differences. What is clear is that, with the perspective of hindsight, many politicians, who claimed that they were acting in the public good, have advocated and instigated policies that later appear to most observers as not having been in the public interest.

The Persistence of Inefficient Equilibrium

Though there are no general propositions concerning the nature of the resource allocations that emerge when the political process is dominated by special-interest groups, most economists believe that such allocations not only violate generally accepted standards of equity and fairness but also are frequently inefficient. That is, the resulting resource allocations generally result in the economy being below the utility possibilities frontier: there are alternative allocations that could make everyone better off.

Why, in the face of this, do individuals not get together and propose one of these Pareto-dominating alternatives, to which, presumably, all would agree? There is no universally agreed-upon answer to this puzzle. Several "partial" answers may be suggestive.

First, as we have already seen, the public interest is a public good. Since the efforts to maintain a good government must come from private individuals, there will be an undersupply of this (as any other) privately provided public good.

Secondly, many of the distributive implications of public programs undertaken at the behest of special-interest groups are far from obvious—and this is deliberately so. It is unlikely, for instance, that the American voters would deliberately vote to transfer resources (give a public gift) to *rich* rice farmers. For these individuals to receive a transfer at the public expense, they must be included in a broader-scale program, of which they are an almost accidental beneficiary. Thus, rich rice farmers become advocates of federal aid to rice farmers, singling out, in their public rhetoric, the benefits that would accrue to poor rice farmers from such a program. A Pareto improvement might, for instance, entail giving each rice farmer a fixed sum, or small rice farmers assistance to move into some other occupation, where their productivity might be higher. But though such direct grants would better serve the distributive goals singled out, they would not receive the backing of rich rice farmers.

ALTERNATIVE SCHEMES FOR DETERMINING THE LEVEL OF PUBLIC GOODS

Since there is a strong presumption that current political processes lead to inefficiencies, the question naturally arises as to whether there are some better schemes. Arrow's impossibility theorem suggests that we are likely to encounter difficulties. We now discuss two proposals that have been put forward for arriving at efficient allocations.

Lindahl Equilibrium

The first is called the Lindahl solution, after the great Swedish economist Erik Lindahl, who first proposed it in 1919.[11] It attempts to mimic, as far as possible, the way that the market works in providing private goods. Market equilibrium for private goods is described by the intersection of the demand and supply curves. All individuals face the same price. The sum of the quantities they demand is equal to the sum of the quantities supplied by firms.

One of the ways that we characterized the efficient level of public goods

---

[11] E. Lindahl, *"Positive Losung, Die Gerechtigkeit der Besteverung,"* translated as "Just Taxation—A Positive Solution" in *Classics in the Theory of Public Finance,* R. A. Musgrave and A. T. Peacock, eds. (New York: St. Martin's Press, 1958).

was the intersection of the aggregate demand curve (formed by adding vertically each individual's demand curve) with the supply curve. The demand curves are generated by asking the individual how much of the public good he would demand if he were to pay so much for each unit produced; that is, in Figure 6.9 if the first individual faced a tax price of, say, p_1, he would demand G^*.

The Lindahl equilibrium is just the intersection of the demand curve for public goods with the supply curve. The Lindahl equilibrium is obviously efficient. In the Lindahl equilibrium all individuals enjoy the same quantity of the public good but differ in their tax prices. In the diagram, the Lindahl equilibrium occurs at G^*, and the first individual pays a tax price of p_1 and the second a tax price of p_2.

The Lindahl equilibrium is Pareto efficient; but we noted earlier that there were, in fact, a whole range of Pareto-efficient resource allocations, in some of which one individual is better off, in others of which another is better off. Almost by definition, there cannot be unanimity about which, among these points, is preferred. The Lindahl equilibrium picks one of the Pareto-efficient points; but individuals who are disadvantaged by this particular Pareto-efficient point will not agree to the use of this mechanism for determining the allocation of public goods; indeed, they might even prefer Pareto-inefficient allocations, so long as the level of utility they obtain is higher.

The most telling criticism of the Lindahl solution is that individuals do not have an incentive to tell the truth because their tax price increases as their

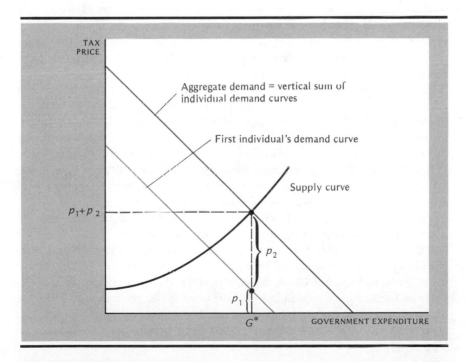

6.9 LINDAHL EQUILIBRIUM The intersection of the aggregate demand curve (formed by adding vertically the individual demand curves) and the supply curve yields a Pareto-efficient allocation.

stated demand does.[12] The question to which we now turn is, are there mechanisms that induce individuals to be honest about their preferences?

New Revelation Mechanisms

We noted earlier that one of the essential problems with public goods is that of preference revelation. In acquiring private goods, individuals reveal their preferences for different private goods. There was no similar mechanism for revealing preferences for public goods. The most obvious political mechanisms either link the individual's statements concerning his attitudes toward the public good to what he must pay, in which case they result in an undersupply (since each individual believes that his statements will have a negligible effect on the supply but a nonnegligible effect on what he must pay, he has an incentive to say that he gets a neglible benefit), or they do not link what he has to pay to what he says, in which case he will have every incentive to exaggerate the benefits.

Recent research has focused on designing simple rules whereby individuals will truthfully reveal their preferences. The rule specifies the relationship between the level of public goods and the tax liability of each individual, and the statements each individual makes concerning his preferences for public goods. (The rule should have the further property that the resulting resource allocation is Pareto efficient).

One such simple rule is the following. Everyone is asked to give his demand curve for public goods, just as in the Lindahl equilibrium. As before, the equilibrium will be at the intersection of the aggregate demand (formed by adding vertically the demand curves of each individual) and the supply curve. For simplicity, we assume that the marginal costs of production of the public good is constant, so the supply curve is horizontal. But now, there is a different rule for determining the individual's tax liability.

The aggregate demand curve of all *others* intersects the supply curve at G_0 in Figure 6.10. This is what the level of public goods would be if the individual said that he got no value out of the public good. He is told that for each unit beyond G_0 that the government produces he will have to pay the difference between the marginal costs of production and the aggregate demand of all others. If the equilibrium entailed an output of $G_0 + 1$, the individual would have to pay AB, the distance between the marginal cost curve and the "others" aggregate demand curve.

The individual is in a position to determine the level of public goods simply by his announcement of how much they are valued to him. Clearly, he will try to increase G to the point where the marginal cost to him of increasing G is equal to his marginal benefit. This can be seen in two alternative ways. First, in Figure 6.10, we have plotted the marginal cost to the individual from each additional unit of production beyond G_0, given others' demands. Since his marginal cost is the difference between the cost of production and others' demand, the marginal cost (CD) is equal to AB. We have also drawn

---

[12] That is, the higher their stated demand (given the demand statements of others), the higher expenditures will be, and the higher the expenditures, the higher the tax price they face.

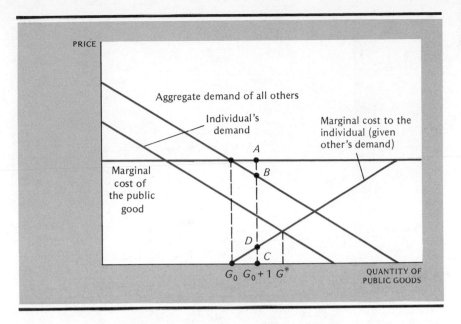

6.10 NEW REVELATION MECHANISM If the individual must pay the difference between marginal cost and others' demands *(AB)* he will honestly reveal his demand.

the individual's demand curve; the individual will wish point G^* to be chosen, where *his* demand curve intersects *his* marginal cost curve.

We now show that each individual has an incentive to reveal honestly his demand for public goods, and when each honestly reveals his demand, the equilibrium is Pareto efficient. To see this, we look at the individual's budget constraint. The individual faces a budget constraint as depicted in Figure 6.11. The extra amount that the individual has to give up for each extra unit of public goods beyond G_0 is the marginal costs minus the others' aggregate demand. Thus he sets his marginal rate of substitution equal to the marginal costs minus the others' aggregate demand (the point E in Figure 6.11). It is clear that the individual has no incentive to misrepresent his preferences. If he asked for any level of public goods other than G^* he would be worse off.

Assume now that each individual honestly announces his demand curve. Recall that in constructing the demand curve, the tax price for each individual (the slope of his budget contraint) was set equal to the individual's marginal rate of substitution. Hence, when the demand curves are added vertically, the sum of the tax prices—that is, the sum of the marginal rates of substitution—equals the marginal cost (the marginal rate of transformation):

$$MRS_1 + MRS_2 + \cdots = MC.$$

In other words, each individual's marginal rate of substitution is equal to the marginal cost minus the sum of the marginal rates of substitution of

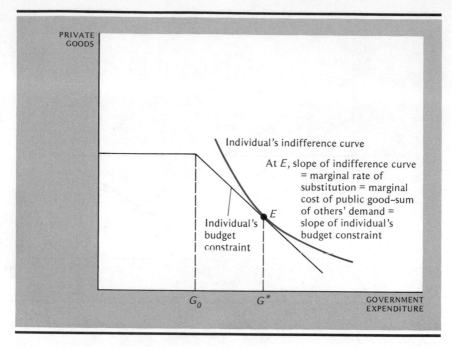

PRIVATE
GOODS

Individual's indifference curve

At E, slope of indifference curve
= marginal rate of
substitution = marginal
cost of public good–sum
of others' demand =
slope of individual's
budget constraint

E

Individual's
budget
constraint

G_0 G^*

GOVERNMENT
EXPENDITURE

6.11 CHOICE OF OPTIMAL G BY INDIVIDUAL If the individual must pay the difference between marginal cost and others' demands, and others have honestly revealed their demands, the allocation to public goods will be Pareto optimal.

others (the sum of their tax prices). For instance, for the first individual,

$$MRS_1 = MC - (MRS_2 + MRS_3 + \cdots).$$

But this is exactly the point we described earlier, where the marginal cost to the individual of further increases in government expenditure (which equaled the marginal cost of production minus the sum of others' demand prices at the given quantity) equaled the marginal benefit to the individual (his marginal rate of substitution). We have just shown that if the individual honestly reveals his demand curve, his own utility is maximized, and the allocation of resources to public goods will be Pareto efficient.

Criticisms of the New Revelation Mechanisms

Economists have investigated alternative mechanisms that induce individuals to reveal the truth, specifying certain relationships between what they say, the taxes they have to pay, and the level of expenditure on the public good. There are a number of closely related mechanisms. All of them have the property that the individual, though only 1 out of 230 million Americans, can have a distinct effect on the outcome.

There is considerable controversy about the relevance of these mechanisms. If they are so good, why are they not used? Several suggestions have been put forward.

Like the Lindahl equilibrium we described earlier, these mechanisms ensure that the condition for a Pareto-efficient allocation—that the sum of marginal rates substitution equal the marginal rate of transformation—is satisfied. But some individuals might prefer another, Pareto-inefficient allocation that gives them a higher level of utility.

The administrative costs of obtaining revelations in this form from each individual might be quite high. Moreover, the mechanisms are sensitive to collusion. In our formulation, each individual took the others' announcements as given. But if two or more individuals can get together and coordinate their announcements, they can usually gain by making announcements that are not truthful. Finally, the mechanisms do not, in general, guarantee a balanced budget. Although the sum of the marginal willingness to pay (marginal rates of substitution) does equal the marginal cost, the total amount paid may well differ from the total costs of the public good.

VALUES AND COMPETENCE

Most of this chapter has been concerned with the political mechanisms by which the levels of public goods are determined. The political mechanism provides a means by which conflicts of values concerning what the government should do with respect to public goods are resolved.

Although conflicts of value are central to many political debates, these are not the only sources of disagreement. In the elections for the local commissioner of sewers, for instance, there is seldom controversy over whether or not clean waste is desirable, although occasionally there is controversy about what are acceptable levels of pollution. Rather, each contestant claims that he or she will be a more efficient manager. That is, public officials play an important role in determining the level of outputs that can be obtained from any given level of inputs. The efficiency of the public sector depends on the competence of public management, and this in turn depends on the competence of the elected officials (on their ability to choose, for instance, good bureaucrats, or their ability to design programs that attain desired objectives). Unfortunately, voters have only limited information on the basis of which to make judgments concerning competency.

SUMMARY

1. The majority voting equilibrium, when it exists, reflects the preferences of the median voter.
2. The majority voting equilibrium does not, in general, result in an efficient supply of public goods; there may be either an undersupply or an oversupply.
3. The majority voting equilibrium exists if preferences are single-peaked.
4. Preferences for a single public good will usually be single-peaked. Preferences will not be single-peaked if: a) there is more than one public good, and the vote is taken over packages, rather than over a single good at a time; b) voting is over a publicly provided private good, for which there exists a private alternative, such as education; or c) voting is over distributional questions, such as the structure of the income tax schedule.

5. A majority voting equilibrium may not exist when preferences are not single-peaked. That is, if there are three alternatives—A, B, and C—A may be preferred by a majority over B, B by a majority over C, and C may be preferred by a majority over A.

6. Arrow's impossibility theorem demonstrates the impossibility of finding an alternative, nondictatorial political mechanism that resolves this problem of majority voting and that satisfies certain other properties that one would desire of any political mechanism (such as the independence of irrelevant alternatives.)

7. In a two-party system, there will be a convergence of positions of the two parties toward that of the median voter.

KEY CONCEPTS

Preference revelation	Voting paradox
Aggregating preferences	Single-peaked preferences
Tax price	Arrow's impossiblity theorem
Median Voter	Lindahl equilibrium

QUESTIONS AND PROBLEMS

1. Assume that all individuals have identical preferences but some individuals are wealthier than others. Assume there is a single public good and a single private good. Show diagramatically how you derive the demand curve for the public good, as a function of the tax price charged the individual. Assume that the demand function is of the form

$$G = Y/p,$$

where Y is income and p is the tax price. This says that when income doubles, the demand for public goods doubles, but when the tax price doubles, the demand is cut in half. Assume that the tax price is proportional to the individual's income (as with proportional taxation). How will the demand for the public goods differ among those with different incomes?

2. In the text, we suggested that for well-off individuals, with uniform taxation, preferences for education were not single-peaked. Why might preferences for local parks and for urban public transportation systems (buses and subways) also not be single-peaked?

3. Is the median voter always the voter with the median income? Give examples.

4. How might the majority voting model be used to explain the growth of government expenditures?
   a) Should changes in median or average income better explain increases in the demand for government services?
   b) What should be the effect of an increase in the costs of producing public good caused by government inefficiency? Would it make a difference if the increase in cost is a result of government paying above-market wages (wages higher than those paid comparable workers in the private sector)? (Does our answer to the last question depend on whether the median voter is a government employee?)
   c) Why might you expect that, if income per capita remains the same but the number of individuals in the economy increases, the demand for public goods would increase?

7

Public Production and Bureaucracy

The government employs approximately 18 percent of the labor force. These employees are engaged in a variety of activities. Some of them are in charge of administering government programs, collecting tax revenues, formulating government regulations and seeing that they are enforced. Others are employed in the production of electricity, in the provision of education, and in the armed services. In this chapter we first examine the kinds of production activities in which the government is involved, including a comparison between patterns of public production in the United States and abroad. We then take up the differences between private and public production. Do these differences provide a basis for making judgments about when the government should produce some commodity and when it should purchase it from the private sector?

There is an increasingly widespread view that the government is extremely wasteful. The Center for Policy Studies of the University of Michigan periodically does a survey in which it asks, "Do you think people in the government waste a lot of money we pay in taxes, waste some of it, or don't waste very much of it? In 1958, 43 percent thought that the government wasted a lot of it. Two decades later, this had increased to 77 percent. We wish to know if there are reasons to *expect* government bureaucracies to be less efficient than the private sector.

PUBLIC ENTERPRISES AND PRODUCTION IN THE UNITED STATES

In the United States, government is involved in the production of both public goods and private goods. Public production occurs at the federal and local levels. In addition, however, the government (both at the federal and local levels) contracts with private firms to supply goods and services, both directly to itself and to individuals. In this section we discuss the role of the government in production of private and public goods, and of private firms in supplying services to the government.

Public Production of Private Goods

There are six major areas in which the federal government produces private goods. For these goods, exclusion is possible (and the government does in fact charge for most of these goods and services) and the extra costs of providing the goods and services to an additional individual are significant. In most of these areas, government production coexists with private production.

1. *Postal Service.* This is one of the few activities that is constitutionally mandated. The delivery of first-class mail is the one area (besides printing money) in which the government maintains an exclusive monopoly. But there has been extensive competition in recent years in other areas of mail delivery. The United Parcel Service now delivers more parcels than does the Post Office; there are scattered local delivery firms, and a number of companies are now actively competing in the express-mail delivery service. Electronic mail delivery promises to be another area of active competition in the near future.

2. *Electricity.* A significant fraction of the electricity in the United States is produced by publicly owned utilities. Some government production is a by-product of its responsibility for controlling rivers; a joint product with flood control is the production of hydroelectric power. The federal government also took an active role in the electrification of the rural parts of the United States (through the Rural Electrification Authority).

3. *Railroads.* Until recently, the United States was one of the few countries in which virtually all railroads were private enterprises. (The government had, however, given extensive subsidies to the railroads, through land grants.) But for a variety of reasons, during the period after World War II, the railroads increasingly found themselves in difficult economic straits, and a number of them went into bankruptcy. The federal government responded to the impending crisis by establishing two enterprises: Amtrak, the national passenger railroad company, and Conrail, a consolidation of the bankrupt Penn Central and a number of other railroads in the Northeast. They have received large government subsidies, though more recently there have been extensive discussions about curtailing, and even eliminating, these subsidies.

4. *Insurance.* The government is involved in a variety of insurance programs, including, among others, flood insurance, crime insurance, insuring bank deposits (the Federal Deposit Insurance Corporation), and disability insurance, life insurance, unemployment insurance, and credit insurance. Many of these insurance programs arose because private firms failed to provide what was perceived to be adequate insurance coverage for certain risks.

5. *Banking and Credit.* In almost every major industrialized country there is a central bank, which serves as a bankers' bank, and plays an active role

in regulating and controlling the banking industry. This central bank is a **153**
**Public Enter-
prises and
Production
in the
United States** government enterprise; the United States is no exception to the pattern. The
Federal Reserve System serves as the Central Bank in the United States.
The governors of the Federal Reserve Board are appointed by the president,
with the approval of Congress.

Though the Federal Reserve Board's activities can be viewed as primarily
regulating the banking system (and controlling the money supply), the federal government is involved in a large number of other activities in the credit
market. Indeed, we noted in Chapter 2 that a substantial fraction of new
loans involve the federal government, either directly, through one of its
agencies, or as a guarantor of the loan.

6. *Land and Resource Management.* The federal government is the largest
land owner in the United States, owning more than one-third of the country.
Much of this land is used to produce timber or for grazing, and under some
of it there are vast mineral resources. Although the federal government has
the responsibility of *managing* these enormous resources, it has for the most
part not actually engaged in production, other than providing national parks
and recreational areas; it leases the land to private firms and individuals to
extract the oil, to mine the coal, to fell the timber, and to graze their cattle.
The Reagan administration proposed in 1980 to increase significantly the
rate at which this land was sold or leased to private individuals, reducing the
amount of land under direct federal management. These proposals have been
the subject of considerable controversy.

The role of government in the production of private goods is greater in
most other countries. Among the industries that are frequently nationalized,
besides railroads, banking, insurance, and power, are steel, coal, and telecommunications.

Public Production versus Public Provision

In addition to these activities, governments in most countries are involved
in the production of a wide range of public goods and publicly provided
private goods, including education, sewage, and health care.

As we noted in Chapter 2, the government *purchases* goods and services
and *provides* them to individuals. In fact, most of the government's production activities are linked with government provision, both of pure public
goods and of publicly provided private goods. The decisions about whether
to produce a good publicly and whether to provide it publicly should, however, be viewed separately. For instance, the government is actively involved
in the production of national defense. But the military purchases most of its
equipment (its airplanes, guns, ships, etc.) from private firms. And it frequently hires private contractors to manage public facilities. The total expenditure for contract services amounted to between $8 and $13 billion in 1978;
indeed, a quarter of the "commercial and industrial" activities (food service,
construction, vehicle maintenance, etc.) were purchased by the government
from the private sector.[1] These are examples of public provision with private
production.

[1] See E. S. Savas, *Privatizing the Public Sector* (Chatham, N.J.: Chatham House Publishers, Inc., 1982),
p. 67.

Though some local communities are involved in the production of private goods, like electricity, which they sell to their citizens, most of what is produced by local governments is again provided directly (and freely) to the citizens: waste disposal, garbage collection, police protection, fire protection. The most important production activity at the state and local level is education.

Again, though there is a close link at the local level between the public production of a good or service and its public provision, it is important to reemphasize that the link is not inevitable. Many communities use private contractors to provide garbage collection. Over the past decade, there has been an ongoing debate over whether the close link between public production and public provision of education should be broken by allowing for increased aid to private schools.

The Bureaucracy: Administering Public Laws and Programs

Perhaps the most important "production activity" of the government is administering public laws and programs. After individuals have voted for their elected representatives, and these representatives have legislated public programs, the public programs have to be administered: detailed regulations have to be promulgated, procedures by which those eligible for funds can apply for them have to be developed, applications have to be reviewed, checks have to sent out, etc. No matter how well-intentioned a program may be, if it is badly designed, inequities and inefficiencies will result. We refer to those collectively responsible for the administration of governemnt program as the government bureaucracy. Figure 7.1 represents, in a schematic way, the links between the electorate and the public program designed to provide services to the electorate.

Changing Patterns in Government Production

The United States has not experienced dramatic changes in the role of government production such as have occurred in many European countries over the past fifty years. In the United Kingdom after World War II, the government nationalized the steel and coal industries and completed the nationalization of the railroads. In France, Francois Mitterrand, a socialist, elected president in 1980, nationalized those parts of the banking system that had not previously been nationalized, as well as parts of a number of other industries. The issue of government control of production has not been a particularly heated political issue in the United States, and the changes that have occurred have occurred gradually. The government's direct involvement in railroads occurred only after the bankruptcy of several private railroads (though its involvement through regulation and, as mentioned earlier, land grants dates back more than 100 years). Similarly, though the government is now extremely active in providing credit, this has not come about suddenly, by nationalizing the banking system, but gradually, by providing a variety of special loan programs aimed at meeting particular needs.

Still, the question of the appropriate role of government in production

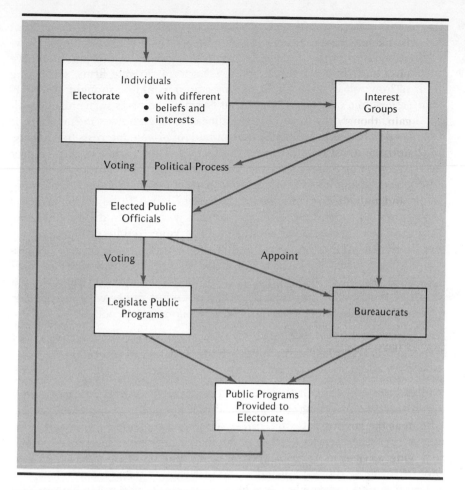

7.1 LINKS BETWEEN THE ELECTORATE AND THE PUBLIC PROGRAMS DESIGNED TO PROVIDE SERVICES TO THE ELECTORATE (1) The electorate elects public officials. (2) The public officials legislate programs and appoint bureaucrats to administer public programs. (3) The bureaucrats provide the services to the electorate, within the context of the programs that have been legislated. (4) Interest groups exert influence at all stages.

remains widely debated: Would some of the services that the government presently provides (such as education) be better provided by private firms? Are there are other services (such as telephones) currently privately provided that might better be provided by a government enterprise?

PUBLIC VERSUS PRIVATE PRODUCTION: DIFFERENCES BETWEEN PUBLIC AND PRIVATE OBJECTIVES

The basic reason that those who advocate an active role for the government in production do so is that they believe that private firms pursue objectives that are not necessarily in the national interest. The major criticism of public production is that it is less efficient.

Private firms pursue the maximization of profits of the owners, and not the welfare of the nation. This is the most widely heard argument for government control of production. To assess the validity of this argument, we must return to the basic discussion of Chapter 4. Private firms, in pursing their narrow self-interest (profit maximization), could be thought of as pursuing the public interest. The fact that competitive firms, maximizing profits, lead the economy to an efficient allocation of resources means there is not necessarily a conflict between the pursuit of private interests (profit maximization) and what is in the public interest. However, when market failures occur, firms' pursuit of profit maximization might not result in an efficient resource allocation. The existence of a market failure does not necessarily imply that the government should intervene. It has to be shown that the government can correct the market failure, without introducing offsetting problems. And when government does intervene, public production may not be the appropriate remedy. Rather than attempting to control production directly, it may try to do so indirectly, by using regulation and/or taxes and subsidies to encourage firms to act in the public interest. The question is not so much which policy is the correct one but rather what are the circumstances under which each of these is the appropriate policy.

Alternative Ways of Reconciling Private and Social Interests

In the United States, regulation is used to control industries like telephones and electricity, in which there is a single firm. In contrast, in most other countries, the government has taken direct control over these industries. The government regulates the prices the firm can charge, it mandates that it provide certain services, and it prohibits the firm from engaging in certain activities. Thus prior to 1983, AT&T was prohibited from competing in areas other than those directly related to the provision of telephone services, but it was required to provide telephones to everyone who was willing to pay the fees set by the government. Even if the telephone company lost money in providing telephone service to a remote farmer, it was required to do so.

The government also uses tax policy to encourage what it views to be socially beneficial actions. To encourage the hiring of disadvantaged teenagers during the summer, the government provides a tax credit. In many other countries, the government provides generous tax subsidies to those firms locating in areas where there is high unemployment.

Advantages of Regulation and Taxation. Those who advocate regulation and taxation as remedies for the market failures believe that they have three major advantages over public ownership. First, they allow for a more consistent and efficient national policy. Assume it is desirable to locate firms in some area with high unemployment. Because of this, nationalized firms are often told to locate in these areas. It is, however, better to provide a general subsidy, with those firms for whom the move to the areas has the least cost taking advantage of the subsidy, than to impose the burden simply on those firms that happen to be nationalized.

Second, the utilization of tax and subsidy schemes allows a clearer estimate of the costs associated with pursuing the given objective. It may be desirable to reduce the level of pollution, but how much is it worth? It may be desirable to locate the firm in an area where there is high unemployment, but how much is it worth? It is often difficult to ascertain the additional costs of government enterprises following these objectives; providing direct government subsidies brings the costs of pursuing these alternative objectives more into the open and thus allows a more rational decision concerning whether the costs are worth the benefits.

Third, there is a widespread belief that incentives for efficiency are greater with private firms, even if regulated. The evidence for this greater efficiency, and the reasons for it, are discussed below.

Advocates of public production claim that these indirect control mechanisms are not completely effective; private firms have more information than the regulators and are able, through one means or an other, to get the regulators to work in the interests of the regulated. Moreover, the government may have a multiplicity of objectives, and it may be difficult to devise a set of regulations that fully reflects these objectives.

Finally, the use of regulation (and tax or subsidy schemes) often has resulted in large distortions, as firms attempt to take advantage of favorable provisions and avoid the impact of unfavorable provisions. There is a widespread belief, for instance, that utility regulations have led to excessive investment by utilities.

Those who advocate no (or very weak) controls believe that proponents of regulation are correct in their view that publicly owned enterprises are inefficient. They also agree with critics of regulation that regulations result in inefficiencies, and that regulation frequently serves the interest of the regulated or of special-interest groups. They go further in arguing that there is no reason to believe that public enterprises act in the "public interest" (rather than in the interests of special-interest groups or of the managers and workers of the public enterprises). In recent years, for instance, there have been frequent complaints of pollution and sex discrimination against public enterprises and governmental agencies.[2] (The relevant question, of course, is whether such complaints are more or less frequent than in similarly situated private firms.)[3]

More generally, those who believe that the government should not intervene in the market believe that any slight advantages that might exist from the possible improved congruence between firms' actions and social objectives resulting from either public ownership or regulation are small compared to the inefficiencies arising from public ownership or regulation.

We will not be able to resolve these disputes in this chapter. What we will attempt to do in the remaining pages is answer three questions:

1) Are there particular market failures that frequently result in government production?

2) Is it true that public enterprises are less efficient than private enterprises?

3) How can we explain these differences in efficiency?

---

[2] See E. S. Savas, *Privatizing the Public Sector*, p. 86.

[3] An interesting reflection of this dichotomy between the actions of public enterprises and "social interests" is the recent attempt by the Socialist government in Greece, headed by Andreas Papandreou (formerly chairman of the economics department of the University of California), to "socialize" the public enterprises.

Market Failures and Public Production: Natural Monopoly

The most important market failure that has lead to public production arises when markets are not *competitive*. As we saw in Chapter 5, a common reason that markets may not be competitive is the existence of increasing returns to scale; that is, the average costs of production decline as the level of production increases. In that case, economic efficiency requires that there be a limited number of firms. Industries where increasing returns are so significant that only one firm should operate are referred to as **natural monopolies.** Examples of natural monopolies include telephones, water, and electricity.

The major cost associated with delivering water is the network of pipes. Once pipes have been installed, the additional costs of supplying water to one extra user are relatively insignificant. It would clearly be inefficient to have two networks of pipes, side by side, one delivering to one home, the next to a neighbor. The same is true of electricity, cable TV, and natural gas.

We represent the average cost curve and the demand curve for a natural monopoly in Figure 7.2. Since the costs of production decline as the level of production increases, it is efficient to have only one firm. In the case depicted, there is a whole range of viable outputs (where the firm makes a profit). The maximum viable output (without subsidies) is where the demand curve intersects the average cost curve.

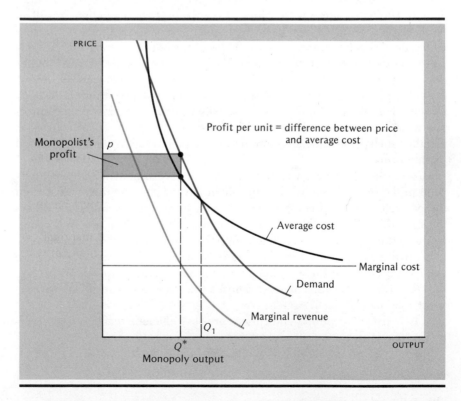

7.2 NATURAL MONOPOLY With no sunk costs and potential entry, a natural monopolist would operate at Q_i, the lowest price consistent with at least breaking even. With sunk costs, the price will be higher. The monopolist unconcerned with the threat of entry operates at Q^*, where marginal revenue equals marginal cost.

In these situations, we cannot rely on the kinds of competitive forces that we discussed earlier to ensure that the industry is efficient. Efficiency requires that price equal marginal cost. But if the firm charges a price equal to marginal cost, it will suffer a loss, since marginal cost is lower than average cost for industries with declining average cost.

One common recommendation in this situation is for the government to provide a subsidy to the industry and insist that the firm charge a price equal to the marginal cost. Such a policy is sometimes referred to as "first-best." It ignores, however, the question of how the revenues required to pay the subsidy are to be raised; it assumes, in particular, that there are no distortions associated with raising this revenue. Moreover, it assumes that the government knows the magnitude of the subsidy that will enable the firm to be viable.

In practice, most governments have *attempted* to make such industries pay for themselves. (They may also be concerned with the equity of making general taxpayers pay to subsidize a private good that is enjoyed only by a portion of the population, or enjoyed by different individuals to different extents.) Thus they have insisted on government-managed natural monopolies operating at the intersection of their demand curve and their average cost curves. This is called the zero profit point, and this policy is sometimes referred to as a second-best policy.

Potential Competition and Efficiency

This zero profit point is precisely the point where natural monopolies may operate, under the assumption that there is effective potential competition. Assume a firm tried to charge a price that exceeded the average cost of production. If it were easy to enter (and exit) from an industry, a firm that tried to capture a profit for itself would instantaneously be threatened with entry, with some firm willing to provide the given service or commodity at a lower price. Under these conditions, the firm could come in and provide the services or commodities at a profitable price, without worrying unduly about the reactions of the original firm.[4] Thus the presence of a single firm does not, in itself, imply that the firm can exercise monopoly power. So long as there are potential entrants, that single firm must charge a price equal to average cost. The market allocation does not correspond to the first-best policy we described earlier: price equals average costs, not marginal cost. But this allocation does correspond to the second-best situation, in which the government does not provide subsidies to industries.

Sunk Costs

All of this changes when there are **sunk costs.** Sunk costs are costs that are not recoverable upon the exit of the firm. Most research and development expenditures represent sunk costs. But a building that can be costlessly con-

[4]In the recent literature in industrial organization, markets with decreasing average costs but no sunk costs, in which price is maintained at a level equal to average costs, are referred to as contestable. See W. J. Baumol, J. Panzar, and R. Willig, *Contestable Markets and the Theory of Industrial Organization* (New York: Harcourt Brace Jovanovich, 1982). For a simple exposition of the theory of contestable markets, see W. J. Baumol, "Contestable Markets: An Uprising in the Theory of Industry Structure," *American Economic Review* 72 (1982): 1–15.

verted into another use does not represent a sunk cost. An airplane, which can easily be sold to another airline, does not represent a sunk cost.

Why are sunk costs so important? They create an essential asymmetry between an established firm and those that are not. The potential entrant is not in the same position as the firm already in the industry, for the firm already in the industry has expended funds that it cannot recover. Under a variety of circumstances, these sunk costs act as a barrier to entry and allow the established firm a degree of monopoly power that it could not exercise in the absence of the sunk cost.

Since virtually all natural monopolies entail important sunk costs, the government cannot simply rely on the threat of potential competition. The fact that a single firm controls a consumer's telephone service, his water, or his electricity gives rise to concern: the monopolist is in a position to exploit the consumer. The consequences of this were seen in Chapter 5, and are reproduced in Figure 7.2. The monopolist who is unconcerned about entry charges a price that maximizes his profits, the price where the extra revenue (the marginal revenue) he gets from selling an additional unit is equal to the extra costs (the marginal costs). His profit per unit of output is the difference between the price he charges and the average costs.

Prices of Multi-Product Regulated and Nationalized Industries. So far, we have focused our attention on a natural monopoly producing a single commodity. If the industry is not to be subsidized, it must charge a price in excess of marginal cost.

On what principle should prices be set when the natural monopoly produces several commodities? Prices, on average, will still need to exceed marginal cost (if the firm is to break even). Should, for instance, the ratio of the price to marginal cost be the same for all the firm's products? Should higher charges on some services be used to subsidize other services?

The U.S. Postal Service, for instance, imposes uniform charges for delivering mail, even though the marginal cost of delivering mail to a rural household in North Dakota may be much higher than delivering a letter in Chicago. If the post office is to break even, there must be a cross-subsidy, a subsidy from one user (product) to another user (product).

The issue is obviously a very political one; the elimination of cross subsidies will adversely affect some individuals and groups. When pricing decisions are made politically, they will attempt to persuade those in charge to lower the prices they face (implicitly raising prices to someone else).

The analysis of pricing decisions involves both efficiency and distributional considerations. Economists have been particularly concerned with the efficiency costs of politically determined pricing policies. When prices are raised on some service, the consumption of that service declines, but a 1 percent price increase for some goods reduces demand more than a similar price rise for other goods. Goods for which demand is more sensitive to price increase are said to be price-elastic. In Figure 7.3A we have drawn an inelastic demand curve, for which a change in price does not result in very large change in consumption, while in Figure 7.3B the demand is very elastic; a change in price results in a large change in consumption.

If a natural monopoly is to break even (without government subsidies), it obviously must charge a price in excess of marginal cost. If the government

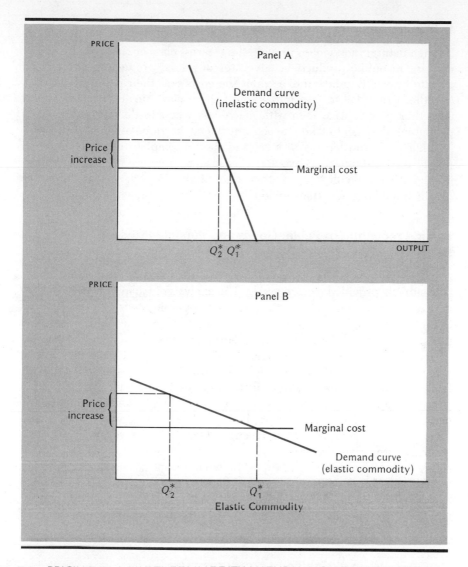

7.3 PRICING IN A MULTI-COMMODITY NATURAL MONOPOLY (A) With an in-
elastic demand, an increase in the price above marginal cost results in a relatively small decline
in output. (B) With an elastic demand, an increase in price above marginal cost results in a
large decline in output.

increased price above marginal cost by the same percentage for all commodities, clearly consumption of goods with elastic demand would be reduced
by more than those with inelastic demand. If it wishes to reduce consumption of all goods by the same percentage, it should increase the price (above
marginal costs) more for commodities whose demand is inelastic than for
commodities whose demand is elastic.[5]

[5]The problem of how to set prices for a multi-commodity public monopoly was first solved in 1956 by
Marcel Boiteux, who served as the director of Electricité de France, the government agency responsible in
France for producing electricity. For an English translation, see "On the Management of Public Monopolies

Public Production and Other Market Failures

Though natural monopolies provide the clearest class of market failures giving rise to public production, advocates of public production cite others: private firms fail to take into account the costs that their pollution imposes on others; they fail to take into account the social gains from employment (and thus may replace men with machines, when to do so is not socially desirable); they fail to take into account the congestion costs associated with locating in a crowded urban area; and they attempt to take advantage of uninformed and unwary consumers. These allegations are serious, but unfortunately, it is difficult to assess their quantitative importance, or the extent to which public production would alleviate these problems.

Public Production of Public Goods and Publicly Provided Private Goods

A rather different set of arguments arises in the cases of pure public goods and publicly provided private goods. The analysis of Chapter 5 showed only that government must finance the provision of public goods, not that it needs to produce them. It can, for instance, *contract* to have the goods or services privately produced. In some cases, contracting may be difficult: it may be difficult to specify precisely the characteristics of the product or service that is to be provided. While it is possible to contract for the delivery of a specific tank or plane, it would be difficult for the government to contract with a private firm to "provide for the national defense." Education, as mentioned earlier, is an activity about which there has been considerable debate concerning suitability of private production. Could local governments write a contract with private schools to produce the kind of education the community wishes? Would it have to supervise what is done so closely that it might as well take direct control? There are, however, some local services—such as refuse collection—for which contracts may easily be drawn up, and for which private production of publicly provided goods is not uncommon.

ARE PUBLIC ENTERPRISES LESS EFFICIENT?

A major ground of comparison between public and private enterprises is that of inefficiency. Stories of government waste, bureaucratic red tape, rigid regulations, and obtuse regulators abound in the popular press.

Subject to Budgetary Constraints," *Journal of Economic Theory* 3 (1971): 219–40. This question of the determination of prices for different commodities turns out to be equivalent to a rather similar question posed some twenty-five years earlier by the great British economist Frank Ramsey. He asked: If the government must raise a given amount of revenue by distortionary taxation, how should it raise that revenue? Should it, for instance, charge a uniform tax on all commodities, so that the ratio of the price to marginal cost would be the same for all commodities? Would there then be no relative distortions? Ramsey showed that, as plausible as that might seem, it was not the correct answer; it was preferable to charge a higher tax on a commodity whose demand was inelastic. Both Ramsey and Boiteaux ignored the distributional issues that are central to most of the political debate. These were introduced into the analysis by M. Feldstein, "Distributional Equity and the Optimal Structure of Public Prices," *American Economic Review* 62 (1973): 32–36 and (in the context of taxation) by P. Diamond and J. Mirrlees, "Optimal Taxation and Public Production," *American Economic Review* 61 (1971): 261–78, and by A. B. Atkinson and J. E. Stiglitz, "The Structure of Indirect Taxation and Economic Efficiency," *Journal of Public Economics* (1972): 97–119 and "The Design of Tax Structure: Direct versus Indirect Taxation," *Journal of Public Economics* 6 (1976): 55–75. See also below, Chapter 19.

In 1984 a presidential panel entitled "Private Sector Survey on Cost Control," headed by a New York industrialist J. Peter Grace, completed an eighteen-month study. It made 2,500 recommendations to eliminate government waste that could save $424.4 billion over three years, 27 percent of which could be achieved simply by administrative action. Among the administrative failures cited were the following:

• The Pentagon has bought standard screws (available in any hardware store for 3 cents) for $91 each. The panel attributes this to lack of competitive bidding and estimates the total loss from this practice to be $7.3 billion.

• Federal employees use 64 percent more sick time than private-sector employees in nonmanufacturing industries. The panel attributes this to sick-leave policy and estimates that the loss over a three-year period is $3.7 billion.

• Replacing out-of-date computers (average age 6.7 years, twice that in the private sector) would save $6.5 billion.

• Improving the Department of Defense inventory management (the present system generates 6 million pounds of computer output annually) would save $6.1 billion.

• Correcting government mailing lists, which sometimes repeat the same address 29 times, would save $96 million.

• The Veterans Administration spends $61,250 per bed to build nursing homes, almost four times the costs of a major private-sector nursing home operator.

• The General Services Administration employs 17 times as many people and spends 14 times as much on management costs as a private-sector company managing comparable space.

Many of the recommendations for eliminating waste were really recommendations for eliminating hidden subsidies to particular groups in the population. Among these:

• Government-subsidized power is sold at one-third market rates. Industrial users in the Northwest pay 2.456¢ per kilowatt hour while private-sector power in San Diego costs 12.086¢ per kilowatt hour. The total savings from eliminating subsidies (over a three-year period) is estimated at $19.8 billion.

• The government is required by law to pay "prevailing wages" on federal construction projects. The law prevents both outside contractors and smaller, more competitive contractors from undercutting large, established local builders. The three-year cost of this practice is estimated to be $5.0 billion.

• Congressional resistance to closing unneeded military bases adds $3.1 billion to the budget over a three-year period.

• Legislation prohibiting competitive bidding on moving household goods to Alaska or Hawaii increases moving costs by up to 26 percent.

The Grace panel's study confirms inefficiency in the public sector. But the government does not have a monopoly on inefficient practices. One could of course, find similar anecdotes concerning inefficiencies in private firms, of the difficulties in collecting money from insurance firms, of bureaucratic red tape in banks. There are incompetent people in all walks of life, and competent people make mistakes. The question is, is there any evidence to suggest that waste is greater in the public sector than in the private sector?

Comparison of Efficiency in the Public and Private Sectors

Unfortunately, there have been few systematic studies of the relative performance of the public and private sectors, and these have to be interpreted
with some caution. On the negative side are such findings as:

• Public housing projects cost about 20 percent more to produce than
comparable private housing.[6]

• Public garbage collection costs about 50 percent more than private garbage collection.[7]

• The cost of privately produced (but publicly financed) fire protection in
Scottsdale, Arizona, was approximately 47 percent less than the cost of publicly produced fire services provided to comparable communities.[8]

But not all studies show that government enterprises perform more poorly
than private. In Canada, there are two major rail systems, one private and
one public; one recent study concluded that there was no significant difference in the efficiency of the two systems.

While some studies show higher hospital costs in government hospitals,
others show lower costs. And in state-run liquor stores, Sam Peltzman of the
University of Chicago found that prices were 4 to 11 percent lower than
those charged by private retailers.[9]

While administrative costs of the social security administration are less
than 2 percent of the benefits paid, private insurance companies frequently
spend as much as 30 to 40 percent of the amount provided in benefits in
administrative and sales costs. One study compared the number of administrators to teachers and researchers in public and private institutions of higher
education and found that there were almost 50 percent more administrators in private schools than in public schools.[10] Moreover, some studies have
shown marked improvements in productivity in the public sector in recent
years. One study, by the Office of Personnel Management, covering 65 percent of federal employees, showed that productivity had increased at an annual
rate of 1.4 percent between 1967 and 1978, slightly higher than the rate of
productivity increase in the private sector.[11]

The same ambiguity in findings has been noted on an international basis.
While the major British nationalized enterprises have suffered (often huge)
losses, many of the French national enterprises have been quite profitable.

One difficulty encountered in such studies is determining "comparabili-
ties": costs for garbage collection in communities in which houses are close
together might differ significantly from costs for garbage collection in com-

[6] R. Muth, *Public Housing* (Washington, D.C.: American Enterprise Institute, 1973).

[7] E. S. Savas, *The Organization and Efficiency of Solid Waste Collection* (Lexington, Mass: D. C. Heath,
1977.)

[8] R. Ahlbrandt, "Efficiency in the Provision of Fire Services," *Public Choice* 16 (1973).

[9] D. W. Daves and L. R. Christensen, "The Relative Efficiency of Public and Private Firms in a Compet-
itive Environment: The Case of Canadian Railroads," *Journal of Political Economy* 88 (1980): 958–76. Cotton
Lindsay, "A Theory of Government Enterprise," *Journal of Political Economy*, October 1976. Hrebiniak and
Alutto, "A Comparative Organizational Study of Performance and Size Correlated in Inpatient Psychiatric
Departments," *Administrative Science Quarterly* 18 (1973). Sam Peltzman, "Pricing in Public and Private
Enterprises: Electric Utilities in the United States," *Journal of Law and Economics* 14 (1971).

[10] Lorraine E. Prinsky, "Public vs. Private: Organizational Control as Determinant of Administrative Size,"
Sociology and Social Research 62 (1978).

[11] See Nancy Hayward and George Kuper, "The National Economy and Productivity in Government,"
Public Administration Review 38 (1978) and U.S. Office of Personnel Management, *Measuring Federal Productivity*, February 1980.

munities in which houses are far apart. Communities that elect to use private services may be different, in some important way, from communities that elect to use public services.

Those enterprises that are run by the government may differ systematically from those that are privately run. Many of the public enterprises in Britain today became public enterprises as a result of bankruptcy: the government intervened to stop the plants from closing by taking over the firms. These firms are government enterprises because they were running at a loss; they are not running at a loss because they are government enterprises.

An example of the caution necessary in evaluating studies comparing public and private performance is provided by the recent study of private versus public schools headed by University of Chicago sociologist James Coleman. He found not only that students in private schools performed better but that such schools were as racially mixed as public schools.[12] However, students attending the private schools have chosen to go there; they (or their parents) have expressed a commitment to education (in their willingness to spend money on it); and the school has the option of rejecting students who fail to perform or are disruptive. Even if one finds that private school students do perform better, one cannot infer that converting any public school system into a privately managed one would improve performance.

Though there is only scattered evidence that public bureaucracies are less efficient than private firms, the belief that this is so is widespread. Instances of public incompetence are very much in the public eye; instances of private incompetence do not draw comparable attention.[13]

Still, it is worth noting that several studies indicate a reasonably high level of "consumer satisfaction" with government bureaucracy. A Harris Poll of those who had had some nonroutine dealings with a federal government agency found that 46 percent found the experience "highly satisfying" while an additional 29 percent found it "only somewhat" satisfying. A University of Michigan study found comparable levels of satisfaction, while an Ohio State University study found high satisfaction levels from about 60 percent of the respondents. These studies (in which individuals evaluate a specific experience) should be contrasted with surveys of general impressions of government efficiency. A Gallup Poll study found that two-thirds of those interviewed thought bureaucrats do not work so hard as the interviewees themselves would in governmental jobs and that the government employs too many individuals.[14]

SOURCES OF INEFFICIENCY IN THE PUBLIC SECTOR

One of the traditional arguments in favor of government control of production is that it would be more efficient than private production. There are problems of coordination among private firms that will frequently lead to

---

[12] Most students in private schools attend inner-city Catholic schools.

[13] Instances of "large" private failures also receive considerable attention. The huge cost overruns on nuclear power plants (with final costs frequently being more than ten times the original estimates cost) are only partially attributable to changing government regulations.

[14] George H. Gallup, *The Gallup Poll: Public Opinion, 1972–77* (Wilmington, DE: Scholars Resources, 1978) and *The Washington Post*, October 1978, p. 16.

excessive investment in one period and insufficient investment in another.[15] The government (in this view) is in a better position to plan for the orderly development of an industry. These concerns have been particularly impor- tant for less-developed countries, and for industries requiring heavy invest- ments. Some economists, such as John Kennith Galbraith of Harvard University, believe that more planning is required. The prevalent view today among American economists about both the merits and the necessity of gov- ernment planning (at least as it has turned out in practice) is somewhat skep- tical. On the one hand, it is pointed out that extensive planning goes on within private firms. On the other hand, there is concern about the ability of government to plan well.

Why should public enterprises in fact behave much differently than pri- vate ones? Over half the shares of British Petroleum are owned by the Brit- ish government. Yet, at least in its day-to-day operations, it looks little different from any other multinational oil company.

Though there may be important differences in how a small firm that is operated by its owner functions and how a large corporation does, what dif- ferences does it make if they are private shareholders or if there is a single shareholder, the government? Managers of public enterprises may attempt to maximize the profits of the public enterprise in much the same way that managers of private enterprises do. The main difference that economists emphasize is incentives, both organizational and individual.

Organizational Incentives

Government enterprises differ from private enterprises in two important ways: they do not need to worry about bankruptcy and they usually do not have to worry about competition.

Bankruptcy. One source of differences in incentives facing public and pri- vate enterprises has to do with the threat of bankruptcy that private firms face, in contrast with the ever-present possibility of subsidies from the gov- ernment for public enterprises.

The possibility of bankruptcy is an important one; it provides a limit to the magnitude of the social losses that an inefficient management can gen- erate in a private enterprise, and a natural mechanism for the replacement of inefficient management teams. It imposes a budget constraint on the firm. Even a generous manager cannot pay his workers much more than the pre- vailing wage without risking the possibility of bankruptcy.

In contrast, government enterprises often run large deficits over extended periods of time. In Britain, for instance, the cumulative deficits of the British Steel Corporation during the period since nationalization have been mas- sive. The possibility of public subsidies has, it is argued, made managers of public enterprises less resistant to union wage demands; in many countries, wages of public enterprises are considerably in excess of wages for corre- sponding workers in the private sector. The same is true more generally for public employees in the United States. Federal wages for males have been

---

[15]The French government pioneered in the use of what is called indicative planning, in which information about production plans is shared among firms but they are left to make their own decisions. In recent years, however, even this limited form of government planning has not been extensively employed.

15 percent above wages for comparable workers in the private sectors; females' wages have been 21 percent higher.[16]

Competition. A second difference between public and private enterprises arises from the absence of competition facing most public enterprises. Competition plays several important roles. First, competition provides the opportunity for choice. Consider the government agency responsible for issuing license plates: frequently the agency fails to take into account the value of time used waiting in line to obtain the license plate. Since that cost does not appear in the agency's budget, while the costs of additional personnel that might be required to reduce waiting times is included, there is an incentive to reduce costs in this way (which actually increases the total social costs of providing the service).

Individuals might be willing to pay more for the service, but they are not offered the opportunity of choice. When there is competition, individuals can reveal their preferences by their acts of choice. The presence of choice *forces* firms to come to terms with the costs imposed on those outside their agency as a result of bureaucratic processes. Thus a bureaucratic insurance firm, which requires extensive paperwork in order to obtain a claim, might find itself losing customers to a less bureaucratic firm. The public bureaucracy behaving in the same way will not receive the same signal.

Albert O. Hirschman of the Institute for Advanced Study has called this method of communicating preferences exit, as opposed to voice (the expression of views through the political process). When individuals have no choice, voice is the only option available, and voice may be an ineffective method of inducing bureaucracies to act efficiently. Thus competition provides a check, a limitation on the inefficiencies associated with public enterprises.[17]

More positively, competition provides an incentive structure: competing enterprises, in their attempt to attract clients, try to find a mixture of services that best meets customer needs. More generally, competition provides a *basis for comparison*. When there is only one agency issuing license plates, it may be difficult to ascertain whether or not the agency is being efficient. Those who are responsible for managing the agency are more knowledgeable about the technology of issuing license plates than outsiders. But when there are several agencies engaged in similar activities, one has a basis for comparison. One can see that one agency has a lower cost than another, and one is then in a position at least to ask why.[18] Even when the comparison of performance is not made explicitly, it is made implicitly by the market and is reflected in the firm's profitability. Competition implies that those firms that are efficient and are able to deliver the kinds of goods and services consumers desire will grow and expand, and that those that are inefficient will decline. These rewards and punishments are meted out by the market, in an impersonal way; managers know this and have a strong incentive to promote effi-

[16] Sharon P. Smith, "Pay, Pensions, and Employment in Government, *American Economic Review*, May 1982, p. 275. See also Paul N. Courant, Edward M. Gramlich, and Daniel L. Rubinfeld, "Public Employee Market Power and the Level of Government Spending," *American Economic Review*, December 1979, pp. 806–17.

[17] A. O. Hirschman, *Exit, Voice and Loyalty: Responses to Decline in Firms, Organizations, and States* (Cambridge, MA: Harvard University Press, 1970).

[18] See B. Nalebuff and J. E. Stiglitz, "Prizes and Incentives: Towards a General Theory of Compensation and Competition," *Bell Journal* 14 (1983): 21–43.

ciency and to be innovative in developing products and services that better meet the needs of consumers.

Individual Incentives

Another important difference between the private and public enterprises lies in the incentive structures facing government employees.

Restrictions on Salary Structure. Managers in public enterprises seldom have pay structures that are as closely related to profits as managers of large private enterprises. For a government enterprise to pay its president, say, five times the salary of the president of the United States is probably unacceptable. How important this restriction is is a question of some debate. It may affect the quality of the individuals it succeeds in hiring, and it may affect the effort the manager exerts. But there are those who claim that managers do the best they can, and financial reward is only part of what motivates individuals; and there are those who argue that there is little evidence that managers make much difference anyway.[19]

Tenure. A second important difference is the ease with which individuals can be fired. It is very difficult to be fired from government jobs. This attribute of security if often cited by potential employees as one of the more desirable features of government employment. Prior to the current civil service system, federal employees served at the whim of the president; part of the spoils of winning the election was the right to appoint ones supporters to government jobs. Today, the only political appointments are the secretaries of each of the departments, and those who serve immediately under them (the undersecretaries, assistant secretaries, and deputy assistant secretaries.) Though the intent of the civil service legislation was to establish a professional administrative system, immune from political pressures, this protection from being fired for political reasons also entails considerable protection from being fired for incompetency.[20]

The combination of the limitations on rewards for good performance and the absence of punishments for bad performance undoubtedly plays an important role in explaining bureaucratic behavior. At the same time, the government may attract to itself individuals who value security highly and who do not view the absence of high rewards as much of a loss, since they would not attain a high salary in the private sector anyway. Changes in the reward structure for these individuals might not elicit a marked change in their behavior.

---

[19] In an often-quoted study, Lieberson and O'Connor showed that changes in management had little significant effect on the performance of the firm. See S. Lieberson and S. F. O'Connor, "Leadership and Organizational Performance: A Study of Large Corporations," *American Sociological Review* 37 (1972): 117–130. See also G. Salanick and J. Pfeffer, "Constraints on Administrator Discretion: The Limited Influence of Mayors on City Budgets," *Urban Affairs Quarterly* 12 (1977): 475–98.

[20] This slightly exaggerates the lack of rewards within the bureaucratic structure: individuals can still be promoted. But the possibilities of promotion become limited in periods in which the growth of government is restricted. Though this may happen in private enterprises as well, individuals who find their promotion possibilities limited leave to other firms; the security of tenure within the civil service and the relatively high pay make exit to private firms relatively unattractive. In these circumstances, incentive problems may become particularly severe.

Over the years, various branches of the civil service have developed different reputations. While some, such as the National Park Service, have developed a positive public image, there is a general view of the federal bureaucracy as entailing inefficiency, lack of innovativeness, inflexibility, blind
attention to following routines, and endless red tape.

In this section, we discuss how bureaucracies differ from other kinds of
organizations and how we can explain certain aspects of bureaucratic behavior.

Differences between Administrative Activities and Other Production Activities

Earlier, we cited several studies comparing public and private enterprises
undertaking similar activities, such as garbage collection. It is important to
remember, however, that a large fraction of government activity is very much
different from these kinds of production activities. Much of government activity
is administrative, or "white" collar. It may be that many of the problems we
associate with bureaucracies arise not because they lie within the public
sector but because of the nature of the duties of bureaucrats.[21] In the economists' typical model of a production activity, there is a well-defined notion
of what the worker is supposed to do, inputs can be observed, outputs can
be observed, and there is a well-defined relationship between inputs and
outputs.[22] None of these conditions holds for much of the administrative
activity within the public sector. The differences between administrative
activity and conventional activity also account for the limited use of incentive
pay structures. It may not be possible to design effective incentive structures
where it is difficult to measure performance.

Difficulties in Measuring Performance. There are some difficulties in
measuring the performance of firms in the private sector. The manager of
the firm may claim that though current profits are low, the firm has taken
decisions that are aimed at maximizing the long-run profitability of the firm.
Nevertheless, the criterion, that of profitability, is clear. In the case of public-sector agencies, however, it is far more difficult to ascertain whether the
agency has been successful. Did students do better as a result of federal aid
to education for the poor? How does one measure this: does one use reading
scores? What are valid tests? And how can one distinguish the contribution
of one particular public program from all the other changes that are going
on in the environment at the same time? In the last few years, these problems have been of considerable concern and have given rise to attempts to
develop systematic evaluation procedures for public programs.

Since outcomes cannot be evaluated precisely, performance is more likely
to be judged on the basis of procedures and process: how well the manager

---

[21] These differences have been emphasized in the work of J. Hannaway, "Supply Creates Demands" paper
presented at Academy of Management Meetings, San Diego, August 1985.

[22] There has been an extensive recent literature dealing with the special problems that arise when inputs
cannot be observed but outputs can. See, for instance, J. E. Stiglitz, "Incentives, Risk, and Information:
Notes towards a Theory of Hierarchy, *Bell Journal of Economics and Management Science*, Autumn 1975,
pp. 552–79.

follows the present routines and how successful he is in dealing with the bureaucracy.

Multiplicity of Objectives. The difficulty of assessing the success of a government official is exacerbated by the multiplicity of objectives associated with most public programs. While profit maximization is the clear objective of private firms, public agencies have to worry about a variety of distributional considerations. The legislation setting up a program frequently lists a number of objectives without specifying how trade-offs are to be made. Individuals within and outside the bureaucracy may differ on how those trade-offs should be made. To some it may be far more important to make sure that everyone who is entitled to some government program gets access to it than it is to make sure than someone who is not entitled to a government program is denied access. Critics of government programs tend to focus only on the latter. But any attempt (with given administrative resources) to cut back on one type of error increases the number of errors of the other type.

Ambiguous Technology. A third characteristic of many government programs that makes them ill-suited for the use of conventional incentive structures is that the relationship between the efforts of the manager and the success of the program is very tenuous. This is particularly true of the newer government programs. The objectives of many of the programs enacted under President Johnson's "Great Society" programs were clear; to reduce, if not eliminate, the extent of poverty in the United States. But the "technology"—how this was to be done—was (and to a large extent remains) unclear. The fact that in bureaucracies there was no clear relationship between inputs and outputs was noted by C. Northcote Parkinson:

> It is a commonplace observation that work expands so as to fill the time available for its completion. . . . Granted that work (and especially paper work) is thus elastic in its demands on time, it is manifest that there need be little or no relationship between the work to be done and the size of the staff to which it may be assigned. . . . Politicians and taxpayers have assumed with occasional phases of doubt that a rising total in the number of civil servants must reflect a growing volume of work to be done. Cynics, in questioning this belief, have imagined that the multiplication of officials must have left some of them idle or all of them able to work for shorter hours. But this is a matter in which faith and doubt seem equally misplaced. The fact is that the number of the officials and the quantity of the work to be done are not related to each other at all. . . .[23]

Parkinson went on to announce Parkinson's Law, which describes the law of growth of public organizations. It was predicated on two hypotheses: "An official wants to multiply subordinates, not rivals; and officials make work for each other."

What Do Bureaucrats Maximize?

Economists begin with the presumption that individuals act in their own self-interest. Thus, to understand the behavior of bureaucracies, one must

---

[23]From C. Northcote Parkinson, "Parkinson's Law," *The Economist*, November 1955, reprinted in E. Mansfield, *Managerial Economics and Operations Research* (New York: W.W. Norton, 4th ed., 1980).

ask, What is it in the interests of the bureaucrats to do? In the preceding section we argued that, for a variety of reasons, bureaucrats are not given incentive structures in which their pay is related very closely to their performance. The question then is, What do bureaucrats seek to maximize? One answer is provided by W. A. Niskanen, a member of the Council of Economic Advisers in the Reagan administration and a former vice-president of the Ford Motor Company.

He postulated that bureaucrats seek to maximize the size of their agency: bureaucrats are concerned with "their salary, the perquisites of office, public reputation, power, patron, age," and all of these are related to the size of their agency. In this view, the bureaucrat attempts to promote the activities of his bureau in many of the same ways that a firm attempts to increase its size. He *competes* with other bureaucrats for funds. Bureaucratic competition replaces market competition.[24]

How Do Bureaucrats Increase the Size of Their Agency? What implications does the Niskanen hypothesis have for the behavior of the bureaucrat (and the bureaucracy)? How does a bureaucrat succeed in increasing his share of the overall budget? There are several mechanisms, and understanding them gives some insights into some of the well-known characteristics of bureaucracies.

First, the bureaucrat seeks to provide desired services. To this extent, the bureaucratic competition provides a healthy function. But the direct clientele of the bureaucrat are not the citizens, who receive the services, but the congresspeople, who vote for the appropriations. Government bureaucrats tend to be particulary attuned to the desires of those congresspeople who serve on the committees and subcommittees that oversee the government agency. Thus some of the alleged bureaucratic inefficiencies are not really inefficiencies arising from the bureaucracy but legislative (congressional) inefficiencies: the bureaucracy is simply responding to the desire of Congress to extend special favors to certain special-interest groups.

It is when competition among bureaucracies becomes limited that the bureaucrats' interest and the public interest may diverge most markedly. Niskanen argues that there has been an increasing centralization within the bureaucracy.[25] The attempts to "rationalize" the bureaucracy, to ensure that two government agencies do not perform duplicative functions, has the disadvantage that it reduces competition.

If we view a bureaucracy as a monopolist in providing some service, and we postulate that the bureaucracy wishes to maximize the size of his agency, then we can obtain a clear prediction concerning what the bureaucrat should

[24] W. A. Niskanen, Jr. *Bureaucracy and Representative Government* (Chicago: Aldine, 1971), p. 38. It should be emphasized that the bureaucrat does not necessarily view himself as pursuing his own selfish interest. The navy admiral who pushes for more aircraft carriers believes that he is doing what is in the national interest, but so does the air force general who pushes for more bombers, and the army general who pushes for more land-based missiles. These individuals come to believe in the worth of the activities in which they are engaged.

[25] Sam Peltzman has criticized this centralization hypothesis as an explanation for the growth of bureaucracy. He compares economies with different degrees of centralization and argues that there is no systematic realization between that and bureaucratic growth. There are other variables that affect bureaucratic size and growth, and it is, unfortunately, difficult to account for all of them. The question is, other things being equal, does an increase in centralization lead to more bureaucratic growth? See S. Peltzman, "The Growth of Government," *Journal of Law and Economics*, October 1980, pp. 209–88. Others have found some relationship between concentration (bureaucratic competition) and bureaucratic size or growth.

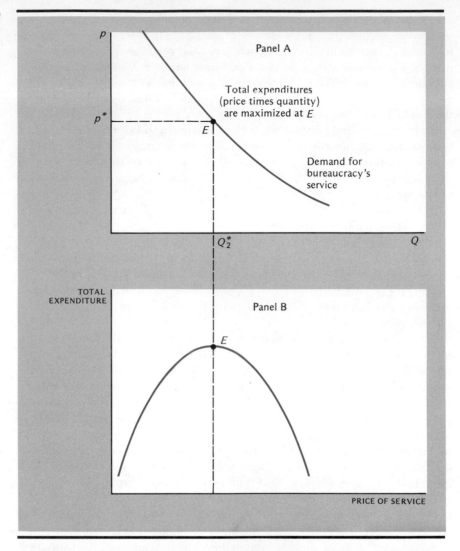

7.4 MAXIMIZING A BUREAUCRACY'S SIZE As the price of the service increases up to p*, total expenditure increases. To maximize revenue, the bureaucrat sets the price of the bureaucracy's service at the point of maximum expenditures, E.

do. If the demand for the service of the bureaucracy is inelastic over some range as the price of the service is increased, total expenditure (price times quantity) increases (see Figure 7.4). In Figure 7.4B we have plotted the total expenditure on the public service as a function of the price charged. Expenditure is maximized at the point E.[26]

[26]Technically, this is the point where the elasticity of demand is equal to unity. The elasticity of demand, it will be recalled, gives the percentage change in demand from a percentage change in price.

$$\text{Elasticity of demand} = \frac{\text{\% change in demand}}{\text{\% change in price}}$$

Thus, if a one percent increase in the price causes a more than one percent reduction in demand, total revenue (the product of price times quantity) is reduced. Demand is inelastic if the quantity demanded is not very sensitive to price.

As the price of the service increases up to p^*, total expenditure increases. The bureaucrat maximizes his revenues at point E. If the bureaucrat could charge what he liked for the public service, or if he wished to maximize expenditures by the public on the services he provides, he would charge price p^*. But the bureaucrat cannot arbitrarily choose a price to charge. The price for the service provided by the bureaucrat is simply the costs per unit of the service delivered. If he wishes to increase the price, he can only do it by decreasing efficiency. If the bureaucrat were a perfect monopolist, it would pay him to increase the degree of inefficiency until the price (costs per unit of delivered service) were increased to p^*.

Several factors are critical in enabling the bureaucrat to do this. First there must be an absence of competition. If there were competition, some other bureaucrat could offer to perform the services at lower costs. Second, the technology must be ambiguous, so that it must be difficult to ascertain whether or not the bureaucrat is being inefficient. How many pieces of paper should a paper processor process per minute? Since this is likely to vary markedly from task to task, no outside standard can readily be set.

Imperfect Information and Budgets. Finally, the bureaucrat often has an important *informational advantage* over legislators. Congressmen usually have limited information concerning what it should cost to perform various services. They do not know how much it should cost to produce a new missile system. At times, when bureaucrats are competing against each other or when the costs of some program seems excessively high, bureaucrats will tend to underrepresent the costs. They know that once the program has been initiated, they will be able to obtain the necessary supplemental funds required to complete it. Military procurement has been particularly marked by cost overruns. At other times, there may be an incentive to exaggerate the costs required to perform some task; the extra resources can then be diverted to some other use.

Indeed, one of the great concerns of a bureaucrat is that it come to be believed that he can do his job at a lower cost. A bureaucrat who failed to spend his entire budget would be in danger of having his budget cut the next year. This is what gives rise to what are called "spend-out problems"—problems using up the congressional appropriation during the final months (days) of the fiscal year.

The bureaucrat can not only misrepresent the benefits and costs associated with his activities; he can also take actions that *affect* those benefits and costs. In particular, it is common for an agency to be given an overall budget; this is the major instrument of control over the agency. The agency, though, may enjoy some discretion within that budget. In particular, the bureaucrat may use this discretion to pursue his own goals (whatever those are) rather than those of the legislators. The threat of cutting back on some part of the expenditure is sometimes employed by public agencies to increase their overall budgets. Thus when the National Park Service had its budget cut, it eliminated its expenditure for lighting the Statue of Liberty in hopes that the ensuing public outcry would lead to a restoration of its budget.

Finally, the bureaucrats may exercise influence over the size of their budgets by presenting a limited set of alternatives. The military may claim that only two types of defense systems are feasible, one very ineffective but costing very little, and the other costing a great deal. (Although there may well be others, these are claimed to be "inferior" in one way or another.) By refusing to present details of the alternatives, they force a vote between two extremes, hoping in doing so to get the high level of expenditure. By controlling the agenda in this way they may seek to increase the size of the budget.[27]

Bureaucratic Risk Aversion

The bureaucrat's desire to increase the size of his budget seems to provide an explanation of many aspects of bureaucratic behavior. There are other aspects of bureaucratic behavior that can best be explained by another important aspect of the incentives facing bureaucrats. Though bureaucrats' pay may not be closely and directly related to their performance, in the long run their promotion is at least partially dependent on observed performance.

A bureaucrat's mistakes are more likely to be noticed than his successes (or at least so he fears). He can absolve himself of responsibility for mistakes by following certain bureaucratic procedures that ensure that all of his actions are reviewed by others. Although this process of group decision making also reduces the claims the individual can make for any success, the bureaucrats seem willing to make this trade-off. We say they are **risk-averse.** This is what gives rise, in part, to the nature of bureaucracies: everything must pass through the appropriate channels (red tape).

Two other factors enhance these bureaucratic procedures. First, many of the costs associated with engaging in risk-averse activities are not borne by the bureaucrats themselves. Rather, they are borne by society as a whole, through the taxes it pays and the costs of delays and paperwork imposed on it in dealing with the bureaucracy. (Indeed, there are those who claim that the bureaucrats may actually enjoy the bureaucratic process.)[28]

Second, the prevalence of set routines that must be followed entailing the approval of any proposal by several different individuals is not only a consequence of bureaucrats pursuing their own self-interest. It follows naturally from the **fiduciary** relationship between government bureaucrats and the funds they allocate. That is, government bureaucrats are not spending their own money. They are spending public resources. It is generally accepted that an individual should have less discretion—should take greater care—in spending the money of others than he might in spending his own money. Again, what is implied by taking greater care is that certain routines are followed; these routines ensure that the funds are spent not according to the whim of any single individual. They also serve the function of reducing the possibility of corruption. Since many individuals must give approval, it is usually not in the power of any individual to give a contract at an above-market price and thus receive a kickback.

Two examples of routines are the use of cost-benefit analyses and environmental impact statements. The intention of following such procedures is clear.

---

[27] See R. Filimon, T. Romer, and H. Rosenthal, "Asymmetric Information and Agenda Control: The Bases of Monopoly Power in Public Spending," *Journal of Public Economics,* February 1982, pp. 51–70.

[28] There are alternative, more psychologically or sociologically based theories of why bureaucrats behave bureaucratically.

On the other hand, because the data on which an assessment can be firmly established are rarely available, the studies often become routine exercises with predictable outcomes. Occasionally they serve as the basis for attempts by opponents of the project to delay the project; by delaying the project, the opponents hope to increase the costs to the point where the project is no longer economically feasible. There is a social loss in these delaying practices.

Reform of the Bureaucracy

Though reforms might improve the incentives facing bureaucrats, these reforms might themselves have disadvantages that outweigh the benefits. Consider the Civil Service Law, which protects civil servants from being fired. It was originally instituted to eliminate the spoils system, in which the winner of the election was entitled to appoint those who would be responsible for administering public programs. The protection from dismissal, combined with the rigidities in the pay scale, means that individuals may have relatively little reward for performing well, and relatively little punishment for performing badly, so long as performance is above a certain minimal level of competence. Though the elimination of job protection might have a beneficial effect on incentives, few advocate this as a resolution of the incentive problem, because politicization of the administrative process would almost inevitably result. There may be, however, reforms in the pay structure and promotion systems that would enhance incentives.

In some cases, the introduction of competition—establishing competing bureaus performing similar tasks—might have a beneficial effect. Recall our earlier discussion where we suggested that one of the major differences between public and private enterprises arose from the absence of competition. It is often alleged that monopolies in the private sector are also frequently characterized by inefficiencies, bureaucratic red tape, etc. Indeed, Daves and Christensen, in their comparison of private and public railroads in Canada, conclude that "any tendency toward inefficiency resulting from public ownership has been overcome by the benefits of competition . . . that the oft-noted inefficiency of government enterprises stems from their isolation from effective competition rather than their public ownership per se."[29] To what extent competition can be extended in the public sector remains a question of continuing debate.[30]

Finally, there are those who believe that the inefficiencies we have noted are an inevitable consequence of our Constitutional system. Harvard political scientist M. P. Fiorina has argued:

> To have an impact a structural reform must change incentives . . . but those structural reforms which would significantly change the incentives facing congressmen and bureaucrats will stand little chance of adoption. . . . The political forces underlying existing equilbria will understandably block any structural reform capable of destroying these equilibria. Unfortunately, such equilibria

---

[29] D. W. Daves and L. R. Christensen, "Relative Efficiency of Public and Private Firms."

[30] Some claim, for instance, that the rivalry between the different branches of the military has been beneficial, while others argue that the competition has prevented them from working together in the national interest.

arise from fundamental features of our constitutional system; only structural reforms aimed at that level can make much of a difference.[31]

SUMMARY

1. In the United States, the government has played an important role in production in several sectors, though its role is far more limited than in most other developed countries.

2. Government enterprises differ from private enterprises in two important ways:
   a) While private enterprises maximize profits, government enterprises may pursue other objectives. The government may, however, be able to use tax and subsidy policies to affect employment, wage, location, and other policies of private enterprises, just as it could if it controlled the enterprise directly.
   b) Public enterprises face different incentives. Some of the differences in incentives arise from the absence of competition and the absence of the possibility of bankruptcy. The limited use of pay incentives and the greater degree of job security may provide part of the explanation of the differences in individuals' behavior.

3. The behavior of the bureaucracy (and individual bureaucrats) plays an important role in determining not only the efficiency with which public goods are provided but what goods are provided and to whom they are provided.

4. There is some limited evidence that governments are less efficient than private enterprises in providing comparable services, though the absence of competition may be central in explaining differences in performance.

5. Bureaucrats face limited financial incentives for performing well; part of this is a result of problems inherent in measuring performance, the uncertain technologies in providing public goods, and the multiplicity of objectives. Bureaucratic behavior may be partly understood in terms of their desire to increase the size of the bureaucracy. Bureaucratic red tape and reliance on routines are partly explained by bureaucrats' aversion to risk.

6. While most European governments have taken over direct control of natural monopolies, in the United States they are regulated. Whether regulation works effectively in the public interest is a question of some debate.

KEY CONCEPTS

Bureaucracy	Sunk costs
Nationalized industry	Risk aversion
Public enterprise	Fiduciary
Indirect control	First-best
Natural monopoly	Second-best
Regulation	Privatization

QUESTIONS AND PROBLEMS

1. In recent years there has been extensive discussion of privatization of public enterprises. The government has proposed selling Conrail and the British government has partly sold off its telephone services. In each of these cases, outline the major arguments in favor of and against privatization. Do you feel differently about the two cases? Why?

---

[31] M. P. Fiorina, "Bureaucratic (?) Failures."

2. Under the Reagan administration, the Department of Interior greatly increased the rate at which it leased offshore oil and gas. This had the effect of significantly reducing the prices that the government received for these leases. (Though the leases are sold by auction, on more than two-thirds of the tracts there was only a single bidder.) Discuss the distributional and efficiency consequences of this policy.

3. The post office claims that one of the reasons it cannot provide services as cheaply as private firms is that it is required to provide services to rural areas but it cannot charge them more than the urban areas. The private companies "skim" the low-cost markets. (Effectively, the urban areas are subsidizing the rural areas.) Discuss the efficiency and equity consequences of this kind of cross-subsidization.

4. Some have argued that if it is desirable, as a matter of national policy, to subsidize rural post offices, the subsidies should be paid out of general tax revenue, not by the other users of the postal system. Discuss the advantages and problems of such an alternative subsidy scheme.

5. There are many private security firms; many large housing developments have police protection provided by a private firm. Yet few towns contract out their police department. Why do you think this is so? What would be the advantages and disadvantages of doing so? Recently, however, many communities have contracted to have their prisons run by private firms. What advantages or problems might you anticipate from this?

6. The military buys most of its equipment from private contractors but does not use private contractors to man its ships or fly its airplanes. What differences in the nature of the services provided might account for these differences?

8

Externalities

In the past two decades, the government has taken an increasingly active role in ensuring the quality of the environment. Legislation restricting automobile emissions has been passed, and standards for admissible levels of air and water pollution by manufacturers have been established. Before any offshore oil wells are drilled, the environmental impact must be assessed, and stringent regulations for the disposal of toxic chemicals have been imposed.

Government activity in this area has clearly had some beneficial effect. There has been a noticeable improvement in the quality of air in major industrial cities such as Pittsburgh and Gary since the passage of the Air Pollution Control Act of 1962. Lakes such as Lake Erie, which once faced the prospect of becoming so polluted that much marine life would be extinguished, have been saved. Still, problems remain: on some days Los Angeles is blanketed by smog in spite of stringent California regulations on air pollution. Dangerous poisons from chemical dumps have threatened many communities, and the question of whether the Environmental Protection Agency was lax in enforcing the law became a political issue in 1982. Acid rain still threatens some of our major forests. Many claim that still more stringent laws are thus required if we are to ensure the quality of the environment for our descendants. Others claim that the costs of many of these attempts to control pollution exceed the benefits, and that the present system of government regulation is both unfair and inefficient.

Air and water pollution are two examples of a much broader range of phenomena that economists refer to as externalities (mentioned earlier, in Chapter 4). Whenever an individual or firm undertakes an action that has an effect on another individual or firm for which the latter does not pay or is not paid, we say there is an externality. This chapter explains what economists mean by externalities, the means by which private markets deal with externalities, the limits of these private mechanisms, and therefore, why government action may be required. Finally, we ask, given that government action to control externalities may be warranted, what is the best method of dealing with them? Should, for instance, the government impose direct regulations, as it has done in the case of automobile emissions? Alternatively, should it subsidize private expenditures to control pollution, as many industry spokespeople advocate? Or should it simply impose a charge for pollution?

EXTERNALITIES: SOME DISTINCTIONS

Economists distinguish among several categories of externalities. Some externalities have a beneficial effect on others and are referred to as **positive externalities;** others have a detrimental effect and are referred to as **negative externalities.** A firm that pollutes the air is imposing a negative externality on all individuals who breathe the air and on all firms whose machines wear out more rapidly in the presence of polluted air.

The beekeeper confers a positive externality on the neighboring apple orchard: as a result of pollination, the greater the number of bees, the more apples in the apple orchard. And the apple orchard confers a positive externality on the beekeeper. The more trees in the apple orchard, the more honey will be produced by the bees. The action of each individual has a direct benefit on the other for which no compensation is received.

Some externalities are generated by *producers,* others by *consumers.* The consequences (the benefits or costs of the externality-generating activity) may be experienced either by producers or by consumers. While most air pollution today is industrial, the major source in Victorian England was home coal fires. An individual who smokes in a nonventilated room causes a negative externality that is keenly felt by nonsmokers. A firm that pollutes a river causes an externality both to consumers who live downstream and to producers whose plants are located downstream. The externality may both lower the profits of the downstream firm and result in its raising its prices.

Some externalities, like those that affect the quality of air, are environmental and thus affect everyone who makes use of the environment. Others are more direct. If I leave garbage strewn over my lawn, only my immediate neighbors experience the externality.

Common resources. There is a particularly important class of externalities referred to as **common resource problems.** The central characteristic is that there is a pool of scarce resources to which access is not restricted. Consider a pond popular with fishermen. The difficulty of catching a fish depends on the number of other fishermen. Each fisherman causes a negative externality on the other fishermen.

An important example is oil pools. Oil is usually found in large pools beneath the ground. To obtain access to a pool, all one needs to do is to buy enough land to drill a well and equipment for the drilling. Of course, the more oil that one well takes out of the pool, the less there is for others to take. The total extra oil obtained as a result of drilling an extra well may, in fact, be negative; drilling an extra well reduces the pressure, and this may reduce the amount of oil that can be extracted from the pool. Again, there is a marked difference between the private returns to drilling a well and the social returns.

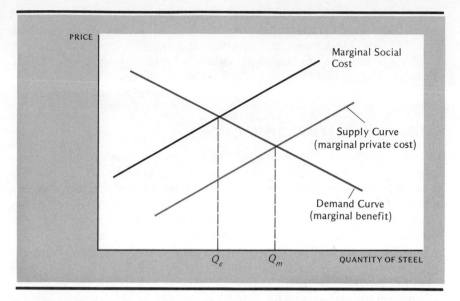

8.1 EXCESSIVE PRODUCTION OF GOODS YIELDING NEGATIVE EXTERNALI-
TIES The presence of a negative externality means that marginal social costs exceed marginal
private costs, and the market equilibrium will entail an excessive production of the commodity.
(Q_m is market equilibrium, Q_e is the efficient level of output.)

THE CONSEQUENCES OF EXTERNALITIES

Whenever there are externalities, resource allocations may not be efficient.
Consider, for instance, a firm that could, by expending resources, reduce its
level of pollution. There would be a large social benefit; but there is no
private incentive for the firm to spend this money. It receives no private
benefit.

When there are externalities, the level of production of externality-generating commodities may be excessive. Figure 8.1 shows conventional demand
and supply curves. We argued earlier that, in the absence of externalities,
the resulting market equilibrium, Q_m, was efficient. The demand curve
reflected the individual's marginal benefits from the production of an extra
unit of the commodity, and the supply curve reflected the marginal costs of
producing an extra unit of the commodity. At the intersection of the two
curves, the marginal benefits just equal the marginal costs. Now, with externalities considered, the industry's supply curve may not reflect marginal
social costs, only marginal private costs—those borne directly by the producers. If the expansion of steel production increases the level of pollution,
there is a real cost to that expansion in addition to the costs of the iron ore,
labor, coke, and limestone that go into the production of steel. But the steel
industry fails to take the cost of pollution into account. Thus Figure 8.1 also
shows the marginal social cost curve, giving the total extra costs (private and
social) of producing an extra unit of steel. This cost curve lies above the
industry supply curve. Efficiency requires that marginal social cost equal the
marginal benefit of increasing output: production should occur at Q_e, the

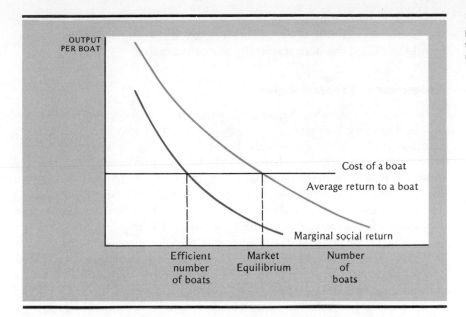

8.2 COMMON RESOURCE PROBLEM LEADS TO EXCESSIVE FISHING The extra output of an additional boat is less than the average output. There will be an excessive number of boats.

intersection of the marginal social costs curve and the demand curve. The efficient level of production is lower than the market equilibrium level.

Similarly, in the common resources problem, marginal social benefits are less than marginal private benefits. Consider a lake in which the total number of fish caught increases with the number of fishing boats, but less than proportionately, so that the number of fish caught per boat decreases as the number of boats increases. The marginal social benefit of an additional boat is thus less than the average catch of each boat; some of the fish that the boat catches would have been caught by some other boat, as shown in Figure 8.2. The private return to an additional individual deciding whether to purchase a boat is simply the average return (once they are on the lake, all boats catch the same number of fish) which is much more than the marginal social return. Thus, while the private market equilibrium entails average returns equal to the cost of a boat (assumed to be constant), social efficiency requires that the marginal social return be equal to the cost of a boat.

There is thus a presumption that when there are externalities, the market equilibrium will not be efficient.

PRIVATE SOLUTIONS TO EXTERNALITIES

One way that the private sector can deal with externalities without the aid of direct government intervention is to **internalize** the externality by forming economic units of sufficient size that most of the consequences of any action occur *within* the unit.

Let us see how this applies to another example we gave earlier, the positive externality between beekeeping and apple orchards. This externality may be internalized by having the owner of the apple orchard also become the beekeeper. It will work, of course, only if the apple orchard is sufficiently large that the bees stay in this one apple orchard.

Assignment of Property Rights

Externalities arise, as we have noted, when individuals do not have to pay for the full consequences of their actions. There is excessive fishing in a common pool because individuals do not have to pay for the right to fish. Externalities can frequently be dealt with by the appropriate assignment of **property rights.** Property rights assign to a particular individual the right to control some assets and to receive fees for the property's use. It was because no one had the property rights controlling access to an entire oil pool that too many wells were drilled. When the oil pool is controlled by a single individual, he has an incentive to make sure that the correct number of wells is drilled. Since economic efficiency is enhanced by having a single firm control the entire pool, any firm could buy the land over the pool from its present owners (at what they would have received from selling the oil) and wind up with a profit. In this view, no outside intervention would be required to ensure that an efficient pattern of property rights emerged.

Even when property rights for a common resource are not assigned to a single individual, the market may find an efficient way of dealing with the externality. Owners of oil wells frequently get together to **unitize** their production, thus making it less likely that too many wells are drilled.[1] And fishermen using the same grounds may get together to devise mutually agreed upon restrictions to prevent excess fishing.

The Coase Theorem. The assertion that whenever there are externalities, the parties involved can get together and make some set of arrangements by which the externality is internalized, and efficiency ensured, is referred to as the **Coase theorem.**[2]

For instance, when there are smokers and nonsmokers in the same room, if the loss to the nonsmokers exceeds the gains to the smokers, the nonsmokers might get together and "bribe" (or, as economists like to say, "compensate") the smokers not to smoke. If the smokers are in a nonsmoking compartment of a train, and the restriction on smoking (which can be viewed as an externality imposed on the smokers by the nonsmokers) takes away more from their welfare than the nonsmokers gain, the smokers will get together and "compensate" the nonsmokers in order to allow themselves to smoke.

Of course, the determination of who compensates whom makes a great deal of difference to the distributive implications of the externality; smokers are clearly better off in the regime in which smoking is allowed unless the smokers are paid not to smoke than they are in the regime in which smoking is banned unless they compensate nonsmokers.

---

[1] Under unitization, the development of an oil or gas reservoir is put under a single management, with proceeds distributed according to a formula specified in the unitization agreement. This unitization is not done to reduce competition (it occurs even among small oil companies who take the price of oil as given, unaffected by their actions) but to increase efficiency.

[2] R. H. Coase, "The Problem of Social Cost," *Journal of Law and Economics* 3 (1960): 1–44.

Social Sanctions

The example of the externality associated with smoking can be used to illustrate another mechanism for the control for externalities: social sanctions and the inculcation of social values. The Golden Rule can be thought of as an attempt to deal with externalities: "Do unto others as you would have them do unto you." Its converse is also important: Do not do unto others as you would not have them do unto you.

This may be roughly translated into the language of economics as "Do cause positive externalities," and "Do not cause negative externalities." As children, we are all made aware of the fact that some of our actions—such as talking loudly at the dinner table—have effects on others, for which we do not have to pay, at least directly, in the form of monetary compensation. There are, however, other sanctions that may be applied. Parents try to induce their children to behave in "socially acceptable ways" (including not generating negative externalities and conferring positive externalities). Although this socialization process does succeed in avoiding many negative externalities at the level of the family, it is less successful in dealing with many of the kinds of externalities that arise in modern society: even the threat of a \$200 fine for littering may be insufficient to induce some individuals to clean up after themselves in a public park. It is not possible to rely solely on social mechanisms for limiting externalities.

Failures of Private Solutions

If the arguments asserting that private markets can internalize externalities are correct, is there any necessity for government intervention? And if these arguments are correct, why is it that cooperative agreements have failed to take care of so many externalities?

There are basically three reasons that government intervention is required. The first has to do with the public-goods problem we discussed in Chapter 5. Many (but far from all) externalities entail the provision of a public good, such as clean air or clean water: in particular, it may be very costly to exclude anyone from enjoying the benefits of these goods. Where nonsmokers get together to compensate smokers for not smoking, it pays any individual nonsmoker to claim that he is almost indifferent to letting others smoke. He will attempt to be a free rider on the efforts of other nonsmokers to induce the smokers not to smoke.

The problems of arriving voluntarily at an efficient solution are exacerbated by the presence of imperfect information. The smokers will try to persuade the nonsmokers that they require a lot of compensation to induce them not to smoke. In any such bargaining situation, one party may risk the possibility of not arriving at a mutually advantageous agreement, in order to get more out of those bargains that are made.

Problems may arise even in cases where markets are well established. Consider the problem of an oil pool, the land above which is owned by several individuals. Though efficiency can be obtained by unitization, if all but one of the owners of land unitize, it may not pay the last owner to join. He knows that production on the unitized portion will be reduced, thus enabling him to increase his production. He will only join if he receives more than a proportionate share of the revenues. But each small owner may believe he can gain by holding out to be the last to join the unitization agreement (or to sell to a large firm attempting to purchase all the small owners). Thus states have found it necessary to pass legislation requiring unitization.

The second reason for government intervention concerns transaction costs. The costs of getting individuals together to internalize these externalities voluntarily is significant. The provision of those organizational services itself is a public good. Indeed, the government may be looked upon as precisely the voluntary mechanism that individuals have set up to internalize the externalities (or to reduce the welfare losses from the externality in some other way).

The third is that the set of property rights that have been established often give rise to inefficiencies. Many of the existing property rights have been established not through legislation but through what is called the common law. When one individual imposed an externality on another, the injured individual brought suit against the first individual. Sometimes these suits were successful, sometimes they were not. Over the years, a set of implicit property rights and rules has been established that defines in a fairly clear way those situations in which an individual suffering an externality can bring suit with some hope of success, and where he cannot. For instance, if a nonsmoker develops a cough as a result of some smokers smoking in the same compartment of a train in which he sits, he cannot sue the smokers with much hope of success. If an individual throws garbage on his neighbor's lawn, the neighbor has a reasonable chance of success in a suit. If an individual burns leaves on the corner of his lot so that the wind blows smoke into his neighbor's house, causing smoke damage to the house, the neighbor has *some* chance of a successful suit.

The advantages of using the government as a vehicle through which the externalities are dealt with are that it saves on transaction costs (an additional organization to deal with each type of externality does not have to be created) and it avoids the free rider problems typically associated with public goods. Among disadvantages of using the government are those we encountered in Chapters 6 and 7: the political mechanism is a far from perfect means for allocating resources, since it is subject to manipulation by special-interest groups. Further, any regulations and rules devised in the public sector have to be enforced by a bureaucracy with all of the limitations noted earlier.

PUBLIC REMEDIES FOR EXTERNALITIES

There are four broad categories of public-sector remedies for externalities: the government can impose fines; it can subsidize expenditures to reduce negative externalities; it can impose regulations to restrict the negative externalities imposed by one group on another; or it can attempt to define, through the legal system, a set of property rights that discourages negative externalities.

Before comparing the merits of these alternative remedies we should first dispel the common fallacy, which asserts that we should never allow an individual or firm to impose a negative externality on others. For example, it is sometimes asserted that a firm should never be allowed to pollute the air and water. In the view of most economists, such absolutist positions make no sense. There is, indeed, a social cost associated with pollution (or any other negative externality), but the cost is not infinite; it is finite. There is some amount of money that people would be willing to receive in compensation for having to live in a community with dirtier air or dirtier water. Thus we need to weigh the costs and benefits associated with pollution control just as we need to weigh the costs and benefits associated with any other economic activity. The problem with the market is *not* that it results in pollution; there is, indeed, a socially efficient level of pollution. The problem instead is that firms fail to take into account the social costs associated with the externalities they impose—in this case, pollution—and as a result, there is likely to be an excessively high level of pollution. The government's task, then, is not to eliminate pollution entirely: that would be a virtually impossible task. Rather, it is to help the private sector achieve the socially efficient level of pollution, to make individuals and firms act in such a way that they are induced to take into account the effects of their actions on others.

In the ensuing discussion we shall focus our attention on pollution externalities. The arguments, however, extend in a straightforward way to other categories of externalities.

Fines

Most economists favor the use of fines as a way of remedying the inefficiencies associated with negative externalities: a pollution charge should be imposed on those who pollute the air or water.

The basic principle involved in the imposition of fines (charges) for controlling externalities is simple: in general, whenever there is an externality, there is a difference between the social cost and the private cost, and between the social benefit and the private benefit. A properly calculated fine presents the individual or firm with the true social costs and benefits of his actions.

Taxes (which can be thought of as fines) and subsidies designed to ameliorate the effects of externalities, to make marginal private costs equal to marginal social costs, and to make marginal private benefits equal to marginal social benefits are called **corrective taxes.**[3]

Consider the example, discussed earlier, of a steel firm polluting the air. We showed that because the firm was concerned only with its private marginal costs, not the social marginal costs (the two differing by the marginal costs of pollution), output of steel would be excessive. By charging the firm an amount equal to the marginal cost of pollution, the marginal private costs and marginal social costs are equated. In Figure 8.3 we have assumed that the amount of pollution is proportional to the level of output, and the marginal cost of each unit of pollution is fixed; hence by imposing a fixed charge per unit of output, equal to the marginal social cost of pollution, the firm will be induced to produce the socially efficient level of output. In the figure,

[3] A. C. Pigou, a great English economist of the first half of this century, argued persuasively for the use of corrective taxes in his book *The Economics of Welfare* (London: Macmillan, 1918). These taxes are sometimes called Pigovian taxes in his honor.

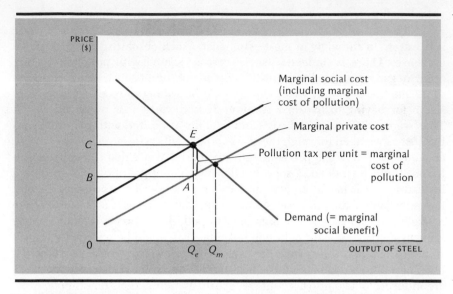

8.3 MARKET EQUILIBRIUM WITH AND WITHOUT FINES In the absence of a tax on pollution, firms will set price equal to marginal private cost. There will be excessive production (Q_m). By setting a tax equal to the marginal pollution cost, efficiency is obtained.

the distance *EA* represents the pollution tax per unit output, and the area *EABC* represents the total pollution taxes paid.

Fines also ensure that the firm spends a socially efficient amount on pollution abatement. Assume that there is a given, known marginal social cost imposed on others by each unit of pollution (measured, say, by the number of particles added to the air per unit of time). It is costly to reduce pollution; at any given level of production, it costs more to reduce pollution more. We assume that the *marginal* cost of pollution control is also rising. This is depicted in Figure 8.4, where we measure along the horizontal axis the *reduction* in pollution (from what it would be if the firm spent nothing on pollution abatement). Efficiency requires that the marginal social benefits associated with further pollution abatement expenditures just equal the marginal social costs, point *P** in the diagram. If the firm is charged a fine, *f**, equal to the marginal social cost of pollution, the private firm will undertake the efficient level of expenditure on pollution abatement. (It also should be clear that firms will undertake the pollution abatement in the least costly—most efficient—manner possible; this may entail not only direct expenditures for pollution control devices but changes in the input mixes and other alterations in the production process.)

Similarly, in those situations where there is a *positive* externality, the government should impose subsidies. There are a few instances where the government does subsidize the consumption of some commodity (often through the tax system) because it believes this will result in a positive externality. For instance, expenditures for the restoration of historical buildings receive extremely favorable tax treatment. This is presumably on the grounds that we all benefit from the preservation of our national heritage. In Figure 8.5 we depict a situation where the price does not correctly reflect the true

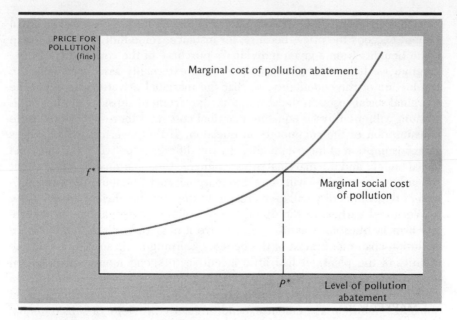

8.4 EFFICIENT CONTROL OF POLLUTION The efficient level of pollution can be attained either by charging firms a fine of f^* per unit of pollution (say, measured by the number of particles added to the air) or by imposing a regulation that firms have a pollution abatement level P^*.

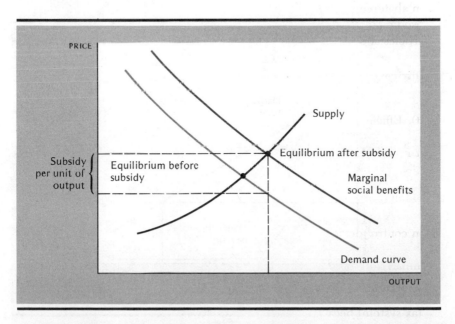

8.5 EQUILIBRIUM WITH AND WITHOUT SUBSIDIES IN THE PRESENCE OF POSITIVE EXTERNALITIES If there are positive externalities associated with consumption of the commodity, there will be too little consumption of it. This can be corrected by imposing a subsidy on its use.

marginal social benefit of an extra unit of the commodity. The marginal social benefit exceeds the price, because, for instance, some individuals may reap some benefits from a given individual's purchase of the commodity. In the diagram we have assumed that there is no externality associated with the production of the commodity, so that the marginal private costs equal the marginal social costs. In the absence of a government subsidy, market equilibrium will entail price equaling marginal cost, and there will be too little consumption of the commodity in question. If the government subsidizes the consumption of the commodity, by the difference between the marginal social benefit and the marginal private benefit, then marginal private benefit (including the subsidy) will equal the marginal social benefit, and consumption of the commodity will be increased to the socially efficient level.

We noted earlier, in the discussion of pollution externalities, that since the firm in question was likely to receive a negligible direct benefit from pollution abatement (most of the benefits accruing to those who live in the vicinity of the plant), it had little incentive to spend money on pollution abatement. There was, from a social point of view, too little expenditure on pollution abatement. Rather than taxing pollution, the government could subsidize pollution abatement expenditures. By providing a subsidy equal to the difference between the marginal social benefit of pollution abatement and the firm's marginal private benefit, the efficient level of pollution abatement expenditures can be attained. This is illustrated in Figure 8.6. (Note that the marginal cost of pollution is directly related to the marginal benefit of pollution abatement.)

This remedy does not, however, attain a socially efficient resource alloca-

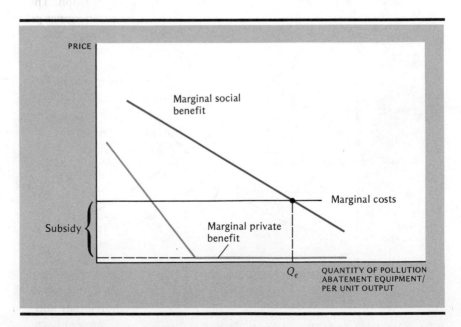

8.6 POLLUTION ABATEMENT SUBSIDIES By subsidizing the purchase of pollution abatement equipment (by the difference between marginal social benefit of pollution abatement and marginal private benefit), an efficient level of expenditure on pollution abatement can be attained.

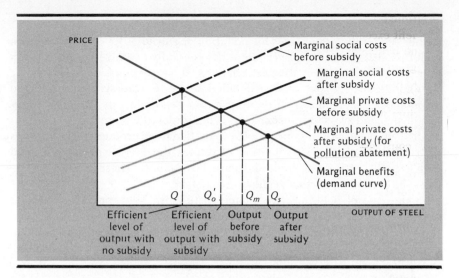

8.7 MARKET EQUILIBRIUM WITH POLLUTION ABATEMENT SUBSIDIES Even after the pollution abatement subsidy, the equilibrium level of output of steel is still inefficient; the firm fails to take into account the extra costs of public subsidies for pollution abatement associated with increased output of steel as well as the marginal social cost of any remaining pollution.

tion. The reason is simple: the total marginal social costs of producing steel include the costs of the government subsidies for pollution abatement. Firms fail to take this into account in deciding on the level of production. Thus, as before, the marginal social cost of production exceeds the marginal private costs. The pollution abatement subsidy reduces the marginal social cost of output, but it also reduces the marginal private costs. There is still an excessive level of production of steel, as illustrated by point Q_s in Figure 8.7.[4]

The reason that polluters prefer subsidies for pollution abatement to fines is clear: profits under the former system are higher than under the latter. The distributional consequences are not limited to the polluting firms and their shareholders. Because output will be smaller under the system of fines, prices will be higher, and consumers of the products of the polluting firm will be worse off. On the other hand, those who have to pay the taxes to finance the subsidies for pollution abatement are clearly better off under the system of fines. It should be emphasized, however, that the choice between subsidies and fines is not just a distribution issue. When both systems are feasible (and ignoring monitoring costs) the system of fines results in a Pareto-efficient resource allocation, while the system of subsidies for pollution abatement does not; that is, in principle, there is a set of taxes that could be imposed on different individuals or firms who benefit from the use of the fine system, the proceeds of which would be distributed as compensatory payments to the polluting firms. This would make all individuals and firms better off than they are under the subsidy-for-pollution-abatement scheme.

[4]If the level of pollution of a firm cannot be directly monitored, a second-best policy may entail a subsidy for expenditures on pollution abatement combined with a tax on output. The tax on output (if set at the appropriate rate) reduces the level of output to the socially efficient level.

Regulation

Rather than using either fines for pollution or subsidies for expenditures on pollution abatement, the government has generally employed regulations in its attempt to restrict negative externalities. It has set emission standards for automobiles. It has put forth a detailed set of regulations relating to the disposal of toxic chemicals. It requires airlines and railroads to set aside certain designated areas for nonsmokers. It has imposed laws requiring oil companies with wells in the same oil pool to unitize their production. It imposes restrictions on fishing and hunting to reduce the inefficiencies associated with excessive utilization of these common resources. These examples illustrate the myriad forms that regulation may take.

In the case of pollution, we should distinguish between two important classes of regulations: those in which the level of pollution is monitored and firms are proscribed from exceeding a certain critical level of pollution and those in which the government regulates the production process. For instance, the government may not allow the use of certain grades of coal; or it may require that the firm employ scrubbers and other pollution abatement devices; or it may require that the firm construct a smokestack of a given height.

When it is feasible to regulate the level of pollution directly, it seems preferable to input regulation. What society is concerned with is the level of pollution, not how the pollution is produced. The firm is likely to know better than the government the best ways of reducing the level of pollution (how to reduce the level of pollution at least cost). Yet the government has relied heavily on input regulations since in some cases it may be easier to monitor inputs than to measure the level of pollution. But this does not provide the full explanation: the choice of regulatory method has also been influenced by political considerations, as we shall see later.

Comparison between Regulations and Fines

The comparison between the use of *regulations* and *fines* corresponds to the comparison between the use of direct controls (a command system) and prices in running the economy. In Chapter 4 we showed how a price system could be used (in the absence of externalities) to implement an efficient resource allocation. Not only is the competitive equilibrium Pareto efficient, but every Pareto-efficient allocation can be sustained through a competitive price mechanism, provided the appropriate transfers are made. Of course, the same resource allocation could have been attained simply by the government imposing it through a set of commands. In situations where there are no monitoring costs, and where all the costs and benefits associated with pollution and pollution control are known, the government can accomplish with regulation anything it can accomplish through fines. Thus if social efficiency requires that no more than so many units of pollutants be added to the air per ton of steel produced, the government can impose this as a regulation rather than setting a level of fines that induces the socially efficient level of pollution.

When input regulations alone are used, the regulator can attain the efficient level of expenditures on pollution abatement. But the efficient level of

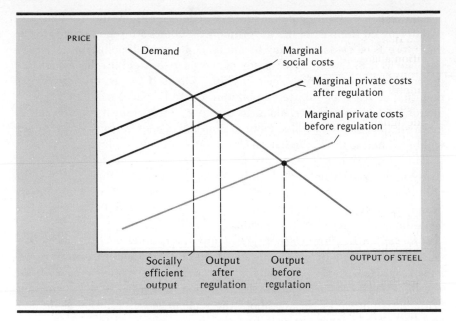

8.8 EFFICIENCY WITH POLLUTION ABATEMENT SUBSIDIES Even with regulations on pollution abatement, there will not be an efficient level of output.

production of the polluting commodity cannot be obtained (except in the extreme case where efficient pollution abatement entails the elimination of all pollution). Thus this system of pollution regulation shares the same deficiency that the system of subsidies for pollution abatement does, but to a lesser extent. In Figure 8.8 we have depicted the regulations as bringing marginal private costs near but still not equal to marginal social costs, so that there is still overproduction of the polluting commodity.

Choice among Fines, Subsidies, and Regulations

So far, our discussion has established that Pareto-efficient resource allocations can be attained by a system of fines but not by regulations or subsidies. On the other hand, the different systems have distinctly different distributive effects. Firms (and their consumers and workers) are more adversely affected by fines than by regulation, and least by subsidies. Though those who gain from the use of a system of fines might, in principle, be able to compensate those who lose, in fact the compensations are seldom made. The potential large differences in the distributive impacts of the different programs are largely responsible for the controversies that have arisen over the appropriate system of pollution control. But there are other issues as well: 1) the alternative methods have different transactions costs associated with implementing them; 2) different information is required for their efficient implementation; 3) they differ in how well they perform in the presence of variability or uncertainty about costs and benefits; and 4) they may differ in the ease with which they can be politically manipulated to serve special-interest groups.

Transaction Costs. Regulation and fine schemes require different kinds of monitoring on the part of the government. Under both schemes it is not in the interests of a steel company to announce how much pollution it is creating. Nor is it in the interests of any of the users of steel (to the extent that the market is competitive), since any fines imposed as a result of excessive pollution or any expenditure on pollution-control devices mandated by regulations are simply passed along to the user. And while it may be in the interests of consumers collectively to monitor, if monitoring is costly none will be willing to do it. We have a classic public-good problem.

The burden of monitoring must fall upon the government. It may be less costly to ascertain whether a firm has exceeded a certain threshold level of pollution than to determine with any precision the exact level of pollution. Simple regulatory schemes require only the first kind of information, while a system of fines requires the second.

Information Requirements. Equally important, different externality control systems require different information for their implementation. It is perhaps reasonable to assume that the government has a fair estimate of the marginal social costs associated with pollution. But it is likely that the government is not well informed about the technology of pollution abatement and control, at least not as well informed as are private firms. This is particularly true in those cases where the pollution control devices have not yet been developed. Neither side has very good information: both are simply making guesses, but since producers know more about the technology of their industries than does the government, their guesses are more likely to be accurate. The private producers have no incentive to reveal their information to the government; rather, they have every reason to try to persuade the government that the technology for pollution abatement will be extremely hard to develop, so that it will be impossible to satisfy stringent regulations. If the government does impose stringent regulations but allows firms several years to develop the requisite technology, they may not have an incentive to comply: they may believe that, if and when the deadline arrives, the new technology has not been developed, it is unlikely that the government will shut down the industry.

The information required to achieve an efficient level of pollution via regulation is even greater than the discussion until now has suggested. If firms have different costs associated with pollution abatement, the efficient level of pollution abatement will differ from firm to firm. To set efficient levels of pollution control, then, the government must know the cost functions of *each* firm in the economy. Since government's knowledge of firms' costs functions is heavily dependent on information provided by the firm, it is clear that firms have an incentive to "fudge" the data.

Note, moreover, that if in the regulatory scheme the government errs in its judgment concerning the costs of pollution control, it will result in an inefficient level of pollution. If the government underestimates the costs of pollution control and sets stringent regulations, firms may spend a considerable amount of resources to comply with the regulations. At the margin, the cost of compliance exceeds the marginal social benefit. In a competitive economy, these costs are passed along to the users of the product.

The system of imposing fines does not suffer from the same informational requirements. The government ascertains what the marginal social costs associated with pollution are. Then the firms decide whether the costs of the pollution control devices exceed the benefits of the pollution control as measured by the penalties imposed for failing to control pollution. There is no longer any gaming between the industry and the government. Of course, if the government incorrectly estimates the marginal social costs of pollution, then inefficiencies will arise, under either a system of fines or a regulatory system.

Nonlinear Fine Schedules

There are many circumstances in which the government may not be able to ascertain accurately the marginal social costs of pollution (or of some other externality). The cost may be an increasing function of the level of pollution. For the government to know the appropriate fine, it must know the equilibrium level of pollution, and this it will not be able to ascertain without detailed knowledge of the technology of the firms. Moreover, the marginal social costs curve may shift from time to time, and more frequently than it is feasible to revise the fine schedule.

In these circumstances, it may be desirable for the government to impose a *nonlinear fine schedule*, or to impose regulations. A nonlinear price system entails having a fine that depends on the level of pollution. The simplest such system is depicted in Figure 8.9. There, the fine for levels of pollution up to some critical level P^* is low, but for pollution levels in excess of that critical level the fine per unit of pollution is high. Ideally, one might like to confront the firm with the entire marginal social cost of pollution schedule,

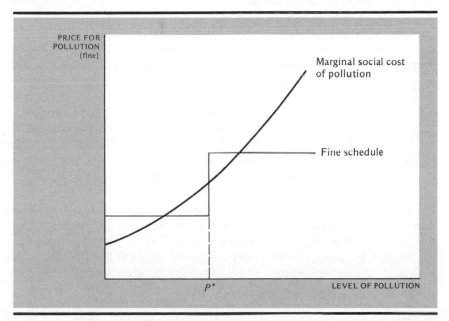

8.9 REGULATIONS AND NONLINEAR FINES A regulatory scheme can be viewed as a limiting case of a fine scheme, where the fine for levels of pollution in excess of P^* is so large that no firm will pollute in excess of P^*.

as depicted in Figure 8.9. Then, at each level of pollution, the firm would face the true marginal social cost. The two-level fine schedule depicted in the figure may be thought of as an approximation of the marginal social cost function. If it should turn out that the pollution control technology results in a very low level of pollution, then the approximating schedule will have resulted in an excessive expenditure on pollution control; if it should turn out that the pollution control technology results in a very high level of pollution (because pollution control is very expensive), then the approximating schedule results in too little expenditure on pollution control.

One possible schedule entails a zero fine up to some critical level, and then an infinite fine beyond that, making levels of pollution greater than P^* impossible. This is essentially a regulation against pollution above the level of P^*. Thus the distinction between fines and regulations is not a clear one. A regulation can be viewed as equivalent to a limiting case of a nonlinear fine system.

Variability in Marginal Costs and Benefits of Pollution Control

The costs of pollution control (and the benefits) may vary from place to place from time to time and from firm to firm. The *marginal* social benefit of pollution control may be quite different in Los Angeles (which is faced with a severe smog problem) from what it is in Montana. The cost of pollution control may be markedly different for one kind of coal than for another. In principle, either a set of regulations or a set of fines should recognize these differences. There should thus be a different set of regulations for each different set of circumstances, or a different level of fines for each community, firm, and date. The informational requirements to implement such a detailed scheme are clearly enormous. In practice, this has resulted in broad sets of regulations that are not adapted well to varying conditions. In localities where there is a belief that the marginal social cost locally is greater, these general regulations are supplemented by local regulations. Thus California has far more stringent regulations on automobile pollution than does the rest of the country, because of the tendency for particulate matter to combine with moist air off the Pacific Ocean to produce smog.

The nature of the variability in costs and benefits plays an important role in the choice between regulatory schemes and fines. If costs of pollution control vary but benefits are certain, fines are preferable to regulations. Firms that are subject to fines will adjust the level of pollution control to the efficient level; regulations will not allow this adjustment. If benefits vary but costs don't, the two systems are equivalent. The fine system will result in a fixed level of pollution, sometimes too high, sometimes too low, just as with a regulatory system. The consequences of a fine are no different from those of a regulatory system in which the government fixed the level of permissible pollution. When both costs and benefits vary, matters are more difficult. There are circumstances in which regulations may be preferable to fines.

Politics and the Choice of the Form of Externality Remedy

Since the costs of the regulations to the firms are not insignificant, the extent of the regulations is a politically charged subject. The form of the regulations that emerge is affected not only by the economic costs (as estimated by a dispassionate observer) but by the power of the various interest groups affected by the regulations. A politically powerful interest group may be able to stave off a set of regulations that would have been imposed had the group been weaker.

More interestingly, a group that is without the political power to stave off some regulations may be strong enough to extend the regulations to rivals, for whom it is not appropriate. This happened in the coal industry. Eastern and midwestern coal is dirty (high sulfur), while western coal is clean. Thus, specifying a maximum level of admissible pollution, or requiring scrubbers only on dirty coal, would give western coal an advantage over eastern coal—as well it should, given that there was an additional social cost of using eastern coal. But when the Clean Air Act Amendment of 1977 was passed, the eastern coal producers teamed up with the environmentalists to lobby for the scrubbers for western coal as well.

There is a widespread feeling among economists that regulatory systems are more susceptible to such political manipulation than are systems of fines.

Problems With Compensation

But while the fine system is Pareto efficient, not all individuals are better off in the fine system than under the two alternative regimes. In principle, however, those who are better off could more than compensate those who are worse off. The difficulty is that this compensation is seldom paid; in many cases it is difficult to identify individually those who should be compensated.

Similar problems arise more generally in determining the appropriate compensation for externalities. Consider, for instance, a steel mill that pollutes the neighboring air. Those who live nearby are clearly worse off as a result of the pollution. But if the steel mill existed before they purchased their houses, the price they paid for their house would have reflected the fact that the air was polluted; they paid less for their house than they otherwise would have. The person who suffered was the owner of the house at the time that the steel mill was constructed (or at the time it was announced that the steel mill would be constructed). In most cases, it would be impossible to find that individual (years may have passed since the steel mill was constructed.) In many cases, the house was not constructed until after the mill was. Then, the person who might have been hurt was the owner of the land; but in most cases, he is likely to have been better off since the building of the mill: the gain in value to his land from its proximity to the mill exceeded the loss from the pollution. When the value of an asset (like land) increases or decreases to reflect the surrounding amenities (the cleanliness of the air), we say that the value of these amenities is **capitalized.**

It is not only consumers of the products of the polluting industry, owners of capital in the polluting industry, and breathers of air near the polluting firm who are affected by the system of pollution control. Workers may be affected as well. Imposing a system of fines may result in some plants closing down. Workers at those plants may become unemployed. They bear the costs of finding other jobs. If costs of finding another job and of moving were negligible, these individuals may not be very adversely affected; but in many instances, these costs are significant, and unemployment compensation only partially reduces the burden imposed upon them. Thus in principle, if a system of fines were to be adopted, these individuals should be compensated.

Because of the difficulties in implementing compensation, compensation is seldom made. Thus the choice of the system by which the effects of externalities are remedied has a direct bearing on the welfare of different individuals; the firms whose profits will be reduced by fines or regulations will oppose them; to them, the fact that fines are Pareto efficient is of little concern. They contend that since imposing a fine lowers the return to previously invested capital, it is "unfair" to those who have invested their capital in the polluting industry to make them bear the full burden of the change in society's attitudes toward pollution.

Legal Remedies for Externalities

There is one great advantage of employing the legal system to deal with externalities. Rather than relying on the government to ensure that externalities do not occur, the injured party, who has a direct, vested interest, bears the responsibility for enforcement. This is obviously informationally more efficient, since presumably the injured party is more likely than the government to know that an injury has occurred.

For this to be effective, however, a well-defined and consistent set of property rights has to be established. Thus the legal system could not be used to deal with the externalities that we noted were associated with common resources; by definition, no one had the right to exclude others from the use of these resources, and it was this that gave rise to the externalities. The process by which property rights have been established through the judicial system on a case-by-case basis has not resulted in the establishment of a consistent and well-defined set of property rights that can deal with the whole array of externalities that arise in modern society. It has, however, two important advantages over the alternative approach to defining property rights, through legislation. It is not as sensitive to interest-group pressures, and the full complexity of the range of externalities that occur in practice often is best brought out through a judicial process.

The judicial process for dealing with externalities has five limitations. First, there are large transaction costs associated with any litigation. Of course, it is not clear whether these are large in comparison to the administrative costs of enforcing a regulatory or fine system. For many externalities, the losses involved may simply be too small to be worth dealing with under any system; since those costs are borne publicly in regulatory or fine schemes, but privately with judicial enforcement, the decision on whether to attempt to eliminate the externality is made efficiently under the judicial enforcement scheme but inefficiently under the other schemes.

Second, since those generating externalities know that litigation is expensive, they may be inclined to generate their externality just up to the point where it pays the injured party to sue—which obviously gives rise to considerable inefficiencies. One way of dealing with this is to impose multiple damages similar to the system of triple damages in antitrust cases; there, when a firm has been shown to have behaved in a noncompetitive way and to have caused, as a result, a loss of profits to his rival, the firm must pay the injured party three times the amount of losses that are deemed to have been sustained. Applied to pollution, this plan would make sure that firms will not induce externalities the losses from which are greater than one-third the cost of litigation.

Thirdly, frequently there is some uncertainty about the extent of the injury, and there is also often some ambiguity about the outcome of most suits. If litigation costs are large, the uncertainty acts as a further deterrent to individuals using the court system to deal with externalities.

Fourthly, the high litigation costs and uncertain outcome of the litigation process imply that there is, in effect, differential access to legal remedies, which conflicts with our usual notion of justice.

Finally, in many cases there is a large number of injured parties; no single individual sustains a sufficiently large loss of welfare to make it worth his while to sue, but the injured parties as a class suffer sufficiently large losses that it would more than compensate them for suing. Once again, there is a free rider problem. It pays any one individual to let the others file suit; and if they are successful, he can file suit on his own using the previous findings as precedents. This will greatly reduce his litigation costs (indeed, usually there will be an out-of-court settlement).

The legal system has attempted to deal with this important free rider problem by establishing a category of suits called **class-action suits.** A lawyer files a suit on behalf of the entire class of injured individuals. If he is successful he collects his fee from all of those within the class, all those who have benefited from the judicial decision. There is not universal agreement about how well this system works; in particular, none of the injured individuals is usually in a position to monitor the legal expenses, and these expenses often seem to be unduly large (or at least so the injured parties claim; the lawyers claim that the high level of legal expenses arises from the particular nature of the cases).

In short, the legal system does provide a framework that can deal with certain categories of externalities. It provides an important remedy for some of those externalities not adequately dealt with through one of the alternative means discussed in this chapter; but the limitations of the judicial process are sufficiently important that it cannot be relied upon to deal with a number of the more important externalities.

SUMMARY

1. Externalities are actions of an individual or firm that have an effect on another individual or firm for which the latter does not pay or is not paid.

2. Sometimes, economic efficiency can be attained without resorting to government intervention by establishing sufficiently large economic organizations that the externalities can be internalized. Alternatively, they may be resolved through cooperative action by individuals.

3. There are some strong incentives for private markets to eliminate any inefficiencies arising from externalities. The assertion that they do is called the Coase Theorem.

4. There are several important limitations on these private solutions to externality problems. We have emphasized two in particular: public-goods problems and transaction costs.

5. There are four methods by which the government has attempted to induce individuals and firms to act in a socially efficient manner: fines, subsidies, regulation, and the judicial system.

KEY CONCEPTS

Positive externalities

Negative externalities

Common resources

Pecuniary externalities

Technological externalities

Internalizing externalities

Unitization of oil fields

Property rights

Coase theorem

Corrective taxes

Capitalization

Class-action suits

QUESTIONS AND PROBLEMS

1. Make a list of the positive and negative externalities that you generate or that affect you. For each, discuss the advantages and disadvantages of each of the remedies discussed in the text.

2. An important class of externalities to which attention has recently been directed are called *information externalities*. The information produced by one individual or firm generates benefits for others. The success of an oil well on one tract of land increases the likelihood of oil being found on an adjacent tract, and hence increases the value of that tract. Can you think of other examples of information externalities? What are the likely consequences, in terms of the efficiency of resource allocations? Discuss the possibilities of private market solutions to these problems.

3. Explain why subsidies for pollution abatement equipment, even if they result in an efficient level of pollution abatement, will not result in an efficient resource allocation. Under what circumstances can regulations lead to an efficient resource allocation?

4. Assume there are two types of communities in the United States, those in which there is a high benefit of pollution control and a high cost of pollution control; and those in which there is a low benefit of pollution control and a low cost of pollution control. Assume that the government must set either uniform regulations (a uniform level of pollution control) or a uniform fine for pollution. Show diagrammatically that a regulatory scheme may be preferable to a system of fines. How does your answer change if communities in which there is a high marginal cost of pollution control happen to be communities in which there is a low marginal benefit; and communities with a low marginal cost of pollution control happen to be communities in which there is a high marginal benefit?

5. Zoning laws, which restrict how individuals can use their land, are sometimes justified as a means of controlling externalities. Explain. Discuss alternative solutions to these problems of externalities.

6. What is the externality associated with an additional individual driving on a congested road? How do tolls help alleviate this externality? How should the toll be set?

PART THREE

EXPENDITURE PROGRAMS

In this part, we show how the theoretical models we developed in previous chapters can be used to analyze a variety of public expenditure programs: national defense, health care, education, welfare, and social insurance. These particular programs were chosen for two reasons. They are among the most important programs: in terms of dollars spent they account for more than two-thirds of federal expenditures as well as of total public expenditures in the United States. And the examination of these particular programs brings out most of the critical issues in expenditure analysis; other programs can be analyzed using the basic framework and tools of analysis that we develop here. The first two chapters are devoted to explaining our basic approach to the analysis of public expenditures: Chapter 9 develops a general framework, while Chapter 10 shows how the benefits and costs of different government programs may be quantified. Chapters 11–14 then apply this framework.

9

The Analysis of Expenditure Policy

The framework for the analysis of public expenditure we will set up in this chapter is intended to provide guidelines. It is not a simple formula that can be applied blindly to all problems but rather a list of considerations that should be raised. Some of these may be more relevant to certain government programs than to others. The kinds of questions we are ultimately interested in addressing are:

Why is there a government program in the first place?

Why does the government program take on the particular form that it takes?

How does the government program affect the private sector?

Who gains and who loses as a result of the government program? Are the gains greater than the losses?

Are there alternative programs which are superior to current government programs (that is, in which all individuals can be made better off)? Are there alternative programs that have different distributional consequences but that at the same time achieve the primary objectives of the program? What are the impediments to the introduction of these alternative programs?

We begin by breaking down the analysis of public expenditures into eight steps.

1. NEED FOR PROGRAM

It is often useful to begin the analysis of a public program by investigating the history of the program and the circumstances under which it arose. Who were the individuals or groups who pressed for its passage, and what were the perceived needs to which it was supposedly addressed?

For instance, when the bill establishing the social security program was passed in 1935, the United States was in the midst of the Great Depression. Up to that time few employers provided adequate pensions for their employees, and the private market for annuities (insurance policies that provide individuals with a given income from retirement until death, regardless of how long they live) was underdeveloped; many individuals had failed to save adequately for their retirement, and many of those had found their savings wiped out by the stock market crash in 1929. The failure to have adequate savings was not as irrational and improvident as it appears to us today; in those days, many individuals continued to work until they died. They needed life insurance to look after their family after their demise but not pensions for themselves. But in the Great Depression, many of these individuals lost their jobs and had no unemployment insurance. It was widely felt that society had to make some provision for them and that it was preferable to do so on a systematic basis rather than just to solve the immediate problems of the time.

2. MARKET FAILURES

The second step in the analysis of public programs is to attempt to relate the need, the source of demand, to one or more of the market failures discussed in Chapter 4: imperfect competition; public goods; externalities; incomplete markets; and imperfect information. In addition, we saw in Chapter 4 that even if the economy is Pareto efficient, there are two further arguments for government intervention: first, there is no reason to suppose that the distribution of income that emerged from the market economy would be viewed as socially equitable; and second, some individuals believe that evaluating each individual's welfare by his own perceptions provides an inappropriate or inadequate criterion for making welfare judgments. There are merit goods, which the government should encourage, and merit bads, which the government should discourage, or prohibit.

In some cases, the nature of the market failure is obvious: national defense is a pure public good, and as we argued earlier, in the absence of public provision, such goods will always be in undersupply. In other cases the answers are not so obvious, and there may not be agreement among economists about the nature of the market failure. While some economists believe that education is a public good, others argue that it is essentially a private good. To find an explanation for its public provision one must look elsewhere: at the distributive consequences of public provision or at education as a merit good, essential for the functioning of a democratic society.

The fact that there is a demand for the public provision of some good or service does not in itself imply that there has been a market failure. Currently, there is widespread concern about the rising cost of medical services. This has led some groups to demand that the government take a more active role in providing health care. There are a number of explanations for the rise in health care costs, one being that health care is a service industry. In most recent years there has been a sharp increase in the price of all services relative to manufacturing goods. Some economists argue that although there have been market failures, there is no reason to presume that government intervention would improve things. Others believe that government programs (including medicare) have made things worse, both by increasing the demand for limited medical resources and by reducing the pressure for cost controls because the government pays most of the cost. Similarly, while some economists view as evidence of market failure the fact that individuals cannot obtain complete insurance coverage for their health risks, others believe that the reason the market does not provide complete coverage is that with it, individuals have no incentive to economize on health expenditures. Thus the government has found that it too has been forced to insist that individuals pay some portion of their health care expenditures.

In short, some of the demands for public provision arise from an inadequate understanding of the market and of the possibilities that the government has for making things better. Identifying whether there is or is not a market failure is an essential step in identifying the appropriate scope for government action.

3. ALTERNATIVE FORMS OF GOVERNMENT INTERVENTION

Once a market failure has been identified, a variety of government actions might address the problem. The three major categories of action are public production; private production, with taxes and subsidies aimed at encouraging those activities the government wishes to encourage and discouraging those activities it wishes to discourage; and private production with government regulation, aimed at ensuring that firms act in the desired way.

The consequences of any government program are critically dependent on the exact nature of the program. Thus if the government decides to bear responsibility for production, it still must decide on how the output is to be allocated. It can charge for the good at market prices; it can charge for the good at something approximating the cost of production, as it typically does for electricity; it can charge for the good, but the charges can be much less than the cost of production, as it typically does for higher education; it can provide the good freely and uniformly, as it does for elementary school and secondary school education. In countries like Britain, where medicine is provided freely, it is obviously not provided equally to all individuals. Needs differ. The decision as to who gets how much of the available supply of medical services is left to doctors (operating within guidelines set up by the government, in consultation with them).

Similarly, if the good is to be privately produced, the government must decide whether to: a) contract directly for the commodity but retain responsibility for distributing the goods; b) provide a subsidy to producers, with the hope that some of the benefits will be passed on to consumers through lower prices; or c) provide a subsidy to consumers. And if some form of subsidy is desired, it must be decided whether it should be provided through the tax system or through a direct grant. If a subsidy is granted, the terms have to be decided upon—e.g., how restrictive eligibility standards should be. All of these possible forms of government action are observed.

Higher Education: An Example

Consider higher education. It is publicly produced: every state has its own system of universities, colleges, and junior colleges. Though direct aid to private universities is limited in the United States, in other countries (such as Canada) it is common, and granted on the basis of the number of students enrolled. In the United States the federal government provides considerable aid to research universities through a variety of programs of support for basic and applied research. Most federal support to higher education, however, takes the form of support to the consumers: the students. Though there have been no general programs of support, there have been two major selective programs. First, since World War II a large number of veterans have attended colleges and universities at government expense; the enticement of this support has been credited as a major attraction for enlistment in the armed forces. Second, federal loans and federally guaranteed loans have been available, particularly to lower- and middle-income individuals, often at subsidized rates.

In recent years there has been extensive discussion of two new programs. The first is to allow individuals, in computing their income taxes, to deduct their educational expenses from their income, or to get a tax credit against their educational expenses. The second is educational vouchers: all individuals would be given a certificate entitling them to, say, $4,000 of education at an approved institution, either public or private. We will discuss education in detail in Chapter 15. At this stage of analysis, the importance of identifying alternative programs cannot be overestimated. Frequently, new programs can be devised that attain the objectives of older programs at less cost and more effectively. "Social innovation" is no less important than technological innovation.

The Importance of Particular Design Features

The detailed provisions of a program, for instance the precise statements concerning eligibility standards, are often crucial in determining the success of the program, its distributional impact, and its efficiency consequences. If the eligibility standards for some government subsidy program, for instance, are defined too broadly, a disproportionate share of the funds may go to those who are not in need. In addition, distortions arise as individuals alter their behavior in an attempt to satisfy the eligibility standards.

Fairness and efficiency require making a number of distinctions which, though clear in principle, are difficult to administer in practice. The distinction between those who are hungry and those who are not may be an important one, but to devise a program to provide food for the hungry requires some easy way of identifying who the hungry are. Too narrow a definition will result in many of those who are needy not receiving aid. Again, a broad set of eligibility standards will result in many individuals who are not needy receiving aid, much to the objections of other taxpayers who are having to contribute to the support of these individuals.

4. EFFICIENCY CONSEQUENCES

Having identified a number of alternative programs, the next step in the analysis is to evaluate them. This entails identifying the efficiency and distributional consequences of the program and assessing the extent to which alternative programs can meet alternative objectives of public policy.

Government programs may result in inefficiencies both in the production of a good or service and in levels of consumption. In Chapter 7 we suggested that whether the government decides to produce a good or service itself, decides to purchase the good or service from private firms but distribute it itself, or decides to have private firms produce it subject to government regulation may have an important effect on the costs associated with producing and delivering the given good or service.

We also suggested that when consumers had an element of choice, the competition among providers was likely both to increase the efficiency with which the goods or services were provided and to make what was produced more responsive to the needs and desires of consumers. These arguments are less persuasive if consumers have limited information concerning the product they are purchasing (such as medical care) or if consumer concern about costs is reduced because the government pays whatever the individual spends, up to some limit.

Private-Sector Responses to Government Programs

One of the central features of a mixed market economy like that of the United States is that the government has only a limited degree of control over it. The private sector may, for instance, react to any government program in such a way as to undo many of its alleged benefits.

The government has long been concerned with the magnitude of fluctuations in the prices of agricultural products. When output is very low, prices rise enormously; and when output is very high, prices fall. Farmers know this, and this provides them with an incentive to put into storage crops whose storage costs are low (like wheat and rice) when the price is low and to sell out of storage when the price is high. This reduces the magnitude of the price fluctuations. It also serves a very useful social function: transferring resources from periods in which they are less valuable (when the price is low) to periods in which they are more valuable (when the price is high). But since storage is not costless, the price fluctuations are not eliminated. The government has been concerned about the magnitude of these price fluctuations. It has attempted to stabilize the prices farmers receive for their crops further by guaranteeing to farmers a minimum price. These programs reduce the incentive for the private sector to store commodities on its own and result in the government having to pay for the storage of enormous amounts of such commodities as butter, cheese, milk, and wheat.

There are further repercussions of the government program: the reduction in risk makes it more attractive to grow crops whose prices are stabilized; the increased output depresses the prices, and to maintain them at their previous average levels necessitates further expenditures by the government and programs to restrict production (paying farmers not to produce). Our example illustrates the importance of considering not only the immediate consequences of a government program but the long-run consequences, after all producers and consumers have adjusted their behavior.

Income and Substitution Effects and Induced Inefficiency

For many programs, it is useful to distinguish between *substitution* effects and *income* effects. Whenever the government program lowers the price of some commodity we say that there is a substitution effect. The individual substitutes the cheaper good for other goods. Tuition subsidies for higher education have a substitution effect: individuals substitute education for other goods they might have spent their money on. On the other hand, grants to individuals that make them better off but do not alter the prices at which they can purchase different commodities have an income effect; the individual changes his expenditure pattern as a result. In many cases, there is both an income effect and a substitution effect, and both alter the individual's behavior. Normally, however, it is only the substitution effect that we associate with an *inefficiency*.

To see this, assume that the government gave an individual food stamps to buy $10 worth of groceries every week. Prior to this, the individual's budget constraint appeared as in Figure 9.1. By giving up $1 of groceries the individual could acquire $1 more of other goods. His budget constraint has shifted up. If the individual now wants to consume more than $10 worth of groceries, he still must give up $1 of other goods for each extra dollar of groceries consumed. There is no substitution effect. There is, however, an income effect. But the effect on food consumption is the same as giving the individual an equivalent amount of income (except in the case where total food consumption prior to the food stamp program was less than $10).

The food stamp program has altered his behavior; he consumes more food than he previously did. But the increase in his consumption of food is less

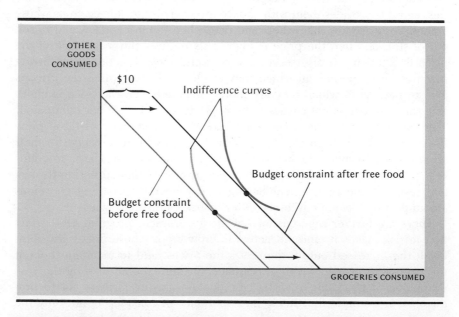

9.1 INCOME EFFECT Giving free food has an income effect but no substitution effect: its effects are identical to giving an individual extra income.

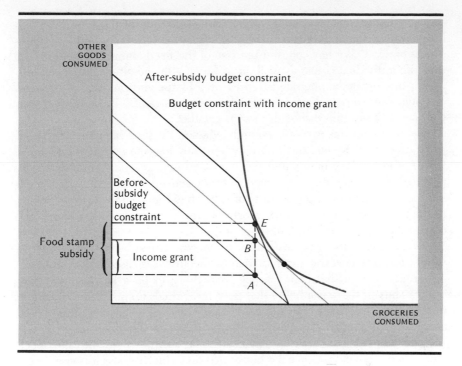

OTHER
GOODS
CONSUMED

After-subsidy budget constraint

Budget constraint with income grant

Before-
subsidy
budget
constraint

Food stamp
subsidy

Income grant

E

B

A

GROCERIES
CONSUMED

9.2 SUBSTITUTION EFFECT When the magnitude of the subsidy depends on the amount of food consumed, there is a substitution effect, and a resulting inefficiency. The poor individual could have been made just as well off with an income grant (or an equivalent food grant) of *AF. BF* measures the cost of the inefficiency.

than $10. And because there is no substitution effect, there is no inefficiency associated with this food stamp program.[1]

Assume, in contrast, that the government had said that it would pay for 10 percent of the first $100 of food purchased; that is, the maximum payment that the government would make to any individual is still $10. This lowers the cost of food for expenditures up to $100. The new budget constraint appears as in Figure 9.2. Now, provided consumption of food per week is less than $100, there is a substitution effect.

The reason we say that this program results in an inefficiency is that we can design an alternative program that leaves the individual just as well off but costs less. This can be seen in Figure 9.2. The true cost of the food—the amount of other goods that society must somehow give up—remains unchanged: for each additional dollar of food consumed, society must give up $1 worth of other goods. The magnitude of the subsidy is thus depicted as the difference between what the individual has to pay and what society has to forego; it is, in other words, the vertical distance between the before-subsidy budget constraint and the after-subsidy budget constraint at the equilibrium level of consumption of groceries. In Figure 9.2 we have also

---

[1]The food stamps simply increase his effective income by $10. Thus the extent to which he increases his consumption of food depends simply on his income elasticity of goods, which specifies the percentage increase in his consumption of food as a result of a 1 percent increase in his income, at a fixed set of prices.

drawn a budget constraint for a food stamp program of the type first analyzed, where the individual simply gets a grant of a fixed amount for expenditure on food. We have chosen the size of the fixed amount to be given so
that the individual is just as well off as he is with the alternative program.
Again, the cost of the program is represented by the vertical distance between
the before-subsidy and after-subsidy budget constraints. But note that now
the size of the required subsidy *(AB)* is smaller.

The reason for this is simple enough: when individuals have to pay the full
price of food at the margin (that is, when they have to pay $1 for $1 more
worth of groceries), they value the increased consumption of groceries by
precisely what they have to forego in other consumption goods. But when
individuals are given a 10 percent subsidy, they then purchase groceries up
to the point where they value $1 worth of groceries at 90 cents, which is the
cost to them of the $1 worth of groceries.

It is important to distinguish between income and substitution effects. In
some cases, the government may wish to encourage or discourage some economic activity; in that case, it may wish there to be a large substitution
effect. Thus, if there is a belief that poor individuals do not attach sufficient
importance to housing, and the government wishes to improve the quality
of housing they purchase, then a program in which the government pays a
fraction of housing expenditures (which has, as a result, a substitution effect)
will be more effective than a flat housing grant, which (unless it is very large)
has only an income effect.

On the other hand, if the government is primarily concerned with how
well off different individuals are, then programs that do not alter *marginal
incentives* are preferable; it does not cause the kinds of inefficiencies we
noted were associated with the substitution effect.

5. DISTRIBUTIONAL CONSEQUENCES

Different individuals are likely to receive different benefits from any particular government program. But it is not always easy to ascertain who really
benefits from a given program. We emphasized in our discussion of the efficiency consequences of public programs the importance of identifying the
private-market responses to the government program. These responses are
equally important in identifying the distributional consequences.

Consider, for instance, the medicare program, government support of
medical care for the aged. The aged clearly benefit greatly from the program;
but to some extent, the federal aid substitutes for money that the elderly's
families would have contributed, and to that extent, the true beneficiaries of
the program are not the elderly but their children.

Similarly, there has been considerable concern that, at least in the short
run, federal subsidies for private housing for the poor simply increase the
price of housing; the true beneficiaries are the slum landlords, not the poor.

Who benefits from a new subway system? At first glance, one is inclined
to give the obvious answer: subway riders. But this may be incorrect. Those
who own houses or apartments near the subway will find that their houses
and apartments are more sought after; the increased demand for these houses

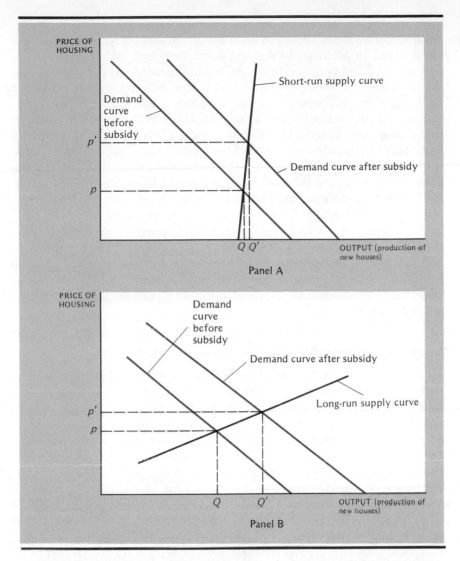

9.3 SHORT-RUN AND LONG-RUN INCIDENCE OF EXPENDITURE PROGRAM
(A) In the short run, a subsidy may increase price more than quantity. Thus landlords may benefit from a housing subsidy given to help the poor acquire better housing. (B) In the long run, the ouput response will be large and the price response smaller.

and apartments will be reflected in the rents that the owners can charge (and hence in the market value of the houses and apartments). The poor commuter finds that he is better off, because of the better subway service, but worse off because of the higher rents, and the two effects are likely to cancel. The true beneficiaries are the property owners near the subway lines.

These examples illustrate once again the importance of taking into account the full effects of the government program, including its effects on market prices. We can illustrate the effect of a government subsidy in Figure 9.3. There we have drawn the demand and supply curves for housing. In the short run (Panel A), the supply of housing is assumed to be very inelastic: it takes some time before new housing can be constructed. Assume the government passed a general subsidy for housing, the effect of which is to increase the demand for housing (the demand curve shifts up). Note that in the figure, almost the entire subsidy is reflected in the increased price of housing; there is very little increase in the actual level of housing services provided. In the long run, of course, the supply response is likely to be larger; hence in Figure 9.3B we have drawn a fairly flat long-run supply curve, showing that a small percentage increase in the price, given enough time, elicits a fairly large increase in the supply of housing. In the short run, the beneficiaries of housing are the current owners of houses; renters find that virtually their entire subsidy is reflected in higher rents (the shift from p to p'). In the long run, however, renters are better off as the quantity of housing supplied (the shift from Q to Q') outweighs the price increase.

When those who benefit from a government program are different from those that the program was intended to help, we say that the benefits have been *shifted*, or that the *actual incidence* (who the benefits actually fall to) is different from the intended beneficiaries. Considerable research in recent years has been devoted to determining the actual incidence of government programs.

Evaluating the Distributional Consequences

As we have noted, different individuals receive different benefits from any particular government program. Although it is obviously not possible to identify how much *each* individual benefits, it may be important to know how individual groups in society are differentially affected. Which groups we focus on may vary from program to program, and benefits may vary within a particular income group. Thus, a program of rebates for heating-oil expenditures for those whose income falls below a particular level obviously benefits the poor more than the rich, but it benefits some poor (those who consume a lot of heating oil, those who live in the Northeast) more than others (those who live in the Sunbelt). If the variability of consumption of heating oil among the poor is very large, this may be viewed as an unfair way of helping the poor, unless those who consume a lot of heating oil are viewed to be particularly deserving of assistance.

In other cases, we may attempt to identify how producers are affected differentially. This is typically the focus of analysis in the evaluation of programs aimed at aiding particular industries, such as government loans to a large defense contractor or agricultural price supports. In still other cases, such as the social security program, we may be concerned with the differential impact on the present elderly versus the impact on the young—the elderly of the future. We refer to these as the *intertemporal distribution effects*—distribution effects over time—of the program. In still other cases, we may wish to identify the regional impact or the impact on cities versus suburbs, or urban versus rural areas.

When the benefits of a program accrue disproportionately to the poor (they receive more than their contribution to the costs of the program through the tax system), we say that the distribution effect of a program is *progres-*

sive. If the benefits accrue disproportionately to the rich we say that it is *regressive.*

There are often controversies about who are the real beneficiaries of a program, and the perspective one obtains on its distributive impact is determined in large part by the group one is focusing on. For instance, government support for higher education is often viewed as enabling the children of the poor to go to college, and thus is viewed to have a positive redistributive impact. But, on closer examination, children of the middle- and upper-middle-classes are more likely to avail themselves of a higher education and whatever government support for it they can obtain. Thus the net benefits accrue disproportionately to the children of middle- and upper-middle-class individuals, and in this perspective, state support appears to be *regressive.* Moreover, it is not clear that parents' income provides the appropriate focus of attention; the beneficiaries of education are not the parents but the children; it is the children who will receive higher wages as a result of the increased level of education.

Let us contrast the distributional consequences of direct state-supported universities (allowing them to charge a low tuition) with those of a loan program. Those who avail themselves of higher education will, on average, have a much higher income than those who do not. Such a system of financing education may thus be more progressive than the current system, where even low-wage high-school dropouts are called upon to provide some support for higher education.

This example makes clear that one's view of the distributional impact of a government program depends not only on what groups one focuses upon but also on the available alternatives to a given program. The relevant choice is seldom this program versus no program but one type of program versus another. Thus, the present state system of aid to higher education *may* be progressive, relative to a totally private education system; but its distributional impact may look less favorable when contrasted with a system of loans for higher education.

Fairness and Distribution

Political discussions commonly focus on the equity aspects of various proposals, with each side claiming that its proposals are more fair. Notions of fairness are, unfortunately, not well defined; different individuals may have conflicting views of what is fair. The middle-class family that loves children but has decided for financial reasons to limit the number of children that they have to two may feel that it is unfair for them to have to support someone else's child simply because that other person has refused to use modern birth control methods. The family that has saved $40,000 to put a child through college may feel that it is unfair that they should not be entitled to receive a government grant or loan, when their next-door neighbors, with the same income (who have put nothing aside for their children's education) enjoy expensive vacations every winter and are entitled to a government grant.

The unmarried person and the family with both spouses working may both think it unfair that their expected returns from social security are so much lower than those of an individual whose spouse does not have a job outside the home. But an individual whose spouse does not work outside the home may feel that it is fair that he receive more, since his family has not had the benefit of a second income.

6. EQUITY-EFFICIENCY TRADE-OFFS

Because of the ambiguities associated with using the term *fair,* we try to avoid it; rather, we focus our analysis simply on identifying the impact of programs. In many expenditure programs, trade-offs exist between the objectives of efficiency and equity. It may be possible to design a more progressive expenditure program, but only at some cost. An increase in social security benefits may be desirable from the perspective of certain distributional goals, but the increased benefits may lead to earlier retirement, and the higher taxes required to finance them may decrease work incentives. Higher unemployment compensation may provide increased income to some who are among the most needy, but unemployment insurance may make an individual feel disinclined to find another job.

Disagreements about the desirability of different programs often arise from disagreements, not only about values—the relative importance of equity versus efficiency considerations—but also about the nature of the trade-offs, how much loss of efficiency would result from an attempt to change the structure of the benefits of some program to make its distributional impact more progressive.

Figure 9.4 shows the equity-efficiency frontier for some hypothetical program and the indifference curves for two individuals. In Panel A, Scrooge is much less willing to give up efficiency for a gain in equity than is his brother, Spendthrift. E_1 represents the point on the trade-off curve that is optimal as Spendthrift sees it, while E_2 is optimal from the point of view of Scrooge. Not surprisingly, Scrooge chooses a point with higher efficiency but lower equity than does Spendthrift. Thus in Panel A, the source of the disagreement about policy is a difference in the values held by the two individuals.

On the other hand, in Panel B we have depicted a situation where the differences about policy arise from differences in judgments concerning the nature of the trade-off. Scrooge thinks that to get a slight increase in equity one must give up a lot of efficiency. He thinks the trade-off curve looks like the colored line. On the other hand, Spendthrift thinks that one can get a large increase in equity with just a slight loss in efficiency.

For instance, if the main reason that unemployed individuals do not obtain jobs is that there are no jobs available—that is, if the likelihood of finding a job is relatively little affected by the size of unemployment compensation, one might be able to increase unemployment benefits with little loss in efficiency. But there is not agreement about the extent to which unemployment insurance lowers the probability of an individual's obtaining a job.

Thus if unemployment insurance has little effect on job search, there is not much trade-off between efficiency and equity, and the frontier is consistent with Spendthrift's perception; while if job search is very sensitive to unemployment compensation, there is a significant trade-off, and the equity-efficiency frontier is consistent with Scrooge's perceptions.

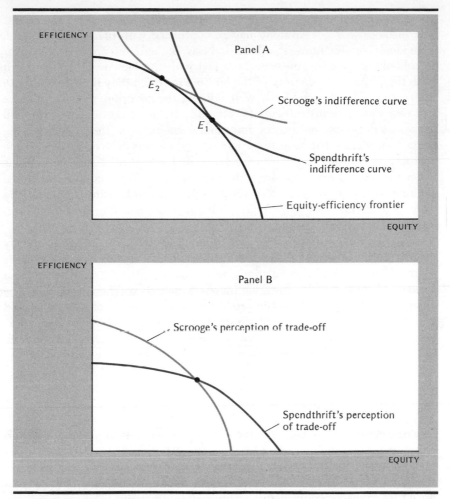

9.4   SOURCES OF DIFFERENCES IN VIEWS CONCERNING PUBLIC PROGRAMS
(A) Scrooge and Spendthrift have the same perceptions concerning trade-offs but differ in values. (B) Scrooge and Spendthrift differ in their perception of the nature of the efficiency-equity trade-off.

It is important to emphasize that the equity-efficiency trade-off is encountered repeatedly in the evaluation of the detailed provisions of any government program. The decision to charge tolls on a bridge means that those who benefit from the bridge (that is, those who use it) have to bear its costs. To many people, this is desirable for equity reasons; it is unfair to make someone who does not drive over the bridge pay for it. But there is an efficiency cost in money and time: the wages of toll collectors and the time of motorists. Moreover, if some drivers are discouraged from using the bridge (when it is below capacity), there is a further efficiency loss from underutilization.

7. PROGRAM EVALUATION

The discussion so far has focused on two bases for evaluating public programs: their effect on economic efficiency and their effect on distribution.

Government policy may be concerned with a broader range of objectives. For instance, the government may be concerned with the extent to which individuals of different racial, ethnic, and class backgrounds are mixed together in schools. It may be concerned not just with the income of the poor but with the physical appearance of the housing in which they live. When these alternative objectives are fairly well defined, the government can still make use of a variety of instruments for attaining them; in particular, it can still make use of private producers, imposing regulations on them, or imposing certain standards that have to be met for individuals or firms to be eligible to receive subsidies. Thus the government has specified that institutions receiving federal grants comply with certain affirmative action regulations. If the government decided to institute a program of housing grants for the poor, it could insist on basic standards for anyone providing housing to individuals receiving a housing grant.

In some cases, however, it may be difficult for the government to specify clearly (and in advance) all of its objectives, or to articulate these objectives in the form of a set of regulations or standards. There is, furthermore, a concern about the extent to which these regulations will be enforced. There is widespread belief that private producers, in the absence of well-articulated and enforced regulations, will simply pursue profit-maximizing behavior, regardless of any stated alternative objectives. There is an argument, in such circumstances, for the government to assume direct responsibility for the activity.

8. POLITICAL PROCESS

In a democracy, many individuals and groups are involved in the design and adoption of any public-expenditure program. These individuals have various objectives and various beliefs about how the economy works. The program that eventually is adopted is a compromise among their views. The compromise that emerges will probably not resemble the views of any one individual and may seem to be inconsistent with any single set of objectives. If two chefs disagree about the appropriate liquid to add to a sauce, one arguing that lemon juice should be added and another that cream should be added, the compromise solution of adding a little of both may be disastrous, with results inconsistent with any culinary objective.

The study of the political process by which a particular expenditure program was adopted may be insightful for two reasons. First, we may be able to understand why the program looks the way it does. We discussed earlier the government program to stabilize farmers' prices. There is a market failure that this program addresses: the inability of individuals to obtain insurance for many of the important risks they face, including that associated with the variability of prices.[2] But a closer examination of the program suggests that if that were the only objective of the program it would be designed in a quite different way. Rather, one of the clear objectives of the program is to transfer resources (income) to farmers from the rest of the population. Yet if

---

[2] Futures markets now enable the farmer to divest himself of some of the risks associated with price variability.

that is the objective, there are more efficient ways of transferring resources to the farmers; outright grants would be preferable to the present program. But *if* the objective were made explicit, if the transfers were made conspicuous, it is not clear that they could get approved. Voters in urban districts might strongly oppose them, while they do not oppose the present form of inefficient subsidies, simply because they are not fully aware of the nature of the transfers.

Particular provisions of public programs are likely to have strong distributional consequences for particular groups in the population. If one group can be suitably organized, they will attempt to induce the political process to adopt provisions that are to their benefit. In Chapter 8 we discussed the regulations providing for scrubbing the smoke emitted from burning coal. These regulations may have an enormous effect on the relative demand for hard (or western) coal and bituminous coal and hence on the incomes of both miners and coal producers in different parts of the country. The shape of environmental legislation and regulation may be affected as much by these particular distributional consequences as by overall efficiency considerations.

This brings us to the second reason why it is important to study the political process by which expenditure programs get adopted. Some programs may be more influenced by political pressures than others. An example is a program with an elaborate set of technical regulations and a variety of detailed provisions. Such a program may be subject to pressure to have those regulations that favor certain well-defined interest groups. When technical expertise is required, it may be difficult to get impartial technical advice. Those who are capable of providing the information often have a vested interest in the outcome. Generals in the armed forces may have the most information about the military strengths of the United States and its potential enemies, but by virtue of their training and their positions, they look at the world with a particular perspective. Even if they do not take positions from a narrow self-interest point of view but really believe that they are making their recommendations on the basis of public interest, the nature of their advice may be very much the same as if they were acting out of self-interest. Thus it is not surprising that we see a navy admiral arguing for aircraft carriers while an air force general pushes for bombers.

Accordingly, in evaluating alternative policies, one needs to take into account the political process, what the legislation might look like after it has been subjected to the political process, and what the consequences of the program will be, knowing that it will be administered by bureaucrats, probably not unlike those administering other government programs, and subject to the same kinds of incentives.

SUMMARY

There are eight major elements in the analysis of public-expenditure programs:

1) identifying a need, the source of demand for the government program;

2) identifying a market failure (if it exists) and ascertaining whether what is at issue is a concern over the consequences of the present distribution of income or the provision of a merit good;

3) identifying alternative programs that might address the perceived problems, noting in particular the importance of particular design features for the determination
of the consequences of the program;

4) identifying the efficiency consequences of alternative programs;

5) identifying the distributional consequences of alternative programs;

6) identifying the trade-offs between equity and efficiency considerations;

7) identifying the extent to which alternative programs achieve public policy objectives; and

8) identifying how the political process affects the design and implementation of public programs.

QUESTIONS AND PROBLEMS

1. Explain how the following particular design features have an important effect on
the consequences of government programs:
   a) The level of income required for eligibility for food stamps is reduced by expenditures on housing.
   b) Whether an individual between sixty-five and seventy used to be eligible for
   social security benefits depends on his income calculated on a month-by-month
   basis.
   c) An ex-spouse becomes eligible for social security benefits only if she has been
   married for at least ten years.
   Can you think of other instances where particular design features have seemingly
   unintended consequences?

2. Who may be the actual beneficiaries of the following government program or proposed programs; that is, taking into account how individuals respond to the government program, who are those who are actually better off as a result of the
program?
   a) medicare
   b) housing subsidies for the poor
   c) education loans extended to those with parents earning in excess of $50,000.
   Can you think of other instances where those who actually benefit from the program may be different from those the program seemingly intended to benefit?

3. In Chapters 11–15, we will use the framework that we have discussed in this
chapter to analyze several different government programs. Before reading those
chapters, see if you can answer the following questions for each program:
   a) What were the original sources of demand for the program? What perceived
   need was the program indended to address?
   b) What are the market failures?
   c) What are the possible forms of government intervention? Are there particular
   design features that have had, or currently do have, an important effect on the
   effectiveness of the program?
   d) What are the major efficiency consequences of the program?
   e) Does the program entail any effective redistribution?
   f) Are there important instances of trade-offs between equity and efficiency in the
   design of the program?
   g) What are some alternatives for meeting the objectives of the program? To what
   extent might they do a better job—e.g., by reducing distortions and increasing
   the equity of the programs?
   h) How has the political process affected the nature of the present program?

10
Cost-Benefit Analysis

The preceding chapter set out the basic framework for the analysis of government expenditure policies. In many cases, the government wants more than a qualitative analysis; it needs a quantitative analysis. It needs to know whether a particular project should be undertaken, whether the benefits exceed the costs.

Should the government build a bridge and, if so, of what size?

Should the government construct a dam and, if so, of what size?

Should the government institute more stringent regulations for inflammability of mattresses?

Should the government institute more stringent regulations for licensing drugs?

Should the government extend the Washington, D.C., subway system?

Should the government declare certain portions of the Cape Cod seashore a national park?

These are all examples of particular projects (regulations, actions) upon which the government must decide. The government must also make decisions concerning entire programs. Should the manpower training program, which attempts to train unskilled and unemployed workers for better jobs, be terminated or extended? What has been the value of its benefits relative to its costs? Has the bilingual education program, which attempts to provide native-language instruction to those for whom English is a second language, been successful—that is, have its benefits exceeded its costs? This chapter describes how the government goes about making these evaluations.

Before doing this, however, it is instructive to consider how a *private* firm makes decisions concerning which projects to undertake.

PRIVATE COST-BENEFIT ANALYSIS

Private firms constantly have to make decisions concerning whether to undertake some investment decision. We can characterize the procedures they follow in four steps.

1. Identify the set of possible projects to be considered. A steel firm wishes to expand its production capacity. There may be a number of ways it could do this; there may be alternative technologies available for smelting iron ore; there may be a number of alternative specialized forms of steel that could be produced. The first stage is then a listing of the various major alternatives.

2. Identify the full consequences of each of these alternatives. The firm is primarily concerned with the inputs for which it has to pay and the outputs it can sell. Thus the firm will determine the labor, iron ore, coal, and other materials required for each production alternative; it will assess the quality of steel that will be produced under each alternative; it will determine the quantity of various wastes that will be produced.

3. Assign a value to each of the inputs and outputs. The firm will have to estimate the costs of various kinds of labor (various skills) over the lifetime of the plant; it will have to estimate the costs of other inputs, such as coals and iron ore. It will have to estimate the prices at which it can sell the steel (which will depend on the quality of the steel produced, which may in turn vary from project to project). And it will have to estimate the costs of disposing of wastes.

4. Add up the costs and benefits to estimate the total profitability of the project. The firm will undertake the project with the highest profit (the maximum difference between benefits and costs)—provided, of course, that profits are positive (taking appropriate account of the opportunity costs, the return the funds could obtain elsewhere). If profits for all contemplated projects are negative, it undertakes no project; it invests the funds elsewhere.

Evaluating costs and benefits at different dates. The procedure described above seems simple and straightforward. Only one part requires some elaboration. The benefits and costs of the steel mill occur over an extended period of time. Surely the firm is not indifferent when it comes to choosing between receiving a dollar today or receiving one in twenty-five years. How are the benefits and costs that accrue at different dates to be valued and compared?

PRESENT DISCOUNTED VALUE

The basic procedure employed by economists (and businesspeople) is based on the premise that *a dollar today is worth more than a dollar tomorrow.* If the firm receives $1 today, it can take it down to the bank, deposit it, and have (if the rate of interest is 10 percent) $1.10 at the end of the year. Thus $1 today is worth $1.10 next year. The firm is just as well off receiving $1 today as $1.10 next year. If the firm invests the $1.10 it will have at the end of the following year, $1.21. Accordingly, the firm is indifferent in choosing between receiving $1 today and $1.21 in two years' time.

To evaluate projects with receipts and expenditures in future years, it multiplies those receipts and payments by a **discount factor,** by a number (less than one) that makes those future receipts and payments equivalent to current receipts and payments. The discount factor is smaller the further into the future the benefit is received. The discount factor for payments in one year is just $1/1+r$, where r is the rate of interest (in our example $r = .10$, so the discount factor is $1/1.1 = .9$); for payments in two years' time it is just $1/(1+r)(1+r) = 1/(1+r)^2$ (in our example it is $1/1.21$). The value *today* of $100 to be received two years in the future is thus $100/1.21 = \$82.6$. We then add up the value of what is to be received (or paid out) in each year of the project. The sum is called the **present discounted value** of the project, often abbreviated as PDV. If R_t is the *net* receipts from the projects in period t, and r the rate of interest, then, if the project lasts for N years, its PDV is given by

$$\text{PDV} = R_o + \frac{R_1}{1+r} + \frac{R_2}{(1+r)^2} + \frac{R_t}{(1+r)^t} \cdots \frac{R_N}{(1+r)^N}$$

Table 10.1 provides an illustration of how this might be done for a hypothetical steel mill lasting five years. (Most steel mills last much longer than that; this makes the calculations more complicated, but the principle is the same.) For each year, we multiply the net receipts of that year by the discount factor for that year. Notice the large difference between undiscounted profits ($1,000) and discounted profits ($169). This difference is likely to be particularly large for long-lived projects entailing large initial investments; the benefits for such projects occur later in time (and are therefore worth less) than the costs, which occur earlier in time.

Table 10.1 HYPOTHETICAL CALCULATION OF PROFITABILITY FOR A FIVE-YEAR STEEL MILL

Year	Benefits	Costs	Net Profits	Discount Factor	Discounted Net Profits
1		3,000	-3,000	1	-3,000
2	1,200	200	1,000	$1/1.1 = .909$	909
3	1,200	200	1,000	$1/(1.1)^2 = .826$	826
4	1,200	200	1,000	$1/(1.1)^3 = .751$	751
5	1,200	200	1,000	$1/(1.1)^4 = .683$	683
Total	4,800	3,800	1,000		169

SOCIAL COST-BENEFIT ANALYSIS

The government goes through basically the same procedures in evaluating a project. There are, however, two critical differences between social and private cost-benefit analyses.

1. The only consequences of a project that are of concern to the firm are those that affect its profitability. The government may be concerned with a much broader range of consequences. It may be concerned with the ecolog-

ical effects of some dam; it may be concerned with the impact of the dam on the recreational uses to which the river can be put.

2. The firm uses market prices to evaluate what it has to pay for its inputs and what it receives for its output. There are two instances in which the government might not use market prices in evaluating projects: a) In many cases market prices do not exist because the outputs and inputs are not sold on the market. There are not market prices for clean air, for lives saved, for the preservation of wilderness in its natural state. b) In other cases, market prices do not represent true marginal social costs or benefits. Recall from Chapter 4 that in the absence of market failures, market prices do reflect marginal social costs and benefits and the government should also use market prices in evaluating its projects. Government action is required, however, precisely because there is some market failure, and the prices the government uses to evaluate its projects must reflect these market failures. Thus if the government is concerned about unemployment, it may not view the individual's wage as a true measure of the marginal social cost of employing that individual. If the government believes that capital markets are not working well, it may not wish to use the market rate of interest in discounting future benefits and costs.

Valuing Nonmarketed Commodities: Consumer Surplus. In this and the next section, we consider some of the problems associated with the evaluation of nonmarketed commodities. We begin with an example where, in principle, the government could charge a price. The government is considering building a bridge. It can charge a toll for the use of the bridge. For each toll, there will be a certain demand for usage of the bridge. Assume that the minimum efficient size of the bridge is such that at a zero price, there is excess capacity, as depicted in Figure 10.1. Thus, the price the government charges (since the marginal cost of using the bridge is then zero) is zero; but clearly, the *value* of the bridge is positive: the bridge enables individuals to save time, and they would be willing to pay for its use. The question is, how much is it worth?

How much better off are individuals as a result of the construction of the bridge? First we construct a **compensated demand curve,** as shown in Figure 10.1. The compensated demand schedule traces out the demand for any commodity as we lower the price when, at the same time, we take away enough income from the individual so that he is no better off at the lower price than he was at the higher price. To see this, think of asking an individual how much he would be willing to pay to use the bridge once, then how much *extra* he would be willing to pay to use the bridge twice and so on. By asking these questions, we are able to trace out the compensated demand curve. We call it the compensated demand curve because at each question, we are asking the individual to compare his welfare when the bridge was not available with the new situation, whether he can use the bridge once, twice, thrice, etc. The level of welfare of the individual is thus kept fixed at the level it was prior to the construction of the bridge. The area under the demand curve between 0 and, say, 5 units clearly gives the total amount that the individual would be willing to pay for 5 units. If the total number of trips taken on the bridge at a zero price is 6, the area under the demand curve

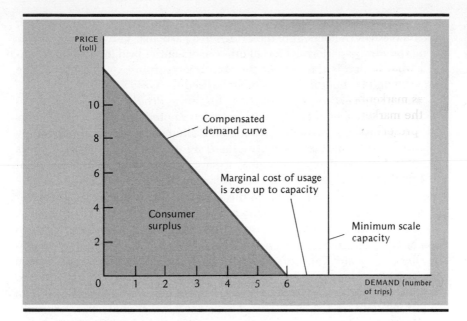

10.1 CALCULATION OF CONSUMER SURPLUS Even at minimum scale, the capacity exceeds the demand at zero price. It still may be desirable to construct the bridge if the consumer surplus (area under the compensated demand schedule) exceeds costs of construction.

gives the total amount that he would be willing to pay for 6 trips and still be just as well off as he was when there was no bridge.

The compensated demand curve needs to be distinguished from the ordinary demand curve; usually as we lower the price of a commodity, the individual is better off; as we raise the price of a commodity, the individual is worse off. Thus at each point along the demand curve, the welfare of the individual is different. Along the compensated demand curve, as we change prices we continuously take away or give income to an individual, to leave him at a fixed level of welfare. If an individual's demand for a commodity (e.g., the number of trips he takes over the bridge) does not depend on his income, then his compensated demand curve and his ordinary demand curves coincide. Otherwise, the two differ as a result of the "income effect" associated with taking away or giving income as compensation.[1] The gain as a result of the bridge construction is the area under the compensated demand curve, and is called the **consumer surplus.** In our example, this may easily be calculated. For the first trip, individuals are willing to pay $10; for the second, only $8 (additional); for the third, $6; for the fourth, $4; and for the fifth, $2. They are willing to pay nothing additional for more than 5 trips. If they were asked, What would you be willing to pay to have unlimited use of the bridge?—i.e., How much could we charge you and leave you just as well

---

[1]There has been some controversy concerning the empirical significance of the "income effect." See, for instance, R. Willig, "Consumer's Surplus Without Apology," *American Economic Review* 66 (1976): 589–97 and J. Hausman, "Exact Consumer's Surplus and Deadweight Loss," *American Economic Review* 11 (1981): 662–76 for two opposing views. Whether economists "should" ignore the income effect or not, in practice, they almost always do, because of difficulties in quantifying the magnitude of the income effect.

off as you were before the bridge was built?—the answer would be $30, which measures the benefit of the bridge to a particular individual. A similar calcuation can be performed for all other users of the bridge. The total benefit of the bridge is the sum of the consumer surpluses of all users. The bridge should be built if these benefits exceed the costs.[2]

Valuing Nonmarketed Commodities: Inference Problems. A central problem in social cost-benefit analysis is, as we have noted, that many of the costs and benefits are not marketed. Though for some commodities produced by the government—such as electricity—there are well-established market prices (which still may not reflect marginal social costs or benefits), there are not markets for lives saved, for clean air, or for unpolluted rivers.

How is the government to value the savings in life resulting from a better program of drug regulation, or tighter standards for mattress inflammability, or seatbelt requirements? How is the government to value the savings in time or comfort provided by a new subway system? How is the government to value cleaner air? These are not easy questions, but techniques have been developed (in some cases they are rather controversial) that provide answers. These techniques entail making inferences about individuals' evaluations from market data and from their observed behavior in other contexts.

Valuing Time: A Constructive Approach. The old adage "time is money" describes the view taken by most economists in evaluating the savings in time resulting from an improved transportation system such as a better subway system or a better road network. The typical approach is to attempt to ascertain the wage rate of those who use the transportation system; under certain ideal conditions, the wage provides a measure of an individual's evaluation of his own time. In simple economic models, an individual is pictured as making a choice between the amount of leisure and the amount of work that he undertakes. As a result of giving up one more hour of leisure, he gets an increase in consumption goods equal to his hourly wage. In equilibrium, he is indifferent when choosing between giving up one more hour of leisure and increasing his consumption by his wage, or reducing his work (increasing his leisure) by an hour and decreasing his consumption by an amount equal to his hourly wage. Thus his wage provides a monetary valuation of his time.

There are some who claim that this provides an overestimate of the value of time: many individuals would like to work more at their wage rate but are unable to find additional employment at that wage; the job restricts the number of hours that they can work. The individual's valuation of his leisure is thus fairly low; the compensation that would be required for reducing an individual's leisure by one hour is, in this view, much less than the wage that the individual receives.

There are others who claim that the wage may provide an underestimate of the value of leisure for some individuals and an overestimate of the value of leisure for other individuals. They point out that, for instance, professors have chosen a relatively low-wage job relative to other options available to them because of the great nonpecuniary benefits associated with the job.

---

[2]This discussion abstracts from a number of other considerations that will be the subject of discussion below, including the assessment of who benefits and who pays the costs.

The value of their leisure exceeds the wage they receive. On the other hand, the wage of the coal miner or the garbage collector includes some compensation for the unattractive features of those jobs and hence represents an overestimate of the value of leisure.

The Valuation of Life. Probably no subject in public cost-benefit analysis has engendered so much emotional discussion as economists' attempts to place a monetary value on life. As distasteful as such a calculation may seem, it is necessary, in a variety of circumstances, for governments to face up to this problem. There is virtually no limit to the amount that could be spent to reduce the likelihood of an accident on a road, to reduce the likelihood of someone dying from some disease, etc. Yet at some point a judgment must be made that the gain from further expenditures is sufficiently small that such additional expenditures are not warranted. An individual who otherwise would not have may die as a result of this decision. Yet we cannot spent 50 percent of our natural income on transportation safety or 50 percent of our national income on health.

There are two methods currently in vogue for estimating the value of life. The first is the *constructive method*—that is, we estimate what the individual would have earned had he remained alive (until his "normal" age of death). To do this, we extrapolate his employment history, comparing it to individuals in similar positions. Some argue that this method provides an overestimate of the economic value of the individual; if one believes that individuals' incomes correspond to their marginal products—what they have added to the production of society—then this method reflects the amount by which national income has been reduced as a result of the death of this individual. At the same time, it does not make any allowance for what it costs society to sustain this individual. His projected income, for instance, might be the result in part of training he would have received at some date in the future. Society has saved itself those educational expenditures, and this ought to be netted out of the loss to society from the death of the individual. The problem is, there seems to be no clear way of determining precisely how much of an individual's expenditures ought to be subtracted to provide an estimate of the economic value of life.

On the other hand, this method suggests that after retirement, an individual's life has a zero value, since there is no loss of earnings. This seems wrong.[3]

There is an alternative, indirect method. In some occupations, there is a much higher probability of death than in others. For instance, the accident rates for coal miners are higher than for college professors, and the death rate for those who work in asbestos factories and who operate jackhammers is much higher than for clerical workers. Individuals who undertake riskier occupations normally require compensation for undertaking these additional risks. By choosing the riskier occupation, they are saying that they are willing to face a higher probability of death for a higher income while they are alive. The second method calculates the value of life by looking at how much extra income individuals need to compensate them for an increase in the

---

[3]The method is also beset by a number of technical problems. For instance, the results are very sensitive to the discount rate employed, and there is no agreement about what this should be.

probability of death. There is considerable controversy, however, about this second method; there are those who believe that it provides a gross underestimate of the value of life; they argue that individuals are not well informed concerning the risks they face.[4] Also, for well-known psychological reasons, individuals attempt to ignore what information they do have concerning the riskiness of their job.[5]

As controversial as the estimates of the value of life may be, it is likely that they will continue to be useful in the evaluation of projects that affect the likelihood of death. There appears to be no alternative if we are to evaluate projects in which a change in death probabilities is a significant consequence. Whether, for instance, there should be higher standards for air quality may depend on the value assigned to the resulting reduction in mortality.

COST-EFFECTIVENESS

An alternative procedure that is widely employed when the benefits of some project are hard to evaluate is called **cost-effectiveness analysis.** An objective is taken as given, and the question is simply, What is the most effective way to achieve this objective? Assume that we wish to avoid the problems associated with valuing life while helping the government assess a variety of ways of reducing highway deaths. We could calculate the costs associated with each of several methods of accomplishing the same goal. Or we might simply show the marginal costs associated with reducing the death rate by each additional individual, leaving it to the legislators to determine which point along the curve should be chosen (and therefore what method of improving traffic safety should be chosen).

When The Occupational Safety and Health Administration considered standards for noise pollution, they did a cost-effectiveness study, calculating how many extra workers would be protected from hearing loss as a result of alternative standards. They then calculated the cost associated with each standard. On the basis of this, they calculated the marginal gross and net costs (taking into account the fact that hearing losses reduce productivity) associated with different levels of protection, as depicted in Figure 10.2. The curve shows that there are significant extra costs of trying to protect additional individuals.[6] On the basis of this, one study concluded, "an effectively administered hearing-protector program could provide most of the benefits at much lower cost in comparison with an industrywide engineering-only noise standard. . . . an 85-decibel hearing-protector standard [has] the relatively reasonable marginal cost of about $23,000 per hearing impairment avoided. . . ." In ordinary English, the study recommended the use of ear plugs rather than drastic changes in plants and equipment requiring to implement the same level of hearing protection.

---

[4] Several studies have attempted to estimate the magnitude of workers' misperceptions and suggest that they may not be too large. See, for instance, W. K. Viscusi, *Risk by Choice: Regulating Health and Safety in the Workplace* (Cambridge, MA: Harvard University Press, 1983).

[5] This is sometimes referred to as "cognitive dissonance." For an application of these psychological concepts to economics, see G. Akerlof, and W. T. Dickens, "The Economic Consequences of Cognitive Dissonance," *American Economic Review* 72 (1982): 307–19.

[6] From J. R. Morrall III, "Exposure to Occupational Noise," in *Benefit-Cost Analyses of Social Regulation,* ed. James C. Miller III and Bruce Yandle (Washington, D.C.: American Enterprise Institute for Public Policy Research, 1979).

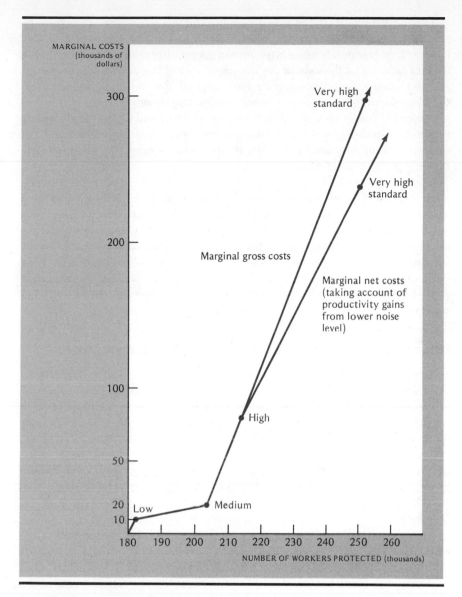

10.2 COMPARISON OF ALTERNATIVE STANDARDS FOR OCCUPATIONAL NOISE EXPOSURE Higher standards cost more and protect more workers. SOURCE: Morrall.

SHADOW PRICES AND MARKET PRICES

Whenever there is a market failure, market prices may not reflect true marginal social costs or benefits. Economists attempt to calculate, in such circumstances, the true marginal social cost or benefits, for instance, of hiring an additional worker or importing or exporting additional goods; they call these "social prices" or "shadow prices." The term *shadow price* is used to remind us that these prices do not really exist in the market but that they are the true social prices, reflected imperfectly in the market price.

The most difficult part of calculating the shadow prices is tracing through the full consequences of a government action in the presence of a market failure. Disagreements often arise among economists about the nature of the market failure and thus about the consequences of the government action.

For instance, some economists have argued that because, in most less developed countries, unemployment is high, the marginal social cost of hiring an individual is very low. But hiring an unemployed worker in the urban sector may induce workers to migrate from the rural sector, leaving the unemployment rate unchanged. In these circumstances, the shadow wage may equal the market wage.

It is, of course, unlikely that a bureaucrat working in some project evaluation office will be able to trace out the full consequences of undertaking a project. He cannot ascertain the appropriate "shadow prices" to use. Thus in some countries in which cost-benefit analysis is widely employed, the minister of planning may instruct his project evaluators on what shadow wage to use (he may be told, for instance, to assume a shadow wage that is 80 percent of the market wage for unskilled labor and 120 percent of the market wage for skilled labor.) In the United States, most cost-benefit analysis has assumed that the market wages are the appropriate wages to use.

DISCOUNT RATES FOR SOCIAL COST-BENEFIT ANALYSIS

In our discussion of private cost-benefit analysis, we noted that a dollar next year or the year after was not worth as much as a dollar today. Hence, income to be received in the future or expenses to be incurred in the future had to be discounted. In deciding whether to undertake a project, we look at its present discounted value. The discount factor private firms use is $1/1+r$, where r is the rate of interest the firm has to pay. The question is, what discount rate should the government use? The discount rate used by the government is sometimes called the *social discount rate*. The central question of concern is the relationship between this and the interest rate faced by consumers, on the one hand, and producers, on the other.

For evaluating long-lived projects, such as dams, the choice of the discount rate is crucial: a project that looks very favorable using a 3 percent interest rate may look very unattractive at a 10 percent rate. If markets worked perfectly, the market interest rate would reflect the opportunity cost of the resources used and the relative evaluation of income at different dates. But there is a widespread belief that capital markets do not work well. Moreover, taxes may introduce large distortions. Thus it is not clear which of the various market rates of interest, if any, should be used: for instance, should it be the rate at which the government can borrow, or should it be the rate at which the typical taxpayer can borrow?

Although no consensus has been reached among economists at a practical level, there is some agreement about the principles. First, one needs to consider how a project will affect the economy, and to whom the benefits (and costs) accrue. Then one weighs the benefits and costs accruing to different individuals using a social welfare function (Chapter 3). One might give less weight to increases in consumption to future generations than to increases in consumption to the current generation, because one believes that, as a result of technological progress, they will be better off on any account.

227
Discount
Rates for
Social
Cost-Benefit
Analysis

This assessment of how projects affect different generations is particularly important for long-lived projects, where the costs may be borne by one generation, and the benefits received by succeeding generations. The assessment of these projects entails a trade-off between individuals of different generations. What is at issue is the **intergenerational distribution** of income or welfare. We can talk about society's marginal rate of substitution of one generation's income for another, just as we can talk of an individual's marginal rate of substitution of consumption in one period for another. The question is, What is the relationship between *society's* marginal rate of substitution and the market rate of interest? The answer depends on how successful the government has been in adjusting the intergenerational distribution of income to reflect society's judgments concerning the appropriate intertemporal distribution.[7]

In the absence of an active government policy, there is no reason that the intergenerational distribution of welfare generated by the market has any optimality properties; there is no reason to believe, in other words, that there will be any systematic relationship between the market rate of interest and society's marginal rate of substitution between this generation's consumption and that of the next generation.[8] Using the market rate of interest may result in too high a discount rate, or too low a discount rate.

Disagreements arise among economists concerning the impact of the project being evaluated, the extent to which the government has used other policy instruments to bring about the appropriate intergenerational distribution of income, and, consequently, how increments to income of different generations should be valued. For instance, some economists are particularly concerned about the extent to which public projects displace (or "crowd out") private projects. These economists tend to argue for using the rate at which firms can obtain financing.[9]

An Example: The Middle Snake River Hydroelectric Project. Several of the issues we have discussed are illustrated by the cost-benefit analysis of a hydroelectric project on the Middle Snake River in the Pacific Northwest, which was conducted in the early 1970s.[10] Four alternative projects were considered. They differed in scale, in location, in the output of electricity

---

[7]Several economists have argued that parents take into account the welfare of their children in making their savings-bequest decisions. In this view, then, in equilibrium, the marginal rate of substitution between their consumption and their children's is simply related to the rate of interest (if they give up one unit of consumption today, their children can get more than one dollar; the amount extra is just the return on their investment; in equilibrium, they must be indifferent when choosing between consuming one more unit today and postponing consumption, giving the extra consumption to their children.) In this view, the social rate of discount can be directly calculated from the market rate of interest, in exactly the same way that it can for a short-lived project affecting a single generation. Indeed it should be noted that if the government decides to transfer more resources to the next generation, parents will decide that they need to transfer less; the change in bequests just offsets the government's action. This argument that public savings is a perfect substitute for private savings requires that there are not limitations on borrowing, all individuals know that they will have children, and all have the same number of children. For a discussion of this view, see R. Barro, "Are Government Bonds Net Wealth?" *Journal of Political Economy* 82 (1974): 1095–117.

[8]We sometimes refer to this marginal rate of substitution as the **social rate of time preference**.

[9]The view that because government investment crowds out private investment, the producer interest rate should be used in project evaluation is sometimes referred to as the *opportunity cost view*. Even if there is "crowding out," it may not, however, be appropriate to use the producer rate of interest, in the absence of an active and effective government policy to redistribute income across generations. If, however, the government imposes a full set of optimal commodity taxes and subsidies, it should use the rate of interest faced by producers. There is considerable controversy, however, over whether these special cases provide much guidance for policy purposes.

[10]I have drawn heavily on L. G. Hines, *Environmental Issues* (New York: W. W. Norton, 1973). For a fuller discussion, see Chapter 7 of his book.

they would generate, in their effects on fish and wildlife and on flood control, and in the extent of the recreational facilities they would provide. Which project was desirable turned out to depend critically on two factors: the discount rate and the evaluation of the effects on the environment. While at a 3¼ percent interest rate several of the plans looked viable, at a 9 percent interest rate only one of the projects had a positive present discounted value—and this was not the project that would have been selected at the lower interest rate.

While a market value can be assigned to the value of the fish, it is more difficult to determine the value of "natural wilderness." John Krutilla argued that the Middle Snake canyon

> may have few, if any, close substitutes. Morever, if the present environment is adversely altered, its reproduction is not possible. In short, while rare phenomena can be reduced in supply, they cannot be expanded by the works of man. They represent irreplaceable assets not subject to reproduction. Now if the supply is thus fixed but the demand for the services of this asset increases, it is an irreplaceable asset with an increasing annual benefit.[11]

He estimated that when the cost of the loss of the free-flowing character of the river was included in the analysis—and the benefits and costs discounted at 9 percent—none of the projects had a positive present discounted value.

Nevertheless, the Federal Power Commission licensed one of the four projects. Environment economist Lawrence Hines argued that that decision was not cost-effective:

> Adding 1,700 megawatts of thermal output instead of hydroelectric output to the Pacific Northwest grid would have an inappreciable effect upon power rates in that region. But adding a dam to the Middle Snake would involve a transcendent aesthetic change. There is no doubt about which is the greater cost.

Curiously enough, benefits of the project turned out to depend on two events that were not anticipated at the time these evaluations were conducted. The enormous increase in the price of energy resulting from the oil crises in 1973 and 1979 vastly increased the benefits from the project. But while demand for electricity was forecasted to rise rapidly, it failed to do so, so that by the late 1970s and early 1980s there was considerable excess capacity. The cost-benefit analysis completely ignored the inevitable uncertainties associated with any long-lived project.

THE EVALUATION OF RISK

The most common mistake is to argue that in the face of risk, the government should use a higher rate of discount. Recall that discount rate relates the value of a dollar at one date to its value at a later date. To see how increasing the discount rate may lead to absurd results, consider a project that, at termination, requires an expenditure (an automobile has to be towed

---

[11]J. V. Kruttilla, *Testimony before the Federal Power Commission on the Middle Snake Issue* (Washington, D.C.: Mimeographed, 1970), p. 29.

to the junk yard). Assume that there is some uncertainty about the magnitude of that cost. We would normally think that this uncertainty would make
the project less attractive than if we knew for sure what the termination costs
were. But consider what happens if we use a higher discount factor to offset
the risk: the present value of those costs is reduced, and the project looks
more, not less, attractive. To use a higher discount rate confuses the evaluation of income at different dates with the evaluation of risk; these are two
separate issues.

To evaluate risks, economists introduce the concept of **certainty equivalence.** Assume there is some risky prospect. The output of the project may
be worth $0 next year or $100; there is a fifty-fifty chance of each outcome.
The *average* value is just $50 ($\frac{1}{2} \times \$100 + \frac{1}{2} \times \$0 = \$50$). If we dislike risk,
however, we would clearly prefer a project whose return was a certain $50.
In fact, we would prefer a project with a smaller average value, so long as
the risk was smaller. If we would be indifferent in choosing between the
risky project with an average value of $50 and a perfectly safe project with a
value of $45, we would say that $45 is the certainty equivalent of the risky
project with mean $50. We could, alternatively, have said that there is a 10
percent risk discount factor—i.e., we deflate the average value by 10 percent to obtain the certainty equivalent. To evaluate risky projects, then, we
simply take the present discounted value of the certainty equivalents.[12]

Thus risky projects have to earn a higher return than safe projects with
the same average return to be acceptable. The extra amount a risky project
must earn to compensate for the risk we call its **risk premium.**

Table 10.2   EXAMPLE OF COST-BENEFIT ANALYSIS FOR RISKY INVESTMENT

Year	Expected Net Benefit	Risk Discount Factor	Certainty Equivalent Net Benefit	Time Discount Factor (10 percent interest rate)	Discounted Value of Certainty Equivalent Net Benefit
1	$-100	1	$-100	1	$-100
2	100	.9	90	.91	81.90
3	100	.8	80	.83	66.40
4	100	.75	75	.75	56.25
5	-50	1.5	-75	.68	-51
Total	150		70		53.55

We illustrate the procedure in Table 10.2, for a five-year project. We have
assumed that the initial investment in the first period is certain, and hence
the risk discount factor is 1. The benefits that accrue in years 2, 3, and 4 are
increasingly uncertain, and hence larger risk discount factors are used in
each of those years. The final year, the project is scrapped; there are large
costs associated with the termination of the project. (Consider the problem
of what to do with a nuclear power plant when its useful life has come to an
end). But these costs are uncertain. Hence our risk discount factor for these
costs is greater than 1. (In contrast, had we employed a higher time discount

[12]This methodology is not perfectly general. It requires that we be able to separate the analysis of risk at
one date from that at other dates. For most practical purposes, however, it is sufficiently general.

rate to take account of risk, these uncertain scrapping costs would not have weighed very heavily on our cost-benefit calculation.)

To obtain the certainty equivalent value at each date, we multiply the expected net benefit by the risk discount factor. Then to obtain the present discounted value of the certainty equivalent net benefit at any date, we multiply it by the time discount factor. To obtain the present discounted value of the certainty equivalent net benefit for the entire project, we add up the discounted certainty equivalent net benefits for the life of the project.

Relationship between the Market Risk Discount Factor and Social Risk Discount Factor. The question is, How should the government evaluate the risks associated with various projects? In some cases, such as the risks associated with electricity generation, it can look to how private markets value risks.

For risks for which there is no comparable private project, matters are more difficult. Some, such as a flood control project, serve to reduce the risks individuals face, and for these projects, the risk premium is negative. Since the government can spread risks over the entire population, when the project does not serve an insurance function (reducing the risks individuals would otherwise face) and when the project is not correlated with income from other sources (that is, the return to the project is neither particularly high nor particularly low when the economy is, say, healthy), the government should employ no risk premium.

DISTRIBUTIONAL CONSIDERATIONS

The benefits of any given public project are not uniformly distributed across the population. Some projects, such as a dam, have benefits that are limited geographically. Other projects, such as the bilingual education program and jobs retraining program, are directed mainly at the poor. The government is clearly concerned about the impact of its programs on the distribution of income. How are these effects to be taken systematically into account, and how can they be quantified?

Two procedures are commonly employed. One is to attach different weights to benefits accruing to different individuals, and the other is simply to compare measures of inequality with and without the program.

Distributional Weights

The procedure for introducing social (distributional) weights into social cost-benefit analysis is straightforward. We divide the population into income groups, the lowest quartile (one-fourth) of the population, the second quartile, etc. We then assess the magnitude of the net benefits (benefits minus costs) that accrue to each of the groups. Next, we determine social weights to be attached to each group. Thus if we attach a weight of 1 to the first quartile, richer individuals get successfully smaller weights. We then multiply the benefits by the weights, to obtain "weighted benefits." Adding these up over all groups yields the net weighted benefit of the project. Note that a project could have a negative net unweighted benefit and a positive net weighted benefit, as illustrated in Table 10.3. Thus the attractiveness of a project may depend critically on how the weights are assigned to different groups.

Quartile of the Population	Net Benefit	Social Weight	Weighted Social Net Benefit	Alternative Social Weight	Alternative Weighted Social Net Benefit
1	100	1	100	1	100
2	+50	1/2	25	.9	45
3	−50	1/4	−12.5	.7	−35
4	−200	1/8	−25	.55	−110
Total	−100		87.5		0

Economists often relate these evaluations to their views of the rate at which the marginal utility of income diminishes. It is generally hypothesized that each additional dollar that an individual obtains increases his welfare, but by smaller and smaller increments. Under this hypothesis, and the additional hypothesis that each individual's utility function is approximately the same, an extra dollar given to a poor individual is worth more than an extra dollar given to a rich individual. The amount depends on how rapidly marginal utility diminishes. In Figure 10.3A the utility function is almost a straight line; the marginal utility of a rich individual is almost the same as that of a poor individual. On the other hand, in Figure 10.3B the utility function is very curved, so that the marginal utility of a rich individual is much less than that of a poor individual. The percentage by which marginal utility decreases as a result of 1 percent increase in income is referred to as the *elasticity* of marginal utility; if this was 1, and skilled workers had a 10 percent higher income, then one would weigh the *change* in consumption of skilled workers by 10 percent less than one weighed the change in consumption of the unskilled workers. If one thought that the elasticity of marginal utility was 2, then one would weigh the skilled by 20 percent less than the unskilled.

Many economists have argued that a "reasonable" number for the elasticity of marginal utility of income is between 1 and 2. They attempt to infer the elasticity of marginal utility from observing individuals' behavior in various circumstances—in particular, their behavior under risk. The greater the elasticity of marginal utility, the more worried individuals are about losses of income. Hence they will buy more insurance. One can make inferences about the degree of risk aversion from the quantities of insurance purchased at different premiums.

Should Distributional Weights Be Used in Cost-Benefit Analysis? There are some who claim that in the actual cost-benefit calculation one should ignore distributional considerations, although one might want to report separately how the project affects different groups. There are others who insist that distributional considerations are central to public-policy evaluation.

There are some grounds for the former position. Supporters of this view contend that if the government wishes to redistribute income it should do so directly. Recall from Chapter 5 that in determining the efficient level of expenditure on a public good there were circumstances in which distributional considerations were shown to be irrelevant; we simply calculated the sum of the willingness to pay of each of the individuals. We did not weight the willingness to pay of a poor individual more than that of a rich individual.

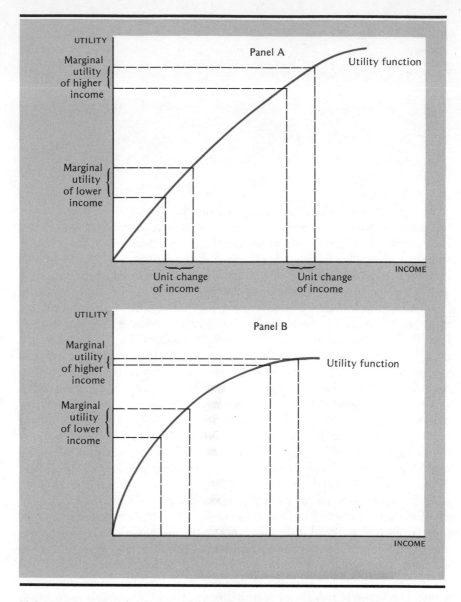

10.3 TWO ASSUMPTIONS ABOUT MARGINAL UTILITY (A) Marginal utility does not change much with a change of income. (B) There is rapidly diminishing marginal utility of income.

But when the government's ability to redistribute income through nondistortionary means is limited, the distributive effects of a government project should be taken into account.

Moreover, there are many public projects (generally not pure public goods) whose object is deliberately to redistribute welfare. In that case, to ignore the distributional consequences in an assessment seems to miss the whole point of the project or program. Thus a major argument for federal support of education is its positive distributive consequences; a cost-benefit analysis of an educational program thus ought to make use of distributional weights.

One need not take a strong stand on this issue: it is relatively easy to calculate the costs and benefits corresponding to any relevant set of welfare weights assigned to different groups.

The Effect of Public Programs on Measures of Inequality

The second basic approach to incorporating distributional considerations in program evaluation is to ascertain the effects of the program on the distribution of after-tax and subsidy income (or welfare). To assess the impact, we need some way of measuring inequality. In the following pages we describe some of the alternative ways that are frequently employed.

Measuring Inequality. We can describe the income (or wealth) distribution in a number of different ways. One way is depicted in Figure 10.4, where we show the proportion of individuals in various income levels. With complete equality, of course, everyone would have the same income; a distribution with a high percentage of individuals with a very low income and a higher percentage with a very high income is, naturally, more unequal than one in which the income is concentrated in the middle. Thus, in Figure 10.4B the income distribution marked *A* is more unequal than that marked *B*.

Lorenz Curves

Another way of describing the income distribution is depicted in Figure 10.5. We rank individuals from the lowest to the highest. We add up the income of the poorest 1 percent of the population, the poorest 2 percent, the poorest 3 percent, etc. We then calculate what percentage of the total

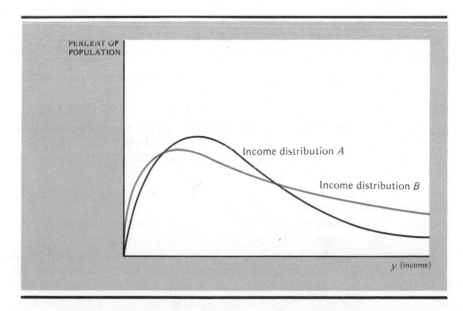

10.4 MEASURES OF INCOME DISTRIBUTION The income distribution specifies the fraction of the population at each income level. Income distribution *A* is more unequal than income distribution *B*, since there is a higher probability of having a very high or a very low income and a smaller chance of having an "average" income.

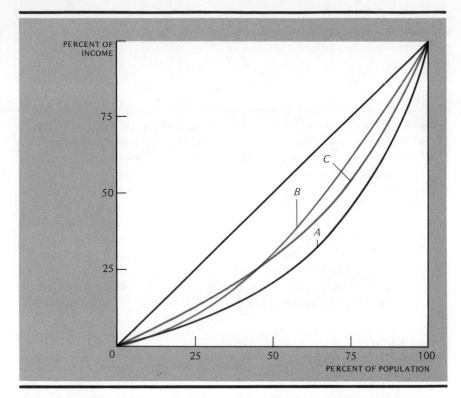

10.5 THE LORENZ CURVE The Lorenz curve gives the cumulative percentage of the total income accruing to the lowest percentiles of the population. *A* corresponds to a more unequal distribution than *B*, since with *A*, the poorest groups have a smaller percentage of total income. Lorenz curves frequently cross. It is not clear whether *B* or *C* is more equal.

income this poorest 1 percent has, what percentage the poorest 2 percent has, etc. We plot these numbers in Figure 10.5. The curves plotting the percentage of national income earned by the various income groups within the population are known as **Lorenz curves.** If there were complete equality, the poorest 5 percent would have 5 percent of the national income. With a great deal of inequality, the poorest 5 percent has a negligible percentage of national income. Curve *A* represents a very unequal distribution, while curve *B* represents a fairly equal income distribution.

More generally, we say that if one Lorenz curve lies inside that of another, the distribution of income corresponding to the second is more equal than the distribution corresponding to the first.[13] Unfortunately, just as we saw earlier that the Pareto principle provides insufficient guidance for most policy purposes, ascertaining whether one Lorenz curve lies inside another is often only of limited usefulness, for two reasons. The first is that frequently the criterion is not satisfied. That is, one Lorenz curve crosses that of the other (*B* and *C* in Figure 10.5). Equally important, we often are called upon to make trade-offs between inequality and mean income. How much is society willing to pay for a reduction in inequality? These are quantitative ques-

[13] See A. B. Atkinson, "On the Measurement of Inequality," *Journal of Economic Theory* 2(1970):224–63 for a more extensive discussion of the concept of greater income inequality.

tions, requiring a numerical measure of inequality. If one Lorenz curve lies inside another, we can say that one income distribution was more unequal than another, but this provides no quantitative measurement of the difference.

Gini Coefficient. One commonly used measure of the difference between income distributions is the Gini coefficient. We showed earlier that the closer to the diagonal that a Lorenz curve is, the more equalitarian is the distribution of income. We can measure the distance from the diagonal by the area between the curve and the diagonal. Twice that area is called the Gini coefficient. When the area is 0, the Gini coefficient is 0, and there is no inequality; when the area is ½, all of the income is concentrated in the wealthiest individual, and the Gini coefficient is 1. Thus the Gini coefficient must lie between 0 and 1. For the United States and most other developed countries, the Gini coefficient is around .3 (and has not changed much in recent decades).

The Poverty Index. Another measure that is commonly employed in policy analysis is the percentage of the population that falls below the poverty line. The poverty line is defined as some "minimal" subsistence level of income. Exactly what that means, of course, is not clear, since individuals at the poverty line in the United States have incomes that far exceed the average level of income of individuals in most poorer countries.

The poverty index, like the Gini coefficient, does not correspond to any utility (or social welfare) function. It has a number of peculiar properties. It does not pay any attention to the extent to which individuals are below the poverty line, or the extent to which they are above the poverty line. It simply counts the fraction of the population that lies below a particular level.

SUMMARY

1. Cost-benefit analysis provides a systematic set of procedures by which the government can assess whether to undertake some projects or program and, when there is a choice of projects or programs, which project or program should be undertaken.

2. Private cost-benefit analysis entails determining the consequences (inputs and outputs) associated with the project, evaluating these using market prices to calculate the net profit in each year, and, finally, discounting profits in future years to calculate the present discounted value of profits.

3. Social cost-benefit analysis involves the same procedures as private cost-benefit analysis, except that a broader range of consequences is taken into account, and the prices at which inputs and outputs are evaluated may not be market prices, either because the inputs and outputs are not marketed (so market prices do not exist) or, due to a market failure, because market prices do not accurately reflect marginal social costs and benefits.

4. When the government makes available a good or service that was not previously available (e.g., constructs a bridge across a river) or provides a public good, the value of the project to an individual is measured by the consumer surplus it generates; this is the area under the (compensated) demand curve.

5. The government has to make inferences (based on market data or observed behavior) concerning the valuation of nonmarketed consequences—e.g., lives and time saved.

6. The rate of discount used by the government to evaluate projects may differ from that used by private firms.

7. To evaluate risky projects, the certainty equivalent of the benefits and costs needs to be calcualted.

8. Distributional considerations may be introduced into evaluations, either by weighing the benefits accruing to different groups differently or by assessing the impact on some measure of inequality.

KEY CONCEPTS

Discounting, discount factor   Social rate of discount
Present discounted value   Intergenerational distribution
Compensated demand curve   Certainty equivalent
Shadow or social prices   Risk discount factor
Consumer surplus   Risk premium
Cost-effectiveness   Distributional weights
Crowding out   Lorenz curve

QUESTIONS AND PROBLEMS

1. Consider a project that costs $100,000 and yields a return of $30,000 for five years. At the end of the fifth year, there is a cost of $20,000 to dispose of the waste from the project. Should the project be undertaken if the discount rate is 0? 10 percent? 15 percent? The interest rate at which the net present discounted value of the project is zero is referred to as the *internal rate of return* of the project.

2. Assume there is uncertainty about the costs of disposing of the waste; there is a fifty-fifty chance that they will be $10,000 and $30,000. Discuss how this uncertainty affects the cost-benefit calculation (if the government is risk-neutral? risk-averse?).

3. Assume now that there are two groups in the population. Each contributes equally to the cost of the project, but two-thirds of the benefits accrue to the richer group. Discuss how this alters the cost-benefit calculation. Under what circumstances will the decision to undertake the project be altered?

4. Assume that the government has a choice now between undertaking the given project and undertaking a larger project. Assume if it spends an additional $100,000 returns will be increased by $25,000 and disposal costs in the final year will increase by $20,000. Which project should be undertaken if the discount rate is 0? 10 percent? 15 percent? In the case where there are two groups in the population, how are your answers affected if two-thirds of the incremental benefits go to the poor (with the incremental costs being shared equally, as before?)

5. Discuss why, under each of these circumstances, a social cost-benefit analysis might differ from a private cost-benefit analysis: a) the unemployment rate is 10 percent; b) the government has imposed a tariff on the importation of textiles; c) the government has imposed a quota on the importation of oil; d) the government has imposed a tax on interest income; e) the government has imposed price controls on natural gas; f) the government has regulated airlines, so that prices exceed the competitive levels.

6. For each of the following projects, what benefits or costs might be included in a social cost-benefit analysis that might be excluded from a private cost-benefit analysis: a) a hydroelectric project; b) a steel mill; c) a chemical plant; d) a project to improve car safety; e) a training program to improve the skills of minority workers in a firm? How might your answers be affected by changes in legislation (e.g., concerning manufacturers' liabilities for automobile accidents, legislation imposing fines on polluters, etc.)?

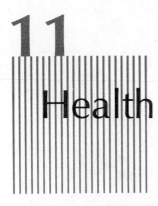

11
Health

Expenditures on health have risen from 6 percent of GNP in 1966 to more than 10 percent today. Federal government outlays have contributed much to this rise: from 1974 to 1984 they increased nearly fourfold. Figure 11.1 provides a detailed look at the increasing expenditures on health care. Though some of this can be attributed to inflation, and some to an increase in population, increases in real per capita expenditures account for 25 percent of the change.[1] Not only have health expenditures taken an increasingly larger share of government expenditures, rising from 5 percent in 1960 to more than twice that by the early 1980s, but the government has taken on increasing responsibility for financing medical expenditures.

Were these events coincidental, or did the government expenditures "cause" the increase in total expenditures and in the cost of medical services? Are we spending too much on health? And are we getting as much "health" as we can for what we spend? Do we have an equitable system for the provision of medical services?

These questions have been at the center of a political debate during the past decade. There is concern that even today some individuals receive inadequate medical services. Prior to 1965, there were two large groups that received much less medical care than others—the aged and the poor. These are now covered by the medicare and medicaid programs, respectively. There remain, however, some gaps, most notably for the unemployed. There is also concern with the rapid rise in hospital costs; since 1967 these have increased at almost twice the rate of inflation.

There is widespread agreement that something should be done. Those who are particularly concerned with gaps in insurance coverage advocate

[1] *Health Care Financing Review* 5 (1984).

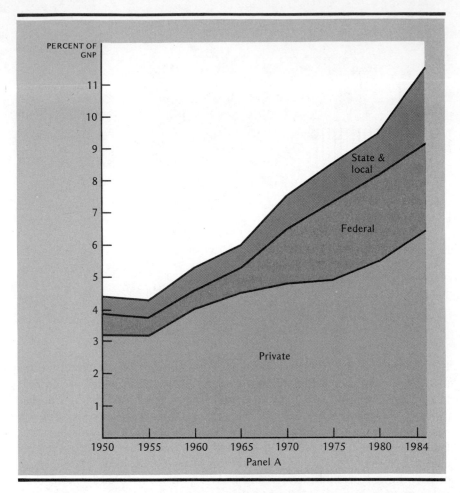

11.1 RISING EXPENDITURES ON HEALTH CARE Panel A shows national health expenditures by source of funds as a percentage of GNP. Panel B shows the increase in federal

greater government involvement in the provision of medical services and have put forward proposals for a national health insurance program. Some of those who are concerned with the high cost of medical care believe government regulation is required.

There are others who believe that the government is more a part of the problem than the solution; they feel that the present system has led to excessive utilization of medical services, that the marginal benefit of medical services is less than its marginal cost.

There is also concern with the budgetary consequences of the present medicare and medicaid programs. There is widespread belief that in the not too distant future, unless something is done, there will be a crisis in medicare. The social security administration has projected the revenues to be received from the tax that is supposed to finance medicare and compared it to the projected expenditures. Under the assumption of no changes in either benefits or taxes, a projected deficit of $5.7 billion in 1988 will grow by 1995 to a deficit of $60.9 billion. The cumulative deficit by 1995 is estimated to

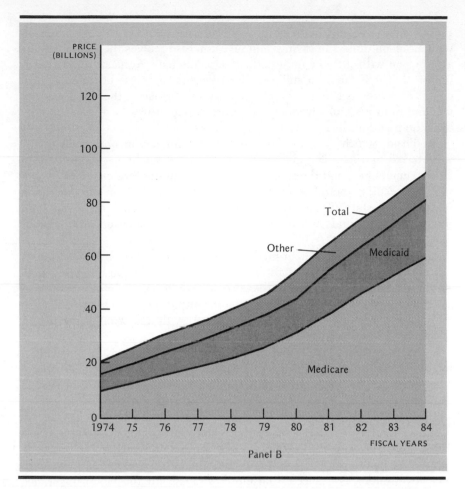

PRICE
(BILLIONS)

120

100

80

60

40

20

0

Total

Other

Medicaid

Medicare

1974 75 76 77 78 79 80 81 82 83 84

FISCAL YEARS

Panel B

outlays for health. SOURCE: *Health Care Financing Review*, 1984; *The Budget in Brief*, FY 1984.

be more than a quarter of a trillion dollars. To break even in the period 1983–2007 it is estimated that tax rates will have to rise between .4 and 2.5 percentage points. (These taxes are part of the social security tax. Currently the rate is 2.9 percent; the increase would bring them to between 3.3 and 5.4 percent.) And to break even in the period 2007–2031, rates will have to go to 8.8 percent. (The entire social security tax, including the part designated to finance retirement, is now only 14.1 percent.)

AN OUTLINE OF GOVERNMENT MEDICAL PROGRAMS

The federal government has played a role in medical expenditures for a long time. For instance, since 1948 the Hill-Burton construction grants have provided for federal support for the construction and renovation of hospitals. But today four programs represent the vast majority of public expenditures in health care, and of these four, two are less than three decades old.

The largest of the programs is **medicare,** which provides medical care for those over sixty-five. Eligibility for medicare is based solely on age; a person with a million dollars in savings and investments receives the same benefits as a person with little or no wealth. Recipients have to make some contribution, but it is far from sufficient for covering the costs of their medical care. The rest comes from a 2.9 percent payroll tax (part of the social security tax) and from general revenues. Medicare expenditures have risen rapidly over the past decade.

Medicaid, which provides for medical care for low-income individuals, was started in 1965. The eligibility standards are set by each state within federal guidelines, and the state and local communities are required to provide between 20 and 50 percent of the funds, depending on the per capita income of the state. These expenditures too have grown at a rapid rate, and the resulting demands on local and state resources have posed serious problems.

Another major government medical program is that run by the Veterans Administration. The VA hospitals provide medical care for those injured while serving in the armed forces; but they provide medical care for other veterans as well. Increases in these VA hospital expenditures have kept pace with those of the medical expenditures in general, with a sevenfold increase in the years between 1962 and 1982.

A fourth category of expenditures, for medical research and teaching, increased rapidly in the 1950s and 1960s but in real terms declined somewhat during recent years (by approximately 20 percent from 1975 to 1982).[2]

TAX EXPENDITURES

These four programs of direct assistance are not the only forms of public support for health care. There are, in addition, two major categories of indirect government assistance. If an employer pays for the health insurance costs of his employee, the expenditure is not treated as taxable income by the employee; nor does it enter the base for the payroll tax. It is *as if* the government simply allowed the individual to deduct all of his expenditures on health insurance.[3] Obviously, this greatly encourages expenditures on health insurance. The extent to which it reduces the effective cost of health insurance depends on the individual's marginal tax bracket—that is, on how much extra tax he would have had to pay if the firm had simply given him the extra income rather than spending it on health insurance. Assume, for instance, that the firm is currently spending $1000 on health insurance for an employee who is in the 25 percent marginal bracket—that is, if his income increases by $1,000, his taxes increase by $250. Accordingly, if the firm had paid the worker the $1,000 directly, his taxes would have gone up by $250. Economists call the $250 a **tax expenditure** because it is the same as if the government taxed income fully but then gave the individual a grant of $250 for each $1,000 that he spent on medical insurance. The individual would, of course, be indifferent when choosing between this system and the current

---

[2] Using the medical care price index.

[3] Individuals, however, are not allowed to deduct their medical insurance premiums; it is only insurance that is paid for by the employer that receives the favorable treatment.

system, and the government (apart from the possibly larger administrative cost) would too. But the budget would look quite different. Revenues would be up, but expenditures would be up by exactly the same amount. Tax expenditures on employer-financed medical insurance amounted to $21 billion in 1983.

The second major category of indirect assistance, or tax expenditures, for health is the income tax deduction for medical expenses. Now, only medical expenses in excess of 5 percent of the individual's income can be deducted, up from the 3 percent it had been for several years before that. The estimated tax expenditure for 1985 in this category is about $3½ billion.

Tax expenditures encourage both health insurance purchases and medical expenditures. They effectively lower the price the individual must pay for insurance, as depicted in Figure 11.2A. The employer is concerned only with the total cost of compensation, what it costs him to employ a worker. The employee who would have purchased $750 worth of insurance anyway is indifferent to having his income reduced by $1,000 and having the employer provide the insurance. But if his employer does this the employer saves $250. Assume the individual supplements the hospital insurance provided by his employer with a $75 accident policy. If the employer decides to provide this policy too, the individual is willing to take up to a $100 wage cut. It obviously pays the employer to provide the insurance.

Consider now a policy that the individual feels is worth only $75 but that costs $95. The individual is willing to pay only $75 for the policy. It still pays the firm to provide the policy, for by offering it, the firm can reduce wages by $100 ($75 after tax is equivalent to $100 before tax), and the policy costs only $95. The tax system effectively reduces the price of hospital insurance by 25 percent. Even if the insurance company is very inefficient and spends considerable resources to administer the program, it still pays the firm to provide the insurance.

The effect of tax deductibility of medical expenditures on the demand for health care can be similarly analyzed. Consider an individual who spends more than 5 percent of his income on medical expenses. If he is in the 25 percent marginal tax bracket and decides to spend an additional $100, it costs him only $75—that is, because he can deduct the $100, his taxes go down by $25, and thus he has $75 less to spend on other goods. If the individual has an income level that puts him in the 50 percent marginal tax bracket, to purchase an additional $100 of medical services costs him only $50. The price of medical services is cut in half. In Figure 11.2B we have drawn a demand curve for medical services. It is clear that by lowering the price by 50 percent, the demand for medical services will be increased.

Insurance also encourages individuals to consume more medical services than they otherwise would, since they have to pay a relatively small proportion of hospital costs and only a fraction of many doctor and other medical expenses. Thus government tax expenditures lead to higher consumption of medical services, both because of the resulting greater insurance coverage and because many of these expenses not covered by insurance are deductible from the income tax.

There is some doubt about how significant these effects are. Their impact depends on how elastic the demand curve is. If the demand is very inelas-

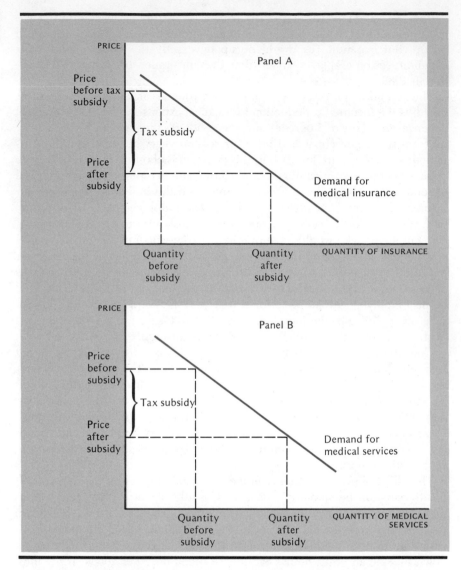

11.2 EFFECTS OF TAX POLICY ON DEMAND FOR MEDICAL CARE AND MEDI-CAL INSURANCE (A) The tax subsidy of medical insurance increases the demand for medical insurance. (B) The tax subsidy on medical expenditures increases the demand for medical expenditures.

tic—if most medical expenditures are not voluntary but are dictated by the health condition—the effect on the demand for medicine is very small. If the demand is elastic, as in cosmetic surgery, where the medical service provided is not essential to the well-being of the individual, then lowering the effective price can have a substantial effect.

The price elasticity of hospital care has been estimated by Martin Feld-stein, who served as Chairman of the Council of Economic Advisors from

All Persons	Income Tax Savings	Medicare*	Medicaid	Total Federal†
Per Capita Government Expenditures				
Poor and near-poor	$ 2	$141	$184	$327
Other low-income	16	99	63	178
Middle-income	43	57	16	116
High-income	90	48	4	142

Total Government Expenditures (billions of dollars)

	$	%	$	%	$	%	$	%
Poor and near-poor	0.1	1	4.3	28	5.6	62	10.0	29
Other low-income	0.5	5	3.1	20	2.0	22	5.6	16
Middle-income	3.5	34	4.7	31	1.3	14	9.5	27
High-income	6.2	60	3.3	21	0.2	2	9.7	28
Total expenditures	10.3	100	15.4	100	9.1	100	34.8	100

Source: Gail R. Wilensky, "Government and the Financing of Health Care," *American Economic Review,* May 1982, p. 205, Table 2.

*Net expenditures (total expenditures less premiums).

†Excludes expenditures from veterans' programs and small federal programs. The definitions of income groups are as follows: The "poor" include those whose family income was less than or equal to the 1977 poverty level as well as those whose income was between 101 and 125 percent of that level. "Other low-income" includes those whose income is 1.26 to 2 times the poverty level, "middle-income" is 2.01 to 4 times the poverty level, and "high-income" is 4.01 times the poverty level or more. For a family of four in 1977, these four groups distribute as follows: less than $8,000 to $9,999, $10,000 to $15,999, $16,000 to $31,999, and greater than $32,000. The percentages of the population in each group are 14, 15, 39, and 32 percent, respectively.

1982 to 1984, at about .7.[4] This means that an individual in the 25 percent marginal tax bracket consumes 17.5 percent ($.7 \times 25$) more hospital services than he would without the subsidy. Other studies have obtained lower price elasticities, between .2 and .7.

There is concern not only about the efficiency consequences of our tax expenditures on the excessive consumption of medical services it induces but also about their equity.

In Table 11.1 we summarize the federal expenditures on health. The table shows that though direct expenditures have a significant redistributive impact, the benefits of the tax expenditures largely accrue to higher-income individuals.[5] The net effect is that the lowest level of total governmental expenditures (including tax expenditures) *per capita* is received by middle-income individuals.

MARKET FAILURES

How do we account for the role of government in the provision of medical services? What have been the market failures? There are different explanations for different categories of federal expenditures.

[4] Martin Feldstein, "Hospital Cost Inflation: A Study in Nonprofit Price Dynamics," *American Economic Review* 61 (1971): 853–72. See also R. Rosett and L. Huang, "The Effect of Health Insurance on the Demand for Medical Care," *Journal of Political Economy* 81 (1973): 281–305.

[5] The importance of the tax deductibility provisions may have been reduced by the tax law changes in 1983, which severely limited these deductions.

Medical research, like other forms of research, is often close to a pure public good. While some innovations, like drugs, can be patented, most discoveries are not patentable, and even when they are, it may be questionable whether it is desirable to do so. The increased prices for these drugs may result in a decrease in their utilization. And there is considerable concern over whether a disproportionate fraction of private research expenditures goes to attempting to invent around a patent—to come up with a drug that is just as good as the patented drug but is not covered under the existing patents.

There are externalities associated with certain diseases, particularly contagious diseases. These may make it desirable to have regulations concerning quarantining and compulsory vaccinations and provide part of the rationale for the Public Health Service.

The expenditures on veterans' medical benefits can be viewed as a delayed form of compensation; though the government provides relatively low salaries to those who serve in the military, it provides medical insurance extending beyond the period of service. This insurance seems particularly justified in connection with service-related medical needs.[6]

The tax deductibility of medical expenses is justified on the grounds that the appropriate basis of taxation is some measure of ability to pay. Medical expenses reduce an individual's ability to pay (if they are involuntary). Thus income minus medical expenditures (in excess of some given fraction of income) may provide a better measure of ability to pay than does income alone. To put it another way, the tax system tries to offset the "unjust tax" imposed on individuals by fate, in the form of medical expenditure.

Finally, medicare arose partly because of the failure of the market to provide adequate insurance for the elderly.

Inequality and the Government Provision of Medical Services

The most important explanation for the increased role of the government in subsidizing medical services arises from the concern about the consequences of inequality. There is widespread belief that no individual, regardless of his income, should be denied access to adequate medical care. If choices have to be made, they should be made on the basis not of wealth but of other attributes, like age, or the likelihood of success of the operation, or perhaps random selection. This view holds that medical services are different from clothes, movies, automobiles, and most other commodities. Just as the right to vote should not be subjected to the marketplace (individuals are not allowed to buy and sell their votes), and just as when there was a draft, individuals were not allowed to buy their way out of their military obligations (though during the Civil War they were) the right to live—access to medical services—should not be controlled by the market. This view is known as *specific equalitarianism*.[7]

Not all economists agree about whether medical services should be treated

---

[6]The principle that employers should be responsible for injuries to workers while on the job has been extended to most workers in the private sector. Employers are required to provide "workers' compensation insurance."

[7]J. Tobin, "On Limiting the Domain of Inequality," *Journal of Law and Economics* 13 (1970): 263–77.

differently than other commodities. Many hold that they should not: those
who have more money and want to spend it on getting health care should be allowed to do so. Those who hold this view often point out that the relationship between medical care and life (death) is very weak; that other factors, such as smoking, drinking, food, and particularly education, seem to play an equally, if not more, important role in determining an individual's life span and other health indicators.[8] In Britain, the government provides free medical care to all individuals and has done so since shortly after World War II. One study of the British experience showed that the National Health Service has not reduced class differences in infant mortality, maternal mortality, or overall life expectancy.

Still, a third view—toward which many Western democracies seem to be gravitating—is that everyone should have the right to a certain minimal level of care. The provision of medicaid can be thought of as reflecting that view. At the same time, those who hold this view are often concerned with the consequences for economic efficiency of alternative methods of ensuring that everyone has access to a certain minimal level of medical care.

Though the concerns we have just sketched out provide part of the explanation for the current role of the government, there may be other market failures, which provide (according to some policy analysts) grounds for government intervention of one form or another. Whether this is the case or not, it is necessary to understand why medical markets differ from conventional competitive markets if one is to assess the consequences of various policy proposals.

Why Medical Markets Do Not Satisfy the Standard Conditions for Well-Behaved Competitive Markets

The standard competitive market theory makes several critical assumptions:

a) There are many sellers, each of which is seeking to maximize its profits.

b) The commodity that is being bought and sold is homogeneous.

c) The buyers are well informed: they know the prices and qualities being sold by all vendors.

Under these conditions, if a firm discovers a better way of producing some commodity, it simply lowers its price, stealing customers away from other producers. Production is always efficient, and prices always reflect the production costs of the most efficient producers.

When these conditions are not satisfied, inefficient producers may survive, and prices may exceed costs of production. For instance, if there is a monopolist, he charges a price at which marginal revenue equals marginal costs. Since marginal revenue is less than price, the monopolist's charges will exceed his (marginal) costs of production.

When the commodity is heterogeneous and individuals are not perfectly well informed, then it is difficult for an individual to tell whether a lower price signals a better buy or a lower-quality commodity. And when consum-

[8]For an articulation of this view, see V. R. Fuchs, "From Bismarck to Woodcock: The 'Irrational' Pursuit of National Health Insurance," *Journal of Law and Economics* 19 (1976): 347–59, or V. Fuchs, *Who Shall Live? Health Economics and Social Choice* (New York: Basic Books, 1975).

Table 11.2 DIFFERENCES BETWEEN MEDICAL MARKETS AND STANDARD COMPETITIVE MARKETS

Standard Competitive Markets	Medical Markets
Many sellers	Only limited number of hospitals (outside of major cities)
Profit-maximizing firms	Not-for-profit
Homogeneous commodities	Heterogeneous commodities
Well-informed buyers	Ill-informed buyers

ers are uninformed about prices, firms may be able to increase their prices above the competitive level with only a limited loss of customers. Unfortunately, none of the conditions required for a well-functioning competitive market is satisfied in medical markets, as we see in Table 11.2.

While there is some presumption that the consumer is reasonably well informed when he purchases a car or a TV (and there are a number of sources from which he can readily obtain information), when individuals go to a doctor, what they are buying, in large measure, is the doctor's knowledge or information. The patient must rely on the doctor's judgment about what medicine is required, whether an operation is advisable, etc. It is far more difficult to appraise various doctors than to appraise various television sets. This is one reason that the government has long taken a role in licensing doctors and regulating the drugs they can administer to their patients.[9]

Limited Competition

Imperfect information has the effect of decreasing the effective degree of competition.[10] A firm selling a standard commodity, like a Zenith television, knows that it can attract customers away from other stores by lowering its price. Customers can easily ascertain where they are getting the best value for money.

By contrast, potential patients who saw a doctor with lower prices than his competitors might infer that he was not in great demand and was therefore trying to attract more customers; but the lack of demand for his services might suggest to them that he was not a good doctor.

By the same token, the heterogeneity of medical services makes price and quality comparisons difficult and thus inhibits the effective dissemination of information. My neighbor may have been pleased with the medical treatment that he obtained from his doctor, but if his medical problems are different from mine, that is no assurance that I will be pleased. And if I hear that one doctor charges more than another doctor, to evaluate whether one is a better buy I have to know precisely what services were performed.

The practices of the medical profession may compound the inevitable limitations of competition resulting from imperfect information. Doctors are not allowed to advertise. In other contexts, restrictions on advertising have been

---

[9] Kenneth Arrow has emphasized the importance of imperfect information in medical markets. See K. J. Arrow, "Uncertainty and the Welfare Economics of Medical Care," *American Economic Review* 53 (1963):941–73.

[10] See, for instance, S. Salop, "Information and Monopolistic Competition," *American Economic Review*, May 1976, pp. 240–45.

shown to raise prices (because they inhibit competition.) Thus, several states
now allow advertising for eyeglasses, and in those states, there has been a dramatic decrease in the price of eyeglasses.

There are other measures by which doctors can attempt to restrict price competition. It has been suggested, for instance, that "lowering fees might provoke one's colleagues to deny a surgeon hospital privileges or seek to damage his reputation."[11]

The fact that doctors often need to consult with each other and that they share hospital facilities (and often other interests) may also reduce competitive pressures. As Adam Smith put it, perhaps too strongly in *The Wealth of Nations*, "People of the same trade seldom meet together, even for merriment and diversion, but the conversation ends in a conspiracy against the public, or in some contrivance to raise prices."

Moreover, there is also limited competition among hospitals. Most smaller communities have only a few hospitals. In the event of an emergency, the individual seldom is in a position to choose from among many. And even when there is time to make a choice, the choice is made not by the individual but by his doctor.

Consequences of Limited Information and Limited Competition

These limitations on information and competition that we have just described mean that the medical market may behave quite differently from markets where competition is more effective. For instance, conventional competition theory would predict that an increase in the supply of doctors would lower the price of medical services. During the past decade the number of doctors has almost doubled; it has increased much faster than demand; yet prices have not fallen. The consequence is extensive underemployment of many doctors, particularly surgeons. As long as a decade ago, Victor Fuchs, one of the nation's leading health economists, cited as evidence for a "surgeon surplus" a comprehensive detailed study of one surburban New York community, in which the typical surgeon had a work load that was only one-third of what experts viewed as a full schedule. (These results were consistent with calculations for the state and country as a whole, dividing the number of operations by the number of surgeons). Indeed, some have argued that increasing the number of surgeons leads to an increase in the number of operations rather than a lowering of price.[12]

Questions of whether an operation is advisable or necessary are, of course, debatable. Most doctors do not recommend operations simply to increase their own income. But in making a professional judgment about whether an operation is desirable, the amount of time that they have on their hands and the pressure from other patients who may need the operation more has an important effect. And the "customers" with limited information are likely to have surgery if their surgeon recommends it.[13]

[11] V. Fuchs, *Who Shall Live?*
[12] Ibid.
[13] Although seeking second opinions before undergoing surgery may improve matters, it is far from a solution. In a community in which there is a larger supply of physicians, "standard practice"—the conditions under which operations are recommended—adjusts.

Malpractice Suits

Another consequence of the fact that consumers are uninformed purchasers is that they are frequently disappointed with what they have purchased. In the case of an individual who purchased a bad brand of TV, this does not have significant consequences. But in the case of medicine, an individual who believes that the doctor has provided him with inappropriate medical care can sue, and in recent years there has been a rash of such malpractice suits. These greatly encourage the doctor to provide excessive care.

The doctor can be sued if he fails to prescribe some drug, even though the probability of its having a beneficial effect is low. If he fails to administer some test, even if the costs relative to the information it yields are high, he can be sued. Since most of the costs of the test or drug are borne by a third party (the insurance company) he has every incentive to administer the test or to prescribe the drug, even though an informed patient would have been unwilling to do so if he had to pay for the test or drug himself.

Both the number of malpractice suits and the size of settlements in the United States have increased rapidly in the past few years. In 1983, 16 malpractice claims were filed for every 100 doctors, 20 percent more than in the previous decade. The value of awards totaled $2 billion in 1983, up 33 percent from the previous year and double the figure for 1980. The American Medical Association estimated that the total costs of tests and treatments prescribed because of fear of a malpractice suit was between $15 and $40 billion in 1983.

Absence of Profit Incentive

The final difference between medical markets and standard competitive markets is the absence of a profit motive: the vast majority of hospitals in the United States are not-for-profit institutions. They view their objective not as minimizing the cost of delivering medical care (or maximizing profits), but as maximizing the quality of medical care they can provide. The consequences of the absence of profit incentives are exacerbated by the manner in which they are reimbursed for their expenses by insurance companies; in most cases hospitals are paid whatever they charge.

Recent changes in the medicare program provide reimbursement to hospitals on the basis of a diagnosis—e.g., the reimbursement for care of a mild heart attack patient is fixed, regardless of the length of stay in the hospital and the hospital's actual costs. While advocates of this new system believe it will provide hospitals with a strong incentive to reduce expenditures, critics worry that it will adversely affect the quality of medical care. Hospitals may refuse to provide care for under-reimbursed diagnoses. They may also be encouraged to discharge patients prematurely because while they may be able to be reimbursed for a return stay, they could not be reimbursed for an extended stay.

INSURANCE

To many people, the major problems with the medical industry relate to insurance. Although an efficient private market for health insurance was slow to develop (major medical insurance covering large medical risks did not become widely available until after World War II), with the encouragement of the tax laws we described earlier, the majority of those working were covered by the early 1960s. This still left some important gaps: the unemployed, the poor, the aged and those suffering catastrophic illnesses. Medicare and medicaid were enacted to remedy the problems of the aged and the poor so that today over 90 percent of the population is covered, either by public programs or by private plans. There have been recurrent proposals to provide some kind of health coverage for the unemployed, though there is none in place now. And even major medical insurance policies frequently have limits on their coverage, so that certain catastrophic illnesses are not covered.

The Importance of Insurance

The basic objective of insurance is to reduce the risks that individuals have to bear, to shift them to those who are more willing (in a better position) to bear these risks.

Consider an individual who faces a 10 percent probability of having an accident that will cost him $1,000 in medical services. We say his average (or "expected") medical expenditures are $.10 \times \$1,000 = \$100$. Without insurance an individual with a $10,000 income faces a 10 percent chance of having only $9,000 to spend on goods other than medicine. If he has the accident, he may find it difficult to meet his house payments, his car payments, etc. Most individuals do not like facing such risky prospects; we say that they are risk-averse. They would prefer paying an insurance company $100 every year, whether or not they have an accident, and having the insurance company pay the costs of an accident if it occurs. If there were no administrative costs, the insurance company would, on average, break even. But most individuals are willing to pay considerably more than $100 to have the insurance company assume the risk. In a competitive insurance market, the insurance will be provided at a premium that allows the insurance company to just break even, taking into account administrative costs; thus, if administrative costs amount to 10 percent of the average payout, the insurance premium will be $110. A very risk-averse individual would have been willing to pay, say, $150 to have the insurance company assume the risks for him. The difference—$40—is the perceived gain from insurance coverage.

The magnitude of the gain from insurance depends on the size of the risk and the extent to which it can be anticipated. For instance, most pregnancies, though very costly, are planned; they do not represent an unpredictable risk. It is only the complications that sometimes attend pregnancy that give rise to a risk.[14]

---

[14] Many standard insurance policies cover the standard pregnancy costs but exclude complications, precisely the kind of risk that should be insured. Similarly, routine doctor's visits are both small in cost and fairly predictable in occurrence. The costs of administering an insurance program to cover such costs far exceeds the benefits from any slight risk reduction. Insurance should not be provided for such risks.

The Consequences of Insurance

Though insurance performs an important role, it has one important consequence: insurance encourages the individual to spend more on medical services than he otherwise would.

If an individual knows that his insurance company will pay 80 percent of the cost of staying in the hospital an extra day, he may decide to stay in an extra day, though he really doesn't need to. And he will not object much if the hospital charges $300 a day for a room rather than $200, knowing that the extra charge will cost him only $20 a day. His doctors will not hesitate to administer even a very expensive drug, with a low probability of providing relief, knowing that his patient will not have to pay the bill.

The provision of insurance has effectively lowered the individual's marginal costs of obtaining additional medical care. If the insurance company pays 80 percent of the individual's medical expenses, an individual can obtain $1 worth of medical services for 20 cents. It is as if the price of medical services is reduced by 80 percent.

Thus the provision of insurance leads individuals to purchase medical services to the point where the marginal return is far less than the marginal social cost of these services; they purchase medical services to the point where the marginal return is equal to their private marginal cost, the extra amount they have to pay, which is a small fraction of the total extra costs.

We illustrate this in Figure 11.3, where we have drawn a demand curve for medical services. The horizontal axis can be interpreted as either the quantity or quality of services. At a lower price, individuals demand more and better medical services. We have also drawn the marginal cost of providing extra (higher-quality) medical services. For simplicity, we have assumed that these costs are fixed. But the individual who has insurance coverage does not have to pay the entire marginal costs, only a fraction of the marginal costs. Assume the insurance policy pays 80 percent of his hospital costs. Then the price he pays is only 20 percent of the value of the resources he uses. This induces him to increase his demand from Q_0 to Q_1. But what is of particular concern is that the value of the extra services consumed is less than the marginal costs. This results in an inefficiency. The gray triangle *ABC* measures the extra amount individuals would be willing to pay for an increase in output from Q_0 to Q_1. The extra cost to society of the increase is the rectangle *ABEC*: the extra costs exceed the extra benefits by the colored triangle *BCE*. The magnitude of this distortion depends again on the price elasticity of medical services. If Feldstein's estimate of a price elasticity of hospital services of .7 is correct, a policy where the insurance company pays 80 percent of the costs increases expenditures by more than 50 percent.

Moral Hazard

The problems arising from the fact that the provisions of insurance affect behavior is sometimes called the problem of **moral hazard.** In current usage, the term has little to do with morals. The term arises from the view that it would be immoral for an individual to undertake an action that would lead to the receipt of an insurance benefit; it would, for instance, be immoral for

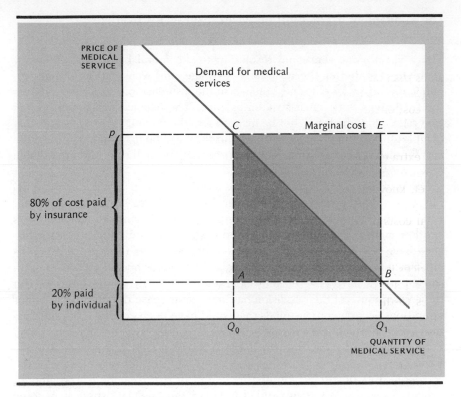

11.3   INSURANCE AND THE COST OF MEDICAL SERVICES Insurance lowers cost of medical services to individuals and increases demand.

an individual to set fire to his house simply to collect his fire insurance. But though such actions might be widely held to be immoral—and indeed are illegal—there is a much broader category of incentive issues, such as the care the individual should take to prevent a fire. The term *moral hazard* has come to refer to this whole broad range of incentive effects.

Insurance affects not only the quantity and quality of medical care that individuals purchase when sick. It also may affect their "health mainte-nance" activities. Because individuals do not have to pay all the cost of an illness, they may take insufficient care to prevent it. Would individuals smoke less, or drink less when they drive, if they had to bear all the economic consequences of their actions?

The fact that the rapid growth of insurance coverage and the rapid increase in health care expenditures have occurred contemporaneously in the United States suggests to some that the provision of insurance has been a major factor contributing to the growth in expenditures. By 1981, 89 percent of hospital expenses and 62 percent of physicians' fees were paid by insurance companies and the government—by parties other than those receiving the medical services. But the fact that there has been an almost equally rapid growth in expenditures in some countries where there has not been a cor-responding increase in insurance coverage casts doubt on the view that insurance is the sole or even a major culprit.

The Fundamental Trade-off between Insurance Coverage and Incentives

There is, in some sense, no resolution to the moral hazard vs. efficiency problem. The better the insurance coverage, the weaker the normal economic incentives for efficiency; the worse the insurance coverage, the stronger the incentives. One must strike a balance. The balance will entail limited coverage; individuals will not be insured for 100 percent of the costs, for that completely eliminates all incentives; but they will be insured for some of the cost for all large risks. (Efficiency requires that on small risks and predictable costs, there should be no insurance.)

Some of the moral hazard problems can be reduced by greater monitoring, to ensure that unnecessary medical expenditures are not undertaken. But whether the increased costs of improved monitoring are worthwhile is another matter. Some of the increased costs associated with medical insurance have been a consequence of misguided attempts to improve monitoring. For instance, to ensure that only relatively serious operations are covered, some policies have covered only operations occurring in the hospital. But the consequence of this provision has been to increase the number of minor operations occurring in hospitals that could have been conducted in the doctor's office at much less expense.

Many accident policies pay a flat fee. These do not give rise to a moral hazard problem (other than that associated with the incentive to avoid the accident). But this greatly limits the extent of risk reduction. The amount provided may be less than needed to cover the medical expenses of some accidents and more than needed for others. Another way to control expenditure is to delegate more discretion to the physician, but not to pay the physician on the basis of fee-for-service (which may lead to an incentive for overprovision). This is the approach taken by health maintenance organizations (HMOs), which charge a fixed fee for each subscriber rather than a fee for each service.

REFORMS IN HOW MEDICINE IS PROVIDED AND FINANCED

There is more agreement that something should be done about the health care system in the United States than there is about what should be done. The proposed reforms attempt to address problems in two areas: reducing medical costs and ensuring that all individuals have access to adequate medical care.

Reducing the Extent of Insurance Coverage

Many economists believe that the moral hazard problem resulting from the extensive provision of insurance is the central factor explaining the rise in medical costs and expenditures. Private markets, in providing insurance, recognize the critical role of moral hazard; they deal with it by providing only limited insurance coverage—for instance, by insisting on what are called **co-insurance** clauses, where the purchaser of the insurance still must pay a significant fraction of the costs. Critics of governmental policy claim that in designing the medicaid and medicare programs, insufficient attention was paid to the problem of moral hazard, and that more extensive co-insurance requirements should be introduced. Moreover, the special tax treatment of employer-financed health insurance programs has led to excessive provision of private health insurance, and removing these tax subsidies would reduce the level of private insurance and again induce individuals to pay more attention to costs.

Those who believe that the demand for medical services is fairly price-inelastic but that the demand is affected greatly by what physicians prescribe believe that requiring individuals to pay even 20 percent or 25 percent of the costs will not go a long way to resolving the problems facing the industry.

Reforming the Manner in Which Hospitals Are Reimbursed

Critics of the medicare and medicaid programs and the major private insurance firm, Blue Cross-Blue Shield, claim that the way that reimbursements—e.g., for hospital expenses—are determined leaves little incentive for efficiency. Reimbursements are based on costs of the hospital, up to some maximum determined by the charges of all hospitals imposed in the previous year. There is no incentive in this system for the hospital to reduce its costs below the maximum reimbursible level. If the fees for different services—the treatment of different diseases—were fixed, each hospital would have an incentive to lower the costs of providing the service, since it could keep any cost savings as profit. This is, of course, the kind of incentive that works in other markets for firms to devise less expensive ways of providing goods and services. Such a system was introduced into the medicare program in 1983.

There are many who do not believe that these incentive structures are appropriate for medical services. First, medical services are so complex that it is difficult to define precisely the service to be associated with each fee. Removing a gallstone may be a simple matter with one patient but complicated with another. Profit-maximizing hospitals will have as much of an incentive to cut corners in the quality of the service they provide as to provide the services more efficiently. Critics are also concerned that the system will encourage hospitals to shut down units for which the reimbursements are below their costs.

Supporters of the programs to provide better incentives for cost saving reply that the supervision of hospitals, both by governmental agencies and by the doctors who use the hospitals, is sufficiently great to limit extensive abuse, and they point to the success of several chains of private-for-profit hospitals in lowering the costs of providing certain services.

The fact that most hospitals are not-for-profit reduces the force of these concerns but also suggests that the range of incentives for improving efficiency may be limited, even with a system that is effective in cost reductions for profit-making hospitals.

Economists who worry about the lack of competitiveness of medical markets and the lack of information of consumers do not think these reforms will significantly improve matters.

Regulation

Some individuals believe that costs can be contained by regulating the amount a doctor can charge for certain services. It may be difficult to devise a scheme that both contains costs and maintains quality. The time (and associated care) it takes a doctor to perform a given procedure is variable; if the public program lowers his reimbursement for some service, he may simply spend less time performing it. If there are some services for which the reimbursement is high relative to the minimum time required to perform that service, doctors may perform more of those services. If the fees provided by public insurance are lower than those offered for similar services in the private market, only low-quality doctors may opt to work for those covered by public insurance. The problems of organizing a national health insurance system on the basis of a fee for services were sufficiently formidable that when the United Kingdom established its system, it chose to reimburse general practitioners on the basis of the number of patients served rather than the number of services performed, and it put specialists on salary.[15]

Changing the Organization of the Medical Industry

Those who believe that the primary determinant of the kinds of medical services consumed is the doctor believe that the appropriate remedy entails improving the incentives facing the doctor; what we should be concerned with is the provision of health, not the provision of medicine. To do this efficiently requires undertaking certain preventive procedures. Health maintenance organizations provide comprehensive medical care on the basis of a fixed fee. Doctors are normally on salary. Advocates believe that these organizations have better incentive than traditional medical services to provide "health" in an efficient way, to provide preventive medicine where it pays, to combine out-patient and in-patient services in the appropriate manner.

Health economist Paul Feldstein of the University of Michigan summarizes studies comparing costs showing that, in these organizations, medical expenditures are 10 percent to 40 percent lower than those for persons with comparable insurance coverage using the fee for service delivery system. Hospitalization rates, in particular, are lower.[16]

Given their seeming advantage, why haven't HMOs become more widespread? University of Chicago economist Reuben Kessel argued that doctors use their monopoly powers to prevent their growth, both by denying access to the hospitals they controlled and by inducing state legislatures to pass restrictive legislation.[17] More recently, there has been some encouragement of HMOs at the federal level.

Increasing the Extent of Coverage

Finally, there are those who believe that the most significant problem is that some individuals cannot now obtain adequate medical services. It is clear

---

[15] See R. Zeckhauser and C. Zook for a good discussion of why regulations are likely to be ineffective as a means of cost control. "Failures to Control Health Costs: Departures from First Principles," in *A New Approach to the Economics of Health Care*, ed. M. Olson (Washington, D.C.: American Enterprise Institute for Public Policy Research, 1981).

[16] P. J. Feldstein, *Health Care Economics* (New York: Wiley, 2d ed., 1983). He also cites a study that there is no significant difference in health status between those in such organizations and those with private coverage. M. S. Blumber "Health Status and Health Care Use by Type of Private Health Coverage," *Millbank Memorial Fund Quarterly*, Fall 1980, p. 649.

[17] R. Kessel, "Price Discrimination in Medicine," *Journal of Law and Economics*, October 1958, pp. 20–53.

255
Reforms in
How Medi-
cine Is Pro-
vided and
Financed

Table 11.3 PHYSICIANS' VISITS PER PERSON PER YEAR BY FAMILY INCOME: 1964 AND 1975

	1964		1975	
Age Group	Income	Number of Visits	Income	Number of Visits
All ages	All incomes	4.5	All incomes	5.1
	Under 4,000	4.3	Under 5,000	6.0
	4,000–6,999	4.5	5,000–9,999	5.2
	7,000–9,999	4.7	10,000–14,999	4.8
	10,000 and over	5.1	15,000 and over	4.9
	Ratio, highest to lowest	1.19	Ratio, highest to lowest	0.82

Sources: Department of Health, Education, and Welfare, National Center for Health Statistics, *Volume of Physician Visits by Place of Visit and Type of Service, United States, July 1963–June 1964,* Vital and Health Statistics, series 10, no. 18 (GPO, 1965), pp. 18, 19, 29, and National Center for Health Statistics, *Health, United States, 1976–1977,* DHEW (HRA) 77-1232 (GPO, 1977), p. 265.
From K. Davis and C. Schoen, *Health and the War on Poverty: A Ten-Year Appraisal* (Washington, D.C.: Brookings Institution, 1978).

from Table 11.3 that medicaid and medicare have enabled the poor who are covered by these programs to obtain medical services; indeed, since the cost to them is nothing, it is not surprising that they seem to avail themselves of doctors even more than do those with higher incomes. But there are some gaps.[18] There are those who believe that the gaps are sufficiently large, that the coverage is so haphazard under the present system that it should be replaced by a system of national health insurance. Such proposals are currently receiving little support, largely because legislators are presently concerned about growth in the federal budget. Serious consideration is being given, however, to legislation that would help fill in the gaps.

SUMMARY

1. Though decisions about health are difficult, resource allocations—choices among alternative uses of funds—must be made. Economic analysis may be useful in making those decisions in a systematic and consistent way.

2. Expenditures on medical services, the costs of medical services, and public expenditures on medicine have all risen rapidly in recent years; medical expenditures represent the third largest category of public expenditures, after defense and education; the government now pays half of all health expenditures.

3. The four major public programs are medicare, medicaid, health care for veterans, and public support for research and development. In addition, there are two major categories of tax expenditures: employer-financed health insurance and tax deductibility of medical expenses exceeding a certain level.

4. The health care industry is characterized by several market failures:
   a) Uniformed consumers;

---

[18] Medicaid has never covered more than two-thirds of the poor; increased eligibility standards have reduced that percentage. In 1983, when unemployment peaked, 11 million people who had employer-provided insurance lost that coverage. See Louise B. Russell, "Medical Care," in J. Pechman, ed., *Setting National Priorities* (Washington, D.C.: Brookings Institution, 1983). A study by the Department of Census showed that 15 percent of the population were not covered by health insurance and were not eligible for government assistance (medicaid, medicare, or veterans). Seventy-five percent of the population was covered by private insurance, mostly provided by their employer. Fifty percent of blacks and 30 percent of Hispanics were not covered.

b) Limited competition;

c) Externalities, associated with contagious diseases; and

d) Nonprofit maximizing behavior.

5. Many economists believe that the rapid increase in medical costs arises from the extensive growth of private insurance plus government programs that cover medical expenses.

6. Those who believe that the medical market is competitive believe that if individuals have to bear a larger fraction of the costs, and if hospitals are reimbursed in a way that provides them with an incentive to be efficient and to reduce costs, costs will be reduced.

7. Some of those who believe that the market is not competitive believe that costs should be controlled by regulation. Most economists, however, are skeptical about the likely success of regulation in a market as complex as that for medicine. Many believe that a change in the methods by which medicine is delivered—in particular, the more extensive use of health maintenance organizations—is the most hopeful way of reducing medical costs.

8. There is concern that there are still some large gaps in coverage, particularly for the unemployed and for catastrophic illnesses.

KEY CONCEPTS

Medicare	Specific equalitarianism
Medicaid	Moral hazard
Tax expenditures	Third-party coverage
Co-insurance	

QUESTIONS AND PROBLEMS

1. In what ways is the purchase of medical services similar to the purchase of a car? In what ways is it different?

2. We have noted that there are extensive disagreements about what should be done about how medical care is provided in the United States. To what extent are these differences due to differences in judgments concerning how the market of medical services functions? Be specific. To what extent are these differences due to differences in values?

3. Consider the "market failures" that arise in medical markets and the proposals currently being debated for altering how medical care should be provided in the United States. Discuss the extent to which each of the proposals is aimed at remedying particular market failures.

4. Discuss the effects on the welfare of different individuals and on their demand for medical services of eliminating the deduction for medical expenses and of extending the deduction to make all expenditures deductible.

5. During the past twenty-five years there has been a marked decline in community-run hospitals and an increase in private (for-profit) hospitals. Are there reasons that hospitals should be particularly well- or badly suited to being run publicly? What do you think accounts for these trends?

6. Critics of malpractice suits claim that they have contributed significantly to the rise of medical costs and argue for legislation that would limit the size of awards, limit lawyers' fees, or otherwise discourage such suits. Many lawyers are concerned that any such legislation would impair the rights of those injured by malpractice to be justly compensated for the damages they have incurred. Discuss the equity-efficiency trade-offs. What do you think should be done?

12
Defense

Defense expenditures represent the largest single item of government spending, constituting more than a quarter of the federal government's budget, if we include the expenditures for veterans' benefits and space research.[1]

Military expenditures, both in real terms and as a percentage of GNP, have varied markedly. Following the Vietnam War, there was a marked reduction in military expenditures; military expenditures began to increase under the Carter administration and were further increased under President Reagan. Though as Figure 12.1 illustrates, real expenditures reached an all-time high for peacetime during the Reagan administration, as a percentage of GNP they were still smaller than during the Eisenhower and Kennedy administrations.

Because such a large fraction of military expenditures is for the procurement of new defense weapons systems, the commitments made in the early 1980s will have implications for defense expenditures in the late 1980s. And because these new military systems will require ongoing expenditures in maintenance and in personnel, they have implications for defense budgets into the 1990s. Even if it were decided today to reduce military expenditures, it might take several years before such a changed policy could have significant effects.

Military expenditures in the United States are large, both as a fraction of government expenditures and as a fraction of national income, when compared to expenditures in most other Western countries. However, the United States percentage is not large relative to the Soviet Union, as Figure 12.2 demonstrates.

The issue of whether we are spending enough (or too much) on defense

---

[1] Veterans' benefits may be thought of as deferred compensation for those who previously served in the armed forces. Much (but not all) of space research is motivated by military considerations.

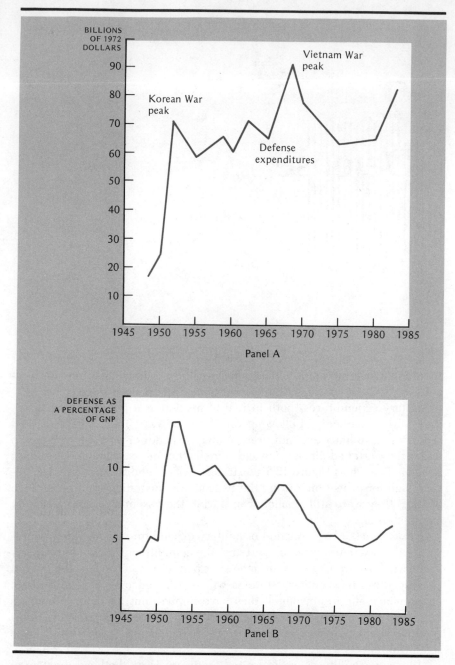

BILLIONS
OF 1972
DOLLARS

Vietnam War
peak

Korean War
peak

Defense
expenditures

Panel A

DEFENSE AS
A PERCENTAGE
OF GNP

Panel B

12.1 U.S. DEFENSE EXPENDITURES Panel A shows national expenditures on defense in constant 1972 prices (using CPI deflator). Panel B shows defense expenditures as a percentage of GNP. SOURCE: *Economic Report of the President*, 1984.

has been one of the most hotly contested political issues in recent years. There are also controversies about whether we are allocating our defense dollars in the best way possible. There have been frequent accusations of inefficiency against the military.

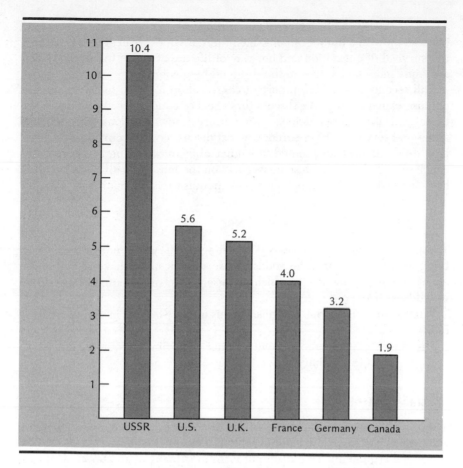

12.2 MILITARY EXPENDITURES AS A PERCENTAGE OF GNP sOURCE: *World Military and Social Expenditures*, 1983.

Defense is one of the few examples of a pure public good. In our discussion of the theory of public goods we suggested that we could decide on how much should be spent on some public good simply by asking individuals for their marginal willingness to pay, how much extra benefit they get out of additional expenditures on a particular public program. Unfortunately, this will not do for defense. Most of us simply do not know how much more protection we buy by spending an extra dollar on defense. We rely on military experts for an assessment of the benefits yielded by further expenditures. But the experts have a natural bias in favor of increased expenditures for the services for which they are responsible.

We rely on experts for judgments concerning the costs of a particular program (say, for a weapons system), for judgments concerning what the program, if successful, would do, and for judgments concerning the responses of others (the Russians) to any action we take. Of course, even if the experts could provide a reliable estimate of the number of lives a particular program would save in a particular contingency, and a reliable estimate of the likelihood of different contingencies, it would not be sufficient to provide a quantitative assessment of the value of a program: we have to know how to place a monetary value on life. Even if one is not loath to do this, it is at best hard to come up with a number upon which there is widespread agreement. And, the survival of our nation and our way of life are at stake; the difficulties of assigning monetary values to these should be obvious.

Still, economics has an important contribution to make to the analysis of defense expenditures. We discuss three sets of issues here. We first discuss the organization of our defense expenditures, how decisions get made and goods and services are procured; we next discuss cost-effectiveness analysis, how different programs aimed at similar objectives can be compared. We conclude the chapter with some remarks on the most difficult question of all: how do we decide how much defense expenditure is enough?

THE ORGANIZATION OF DEFENSE

Those responsible for decisions concerning military expenditures and how the government obtains the goods and services it needs have an important effect on the efficiency with which defense dollars are spent. In this section we address three questions:

What should be the role of civilian versus military experts in shaping defense policy?

How have military procurement practices contributed to inefficiency?

How should the military obtain the personnel it needs?

Civilian Control

There has been a continuing controversy over the extent to which there should be civilian involvement in military decision making.

Several arguments have been put forth in support of greater civilian control. The first is that each branch of the armed forces seems to pursue its own interests. The navy may place greater emphasis on obtaining more aircraft carriers than on obtaining transport ships (the primary benefit of which is to make the army more effective).

Even within each of the forces, established interests may resist new developments that detract from their power. For instance, though the navy recognized the value of Polaris missiles, many of the admirals were afraid that an increased expenditure on Polaris missiles would decrease other naval expenditures, and this initially led them to have limited enthusiasm for the new system. It was Secretary of Defense Robert McNamara who pushed for an increase in the rate of delivery of Polaris missiles, from three to ten Polaris submarines a year.

The limited coordination between the services had often worked to the detriment of the United States. A famous example of this occurred during the Spanish-American War. The capture of Santiago was delayed four weeks because the army commander, General Shafter, and the naval commander, Admiral Sampson, could not agree on a joint plan of action.[2] In more recent years, failure of the navy and air force to agree on specifications for new aircraft has led to greatly increased costs.

[2]See F. E. Chadwick, *Relations of U.S. and Spain, the Spanish-American War* (New York: Scribner's Sons, 1911).

Though the Joint Chiefs of Staff, consisting of a representative from each of the services, attempt to overcome these problems through coordination, they have had limited success. Each of the chiefs feels loyalty toward his own service. General LeMay, while chairman of the Joint Chiefs of Staff, put it this way in testimony before Congress: "I make no claim to objectivity. It is well known that I am partial to air power as a defensive arm of our country. However, I have been and shall continue to be as fair to the other services as my experience will permit."[3]

The staff of the Joint Chiefs has the further problem that upon the completion of the term of service with the Joint Chiefs they return to the service from which they came. Their chances of promotion undoubtedly depend to some extent on how well they have served their own service.

Thus, the advocates of civilian control believe that only a strong secretary of defense can perform the vital role of objectively evaluating the merits of alternative requests for funds. Those who oppose civilian control believe that civilians lack the expertise and experience with which to make such military judgments.

Defense Procurement

As we noted in Chapter 7, the Defense Department purchases a large fraction of its goods from private contractors. Most of these purchases are not made in a conventional competitive market, in which there are many suppliers and many buyers. There is one large buyer—the United States government. There are a few (and often only a few) potential suppliers: for aircraft, for instance, Lockheed, Boeing, and McDonnell-Douglas compete against each other.

To ensure that it obtains the best price, the government usually resorts to competitive bidding; different contractors tell the government what they require to deliver, say, 1,000 tanks of a given specification, and the government purchases the tanks from the lowest bidder. Frequently, however, there are major **cost overruns**—that is, the costs exceed what the producer originally estimated these costs to be. Sometimes the contract between the government calls for these costs to be shared by the government and the private contractor; such contracts are called **cost-sharing contracts.** Even when the contract does not explicitly call for sharing the costs of the overrun, the government absorbs all or a significant fraction of the additional costs. The contractor may claim that the cost overruns are a result of changes in the design specification; such changes almost always accompany the development of a new weapon, particularly when the development occurs over a period of several years, and it is frequently difficult to ascertain the extent to which the cost overruns are in fact a result of the design changes. In other cases, the private contractor simply says that he cannot complete the contract without further funds; the government then has the choice of losing all that it has already spent or negotiating a settlement with the contractor. And even if the government were to sue the contractor for breach of contract, the delays in the development and deployment of the weapons could be very costly.

[3] General Curtis E. LeMay, *America Is in Danger* (New York: Funk and Wagnalls, 1968), p. xii.

The military has been greatly criticized for its procurement procedures. The prevalence of cost overruns means the public or its representatives in Congress seldom has an accurate view of the cost of a ship, a defense system, a tank, etc. at the time it makes a commitment to purchase them. It also means that the government seldom knows whether it has, in fact, let out the contract to the lowest-cost producer;[4] all that it knows is that it let out the contract to the firm that bid the lowest.

What are the reasons for these cost overruns? In the case of new weapons, errors in estimating costs are common. But why should there be a bias in these errors? That is, why should there be a systematic tendency to underestimate the costs? Part of the reason has to do with the competitive bidding process; potential contractors know that they have to produce a low bid to win. The system of cost sharing (implicit or explicit) means that there is relatively little penalty associated with bidding too low. There is, however, a penalty associated with bidding too high, particularly when other firms are bidding low (using, say, their most optimistic estimates of costs): the high-bidding firm will fail to get the contract. Moreover most of the technical expertise, the ability to judge the reasonableness of the estimates, resides in those who have a vested interest in the outcome—the defense contractors who are bidding and the military officers who would like to have the best possible defense system for their service branch.

The system of cost sharing has a further disadvantage in addition to reducing the penalty for under bidding: the winner of the contract has little incentive to be efficient. Indeed, some contracts are of a cost-plus form; that is, the government pays whatever it costs to develop the weapons plus, say, 10 percent. Such contracts provide incentives to be inefficient; the more the firm spends, the more it gets from the government.

Why does the government engage in cost-sharing contracts, with all their obvious disadvantages? Why, even when there are not explicit provisions for cost sharing, does the government agree to pay at least part of the cost overruns?

Part of the reason for cost sharing is the uncertainty inherent in the development of a new weapons system. The best that a firm can do, as we have said, is to provide an estimate of these costs. If there were a **fixed-fee contract** (a contract where the contractor got paid a fixed amount, regardless of the eventual cost), the contractor would have to bear considerable risk; even if he were very efficient, there is some chance that he will encounter difficulties in the development of the system that increases his costs way beyond the fixed fee he is receiving, in which case he may incur an enormous loss. If firms (or their managers) are *risk-averse* and insist on being compensated for bearing risks, they will all put in high bids, representing their estimate of the actual costs plus a fee for bearing the risk. The government is in a better position to bear the risk. By agreeing to a cost-sharing contract, it absorbs much of the risk, but at the same time it reduces the incentives for efficiency.

Though this provides an important rationale for cost-sharing contracts,

---

[4]Notice that at the time the cost overruns occur, what limited competition there was before the contract was let no longer exists: it would, in general, be costly or impossible for the government at that point to turn to other potential suppliers.

some critics of the Pentagon argue that other forces are at work when the government agrees to pay all or part of a cost overrun. A large number of military officers upon their retirement from the armed forces take up positions in private industry, and in particular with defense contractors. Critics say that this provides an incentive for these officers to be accommodating to the requests of the defense contractors.

Supporters of the current system, though admitting that it is far from perfect, point out that there is a healthy level of competition among defense contractors and that this competition provides at least some limit to the extent of inefficiency. Any contractor who performed persistently worse than other firms would find itself having difficulty obtaining contracts.

The Draft versus the Volunteer Army

The government frequently has obtained labor for its military services in a way quite different from that by which other employers obtain labor: it forces young men to serve in the armed forces. Most countries resort to the draft during war, and many countries (for instance, Greece and Switzerland) employ the draft also in peacetime. In the aftermath of the Vietnam War, the draft was abandoned in the United States and an all-volunteer army was established.

The fact that individuals are forced to go into the armed forces means that the salary paid to these individuals is less than the "market" wage for that kind of activity. The draft can thus be viewed as a tax levied on selected individuals in the population. The tax is inequitable and introduces inefficiencies. It is inequitable because it is only levied upon a selected group within the population, able-bodied males between the ages of eighteen and twenty-six. And not all individuals within this group are selected. During the early years of the Vietnam War, individuals could obtain exemptions if they attended school or if they were in certain occupations. There was a strong bias in these exemptions: more sons of the middle class obtained them than those of the poor.

The draft introduced two inefficiencies. For some individuals, the opportunity cost—in terms of foregone wages—of going into the military was much smaller than for others. (That is their productivity in other occupations was much lower). Markets serve the important function of allocating workers of different abilities to their most productive uses. The draft does not take into account individuals' opportunity costs. The effective tax on some individuals is thus much higher than on others.

Secondly, the draft may result in the military not taking into account full costs of its alternative programs. Because the draft makes manpower less expensive than it would be if the required high wages were paid to recruit workers, the military may not make the appropriate trade-offs between the use of men and machines.

But those who favor the draft and oppose the volunteer army put forward several arguments. First, they are concerned with the inequities associated with a volunteer army. Since the poor (with limited alternative opportunities) will be attracted into the army, the burden of a war will fall more upon the poor. Holders of this view maintain certain rights and obligations should not be distributed according to the market place. We referred to this view in the last chapter as *specific equalitarianism*. The obligation to fight and die for one's country is one of these obligations.

Secondly, critics of the volunteer army are concerned with the effectiveness of the armed forces. If only those with low opportunity costs serve, the quality of the armed forces is likely to be low. There is an obvious solution to this problem: any employer faces a similar problem and responds by increasing the wage to the point where he has an applicant pool with a sufficiently large number of good applicants that he can obtain the quality he wishes. But if Congress is sufficiently shortsighted that it fails to allocate enough funds for military wages, our national defense may suffer from the low quality of personnel.

COST-EFFECTIVENESS ANALYSIS

One of the ways by which the Defense Department has attempted to increase the efficiency of how the defense dollar is spent is to employ cost-effectiveness analysis. This entails a detailed comparison of alternative ways of achieving the same objective. Cost-effectiveness analysis was popularized by Robert McNamara, who was Secretary of Defense under presidents Kennedy and Johnson. Many military officers objected to cost-effectiveness analysis because they believed that military judgments concerning the relative merits of alternative defense programs could not be reduced to a simple (or even complicated) set of economic calculations.

One example of cost-effectiveness analysis is provided by economist William Kaufman, of M.I.T. and the Brookings Institution.[5] The problem he considers is how best to prepare for a Soviet offensive directed simultaneously at central Europe and the Persian Gulf. He estimates that it might be necessary to deliver 800,000 tons of material to the two theaters within thirty days. He also estimates that the current airlift capacity is no more than 200,000 tons. The 1984 budget requested fifty C-5B aircraft at a cost of $6.4 billion. This could increase capacity by about 70,000 tons, leaving a shortfall of 530,000. He argues that a more cost effective method of delivering the material is the construction of fast sealift ships. He calculates that thirty-two such ships, combined with the eight already available, could deliver the full 800,000 requirement within thirty days.

Similarly, there are alternative ways of ensuring a **second-strike capability,** the ability of the United States to retaliate after a surprise attack against us. We could construct a new MX missile system, or we could expand our submarine-based Polaris missile system. For each missile system, we can estimate the number of such missiles that would be destroyed in a first strike by the Soviet Union. We could then calculate the cost—per megaton of second-strike capacity, say—for each alternative. The one that is lower is the more cost-effective.

Multiple Objectives. In many cases, however, a given weapons system serves multiple objectives. The airlift capacity would be of particular value

[5]W. W. Kaufmann, "The Defense Budget," in J. A. Pechman, *Setting National Priorities* (Washington, D.C.: Brookings Institution, 1983).

in delivering small amounts of tonnage to a distant theater on short notice.
But Kaufman claims "that this is hardly an argument for expanding the current airlift force. The same effect can be achieved by forces deployed in Europe and the Arabian Sea and prepositioned equipment in the two theaters—both of which already exist—combined with current airlift."

A similar issue arose in discussions concerning the air force's proposed B-70 bomber. This was intended to replace the B-52 as the principal United States bomber. Its major mission was to drop nuclear bombs on predesignated targets. McNamara argued that the same objective could be accomplished at less cost by missiles; and indeed, he contended that missiles had certain advantages: they required less time (fifteen to thirty minutes, as opposed to two to three hours) to reach most targets, and the bombers are more vulnerable on the ground than either Minutemen missiles in underground silos or mobile missiles like those in the Polaris submarine.

No two defense systems are ever identical, and proponents of the bombers claimed that they could perform other functions better than the missiles. In particular, the air force generals who advocated the B-70 bomber claimed that the bomber had a reconnaissance potential that missiles did not have. This would enable the more effective destruction of Soviet missiles remaining after our initial strike. Assuming that the B-70 enabled the destruction of all intercontinental ballistic missiles, it would still not be able to destroy the submarine-launched missiles. Thus, from buying the B-70s, the net reduction in deaths would be small: under one set of assumptions (in which the United States struck first) the number of Americans killed would be reduced from between 60 and 90 million to between 45 and 75 million; under another set of assumptions, if the Soviet Union struck first, the number of Americans killed would be reduced from between 80 and 150 million to 70 and 135 million. Thus McNamara claimed that even under the most "favorable" conditions, the B-70 bomber's secondary mission had limited value, not worth the $10 to $15 billion estimated cost.

Alternative Scenarios. These examples illustrate the kind of analysis that is essential in assessing the value of a weapons system. An important part of this analysis involves the consideration of alternative scenarios—e.g., an attack on one front with conventional weapons, with some warning, an attack on one front with no warning, an attack on two fronts with conventional weapons, or a nuclear attack. We then attempt to ascertain how, say, a new weapons system or increased expenditure on naval ships would affect the outcomes in each of these scenarios. For instance, we might calculate the additional second-strike capacity (that is, the megatons of deliverable nuclear weapons) we would have after an attack by the Soviet Union resulting from a new missile system. Or we might calculate the additional number of troops that we could deliver overseas in thirty days after the outbreak of a one-front war as a result of purchasing so many air transport planes.

Thus one defense system may be more effective in one scenario, another in another. Spending more (purchasing both systems) may increase our defense capabilities, but that is hardly an answer: we need some assessment of the likelihood of alternative scenarios and the consequences under each of the additional defense expenditures. On the basis of this, one may be able to make some judgments about how much is enough.

Trade-offs in Allocating Defense Dollars

Cost-effectiveness analysis can be used to help ensure that defense dollars are not wasted. But there are many decisions where it is of only limited usefulness. A question that arises repeatedly is how much of our defense budget should be spent in preparation for conventional wars. We can obtain greater protection against conventional attacks (by increasing, say, our expenditures on conventional weapons) at the expense of decreasing our protection against a nuclear attack. For a given amount of resources, we cannot, in general, obtain more of one type of protection without sacrificing some amount of the other kind of protection. Different individuals may prefer different points on this feasibility locus depending on their judgments concerning the likelihood of the two types of wars.

Some Problems in Allocating Defense Expenditures

Ends versus Means. Quite often in defense discussions there is a confusion between ends and means. Acquiring various weapons systems should not be viewed as an end in itself but as a means of attaining certain defense objectives—e.g., the destruction of a certain fraction of the Russian arsenal in the event of a first strike by the Soviet Union. In this calculation, the least expensive missile is not necessarily the most effective. Assume, for instance, that Polaris missiles are twice as expensive as land-based missiles but that, in a first strike, 75 percent of the land-based missiles are destroyed, while none of the Polaris missiles are destroyed. In order to have one land missile available after the strike, we need to construct four missiles. The total "effective" cost of the submarine-based missile is half that of the land-based missile.

Full Cost Accounting. Another error frequently encountered in defense analysis is the failure to account for all the costs of a defense system. These include not only the research and development costs but personnel and the expenditures required to maintain the defense system.

Without this full cost information, it is difficult to make efficient choices. There may be a bias in favor of projects with low capital costs but high maintenance and personnel costs.

Technologically Driven Innovation. There is a strong desire by many in the military establishment to have the most modern weapons. This appears almost as an end in itself. New defense systems are developed to take advantage of technological breakthroughs, and old weapons may be discarded simply because more advanced weapons systems might be available.

Economists argue that newer equipment is not necessarily more cost-effective. The question of whether or when to phase out old technologies and adopt new ones should be related to the overall objectives of defense. Newer equipment may not be as reliable and may require more maintenance expenditures.

HOW MUCH IS ENOUGH?

The final question to which we turn—How much should we spend on national defense?—is a more difficult question to answer than the question of how to allocate a given defense budget.

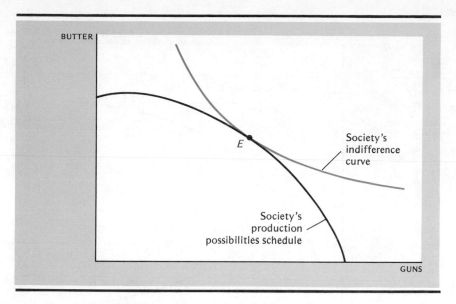

12.3 SOCIETY'S PRODUCTION POSSIBILITIES SCHEDULE Society can only obtain more defense (more guns) by giving up on other goods (butter).

Are we spending too much on national defense? Spending more money on defense may have positive benefits; it may increase the probability of survival in the event of an attack.

We are concerned here with how to make those judgments in a systematic way. This is the traditional choice between guns (national defense) and butter (other goods) represented by the production possibilities schedule, as illustrated in Figure 12.3. One can obtain more national defense, but only at the expense of sacrificing other goods. An indifference curve represents combinations of guns and butter that society is indifferent in choosing from among. Society is willing to sacrifice some butter for more defense. As we give up more butter, we require larger and larger increments in defense to leave us indifferent. Higher indifference curves (giving more guns and butter) obviously represent higher levels of welfare. The highest level of welfare that is attainable is at point *E*, where the indifference curve is just tangent to the production possibilities schedule.

This is a good way of thinking about the trade-offs that society must face. Unfortunately, it is not very helpful in answering the question of how much is enough. To apply this analysis to defense spending, we have to know how much extra protection we get from increased military spending.

The Value of Marginal Analysis

We argued in our analysis of how to allocate a given defense budget that one needs to consider the effect of the expenditures on various defense objectives. In evaluating whether we should spend more on defense, we similarly need to know how much *extra* "protection" do we get from an extra expenditure of $1 billion.

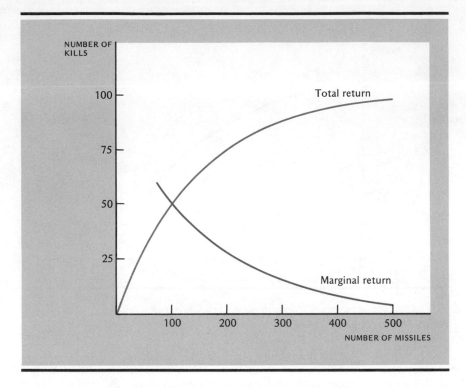

12.4 THE ROLE OF MARGINAL ANALYSIS IN DEFENSE The relevant question is not whether we should have 500 missiles or no missiles, but how many extra kills we get from each additional missile. There may be sharply diminishing returns.

The following example, provided by Charles Hitch, who was assistant secretary of defense under McNamara, illustrates the role of marginal analysis.[6] Assume each missile has a 50 percent probability of success in killing its target. We have 100 targets that we would like to destroy. If we sent 100 missiles at the targets, we would "achieve an expectancy of 50 kills, 200 missiles—75 kills, 300 missiles—87 kills," as depicted in Figure 12.4. There are clearly very strong diminishing returns. While the first 100 missiles give us 50 kills, increasing the number of missiles from 400 to 500 increases the number of kills by only 3. We need to ask ourselves not whether it is worth the cost of 500 missiles to get 97 kills but whether it is worth the cost of 100 additional missiles to get 3 extra kills.

This kind of analysis is not easy. But by relating the expenditures to the objectives, and by showing what one gets from additional expenditures, one can hope to make more rational decisions concerning how much is enough.

In making these assessments, however, one set of considerations is particularly hard to evaluate: deterrence.

[6]From C. J. Hitch, *Decision Making for Defense* (Berkeley, CA: University of California Press, 1966), pp. 50–51.

The calculations described above are all made on the basis of a given size of enemy forces (current plus projected increases). But an essential aspect of defense analysis is that the behavior of our enemies is affected by our military expenditures, in two important ways. First, if we spend more, then they are likely to spend more; the net gain in our advantage cannot be calculated assuming that they do not respond at all. It is even possible that increased expenditures result in our net advantage being reduced: for every dollar we spend, they may spend more than a dollar. The belief that we can gain from further expenditures is thus partly based on the assumption that the Soviet Union will not be able or willing to fully match our expenditures. This is, of course, debatable: while their national income is much smaller than ours, their ability to suppress consumption of their citizens is greater than ours.

But there is also the belief that the Soviets will be affected in another way by our military strength: they will be less likely to undertake hostile actions. Thus the probabilities of the different scenarios, a conventional war or a nuclear war, will be affected by our military capabilities. This has played an important role in recent military debates. Those who have advocated increased military spending have argued that an enhanced second-strike capability reduces the likelihood of an attack. Critics of increased military spending have argued that once one has assured oneself a very high probability of effectively destroying the enemy with a second-strike capability, further increments to that capacity have little additional deterrent value; they believe that given our current arsenal of weapons, further increments have little value.

Critics of increased military expenditure further claim that there are circumstances in which such spending may actually increase the likelihood of an attack. This argument has played an important role in the debate over defensive nuclear weapons. Assume Russia believed that in ten years time, we would have constructed a defensive system that would make us invulnerable, and that they would not be able to develop a corresponding system for another fifteen years. Russia could believe that it would then be in the interests of the United States to attack during the period during which they were vulnerable but we were not. But then, Russia, anticipating this, would have every incentive to launch a preemptive strike, before our defense capacity is put into place.

Economists have relatively little to say about these questions. They can analyze "rational" responses, using a technique of analysis called game theory, originally explored by economist Oskar Morgenstern of Princeton and by mathematician John von Neumann, of the Institute of Advanced Studies. But there are no assurances that the Soviet Union will respond rationally to our actions. There are disputes about what motivates the leaders of the Kremlin and what they believe are the intentions of the United States. It is largely because these responses play such a critical role in the assessment of the benefits that accrue from alternative defense policies that economists have made only a limited contribution to the debate over how much is enough.

SUMMARY

1. Advocates of greater civilian control of the Department of Defense are concerned with the lack of coordination among the services and the biases in decision making that result when excessive reliance is placed on experts with vested interests.

2. In choosing among alternative uses of defense funds, cost-effectivenss analysis is useful in ensuring that the best weapons systems are employed to attain given objectives.

3. Frequently, however, there is a multiplicity of objectives. We need to ascertain the marginal benefit of additional funds spent in different ways assuming different scenarios and different objectives.

4. In evaluating alternative weapons systems, it is important not to confuse means with ends and to take full account of the long-run costs (including maintenance and personnel) associated with each weapons system.

5. The procurement systems often employed by the military entailing cost-plus contracts may have contributed significantly to high costs.

6. The draft can be viewed as a selectively imposed tax. Though there are both equity and efficiency arguments in favor of the volunteer army, there are some who believe that a volunteer army is inequitable.

7. In evaluting alternative defense programs, it is important to focus on the extra benefits attained from an extra expenditure—to employ, in other words, marginal analysis.

KEY CONCEPTS

Civilian control	Cost-sharing contracts
Deterrence	Fixed-fee contract
Cost overrun	Full cost accounting

QUESTIONS AND PROBLEMS

1. Assume the government has decided to install a missile system designed to provide a second-strike capability with 100 missiles. It is now considering whether to increase the number to 110. Assume you are on the congressional committee that must approve the increased expenditure. List some of the questions you might ask to ascertain whether the increased expenditures are desirable.

2. Should military officers and defense department officials be proscribed from working for private defense contractors for a period of several years after termination of their governmental service?

3. In what ways is the purchase of a hammer by the military different from the purchase of an MX missile system? How does this affect government procurement policies in these two areas?

4. In what ways is the purchase of a hammer by the military different from the purchase of labor services? How does this effect government procurement policies in these two areas?

5. "The problems of defending our country have become so technical and complex that they should be left to the military experts. The government should simply decide how much it wishes to spend on defense and leave the problem of allocating the expenditures to the military." Discuss.

13
Social Insurance

Although modern governments have long taken some responsibility for providing for the needy, during the past fifty years this has come to be viewed as one of the primary functions of government. In 1983, social insurance and welfare expenditures represented more than 40 percent of the federal government's budget.

Of the major social insurance programs, by far the largest, is the old-age, survivors', and disability insurance (OASDI), enacted in 1935. This is usually referred to as social security and is intended to provide a basic standard of living to the aged, the disabled, and their survivors. As Table 13.1 indicates, in twenty years this program has more than tripled in *real* terms, going from 23.5 billion 1973 dollars in 1963 to 74.9 billion 1973 dollars in 1983. The second largest program, medicare (technically, social security includes both the medicare and OASDI programs), provides medical care for the aged and was discussed in detail in Chapter 11. Unemployment insurance, also enacted in 1935, is intended to provide income to individuals during short-term spells of unemployment (as its name suggests). Other social insurance programs

Table 13.1 EXPENDITURES IN MAJOR SOCIAL INSURANCE PROGRAMS

	Real Expenditures (billions of 1973 dollars)		
	1963	1966	1983
Social Security (OASDI)	23.5	28.6	74.9
OASI	21.6	26.0	66.7
Disability Insurance	1.9	2.6	8.2
Unemployment Insurance	4.1	2.5	9.2
Medicare	—	1.4	25.6

Source: Social Security Bulletin, Annual Statistical Supplement, 1982. Survey of Current Business, 1984.

include worker's compensation, which provides money to individuals who are injured on the job, disability benefits for veterans, retirement benefits for railroad workers, and funds for coal miners suffering from black lung. Until 1983 government employees were not included in the social security program; there are separate retirement programs for civilian and military employees. The programs for government employees and veterans should probably be viewed as deferred compensation rather than as social insurance programs.

In many ways, these programs provide insurance to individuals against particular risks that they face just as private insurance does. Thus medicare covers medical expenditures of the aged, just as a private health policy would. There is one important difference: with private insurance there is a close relationship among the payments of the individual, the risks he faces, and what he receives. Thus the premium for a health insurance policy would depend on factors affecting the health condition of the individual, such as his age. The amount that an individual received back from an *annuity* (a private insurance policy providing a certain income every year after the individual reaches, say, sixty-five) on average is effectively just what he puts in (plus accumulated interest). This is not true of social insurance. Social insurance programs provide insurance *and* redistribute income. Confusion between these two roles has been a major impediment in the evaluation and reform of social insurance programs. In this chapter we shall discuss the major issues facing the social security (OASDI) insurance program.

PROBLEMS FACING THE SOCIAL SECURITY SYSTEM

In 1983 the social security system was in a crisis, for the second time in five years. The program was running out of funds. Though there was a short-term problem, the long-term problems were even greater. The long-term deficit—the difference between expected revenues and expected benefits—was according to some estimates well over one trillion dollars.[1] One pessimistic projection suggested that to cover current commitments for social security and health benefits would necessitate raising the payroll tax to 48 percent, while even optimistic projections suggested that the tax rate would have to be increased to 18 percent.[2]

There were three possible solutions: social security taxes could be increased, its benefits could be reduced, or funding from general tax revenues could be directed to finance the social security system. All three prospects seemed unattractive. To reduce benefits seemed unfair to those who were counting on social security for their retirement; it was as if the government was reneging on a promise. Social security taxes were already scheduled to increase, and further increases seemed politically unpalatable. Using general tax revenues was opposed by many in principle and as a practical matter did not

---

[1] This was about the size, at the time, of the entire privately held national debt. The estimate depends on a number of assumptions concerning the rate of interest, productivity changes, and demographic (that is, population) changes, as we shall see below. The Social Security Administration provides a range of estimates. Under alternative assumptions, the deficit was projected to be even larger. For a discussion of the alternative assumptions, see L. H. Thompson, "The Social Security Reform Debate," *Journal of Economic Literature*, December 1983, pp. 1425–67.

[2] Michael Boskin, *The Social Security System* (New York: Twentieth Century Fund, 1984).

help much, since there already was a large deficit that had to be dealt with. Ronald Reagan appointed a presidential commission, headed by the former chairman of the Council of Economic Advisers, Alan Greenspan, to offer a set of recommendations to resolve the problem. We will see how the problem arose and how it was at least temporarily resolved.

This financial crisis, however, is not the only source of concern about the social security system. There are concerns about the equity of the system and about its effects on economic efficiency. Before turning to a detailed examination of these questions, however, we first must look at the structure of the system.

THE STRUCTURE OF THE SOCIAL SECURITY SYSTEM

The social security retirement program is the largest government program aimed at providing for the elderly, as illustrated in Figure 13.1. It is financed by a payroll tax, set in 1983 at 13.4 percent on the first $35,700 of income. The base rises with inflation and the rate is scheduled to rise to 15.3 percent by 1990. (See Table 13.2.) According to the law, half the tax is paid by individuals and half by their employers; but most economists believe that this is simply a legal fiction. The consequences of the tax are *essentially the same* as they would be if the individual were responsible for paying all of it. What difference should it make who mails the check to the government?[3]

The system is organized on a pay-as-you-go basis; the payroll taxes of those

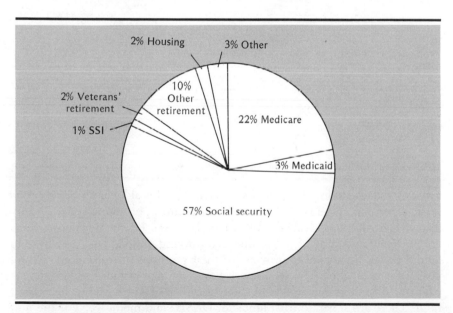

13.1 FEDERAL OUTLAYS BENEFITING THE ELDERLY: FISCAL YEAR 1982 SOURCE: U.S. Dept. of Commerce, Bureau of the Census; *America in Transition: An Aging Society*, p. 13.

---

[3]Employers are concerned only with their total labor costs, including any employment taxes; employees are concerned only with their net after-tax income. The government's revenue is simply the difference between the two, and it makes little difference who the government says is paying the tax. For a more extensive discussion, see Chapter 17.

Table 13.2 SOCIAL SECURITY TAX RATES AND BASE HAVE INCREASED RAPIDLY OVER THE PAST FIFTY YEARS

Tax rates from 1983 and beyond are scheduled in existing law.
Employers and employees pay these taxes.

	Annual Earnings Base	Tax Rate	Maximum Tax
1937	$3,000	1.0%	$30.00
1950	3,000	1.5	45.00
1951	3,600	1.5	54.00
1954	3,600	2.0	72.00
1955	4,200	2.0	84.00
1957	4,200	2.25	94.50
1959	4,800	2.5	120.00
1960	4,800	3.0	144.00
1962	4,800	3.125	150.00
1963	4,800	3.625	174.00
1966	6,600	4.2	277.20
1967	6,600	4.4	290.40
1968	7,800	4.4	343.20
1969	7,800	4.8	374.40
1970	7,800	4.8	374.40
1971	7,800	5.2	405.60
1972	9,000	5.2	468.00
1973	10,800	5.85	631.80
1974	13,200	5.85	772.20
1975	14,100	5.85	824.85
1976	15,300	5.85	895.05
1977	16,500	5.85	965.25
1978	17,700	6.05	1,070.85
1979	22,900	6.13	1,403.77
1980	25,900	6.13	1,587.67
1981	29,700	6.65	1,722.35
1982	32,400	6.7	2,170.80
1983	35,700	6.7	2,391.90
1985	*	7.05	
1986	*	7.15	
1990	*	7.65	

*Wage base will automatically increase with growth in average wages.

working today pay for the benefits received by the elderly today. By contrast, a pension system in which each age group's pension is supported by its own contributions is called a fully funded system. Private pension systems are normally fully funded; while they are working, individuals contribute to a fund that is then used to provide for their pensions in retirement. In any year, of course, the social security system may take in more or less than it pays out. The difference is added to (or taken out of) the social security trust fund. There are separate trust funds for OASDI and medicare. For the first two decades of its existence, social security revenues exceeded benefits; by 1970, the trust funds amounted to more than $40 billion. But in the past fifteen years, payments have exceeded revenues; by 1983, the OASDI fund was essentially depleted, and the medicare insurance fund was rapidly on its way to depletion. It should be emphasized, however, that the trust fund is not like a pension fund; the payments to future social security beneficiaries are not supposed to come out of the trust fund. With a private pension fund, the employer is supposed to set aside enough money while the worker is working to pay the benefits that have been promised. On the other hand, the trust fund is simply a buffer stock, to ensure, for instance, that if the economy went into a recession, causing revenues to decline, the system would still be able to meet its obligations.

Individuals are eligible to receive benefits at the age of sixty-two. However, if they wait to retire until sixty-five, they receive a higher payment. Payments are not increased if retirement is postponed beyond sixty-five.[4] The amount of payments depends on the contributions of the individual; in general, the greater the contributions, the greater the receipts, although the relationship is a complicated one.[5]

Originally, the social security system covered only a fraction of the working population, with agricultural workers, the self-employed, government employees, and employees of nonprofit institutions excluded. Over the years, the coverage has been extended so that today, the only employees not covered are those of local and state government.

Until 1983, social security payments were tax-exempt. Now, 50 percent of the benefits are taxable for individuals with more than a $25,000 income (or married couples with an income in excess of $30,000).

The growth of the system can be represented in several different ways. The number of beneficiaries of OASDI has increased from 3.5 million in 1950 to 32.3 million in 1983; this is a reflection of the general increase in population, of an increased proportion of elderly people within the population, of earlier retirements by the elderly, and of the broadening coverage. The number of beneficiaries of disability insurance increased from one-half million in 1960 to 4.7 million in 1980, though tighter eligibility standards reduced the number to 4 million by 1983.

While the beneficiaries of OASDI increased 10-fold in 33 years, the benefits increased *150-fold*, from 1 billion dollars to 149.1 billion. In real terms, this was still an impressive growth (in constant dollars, from 1 billion to 36.1 billion).

There has been a concomitant increase in taxes, from 2 percent of earnings up to $3,000, for a maximum payment of $60 in 1937, to the 1983 level of 13.4 percent earnings up to $35,700 for a maximum tax of $4,783.80 (2.9 percent goes to pay for medicare; the residual, for OASDI, still represents an impressive growth).

THE CAUSE OF THE CURRENT CRISIS IN SOCIAL SECURITY

Because the social security program is funded on a pay-as-you-go basis, the financial viability of the system depends on the ratio of those working to those retired. During the past twenty-five years, there have been three marked changes. First, age span has increased. Those who reached age sixty-five in

---

[4] Under the 1983 law, benefits of those who retire between sixty-five and seventy will gradually rise, so that by 2000, the present discounted value of benefits will be the same regardless of the age of retirement. (For a definition of present discounted value, see Chapter 10.)

[5] In 1983, the basic benefit was 90 percent of the first $254 of the worker's averaged indexed monthly earnings (AIME), plus 32 percent of the next $1,274 of AIME, plus 15 percent of the AIME over $1,528.

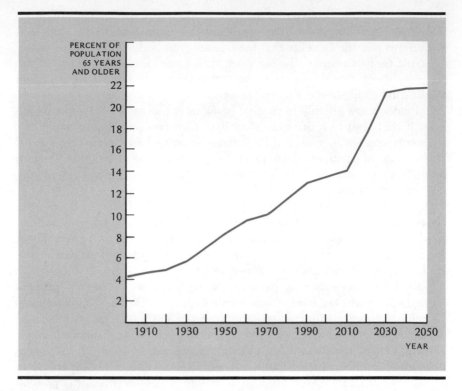

13.2 GROWTH OF THE OLDER POPULATIONS, ACTUAL AND PROJECTED:
1900–2050 SOURCE: *America in Transition*, p. 3.

1930 could expect to live to age seventy-seven; by 1950 women could expect
to live to age eighty-eight while men could expect to live to age eighty-one.
Second, birth rates have fallen; the average woman now has fewer than two
children. Finally, labor force participation of men over sixty-five (the percentage of those who work) has dropped dramatically, from 45 percent in
1950 to 20 percent in 1980.

The consequences of these changes, as Figure 13.2 shows, is that there
has been a marked increase in the fraction of the population sixty-five and
over, from less than 7 percent when social security was enacted, to 12 percent today; and the ratio is expected to increase to more than 20 percent
within fifty years. Even more marked has been the change in the ratio of
those working to social security beneficiaries. Figure 13.3 shows how it has
declined from 16.5 in 1950 to slightly more than 3 today; further declines to
2 are expected over the next fifty years.

There is another important determinant of the viability of the system. The
payments to the old are related to their wages. They increase with inflation.
If the wages of the young (adjusted for inflation) increase, then their income
is larger, relative to the receipts of the beneficiaries. Over the past fifty
years, wages have increased faster than inflation, reflecting the continuing
rise in productivity. But during the past decade, there has been a slowdown
in the rate of increase in productivity, and, correspondingly, real wages have
failed to rise.

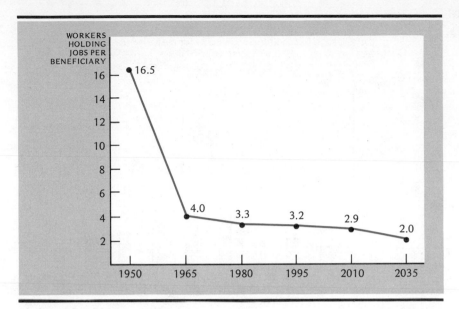

13.3 WORKERS PER SOCIAL SECURITY BENEFICIARY There has been a marked decline in workers per social security beneficiary. SOURCE: *The New York Times*, February 4, 1983.

The future viability of the system depends on whether the trends of recent years are continued. If productivity increases remain low, if birth rates remain low, if people continue to live longer, then the obligations to those who will retire in twenty-five years will be large relative to income of the working population at that time: the system may be in for trouble. Thus the Social Security Administration makes alternative estimates of its long-range financial status. Its "intermediate estimate" (neither optimistic nor pessimistic) is that under current legislation, during the period 2032–2056, social security taxes would have to be raised to almost 20 percent.[6]

For the short run, however, the Social Security Administration estimates that for the next twenty-five years there will be a slight surplus (for OASDI; this slight surplus is more than offset by the deficit in medicare.)

Unfortunately, as we have noted, the performance of the system is very sensitive to the estimates of productivity, labor force participation, and demographic changes. The Social Security Administration thought that the minor adjustments it made in 1977 were sufficient to ensure the viability of the system over the indefinite future but discovered that within five years the system was once again in crisis.

Though the ratio of social security beneficiaries to those working has increased—and will continue to increase—markedly, the same demographic changes that placed a higher burden on the working may make them better able to bear this burden: they will have fewer children to support.[7] Still, to

[6]If the medicare deficit is also corrected, the tax would have to almost double, to 29 percent. Recall that these are "intermediate" estimates. Pessimistic estimates put the required tax rate at 48 percent.

[7]The net effect is that while in 1960 there were 91.5 individuals either under nineteen or over sixty-five, for every 100 individuals between twenty and sixty-five by the year 2000, this will be reduced to only 70.5.

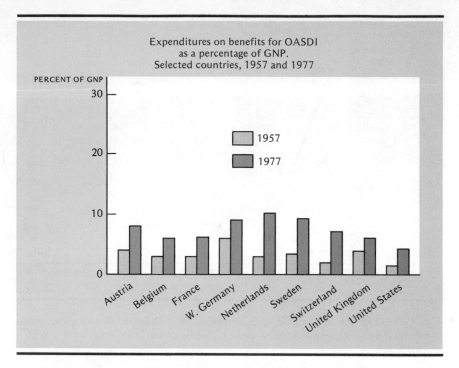

13.4 EXPENDITURES ON BENEFITS FOR OASDI AS A PERCENTAGE OF GNP—
SELECTED COUNTRIES, 1957 AND 1977 Expenditures in the U.S. are less (as a fraction
of GNP) than in other countries. Data for Belgium and France do not include disability benefits.
SOURCE: *Social Security in Europe: The Impact of an Aging Population* (Washington, D.C.:
Government Printing Office, 1981).

support the aged may require large increases in the tax rate, and these may
have significant (and deleterious) effects on the economy.

Comparison between the United States and Some European Countries.
The problems facing the United States are similar to those facing many
European countries. Indeed, in many European countries, expenditures on
social security are not only much larger than in the United States, but they
have grown more rapidly, as we see in Figure 13.4. As a result, payroll taxes
(earmarked, as in the United States, for social security) are high: 35 percent
in the Netherlands and 25 percent in Italy, for instance. There has been
increasing concern within these countries about the incentive effects of such
high tax rates (particularly when combined with high income tax rates).

SOCIAL SECURITY, PRIVATE INSURANCE, AND
MARKET FAILURES

Prior to 1935, private markets provided life insurance but not retirement
insurance. Few firms provided much in the way of pensions.

The Great Depression caused a crisis: there were many aged thrown out
of work who had little prospect of being rehired and no means of support.
The social security system was intended to ensure that all of the aged had at
least a minimal level of support.

In the past fifty years, however, there have been marked improvements in private markets. Now, many workers are covered by private pensions. The government has taken steps to ensure the financial soundness of private pension programs.[8] But these private insurance policies still are deficient in several respects.

279
Social Secu-
rity, Private
Insurance,
and Market
Failures

High Transaction Costs. To provide for their retirement, individuals can purchase annuities from private firms. Annuities pay a fixed amount every month from some age (usually sixty-five or seventy) until the individual dies, no matter how long he or she lives. Under most private annuity programs, however, the expected rate of return obtained does not appear to be very good—far lower than market rates of interest. This is partly because of high administrative costs (including in many cases substantial commissions for the salespeople). While administrative costs for social security are less than 2 percent of benefits paid, private insurance companies spend one dollar in administrative costs, dividends (profits), and taxes for every two dollars in benefits paid.[9] The trade-offs are clear: it is administratively less expensive to provide a uniform retirement program for all individuals than to have a large number of competing programs available, among which the individuals can choose. So long, however, as the level of retirement benefits is relatively low, few individuals are being forced to save more for retirement than they would like; there is no significant welfare loss from the provision of a reasonably low level of benefits. This argument does not hold, however, if the benefits are substantial.

The concept of **replacement rates** is sometimes used to assess the magnitude of social security benefits. The replacement rate is defined as the *ratio* of the social security benefit to pre-retirement income. A replacement rate of unity means that an individual retiring would suffer no loss in income, assuming there were no private pensions. Replacement rates in 1983 were close to one (and in some cases exceeded 1) for low-income workers with an uninsured spouse, but were much less than unity for high-income workers, as Table 13.3 shows.

Lack of Indexing: The Inability of Private Markets to Insure Social Risks. A major difference between private insurance policies and the social security program is that social security benefits are indexed; they increase with inflation. The closest private policies have come to indexed benefits was annuities whose benefits were linked with the performance of the stock market. When these insurance policies were introduced, it was thought that they would provide a hedge against inflation; the stock market would go up with

Table 13.3 REPLACEMENT RATES: 1983

Earnings Each Year	Single Earner	Worker with Uninsured Spouse Aged Sixty-Five
Half-time Minimum Wage	.9	1.35
Full-time Minimum Wage	.63	.95
Average Covered Earnings	.46	.69
Maximum Taxable Earnings	.26	.39

Source: L. H. Thompson, "Social Security Reform Debate," p. 1429.

---

[8]The government not only regulates private pensions but provides insurance.

[9]Charles T. Goodsell, *The Case for Bureaucracy*, (Chatham, NJ: Chatham House Publishers, 1983), p. 52.

prices in general. As it has turned out, however, between 1974 and 1982 the stock market failed to keep pace with inflation.

The risks of inflation are an example of an important class of risks referred to as **social risks.** These are risks that society as a whole faces. It is difficult for any private insurance firm to bear such risks. Aside from exceptional circumstances such as war, the deaths of different individuals are "independent" events. The firm that insures a large number of individuals can predict fairly accurately the number of individuals that will die each year. But if there is a war, the number may be much larger. Thus most insurance policies exclude the coverage of death in a war. Similarly, if a policy insured against inflation, it would find that if the inflation rate increased much faster than it had expected, it would bear a loss on all of its policies; it might well find that it was not able to meet all these commitments at the same time. There is no market for insurance against inflation.

The Advantages of Public Risk Absorption. There are two major distinctions between the ability of the government and that of private firms to provide insurance for social risks. First, the government is in a position to meet its obligations, by raising taxes. Secondly, the government can engage in risk sharing across generations. The costs of a war, for instance, can be shared by the current generation and future generations; through reducing investment during the period of war and through subsequently imposing taxes on the young for the benefit of the old, the costs of the war can effectively be shared by the generation that is working during the period of war and subsequent generations. If the economy experiences a particularly bad episode of inflation this decade, it can transfer some of the burden of that onto younger, working generations. As important as intergenerational risk sharing may be in practice, it has provided little of the official rationale for social insurance programs.

Adverse Selection, Differential Risks, and the Cost of Insurance

A third major problem with private insurance arises from the fact that different individuals have different life expectancies. A firm selling a life insurance policy does not want to insure people who are likely to die; if it knows that they are likely to die, it will insist on charging a high premium. For someone over the age of sixty-five or someone with a heart condition, these premiums may be particularly high. On the other hand for private insurance firms selling an annuity, the concern is just the opposite: they only want to insure people who are unhealthy, who are likely to die soon. Since women live longer than men, insurance companies in the past charged women lower life insurance premiums but higher premiums for annuities.

The fact that individuals differ in their life expectancies thus implies that, to the extent that these differences can easily be identified, economic efficiency requires that private insurance firms will have to charge premiums reflecting them. There are those who believe that this is unfair: if someone is unlucky enough to have bad health, it is bad enough, but to charge him a higher premium for his life insurance is adding insult to injury.

If private insurance firms cannot discriminate among individuals of different risks, quite another problem arises. In competitive equilibrium, the premiums must reflect the *average* risk of those who purchase the policy (for life insurance or annuity, this corresponds to the average life expectancy). But this means that good risks are in effect subsidizing the poor risks. With annuities, those who die young subdize those who live a long time; with life insurance, those who live a long time subsidize those who die young. This means, in turn, that good risks, on average, get back less from the insurance company than they put in. To them, insurance is a bad gamble. But if such individuals are not very risk-averse, they will not buy insurance. When the best risks no longer purchase insurance, the premiums must increase. This process, by which only the worst risks purchase private insurance, is called **adverse selection.**[10] Adverse selection may provide part of the explanation for high premiums charged for annuities. The government can force all individuals to purchase the insurance to avoid the problem of adverse selection. In doing so, it is engaging in some redistribution; good risks are paying more than they "ought to"; bad risks less than they "should."

Moral Hazard and Social Security

There is another reason why private insurance firms often offer only limited insurance. Insurance may reduce the individual's incentive to avoid the insured-for event; we referred to this as **moral hazard** in Chapter 11.

Individuals, in contemplating making provisions for their eventual retirement, face two important sources of risk.[11] The first is that they do not know how long they might live after retirement. An individual who did not buy an annuity would have to husband his resources carefully; he would have to worry about the possibility that he will live longer than average. In insuring this risk, no significant moral-hazard problem arises. But a moral-hazard problem does arise in the second risk, for which social security provides insurance; individuals do not know how well they will be able to work at the age of sixty-two or sixty-five or seventy. Some individuals are healthy and their skills have not become obsolete; they continue to work well beyond seventy. Others are incapable of working; they become disabled. But many individuals are in an in-between state at sixty-two or sixty-five; they are not medically disabled, but they are finding it increasingly difficult, or less enjoyable, or less productive, to work. When they are younger, individuals like to purchase insurance against the possibility that they will fall in this gray area, not so disabled as to qualify for a medical disability but not so well off that they can easily continue working. Social security provides that insurance: it enables an individual who wishes to retire at sixty-two to do so. But the better the "insurance," the larger the fraction of working income that social security replaces, and the less strong the incentive to work; with full replacement, even an individual who is in perfect health and is highly productive might be induced to retire. This is the central moral-hazard problem associated with social security.

The failure of the private market to provide complete insurance should not be viewed as a capricious consequence of rapacious insurance companies

---

[10] For a more extended analysis of the effects of adverse selection in insurance markets, see M. Rothschild and J. E. Stiglitz, "Equilibrium in Competitive Insurance Markets," *Quarterly Journal of Economics* 90 (1976): 629–50.

[11] Other than the risk of inflation, which we have already discussed.

trying to exploit the hapless consumer, but rather as a rational response to a critical economic problem, of providing at least some incentives to the insured. To the extent that this provides an explanation of the limitations of insurance provided by the private market, there is no reason to believe that the government can do any better: the trade-offs between risk reduction and incentives remain the same. In other words, concerns about the moral-hazard problem provide a limitation on the extent of insurance that can be provided, privately or publicly.

Retirement Insurance as a Merit Good

Even where there are good insurance markets, there remains a rationale for government action: if society believes that it cannot countenance an older individual suffering because he has failed to make adequate provision for his retirement years, and if a number of individuals fail to make adequate provision for their retirement on their own, there is an argument for *compelling* individuals to do so. For those who do make provision for their retirement may feel that it is unfair that they should have to bear the burden of those who could have made adequate provision for their retirement but simply had insufficient foresight to do so. In this view, retirement insurance (or life insurance) is a merit good, one that a paternalistic government forces on the individual for his own good. But it is different from many other merit goods, because a significant part of the costs of the individual's failure to purchase the good is borne by others. However, to the extent that this provides the rationale for social insurance, it suggests only that the government require individuals to obtain insurance, not that the government should require that individuals purchase the insurance from the government itself.

EQUITY ISSUES IN THE DESIGN OF SOCIAL SECURITY

Social security is a combination of a (forced) retirement savings program, an insurance program, and a redistribution program. Looked at simply from the perspective of a savings and insurance program, fairness would dictate that the returns received by different individuals correspond to their contribution. Any insurance program entails, of course, some individuals (those for whom the insured-against event occurs) receiving more than they contribute. Here, in this context, we would expect that those who live longer, or who need to retire earlier, would receive more than they contribute; fairness here means that the "expected" receipts for any individual correspond to his contributions.

If one looked at social security from the perspective of a redistribution program, one would assume that fairness dictates that there be transfers to those who are less well off; the poor should get back more than they contribute.

Intergenerational Equity

The current social security system represents a transfer of resources from the current young to the current old, a transfer for which they may not be subsequently compensated. A single, middle-income male who retired in 1970 will have received, on average, by the time he dies, a net transfer of more than $25,000; for those retiring in 1980, the transfer is estimated to be slightly smaller, $24,000. Those of later generations will pay more than they get back: a single male retiring in the year 2010 will pay over his lifetime more than $69,000 more than he gets back, and for someone retiring in the year 2020 (someone who is thirty in 1985), the difference *will have increased to $88,000.* [12]

Is this intergenerational redistribution desirable? The question of transferring income from the current working generation to the current elderly entails an analysis of the same issues involved in redistribution at one point in time. During the past fifty years, there has been a marked increase in the standard of living of most Americans. If this continues, a redistribution of income from the current working generation to the current aged is equitable, since the current working generation, over their lifetime, will in any case (even after this distribution) still be better off than the current aged. But during the past ten years there has been a marked slowdown in the rate of productivity growth; in some years there have even been decreases in per capita income. If this more recent pattern continues, the grounds for redistributing income from the current working generation to the current aged are much weaker. The problem is that it is impossible to predict with any reliability what will happen to per capita incomes over the next fifty years.

Intragenerational Distribution

A second set of issues concerns the distributive effect of social security *within* a generation. At the present time, all retirees get back considerably more than they put in. One of the objectives of the social security system was to provide a minimal level of income even to the poorest. The social security system has succeeded in greatly reducing poverty for those over sixty-five. Using the standard poverty index, in 1959, 35 percent of those over sixty-five were in poverty; by 1981 this was reduced to 15 percent. [13]

The social security system transfers different amounts to aged individuals of different circumstances. The ratio of the amount received to the amount contributed is higher for low-income individuals than for high-income individuals. At the same time, the actual amount transferred—the size of the social security bonanza—is largest for the better off. While the average lifetime transfer (the difference between what they receive and what they contribute) for those in the poorest quarter of the population was $34,042 in 1979, for the richest quarter it was one-third greater, almost $46,000. [14] Although all the current retirees have benefited, "to them that have, more shall be given." The ratio of receipts to benefits also differs markedly according to marital status, and whether both the husband and wife worked or only one worked.

[12] All numbers represent present discounted values, valued in real 1980 dollars, at age sixty-five. See M. Hurd and J. B. Shoven, "The Distributional Impact of Social Security," *National Bureau of Economic Research Working Paper* no. 1155, June 1983.

[13] Bureau of the Census, *America in Transition: An Aging Society* (Washington, D.C.: U.S. Dept. of Commerce, Current Population Report Special Studies Series, P–23, no. 128), p. 10.

[14] All expressed in present discounted value terms.

Concern has been expressed that the current social security system interferes with economic efficiency in two important ways: it reduces capital formation and it induces early retirement.

Savings

There is widespread belief that provision of social security reduces what individuals need to save for their retirement. As a result of this reduction in savings, there is less capital formation, and this may have a deleterious effect on the growth in productivity. Future generations will be worse off. Some critics of social security, such as Martin Feldstein, claim that it may have reduced capital accumulation in the United States by as much as one-third.[15] They attribute at least some of the marked differences in growth rate between Japan and the United States to differences in savings rates, and much of the difference in savings rates in turn is attributed to the differences in social security systems: Japan makes very limited public provision for the aged.

Supporters of social security, though admitting the theoretical possibility that social security may have depressed savings, doubt the quantitative importance of the depression. They point out, for instance, the marked growth of pension funds that occurred after the introduction of social security. One explanation for this is that social security enables individuals to retire earlier; but because it does not fully replace earnings, individuals are induced to save on their own account to make up the difference. Moreover, supporters of our current social security system contend that to the extent that there is a depressing effect, the government can, through other actions, offset these effects. It can stimulate investment, for instance, by investment tax credits. By reducing government deficits it can ensure that a larger fraction of savings goes into private capital formation rather than into the holding of government debt. Feldstein believes that the social security system's depressing effects on savings are so large that these actions, while ameliorating the effects of social security, cannot fully offset them.

Early Retirement

Social security also has an effect on labor supply: it induces individuals to retire earlier than they otherwise would. We noted earlier the large decline in the labor force participation of those over sixty-five during the past two decades; this has occurred at exactly the same time that there has been a large increase in social security benefits. (During the period 1970–1972, real social security benefits were increased by 28 percent; in the period between 1968 and 1976, real benefits increased over 50 percent). Michael Hurd of the State University of New York at Stony Brook and Michael Boskin of

---

[15]There is considerable controversy concerning Feldstein's results, involving a number of technical issues. Different studies have obtained different results. S. Danziger, R. Haveman, and R. Plotnick ("How Income Transfers Affect Work, Savings and the Income Distribution," *Journal of Economic Literature*, September 1981) conclude in their survey that the transfer programs (in which the effect of social security is dominant) ". . . have depressed annual private savings by 0–20 percent relative to their value without these programs, with the most likely estimate lying near the lower end of this range."

Stanford University argue that the decline in labor force participation was, indeed, due largely to real increase in social security benefits.[16]

Earlier, we pointed out that government programs have both income effects and substitution effects. Inefficiencies are associated with substitution effects. Both of these effects arise in the case of social security. The large transfer of resources to the elderly has an income effect; the retired individuals take some of this increased income in the form of extra leisure: early retirement. In addition, however, there is a substitution effect.

There is, however, considerable controversy about the size, and even direction, of the substitution effect. As individuals work longer, their total contributions to social security increase; they are taxed on their additional income. Their benefits per year are also increased. The question is, do they increase *enough* to compensate for the increased payments? At present the adjustment is not enough, but as a result of the reform bill of 1983, by the year 2008, on average, there will be a full adjustment. But in recent years, there has been an effect encouraging workers to stay on: the magnitude of social security benefits depends on individuals' contributions in previous years. In 1937 their contributions were limited to the first $3,000 of their income; in 1983 they were made up to $37,500. Thus the way social security benefits are calculated means that an individual with, say, a $40,000 income may now experience a significant increase in benefits by staying at work an additional year or two.[17]

Note that there is a distortion whether individuals are subsidized or taxed. The fact that some individuals are subsidized and some taxed does not result in the distortions netting out: the total distortion is not simply related to the average value of the marginal subsidy or tax.

Some of this distortionary effect is an inevitable consequence of the provision of retirement insurance. We could reduce the distortion, but only by, in effect, providing less insurance. There is not agreement about whether such a change is desirable.

THE 1983 RESPONSE TO THE CRISIS IN SOCIAL SECURITY

The financial viability of the social security system posed a political dilemma. The solution proposed by the presidential commission headed by Alan Greenspan did not involve a careful balancing out of the trade-offs, either those involving efficiency or equity considerations; rather, it entailed a mix-

[16] There is, however, some controversy about these results. One survey by Olivia S. Mitchell and Gary S. Fields concluded, "Clearly, no empirical conclusions can be drawn about the effects of Social Security on retirement," while Danziger, Haveman, and Plotnick ("Income Transfers") argue that social security has been at most responsible for one-half of the decline in labor force participation by older men since 1950 (a reduction in total work hours in the economy of 1.2 percent). See O. S. Mitchell and G. S. Fields, "The Effects of Pensions and Earnings on Retirement: A Review Essay," in *Research in Labor Economics*, vol. 5, ed. Ronald G. Ehrenberg (Greenwich, CT: JAI Press, 1982), pp. 115–55.

[17] Some economists have argued that the relationship between benefits and taxes is so loose (and so complicated) that individuals simply treat the social security system as a tax-transfer system; thus, in their decision about how much labor to supply, they take account of the payroll taxes they pay but not of any incremental benefits they receive. For a discussion of the whole set of issues, see M. Feldstein, "Facing the Social Security Crises," *Public Interest* 47 (1977): 88–100; A. B. Laffer and R. D. Ranson, "A Proposal for Reforming the Social Security System," in *Income Support Policies for the Aged*, ed. G. S. Tolley and R. Burkhauser (Cambridge, MA: Ballinger, 1977); A. Munnell, *The Future of Social Security* (Washington, D.C.: Brookings Institution, 1977); and A. Blinder, R. Gordon, and D. Wise, "Reconsidering the Work Disincentive Effects of Social Security," *National Tax Journal* 33(1980):431–32.

ture of "quick fixes" and long run compromises. The means by which the short-run problems were alleviated included: postponing a scheduled cost-of-living increase, accelerating scheduled increases in social security taxes, extending social security coverage to new federal employees, and (perhaps most controversial) taxing social security benefits of high-income individuals. The extension of coverage increases revenues more in the short run than in the long run; the effect of such a change on the long run depends on whether these individuals will be getting back more than they are putting in; if they do, then it exacerbates the long-run problem.

In addition, to improve the long-run viability of the system, the retirement age will be raised gradually from sixty-five to sixty-seven. That decision involves two trade-offs. Implicitly, there was a decision concerning the intergenerational distribution of income. It entailed a decision to place the burden of the adjustment on future generations. (Note that even prior to this decision, while current recipients were receiving a large net transfer from the government, future recipients would be paying a large transfer *to* the government. It is interesting that many younger economists thought this unfair.)

Secondly, it entailed a judgment about the insurance-incentive trade-offs. The individuals who will be particularly disadvantaged by the change in the retirement age are those who find working at sixty-five particularly difficult. The younger generation is, in effect, receiving less insurance against this prospect. On the other hand, this should have the effect of reducing the distortions associated with productive individuals being induced to retire earlier than they otherwise would. Proponents of this change argued that if sixty-five was the appropriate retirement age thirty years ago, then the changes in health—which result in individuals living longer—suggest that today the retirement age should be somewhat higher.

SOME CURRENT EQUITY AND EFFICIENCY ISSUES

In recent years, several features of the social security system have come under extensive criticism, because they are felt to give rise to inequities and inefficiencies. For instance, beneficiaries who are between the ages of sixty-five and seventy have their benefits reduced if they work. For every two dollars they earn, above a certain amount, they lose one dollar of benefits.

While pensions are subject to taxation, until 1983 social security benefits were exempt. (Beginning in 1984, high-income individuals were taxed on half of their social security benefits.)

A particularly vexing problem in the design of the social security system is the treatment of married versus single individuals. Consider two individuals, Bob and Joe, who had the same income when they worked and thus paid the same amount in social security taxes. Bob is married, but his wife never worked outside the house. Joe is not married. The total amount that Bob will receive is much greater than the amount that Joe will. Why, single individuals ask, should they be asked to support married couples? One proposal for addressing this seeming dilemma, as well as several other of the problems facing social security, is the Personal Security Account.

The Personal Security Account proposal was put forward by several prominent young economists, Michael Boskin and John Shoven of Stanford and Laurence Kotlikoff of Boston University, as a way of remedying some of these inequities. We noted earlier that the social security system combines a transfer program and insurance-retirement program. Essentially, their proposal separates these two functions. Each individual would have his own account. The government would provide an inflation-indexed return on tax contributions. The level of insurance benefits would be determined on an actuarial basis that provides all families with identical rates of return on their contributions. The contributions would be used to purchase five separate categories of insurance policies: (1) old-age benefits for household heads and their spouses; 2) survivor benefits for spouses; 3) survivor benefits for children; 4) disability benefits; and 5) old-age health insurance.[18]

Such a proposal would eliminate the seemingly capricious patterns of transfers that characterize the present social security system. It would also enable the system to be put on more sound financial footing.

ALTERNATIVE PERSPECTIVES

In this chapter, we have mainly viewed the social security program as an insurance and savings program. It is, of course, more than this: it is also a transfer program. Some economists (notably Joseph Pechman of the Brookings Institution) think of it primarily as a transfer program. To them, the link between the payroll tax and the social security system is of no substantive significance; there is (in general) no reason to tie particular programs to particular revenue sources.

For others, the link between the two is important, for three reasons. Many of the early advocates of social security believed that it was important that individuals believe that they are getting what they paid for, that there was not a public handout. Many individuals would find it demeaning to take a public handout. (Thus the confusion in the present system—between the different functions of social security, its role in insurance and savings, and its role in transfers—is viewed to be an advantage.) Moreover, if individuals perceive themselves as "purchasing" retirement benefits with their social security contributions, the distortions associated with the payroll tax will be reduced.

Others have been concerned that the political process might lead to excessively generous social security programs; some check on these redistributive programs is required. Having a clearly identified tax that must be raised when social security benefits are raised provides such a check.

SUMMARY

1. The market failures that give rise to the government provision of social insurance include the failure to provide insurance for many of the most important risks facing individuals, the high transaction costs associated with the private provision of

---

[18]The proposal was presented to the National Commission on Social Security Reform, August 29, 1982.

insurance, the failure to provide insurance against social risks, and the problem of adverse selection when markets cannot differentiate among individuals with different risk.

2. The social security retirement program serves three functions: it is a forced savings program, an insurance program, and a transfer program.

3. The social security program has an effect on labor supply, through its effect on induced retirements and on capital formation. There is dispute about the significance of these effects.

4. Changes in demography, in birth rates and life expectancy, in labor force participation among the aged, and in the rate of growth of productivity all contributed to recent financial crises facing the social security system.

KEY CONCEPTS

Transaction costs
Replacement rates
Social risks
Indexing

Adverse selection
Intergenerational equity
Intragenerational distribution
Moral hazard

QUESTIONS AND PROBLEMS

1. For each of the major aspects of the social security program (retirement insurance, survivors' insurance, disability insurance) describe the market failures that gave rise to the program or that might be used to justify its continuation. Assume you were asked to design a program that was to address only one of the market failures. For as many market failures as you can, describe an alternative program to the present system and explain its advantages and disadvantages over the present one.

2. List the risks against which the social security program provides insurance. In which of these instances do you think providing insurance affects the likelihood of the insured-against event occurring?

3. What are the theoretical reasons that social security might be expected to decrease savings? Are there any theoretical reasons why social security might be expected to increase savings? Why might a tax on interest income lead to later retirements? Under what circumstances might such a tax be desirable?

4. Discuss the equity, efficiency, and other allocative effects of the following recent and proposed changes in the social security system, and, where appropriate, provide alternative reforms directed at the same objective:
    a) terminating support of children of deceased workers at age nineteen, whether they are in school or not;
    b) tougher standards for eligibility for disability payments;
    c) increasing the age for eligibility for social security;
    d) increasing benefits for those who retire later so that they receive the same expected present discounted value of benefits, regardless of age of retirement;
    e) exempting those over the age of sixty-five from paying social security taxes.

5. To what extent could the purposes of the social security program be served by a law that required individuals to purchase retirement insurance from a private firm? Discuss difficulties with such a proposal, and what kinds of regulations might be required to avoid these difficulties.

14

Welfare Programs and the Redistribution of Income

There is consensus among Western democracies that no individual should be allowed to go hungry, go without housing, or go without any of the other basic necessities of life simply for want of income. The view that it is the responsibility of the federal government to provide these basic necessities dates in the United States to Franklin Roosevelt's New Deal.

In 1965, President Johnson launched his War on Poverty. He believed that it was the responsibility of the government not only to care for the needy, but to eliminate the root causes of poverty.

We call programs that provide assistance to the poor **transfer** or *welfare* programs. Responsibility for welfare traditionally resided at the state and local levels, but the federal government has taken on an increasingly large role. Even today, however, the states and localities are responsible for "general assistance," and their total expenditures are significant: $30 billion in 1983. Federal outlays for "welfare programs" in that year amounted to in excess of twice that amount.

There are two sets of federal welfare programs. The first set provides *cash* benefits to individuals in particular categories. **Aid to Families with Dependent Children** (AFDC) provides funds to families in which there is no earner, and **Supplemental Security Income** (SSI) provides funds for aged and disabled individuals with low incomes (it supplements social security benefits).

The second set of programs provides benefits for specific purposes: medicaid provides free medicine to low-income individuals and food stamps provide food at below-market prices. The housing assistance programs provide

subsidized housing.[1] These benefits are called **in-kind benefits** (as distinguished from cash benefits). In some cases, the government actually provides the goods (as with public housing, public health clinics, and free cheese
and butter to the poor), but in most cases the individual purchases the commodities from private sellers, with the government paying all or part of the
cost (as with medicaid or food stamps).

In the eighteen years from 1965 to 1983, welfare expenditures increased
almost seventeenfold and, as a percentage of gross national product, more
than tripled. Most of this increase was accounted for by an increase in the
number of recipients; AFDC beneficiaries increased from 4.3 million in 1965
to 10.7 million; food stamp recipients from 400 thousand to 21.7 million, and
SSI recipients from 2.7 to 3.9 million. The medicaid program, which was
just starting in 1965, had grown to the point where 10 percent of the population (21.5 million people) were recipients. (While the magnitude of transfers per recipient for public assistance increased hardly at all in real terms,
social security benefits—in real terms—increased by more than 55 percent
in the same interval.)

These programs, designed to transfer income to the poor, have been the
subject of considerable controversy. There are those who believe that their
structure has weakened incentives of the poor to seek employment, that it
has contributed to the break-up of families and to a sense of dependency
among the poor. On the other hand, there are those who believe that the
level of support is too small, that it is not sufficient to allow the poor to break
out of the vicious circle of poverty. For instance, because of their low income,
they obtain low levels of medical care, nutrition, and education, and this
leads to a low level of productivity; and the low level of productivity in turn
results in their receiving low wages.

As usual, there are efficiency and equity issues: What are the distortions
associated with such transfers? Are there provisions of the current system
that exacerbate the inefficiencies? How effective has the present system been
in reducing inequality? Could we achieve the same distributional objectives
at lower cost with an alternative welfare system? These are among the questions we will address in this chapter.

WELFARE PROGRAMS AND SOCIAL INSURANCE

In our discussion, we distinguish between welfare programs and social insurance; the latter include the social security programs and were the subject of
the previous chapter.

The distinction, however, is not a clear one. We noted in the previous
chapter that most of the social security programs do entail considerable
redistribution; they combine insurance and transfer programs.

Moreover, welfare programs can be thought of as insurance against the
kinds of contingencies that we, or our children, might face: "There, but for
the grace of God, go I." If one did not know whether one was going to enter

---

[1]As we noted in the previous chapter, the medicare and social security programs can be thought of as
being partially transfer programs. The government typically classifies veteran disability and pension payments as public assistance. It is more appropriate to think of these payments as deferred compensation for
military service, and hence we do not include those expenditures.

the world poor or rich, one might well want the government to provide some "insurance" against the possibility of the former occurring—i.e., one might want the government to increase the welfare allocations, the consumption of the poor, at the expense of the rich. It is in this sense that programs aimed at the redistributing of income can be viewed as insurance programs.

CASH VERSUS IN-KIND REDISTRIBUTION

Much of the provision of welfare is in the form of the public provision or subsidization of particular commodities—food, housing, medical care. Many people believe that it would be preferable for the government simply to provide welfare in cash. The present system is criticized on three grounds:

1) It is administratively costly; each of the programs has to be run separately; several different agencies have to determine the elegibility of each individual for the program. Eligibility standards determine who is qualified to receive aid under the given program. These eligibility standards are based primarily on income, but adjustments for family size and other circumstances are generally made. Programs that provide aid to particular groups of individuals are called **categorical aid** programs. When income is a major element in determining eligibility, the programs are said to be **means-tested.**

2) It introduces inefficiencies in resource allocations when there are substitution effects; and when there are not substitution effects, the consequences are not different from those of a direct transfer of income.

3) It is inappropriate for the government to attempt to distort individuals' consumption decisions.

In the following sections, we examine in detail the last two sets of criticisms.

Inefficiencies from In-Kind Redistributions

Consider food stamps, one of the more rapidly growing programs. It began in 1964, when Congress enacted the Food Stamp Act. Federal outlays grew from $30 million in that year, to $2.86 billion a decade later, to $14.2 billion in 1983; the number of participants increased from 400,000 in 1964, to 13.5 million a decade later, to 21.7 million in 1983 (See Figure 14.1).

To get food stamps, one has to have a sufficiently low net income (income minus certain allowable deductions). The deductions, discussed in greater detail below, are such that a family of four could have a total income in excess of $12,000 in 1982 and still receive some food stamps. In 1982 the maximum in food stamps that could be received (someone with zero net income) was $233 per month.[2]

---

[2] Both the amount received and the eligibility standards are adjusted annually for changes in the cost of living. The amount received is the difference between 30 percent of an individual's net income (after allowance for certain expenses) and the cost of a nutritionally adequate diet ($233 per month for a four-person household in 1982), provided the individual meets certain eligibility standards. To be eligible, a family (without anyone over the age of sixty-five) must have less than $1,500 in disposable assets and a gross income below 130 percent of the poverty guidelines for the household size. To calculate net income, the following deductions from income for households without an aged individual are made: a) 18 percent of earned income; b) a standard deduction, which in 1982 was $85; c) child-care expenses, with a limit of $115 a month; and d) total shelter costs including utilities in excess of 50 percent of income (after subtracting the above deductions), limited to $115. If there is an aged individual, a further allowance is made for medical expenses, and there is no limit on the deduction for shelter costs.

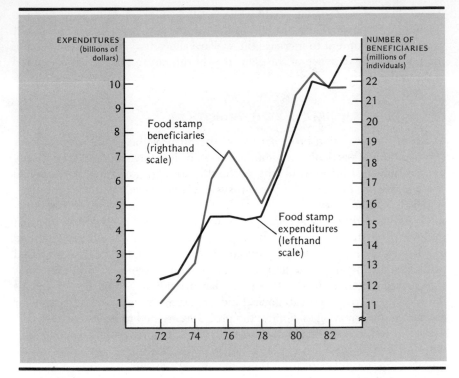

14.1 THE FOOD STAMP PROGRAM There has been rapid growth in the food stamp program. SOURCE: *Social Security Bulletin, Annual Statistical Supplement,* 1982, *Survey of Current Business,* 1984.

To see the effects of the food stamp program, we have drawn the budget constraint in Figure 14.2 before the food stamp program and after it. For simplicity, we consider an individual who initially had $1,000 and now receives $100 in food stamps. His new budget constraint is parallel to the old. If he consumed only food, his consumption of food would go up by $100. For every dollar less he spends on food, he has one dollar more to spend on other goods. Notice that a cash subsidy at $100 would have shifted his budget constraint in exactly the same way, except that with the cash subsidy he could have consumed $1,100 of other goods; with the food subsidy, he can still only consume $1,000 of other goods.

In Figure 14.2A the individual consumes more food than his food stamp allotment. There is then no substitution effect, only an income effect. The effect of the program is identical to a cash subsidy of $100. In Figure 14.2B the individual consumes just the amount of the food stamp allotment. We have drawn the budget constraint of an equivalent grant of cash. The individual would have consumed less food, but he would have been better off. There is a clear substitution effect: the fact that food is free induces individuals to consume more than they would if they had to pay for it. But there is a cost: individuals are worse off than they would have been if they had been given an equivalent cash grant. To put it another way, if we had given a

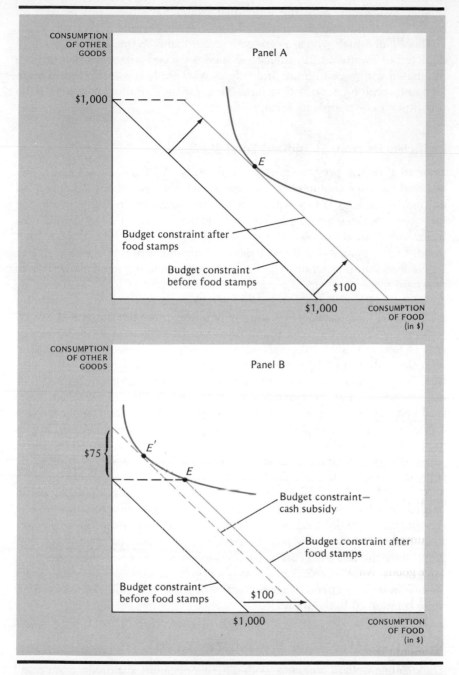

14.2 THE EFFECT OF FOOD STAMP PROGRAMS (A) If the individual consumes more than his food stamp allotment, there is no substitution effect, just an income effect; the effect of the food stamp program is no different from a $100 cash subsidy. (B) This individual purchases no food beyond his food stamp allotment. If he were given a $100 cash subsidy, he would consume less than $100 in food. A cash subsidy would make the individual better off. Alternatively, the government could give the individual a $75 cash subsidy and he would be just as well off.

smaller cash grant, $75, the individual would have been just as well off receiving $100 in food stamps, and the government would have saved $25.

Those individuals who are very poor are probably in the situation we have depicted in Figure 14.2B: their food stamps exceed what they would have purchased with a cash grant. Individuals who are better off consume more food and receive fewer food stamps. Thus for these individuals there is no substitution effect, only an income effect.

Inefficiencies from Subsidized Food Stamps

Prior to 1979 the program worked differently. All families of a given size received the same allotment of food stamps, but the price they paid depended on their income. A family with zero income would pay nothing; as income increased, families would pay a larger fraction of the value of the stamps. Effectively, individuals were allowed to purchase food below the market price. Figure 14.3 shows the individual's budget constraint before and after such a food stamp program. The food stamp program depicted allows him to purchase more food, up to a certain maximum limit of $200, assuming he pays 50¢ for $1 of food stamps. We have also drawn the budget constraint with a flat cash subsidy of $60; as depicted, this gives the individual exactly the same utility as the food stamp program. In Figure 14.3A, because the cost of food is reduced the individual consumes more food than he would with the cash grant; the program is successful in increasing food consumption. But this is an inefficient transfer. The cost of the program is the difference between what the individual pays for food and the market cost of the food consumed. Since the individual consumes $150 of food, he receives a $75 subsidy. The cash subsidy, which shifts the budget constraint up in parallel, would leave the individual just as well off but would cost the government less. In our example, a $60 cash subsidy is equivalent (in its effect on individual welfare) to a $75 food stamp subsidy.

Figure 14.3B depicts a situation in which the maximum amount individuals can purchase with food stamps is sufficiently small that it does not meet the individual's entire food desires. If the individual wishes to consume more than $200 worth, he must pay the full price once his food stamps run out. Now, since the marginal cost of purchasing food is the same (the *slope* of the budget constraint is the same as it was before the food stamp program), there is only an income effect. The program's effects are no different than if $100 were transferred to the individual.

INCENTIVE EFFECTS OF ELIGIBILITY STANDARDS

The differing welfare programs, with differing eligibility standards, often result in distortions in individuals' incentives to work. In some cases, such as in most housing programs, as the individual's income rises above a certain threshold, he becomes ineligible. If an individual's income is below the threshold, he is eligible for public (subsidized) housing; if it is above, he is not. Assume that the value of the subsidy is worth, say, $1,000. That means that by earning an extra dollar, which puts him above the threshold, the

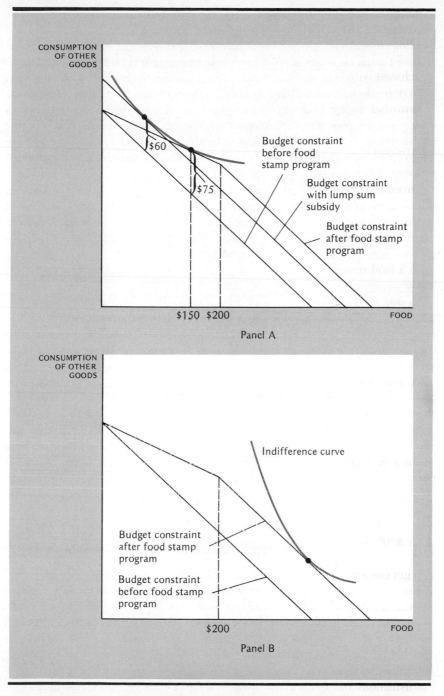

CONSUMPTION OF OTHER GOODS

$60

$75

Budget constraint before food stamp program

Budget constraint with lump sum subsidy

Budget constraint after food stamp program

$150 $200

FOOD

Panel A

CONSUMPTION OF OTHER GOODS

Indifference curve

Budget constraint after food stamp program

Budget constraint before food stamp program

$200

FOOD

Panel B

14.3 THE EFFECT OF A FOOD STAMP PROGRAM WHERE FOOD STAMPS HAVE TO BE PURCHASED In Panel A there is a substitution effect; in Panel B there is only an income effect. Up to $200 worth of food, the individual has to give up only 50 cents for each $1 of food. He must give up $1 of other goods for each dollar's worth of food beyond $200.

individual's net income, including the subsidy, is actually reduced by $999. Effective tax rates above 100 percent discourage work.

Even when there are not rigid thresholds, the extent of benefits often is reduced as income increases. This has the same effect that a tax has. In the food stamp program, the allotment of food stamps decreases by $30 for each $100 increase in income. This is an effective marginal tax rate of 30 percent.

Note that the food stamp program alone has an unambiguously deleterious effect on work incentives. The food stamp program makes individuals better off; it has an income effect: since individuals are better off, they wish to consume more leisure. The food stamp program also has a substitution effect; it reduced the marginal return to working by 30 percent.

This is bad enough, but its effects are compounded by the presence of other taxes in the system. Thus, if the individual has to pay a 7 percent payroll tax, a 2 percent state income tax, and a 14 percent federal income tax, his total effective marginal tax rate is 52 percent, as high as many high-income families and a likely deterrent to effort.[3]

Eligibility Standards for Food as a Housing Subsidy

The eligibility standards may affect not only individuals' work incentives but other aspects of consumption. In the food stamp program, for instance, families are allowed to deduct housing costs in excess of 30 percent of their income in calculating the net income that will determine their food stamp allotment. Consider a family that is spending more than 30 percent of its income on rent and more than its food stamp allotment on food. If it decides to move into a bigger apartment, costing, say, $100 more a month, it reduced its net income for eligibility for the food stamp program by $100; this increases the amount of food stamps it gets by $30. Thus the net cost to the family of increasing its housing expenditures by $100 is only $70. It is as if the government were subsidizing housing. Indeed, for this family, the only substitution effect associated with the food stamp program is on housing; there is no substitution effect on food.

SHOULD THE GOVERNMENT INTERFERE WITH INDIVIDUALS' FREE CHOICES?

Critics of in-kind welfare payments criticize these programs for being paternalistic. In the view taken in the previous section, if providing in-kind subsidies does alter behavior from that associated with a transfer system, it causes an inefficiency; the same levels of utility of recipients could be attained at lower cost to the government. But there is another view that this is precisely what the government is attempting to do: it wants to ensure that the money that is transferred is spent on "good" uses, on housing, food, and medicine. What society cares about, in this prospective, is not so much the welfare of the recipients as the outward manifestations of poverty, the slums, malnu-

---

[3] We should actually include the employer's social security tax as part of the tax paid by the individual; this would raise the effective marginal tax rate to close to 60 percent. On the other hand, if the social security benefits to which the individual is entitled increase as a result of his increased income, the net tax could be lower than 52 percent. For most young individuals the value of the incremental social security benefits is negligible.

trition, etc., that result from it. Some economists find this paternalistic view of the government objectionable; they argue that it violates the principle of consumer sovereignty. Others point out that one of the main objectives of many of these programs is to improve the welfare of the children of the poor; cash grants may not be as effective in doing this as certain in-kind benefits.

Earlier, we encountered the view, called specific equalitarianism, that contends that society may have views not only about the distribution of purchasing power in general but about access to particular goods, services, and rights. The right to a minimal level of medical care, food, and shelter ought to be viewed as a nontransferable right.

CATEGORICAL VERSUS BROAD-BASED AID

A second major controversy has been associated with whether aid should be given to all poor or only to the poor falling into certain categories. Thus the supplementary security income program has focused on transferring income to the aged poor, and AFDC has focused on transferring income to low-income families with dependent children.

Categorical aid (whether in-kind or cash) is more expensive to administer than broad-based aid, primarily because of costs associated with ascertaining eligibility for the program. For instance, in recent years, administrative costs per beneficiary for the supplemental income program have averaged three and one-half times more per beneficiary and seven times more per dollar of benefit payments than administrative costs for the Old Age and Survivors' Insurance Program.

Besides considerations of administrative costs, there are two efficiency issues and one equity issue that arise in comparing categorical versus broad-based aid. Categorical aid may have the effect of inducing individuals to fall into the benefited category; it may have a distortionary effect. This is not true of social security: individuals do not become older faster simply to take advantage of the program. But there are allegations that AFDC has contributed to the break-up of families; the departure of a low-wage father may increase total "family" income by making it eligible for AFDC. During the past decade, there has been a marked increase in the number of children born in families without a father. Whether there is a causal connection remains a subject of dispute.[4]

The major advantage that categorical aid has over broadly based programs is that, under certain circumstances, it can provide more effective redistribution, with less loss in efficiency. It can enable the targeting of aid to the most needy, who, at the same time, will not have adverse incentive responses. We have repeatedly emphasized the trade-offs between equity and efficiency considerations in the design of redistribution programs. Providing a high level of basic income through a transfer program that then declines as the individual's income from wages or other sources increases may discourage work. This will normally imply that a lower level of redistribution is more desirable for individuals whose response to incentives is large than for

---

[4] For instance, the illegitimate birth rate (births per 1,000 married females) almost quadrupled from 1940 to 1970, from 7.1 to 26.4, while the divorce rate (divorces per 1,000 married females) almost doubled, from 8.8 to 14.9. From *Historical Statistics*, Series B29 and B217.

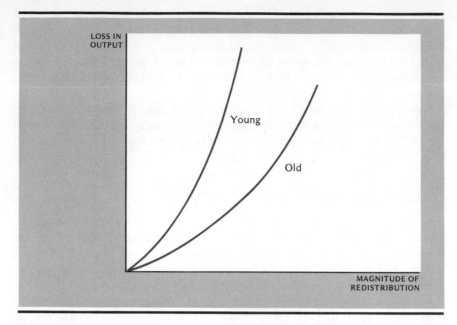

14.4 THE ADVANTAGE OF CATEGORICAL PROGRAMS The loss in output for any given increase in equality may differ across different groups. This may make it desirable to design redistributive programs aimed at different groups.

individuals whose response to wage incentives is small (e.g., those over seventy).

Figure 14.4 depicts a relationship between the magnitude of redistribution and the loss in output for two different groups (the working population and the aged). The greater the redistribution, the greater the loss in output. But because the loss in output for the aged is smaller (for each increase in the extent of redistribution), it is desirable to have a more redistributive program for the aged. By having different programs for groups with different characteristics, one can obtain a more effective redistribution of income.

There is an equity argument against categorical programs; there are those who believe that the government should not discriminate in favor of or against particular groups in the population. Two individuals who are equally poor should receive the same amount from the government, whether they are young or old. There should not be "favored" categories. Admittedly, older individuals may have more medical expenses, and one might want to adjust the transfers to take this into account; but this is already effectively done through medicare.[5]

The Negative Income Tax

There are many who believe that the present system of categorical aid and in-kind aid should be replaced by a single cash-based welfare system, which

---

[5]Some object to means-tested programs because they are believed to be demeaning to recipients. As a result, many who are eligible do not take advantage of the benefits, and thus the programs are less successful in attaining their objectives.

should be integrated into the income tax system. The proposal has been called the **negative income tax.**

All individuals would be required to file a tax return, but just as only individuals above a critical threshold would have to pay income taxes, those below that critical threshold level would receive a check from the government. Consider a tax regime in which everyone receives a check from the government of, say, $1,000 per year but then pays to the government, say, one-third of each dollar that he earns. Those with an income of less than $3,000 would receive something net from the government; those with an income greater than $3,000 would pay to the government more than they receive. Those who favor this system argue not only that it is administratively simpler but that it is less demeaning than the present system, which forces individuals to present evidence to several agencies concerning their low income. Furthermore, advocates claim that the implicit tax rate associated with the present tax system either discourages work or encourages dishonesty. Since an individual's eligibility for benefits declines markedly with an increase in income, the net increase in his consumption from an increase in income may be very limited. As a result, in some types of work, such as household services, the practice of not reporting income is very widespread. It is debatable, of course, whether switching to a negative income tax would alter this.

There were a large number of studies conducted in the 1960s and 1970s to ascertain the effect of our current system of welfare and proposed reforms on work effort and to quantify the associated inefficiencies. There is more of a consensus that effects on work effort are small for general assistance, SSI, food stamps, and housing assistance[6] (0.1 percent for SSI, 0.3 percent for food stamps and housing assistance) than there is for AFDC.[7] The magnitude of the welfare losses is also a subject of debate. We discuss how these welfare losses are measured in greater detail in Chapter 18.

Because welfare benefits may be sharply reduced as income is increased, many low-income individuals face high implicit tax rates.

Supporters of the negative income tax also argue that its further advantage is that it allows individuals to spend money in a way that reflects their own preferences; it does not distort their expenditure patterns in the way that the present welfare system does with in-kind aid.

Though the idea of a negative income tax has received widespread support, it has faced one serious problem: to provide what is viewed by many as a minimal level of support requires a high marginal tax rate. The present system, as we have said, entails a high effective tax rate on the very poor; switching to a negative income tax would lower the tax rate on these individuals but increase the tax rate on middle-income individuals. Not only would this be politically unpopular, but there is a view that it might have serious incentive effects. Advocates of the present system claim that 1) incentive effects among many of the recipients of welfare in our present system are

[6]S. Danziger, R. Haveman, and R. Plotnick, "How Income Transfers Affect Work, Savings and the Income Distribution," *Journal of Economic Literature*, September 1981, p. 996.

[7]For instance, J. Hausman ("The Labor Supply," in *How Taxes Affect Economic Behavior*, ed. J. H. Aaron and J. Pechman [Washington, D.C.: Brookings Institution, 1981], pp. 27–72) obtains estimates thirty-seven times as large as those obtained by R. Moffitt, "An Economic Model of Welfare Stigma," Rutgers University mimeo, 1980.

relatively small; a significant fraction of the recipients are individuals, like the aged and disabled, who would not enter the labor force or work much even if the implicit tax rate were reduced; 2) incentive effects on middle-income individuals may be more significant; 3) the recipients of welfare are much less productive than those in the lower-middle-income ranges who would face an increase in marginal tax rates under the negative income tax proposals; and 4) since there are many more individuals in these lower-mid-dle-income ranges than there are poor individuals on welfare, we should be particularly concerned with the incentive effects of such a change in tax structure.

HOW EFFECTIVE HAS OUR PRESENT WELFARE SYSTEM BEEN IN REDUCING POVERTY?

How effective have the major transfer programs of the past two decades been in decreasing inequality? Answering this question is not as easy as it might seem. It depends on what one measures.

There is a consensus that the programs have made a significant effect in reducing poverty, though the social security program has played a more important role than the cash welfare programs. One study contended that cash welfare payments reduced the number in poverty by 10 percent in 1978, while social insurance programs reduced it by 38 percent.[8] Because of difficulties in valuing the in-kind transfers, there is some disagreement about the role of these transfers in reducing poverty, with estimates ranging from 71 percent to 41 percent.[9]

The high unemployment rate in 1982 and the cutback in welfare payments during the Reagan administration resulted in a marked increase in the number of those in poverty between 1979 and 1982. The number rose from 26.1 million to 28.2 million. When in-kind benefits are included, the number of those in poverty is reduced by one-quarter; it rose from 15.1 million in 1971 to 22.9 million in 1982, according to the U.S. Census Bureau.

On the other hand, the transfer programs seemed to have had a much smaller effect on standard measures of overall inequality, such as the Gini coefficient.[10] Most of the studies suggest a reduction of the Gini coefficient from cash transfers (including social insurance) of between 10 percent and 20 percent.[11] The in-kind transfers had a much smaller effect, ranging from 2.3 percent to 8.3 percent.

But while the transfer programs seem to reduce inequality there has not been a marked change in the degree of inequality during the past decade (again, as measured, say, by the Gini coefficient, or by the fraction of total

[8] S. Danziger and R. Plotnick, *Has the War on Poverty Been Won?* (Madison, WI: Institute for Poverty Research, 1981).

[9] The larger number is for 1975, from M. Paglin, "The Measurements and Trend of Inequality: A Basic Revision," *American Economic Review*, September 1975, pp. 598–609; while the smaller number is for 1976 and is from W. C. Hoagland, "The Effectiveness of Current Transfer Programs in Reducing Poverty," paper presented at the Middlebury College Conference on Welfare Reform, April 1980. For a review of studies conducted through 1981 see S. Danziger, R. Haveman, and R. Plotnick, "Income Transfers." The two studies cited evaluate the benefits to the recipients at the cost to the taxpayer.

[10] For a definition of the Gini coefficient, see chapter 10.

[11] See S. Danziger, R. Haveman, and R. Plotnick, "Income Transfers."

income received by the lowest fifth of the population). The transfer-redistri-
bution programs seem merely to have offset an increase in the before-
tax/before-transfer inequality in income. The forces that have led to this
increase in before-tax/before-transfer inequality are complex and not well
understood.

301
**How Effective
Has Our Pres-
ent Welfare
System Been
in Reducing
Poverty?**

One question that has been raised is the extent to which the government
programs have *caused* the increase in before-tax/before-transfer inequality.
If, for instance, individuals are induced to retire early as a result of social
security, there will be more individuals in the population with zero before-
tax/before-transfer incomes. The government programs may also have contributed to the formation of low-income households: older people with low
income previously may have lived with their children; with the higher social
security payments, they may decide to live on their own. In the data, the
number of households with low income has increased. But these individuals
may well be better off than when they were living with their children.

This example also raises another question concerning the effectiveness of
government redistribution programs: the extent to which they have substituted for private transfers. The elderly formerly received more income from
their children; if for each extra dollar that social security gives an elderly
person his children feel they can reduce what they give him, the net beneficiary of the social security program is not the elderly but the younger individuals who are supporting them. (From this perspective, then, what is at
issue is not so much the level of support for the elderly but rather whether
there should be individual or collective responsibility for their support, and
the economic and social consequences of alternative arrangements.)

A factor that has undoubtedly contributed to the change in the before-tax
income distribution is the change in the fraction of the population over age
sixty-five (which we discussed in the previous chapter). Their needs (apart
from medical, which are taken care of by medicare) may well be less than
those of an individual with four children, two of whom are going to college.
A sixty-five-year-old individual who is living alone and receives $10,000 may
be (from a material point of view) no worse off than a family of six with four
children and an income of $25,000. The data, unfortunately, do not make
adjustments for these differences in circumstances, and economists disagree
about how this should best be done. It is worth noting, however, that inequality
within families facing similar situations is smaller than inequality among the
population as a whole.

Most economists would argue that one ought to focus on lifetime inequality; there are systematic variations in earnings over an individual's lifetime;
the individual's income usually begins low, increases over his middle years,
and then declines again as the individual goes into retirement. There may
be, in addition, short-term fluctuations: the individual may, for instance, go
through a short period of unemployment; a self-employed individual's income
will normally go down as the economy goes into a recession. But individuals
use savings to smooth out these variations in their income to provide for
periods in which their anticipated consumption will exceed their anticipated
income (such as retirement, or during the years in which their children go
to college). Focusing on the inequality of income in any particular year exaggerates the true extent of inequality in our society.

Finally, we should note that income may not provide the only index of inequality. Better nutrition and better care among the poor will be reflected in better health; during the past decades there have been marked changes in the differences in some important health indicators between the poor and the rich. One study showed that indeed mortality rates (the probability of dying in a given year) increased with income; this is explained by adverse diet, lack of exercise, and increased stress.[12] Another study concludes, "Strong evidence suggests . . . that reductions in mortality have been concentrated disproportionately in the lower income classes."[13] Moreover, access to medical care now no longer seems to be strongly dependent on income. Ten years after the introduction of medicare and medicaid, the average number of physician visits per person per year for all groups was 5.1: for those with an income under $5,000 it was 6.0, and for those with an income over $15,000 it was 4.9.[14]

SUMMARY

1. Transfer programs represent one of the fastest-growing areas of government expenditure. Many of the social insurance programs have a large transfer component in them.

2. The in-kind redistributive programs have several disadvantages: a) they are administratively costly; b) in some cases, they have only an income effect, in which case their effect on consumption is the same as cash subsidies; in other cases, they have a substitution effect, and in those cases, the government could provide the same level of welfare to the poor at less cost through a cash subsidy; c) the effect of payment-in-kind eligibility standards is to discourage work and, when compounded with payroll and federal and state income taxes, result in very high marginal tax rates; d) the structure of eligibility standards provides unintended results; for instance the food stamp program subsidizes the consumption of housing; and e) they are paternalistic.

3. Categorical programs have similar disadvantages: a) they are administratively costly; b) they are viewed by some as inequitable, since individuals of the same income are treated differently; and c) they are sometimes distortionary, as individuals attempt to qualify within high-subsidy categories. However, when groups differ in their labor-supply responses (or other responses) to government programs, the government may be able to obtain a higher degree of redistribution, for the same loss of inefficiency, by providing categorical aid.

4. The negative income tax is a proposal to integrate the welfare programs with the income tax system, providing only cash subsidies; it would eliminate the present program of categorical aid. The main concern is whether it could provide an adequate "minimum" standard of living to the very poor, without at the same time imposing very high marginal tax rates on middle-income individuals.

5. The transfer programs of the past two decades have reduced the number of individuals in poverty, and they have had some effect in reducing measures of overall inequality. At the same time, however, there has been an increase in the extent of before-tax/before-transfer inequality.

---

[12] R. Auster, Levelson, and Sarachek, "The Production of Health," cited in P. Feldstein, *Health Care Economics* (New York: Wiley, 2nd ed., 1983), p. 22.

[13] K. Davis and and C. Schoen, *Health and the War on Poverty* (Washington, D.C.: Brookings Institution, 1978).

[14] Source: National Center for Health Statistics, Health, United States, 1976–1977, DHEW (HRA) 77-1232 (GPO, 1977), p. 265.

KEY CONCEPTS

Transfers
Aid to Families with Dependent Children
Supplemental security income
Negative income tax
In-kind benefits

Categorical aid
Means tests
Eligibility requirements
Specific equalitarianism

QUESTIONS AND PROBLEMS

1. It has sometimes been suggested that the government should restrict the use of food stamps to "healthy" foods. Discuss the merits of this proposal. Assuming that it would be easy to distinguish between "healthy" and "unhealthy" foods, describe the effect of such a restriction on an individual's consumption of the two kinds of foods.

2. Consider a welfare program (such as housing) with an eligibility standard that requires that an individual's income be below some threshold level. Draw the individual's budget constraint with and without the subsidy (put labor on one axis, consumption on the other).

3. Consider a welfare program (such as food stamps), the magnitude of the benefits of which decreases as an individual's income increases. Draw the individual's budget constraint with and without the subsidy, and use the diagram to illustrate how work incentives are reduced and how a fixed dollar subsidy could lead the individual to the same level of utility at lower dollar cost.

4. There have been proposals for the use of government subsidies to help poor individuals purchase private housing (just as the government's food stamp program helps them purchase food). Discuss the merits of the private versus public provision of housing.

5. Several different proposals have been put forward concerning how housing subsidies should be provided. Discuss the merits of: a) the government's paying a given fraction of the family's housing expenditures, up to some maximum, with the percentage depending on the family's income; and b) the government's paying a fixed dollar amount of housing allowance, the amount depending on the family's income. In both cases, discuss the appropriateness and consequences of adjustments to reflect the family's expenditures on medicine; on food.

6. Assume you were particularly concerned with the welfare of children. How would this affect the kinds of welfare programs you might support or how you might design your welfare programs?

15
Education

Some of the most heated political controversies in recent years have revolved around education, the third largest single item of expenditure in the public sector, behind national defense and social security. The debates have involved how education should be both financed and produced. Should the federal government take a larger role in the financing of education? Should there be public support for private schools? Should tuition be charged at state universities? How should the funds that are available be allocated between remedial education for the disadvantaged and accelerated education for the gifted?

Underlying the debate are the following basic questions: What is the most efficient way of providing for the education of America's youth? What should be the relative roles of government and the private sector in the production and financing of education? What are the trade-offs between equity and efficiency? Are we spending enough (or too much) on education, and are we spending it well?

Several recent studies have suggested that all is not well with American education. While quantitative measures are hard to come by, one often-cited indicator is the marked decline in average Scholastic Aptitude Test (SAT) scores for college-bound seniors (from a verbal score of 445 in 1973 to 426 in 1982, and a math score of 481 in 1973 to 467 in 1982).[1] By way of comparison, Japanese students are alleged to spend more time in school and to perform better on standardized tests than their American counterparts.[2]

[1] Oversight on Teacher Preparation: Hearing before the Subcommittee on Postsecondary Education, November 17, 1983. There has been a slight increase in SAT scores since 1981.

[2] For instance, in the United States, the school day is typically about six hours, and the school calendar 180 school days; and of the six hours, only 50 percent to 60 percent are spent on instruction (N. Karweit, *Time-On-Task: A Research Review* [Baltimore: Center for Social Organization of Schools, Johns Hopkins University, 1983]). In Japan, the school year is 240 to 250 days a year, students typically go to school almost seven

There are indications that the quality of grade-school teachers has declined significantly in the past decades. While the SAT scores of those going into grade-school and high-school teaching have always been below average, math scores sank from 449 in 1973 to 419 in 1982. (The decline should, perhaps, not be so surprising, given the decline in real salaries of 15 percent during this decade.)

Not surprisingly, there is more agreement that something is wrong than about what should be done, or who should take responsibility for doing it. In this chapter we address a few of the recent proposals for reforms in our educational system. We review the present structure of American education and survey some of the arguments for why education should be publicly provided.

THE STRUCTURE OF EDUCATION IN THE UNITED STATES

Traditionally, elementary- and secondary-school education have been the responsibility of local communities. They financed it (usually with property taxes), hired the teachers, and determined the curriculum. The states have taken an increasing role in financing education; in 1978–79 for the first time, revenues from state sources exceeded revenues from local sources (as we see in Figure 15.1). In the past two decades there has also been a marked increase in federal support, mostly for special programs such as aid to schools where there are a large number of disadvantaged children. While in 1982–83 the federal government provided on average nine percent of the funds, in Mississippi it provided almost 25 percent of the funds, and in Colorado it provided less than 6 percent of the funds. States provided on average 50 percent of the nonfederal funds, but this varied from 99 percent in Hawaii (where there are no local school districts) and 79 percent in Kentucky to 7 percent in New Hampshire.

At the same time, the states have taken an increasingly active role in setting certain minimum standards—the number of days students must be in school per year, the lowest age at which children may drop out of school, the minimum education requirements for teachers employed in public schools (they often specify not only that the teachers, for instance, have a college degree, but also that they have taken a specified number of courses in pedagogy). They also play a role in the determination of the curriculum. Many states require courses in American history in the eleventh grade and adopt certain approved lists of textbooks, from among which the local community must select those books used.

The federal government has not attempted to set standards or curricula. But following the Supreme Court decision of *Brown* v. *Board of Education* in 1954, in which the court ruled that so-called separate but equal educational facilities for blacks and whites were not constitutional, the federal government has taken an active role in promoting integration.

---

hours a day and three and one-half hours on Saturday, and they spend 85 percent of their time on instruction. (D. P. Schiller and H. J. Walberg, "Japan: A Learning Society," *Education Digest*, October 1982). Beyond this, a sizable fraction attend after-school programs (about 75 percent of fourth, fifth, and sixth graders).

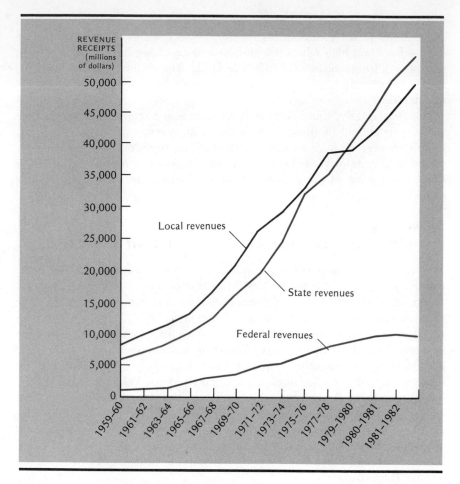

15.1 REVENUE RECEIPTS OF PUBLIC ELEMENTARY AND SECONDARY SCHOOLS
There has been a steady increase in the relative role of state support for public education.
SOURCE: *Digest of Education Statistics, 1982, 1983–84.*

One of the consequences of local control is that many rich communities have spent far more on education than most poor communities. The range in educational expenditures per student has been enormous, even within a single state. In New Jersey, for instance, school district expenditures per student ranged from roughly $2,025 to roughly $5,347 in 1980–81, a difference of 65 percent.[3] The variation is even larger in some other states, and between states.[4]

More than 88 percent of all elementary- and secondary-school students attend public schools. Of those who go to private schools, the vast majority

[3] Margaret E. Goertz, *Money and Education in New Jersey* (Princeton, NJ: Educational Testing Service, 1981).

[4] One study showed that, in 1969–70, in Texas the highest-spending district spent more than fifty-six times the amount spent by the lowest-spending district. Even in the states with the smallest differences, the high-spending districts spent 50 percent to 60 percent more (South Carolina, North Carolina, Maryland). In New York, the high-spending district spent eleven times the amount spent by the low-spending district, and in California, almost eight times the amount. From R. D. Reischauer and R. W. Hartman, *Reforming School Finance* (Washington, D.C.: Brookings Institution, 1973).

(63 percent) go to Catholic parochial schools. Private institutions play a much more important role in higher education. Though a majority of higher education degrees at the bachelor's, master's and doctor's levels are earned at public colleges and universities, almost two-thirds of first professional degrees are earned in private universities. There have not been dramatic changes in the relative role played by private and public schools over the past decade.

In the 1970s the federal government took an increasingly active role in providing aid to higher education, not to institutions but directly to students, mainly in the form of low-interest loans. There were, however, significant cutbacks during the Reagan administration.

FEDERAL TAX SUBSIDIES TO PRIVATE AND PUBLIC SCHOOLS

The personal income tax may have important effects on the demand for public and private education. Expenditures of state and local communities for education (as well as for other purposes) are implicitly subsidized because state and local taxes are deductible on federal income tax returns and interest on state and local bonds is exempt from federal taxations. This means that if my community taxes me $1,000 to support public schools, the cost to me is far less than $1,000. If I am in the 50 percent marginal tax bracket (so that I pay 50 percent for each additional dollar of taxable income to the federal government), then by deducting $1,000, my federal taxes are reduced by $500. The *net* cost to me of $1,000 spent on public education is only $500. In contrast, if I spend $1,000 on private education, it costs me $1,000 that I could have spent elsewhere.

The total value of tax expenditures for education in 1983 was approximately $15 billion, as Table 15.1 shows. Most of these expenditures arose from the deductibility of state and local taxes from federal income tax. Since the value of the tax deductions is greatest for higher-income individuals, this form of support for education is, in effect, *regressive;* that is, it benefits higher-income individuals more than lower-income individuals.

At the same time, the tax system serves to discourage private expenditures on education.[5] If I spend $1,000 in tuition to send my child to a private

Table 15.1 TAX EXPENDITURES ON EDUCATION, 1983 (in millions of dollars)

Subsidy to state and local education from deductibility of state and local taxes and tax exemption of interest on state and local bonds	$13,372
Subsidies to private education and higher education	
Exclusion of interest on state and local student bonds	175
Exclusion of scholarship and fellowship income	415
Deductability of charitable contributions (education)	770
Subtotal	$ 1,360
Total Subsidies	$14,732

Source: Calculated from J. A. Pechman, *Federal Tax Policy* (Washington, D.C.: Brookings Institution, 1983), and *The New York Times,* March 26, 1984, p. 11.

---

[5] But the tax deductibility of gifts to private schools (which are treated as charities) strongly encourages private education.

school, not only do I pass up the already-paid-for public education, but the expenditure is not even tax-deductible. Furthermore, the return to the education, which occurs later in the form of higher wages, is taxed. The tax system thus discourages private spending on education.

WHY IS EDUCATION PUBLICLY PROVIDED?

The public role in the provision of education has been so pervasive in the United States that it is generally taken for granted. In other countries, however, while the government may provide funds to educational institutions, much of the education itself is provided by private, particularly religious, schools.

Is There a Market Failure?

Education is not a pure public good. The marginal cost of educating an additional child is far from zero; indeed, the marginal and average costs are (at least for large school districts) approximately the same. And there is no difficulty in charging an individual for use of this service.

Those who seek to justify public education in terms of a market failure focus on the importance of externalities; it is often claimed, for instance, that there are important externalities associated with having an educated citizenry. A society in which everyone can read can function far more smoothly than a society in which few can read. But there is a large private return to being able to read, and even in the absence of government support, almost all individuals would learn this and other basic skills. Indeed, most individuals would go far beyond that. The question is, given the level of education that individuals would privately choose to undertake were there no government subsidy, would further increases in education generate any significant externalities? There is no agreement concerning the answer, but the case for government support based on these kinds of externalities seems, at best, unproved.[6]

There may be other important externalities associated with education; public education may have played an important role in integrating new immigrant groups into American culture. Public education may have been essential in making the melting pot work. The benefits of this accrued not only to individuals but to the nation as a whole.[7]

Distribution

The primary justification for public support of education arises from concern about the distributional implications of the private provision of education.

---

[6]See, for instance, D. M. Windham, "Economic Analysis and the Public Support of Higher Education: The Divergence of Theory and Policy," in *Economic Dimensions of Education*, A Report of a Committee of the National Academy of Education, May 1979.

[7]There are other externalities associated with the educational process: students learn from each other; good students may learn more from being with other good students than from being with bad students. These externalities have important consequences for questions like, Should students be ability-tracked? Should special schools be set up for the very able? These questions are important, not only in discussing how public schools should be organized but in assessing proposals for more parental choice, particularly through public support of private schools.

Richer individuals will want to spend more on the education of their young, just as they spend more on cars, homes, and clothes. There is a widespread belief that the life-chances of a child should not depend on the wealth of his parents or the happenstance of the community in which his parents live. The prospect of upward mobility, that one's children will be better off, has provided much of the political support for public education and may have played an important role in the political stability of the United States. The immigrants who came to the United States at the turn of the century, though poor, did not feel permanently disadvantaged: they had hopes for their children's prospects. Those prospects, however, often depended on access to good schools.

Imperfect Capital Markets

These concerns about "equity" may explain why the government has taken an active role in providing education at the elementary- and secondary-school levels, but they do not fully explain the role of the government in higher education. If capital markets were perfect, individuals for whom education is beneficial, for whom the return to education exceeds the cost, have an incentive to borrow to finance their higher education. But private lenders are not, for the most part, willing to lend to finance education, and hence those without funds of their own (or their parents') would be denied access to higher education without some assistance from the government.[8] Most of this assistance has taken the form of free, or at least subsidized, education in state universities and colleges. More recently, however, the federal government has attempted to attack the problem directly, by making available grants and loans (often subsidized) and by guaranteeing loans (so that private lenders are willing to extend credit) for higher education.

Current Issues

The concern for equality of opportunity has led to almost universal agreement that the government should play some role in the provision of education. Less certain is what its role should be. Currently, it ties both the production and financing of grade-school and high-school education together. If students wish to receive public support, they must go to public schools. They can choose to go to private schools, but they receive little, if any, public support. The issues currently facing education include:

Should this link between production and financing be broken? Should there be public support for private schools?

How much should be spent on public schools?

How should the funds that are available for public elementary and secondary schools be allocated among competing uses?

How much and what kind of support should be provided for higher education?

---

[8]There are good explanations for this: banks are concerned about the difficulty of getting repaid. The substantial difficulties that the government has had in getting loans to students repaid is consistent with these concerns.

There are those who believe that a greater reliance on the market (private production) would result in greater efficiency, with little loss (and possibly a gain) in equity, while others believe that the loss in equity would be substantial. In the following sections we review some of the central arguments and proposals for reform.

HOW SHOULD PUBLIC EDUCATIONAL FUNDS BE ALLOCATED?

Every school district faces the problem of how it should allocate its educational budget. It can allocate more funds for special education, for remedial classes for the disadvantaged, or it can allocate more funds for accelerated classes for the gifted. As we allocate more funds to any one individual, there is some increase in that individual's productivity. This is the return to education.

If we wished to maximize national output, if efficiency alone were our goal, we would allocate funds so that the extra increase in productivity from spending an extra dollar on one individual would be the same as the extra increase in productivity from spending an extra dollar on another. If very able individuals not only reach a higher level of productivity than others at each level of education but also benefit more from education, so that the *marginal* return to education is higher, such a policy entails spending a greater amount on the education of the able than on that of the less able. To some this seems unfair; these individuals believe that the government should ensure that there is equality of expenditure in public education. But when educational expenditures are equalized, those who are more able—or who have home backgrounds that give them an advantage—will still be better off. Accordingly, there are some who believe that government should engage in **compensatory education;** it should attempt to equalize not input (expenditure) but output (achievement). It should attempt to compensate for the background disadvantages facing some groups in our society. One of the major federal programs is directed specifically at encouraging local communities to provide such compensatory education.

As we allocate more and more funds (of a fixed budget) to the less able, and less and less to the more able, total output falls, since the marginal return to education (under our assumption) for the less able is smaller than for the more able. There is thus a trade-off between efficiency and equality, as depicted in Figure 15.2A. What point one chooses on this locus depends on one's values, on how one is willing to trade off efficiency versus equality.

There are some who maintain, however, that the trade-off curve does not look as in Figure 15.2A but as in Figure 15.2B; that is, some movement toward compensatory education may actually increase national output. In this view, those who are advantaged have a higher output than the disadvantaged at each educational level, but the *marginal* return to further education for the more able is actually lower than for the less advantaged. This implies that we can get both more efficiency (higher output) and more equality by having at least some degree of compensatory education. Unfortunately, there is little empirical evidence to support one view versus the other.

Note that the differences in the education-productivity relationship between one individual and another may be the result either of differences in innate

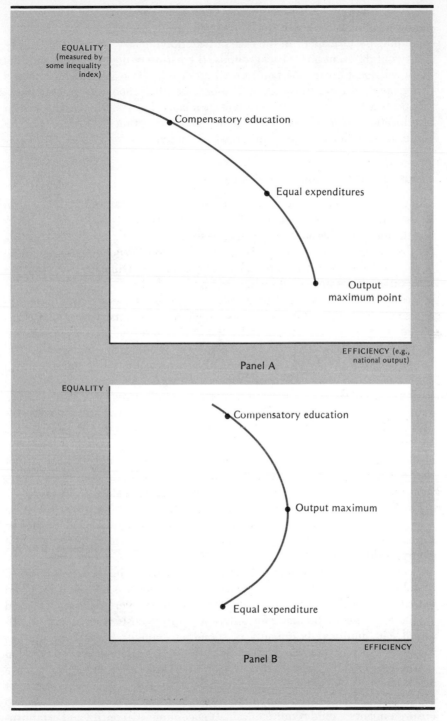

15.2 EQUITY-EFFICIENCY TRADE-OFFS IN EDUCATION EXPENDITURES (A) There may be important equity-efficiency trade-offs in the allocation of educational expenditures. (B) Under some circumstances, providing more expenditures for the less advantaged both increases efficiency (increases national output) and reduces inequality.

ability or differences in environment (home background). There is a long-standing controversy about the relative contribution of these two factors in explaining performance. In the case of two individuals with the same innate ability but different home backgrounds, the nature of the education-productivity relationships may depend on whether education in the home (home background) is a **substitute** for or a **complement** to schooling. If home background is a complement to schooling, it means that it increases the return to education. If it is a substitute, the more education that occurs in the home, the smaller the return to formal education.

Reforming the Financing of Education

The discussion so far has been concerned with the allocation of funds within a school district among students of different backgrounds and abilities. During the past two decades, there has been considerable debate concerning another aspect of resource allocation to education: Expenditures per pupil in some communities is much higher than in others. Different communities have different resources with which to finance education. In addition, different communities have expressed different "tastes" for education. Communities with the same resources may spend different amounts. (These differences can at least be partly explained by the use of the kinds of voting models discussed in Chapter 6. We might expect a community with mostly aged individuals to have less commitment to education than a community with similar resources per student where most voters have school-aged children.)

In 1971, California's Supreme Court ruled in *Serrano* v. *Priest* that the existing manner in which public schools were funded was unconstitutional. The California court held that the "right to an education in public schools is a fundamental interest which cannot be conditioned on wealth." Relying on local property taxes to finance education did that. The ruling required that the state devise an alternative method of financing education. Subsequently, there have been similar decisions in a number of other states.

On the other hand, in 1972 the United States Supreme Court ruled, in *San Antonio Independent School District* v. *Rodriguez*, that local funding in Texas did not violate the "Equal Protection Clause" of the Constitution (the Fourteenth Amendment).

These decisions have focused attention on several important questions: Should spending be the same in every community? Or is all that is required is that a minimal level of education be provided in every community? And should adjustments be made for differences in the costs of education in different communities? Is equality of spending enough? Some communities might use the funds to develop better athletic facilities, others to develop better programs for basic-skills development, others might allocate more funds to special educational programs. The result is differences of treatment of similar individuals who happen to reside in different communities. But to ensure equality would require eliminating community control and establishing a centralized educational system within each state.

What is at issue are not only the basic trade-offs of equity and efficiency; some individuals believe that every parent should have the right to make decisions concerning his child's education. With local control of education, parents at least feel that they can have some influence over the outcomes. Thus local autonomy of schools has become to many almost a principle in its own right; some individuals might still favor local control, even if it could be shown that central control was both more equitable and more efficient. To others, what is at issue is a trade-off between the rights of parents (to decide about their children's education) and the rights of children (to equality of opportunity, regardless of who their parents are).

The states have responded to these concerns by attempting to increase equality while retaining at least some degree of local autonomy. In New Jersey, for instance, the state has broadened its role in financing education (with poorer districts getting much more aid than better-off districts); it has set minimal educational standards that all districts must attain (when Trenton failed to meet these standards, and failed to take what the state thought was appropriate action to remedy the deficiencies, the state took over the school district); and it has placed ceilings on the amount that higher-spending school districts can spend.

Limitations on Equality Imposed by Parental Choice

Some of these attempts to attain greater equality, such as the ceilings on expenditures by richer school districts, have been criticized as self-defeating. What is of concern is not just the degree of inequality within public schools but the total extent of inequality in our society. So long as the government is not willing to prohibit individuals from going to private schools, any attempt to introduce too much equality into the public educational system will result in individuals transferring to private schools.

In England there have been periodic proposals for the government actively to discourage the private schools, on the grounds that private education leads to social stratification (only the upper and upper-middle classes sending their children to private schools). But in the United States, restrictions on private schools might well be unconstitutional, in any case, though there has been controversy about whether private schools should receive public support, which we discuss below, there have been no suggestions that the private schools be actively discouraged.

Those who can afford to send their children to private schools may be induced to do so if they believe that the public schools are not providing an adequate level of education for their children. In narrow economic terms, parents may ascertain that the return to investing in their children exceeds the return to investing in other assets.

Education as a Screening Device

The view of education that we have presented so far is referred to as the **human capital** view. Education is an investment in individuals, which yields a return, just like any other capital investment.[9]

---

[9]There is a huge literature on the human capital view of education. See, for instance, Gary Becker, *Human Capital: A Theoretical and Empirical Analysis with Special References to Education* (New York: National Bureau of Economic Research, Columbia University Press, 2nd ed., 1975).

An alternative view holds that one of the important functions of education is to identify the abilities of different individuals. Those who go to school longer get a higher wage and are observed to be more productive; but this is not because the schools have increased the productivity of these individuals. Rather, the schools have identified those who are the most productive individuals. The school system is viewed as a **screening device,** separating the very able from the less able.[10]

If this view is correct, or even if a part of the returns to education represent the identification of those who are more productive, there may be much less of a trade-off between efficiency and equity than would be the case if the primary reason that those who receive more education receive a higher wage is that they are made, by the education, more productive. On the other hand, if this screening view is correct, it may be more difficult to attain equality of outcome (achievement) within the public school system. First, the expenditures on education may have relatively little effect on productivity; and second, if the school systems fail to identify the very able, those who believe that their children are in this category will pursue other means to signal ability, such as sending them to private schools. Even were the government successful in reducing inequality among those graduating from public schools, there might remain inequality between graduates of public and private schools.

Note that both the screening and human capital views are consistent with the systematic correlation between the level of education and wages: the average wage of the better educated is higher than that of the less educated.

PUBLIC SUPPORT FOR PRIVATE SCHOOLS

In recent years there has been increasing political support for financial aid to private schools. Traditionally, most private schools in the United States have been affiliated with religious institutions, and thus the controversy over aid to private schools has ben closely related to issues of state support for religion, which is explicitly barred by the Constitution. In the last few years, the issue has ceased to be viewed primarily in this light. Most of the proposals involve financial assistance directly to the students rather than to the institution and thus sidestep the issue of state support of religious education (though the consequences may be much the same).

Tuition Tax Credits

There have been two major proposals for aid to private schools. The first of these is a tuition tax credit. Parents who pay for tuition in private schools would receive a credit against their income tax of a certain percentage of their expenditures. The proposals most commonly discussed do not allow individuals with income above a certain level to take the credit. Were such a proposal to be adopted, it would be another example of a tax expenditure.

---

[10]This view has been put forward by J. E. Stiglitz, "The Theory of Screening Education and the Distribution of Income, "*American Economic Review* 65(1975):283–300, A. Michael Spence, "Job Market Signaling," *Quarterly Journal of Economics* 87(1973), and K. J. Arrow, "Higher Education as a Filter," *Journal of Public Economics* 2(1973): 193–216.

The government could just as well not have given a tax credit but simply sent a check of a certain amount to those who have children enrolled in private schools (with the amount depending on the amount spent on a private school, and perhaps on the income of the parent). The expenditures on private education would then be an explicit item in the federal budget. Giving aid in the form of a tax credit has, however, two disadvantages over direct grants. First, it does not provide aid to the very poor, who pay little or nothing in income taxes. Second, it makes the implicit expenditure on private education less obvious, less open. (This may, in fact, be one of its desirable characteristics from the point of view of supporters of aid to private education.)

School Vouchers

A second major proposal is called the **school voucher** system.[11] Each child would be given a voucher, a piece of paper, which he could use at any school he wished.[12] He would turn over the voucher to the school, and the government would then send the school a fixed dollar sum. The school might or might not charge a fee in addition to the voucher. Public schools would, in this view, have to compete directly with private schools. Public schools would have to raise their revenue by persuading students to attend, just as private schools would. If parents valued the kinds of programs provided by the public school and the mix of students going there, then the public schools would do well.

In the view of supporters of the school voucher scheme, this competition would force public schools to be more responsive, and the competition would lead to greater innovation in education. In the view of voucher critics, the scheme would lead to a more socially and economically stratified society, with the children of wealthy and well-educated parents going to one school and the children of poor and less well-educated parents going to other schools. Though regulations to prevent racial discrimination might be easily enforced, regulations to ensure the absence of socioeconomic stratification might be difficult to implement. Finally, questions are raised about discipline problems: Would schools be prohibited from turning down students? Would they be allowed to expel them? Would public schools become a repository for students not acceptable elsewhere? Could one devise a system of giving schools that take children with discipline problems "bonuses"?

Though the plan has received extensive attention, no state has yet adopted it even in a modified form. There was a limited voucher experiment in one school district in San Jose, California. One study, after examining the results of that experiment, concluded that

> education vouchers stand little chance of succeeding in American elementary and secondary schools. [Parents eventually] learn about their alternatives and the rules governing choice. But there is still some question about the social

---

[11] For a survey of the issues, see G. R. LaNoye, *Educational Vouchers: Concepts and Controversies* (New York: Teachers College Press, 1972).

[12] Note that the GI bill, which provided educational benefits for veterans, was essentially a voucher program. They could use their vouchers at any qualified educational institution.

consequences of parents' or students' program choices. Specifically, there is some concern that parents pick programs which reinforce their class-related social values, so that poor children have little opportunity to acquire the beliefs, attitudes, and social competencies necessary for social mobility to the middle class. . . .[13]

AID TO HIGHER EDUCATION

There has been a long tradition of government aid to higher education. At the time many states were established, the state constitutions provided for the founding of a state university. Often a considerable amount of land was set aside and the proceeds from the sale of this land were to be devoted to the use of higher education. Then in 1864 Congress passed the Morrill Act, establishing what are called the land-grant colleges, for the study of agricultural and other technical subjects (such as mining). The extension services provided by the states' agricultural colleges have played an important role in the improvement of agriculture in the United States. The state universities, colleges, and junior colleges have enabled many students who would not otherwise have been able to afford a college education to get one.

The present system has been criticized on both equity and efficiency grounds. A major justification of government support has been that it leads to a more egalitarian distribution of income. But critics claim just the opposite: the major beneficiaries of government support for higher education are the advantaged. Since the average income of those who go to college will be higher than those who do not, aiding them (by subsidizing higher education) in effect constitutes aid to the better off. The net effect of the aid on income distribution is ambiguous: since the wealthier tend to pay more taxes, they bear a larger share of the costs, and receive a larger share of the benefits.[14]

Moreover, the subsidy to education results in excessive "consumption" of higher education. In deciding on whether to stay in school longer, individuals compare the increment to their income with the extra costs (including the *opportunity* costs—their foregone earnings—while they are in school) they have to bear. Since those costs are less than society's cost (by the amount of the subsidy), some individuals will stay in school even though the extra returns fall short of marginal *social* costs.

Thus if individuals could borrow to finance their education but had to pay the full costs of their schooling, they would balance the benefits and costs and make efficient decisions. Poor individuals of a given ability would be just as able to go to universities as the child of a rich parent.[15] If individuals

---

[13] Gary Bridge, "Citizen Choice in Public Services; Voucher System," in *Alternatives for Delivering Public Services,* ed. E. S. Savas (Boulder, CO: Westview Press, 1977).

[14] One study by W. L. Hansen and B. Weisbrod of the University of Wisconsin suggested that the net impact was regressive. The average income of those with children at the University of California was more than 50 percent greater than those with no children in public higher education in California and a third greater than those with children in junior college. The subsidy for those with children in junior colleges represented 12 percent of their income, while the subsidy for those with children in the University of California represented 41 percent of their income. See W. L. Hansen and B. A. Weisbrod, *Benefits, Costs, and Finance of Public Higher Education* (Chicago: Markham Publishing Co., 1969).

[15] Universities may provide "consumption goods"—tennis courts, swimming pools, good conversation—in addition to yielding an investment return. Children of rich parents are likely to consume more of such "consumption goods" just as they consume more of other consumption goods.

could borrow, no one for whom higher education was worthwhile would be denied access to it.

In this view, then, the problem is one of inability to borrow (a market failure), and the appropriate remedy is for the government to provide (or guarantee) loans. Advocates of student loan programs claim that they are more equitable than tuition grants and encourage economic efficiency. Proponents of subsidies (tuition grants), at least for the children of the poor, believe that the inefficiencies associated with "excessive" purchase of education are minimal—the schools tend to weed out those who cannot benefit from the education, and the subsidy is small relative to the total costs (which include the earnings foregone while the individual is in school). They believe that unsubsidized loans will discourage the children of the poor from getting a higher education (particularly since there is always a risk concerning whether the investment will pay off in terms of higher wages; if it does not, they are still saddled with a large loan to repay).[16] In this view, subsidies are critical in encouraging upward mobility among the poor. Advocates of subsidies for children of the poor believe that these dynamic effects, the effects on mobility, are of central concern.

SUMMARY

1. The past thirty-five years have seen marked changes in the structure of education in the United States. There has been increased federal involvement, and a larger fraction of funds are provided by the states.

2. Education is not a pure public good, nor do externalities provide a persuasive justification for the role of the government. The two major justifications for public support of education are the belief that the quality of education obtained should not be solely dependent on the resources of the child's parents and imperfections of capital markets.

3. There may be important trade-offs between equity and efficiency in the provision of education. Attempts to provide compensatory education, in which the government attempts to offset the disadvantages that children from a poor background face, may reduce net national output. Whether compensatory education has this effect depends on a technological issue about which there is not agreement: whether the marginal product of education is greater or less for individuals with disadvantaged backgrounds.

4. So long as parents have the option of sending children to private schools, there is only a limited degree of equality that can be obtained through the public school systems.

5. Though education is not the only determinant of an individual's future wages, there is a systematic correlation between the level of education and wages; there is, however, controversy concerning the explanation of this correlation. Some claim that it is primarily due to the increased skills that children obtain at school (the human capital view), while some claim that it is due to the schools' identifying the very able and differentiating them from the less able (the screening view).

---

[16] If there were perfect risk markets, individuals might be able to divest themselves of this risk. The absence of good risk markets can be viewed as another market failure; this market failure, in turn, can be related to problems of imperfect information. To remedy the risk problem, some have proposed a "contingent repayment loan program" in which the amount repaid would depend on the future income of the individual. Yale University actually instituted such a plan.

6. There has been increasing public support for government aid to private education, either through tax credits or through a voucher scheme.

7. The government has long played an active role in higher education, though its dominance is not as great as at the elementary- and secondary-school levels. Some believe that government aid to higher education is regressive in its effects, since those who benefit from college are likely to have higher incomes.

KEY CONCEPTS

Tax expenditures   Human capital
Compensatory education   Education as a screening device
                                        School vouchers

QUESTIONS AND PROBLEMS

1. Discuss the equity and efficiency arguments for raising tuition at state universities. To what extent do your answers depend on whether there is a good college loan program available?

2. Discuss the equity and efficiency arguments for providing college loans at subsidized interest rates.

3. List some characteristics of our educational institutions that seem to be more consistent with the signaling-screening view of education than with the human capital view.

4. What might you anticipate to be the consequences of eliminating the deductibility of state and local taxes from the federal income tax for: a) the level of expenditures per pupil in public schools and b) the mix of public and private schools in the country? If the price elasticity of the demand for education is unity, what should be the effect on the demand for education in a community in which the median voter is in the 50 percent marginal tax bracket? in the 25 percent tax bracket?

5. It is important to remember that the property tax per student is often as high in industrial centers as it is in the suburbs. Why might you still expect that expenditure per pupil would be lower in the industrial centers than in the suburbs?

6. An important study headed by James Coleman found that private schools were both more effective educationally and more integrated racially.[17] Assuming the results are valid, can you suggest arguments for why this might be so? Discuss the difficulties in drawing policy conclusions from such a study.

[17] J. S. Coleman, T. Haffer, and S. Kilgore, *Achievement in High School: Public and Private Schools Compared* (New York: Basic Books, 1981).

PART FOUR

TAXATION: THEORY

This and the next part of the book are concerned with taxation. This part develops the general theory of taxation, and the next examines in some detail taxation in the United States.

While Chapter 16 sets out the general principles of taxation, Chapter 17 discusses who bears the burden of taxation. Chapter 18 analyzes the effects of taxation on economic efficiency, and Chapter 19 shows how equity and efficiency considerations may be balanced off against each other.

16

Taxation: An Introduction

Taxation is unlike most transfers of money from one individual to another: while most other transfers are entered into voluntarily, taxation is compulsory. In Chapter 4 we saw some of the reasons why the contributions to support public services need to be compulsory: because of the free rider problem, unless support for public goods is made compulsory no one will have an incentive to contribute. We showed, in particular, that all individuals might be made better off by voluntarily agreeing to being compelled to contribute to the support of public goods. Yet the ability to compel individuals to contribute to the support of public goods may also provide the government with the ability to compel individuals to contribute to support some special-interest group: the government has the power to force one group to give up its resources to another group. This forced transfer has been likened to theft, with one major difference: while both are involuntary transfers, transfers through the government wear the mantle of legality and respectability conferred upon them by the political process. In some countries and at some times, the distinction becomes, at best, blurred. The political process becomes detached from the citizenry and is used to transfer resources to the groups in power.

The difficulty arises in distinguishing the legitimate from the illegitimate uses of the power of taxation. Concern about these issues was central to the founders of the Republic. The rebellion that became the revolutionary war is often dated to the Boston Tea Party, which was motivated by a concern that unjust taxes were being levied on the colonies: the slogan "Taxation without representation is tyranny" provided one of the central motifs of the revolution.

BACKGROUND

Taxes have existed virtually as long as there have been organized governments. The Bible said that a tithe (one-tenth) of the crops should be set aside
for purposes of redistribution and for the support of the priesthood. It was
not clear what the enforcement mechanism was, and the Bible does not
report on the extent of tax evasion. In the Middle Ages, individuals provided
services directly to their manor lords; these were effectively taxes but they
were not monetized. The fact that they were forced to provide these services
meant that they were, to some extent, slaves. Some have argued that the
fact that modern taxes are **monetized**—individuals are not compelled to provide services (except in the special case of the draft) but to provide money—
should not obscure the underlying relationships. An individual who must
give the government, say, one-third of his income is, effectively, working
one-third of the time for the government. One important advantage of this
monetization ought to be apparent: the government would face an enormous
managerial problem if each individual had to work four months a year for
the government.

There are, however, two critical distinctions between feudal levies and
modern taxes. In the former case, individuals were not allowed to leave their
manor (without the permission of their lord). The fact that (outside the Soviet
bloc countries) individuals are allowed to choose where they wish to live,
and therefore the jurisdiction that will impose taxes upon them, is a critical
distinction. Second, while under the manorial system individuals were compelled to work, in modern taxation individuals are compelled only to share
what they receive from working (or what they receive from investing, or
what they spend) with the government. They can choose to pay less if they
are willing to work less and receive less for themselves. Still, taxes remain
essentially compulsory.

In the United States, concern about the possibility that the power to tax
might be abused led to certain constitutional restrictions on the kinds of
taxes that could be imposed.[1] For instance, because an export tax was felt to
be a selective levy against the producers of a particular commodity, such
taxes were explicitly barred by the Constitution. Other provisions of the
Constitution attempted to ensure that taxes would not be imposed in a discriminatory manner (the uniformity clause, which says the taxes must be
imposed in a uniform way, and the apportionment clause, which says that
direct taxes have to be apportioned among the states on the basis of population). These constitutional restrictions were interpreted to imply that the
government could not impose an income tax. It was not until a constitutional
amendment was passed in 1913 that the federal government could impose
such a tax.

The restrictions imposed reflected the experiences the colonies had with
the use (or, as they saw it, abuse) of what they viewed as discriminatory
taxes levied by the British government. The writers of the United States
Constitution did not and probably could not have anticipated all of the forms
of discriminatory taxation. Thus in spite of the safeguards that the founders

[1] See Chapter 2.

of the Republic attempted to provide through the Constitution, issues of
taxation have been among the most divisive issues facing the country. In the
early nineteenth century there was, for instance, considerable controversy
over tariffs.[2] Tariffs on industrial goods, though they raised revenues, also
served to protect the industrial North; but while the North may have benefited from these tariffs, the South suffered by having to pay higher prices for
the protected goods.

323
Changing Pat-
terns of Taxa-
tion in the
United States

CHANGING PATTERNS OF TAXATION IN THE UNITED STATES

The passage of the Sixteenth Amendment in 1913, establishing the income
tax, marked a turning point in the structure of taxation in the United States.
Prior to that, the principal sources of federal revenues were excise taxes and
customs duties. In the past sixty years, these have dwindled in importance,
and income taxes (individual and corporate) have become the principal source
of revenue the United States.

Table 16.1   RECEIPTS OF THE FEDERAL GOVERNMENT, 1985 (estimates)

Individual income tax	328.4
Corporate profits tax	76.5
Excise taxes	38.4
Customs duties	9.4
Social security taxes	270.7
Estate taxes	5.6
Miscellaneous	16.0
Total	745.1

Source: Economic Report of the President, 1984.

Table 16.1 shows the receipts of the federal government from various
sources, while Table 16.2 shows the changes in the relative importance of
various taxes during the past half-century. In particular, we see: a) a marked
increase in the relative importance of taxes on individuals and corporations

Table 16.2   PERCENT OF TOTAL REVENUES FROM VARIOUS SOURCES

	1902	1940	1960	1980	1985
Individual income tax	—	16.9	44	47.2	44.1
Corporation tax	—	19.8	23.2	12.5	10.2
Sales and excise taxes	47.6	31.6	12.6	4.7	5.2
Customs	47.4	5.8	1.2	1.4	1.3
Payroll tax	—	14.2	15.9	30.5	36.3
Estate and gift	1.0	6.3	1.7	1.0	.8

Sources: 1902–1940: U.S. Bureau of the Census; Heightened Statistics for the U.S., Colonial Times to 1957,
        pp. 724, 727, 729.
    1960–1980: J. Pechman, Federal Tax Policy (Washington, D.C.: Brookings Institution, 1983),
        p. 353, derived from Office of Management and Budget.
    1985 (estimates): Economic Report of the President, 1984.

---

[2]Tariffs are taxes imposed on imported goods.

(called *direct* taxes) and the decrease in relative importance of taxes on commodities (called *indirect* taxes); b) within direct taxes, a marked decrease in the role of the corporation tax and a marked increase in the role of payroll taxes; and c) within indirect taxes, a decline in the relative importance of customs duties.

These trends have not, however, been universal: in Europe, during the past two decades there has been increasing reliance on what is called the **value-added tax,** which is effectively a national sales tax. The value-added tax is a tax imposed on the value added by an enterprise—that is, the value of its sales minus what it purchased from other firms. There has been some discussion in the United States concerning the introduction of such a tax. Only Australia relies more heavily than the United States on the individual income tax, getting almost half of its revenues from this source.

These reversals in the relative importance of various taxes have not been the only changes that have occurred in the past fifty years. Another extremely important change, which we discussed in Chapter 2, is the increasing share of national output that is collected in taxes, in all major countries. The share ranged, in 1981, from between 27 percent for Japan to 51 percent for Sweden. In the United States, tax collections have amounted to somewhat over 30 percent of national output.

These two trends—the increased share of national income collected in taxes and the increased relative importance of income taxes—have required a marked increase in the tax rates on individual income over the past fifty years. Particularly significant are the increases in the marginal tax rates, the extra tax an individual must pay as a result of earning an extra dollar of income. As we shall show, many of the inefficiencies associated with the tax system arise from high marginal tax rates. While the top bracket when the income tax was first imposed was only 7 percent, and one had to have an income of over $500,000 to face that rate, the top rate rose rapidly, to 77 percent in 1918 (during World War I), then declined to 24 percent in 1929; it then rose rapidly during the depression and World War II, reaching a top rate of 94 percent in 1944 for incomes over $200,000. The maximum rate remained over 90 percent from 1951 until President Kennedy cut tax rates in 1964 (when it was reduced to 77 percent). In 1981 President Reagan cut the maximum tax rate to 50 percent.

Similarly, the personal "first-bracket rate" (the lowest rate paid by individuals subject to taxation) increased from 1 percent in 1913 to a high of approximately 20 percent during the period 1951–1963, then gradually fell to the current level of 11 percent.

The total income which an individual can earn before he has to pay any taxes has increased roughly in proportion to the cost of living during the past forty years. But between 1979 and 1985 the poverty level increased faster than the exemption level, so that by 1985 the exemption level was considerably less than the poverty level, as we see in Figure 16.1. (Recall from Chapter 10 the definition of the poverty level.)

A relatively small fraction of the population had to pay taxes in the early days of the income tax. Now, over 100 million tax returns are filed every year. In earlier chapters we noted the critical role played by the median

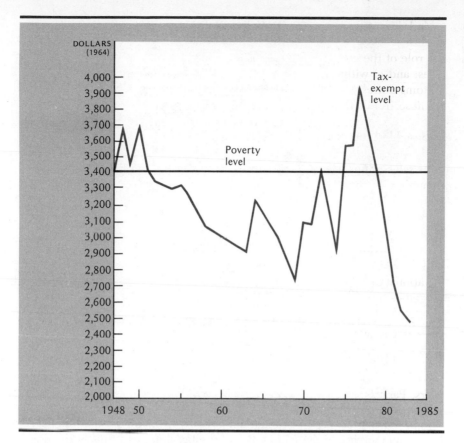

16.1 POVERTY LEVEL AND TAX-EXEMPT LEVEL OF INCOME FOR A FAMILY OF FOUR IN 1964 PRICES Since 1979, the tax-exempt level for the personal income tax has dipped well below the poverty level. SOURCE: J. A. Pechman, *Federal Tax Policy* (Washington, D.C.: Brookings Institution, 1984).

voter and the marginal tax rate he faces.[3] As Table 16.3 shows, this rate has increased markedly in recent decades. The first part of the table shows the marginal tax rates for 1965–1980. The third shows what they *would have been* had the tax laws not changed in 1981. The second part shows the marginal tax rates under the 1981 tax law. The marginal tax rate faced by the median voter between 1965 and 1980 increased from 17 percent to 24 percent. Even more marked was the increase in the marginal tax rate paid by someone at twice the median income, from 22 percent to 43 percent. One of the concerns that led to the tax bill in 1981 was that, with inflation, without a change in the tax law, the marginal tax rates faced by the median individual would increase even further, to a projected 32 percent in 1984. Under the bill, the tax rate paid by the median voter in 1984 was kept almost the same as that in 1981 (while that paid by the individual who had twice the median income was slightly reduced).

[3] Recall the definition of "median" from Chapter 6: half of all individuals have an income greater than the median, half less than the median.

Table 16.3 MARGINAL PERSONAL INCOME TAX RATES FOR FOUR-PERSON
FAMILIES, SELECTED YEARS, 1965–84 (percent)

| | *Family Income* | | |
Year	*One-Half Median Income*	*Median Income*	*Twice Median Income*
1965	14	17	22
1970	15	20	26
1975	17	22	32
1980	18	24	43
	Under Economic Recovery Tax Act of 1981		
1981	17.8	27.7	42.5
1982	16	25	39
1983	15	23	40
1984	16	25	38
	Under Old Law		
1981	18	28	43
1982	18	28	43
1983	18	28	49
1984	21	32	49

Excludes social security taxes and state and local income taxes.
Source: Department of the Treasury, Office of Tax Analysis.

Tax Avoidance and Tax Reform

The past fifty years have been marked not only by an increase in the tax rate
but by an increase in the complexity of the tax code, and thus in the opportunities for tax avoidance. Although the concept of "income" seems simple
enough in theory, in practice, defining what is and is not income turns out
to be a very difficult matter. The government has made matters worse for
itself by taxing different kinds of income at different rates and by allowing a
variety of deductions. Each distinction introduced by the tax law necessitates a set of careful legal definitions; and when the legal distinctions do not
correspond well to sound economic distinctions, there are clear incentives
to make sure that income is received in a form that is taxed at a low rate.

The motive for introducing many of the distinctions may have been quite
reasonable. For instance, medical expenses are deductible; there may be
feelings that those who are sick and have to pay high medical bills should be
treated differently than those who are not sick. But no matter how good the
motive, the consequences, in terms of the complexity of the tax code and
the opportunity for tax avoidance to which it gives rise are subjects of widespread concern.

In addition, these special provisions have incentive effects. As we saw in
Chapter 11, the deductibility of medical expenses may induce individuals to
spend more, for instance, on medical care than they otherwise would. The
recognition of these incentive effects of taxation has had a further consequence: there has been an increasing use of the tax system to encourage
activities that are thought to be socially desirable. Among the examples of

this are the energy tax credit (to encourage energy conservation) and the investment tax credit (to encourage individuals and firms to invest more).[4]

The increase in taxes combined with the provisions for special treatment of certain categories of income has had, in turn, some extremely important consequences: there has been a marked increase in tax avoidance activities. In particular, tax shelters have grown enormously in popularity; these are investment schemes by which individuals can reduce their tax liabilities. (We discuss some of the tax shelters in Chapter 24.) Although these schemes have undoubtedly enabled some individuals to reduce their tax burdens, they have also provided a good source of income for the tax accounts, tax lawyers, and brokers who have put together the tax shelter schemes.

Not all individuals have equal access to these tax shelters; they have provided greater relief from taxation on capital—that is, on interest, capital gains, etc.—than on wages. For some individuals who are in a position to take advantage of the better tax shelters, the effective tax on capital may be negative. Salaried individuals—such as schoolteachers—may have little opportunity for tax avoidance, or perhaps more accurately, they may perceive themselves as having little opportunity for tax avoidance. In fact, many of their fringe benefits, such as health insurance and pensions, are provided in the form that they are so as to avoid taxation of this form of compensation.

A vicious cycle has developed: because of the variety of deductions and special provisions to raise the requisite revenue, tax rates need to be higher than they otherwise would be. This increases the incentive to find loopholes and to obtain special treatment, further reducing the tax base and necessitating further increases in tax rates.

There has thus been an increasing perception that the present tax system needs to be reformed. Some are concerned that the high tax rates lead to serious economic inefficiencies and have contributed to the low rate of savings and investment in the United States, and thus to the slowdown in the rate of increase of productivity. Others are concerned with what they perceive as the gross inequities associated with the present tax system. As President Reagan expressed it when arguing for his tax reform bill, there is not a level playing field.

But while there seems to be a consensus that the tax system ought to be reformed, there is no consensus on how it ought to be reformed. Indeed, when Congress has been able to pass a reform bill there has often been disagreement on whether it has improved matters or made them worse; the Tax Reform Bill of 1976 was widely referred to as "The Lawyers' and Accountants' Relief Bill of 1976." President Reagan's proposals for tax reform have been hotly debated in Congress, with some critics claiming that he had on certain critical issues caved in to special-interest groups (for instance, with taxation of oil and gas), and others holding that he had not gone far enough in meeting their special needs.

Why is it so difficult to design a fair and efficient tax system? Are there not some simple principles, some unambiguous criteria by which we can

---

[4]For a discussion of this use of policy, see Charles Schultze, *The Public Use of Private Interests* (Washington, D.C.: Brookings Institution, 1977). Charles Schultze, currently at the Brookings Institution, served on the Council of Economic Advisers and as director of the Office of Management and Budget.

evaluate alternative tax systems? There are some basic principles, but because there are more than one, there are trade-offs. Reasonable people may differ concerning how much weight should be given to various considerations.

THE FIVE DESIRABLE CHARACTERISTICS OF ANY TAX SYSTEM

It is widely believed that a "good" tax system ought to have:

1) Economic efficiency: the tax system should not interfere with the efficient allocation of resources.

2) Administrative simplicity: the tax system ought to be easy and relatively inexpensive to administer.

3) Flexibility: the tax system ought to be able to respond easily (in some cases automatically) to changed economic circumstances.

4) Political responsiveness: the tax system should be designed so that individuals can ascertain what they are paying so that the political system can more accurately reflect the preferences of individuals.

5) Fairness: the tax system ought to be fair in its relative treatment of different individuals.

ECONOMIC EFFICIENCY

A persistent concern in recent debates over tax policy is whether the present tax system discourages savings and work and whether it has distorted economic efficiency in other ways. For instance, the large increase in the number of Arabian horses in the United States over the past two decades has been attributed to a peculiar loophole in the tax structure. The special treatment of gas and oil may have led to excessive drilling. Railroad box cars were used for a while as a tax shelter, until a glut of these developed.

The history of taxation is dotted with other examples of distortionary effects. As we mentioned in Chapter 1, the result of the window tax imposed in Britain was that houses without windows were constructed. Modern England provides other examples: three-wheel vehicles, though perhaps slightly less safe, and not much less costly, than four-wheel vehicles, were taxed more lightly than the latter. Hence many individuals chose them in preference to the more conventional four-wheel vehicle. Vans (station wagons without windows) were taxed more lightly than station wagons with windows, and again, many individuals were motivated to purchase these vehicles, but not by a preference for darkness in the rear of their vehicle.

Behavioral Effects of Taxation

Most of the efficiency effects of taxation are far more subtle and difficult to assess. Income taxation may affect the length of time an individual stays in school by affecting the after-tax return to education, the choice of jobs (because for some jobs, a larger fraction of the return comes in untaxed "fringe benefits"), whether an individual enters the labor force or stays at home to take care of children, the number of hours a taxpayer works (when he or she has discretion over that), whether he or she takes a second job and the effort put into the job, the amount that the individual saves and the form savings take

(the choice between bank accounts and the stock market), the age at which
an individual retires, and whether he works part time beyond the age of sixty-five.

The effects of taxation are not limited to decisions concerning work, savings, education, and consumption. While there is some question of the extent to which the tax system affects whether individuals get married or divorced, there is little doubt that it affects the timing of these decisions. For instance, the United States tax code considers a couple married for the entire calendar year even if the wedding is held on December 31. So a working couple who earn similar incomes, choosing between a December and January wedding date, are strongly encouraged by the income tax to choose January. The reverse is true for divorce. Taxation affects risk taking, the allocation of resources to R&D, and, in the long run, the rate of growth of the economy. It affects not only the level of investment of firms but the form of the investment (the durability of the goods). It affects the fraction of national savings that is allocated to housing, to other structures, and to equipment. It affects the rate at which our natural resources are depleted. There is hardly an important resource allocation decision in our economy that is not affected in some way or another by taxation.

Financial Effects of Taxation

Sometimes, taxation affects the form that a transaction takes more than its substance. For instance, in real terms it may make little difference whether an employer gives an employee money to purchase a Blue Cross health insurance policy or whether the employer purchases it for him. In tax terms, it makes a great deal of difference. In the former case the individual receives "income" upon which he is taxed; in the latter case the "fringe benefit" is not taxed. Similarly, in real terms it makes little difference whether I save directly for my retirement or whether my employer takes some of my salary and invests it in a (fully funded) pension plan. But the tax implications are quite different, and as a result individuals are induced to save through the pension plan rather than directly. These financial effects may, of course, have in turn further real effects on the economy: pension plans, because of the restrictions imposed on them, may invest their funds differently than the way an individual saving for his retirement might invest them. The restriction of individual choice resulting from the provision of these fringe benefits may, itself, have economic consequences.

Similarly, since dividends, capital gains (increases in the price of a stock), and interest are all treated differently, the tax structure may have a significant effect on the *financial* structure of United States corporations; for instance, on firms' decisions on whether to finance additional investments by borrowing or issuing new shares.

Distortionary and Nondistortionary Taxation

Any tax system influences behavior. After all, the government is taking money away from an individual, and we would expect him to respond, in some way, to this lower income. When we say that we want the tax system to be nondistortionary, we clearly do not mean that we want the individual not to react at all.

A tax is **non-distortionary** if, and only if, there is nothing an individual can do to alter his tax liability. Economists call taxes that are nondistortionary **lump sum taxes.** Distortions are associated with the individual's attempt to lower his tax liability. Virtually all of the taxes imposed in the United States are, in this sense, distortionary. A head tax—a tax one has to pay regardless of income or wealth—is a lump sum tax. A tax that depends on nonalterable characteristics (age, sex) is also a lump sum tax.

Any tax on commodities is distortionary: an individual can simply change his tax liability by reducing his purchases of the commodity. Any tax on income is distortionary: an individual can simply reduce his tax liability by working less or by saving less.

In Chapter 18 we shall show that distortionary taxes are inefficient, in the sense that the government could raise more revenue, with the same effect on the welfare of individuals, by imposing lump sum taxes; or equivalently, the government could raise the same revenue and increase the welfare of individuals.

Corrective Taxation

So far, our discussion has emphasized the negative aspects of taxation: that we should attempt to design a tax system not to interfere with economic efficiency, nor to distort resource allocations. Taxation can sometimes be used in a positive way, to correct some market failure. Recall our discussion in Chapter 8, where we showed that taxation could sometimes be used to correct for externalities. **Corrective taxes** (as these taxes are called) both raise revenue and improve the efficiency of resource allocations. Some economists believe that the market, by itself, will supply too little risk taking, that the government ought to take deliberate actions to encourage entrepreneurship. This argument is sometimes used to justify the special treatment afforded capital gains, the increment in value of assets such as stocks, land, and other real estate (they are taxed at 40 percent of the rate imposed on ordinary income.)[5]

General Equilibrium Effects

The imposition of a tax such as that on wages or on the return to capital alters the equilibrium of the economy. A tax on interest may reduce the supply of savings and, eventually, the stock of capital; this in turn may reduce the productivity of workers and their wages. We refer to these indirect repercussions of the tax as its **general equilibrium effects.**

General equilibrium effects have important distributional consequences, sometimes in a direction quite the opposite of the intent of the legislation. A tax on capital may reduce the supply of capital, increasing the return to

---

[5] In Chapter 22 we discuss the extent to which such favorable tax treatment does encourage risk taking and whether it is the most effective way of doing so.

capital; in some instances, the degree of inequality may actually be increased by such a tax.

Announcement Effects

The economy does not instantaneously adjust to a new tax. Often, the long-run distortions are much greater than the short-run distortions, as the economy is able to respond more fully to the new situation.

But some of the effects of the tax may be felt even before the tax is imposed, simply upon the announcement of the tax. When an announcement is made concerning the future tax treatment of an asset, it has an immediate impact on the value of an asset. If it is believed, for instance, that a particular category of assets (say, housing) is about to be subjected to greater taxation (.e.g., the interest deduction on mortgages is about to be eliminated), then the price of that category of assets may fall markedly. Owners of those assets at the time the announcement is made will (perhaps unfairly) bear the major burden of the tax.

It is these announcement effects (or impact effects), which may be quite significant, that have given rise to the saying that "an old tax is a good tax." Not only may the announcement effect present serious equity problems, but the anticipation of it can have a significant distortionary effect on the supply of assets. Discussions about eliminating the deduction of interest for mortgages may lead home owners to be worried about a significant capital loss, were they to invest in housing, and hence their demand for housing investments may be seriously reduced.

ADMINISTRATIVE COSTS

There are significant costs associated with administering our tax system. There are direct costs—the cost of running the Internal Revenue Service—and indirect costs, which taxpayers must bear. These indirect costs take on a variety of forms: the costs of time spent filling out the tax forms, costs of record keeping, and the costs of accountants and tax lawyers. Joel Slemrod of the University of Minnesota has estimated, for instance, that the indirect costs are at least five times greater than the direct costs.

The administrative costs of running a tax system depend on a number of factors. First, they depend on what records would be kept in the absence of taxation. Businesses need to keep records for their own internal management purposes; the advent of high-speed computers has greatly reduced the costs of record keeping for large corporations. Thus the tax system imposes a relatively small additional burden on large corporations for reporting wage income of their employees. At the other extreme, individuals hiring household help typically do not need to keep detailed records of the wages they pay to their employees. Although they are required to do so by law, most such individuals probably do not report wages of household help; those who do find it very burdensome; the same holds for many small businesses.

The record keeping required for capital gains taxation is particularly onerous because the records often have to be kept over a long period of time. An extreme case of this is the tax levied on capital gains on owner-occupied homes. Individuals are allowed to postpone their taxes, so long as they purchase a more expensive house. Consider an individual who, at the age of twenty-five, in 1935, bought a house for $20,000, sold it when he was thirty-five for $40,000, and then purchased a new house for $50,000. He kept this for another thirty years and then sold it for $80,000. Assume he spent $1,000 in 1936 for a new roof, $1,000 for a new furnace in 1937, $8,000 for a new bathroom in 1962, and $5,000 for a new electrical system in 1970. When he finally sold his house in 1985, he would have to pay a tax on $80,000 less his total previous expenditures ($45,000—his initial $20,000 plus the $10,000 extra he had to put in when he moved into a new house in 1945, plus $2,000 in improvements to his old house, plus $13,000 in improvements to his current house). That is, he has to pay tax on a capital gain of $35,000. But he has to substantiate all his earlier expenditures; he must keep records of all the improvements to all of his houses since the first house he purchased at the age of twenty-five. Needless to say, tax enforcement in this area is relatively lax: many individuals simply fail to report any capital gains at all.

Second, the administrative costs are closely related to the complexity of the tax code. Much of the cost of administering the income tax system comes from special provisions with the tax code; the deductibility of certain categories of expenditures (medicine, charity, interest) requires that records be kept on these expenditures.

Third, differentiation of rates across individuals (with some individuals paying a much higher rate than others) and across categories of income (capital gains are taxed at 40 percent of that imposed on ordinary income) gives rise to attempts to "shift" income, to members of one's family with lower tax rates or to categories of income that are more lightly taxed. Doing this costs money; and stopping individuals from doing this—designing and enforcing provisions of the tax code that prohibit such shifting—costs money.

Fourth, taxing some categories of income may be more expensive than taxing others. There is widespread belief that the administrative costs associated with imposing taxes on capital are much larger than those associated with taxing labor.

FLEXIBILITY

Changes in economic circumstances require changes in tax rates. For some tax structures these adjustments are easy; for some they require extensive political debate; for still others, they are done automatically.

Automatic Stabilization

For instance, as the economy goes into a recession, a reduction in revenues may be extremely desirable, for it can provide needed stimulus for the economy. When prices are stable, the United States income tax shows a high level of "automatic stabilization" as a result of its progressive structure. When incomes drop, as a result of a recession, the average tax rate is reduced—individuals face lower tax rates because their incomes are lower. On the other hand, when income increases, the average tax rate increases. However, in periods of stagflation—where the economy is in a recession but there is still inflation—the average tax rate increases, even though a lower rate might help the economy move out of the recession.

Political Difficulties of Adjusting Rates

When it is considered desirable to change the tax rate, attempts to adjust the United States income tax are often beset by intense political debate. Given the complexity of the tax code, which rates ought to be adjusted? Should all rates be increased proportionately, or are the rich or the poor already bearing a disproportionately large share of the burden of taxation, so that their taxes should be increased less than proportionately? Indeed, it is not even clear how to assess the fairness of a reform proposal. Is a tax reduction of the same dollar amount for individuals at different income levels or the same percentage amount fairer? Should one focus on the average tax rate individuals pay or on their marginal tax rates? Is a tax reform that lowers the average rate faced by a "typical" family with one earner but increases the average rate on a two-earner family fair? Should the tax rate on capital be decreased, to encourage more savings, or increased, because capital owners are in a better position to bear the tax? These are controversies that beset both the evaluation of the 1981 tax reforms and the assessment of the fairness of Reagan's 1985 proposals.

A political compromise among various interest groups must be reached, and this often takes time.

The flexibility of the income tax should be contrasted, for instance, with that of the property tax. This is beset by a number of administrative problems, not the least of which is the difficulty of assessing the value of various pieces of property. Still, it has one advantage: adjustments in the tax rates are made annually in a simple manner as the revenues required for the provision of local public services change.

Speed of Adjustments

Finally, an important aspect of the "flexibility" of a tax system for purposes of stabilizing the economy is timing: the speed with which changes in the tax code (once enacted) can be implemented and the lags in the collection of funds. If fluctuations in the economy are rapid, the lags may limit the efficacy of, say, the income tax, in stabilizing the economy. In Panel A of Figure 16.2 we have shown how, in an idealized economy, income might fluctuate over time. (Actual economies never fluctuate this regularly). Panel B shows what the movements of tax revenues over time might look like if there were no lags in tax collection. In this case, the fact that tax revenues are low in the depth of the recession means that consumers have more to spend, and this spending will provide an important stimulus for the economy.

Now see what happens if there is a lag in the collection of the tax revenues, as illustrated in Panel C. Government revenues reach a peak (say, at point E) when the economy is already on the downturn (national income is falling); the government should be providing a stimulus for the economy just at this point, to get it going again; instead, the fact that tax revenues, are at

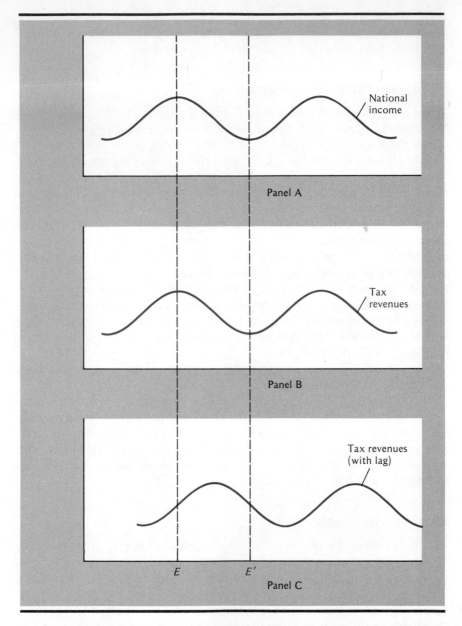

16.2 **STABILIZING GNP WITH TAXES** In an idealized economy, one might be able to match tax increases and decreases with fluctuations in GNP. Lags in the implementation of tax programs, however, can put well-intentioned tax policies out of sync, actually exacerbating the fluctuations.

their maximum implies that taxes are having a dampening effect. The opposite occurs as the economy heads out of a recession, say, at point E' in the figure. The government might like to restrain the economy so that it will not go into an inflationary spiral. Instead, since tax revenues depend on income in the previous year, when income was very low, tax revenues will be low, and consumer spending will thus be abetted by the lower tax.

In recent years the government has passed several pieces of legislation aimed at making businesses more "responsible" to their customers, restricting their ability to take advantage of the uninformed consumer. The Truth-in-Lending Act, requiring that a lender present the complete cost of borrowing in a form such that the borrower can easily compare proposals from other lenders, is perhaps the most noted example of this kind of legislation. There is a feeling among many economists that it is equally desirable for the government not to try to take advantage of uninformed citizens.

In this view, those taxes where it is clear who pays are better than taxes where the burden is not so apparent. Thus the income tax is a good tax and the corporation tax is a bad tax. We know that individuals pay the income tax. But not even economists can agree on who really pays the corporation tax, whether it is effectively a tax on stockholders or consumers.

Sometimes it seems as if the government misrepresents the true costs of the services it provides. For instance, there is widespread agreement that there is no meaningful distinction between the part of the social security tax that is paid by the employer and the part paid by the employee. (According to law, half is paid by each.) The employer is only concerned with the total costs of his employee, the employee only with his take-home pay. No one's economic behavior should be affected if it were announced that the entire tax was to be borne by the employee, were employers to give an equivalent pay raise to their employees to cover the increased tax. Would workers' attitudes toward social security be altered if they thought they had to bear the entire costs?

In some cases there is an almost deliberate attempt to persuade individuals that the cost of government is less than it is. Just as businesses find that they can sell cars more easily if they describe the cost as "only $340 a month for a short 40 months" than if they describe it as "$13,600 paid over 3½ years," so, too, governments sometimes show a preference for tax systems in which individuals never fully reckon the cost of government. One of the arguments put forward for sales taxes is that they are less noticed than other taxes, such as income taxes. Individuals never calculate the *total* amount they pay to the government.

A politically responsive tax structure is also one in which changes in taxes come about as a result of legislated changes, and where the government must repeatedly come back to the citizenry for an appraisal of whether the government is spending too much or too little. Steeply progressive tax rates (rates that rise as incomes rise) result in government's tax revenues in *real* terms (as a share of, say, national income) rising in inflationary times, as they did between 1975 and 1980. These increases in taxes were never directly legislated: indeed, many would argue that it would have been unlikely for Congress to have imposed directly, say, a 10 percent increase in taxes in 1980, although inflation had exactly this effect.

Though political responsiveness, as we have defined it, is widely viewed to be desirable, concerns have often been expressed about how a tax system may be misused in a democratic system to pursue interests of special minority groups, or even by a majority to pursue their interests to the disadvantage of the minority. Thus the Constitution imposed several constraints on the taxes Congress could impose, which we discussed in Chapter 2. Over the years, many of these constraints have been removed, either by constitutional amendment (one of which allowed the income tax) or by more liberal court interpretations. In 1984, for instance, the Supreme Court ruled that the windfall profits tax on oil companies, which exempted Alaskan oil from the North Slope, was not in violation of the provision of the Constitution requiring uniform taxation across the states (though lower courts had ruled that it was).

FAIRNESS

Most criticisms of tax systems begin with their unfairness. It is, however, difficult to define precisely what is or is not fair, as we shall see. There are two distinct concepts of fairness: horizontal equity and vertical equity.

Horizontal Equity

A tax system is said to be **horizontally equitable** if individuals who are the same in all relevant respects are treated equally. The principle of horizontal equity is so important that it is, in effect, enshrined in the Constitution as the Fourteenth Amendment (the Equal Protection Clause). Thus a tax system that discriminates on the basis of race, color, or creed would, in the United States, generally be viewed to be horizontally inequitable (and unconstitutional). Although the underlying idea is clear enough, there are two fuzzy notions in our definition: What does it mean for two individuals to be identical in all relevant respects? And what does it mean for two individuals to be treated the same?

What Does It Mean for Two Individuals to Be Identical? Consider twins who are identical in every respect except that one likes chocolate ice cream and only chocolate ice cream, while the other likes vanilla ice cream, and only vanilla. For simplicity, we assume that chocolate and vanilla ice cream cost exactly the same amount. Is the tax system treating the two individuals in a horizontally equitable manner if it taxes vanilla and chocolate ice cream at different rates? One ends up paying more in taxes than the other, and in this sense the tax system appears to be unfair. But the twins faced the same "opportunity set." The chocolate lover could have bought vanilla ice cream if he had wanted (or vice versa). The tax system did not discriminate; it did not differentiate between individuals.

If we say that the differences in taste are an important economic difference, which the tax system may well take into account, then we can say that the principle of horizontal equity does not apply here. The twins are not identical in all relevant respects. Carried to this extreme, the principle quickly becomes vacuous: no two individuals are ever identical. What are to be acceptable distinctions? Unfortunately, the principle of horizontal equity gives us little guidance on how to answer this question.

One's first intuition might be that all distinctions are inadmissible: age, sex, and marital status should all be irrelevant. In fact, at present we make a distinction on the basis of age (those over sixty-five are allowed an extra exemption) and marital status (two individuals with the same income getting married pay more in taxes than they did before marriage). Congress has felt that those distinctions are relevant.

Perhaps it does so because it is believed that individuals in these circumstances differ in their ability to pay. But if these are admissible bases for differentiation, are there other admissible bases? For instance, does the fact that the economic costs associated with taxing different groups differ provide legitimate grounds for differentiation? In a later chapter we shall show that the inefficiencies arising out of a tax system depend on the magnitude of the responses to the tax. In households with two workers, the worker with the lower wage (usually the woman) displays much more sensitivity to the wage than the primary worker; while income taxes have almost no effect on the amount of labor supplied by the primary worker, they may have large effects on the secondary worker. Thus if the government were concerned with minimizing the inefficiencies arising out of the tax system, it would impose a lower tax on the secondary workers. Is this fair?

What Does Equality of Treatment Mean? The following example illustrates the difficulty of even defining the meaning of equality of treatment. Assume we could agree that a man and a woman who had received the same income over their working lives should be treated equally. What is meant by "equal treatment" of sexes for purposes of social security? Should the ratio of the benefits received to the contributions paid in be the same for the man as for the woman, or should the annual benefit be the same? Women live significantly longer than men, so these two are clearly different. If women receive the same annual benefit as men, the total expected value of their benefits will be much greater than for men. Many would view this to be unfair.

Vertical Equity

While the principle of horizontal equity says that individuals who are essentially identical should be treated the same, the principle of **vertical equity** says that some individuals are in a position to pay higher taxes than others, and that these individuals should do so. There are three problems: determining who, in principle, should pay at the higher rate; implementing this principle—that is, writing tax rules corresponding to this principle; and deciding, if someone is in a position to pay the higher rate, how much more he should pay than others.

Three criteria are commonly proposed for judging whether one individual should pay more than another: some individuals may be judged to have a greater ability to pay; some may be judged to have a higher level of economic well-being; and some may receive more benefits from the government.

Even if agreement were to be reached on which of these criteria should be employed, there would be controversies concerning how to measure ability to pay, economic well-being, or benefits received. In some cases the same measures—such as income or consumption—might be used to judge ability to pay *and* economic well-being.

Ability to Pay versus Economic Welfare. The following examples may help illustrate why there is no agreement concerning what is the appropriate basis for taxation.

Consider first the view that those who are better off should contribute more. The critical question is how we are to tell whether one person is better off than another. Consider one individual who is an obsessive worker, who receives no enjoyment from his work. He is unhappy, his wife and three children have just been killed in an automobile accident, and he has been told that he will die of cancer in two years. Another individual is a happy beachcomber, young and attractive, with no source of income. There may be widespread agreement that the second individual is "better off" than the first, yet the tax system will tax the first at a higher rate than the second. It is apparent that a tax system must be based on a narrowly defined notion of welfare; it cannot attempt to measure overall well-being, and, as such, it must be inherently unfair.

This should be contrasted, for instance, with the allocation of tasks and goods within a family. There, it is possible for us to make overall assessments of both needs and capabilities. We may spend more on a child who has an unhappy experience, trying to compensate for it. There is more complete information than could ever possibly be available to the government.

Consider now the example of Joe Smith and his twin brother Jim, who have identical abilities and education. Joe decides to take a job as a high-school teacher of economics. He teaches six hours a day and the rest of the time he spends fishing, swimming, and sailing. He is very happy. Not surprisingly, his pay is very low. Jim becomes an economic consultant. He works seventy hours a week and has no time for fishing, swimming, or sailing. Their economic opportunity sets, what they could have done, are identical. (Jim and Joe have the same earning ability.) Yet they have made different choices. One has a high income, one a low income. Is it fair that Jim should pay far higher taxes than Joe? Joe believes that it is not economic opportunities that provide the fair basis of taxation but the extent to which individuals have seized advantage of whatever opportunities society has offered—in short, actual income provides the appropriate basis of taxation. Jim believes that it is not actual income that should be relevant but earning ability.

This example illustrates two points: first, while on philosophical grounds Jim and Joe differ on whether economic welfare or ability to pay would ideally be the appropriate basis of taxation, in practice, similar measures (e.g., income, potential income, consumption) will be employed. Secondly, even if they agreed that ability to pay provides the appropriate basis of taxation, controversy will remain concerning whether this is best measured by actual income or potential income. In practice, of course, it is virtually impossible to base a tax system on what individuals could have done. In the United States, we use income (with a variety of adjustments, to be discussed later) as the basis for measuring economic welfare. Some individuals believe that the wage rate provides a better indication of the individual's economic opportunity set than income, since the income tax makes those who choose to work longer hours pay more.

Consumption as a Basis of Taxation. But there is a widespread view that neither of these is a "fair" base of taxation. Both correspond to the individual's contribution to society, the value of his economic output. Is it not fairer to tax individuals on the basis of what they take out, not what they contribute, which is to say, on the basis of consumption rather than income?

Income and consumption differ by savings.[6] That is, income *(Y)* is either consumed *(C)* or saved *(S)*;

$$C + S = Y, \text{ or}$$
$$C = Y - S.$$

Thus a major issue is really whether savings ought to be exempt from taxation. It can be shown that this is equivalent to questioning whether the return to savings (interest, dividends, and capital gains) ought to be exempt from taxation. The following example illustrates again the conflicting views of equity.

Consider another pair of identical twins, whom we shall refer to as Prudence and Spendthrift. They both earn the same income during their lifetimes. Prudence, however, saves 20 percent of her income during her lifetime, accumulating a sizable nest egg for her retirement. Spendthrift, on the other hand, always spends what she receives and, when she reaches retirement, applies for welfare. Under the present income tax, Prudence pays considerably higher taxes than Spendthrift (since Prudence must pay taxes on the interest that she earns on her savings), while she receives fewer benefits. Prudence views the present tax system as unfair, since their economic opportunity sets were, in fact, identical.

She asks, 'Should the government force me to be my sister's keeper, if my sister does not choose to help herself?" Is it unfair to punish Prudence with additional taxation and reward her high-living sister? Her sister replies that it makes no difference: as they approach retirement their incomes differ. The fact is that Prudence's income is considerably in excess of Spendthrift's, and she is therefore better able to pay for the support of the government. Prudence's position—that consumption is a more equitable basis for taxation—is receiving more support today, particularly in light of the low rate of savings.

The Benefit Approach

We noted earlier that one argument for the use of consumption as the appropriate basis for taxation is that it seems fairer to tax individuals on the basis of what they take out of the economic system. Some economists have argued that individuals should contribute to the support of the government in proportion to the benefit they receive from public services. The principles of charging for public services should be analogous to those used for private services. And taxes can be viewed as simply the "charge" for the provision of public services.

In a few cases, the benefit approach is explicitly adopted: fees (taxes) are charged for the use of bridges and some toll roads. Using gasoline taxes to finance roads can be thought of as a simple mechanism for relating benefits (road usage, as measured by gasoline consumption) to taxes.

Economists have not, for the most part, been attracted to the benefit

---

[6] And bequests and inheritances. These involve a rather more complicated set of issues, discussion of which we postpone to a later chapter.

approach to taxation, largely because of the fact that it is impossible to identify the magnitude of the benefits received by different individuals. We all
receive some benefit from defense expenditures, but how are we to appor-
tion the relative benefits among different individuals? For many categories
of expenditures, assessments of benefits is essentially impossible.[7] A second
objection raised against benefit taxes is that they are distortionary. Basing
taxes on usage of a public facility (like a bridge) may discourage its use and
lead to an inefficient allocation of resources.

There are often equity-efficiency trade-offs involved in levying benefit taxes
(in those cases where it is possible to do so). In the absence of benefit taxes,
it is impossible to ascertain who benefits from a public facility such as a
bridge; if the bridge is financed out of general revenues, those who do not
use the bridge are worse off. It seems unfair to them that they should subsidize those who use the bridge.[8]

Alternative Bases of Taxation

The principle of vertical equity says that those who are better off or have a
greater ability to pay ought to contribute more than others to support the
government; the principle of horizontal equity says that those who are equally
well off (equal ability to pay) should all contribute the same amount. Our
discussion of both principles has focused on the difficulties of determining
whether an individual is better off than another, as well off, or worse off.
How should we adjust for the myriad of differences in circumstances facing
different individuals? We consider three examples. In all three cases, present tax laws make some adjustments for these differences in circumstances.
There is, however, some controversy about whether the adjustments are
appropriate.

The first example has to do with health. It is clear that an individual who
is sick and has an income of $10,000 is different from an individual who is
well and has the same income. The individual who is sick, most of us would
say, is worse off (other things being equal) than the one who is well. Being
sick or well is not readily observable: it is accordingly difficult for the tax
code to make adjustments for health status. But there is a surrogate: medical
expenditures. Those who spend more on hospital bills are, on average, worse
off than those who have no hospital bills. The current tax law does allow for
the deduction of medical expenses in excess of 5 percent of the individual's
income.

The second example has to do with marriage. Individuals who are married
differ from those who are not. Surveys by sociologists indicate that married
men, for instance, are happier; whether much credence should be placed on
such evidence or not, the fact is that married men do live longer and are, on
average, in better health. This would suggest that a married man with a

---

[7] In Chapter 6 we showed how, under certain idealized circumstances, we could design mechanisms that
induce individuals to reveal honestly their true marginal evaluations.

[8] The issue of government subsidies of public transportation systems, such as subways and trains, is currently a heated source of controversy in many metropolitan areas.

given income is better off than an unmarried man with the same income.
Does the principle of vertical equity imply that the married man should pay
higher taxes? The present tax structure does discriminate against married
individuals' where the husband and the wife have similar incomes (though
probably not for the reasons just given).

The third example has to do with the tax treatment of children. Consider
two married couples with identical incomes. They both would like to have
two children; one of the couples is infertile, the other is blessed with two
children. Clearly, the couple with the two children is better off than the
infertile couple. The principle that those who are better off should pay more
taxes would suggest that this couple should pay more taxes; in fact, the tax
law results in the couple with children paying lower taxes.

Limitations on the Principles of Vertical and Horizontal Equity. The analysis
so far has shown that though the principles of vertical and horizontal equity
seem, at first, to provide "reasonable" bases for designing a fair tax system,
they are, in fact, of only limited help. The difficult questions—how do we
tell which of two individuals is better off or which has a greater ability to
pay, and what do we mean by equality of treatment?—are left unanswered.
Furthermore, the principle of vertical equity does not tell us how much
more someone who is better off should contribute to the support of the government; all it tells us is that he should pay more.

Because of these difficulties, economists have looked for other principles
on which to base a "fair" tax.

Pareto-Efficient Taxation and Social Welfare Functions

A somewhat different approach recasts the problem of the design of tax
structures into a standard welfare economics problem, as discussed in Chapter 3. First, it attempts to define (given the tools and information available
to the government) what are the set of Pareto-efficient tax structures—i.e.,
tax structures such that no one can be made better off without making someone else worse off. It then seeks to choose from among these Pareto-efficient
tax structures using a social welfare function. The advantage of this approach
is that it separates efficiency considerations from value judgments. Almost
all would agree that if we could find a tax structure in which everyone was
better off (or some better off and no one else worse off) it should be adopted.
On the other hand, we often have to choose from among alternative tax
systems, none of which Pareto-dominates the other; in one tax system the
poor may be better off, the rich worse off. But are the gains to the poor
sufficiently large to justify the losses to the rich? The answer depends on
value judgments, over which reasonable people may differ.

Economists have made use of two special social welfare functions: the utilitarian (social welfare equals the sum of all individuals' utilities) and the
Rawlsian (social welfare equals the utility of the worst-off individual). Using
a social welfare function, one can say not only by how much taxes should
increase with income but also, for instance, whether or under what circum-

stances a deduction for medical expenses should be allowed.[9] We now explore briefly what each of these two social welfare functions implies for tax design.

Utilitarianism. Traditionally, utilitarianism was thought to provide a rationale for progressive taxation, the taxation of rich individuals at higher rates than poor individuals. Under utilitarianism, taxes should be such that the marginal utility of income—the loss in utility from taking a dollar away from an individual—should be the same for all individuals.[10] If the marginal utility of income of Jim exceeds that of Joe, reducing Jim's tax by a dollar and increasing Joe's by a dollar increases total utility (social welfare), since the gain in utility to Jim exceeds the loss to Joe. Since taking a dollar away from a rich person causes him less loss of welfare than taking a dollar away from a poor person, utilitarianism seemed to provide a basis for progressive taxation.

But the very stringent assumptions underlying the analysis are far from universally accepted. In particular, if individuals' income depends on their work (effort), and if raising taxes on those earning higher incomes leads to a reduction in their work (effort), it is possible that this actually reduces the government's tax revenue, or that the marginal loss to the individual per dollar raised by the government may be very large. The earlier argument assumed, in other words, that income would not be affected by the imposition of taxes; it is now widely recognized that it may be. When it is, utilitarianism requires that we compare the loss in utility from an increase in a tax with the gain in revenue. We require that

$$\frac{\text{change in utility}}{\text{change in revenue}}$$

be the same for all individuals. If some group of individuals has a very elastic labor supply (that is, as tax rates are increased they greatly reduce their labor supply), an increase in the income tax rate yields relatively little revenue, so they should not be taxed very heavily.

Utilitarianism was also once thought to provide a basis for the principle of horizontal equity. If everyone had the same utility function, individuals with the same income should be taxed the same. Assume that one individual faced a higher tax than another with the same income. Because of diminishing marginal utility, his marginal utility would be higher than the other. Raising the tax on the individual with a *low* tax rate by a dollar causes him less loss in utility than the gain in utility from lowering the tax on the individual with the high tax rate. Again, this argument would be correct if income were unaffected. But it is, so the argument may no longer be valid.

---

[9]To make utilitarianism (or Rawlsianism) operational, one must make additional assumptions, as we noted in Chapter 3. It is conventionally assumed that all individuals have the same utility function (at each level of income all individuals benefit equally by an extra dollar), and that they exhibit diminishing returns (an extra dollar is worth less at progressively higher levels of income). The reader should also review the caveats noted in Chapter 3 concerning making interpersonal utility comparisons. The difficulties of engaging in serious policy discussions without recourse to some comparisons should also be recalled.

[10]Thus under utilitarianism taxes are not *directly* related to the benefits one receives from a tax, or to the *level* of economic welfare. An individual who loses a limb may be less happy but also less able to enjoy a marginal increment in his income.

The argument that utilitarianism may imply horizontal inequity is perhaps best related by the story of the shipwrecked crew who have only enough food for all but one of their members to survive. In that case, equality would imply that all individuals die, clearly a worse situation (from a utilitarian point of view) than one in which only one dies.[11]

Rawlsian Social Welfare Function. Several economists and philosophers believe that the utilitarian approach is not sufficiently equalitarian, that it does not pay sufficient attention to inequality. In Chapter 3 we discussed the view of John Rawls that society should only be concerned with the welfare of the worst-off individual, that it ought to design the tax system (and other social policies) so as to maximize his welfare. This social welfare function, maximizing the welfare of the worst-off individual, has some simple and direct implications for tax policy: increase the tax rates on all individuals (other than the worst-off individual) to the point where the tax revenues one gleans from them are maximized. This does not necessarily imply that very rich individuals should be taxed at 80 percent or 90 percent of their income, or even that marginal tax rates should always increase with income. It may turn out that those with very high incomes have labor supplies that are more sensitive to tax rates than middle-income individuals.

There are those who argue that not even the Rawlsian criterion is sufficiently equalitarian. A change that makes one person better off but leaves everyone else unaffected, including the worst-off individual, might still be socially undesirable if the person who is made better off is, say, particularly rich. In this view, inequality itself is a social evil or gives rise to social evils. Differences in levels of wealth may give rise, for instance, to social tensions. Inequality of goods leads, in many political situations, to inequality in political power, and this may be used, eventually, to the advantage of the well off at the expense of the poor.

What Economists Can Contribute to Discussions of Fairness. Although economists (or philosophers) have not resolved the basic issues concerning the choice of the appropriate bases for judging fairness, there is still much that can be said. It is important, for instance, to be able to describe the full consequences of any tax, and these are seldom simply described by the amounts of tax each person pays directly. We can attempt to describe how various groups in the population are affected by different tax programs. In all tax systems there are certain groups that seem to pay less than their fair share—given any reasonable concept of fairness. We then need to ask, Why are they treated differentially? It may be (as we shall see in our later discussion) that to treat them fairly would necessitate introducing other, even worse inequities into the tax code. Tax systems must be based on certain *observable* variables, variables such as income or expenditures; as we noted earlier, many of the concepts involved in our more general philosophical discussions (e.g., welfare) are not directly measurable; even income, as we shall see later, is not as well defined as might seem to be the case at first. Thus many

[11] Similarly, it can be shown that, under plausible conditions, utilitarianism requires that with distortionary taxes individuals who appear to be essentially identical should be treated differently. A more formal exposition of the argument is presented in J. E. Stiglitz, "Utilitarianism and Horizontal Equity: The Case for Random Taxation," *Journal of Public Economics* 21(1982): 257–94.

of the seeming inequities involved in our tax system are simply consequences of the inherent difficulties of translating what seem like well-defined
concepts into the precise language required by any tax law.

In other cases, by considering carefully how different provisions of the tax
code and changes in those provisions affect different groups we can obtain
some insights into why one group may claim one set of provisions unfair
while another group claims that to change those provisions is unfair. We can
attempt to distinguish those cases where fairness is used simply as a term to
cover up a group's pursuit of self-interest and those cases where there is
some reasonable ethical or philosophical position underlying claims for equitable treatment.

SUMMARY

1. The five attributes that a good tax system should have are:
   economic efficiency;
   administrative simplicity;
   flexibility;
   political responsiveness;
   and fairness.
2. The two major aspects of fairness are horizontal equity and vertical equity.
3. While some argue that taxes should be related to the benefits received, others
   contend that taxes should be related to the individual's ability to pay; still others
   believe they should be related to some measure of well-being. There is further
   disagreement about how best to measure ability to pay or economic well-being.
   Any tax system must make use of easily observable variables, like income or consumption. Some contend that it is fairer to tax individuals on what they take out
   of the system (consumption) than on what they contribute (their income).
4. The utilitarian approach argues that the tax system should be chosen to maximize
   the sum of utilities. The Rawlsian approach argues that the tax system should be
   chosen to maximize the welfare of the worst-off individual.

KEY CONCEPTS

Distortionary taxes   General equilibrium effects
Nondistortionary taxes   Horizontal equity
Lump sum taxes   Vertical equity
Corrective taxation   Benefit approach
                                  Announcement effects

QUESTIONS AND PROBLEMS

1. Discuss how your views concerning the tax treatment of children might be affected
   by whether: a) you lived in a highly congested country or in an underpopulated
   country; b) you viewed children as a consumption good (for their parents), like
   other consumption goods. Discuss both efficiency and equity considerations.
2. With a progressive tax structure, such as that in the United States, it makes a
   great deal of difference whether husbands' and wives' incomes are added together
   or whether each is taxed separately. Discuss some of the equity and efficiency
   considerations that bear on the tax treatment of the family.

3. Does utilitarianism necessarily imply that tax structures should be progressive?

4. Consider an individual who has lost a leg but, with a new artificial leg, has the same earning power he had before. How should his taxes differ from a similar individual who has not lost his leg: a) under utilitarianism; b) under a Rawlsian social welfare function; c) if you believed that ability to pay provided the appropriate basis for taxation?

5. The government has recently passed a number of pieces of legislation aimed at ensuring that firms do not take advantage of the limited information of consumers. What might be meant by a "truth in taxation" bill? What might be the advantages of and the problems with such a bill?

6. "Since the needs, other than medical, of the aged are typically not as great as those of younger individuals, who have children to support, if the government provides free medical care to the aged, it should simultaneously subject the aged to higher income tax rates." Discuss the equity and efficiency consequences of doing this (consider alternative views of equity.)

17

Who Really Pays the Tax: Tax Incidence

When Congress or a state legislature enacts a new tax, the debate usually includes some opinions about who should pay for running the government or for the particular program being supported by the tax. For example, when Congress adopted the social security tax to pay for the social security system, it levied half the tax on the employer and half on the employee. It thought that the employer and employee should share in the costs of the social security system. But economic reality, unfortunately, does not always follow the laws passed by legislators. The division of the tax burden does not in fact depend at all on how Congress legislated tax rates. We use the term **incidence** to describe who effectively pays the tax.

When a tax is imposed on an industry, and the price rises so that part of the incidence of the tax is borne by consumers, we say that the tax has been **shifted forward.** If the price rises by less than the amount of the tax, we say that it is partially shifted forward. If the price rises by exactly the amount of the tax we say that the tax is fully shifted. If the price rises by more than the amount of the tax—a possibility that we shall note in the case of a monopoly—then we say that there is greater than 100 percent shifting.

If, as a result of the tax, the demand for factors used in the industry declines, and hence the price of those factors declines, we say that the tax has been **shifted backward.**

Consider, for instance, the tax on corporations. These taxes are popular, because it is widely believed that the firm and its shareholders have to pay the tax. But if firms raise their prices as a result of the tax, the tax is effectively paid by consumers. If, as a result of the tax, demand for labor falls and wages fall, the tax is partially paid for by workers, not investors. If the tax makes investing in the corporate sector less attractive, capital will move out of the sector, driving down the return to capital elsewhere. Thus part of the burden of the corporate tax may be felt by capital as a whole, not just capital in the corporate sector.

A tax system in which the ratio of tax payments to income rises with income is called progressive; a tax system in which the ratio of tax payments to income falls with income is called regressive. For instance, a cigarette tax is usually viewed as regressive; the fraction of a lower-income individual's income that is spent on tobacco is higher than the fraction spent by a higher-income individual.

Clearly, whether the U.S. tax system is progressive or regressive depends on the incidence of the various taxes. If the social security tax levied on employers is effectively paid by employees, the effective tax on workers is higher than if it is really paid by employers. If the corporation tax is shifted forward onto consumers or back onto workers, the corporation tax is not as progressive as it would be if it were not shifted (indeed, it is even possible that the corporation tax is regressive).

WHO BEARS THE BURDEN OF TAXES IN THE UNITED STATES

Joseph Pechman and Benjamin Okner of the Brookings Institution have attempted to estimate who bears the burden of taxes in the United States. They assumed that all taxes imposed directly on labor or on capital are not shifted (including property taxes). They considered alternative sets of assumptions concerning the corporation tax and the social security tax. In Case A, half the corporation tax is borne by stockholders, half by owners of property in general (as owners of corporations find that their after-tax return is lowered, they shift their investments in other directions, lowering the return to other forms of capital). Moreover, consistent with most economic theory, they assumed that the employers' share of the social security (payroll) tax is borne by workers. In Case B, half of the corporation income tax is assumed borne by consumers and half by property owners in general; and three-fourths of the payroll taxes are borne by workers, the rest by consumers.

Even with simplifications, the calculations are extremely difficult. One has to trace through how much individuals at different incomes spend on items subject to sales tax or produced by corporations, how much property that is subjected to taxation is owned by individuals with different incomes, what dividends are received by individuals at different income levels, and how these dividend receipts are affected by the corporation tax.

There are a number of ways of reporting the results. One way is to ask what fraction of income is paid in taxes by individuals at different points in the income distribution. We call this their effective tax rate. The results for 1985 are shown in Figure 17.1. In Case A (the black curve) there is a slight degree of progressivity to the tax system as a whole: those in the bottom tenth of the income distribution paid 21 percent of their income in taxes, those in the fifth tenth, 23 percent, and those in the top tenth, 25 percent. In Case B (the colored curve) the highest taxes paid were by those in the lowest tenth and the lowest taxes by those in the top tenth.

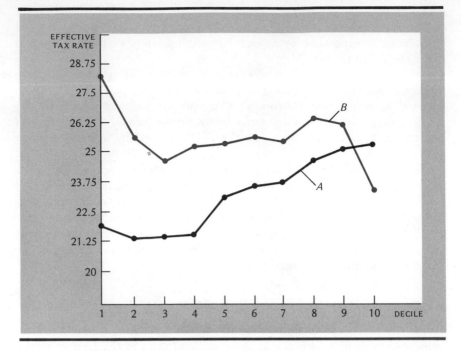

17.1 EFFECTIVE TAX RATES, 1985 Case A: Workers bear all of payroll tax; half of corporate tax borne by shareholders, half by property owners in general. Case B: Workers bear three-quarters of payroll tax; consumers bear one-fourth; half of corporate tax borne by consumers, half by property owners in general. SOURCE: J. A. Pechman, *Who Paid the Taxes, 1966–1985* (Washington, D.C.: Brookings Institution, 1985).

While in Case A effective tax rates have increased in recent years for the poor and have decreased for the rich, in Case B the change in the effective tax rates of the lowest and highest decile is insignificant.

How do we reconcile the apparent lack of progressivity with the widespread view that our tax structure is progressive?

The income tax is progressive. But the progressive effects of the income tax are offset by the regressive effects of sales tax and, to a lesser extent, the payroll tax. The critical difference between Case A and Case B arises from the corporation income tax. Under the first set of assumptions, the tax is very progressive (representing a tax on the poorest tenth of the population of about ½ of 1 percent and a tax on the upper most tenth of 5 percent; but under the second set of assumptions it is regressive, with the poorest tenth paying a 4 percent effective tax rate and higher-income groups paying rates varying from 2.7 percent to 3.3 percent.

The tax system obviously affects individuals differently, depending, as we have discussed, not only on income but on other important circumstances. Consumption patterns of aged and young, home owners and renters, urban and rural, single and married individuals differ; hence their effective tax rates differ.

Unfortunately, up-to-date figures breaking down the effective tax rates for different groups are not available. Table 17.1 presents results from an earlier

Table 17.1 EFFECTIVE FEDERAL, STATE, AND LOCAL TAX RATES BY POPULATION SUBGROUPS, BY POPULATION DECILE, 1966 (all of payroll tax borne by workers; half of corporate tax borne by shareholders, half by property owners in general)

| Population Decile | All Families | Age of Family Head | | Home Owners | Renters | Urban Residents | Rural-farm Residents | Single Persons | Marital Status and Family Size | |
| | | Under 65 | 64 and Over | | | | | | Married Couples | |
									No Children	Two Children
First[a]	27.5	29.1	26.1	28.7	26.9	26.3	30.3	27.8	29.4	38.8
Second	24.8	26.0	23.4	25.7	24.1	24.7	25.3	27.4	24.6	25.8
Third	26.0	26.7	24.5	25.9	26.2	25.9	26.5	30.1	25.4	25.6
Fourth	25.9	26.2	24.1	25.4	26.3	25.9	25.9	30.7	26.3	24.7
Fifth	25.8	26.0	24.6	25.4	26.3	25.7	26.1	30.3	26.7	24.9
Sixth	25.6	25.8	24.1	25.3	26.1	25.6	25.5	29.7	26.4	25.1
Seventh	25.5	25.5	25.3	25.2	26.2	25.6	25.1	29.1	26.6	24.6
Eighth	25.5	25.6	25.1	25.2	26.6	25.6	25.2	31.2	27.1	24.7
Ninth	25.1	25.2	24.7	25.0	25.8	25.3	23.9	29.9	26.7	24.3
Tenth	25.9	25.5	27.5	25.9	26.0	26.5	23.3	29.3	26.5	25.5
All deciles[b]	25.9	25.9	25.9	25.6	26.9	26.0	25.5	30.2	26.8	25.2

[a]Includes only units in the ninth to tenth percentiles.
[b]Includes negative incomes not shown separately.
Source: J. Pechman and B. Okner, Who Bears the Tax Burden (Washington, D.C.: Brookings Institution, 1974).

study. Notice that, on average, differences among groups are not large, except for one group: single individuals are taxed at a higher effective rate than married individuals. This discrimination in the tax system has been a subject of considerable debate.

Finally, according to Pechman and Okner's calculations, under the first set of incidence assumptions, the average tax rate on labor was 17.6 percent while that on capital was almost twice as high, 34.1 percent. Under the second set of incidence assumptions, the tax rate on capital income was still considerably higher (at 21 percent) than the tax on labor.[1]

There are two important lessons to be learned from this kind of study. First, it is clear that the burden of taxes can be markedly different from that legislated; and second, it should be clear that the determination of the burden is a fairly complicated matter, and that there is likely to be considerable disagreement over it, even among experts. We have illustrated this by presenting two sets of results, under different assumptions. But even these do not fully span the controversy concerning the burden of taxation. Their analysis assumed, for instance, that before-tax wages were unaffected by taxes. How these are affected is one of the central concerns of the remainder of this chapter.

TAX INCIDENCE IN COMPETITIVE MARKETS

We begin our analysis by considering a competitive market. The basic principles may be illustrated by the demand-and-supply diagram for beer shown in Figure 17.2. The demand curve tells us how much of a commodity is demanded, at each price, while the supply curve tells us how much of the commodity is supplied at each price. Consider, as an example, the effect of a tax on beer. The equilibrium before the imposition of taxes is depicted by point E_0. It occurs at the intersection of the demand and supply curves. For simplicity, we have assumed that 1 million bottles of beer are produced in equilibrium, at a price of $1 each.

Assume now that the government imposes the tax on producers. For each bottle of beer the producer manufactures, it must pay the government 10 cents. This means that for the producer to receive $1 a bottle after tax, he must receive before taxes $1.10. What the manufacturer is concerned about is his net receipts (after paying taxes). Hence he will be willing to supply the same amount (that he previously supplied at $1) at a price of $1.10 per bottle. The supply curve thus shifts up. The new equilibrium price is increased, but it does not increase by .10. In our example, the price rises to $1.05. The price received by the producer is thus 95 cents. In spite of the fact that the tax was nominally imposed on producers, consumers are forced to pay a part of the increased cost resulting from increased taxes, through higher prices.

The amount by which the price rises—the extent to which consumers bear the tax—depends on the shape of the demand and supply curves. In two

---

[1] The tax rate on labor was calculated from the sum of wages, salaries, wage supplements, 86 percent of nonfarm business income, and 71 percent of farm income; capital income was calculated from the sum of interest, corporation profits before taxes, rents, royalties, capital gains, 14 percent of nonfarm business income, and 29 percent of farm income. These calculations ignore some of the complexities of the capital tax, which makes it difficult to assess the effective tax rate.

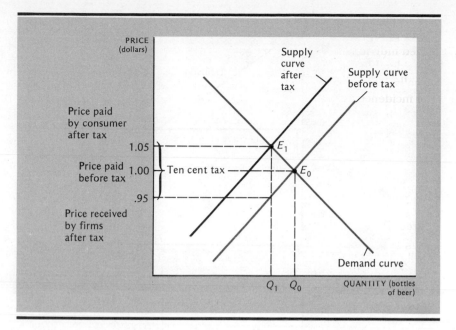

17.2   EFFECT OF TAX ON PRICES AND QUANTITIES The tax shifts the supply curve up by the amount of tax. This lowers the quantity consumed and raises the price paid by consumers.

limiting cases, the price rises by the full 10 cents, so the entire burden is borne by consumers. This occurs when the supply curve is perfectly horizontal, as in Figure 17.3, Panel A, or when the demand curve is perfectly vertical (individuals insist on consuming a fixed amount of beer, regardless of price), as in Panel B.

There are also two cases in which the price paid by consumers does not rise at all; the tax is borne entirely by producers, shown in panels C and D. This occurs when the supply curve is perfectly vertical—the amount supplied does not depend at all on price—or when the demand curve is perfectly horizontal.

This suggests a general principle: the steeper the demand curve or the flatter the supply curve, the more the tax will be borne by consumers; the flatter the demand curve or the steeper the supply curve, the more the tax will be borne by producers. We measure the steepness of a demand curve by the **elasticity of demand;** the elasticity of demand gives the percentage change in the quantity of the good consumed due to a percentage change in its price. We thus say that the horizontal demand curve, where a small reduction in the price results in an enormous increase in demand, is infinitely elastic; and we say that the vertical demand curve, where demand does not change at all with a reduction in price, has zero elasticity.

Similarly, we measure the steepness of the supply curve by the elasticity of supply; the elasticity of supply gives the percentage change in the quantity of the good supplied due to percentage change in its price. We thus say that a vertical supply curve, where the supply does not change at all with a

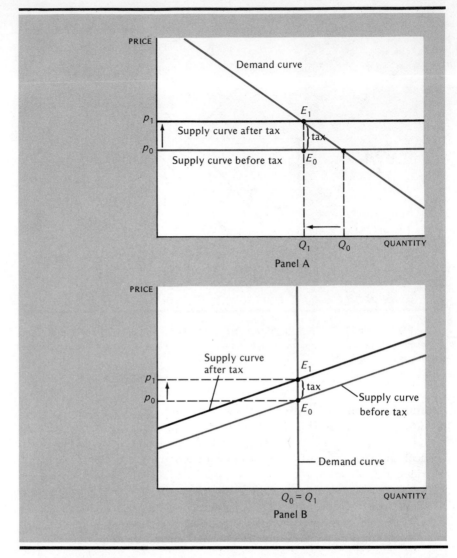

17.3   ELASTICITY OF SUPPLY AND DEMAND (A) Perfectly elastic supply curve: with
a perfectly elastic supply curve (horizontal supply curve), the price rises by the full amount of
the tax; the entire burden of the tax is on consumers. (B) Perfectly inelastic demand: with a
perfectly inelastic demand curve the price rises by the full amount of the tax; the entire burden

change in price, has zero elasticity, while a horizontal supply curve has infinite elasticity.

The more elastic the demand curve and the less elastic the supply curve,
the more the tax is borne by producers; the less elastic the demand curve
and the more elastic the supply curve, the more of the tax will be borne by
consumers.

*Does It Make a Difference Whether the Tax Is Levied on Consumers or
Producers?* Consider now what would happen if Congress passed a beer tax
but this time said that consumers would have to pay the tax. For each bottle

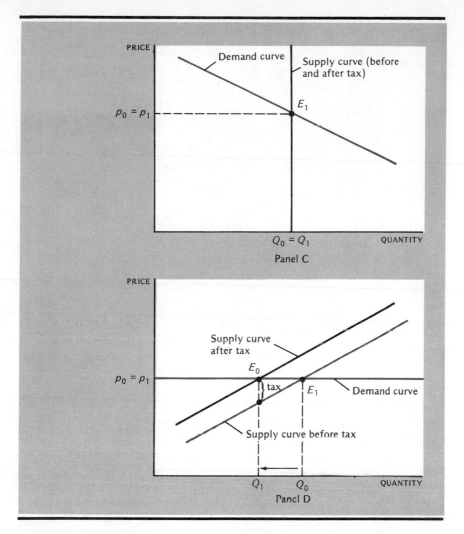

of the tax is on the consumers. (C) Perfectly inelastic supply curve: with a perfectly inelastic supply curve, the price does not rise at all; the full burden of the tax is on producers. (D) Perfectly elastic demand: with a perfectly elastic (horizontal) demand curve, the price does not rise at all; the entire burden of the tax is on producers.

of beer purchased, consumers would have to pay a 10-cent tax. What consumers care about, of course, is not who receives the money they pay. They simply care about the total cost of the beer.

The effect of this tax is displayed in Figure 17.4. If we now interpret the price on the vertical axis of the diagram to be the price received by the manufacturer (rather than the price paid by the consumer), the tax on consumers can be presented by a downward shift in the demand curve, by the amount of the tax. That is, if the manufacturer receives p_1, the consumer must pay $p_1 + t$, and the level of demand is Q_1, just as it would be if, in the before-tax situation, manufacturers had charged $p_1 + t$. It should be apparent

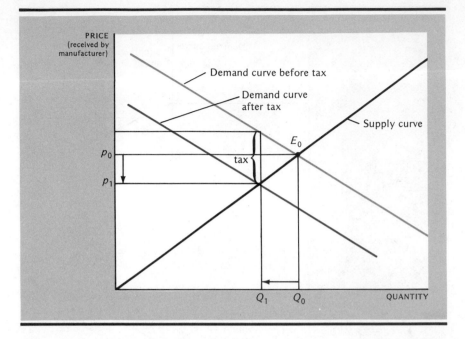

17.4 ALTERNATE VIEWS OF A TAX The effects of a tax can be viewed as either a downward shift in the demand curve or an upward shift in the supply curve (compare with Figure 17.2).

that it makes no difference whether Congress labels the tax a tax on the producers of beer or a tax on the consumers of beer.

Analysis of the Effect of the Tax at the Level of the Firm. The analysis so far has focused on the impact of the tax on the industry equilibrium. It is useful to see how the tax affects the behavior of the individual firm. In Figure 17.5, before the imposition of the tax, the firm faced the price p_0 and had a rising marginal cost schedule, MC. It maximized its profits by setting its price (what it got from producing an extra unit of output) equal to marginal cost (the extra cost of producing an extra unit of output).

Now the government imposes a tax of t per unit of output on the firm. The cost to the firm of producing an extra unit is now $MC' = MC + t$, its marginal production cost plus the tax; it will thus reduce its output to Q'_0. But when all firms reduce their output, prices rise. The new equilibrium entails a price p_1 and an output of Q_1, where the new price is equal to marginal production cost plus tax.

Tax Incidence and the Demand and Supply for Labor

The basic principles we have just derived apply for all taxes in competitive markets. In Figure 17.6A we have depicted the demand and supply curve for labor. It makes no difference whether we say that a tax on labor is imposed on the consumer (in this case, the firms who pay for the use of labor) or on producers (in this case, the individuals who are selling their labor services). The incidence of the tax is the same. The distinction made by Congress, that

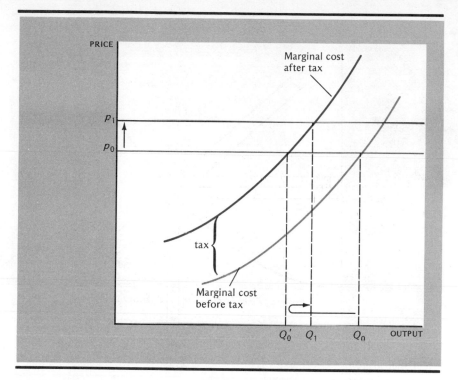

17.5 THE EFFECT OF A TAX ON MARGINAL COST Equilibrium for a competitive firm occurs at the point where price equals marginal cost. The tax shifts the effective marginal cost schedule up.

half of the social security tax should be paid by the employer and half by the employee, makes (for our purposes) absolutely no difference. The consequences would have been the same had Congress said that firms must pay the entire tax or that individuals must pay the entire tax.[2]

Who effectively pays the tax depends on the elasticity of demand and supply for labor. If, as is frequently claimed, the supply of labor is relatively inelastic (i.e., almost vertical), most of the burden of the tax falls on workers, regardless of the legal incidence of the tax.

Some economists believe that the supply curve of labor actually is backward-bending, as illustrated in Figure 17.6B. As the wage rises above a certain level, the supply of labor actually decreases. Individuals decide that, at the higher standards of living that they can attain with the higher wages, they prefer to work less. Thus higher wages reduce the supply of labor rather than increase it. In this case a tax on labor may result in a reduction in the wage rate that is greater than the tax itself, as the decrease in wages induces a larger labor supply, which drives down the wage.

---

[2]There may be a short-run difference. If Congress had said that firms had to pay the entire tax, it is unlikely that they would have responded by lowering wages they paid workers by a corresponding amount.

There are also some differences arising out of the income tax. While the employee's contribution to social security is included in his income (upon which he must pay income tax), the employer's contribution to social security is not. Also, if the individual works for more than one employer, if he pays more than the maximum social security, he can claim a refund of the excess, but the employer is not entitled to any refund.

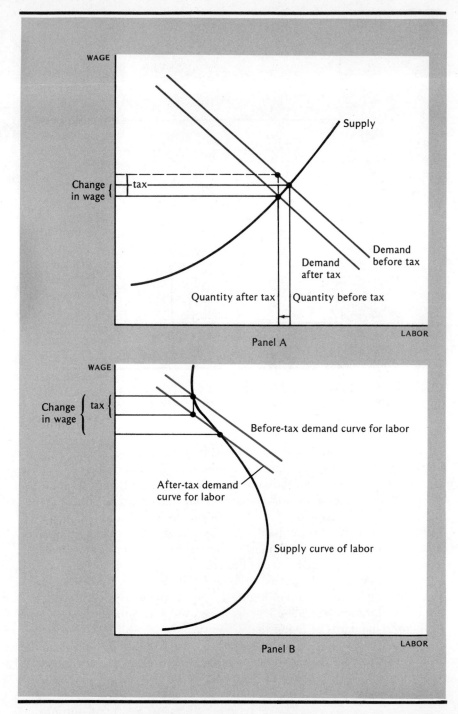

17.6 COMPARING THE EFFECTS OF A TAX ON THE DEMAND FOR LABOR
(A) The effect of a tax on labor is to shift the demand curve for labor down. A tax on labor will
lead to a lower wage and a lower level of employment. (B) With a backward-bending supply
schedule, the wage may fall by more than the amount of the tax.

As we have noted, if the supply elasticity is zero the tax is borne fully by the industry (firm) upon whom the tax is levied.

The supply elasticities of almost all factors (other than labor) or commodities are positive. One exception is the supply of unimproved land. Thus if a tax is imposed on unimproved land, the total burden of the tax will reside on the owners of the land. Unfortunately, it is difficult to distinguish between the value of improved land and unimproved land. In many parts of the United States, for instance, land in the wilderness, with no access to roads, sewers, or water, is almost valueless. How much of the value of land in urban areas can be attributed to "improvements" (so we can attribute the residual to the value of the unimproved land) is difficult to ascertain.

The long-run supply of oil may be fairly inelastic, and hence a tax on oil may be borne primarily by the owners of oil deposits. Since a disproportionate share of the world's oil is owned by those outside of the major consuming nations, the consuming nations have strong incentives to impose such taxes. Of course, owners of oil wells in the United States actively resist these taxes, and they are a sufficiently powerful lobby group to have done so quite successfully. In the United States taxes on oil are far less than those in most Western European nations.

This analysis applies to taxes imposed on the users of oil as well as on producers directly. As we have seen it makes little difference what the legal imposition of the tax is. Thus a tax on gasoline is likely to be borne largely by the owners of oil wells. This is equally true when there are several factors of production. To produce refined gasoline, for instance, requires inputs of labor and capital, in addition to the inputs of crude oil. But the oil industry, while large, is only one of the many users of labor and capital, and thus the imposition of a gasoline tax is not likely to have a significant effect on the price the oil industry has to pay for its labor or capital. If the price of gasoline falls, the full burden of the decline lies on the owners of the crude oil. (In the short run, there may be some excess capacity of refineries, and a small portion of the burden may lie on the owners of capital in the oil industry. In the long run, however, refinery capacity will adjust to the lower level of demand.)

TAX INCIDENCE IN MONOPOLISTIC VERSUS COMPETITIVE ENVIRONMENTS

The analysis in the preceding sections assumed that the market (for beer) was competitive. The effect of the imposition of a tax depends critically on the nature of the market. If the industry is a monopoly (or acts collusively, so that its behavior is similar to that of a monopoly), the effect of the tax could be markedly different.

In the absence of a tax, a monopolist will choose that level of output such that the cost of any further increase in output (the **marginal cost**) is just equal to the benefit. If he produces an additional unit of output, the additional revenue he would receive is called his **marginal revenue.** The monopolist thus sets his marginal cost equal to his marginal revenue. Figure 17.7 depicts

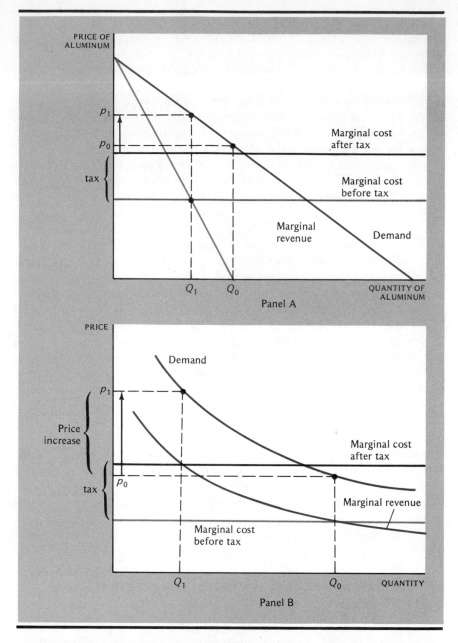

17.7 TAXING A MONOPOLY (A) With linear demand and supply curves, the price paid by consumers rises by exactly half the tax: consumers and producers share the burden of the tax. (B) With constant elasticity demand curves, the price rises by more than the tax.

the demand curve for aluminum, the marginal revenue curve, and the marginal cost of production. The monopolist chooses as his level of output the point where the marginal cost and marginal revenue curves intersect.

The marginal revenue curve lies below the demand curve. It represents the extra revenue the firm receives from selling an extra unit of output as the price it receives for that extra unit, minus the loss it sustains on the other units it sells, because as it attempts to sell more, it must lower the price.

A tax on aluminum can be viewed simply as an increase in the cost of production, which is to say a shift upward in the marginal cost curve. This will reduce output and increase the price.

Relationship between the Change in the Price and the Tax. In the case of a competitive industry, we showed that the price increased by an amount that normally was less than the tax and that the magnitude of the price increase depended on the demand and supply elasticities. The results for a monopolist are more complicated.

First, the steeper the marginal cost curve, the smaller the change in output and hence the smaller the increase in price. With a perfectly vertical marginal cost schedule, there is no change in output and no change in price; the tax is borne by producers. This result parallels that for competitive markets. On the other hand, with a horizontal marginal cost schedule, the extent to which producers or consumers bear the tax depends on the *shape* of the demand curve. (In competitive markets, the consumer bears the entire tax.) Panels A and B of Figure 17.7 illustrate two possibilities. With a linear demand curve, the ratio of marginal revenue to price decreases with output, and the price rises by exactly half the tax; with a constant elasticity demand curve (where a 1 percent increase in the price results in, say, a 2 percent reduction in the demand, regardless of the price level) the ratio of marginal revenue to price is constant. Hence if marginal revenue increases by t, price must increase by even more: the increase in price always exceeds the magnitude of the tax. There is more than 100 percent shifting onto consumers.[3]

Ad valorem versus Specific Taxes. There is another important difference between the taxation of competitive and monopolistic industries. In the case of competitive industries, the form in which we levy the tax makes no difference. We can choose between a *specific tax,* which is specified as a fixed amount per unit of output, or an ad valorem tax, which is specified as a *percentage* of the value of output. All that matters for determining the effect of the tax is the magnitude of the difference (in equilibrium) between the price received by producers and the price paid by consumers, what we refer to as the wedge between the two.[4]

In the case of monopolistic industries, however, the effects of an ad valorem and a specific tax are markedly different. In our discussion of beer we chose a specific tax and represented its effect as an upward shift in the marginal cost curve. We could have also represented it as a downward shift in the demand curve, where the vertical axis now represents not the price paid

---

[3]The marginal revenue *(MR)* is related to the price by the formula

$$MR = p(1 - 1/\eta^d) \text{ where } \eta^d > 1.$$

Since $MR = MC$ (marginal cost) $+ t$ (the tax),

$$p = \frac{MC + t}{1 - 1/\eta^d}.$$

An increase in the tax by 10 cents increases price by $(1/1 - 1/\eta^d) \times 10$¢. If $\eta^d = 2$, the increase in the price is 20 cents.

[4]For administrative reasons, the two taxes may be markedly different. In general the same tax must be applied across a wide variety of commodities. If the tax is on a per unit of output basis, then it represents a higher percentage tax on lower-quality units and thus serves effectively to discourage the production of these lower quality (lower priced) items. This is why there is some preference for the imposition of ad valorem taxes.

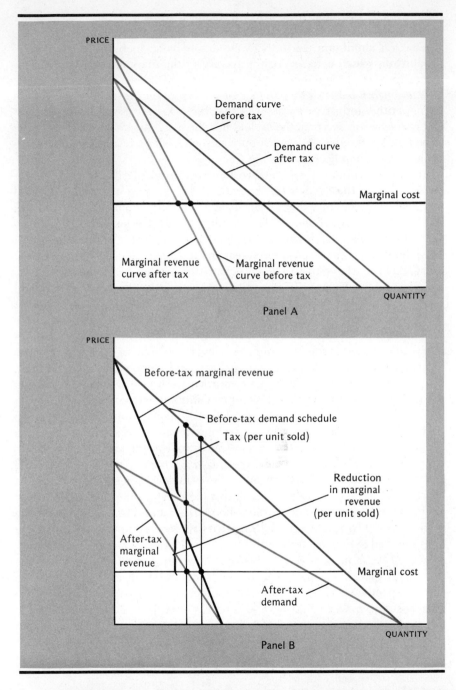

PRICE

Demand curve
before tax

Demand curve
after tax

Marginal cost

Marginal revenue
curve after tax

Marginal revenue
curve before tax

QUANTITY

Panel A

PRICE

Before-tax marginal revenue

Before-tax demand schedule

Tax (per unit sold)

Reduction
in marginal
revenue
(per unit sold)

After-tax
marginal
revenue

Marginal cost

After-tax
demand

QUANTITY

Panel B

17.8 COMPARING THE EFFECTS OF A SPECIFIC TAX AND AN AD VALOREM
TAX ON A MONOPOLIST (A) The effects of a specific commodity tax on a monopolist can
be viewed either as a shift upward in the marginal cost schedule (as in the earlier diagrams) or,
as here, a shift downward in the demand and marginal revenue schedules. (B) Analysis of the
effects of an ad valorem tax on a monopolist. For any given tax revenue, output is higher with
an ad valorem tax than with a specific tax.

by consumers by the price received by the producers. This is shown in Figure 17.8, Panel A.

With an ad valorem tax, if an individual pays a price p for a commodity, the amount received by the producer is $p(1-\hat{t})$ where $\hat{t}$ represents the ad valorem tax rate. Thus the tax paid is a function of the market price. If the price were zero, there would be no tax paid. The effect of the tax is to rotate the demand curve as in Figure 17.8, Panel B, rather than to shift it down uniformly, as depicted in Panel A. Thus a specific tax lowers the marginal revenue received by the firm by the amount of the tax; the ad valorem tax reduces the marginal revenue by less than the tax (the marginal revenue is $(1-\hat{t})MR$—that is, it is reduced by $\hat{t}MR$, while the revenue received by the government is $\hat{t}p$. Since prices exceed marginal revenue, the marginal revenue is reduced by less than the tax). Hence for any given level of equilibrium output, the ad valorem tax raises more revenue; or equivalently, for any given tax revenue, output will be higher with an ad valorem tax.

EQUIVALENT TAXES

In the discussion so far, we have pointed out that taxes that appear legally to be different—a tax on employers to finance social security and a tax on employees; a tax on the producers of beer or a tax on consumers of beer—are really equivalent. There are many other examples of what appear to be very different taxes (and from an administrative point of view *are* different taxes) that are, from an economic point of view, equivalent.

Income Tax and Value-Added Tax

The most obvious such example follows from the basic identity between national income (what all the individuals in our society receive) and national output (what they all produce). Since the value of income and the value of output must be the same, a uniform tax on income (that is, a tax that taxes all sources of income at the same rate) and a uniform tax on output (that is, a tax that taxes all outputs at the same rate) must be equivalent. A comprehensive uniform sales tax is a uniform tax on output and is thus equivalent to a uniform income tax.

The production of any commodity entails a large number of steps. The value of the final product represents the sum of the *value added* at each stage of production. We could impose the tax at the end of the production process or at each stage along the way. A tax at the end of the production process is called a sales tax. A tax imposed at each stage of the production process is called a value-added tax. Thus a uniform value-added tax and a comprehensive uniform sales tax are equivalent; and since a uniform sales tax and a uniform income tax are equivalent, a uniform value-added tax and a uniform income tax are equivalent.

The value-added tax is used in most European countries, and there has been some discussion about introducing such a tax into the United States. Since a uniform value-added tax is equivalent to a uniform (proportional) income tax, replacing our current income tax system with a value-added tax would be equivalent to replacing it with a proportional income tax system.

Equivalence of Consumption and Wage Taxes. Similarly, it can be shown that a uniform tax on wages and a uniform tax on consumption are equivalent.[5] To put it another way, a consumption tax is equivalent to an income tax in which interest and other returns to capital have been exempted. (Our present tax system, in which part of the return to capital is tax exempt and part is taxed at a lower rate than wages, can be viewed as somewhere between a consumption tax and an income tax.)

The equivalence may be seen most clearly by comparing the lifetime budget constraints of an individual (with no inheritances or bequests). For simplicity, we divide the life of the individual into two periods. We assume his wage income in the first period is W_1 and his wage income in the second is W_2. The individual has to decide on how much to consume the first period of his life, while he is young, and how much while is is old. If he reduces his consumption today by a dollar and invests it, next period he will have $1 + r$ dollars, where r is the rate of interest. With a 10 percent interest rate, he will have $1.10. The budget constraint is a straight line, depicted in Figure 17.9.

Consider now what happens to his budget constraint when a wage tax of 20 percent is imposed. The amount that he can consume shifts down. The *slope* of the budget constraint remains unchanged: it is still the case that by

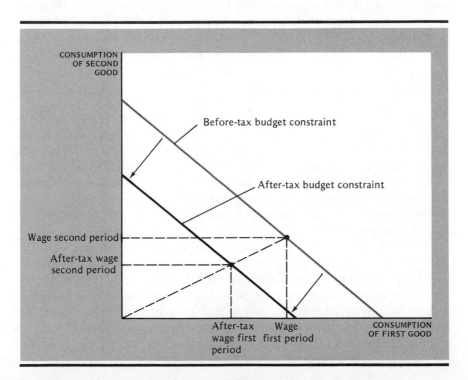

17.9 COMPARING THE EFFECTS OF THE CONSUMPTION TAX AND THE WAGE TAX A consumption tax and a wage tax have exactly the same effect on the individual's budget constraint.

[5] We ignore, for the moment, the effects of bequests and inheritances on consumption.

giving up today a dollar of consumption, he can get $1.10 next period. The new budget constraint is also depicted in Figure 17.9.

But a tax on consumption also shifts his budget constraint in. The slope of the budget constraint again remains unchanged. If the individual spends $1 less today, he has $1.10 more to spend next period. When he spends a $1 today, he gets 20 percent fewer goods because of the tax; but when he spends a $1 tomorrow, he also gets 20 percent fewer goods because of the tax. The trade-off between spending today and spending tomorrow remains unchanged. A wage tax and a consumption tax are equivalent.[6] The timing of the revenues to the government differs between the two taxes, and this may be important if capital markets are imperfect. There are, again, several ways that we can impose these equivalent taxes. We could impose a tax on wage income only, exempting all interest, dividends, and other returns on capital. Or we can tax consumption, which can be calculated by having the individual report his total income minus total savings.

TAX INCIDENCE UNDER PARTIAL AND GENERAL EQUILIBRIUM

So far, we have shown that what is important in determining who bears the burden of any tax is not who Congress says should bear the burden of the tax, but: a) certain properties of demand and supply; and b) the nature of the market, whether it is competitive or monopolistic.

There are several other important factors that need to be taken into account in any complete incidence analysis. First, there is an important distinction between a tax in a single industry and a tax affecting many industries. In our earlier analysis we considered a tax on a small industry (beer). The presumption is that such a tax will not, for instance, have any significant effect on the wage rate. Though the reduction in the demand for beer will reduce the demand for labor in the beer industry, the assumption is that this industry is so small that workers released from their jobs can find employment elsewhere without any significant effect on the wage rate. We refer to this kind of analysis, where we assume that all prices and wages (other than those on which attention is explicitly focused) remain constant, as **partial equilibrium analysis.**

Unfortunately, many taxes affect many industries simultaneously. The corporate income tax affects all incorporated businesses. If the effect of the tax is to reduce the demand for capital in this sector, the capital released cannot be absorbed by the rest of the economy (the unincorporated sector) without reducing the return to capital there. We cannot assume that the return the corporate sector must pay to obtain capital is independent of the tax imposed on that sector. To analyze the impact of such a tax requires an analysis of the equilibrium of the entire economy, not just the industries on which the tax has been imposed. We call such an analysis a **general equilibrium analysis.** There are many instances where the general equilibrium impact of a tax may be markedly different from the partial equilibrium effect. Thus

---

[6] If there are bequests and inheritances, a wage-plus-inheritance tax is equivalent to a consumption-plus-bequest tax. These equivalency relations require a perfect capital market but are true even if there is risk. See A. B. Atkinson and J. E. Stiglitz, *Lectures in Public Economics* (New York: McGraw-Hill, 1980).

if capital can be shifted relatively easily from the incorporated to the unin-corporated sectors of the economy, the tax on corporate capital must be borne equally by capital in both sectors of the economy; they both must have the same after-tax return.

A similar distinction must be made between the incidence of the tax in the long run and in the short run. In the short run, many things are fixed that, in the long run, can vary. While capital presently being used in some industry (like steel) cannot easily be shifted for use into another, in the long run new investment can be shifted to other industries. Thus a tax on the return to capital in the steel industry may have markedly different effects in the long run than in the short run.

If savings are taxed, the short-run effect may be minimal; but in the long run, it may discourage savings, and this may reduce the capital stock. The reduction in the capital stock will reduce the demand for (and productivity of) labor, and this, in turn, will lead to a lowering of wages. As a result, the *long-run incidence* of a tax on savings (or capital) may be on workers, even if the *short-run incidence* is not.

The nature of these general equilibrium effects may differ markedly depending on whether the economy is closed (does not trade with other countries) or open. If a small, open country like Switzerland imposed a tax on capital, the before-tax rate of return would have to fully adjust to offset the tax (or else investors would withdraw their funds from Switzerland and invest elsewhere); the tax would be borne by other factors. Effectively, the supply schedule for capital is infinitely elastic. The same analysis applies, of course, to any state within the United States.

The distinction between short-run and long-run effects is important, because governments and politicians are often shortsighted. They observe the imme-diate effect without realizing that the full consequences of the tax may not be those that they intended.

The final aspect of incidence analysis that we need to discuss is this: it is almost never possible for the government to change only one policy at a time. There is a basic government budget constraint, which says that tax revenues plus the increase in the size of the deficit (increased borrowing) must equal government expenditures. If the government raises some tax rate, it must either lower another, reduce its borrowing, or increase its expenditure. Different combinations of policies will have different effects. We simply cannot ask the question, What would happen if the government increased income taxes? We need to specify whether the income tax is to be accompanied by a reduction in some other tax, an increase in government expenditure, or a reduction in government borrowing. (Often the accom-panying change is taken to be understood but not made explicit; if taxes are not raised, there will be a larger deficit.)

We call the analysis of a tax increase accompanied by a decrease in some other tax **differential tax incidence analysis;** we call the analysis of a tax increase accompanied by an increase in government expenditure a **balanced budget tax incidence** analysis.

Sometimes we are interested in analyzing combinations of policies that leave some important economic variable unchanged. Thus a tax increase may lead to a reduction in the level of aggregate demand and to a lowering of

national income (when income is demand-determined). We
distinguish the effects of a tax program on the level of nationa
the effects that this may have, say, on its distribution) from th
of the tax itself; we thus may look at combinations of policies
level of national income unaffected.

Similarly, many taxes have an effect on the level of capita
The change in capital stock in turn may lower wages. Again
to distinguish the direct from the indirect effects of a tax r
impact on capital accumulation. This is particularly the cas
that other instruments can be used to offset these effects. If an inheritance
tax reduces capital accumulation, it may be possible to undo the effects by
providing an investment tax credit. We may examine a set of policies the
effect of which is to leave capital accumulation unaffected; we call incidence
analysis of this sort **balanced growth incidence analysis.**

Assessing the Total Impact of a Tax Increase

What the government does with the revenue raised by an increase in taxes
determines the consequences. Consider the alternatives: it can either buy
consumption goods or capital goods, or it can use the proceeds of the tax to
reduce the government debt. If it buys consumption goods, and if those
consumption goods it supplies are at least partial substitutes for private consumption goods, the tax will discourage current private consumption
(encourage saving); this will be true whether the individual is a lender or a
borrower. If it buys a capital good, which will increase future consumption,
and if this government-provided future consumption is at least a partial substitute for future private consumption, then the tax will discourage savings
and encourage private (current) consumption. Again, this will be true for
both borrowers and lenders.

If the government uses the tax revenues to reduce the debt, it makes
possible the reduction of taxes in future years. If those who benefit from the
future tax reduction are the same as those who pay the tax today, a small
increase in a *lump sum* tax today simply decreases savings by an amount
equal to the decrease in the supply of outstanding government bonds. Although
savings are decreased, what is available for investment in other than government bonds remains completely unchanged. An interest income tax has the
additional *(substitution)* effect of encouraging current consumption at the
expense of future consumption: it decreases what is available for investment
in other than government bonds.[7] The substitution effect is, in this case, the
only effect of the tax.

There are two major criticisms of this view. First, it assumes that individuals can see through the public veil; that they know the consequences of
various government decisions, and that they integrate this knowledge into
their private decision making. There is considerable skepticism about the
extent to which this occurs.

---

[7]The analysis extends to cases where there is uncertainty, but there are important qualifications, some of
which we note below. See J. E. Stiglitz, "On the Relevance or Irrelevance of Public Financial Policy: Indexation, Price Rigidities and Optional Monetary Policy," in R. Dornbush and M. Simonsen, eds., *Inflation,
Debt and Indexation* (Cambridge, MA: M.I.T. Press, 1983), pp. 183–222.

here have been some attempts to test explicitly for the extent to which individuals can see through the public veil. For instance, if two towns were essentially identical but one had a greater outstanding debt, the market value of land in that town should be correspondingly lower (assuming that the town finances its activities through a tax on property). These tests indicate that individuals see through the public veil very imperfectly.

The second criticism is that, if the time of the future benefit (tax reduction, consumption provided by current investment) is far enough into the future, the individual who benefits is different from the individual who pays the tax today. There is an important element of **intergenerational redistribution.** Thus a tax increase today used to reduce taxes for some later generation does result in the current generation reducing its current consumption. Robert Barro, of the University of Chicago, has maintained that even in these circumstances, current consumption may not be affected. He believes that the current generation cares not only about its own consumption but about its children's welfare, and its children care about their children's. As a result, it is *as if* there is a single individual (or, more accurately, dynasty) extending over an indefinite period. If the government taxes the current generation, say, to build a dam that will benefit future generations, the current generation reckons that it need leave a smaller bequest to that future generation. Though there may be some truth in this argument, so long as *some* individuals do not have descendants or do not care about their descendants, an increase in current taxation will not be fully offset: there will be some reduction in current consumption.[8]

A further limitation on this result is that individuals cannot borrow at the same terms as the government and cannot take perfectly offsetting actions.

Thus, though firms and households often can, and do, take actions that partially offset those of the government, they seldom can do so perfectly.

SUMMARY

1. It makes no difference whether the tax is legally imposed on the producers of a commodity or on the consumers. What does make a difference are the demand and supply elasticities, and whether the market is competitive or noncompetitive.

2. In a competitive market, if the supply is completely inelastic or demand completely elastic, the tax is borne by producers; if the supply is completely elastic or demand completely inelastic, the tax is entirely borne by consumers.

3. A tax on a monopolist may be shifted more than 100 percent—that is, the price paid by consumers may rise by more than the tax.

4. A tax on output (a uniform sales tax), a proportional income tax, and a uniform value-added tax are all equivalent. A uniform tax on wages and a uniform tax on consumption are equivalent.

5. Empirical studies of who bears the burden of taxes show that the degree of progressivity of the tax structure depends critically on assumptions concerning the

[8]See R. J. Barro, "Are Government Bonds New Wealth?" *Journal of Political Economy* 82 (1974): 1095–1117. The article has given rise to a considerable literature. The argument has a long tradition. J. M. Buchanan, "Barro on the Ricardian Equivalence Theorem," *Journal of Political Economy* 84 (1976): 337–42 traces it back to Ricardo (D. Ricardo, *Principles of Political Economy and Taxation, Works and Correspondence,* ed. Piero Sraffa [Cambridge: Cambridge University Press, 1951]). In its modern reincarnation, it was put forth independently in 1965 by Robert Hall (now of Stanford, at the time a graduate student at M.I.T.).

incidence of taxes. While under one set of assumptions, the current United States tax structure has some progressivity, under another set, there is relatively little progressivity.

6. The general equilibrium incidence of a tax, taking into account repercussions in all industries, may differ from the partial equilibrium incidence. The incidence of a tax may be different in the long run than in the short run.

7. It is almost never possible for the government to change one policy at a time. Differential tax incidence focuses on the consequences of substituting one tax for another.

KEY CONCEPTS

Incidence	Marginal cost
Shifting forward	Partial equilibrium analysis
Shifting backward	General equilibrium analysis
Elasticity of demand	Differential tax incidence analysis
Elasticity of supply	Balanced budget tax incidence
Ad valorem tax	Balanced growth incidence analysis
Specific tax	Intergenerational redistribution
Marginal revenue	

QUESTIONS AND PROBLEMS

1. Consider a small town in which workers are highly mobile (i.e., can be induced to leave the town if opportunities elsewhere improve slightly). What do you think the incidence of a tax on wages in that town would be, compared to the incidence in a town in which workers are immobile?

2. Consider a small country, in a world in which capital is highly mobile (i.e., capital will flow into the country quickly if the return offered is greater than elsewhere and will flow out if the return offered is less than elsewhere). What do you think the incidence of a tax on the return to capital would be in such a country?

3. It is frequently asserted that taxes on cigarettes and beer are regressive, because poor individuals spend a large fraction of their income on such items. How would your estimate of the degree of regressivity be affected if you thought: these commodities were produced: a) by competitive industries with inelastic supply schedules; (b) by a monopoly with a linear demand schedule; (c) by a monopoly facing a constant elasticity demand schedule?

4. It is often asserted that gasoline taxes used to finance highway construction and maintenance are "fair" because they make those who use the roads pay for them. Who do you think bears the incidence of such taxes?

5. If you believed that a proportional consumption tax was the "best tax," what are various ways in which you could levy it? Might there be differences in administrative costs associated with levying such a tax in different ways?

6. In what ways may the actual incidence of a government expenditure program differ from the "legislated intent"? Why might the effects be different in the short run and in the long run? Illustrate with examples drawn from Part III of the book, or with a discussion of the effects of government farm programs. Similarly, discuss how the short-run and long-run effects of a regulatory program, such as rent control, may differ from one another.

18

Taxation and Economic Efficiency

All taxes affect economic behavior. They transfer resources from the individual to the government; as a result, individuals must alter their behavior in some way. If they do not adjust the amount of work they do, they must reduce their consumption. They may work more, enjoying less leisure; by working more, they need reduce their consumption less.

No matter how individuals adjust, an increase in taxes must make them worse off.[1] But some taxes reduce individuals' welfare less, for each dollar of revenue raised, than do other taxes. In Chapter 16 we defined a lump sum tax as one that is imposed on an individual and that could not be affected by any behavior of the individual. Since there was nothing the individual could do to affect his tax liability, we said such taxes were nondistortionary. Lump taxes affect the individual's behavior: they might reduce the individual's demands for some commodities or induce individuals to work harder. These effects were purely associated with the fact that the individual had less income to spend and were thus called income effects. Because lump sum taxes are nondistortionary, they raise the most revenue for any given loss in welfare of individuals.

This chapter is concerned with several questions: What determines how individuals adjust to the taxes imposed upon them? What determines the magnitude of the welfare losses arising from the use of distortionary taxation?

---

[1]This ignores, of course, the benefits that may accrue from the increased government expenditures that result from the increased taxes. Throughout this chapter we also ignore general equilibrium effects; before-tax wages and prices will be assumed to be unaffected by the imposition of a tax.

Finally, how can we *measure* the inefficiency associated with the use of distortionary taxation?

TAXES ON LABOR

Consider the individual's before-tax budget constraint depicted in Figure 18.1. As the individual works more, he obtains a higher income, which enables him to purchase more consumption goods. For simplicity, we assume there is a single consumption good and the individual cannot save.

The budget constraint shows the alternative levels of consumption and labor that are possible. In this example, the individual gets paid $5 an hour. If he works 30 hours a week he gets $150. If he works 40 hours a week he receives $200, and if he works 50 hours a week he receives $250.

The figure also shows the individual's before tax indifference curve for work and consumption, giving the combinations of work and consumption goods among which the individual is indifferent. The individual is indifferent, for instance, when choosing among working 30 hours a week and receiving $175, working 40 hours a week and receiving $200, and working 50 hours a week and receiving $500. Note that the individual requires a much larger increase in his weekly income to compensate him for increasing his work from 40 to 50 hours than for compensating him for increasing his work from

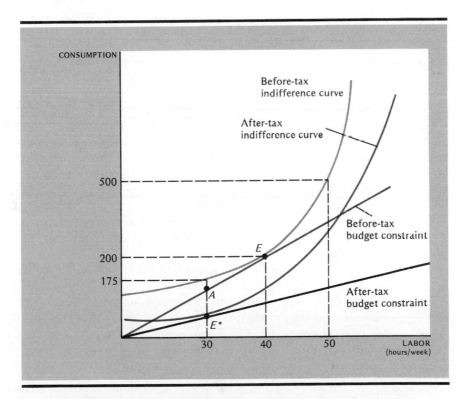

18.1 EQUILIBRIUM BEFORE AND AFTER TAXES The effect of the tax is to shift the budget constraint down, and thus the equilibrium changes from E to E*.

30 to 40 hours. As he works more and more, his leisure becomes more valuable; and as he gets more and more goods, extra units of consumption become less valuable. That is why he requires larger and larger increases in consumption to compensate him for successive increases in his labor supply.

In the absence of taxation, the individual would choose that point on his budget constraint where his indifference curve is tangent to his budget constraint, point E in Figure 18.1.

At E, the individual requires precisely $5 extra compensation for working an additional hour and receives $5 extra for working an extra hour. In other words, the slope of the individual's indifference curve (his *marginal rate of substitution*) is just equal to the slope of his budget constraint, his wage. (The slope of the budget constraint specifies how much his consumption increases in response to an increase in his labor supply; in our example, for each extra hour the individual works he gets an extra $5.)

Income and Substitution Effects of Taxation

We now examine how taxes alter this. Assume that there is a proportional income tax. That is, a given fraction of the income the individual earns must be turned over to the government. This shifts his budget constraint down, as depicted by the after-tax budget constraint in Figure 18.1. There is now a new equilibrium, denoted by E^*. The tax revenue is the vertical distance, at E^*, between the after-tax and the before-tax budget constraints, E^*A. The before-tax budget constraint gives the individual's income—before tax—at the labor supply corresponding to E^*. The after-tax budget constraint gives his level of consumption. The difference is just what he pays in taxes.

In our example, we have imposed a 50 percent tax, and the individual, as a result of the tax, has reduced his labor supply from 40 hours a week to 30 hours a week. Thus, the government's tax revenue is $30 \times \$2.5 = \$75$.

Any tax on income has two effects. First, it makes the individual worse off. As a result of being worse off, the individual will consume less and work harder. This is referred to as the **income effect** of the tax. The second effect is that the return for working is reduced; for each hour the individual works, he used to receive a wage of w; now he receives a wage of $w(1-t)$, where t is the tax rate; that is, his return for working is reduced by the amount of the tax. Since the individual's return for his labor is reduced, he has less incentive to work. We refer to this as the **substitution effect** of the tax; he substitutes leisure for consumption goods.

In Figure 18.2 we illustrate the two effects. We first observe that if we shift the individual's budget constraint down in a parallel way (from OA to CO), keeping the slope—representing the increased consumption for working an extra hour, the wage—fixed, we increase labor supply. This is the movement from point E to $\hat{E}$. Because the individual is poorer, he consumes fewer goods and less leisure.[2] Next, we observe that if we rotate the budget

---

[2] We say that a good is "normal" when, as the budget constraint shifts down parallel at fixed wages and prices, consumption decreases. Similarly, we say that leisure is a normal good when leisure decreases. Throughout most of the remaining analysis, we shall assume that leisure and consumption goods are "normal."

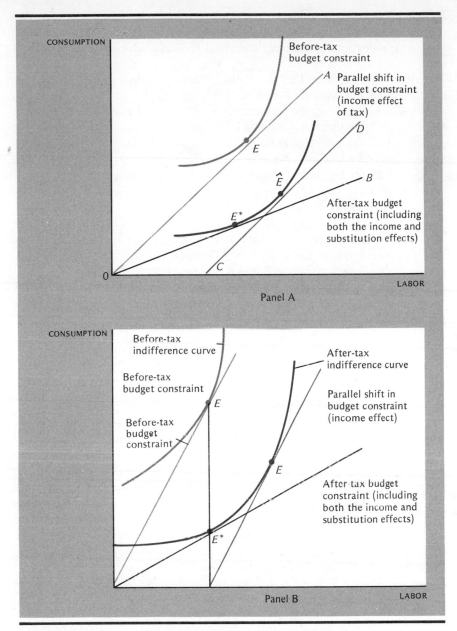

18.2 THE INCOME AND SUBSTITUTION EFFECTS (A) The income effect normally leads to increase labor supply. The substitution effect always leads to decreased labor supply. The net effect is ambiguous. (B) In this example, income and substitution effects exactly cancel; the tax has no effect on labor supply.

constraint—keeping the individual on the same indifference curve (from CD to OA)—labor supply decreases. This movement from $\hat{E}$ to E^* is the substitution effect. Because the wage is lower, at any given level of utility individuals substitute leisure for consumption goods: they work less.

In the case of a proportional income tax, the substitution effect and the income effect work in opposite directions. While the income effect leads the individual to work more, the substitution effect leads the individual to work less. It is impossible to say, on theoretical grounds, which effect will dominate.

In Panel A of Figure 18.2 the substitution effect dominates the income effect, so that the individual reduces his labor supply. In Panel B we have depicted a case where the two effects exactly cancel each other, and the labor supply is unaffected.

Notice that the effect of imposing a proportional wage tax is exactly the same as the effect of lowering the wage. Thus the question of whether a (proportional) tax increases or decreases labor supply is equivalent to asking whether the labor supply curve is upward sloping or backward bending. In Figure 18.3, Panel A, higher wages induce more labor; the substitution effect dominates the income effect. In Panel B, for sufficiently higher wages, the income effect dominates the substitution effect: further increases in wages lead to lower levels of labor supplied. Thus, in Panel A a proportional tax reduces labor supply, while in Panel B it increases it.

Economists measure the extent to which labor supply is affected by the elasticity of labor supply. This gives the percentage change in the labor supply from a percent change in the wage:

$$\text{Elasticity of labor supply} = \frac{\%\ \text{change in labor supply}}{\%\ \text{change in wage}}.$$

If a 1 percent increase in the wage increases the labor supply by 3 percent, we say that the elasticity of labor supply is 3. If a 1 percent increase in the wage increases the labor supply by ½ percent, we say that the elasticity of labor supply is 0.5. There is not agreement among economists about the magnitude of the labor supply elasticity; the consensus is that for men the labor supply elasticity is very small.[3] Apparently, income and substitution effects just about cancel each other. On the other hand, there is a consensus that for women the labor supply response is positive, and much larger than for men.[4] If the female labor supply elasticity is taken to be around 1, then a 25 percent tax would reduce the amount of labor supplied by women by 25 percent. As changes in the role of women in the workplace occur, corresponding changes in labor supply elasticities may occur, but these are not yet well reflected in the data.

Distortionary Effects of Wage Taxation

We have seen that a tax on wages may not have a significant effect on (male) labor supply. Does this mean that such a tax is nondistortionary? As we shall now show, the answer is no. Even if an individual has not changed his supply

---

[3] Some representative numbers are summarized in J. Hausman, "Taxes and Labor Supply," *Handbook of Public Economics,* ed. A. Auerbach and M. Feldstein (Amsterdam: North Holland, 1985). The (uncompensated) wage elasticities in the studies cited ranged from −.13 to .09.

[4] Hausman cites estimates for wives' supply wage elasticities ranging from −.3 to 2.30. His own study ("Labor Supply," in H. Aaron and J. Pechman, eds., *How Taxes Affect Economic Behavior* [Washington, D.C.: Brookings Institution, 1981]) provides an estimate of .91.

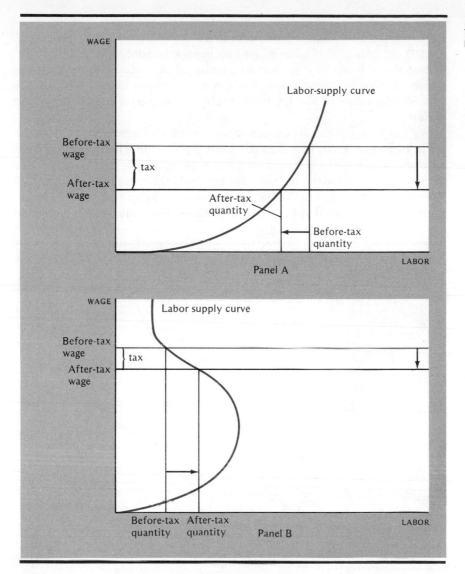

WAGE

Labor-supply curve

Before-tax
wage

tax

After-tax
wage

After-tax
quantity

Before-tax
quantity

Panel A

LABOR

WAGE

Labor supply curve

Before-tax
wage

tax

After-tax
wage

Before-tax   After-tax
quantity   quantity   Panel B

LABOR

18.3 THE EFFECTS OF A TAX ON THE SUPPLY OF LABOR (A) With a positively sloped supply curve, tax reduces labor supply. (B) With a backward-bending supply curve, at some wage levels a tax increases labor supply.

of labor, we could have obtained the same revenue, at lower loss of welfare to the individual, had we imposed a lump sum tax.

Recall the definition of a lump sum tax: it is a tax whose magnitude does not depend on anything that the individual does. A lump sum tax would require each citizen to pay a given amount to the government—say, $100 per week—regardless of income. It simply shifts the individual's budget constraint downward, as depicted in Figure 18.4. The slope of the budget constraint is unchanged: the individual still receives the same extra consumption for working an extra hour. (In our example, with a $5 wage rate, for each extra hour the individual works, he still receives $5.) If he works 40 hours a week, his before-tax income is $200. But his after-tax income is $100. If he works 50 hours a week, his before-tax income is $250, but his after-tax income is $150. At each level of labor supply, his income is reduced by exactly $100.[5] Notice that a lump sum tax has an income effect: because individuals are worse off, they consume fewer goods and less leisure (hence work more). Indeed, the effect of the tax is precisely the *income effect* we described earlier.

We can compare the effects of a lump sum tax and a proportional income tax in two ways. First, how does the labor supply with a lump sum tax compare with that under a proportional income tax, assuming that we choose the tax rate so as to leave the individual at precisely the same level of utility (on the same indifference curve) that he had with the lump sum tax? This comparison is also depicted in Figure 18.4. With the lump sum tax the individual

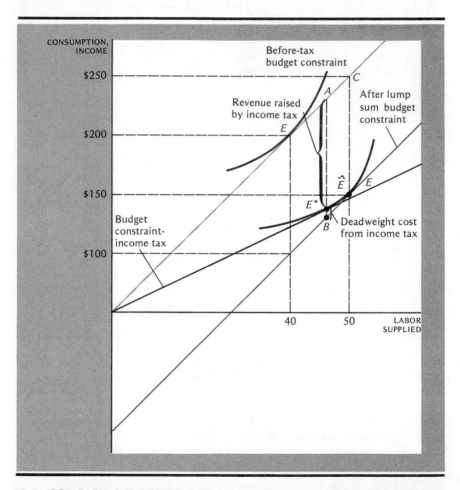

18.4 COMPARING THE EFFECTS OF A LUMP SUM TAX AND A PROPORTIONAL INCOME TAX With a lump sum tax the individual chooses $\hat{E}$; with the income tax the individual chooses E^*.

---

[5]In this simple exposition, we ignore what happens if the individual's income is less than the amount of lump sum tax that has been imposed.

chooses point $\hat{E}$; with the income tax the individual chooses point E^*. It is clear that with the income tax there is less labor supplied; this is precisely the substitution effect we identified earlier.

We now wish to compare the amount of revenue raised by the government. The amount of revenue raised is measured by the difference between the before-tax and after-tax budget constraints, at the level of labor actually supplied. The revenue raised by the income tax is the distance AE.

For the lump sum tax, the distance between the before- and after-tax budget constraints is the lump sum tax and is the same no matter what the amount of labor supplied. Thus the distance $\hat{E}C$ is equal to the distance AB, and both equal the revenue raised by the lump sum tax. It is apparent from the figure that with a lump sum tax, the government raises more revenue than with an income tax. The extra revenue is depicted by the distance E^*B in Figure 18.4.

The Magnitude of the Deadweight Loss

The difference between the revenue raised by a lump sum tax and the revenue raised by an income tax (both of which left the individual at the same indifference curve) is called the **deadweight loss** associated with the income tax. We also refer to the deadweight loss as the **excess burden** of the tax. It is a measure of the inefficiency of the tax system. In Figure 18.4, the deadweight loss is given by the distance E^*B.

The magnitude of this deadweight loss is determined by the magnitude of the substitution effect. Figure 18.5 replicates the part of Figure 18.4 showing the deadweight loss. We have drawn the after-tax indifference curve of two individuals. For one, the substitution effect is much smaller (the indifference curve is steeper) than for the other. As a result, the deadweight loss, E^*B, is much smaller (contrast E^*B with E^*B').

For small taxes, there is a simple formula for the magnitude of the deadweight loss (DWL) from a tax t:

$$\frac{\text{Deadweight loss}}{\text{Tax revenue}} = \frac{1}{2}\, t\eta_u^s,$$

where η_u^s equals the percentage change in labor supply from a percentage change in the wage, keeping the individual on the same indifference curve. This measures the magnitude of the substitution effect. It is called the **compensated elasticity of labor supply.** The term "compensated" is used to remind us that the individual is being kept on the same indifference curve as we change the wage. The ratio of the deadweight loss to tax revenue is just one-half times the tax on labor, times the compensated elasticity of labor supply.

We can write the formula for the deadweight loss in a slightly different way. The revenue raised by the tax is just the tax times the hourly wage w times the hours of labor supplied L, or tax revenue $= twL$. Hence

$$\text{DWL} = \frac{1}{2}\, t\eta_u^s \times \text{revenue}$$
$$= \frac{1}{2}\, t\eta_u^s \times twL$$
$$= \frac{1}{2}\, t^2\eta_u^s wL.$$

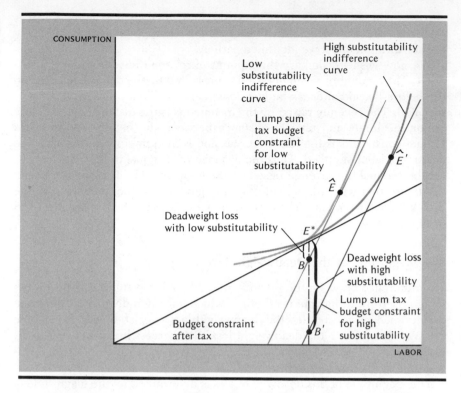

18.5 THE EFFECT OF THE SUBSTITUTION EFFECT ON THE DEADWEIGHT LOSS FROM A TAX The greater the substitution effect, the greater the deadweight loss from a tax.

Notice that the magnitude of the deadweight loss increases with the square of the tax. We say that a tax is "distortionary" whenever there is a deadweight loss. *Large taxes cause much larger distortions than do small taxes.*

Distortion with Inelastic Labor Supply

We now return to our original question: Is there a distortion associated with an income tax, if the labor supply elasticity is zero, so that the number of hours worked remains the same after the tax as before? The answer is yes, and the magnitude of the distortion is proportional to the *compensated* labor supply elasticity. Unfortunately, there is far more disagreement about the magnitude of the compensated labor supply elasticity than there is about the magnitude of the labor supply elasticity. One study, by Jerry Hausman of M.I.T., estimated it to be 0.764, while other studies estimate it to be much smaller. (Robert A. Moffitt, of Brown University, for instance, provided an estimate of 0.05.) With a 25 percent income tax, using Hausman's estimate, the deadweight loss is almost 10 percent (9.55 percent) of revenue raised, while under Moffitt's estimate it is only 2 percent of revenue raised.

COMMODITY TAXATION

A similar analysis applies to a tax imposed on one commodity. Assume that the individual's income is fixed, and he can choose between purchasing two

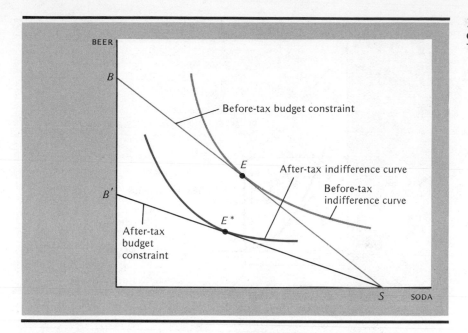

18.6 EQUILIBRIUM AFTER THE IMPOSITION OF A TAX ON BEER Here the income effects and the substitution effects reinforce each other and shift the equilibrium from E to E^*.

commodities, soda and beer. Suppose now that the government imposes a tax on beer. What will be the effect? Figure 18.6 shows the before-tax budget constraint. This gives the various combinations of soda and beer that the individual can purchase. If he spent all his income on soda, he could purchase the amount S; if he spent all his income on beer, he could purchase the amount B. The tax on beer shifts the budget constraint as depicted in Figure 18.6. He can still, if he wishes, spend all his income on soda, in which case he obtains S units of soda. But beer is now more expensive, so he can purchase less of it with his income.

Initially, the individual allocated his income by choosing point E on his budget constraint. This is the point of tangency between the budget constraint and the indifference curve. After the imposition of the tax, there is a new equilibrium, at point E^*. Again, we can decompose the effects of the tax into two parts. The income effect reduces the demand for beer. In addition, however, the tax has increased the price of beer relative to the price of soda, so the substitution effect will discourage the purchase of beer. Now, both the income and the substitution effects reinforce each other: they both lead to a reduction in the demand for beer. But the distortionary effect of the tax is only associated with the substitution effect.

To see this, we again contrast the effect of the beer tax with that of a lump sum tax. A lump sum tax represents a reduction in the amount of income the individual can spend on either commodity: it is depicted in Figure 18.7A as a parallel shift in the budget constraint. The relative price of the two commodities remains unchanged. If we measure the tax in terms of beer, the tax revenue is represented by the vertical distance between the before-tax and after-tax budget constraints. In Figure 18.7A we have contrasted the

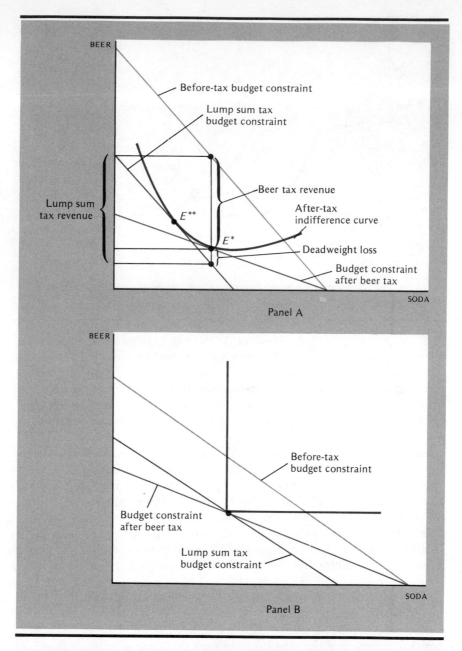

18.7 THE SHAPE OF THE INDIFFERENCE CURVE AND THE DEADWEIGHT LOSS
(A) A lump sum tax generating same (after-tax) utility as a proportional beer tax raises more revenue and leads to higher consumption of beer (but less than in the before-tax taxation). The difference in revenues is the deadweight loss associated with the tax. (B) With L-shaped indifference curve, there is no substitution effect and hence no deadweight loss.

revenues raised by a beer tax with those raised by a lump sum tax, with equal effect on the level of utility. It is clear from the figure that the lump sum tax raises more revenue (and leads to a higher level of consumption of beer) than does the beer tax. The difference between the two is a measure of the inefficiency resulting from the tax—the deadweight loss associated with the tax.

In Figure 18.7B we show the special case where the individual has L-shaped indifference curves. There is then no substitution effect. At a fixed level of utility, a change in the price has no effect on the level of consumption of beer and soda. Consumption with a lump sum tax and a beer tax (which leaves individuals on the same indifference curve) is identical. In that case, the revenue raised by the lump sum tax and by the beer tax is also identical. There is no distortion associated with the beer tax. If it is very difficult to substitute soda for beer—i.e., if the indifference curves, though not L-shaped, are very curved—the distortion associated with the tax is very small. The magnitude of the distortion can vary from commodity to commodity. Some individuals believe that for those addicted to alcohol the indifference curves between food and alcohol are also close to L-shaped, so that the substitution effect is small. Therefore, the deadweight loss is small. For most other commodities, there is a reasonable degree of substitution possibility, and hence taxes imposed on these commodities will have distortions associated with them.

Present and Future Consumption

The individual's allocation of his income between consumption this period and consumption in the future is very much like his decision about allocating his income among two different commodities.

Consumption today can be viewed as one commodity; consumption in the future can be viewed as another commodity. By giving up one dollar of consumption today, the individual can obtain $(1 + r)$ of extra consumption dollars next period, where r is the interest rate. That is, if the individual saves the dollar and deposits it in a bank, he gets back at the end of the period his dollar plus the interest it has earned. This $1 / 1 + r$ is the price of consumption tomorrow, relative to consumption today.[6]

If the individual neither borrowed nor lent money, he would consume whatever his wages were in the two periods. We denote the wages in the initial period by w_0 and wages in the next by w_1. This point is denoted by point W in Figure 18.8. By borrowing, the individual can consume more today, but at the expense of less next period. By saving, the individual can consume more next period, but at the expense of less consumption this period.

The individual thus faces a budget constraint. He can either have C units of consumption today, or $(1 + r)C \equiv \bar{C}$ units of consumption tomorrow, or any point on the straight line joining the two points, as depicted in Figure 18.8. The individual has an indifference curve between present consumption and future consumption, just as he has an indifference curve between beer and soda; the indifference curve gives those combinations of current and future consumption that leave the individual at the same level of utility. The individual is willing to consume less today in return for more future consump-

---

[6] Recall our discussion of present discounted value from Chapter 10. The individual's budget constraint can be interpreted as saying the present discounted value of consumption equals the present discounted value of his wages (ignoring bequests and inheritances).

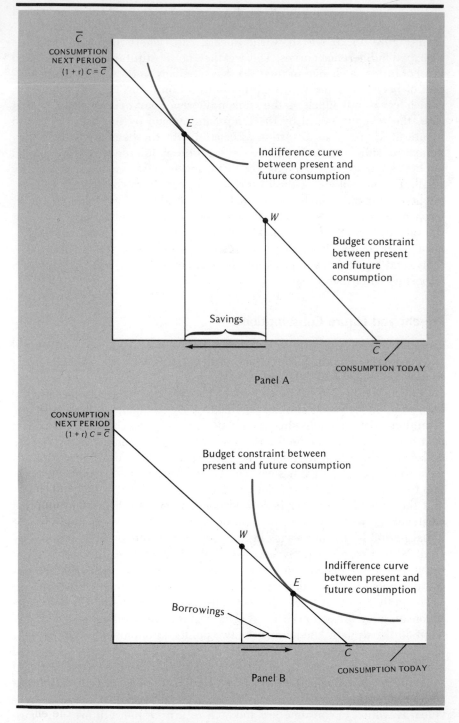

18.8 CONSUMPTION, SAVINGS, AND BORROWINGS The individual's allocation of his income between consumption this period and next period. In Panel A the individual saves, while in Panel B he borrows.

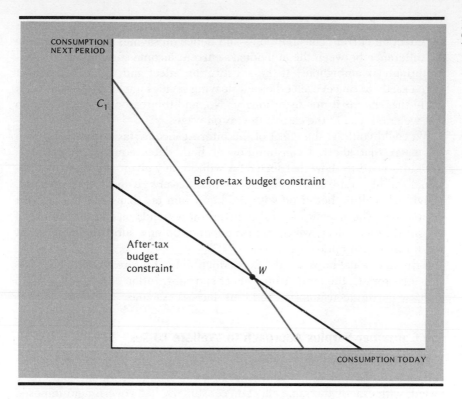

CONSUMPTION NEXT PERIOD

C_1

Before-tax budget constraint

After-tax budget constraint

W

CONSUMPTION TODAY

18.9 THE EFFECT OF AN INTEREST INCOME TAX An interest income tax (with deductibility of interest payments) rotates the budget constraint around the point W. Lenders are worse off, borrowers are better off.

tion. As his present consumption gets smaller and smaller, he becomes less willing to give up more; and as his future consumption gets larger and larger, the extra benefit he gets from each additional unit of future consumption gets smaller and smaller. Thus the amount of increased consumption next period required to compensate the individual for a reduction by one unit in current consumption becomes larger and larger. That is why the indifference curve has the shape depicted. The individual chooses that point on his budget constraint where his indifference curve is tangent, denoted by point E.

In Panel A of Figure 18.8 we illustrate a situation where the individual wishes to consume less than his wage income the first period and saves the rest, while in Panel B the individual wishes to consume more than his wage income the first period and borrows the difference.

Consider now the effect of a tax on interest income combined with tax deductibility of interest payments, as is the practice in the United States. Figure 18.9 shows how the tax rotates the budget constraint around point W. If the individual saves, he is worse off. We can again divide the effects into an income effect and a substitution effect. Because the individual is worse off, he normally will reduce his consumption of both commodities— i.e., he will *save* more. But because future consumption has become more expensive relative to current consumption, the individual's substitution effect discourages future consumption and encourages current consumption. The net effect on current consumption—and hence on savings (savings is simply the difference between the individual's current income and his current consumption)—is ambiguous. If the substitution effect and the income effect were exactly to cancel each other out, leaving savings unchanged, would this imply that the tax is nondistortionary? No, and the reasoning is identical to that we employed in the case of the tax on wages.

We could contrast the effect of the interest income tax with a lump sum tax, a tax that affected consumption at both dates equally. Again, it is straightforward to show that such a tax will, for any given effect on the individual's utility, raise more revenue; or that for any given level of revenue, individuals will be better off with the lump sum tax than with the interest income tax. The magnitude of the distortion depends on the magnitude of the substitution effect, which in turn depends on how substitutable current and future consumption are.

If the individual borrows, the tax deductibility of interest makes the individual better off; then the income effect and substitution effect both work to increase current consumption and thus decrease savings.

The Consumer Surplus Approach to Welfare Losses

In the preceding section we measured the inefficiency from the imposition of a distortionary tax as the additional revenue that government could have raised, with exactly the same effect on consumers, had government imposed a lump sum tax.

The concept of consumer surplus, which we discussed in Chapter 10, is often employed for calculating the loss associated with a distortionary tax.

Assume we have imposed a tax of 30 cents a bottle of beer, and, with the tax, the individual consumes 10 bottles a week. We ask the individual how much he would be willing to give to the government if the tax were eliminated. In other words, what lump sum tax would leave him indifferent to the current situation. He would be willing to pay more than 30 cents × 10 per week. The extra revenue that such a tax would generate is the deadweight loss associated with the use of a distortionary tax system.

We now show how to calculate the deadweight loss using a consumer's **compensated demand curve.** The compensated demand curve gives the individual's demand for beer, assuming that as the price is lowered, income is being taken away from the individual in such a way as to leave him on the same indifference curve. We use the compensated demand curve because we wish to know how much more revenue we could have achieved with a nondistortionary tax, still leaving the individual just as well off as he was with the distortionary tax.

Assume initially the price of a bottle of beer is $1.50, including a .30 cent tax per bottle, and the individual consumes ten bottles a week. We then ask him how much extra he would be willing to pay to consume 11 bottles a week. He is willing to pay only $1.40. The total amount that the individual would thus be willing to pay us as a lump sum tax if we lowered the tax from 30 cents to 20 cents is 10 cents × 10 bottles he previously purchased, or $1.00 (the area *FGCD* in Figure 18.10A).

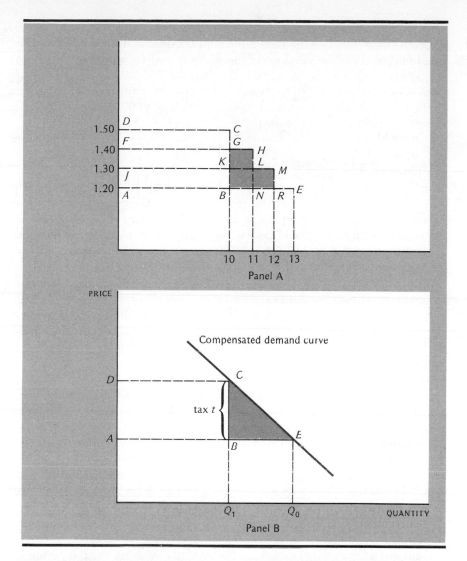

18.10 USING COMPENSATED DEMAND CURVES TO MEASURE DEADWEIGHT
LOSS Government revenue is area *ABCD*. Consumer surplus—the measure of the deadweight
loss—is shaded area. In Panel A, we show how much the individual would be willing to pay
to have the price of beer reduced from $1.50 to $1.20 (keeping him at the same level of utility).
The difference between this and the tax raised (the area *ABCD*) is the deadweight loss.

We now ask him to assume he is in a situation where we levied a $1.00
lump sum tax and charged $1.40 each for 11 bottles of beer. How much *extra*
would he be willing to pay for one extra bottle? Assume the individual said
$1.30. We can now calculate the total lump sum tax that an individual would
be willing to pay if the price were reduced from $1.50 to $1.30. He would
be willing to pay 20 cents a bottle for the first 10 bottles (the area *JKCD*) and
10 cents for the next (the area *GKHL*), for a total of $2.10.

Finally, we ask him to assume he is in a situation where we levied a $2.10
lump sum tax and charged $1.30 each for 12 bottles. How much extra would

he be willing to pay for one extra bottle? Assume the individual said $1.20. We could now calculate the total lump sum tax that an individual would be willing to pay for the elimination of the 30 cents' tax. He would be willing to pay 30 cents on the first 10 bottles (the area *ABCD*), 20 cents on the next bottle (the area *GBHN*), 10 cents on the twelfth bottle (the area *LMNR*), for a total of $3.30. The tax revenue from the tax was $3.00 (the area *ABCD*). The deadweight loss is 30 cents (the shaded area).

Measuring the Deadweight Loss

More generally, the amount that an individual would be willing to pay to have the price reduced by 1 cent is just 1 cent times the quantity consumed. As we lower the price, the quantity consumed increases. In Figure 18.10B the total an individual would be willing to pay to have the price reduced from *D* to *A* is the area *AECD*, which takes account of the change in the quantity consumed as the price is reduced. But of that, *ABCD* is the tax revenue (the tax *AD*, times the quantity consumed at the price, including the tax, *AB*). Hence the deadweight loss, the difference between the two, is just the triangle *BCE*. This is sometimes referred to as the Harberger triangle, after Arnold Harberger of the University of Chicago, who made extensive use of such triangles in calculating the deadweight losses associated with various taxes.[7]

As we noted in Chapter 10, consumer surplus calculations are widely employed to evaluate government programs, as well as to measure the inefficiencies associated with various taxes.[8] They have also been widely criticized. These criticisms have as much to do with how the calculations are done in practice as with the theory. Note in particular that our formula made use of the *compensated* demand elasticity; moreover, our calculation of the area assumed either that the demand curve was linear or that the tax was small enough that a linear approximation was reasonably accurate. If we are calculating the deadweight loss associated with an income tax with 50 percent marginal tax rates, the approximation must be used with considerable caution.

Our analysis has also focused on the effects of the tax on the sector in which it is levied; any tax may also have repercussions for other sectors. Whenever the tax rates in these other sectors are not zero (or there is imperfect competition in these other sectors), we have to pay attention to these repercussions. Assume, for instance, that the government has a tax on both beer and cigarettes. Assume that individuals drink more beer when they are smoking. If the government increases its tax on cigarettes, it may reduce beer consumption, and this may reduce both the revenue raised by the beer tax and the deadweight loss arising from the tax on beer. In the next chapter we discuss briefly how these interactions may be taken into account in designing the optimal tax structure.

---

[7]See, for instance, A. Harberger, "Taxation, Resource Allocation and Welfare," in *The Role of Direct and Indirect Taxes in the Federal Revenue System*, ed. J. Due (Princeton, NJ: Princeton University Press, 1964).

[8]For some recent discussions on the use of consumer surplus, see J. Hausman, "Exact Consumer Surplus and Deadweight Loss," *American Economic Review* 11 (1981): 662–76; R. Willig, "Consumer Surplus Without Apology," *American Economic Review* 66 (1976): 589–97.

The analysis of this chapter has focused on the distortionary effects of a tax on consumers. In our earlier calculations we assumed that supply curves were horizontal, so the entire burden of the tax was on consumers (see Chapter 17). A similar analysis applies to distortionary taxes on producers. Assume, for instance, we had a tax on some input, such as steel, into an industry (automobiles). We can ask what lump sum we could impose on the industry that would have the same effect on profits as the tax on steel.[9] The difference in revenues raised by the lump sum tax and the tax on steel is the deadweight loss from the tax. The magnitude of the deadweight loss will depend on the possibilities of substitution. If the firm cannot substitute any other input for steel (even partially), the tax on steel is no different from a tax on output. There is no distortionary effect on the input mix and hence no deadweight loss associated with a change in the input mix.

Similarly, assume we had a tax on the output of some industry with an upward-sloping supply schedule. We could ask the firm what lump sum tax would have the same effect on profits as the tax on output.

The magnitude of the deadweight loss is measured by the **producer surplus.** Recall how a supply schedule is constructed. At each price, firms produce up to the point where price equals marginal cost. If the supply schedule is upward-sloping, the marginal cost rises as production rises. The magnitude of the deadweight loss is measured by the **producer surplus.** Recall how a supply schedule is constructed. At each price, firms produce up to the point where price equals marginal cost. If the supply schedule is upward-sloping, the marginal cost rises as production rises. The area between the supply curve and price measures the total profits (excluding any fixed costs of establishing the firm). Changes in this area thus measure changes in profits.

Consider the following example. What happens to profits as price increases from 1 to 4 and output increases from 1 to 4? The first unit of output costs $1; the next, $2; the third, $3; and the fourth, $4. If we pay the firm $4, so it produces 4 units, the firm gets $3 more than marginal costs for producing the first unit, $2 more than marginal costs for producing the second unit, and $1 more than marginal costs for producing the third unit. The total profits are $3 + 2 + 1 = \$6$.

This can be seen more generally in Figure 18.11. Assume initially the producer is receiving the price p. Then a tax is imposed that lowers the amount he receives to $p - t$. In the initial situation, his total profits are given by the area OBC.[10] Now, his profits are reduced to OGE. The change in his profits is the area $EGBC$. But of this change, part accrues to the government as tax revenue; the rectangle $EGHC$. The tax on producers has resulted in producers' profits being reduced by more than government revenue has increased. The difference between the two is the deadweight loss associated with the tax. It is simply the shaded area BGH. To put it another way, the

---

[9] This is not, of course, the only deadweight loss arising from the input tax. Since it increases the marginal cost of production, it will result in an increase in the price consumers pay, and there will be a deadweight loss.

[10] More accurately, the shaded area measures the difference between revenues and total variable costs. To calculate profits, we need to subtract fixed costs.

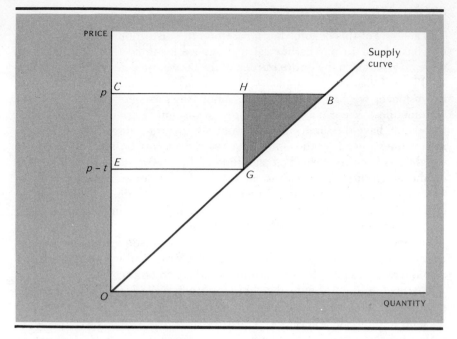

18.11 THE DEADWEIGHT LOSS OF A TAX ON PRODUCTION *BGH* measures the deadweight loss of a tax on production.

government could have imposed a lump sum tax on the firm, which left price at p and which left the firm at the same level of profits as it had with a price of $p-t$. That lump sum tax would have generated higher revenues, by the amount BGH, than the tax on the output of the firm.

It is clear that the steeper—the more inelastic—the supply schedule, the smaller the deadweight loss. In particular, we can, as before, show that for small taxes the deadweight loss increases with the square of the tax rate and with the supply elasticity.

SUMMARY

1. The imposition of a tax that is not a lump sum tax introduces inefficiencies. The magnitude of the inefficiencies is measured by the deadweight loss, the difference in revenues that could be obtained from a lump sum tax, as compared to a distortionary tax, with the same effect on the level of welfare of consumers.

2. The effect of any tax can be decomposed into an income effect and a substitution effect.

3. There is an income effect associated with a lump sum tax but no substitution effect. Thus the magnitude of the distortion associated with any tax is related to the magnitude of the substitution effect. The greater the substitution effect, the greater the deadweight loss.

4. For an income tax, the income effect leads to an increase in the amount of labor; the substitution effect to a decrease: the net effect is ambiguous. However, even

if the income tax leaves the amount of labor supplied unchanged, there is a distortion associated with the income tax.

5. For a tax on a commodity, both the income effect and the substitution effect usually lead to a reduction in the level of consumption of that commodity.

6. For an interest income tax as viewed by a saver, the income effect typically leads to an increase in savings and the substitution effect leads to a decrease in savings: the effect is ambiguous. But even if the net effect is to leave savings unchanged, there is still a distortion associated with the interest income tax. For borrowers, the income effect and the substitution effect both lead to an increase in borrowing (assuming that interest payments are tax-deductible). Now the effect is unambiguous.

7. The deadweight loss may be measured by the area under the compensated demand schedules, as the change in the level of consumer surplus associated with the tax minus the tax revenue. One must, however, exercise caution in using this method for estimating the deadweight loss associated with a tax.

8. There is also a deadweight loss associated with the reduction in the price received by producers. The reduction in profits exceeds the revenues received by the government.

9. For small taxes, the magnitude of the deadweight loss is proportional to the square of the tax and increases with the (compensated) elasticity of demand and with the elasticity of supply.

KEY CONCEPTS

Income effects
Substitution effects
Deadweight loss
Excess burden

Compensated elasticity of labor supply
Compensated demand curve
Consumer surplus
Producer surplus

QUESTIONS AND PROBLEMS

1. If savings does not respond to changes in the interest rate, does it mean that there is no deadweight loss associated with the taxation of interest?

2. Under what circumstances will a government tax or subsidy have income and substitution effects that: a) strengthen each other? b) offset each other?

3. Instead of representing the individual's decisions as a choice between consumption and work, as in figures 18.1 and 18.2, they could have been represented in terms of a choice between consumption and leisure. Draw the indifference curves, and identify the income and substitution effects resulting from a change in the tax rate on labor.

4. Compare the effects of an income tax and a lump sum tax raising the same revenue. In particular, show that the individual's utility is higher with the lump sum tax than with the income tax.

5. Compare the effects of a proportional income tax and a progressive flat rate income tax (i.e., one in which there is a lump sum grant from the government of, say, $3,000, and then a constant marginal tax rate on all income). In particular, show that if the two taxes raise the same revenue, and all individuals have the same income, utility will be higher with the proportional tax.

19

Optimal Taxation

In the previous chapter we observed that there may be a significant welfare loss associated with the imposition of any tax other than a lump sum tax. Two questions immediately arise. Why, if this is the case, do we not just impose a lump sum tax? And if we are to impose distortionary taxes, is there some way that they can be imposed to minimize the deadweight loss? These questions have been at the center of much of the theoretical research in taxation during the past two decades. The research has produced some remarkably simple and insightful answers, answers that may help to design better tax systems in the future.

THE FALLACY OF COUNTING DISTORTIONS

Before turning to these questions, we need to dispose of an argument that has misled a number of distinguished economists. It makes no sense simply to count the number of distortions introduced by the tax system. For instance, some economists have argued that we should have a tax on labor income but on no other goods (say, on cigarettes, alcohol, or luxuries), because one distortion is better than several distortions. This conclusion would be correct if there were no distortions associated with the income tax. But we showed in the previous chapter that an income tax is usually distortionary, and it is not necessarily the case that one large distortion is better than several smaller distortions. Indeed, the analysis of the preceding chapter showed that the deadweight loss from a tax was proportional to the square of the tax rate. This *suggests* that it may be better to have a number of small taxes than a single large tax.

The same fallacy was held to by those who argued that it is better not to tax interest income but rather just to impose a tax on wage income, because

taxing interest income introduces an additional distortion into the economy.
Again, though the conclusion concerning the desirability of not taxing interest income may or may not be correct, the argument is fallacious. One cannot simply count the number of distortions to arrive at the desirable tax structure.

THE SECOND-BEST FALLACY

On the other hand, it is important to guard against an equally dangerous fallacy. The example we have just given, that two distortions may be better than one, illustrates a general proposition that, whenever there are inefficiencies (distortions) in several markets, removing one of them may not improve matters. In earlier chapters we characterized Pareto-efficient resource allocations. All of the required conditions are seldom satisfied. And it may be virtually impossible to remove all the distortions in all sectors. The theory of the second best is concerned with the design of government policy in situations where the economy is characterized by some important distortions that cannot be removed.[1] (This is in contrast to "first-best" economies, where all the conditions for Pareto efficiency can be satisfied.) Thus second-best considerations say that it may not be desirable to remove distortions in those sectors where they can be removed. The theory of the second best is often interpreted fallaciously as saying that as long as there are some distortions, economic theory has nothing to say. This is incorrect, as we shall shortly show. Economic theory can tell us under what circumstances two small distortions are preferable to one large one, when it is better to have inefficiencies in both consumption and production, and when it is better not to have inefficiencies in production. Second-best theory tells us that we cannot blindly apply the lessons of first-best economics; finding out what we should do in such circumstances is often a difficult—but not impossible—task.

OPTIMAL REDISTRIBUTIVE TAXATION

In Chapter 16 we discussed two fundamental principles of taxation, economic efficiency and equity. We are concerned in this chapter with *efficient* tax structures, those that raise a given revenue and obtain given distribution objectives, at least cost in loss in efficiency. As always in economics, there are trade-offs: if the government wishes to pursue policies providing more redistribution, it does so at a cost of greater economic inefficiency (greater deadweight loss). The **optimal tax** structure is the one that maximizes social welfare, in which the choice between equity and efficiency best reflects society's attitude toward these competing goals. In this section we describe why distortionary taxes are imposed, why there is a trade-off between redistribution and economic efficiency, and how we can analyze the choice among alternative tax structures.

---

[1] Early formulations of the theory of the second best include those of James Meade, *Trade and Welfare: Mathematical Supplement* (Oxford: Oxford University Press, 1955) and R. G. Lipsey and K. Lancaster, "The General Theory of Second Best," *Review of Economic Studies* 24 (1956–7): 11–32.

Why Impose Distortionary Taxes?

If the government had perfect information about the characteristics of each individual in our society, there is a strong argument that it would not impose distortionary taxes. Individuals who can more easily pay taxes should, it is widely believed, pay more in taxes than those who cannot easily pay. If the government could ascertain who had greater abilities, and who therefore was in a better position to pay taxes, it would simply impose higher lump sum taxes on those individuals.

But how can abilities be measured? Consider a family. Parents often believe that they have good information concerning the abilities of their children. A parent who has two children, one of whom has a great deal of ability but chooses to become a beachcomber, and the other of whom has limited ability that he uses to the fullest, is more likely to provide financial assistance to the latter than the former; the assistance is made not on the basis of income—the beachcomber may in fact have a lower income than a hard-working but low-ability brother.

The government, however, is not in the position of the parent who can observe the ability and drive of his children. The government can only base its tax on observable variables, such as income and expenditure (and even these, as we shall see, are not easily observable). The choice facing the government is either to have a uniform lump sum tax, one that individuals pay regardless of what they do or their abilities, or to have a tax that depends on easily measured variables, such as expenditures or wages, and such a tax is inevitably distortionary. An income tax does not always succeed in taxing those we might think ought to be taxed—it treats equally the individual who has low ability but works extremely hard and the individual who is of high ability, and takes it easy, provided the two have the same income. Still, most people believe that those who have a higher income ought to pay a higher tax because those with a higher income are, *on average*, more able or have had better than average luck.

The Trade-off between Inequality and Inefficiency

If everyone were identical, there would be no reason to impose distortionary taxes. It would be far simpler administratively and more efficient (in terms of minimizing deadweight loss) simply to impose a uniform lump sum tax. The use of distortionary taxes is an inevitable consequence of our desire to redistribute income, in a world in which the government can observe the characteristics of individuals only imperfectly.

There is thus a trade-off. We can impose a more progressive tax, one that redistributes more income or lays a larger fraction of the burden of taxation on the rich—but we do so at the expense of a loss in economic efficiency. The trade-off is depicted in Figure 19.1, with the magnitude of the deadweight losses from the tax on the vertical axis and some measure of the degree of inequality in income in the economy on the horizontal axis. The government can reduce the degree of inequality but only at the expense of larger increments in the deadweight loss.

It may be useful to think of society as choosing a point along this trade-off

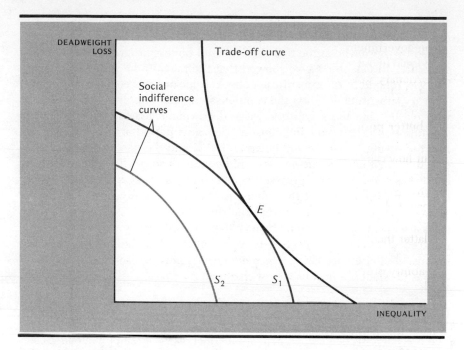

19.1 THE EQUITY-EFFICIENCY TRADE-OFF The indifference curve gives those combinations of deadweight losses and inequality among which society is indifferent. It is willing to accept some increase in inefficiency (in deadweight loss) for some reduction in inequality. The optimal tax structure maximizes society's welfare. It is represented by the point *E* on the trade-off curve where the indifference curve between deadweight loss and inequality is tangent to the trade-off curve

curve. Society also has indifference curves between inequality and deadweight loss, but unlike the usual indifference curves between two goods, this indifference curve is between two bads. Society is willing to accept a larger deadweight loss in return for some reduction in inequality. But as inequality becomes smaller, the amount of additional deadweight loss that it is willing to accept for any given reduction in inequality is reduced. Note that since both inequality and deadweight loss are bad, social welfare increases as we move down in the diagram. Social welfare is higher on the (social) indifference curve S_2 than on S_1.

The optimal tax structure is defined as that tax structure that maximizes society's welfare. It is represented by point *E* on the trade-off curve where the indifference curve of society between deadweight loss and inequality is tangent to the trade-off curve.

Different societies might choose different points on the trade-off curve if they had different attitudes toward inequality. Similarly, we can view much of the political debate concerning how progressive the tax structure should be—that is, how much more taxes high-income individuals should pay than low-income individuals—as one involving differences in values, in how much deadweight loss one is willing to accept for a given decrease in inequality.

There may be disagreements not only about values but also about the empirical question of what the trade-offs are. Those who advocate the desirability of more progressive taxes tend also to argue that the cost, in terms of the deadweight loss, of reducing inequality is smaller than the cost perceived by those who argue that there should be less progressivity to the tax structure. In Chapter 18 we showed that the magnitude of the deadweight loss was related to the substitution effect. If leisure and consumption goods are very substitutable, then the compensated labor supply schedule will be very elastic, and there will be a large deadweight loss from a wage tax. If consumption this period and consumption next period are very substitutable, the savings schedule will be very elastic, and the deadweight loss associated with an interest income tax will be large. Those who believe that the deadweight losses are small are often referred to as *elasticity optimists;* they believe, for instance, that the (compensated) labor supply elasticity and the savings elasticity are low, so that the distortions associated with high tax rates are low; while those who believe that the distortions are large are often referred to as *elasticity pessimists;* they believe that the labor supply and savings elasticities are large. The evidence supporting each view is ambiguous, as we shall see in subsequent chapters.

Why Does More Progressivity Imply More Deadweight Loss?

The preceding section argued heuristically that, as we attempt to attain greater equality with our tax system, the deadweight loss increases. Panels A and B of Figure 19.2 illustrate this general proposition by contrasting two tax schedules. The first is a proportional income tax, in which the tax liability increases simply in proportion to income (this is also called a flat-rate income tax, because tax liability is the same percentage of income for all individuals, no matter how large or small their income). The second is a progressive **flat rate income tax,** which imposes a tax at a flat rate on the difference between the individual's income and some critical level of income, $\hat{Y}$. Individuals whose income falls below the critical income receive a grant from the government equal to the tax rate times the shortfall between their income and the critical level. Notice from Panel A of Figure 19.2 that the marginal tax rate for the progressive flat tax, the extra tax an individual pays or receives on an extra dollar of income, is constant. The *average* tax rate, the ratio of the total tax payments to the individual's income, however, increases with income. This is why we call the tax progressive.[2]

Because, as we have depicted it, the progressive flat tax provides for a payment to individuals whose income falls short of the critical level, we sometimes refer to that portion of the tax schedule below $\hat{Y}$ as a *negative income tax.*[3]

The progressive flat tax can be thought of as a combination of a uniform lump sum grant to all individuals and a proportional income tax. If the gov-

[2]Usage is not standardized. Some prefer to reserve the term *progressive* for tax structures where the *marginal* tax rate increases. Nothing important hinges on these semantic points. Notice that a flat-rate tax combined with a lump sum tax is regressive, in the sense that the average tax rate decreases with income. For a more general discussion of the definition of progressive and regressive tax structures, see A. B. Atkinson and J. E. Stiglitz, *Lectures on Public Economics* (New York: McGraw-Hill, 1980), Chapter 2.

[3]In some proposals, those with income above $\hat{Y}$ are taxed on the difference between their income and this critical level, but those below the critical level neither pay taxes nor receive a rebate.

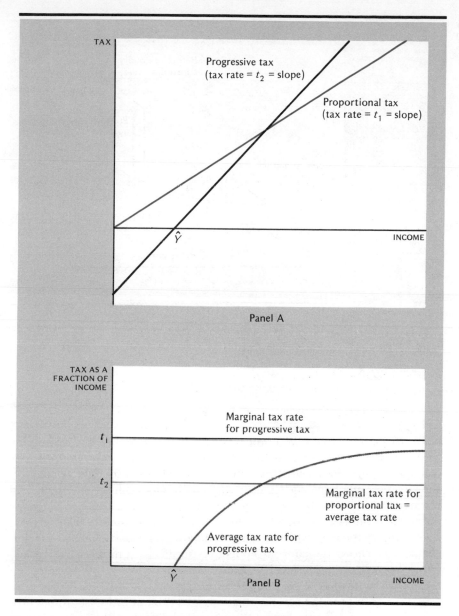

19.2 FLAT-RATE INCOME TAX SCHEDULES Panel A compares the tax schedule of a proportional flat-rate income-tax with that of a progressive flat-rate income tax. Panel B compares average and marginal tax rates for these two taxes.

ernment is both to finance its public goods and other public expenditures *and* pay everyone a uniform lump sum grant, the revenue raised must be higher, so the marginal tax rate must be higher than with just a proportional tax. But the deadweight loss is simply associated with the magnitude of the marginal tax rate. Hence the greater the lump sum grant, the more progressive the tax structure, and the greater the deadweight loss.

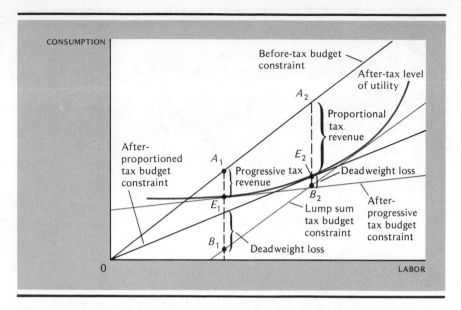

19.3 DEADWEIGHT LOSS FROM PROGRESSIVE FLAT-RATE TAX The revenue raised by a proportional tax (A_2E_2) is much greater than the revenue raised by a progressive tax (A_1E_1), with an equal effect on the individual's utility.

To compare the effects of a proportional and a progressive tax, we employ the same kinds of diagrammatic techniques we employed in the previous chapter. Figure 19.3 shows an individual's before-tax budget constraint, showing how much income (consumption) he has for each level of work, and his indifference curve between consumption goods and work. It also depicts his after-tax budget constraint, assuming that the government takes a given fraction of his income, which is to say it imposes a proportional tax. Finally, Figure 19.3 shows the after-tax budget constraint for a progressive flat tax, which has an exemption level $\hat{Y}$. Those with an income above $\hat{Y}$ are taxed; those with an income below $\hat{Y}$ are subsidized.

We now compare the revenue that the government can raise from a progressive income tax that leaves the given individual at the same level of utility with the revenue that can be raised with a proportional income tax. The revenue raised by the tax is the vertical distance between the before-tax budget constraint and the after-tax budget constraint at the level of work that the individual chooses to put forth. Thus, in Figure 19.3, the tax revenue from the proportional income tax is A_2E_2, while the tax revenue from the progressive tax is A_1E_1, much less. There is an additional deadweight loss resulting from the progressivity; B_1E_1 is much greater than B_2E_2. This is not surprising. We argued before that the deadweight loss is associated with the substitution effect, the change in the hours worked (or, for other taxes, the pattern of consumption) resulting from the lowering of the after-tax wage below the true productivity of labor. Because the marginal tax rate is higher, the substitution effect is larger with a progressive income tax than it is with a proportional income tax, and thus the deadweight loss is larger.[4]

Relationship between Deadweight Loss and Redistribution

We now turn to see how, as we attempt to redistribute income further, we increase the deadweight loss. As we argued before, a progressive flat rate tax can be viewed as a combination of a proportional tax and a lump sum grant. As we increase the lump sum grant, we must raise the tax rate.

Assume we have two groups in the population, one below the exemption level and one above. As we increase the lump sum grant, the group below the exemption level is better off, the group above the exemption level is worse off: inequality has been reduced. But both groups face higher marginal tax rates, and hence the deadweight loss associated with both groups has increased.

There may be a maximum of redistribution that is feasible. As we increase the marginal tax rate, the upper-income individuals eventually may start to reduce the labor supply; they may reduce it enough that the revenue raised by the tax on them is reduced. In that case, the lump sum grant would have to be reduced.

The Utility Possibilities Curve and Distortionary Taxation

We can depict the choices facing society in a slightly different way. In Chapter 3 we derived the utility possibilities frontier for the economy, showing the maximum level of utility for Group 1 that can be obtained for each level of utility of Group 2. We did that under the assumption that we can impose different lump sum taxes on different individuals. Now we recognize that this is not possible. We have to derive a new utility possibilities schedule taking into account the distortions that arise out of our attempt to redistribute income. Two utility possibilities schedules are shown in Figure 19.4. The gray one assumes the lump sum tax option and the black one makes the more realistic assumption of distortionary taxation. The two curves coincide at the point along the original utility possibilities schedule that would emerge as Pareto optimal in competitive equilibrium, with no redistributive taxes— point C. (If there are public goods to be financed by the taxation, then the two curves coincide at the competitive equilibrium corresponding to a *uniform* lump sum tax on the two groups of individuals.) Everywhere else, however, the distortionary tax utility possibilities schedule lies inside the lump sum tax utility possibilities schedule. If the method of redistributing income that we have available is a progressive flat-rate income tax, we can easily derive the utility possibilities schedule. For each level of exemption, we find the level of tax rate that raises the required revenue. We then plot the levels of utility that the two groups attain. As we increase the level of exemption,

---

[4] In Figure 19.3 it is clear that the marginal tax rate is higher (the slope of the budget constraint is smaller) for the progressive tax than for the proportional tax. This is always the case: if the tax rate were the same or lower, clearly the individual would be better off with the tax system with a lump sum grant than with one without it. He could not be on the same indifference curve.

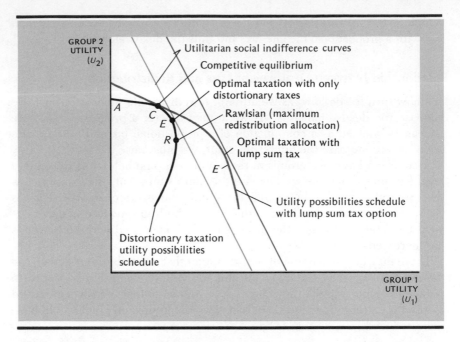

19.4 UTILITY POSSIBILITIES SCHEDULES WITH LUMP SUM AND DISTORTIONARY TAXES Optimal tax corresponds to the point E: society finds that point on the utility possibilities schedule that maximizes social welfare. This is the tangency between the social indifference curves (which with utilitarianism are linear) and the utility possibilities schedule.

the utility of the lower-income group increases and that of the higher-income group decreases.

It is clear that the utility possibilities curve is affected by what information is available and by the methods available for the redistribution of income.

Any tax structure that (given the available information and tax instruments) gets the economy to a point on the utility possibilities schedule is a Pareto-efficient tax structure.[5] Under certain circumstances, for instance, it can be shown that if the government can impose taxes on wages and on the consumption of different commodities, it should in fact impose taxes only on wage income. This is true regardless of one's attitudes toward inequality; that is, a system that imposes taxes on different commodities at different rates is Pareto inefficient.[6]

Society's first problem (after determining the possible set of taxes) is thus to determine what are the Pareto-efficient tax structures. Having done this, the second problem is choosing among alternative Pareto-efficient tax struc-

---

[5] The term *constrained Pareto-efficient* is sometimes used to describe such tax structures to remind us of the limitations imposed by information imperfections. For a more detailed description of Pareto-efficient tax structures see J. E. Stiglitz, "Self-Selection and Pareto-Efficient Taxation," *Journal of Public Economics* 17 (1982): 213–40.

[6] What is required is that the sole source of differences among individuals is their differences in productivity and that their marginal rate of substitution between two different commodities does not depend on the amount of leisure they enjoy. See A. B. Atkinson and J. E. Stiglitz, "The Design of Tax Structures," *Journal of Public Eonomics* 6 (1976): 55–75.

tures. This is equivalent to deciding on a point along the utility possibilities schedule.

Earlier, we called the tax structure that maximizes society's social welfare the optimal tax structure. The optimal tax structure thus will depend on: a) society's social welfare function and b) the information available to the government and, correspondingly, the kinds of taxes that can be imposed. If the government could identify the abilities of each individual and could levy lump sum taxes on each according to his ability, the income tax would not be part of a Pareto-efficient tax structure (and it would not be part of an optimal tax structure).

The relationship between the optimal tax structure and the social welfare function is easy to see in Figure 19.4. A utilitarian would maximize the sum of the utilities of the two groups; that is, the social indifference curves, giving those combinations of U_1 and U_2 among which society is indifferent, are linear. Society is willing to give up some welfare of Group 1 for an equal increase in the welfare of Group 2. The utilitarian optimal tax structure, given that the government can only infer the differences in ability from observations of income, is depicted as point E. (If government could distinguish between people of different ability, so that it could impose differential lump sum taxes, then E' corresponds to the optimal tax structure.)

Rawlsian Taxation

Notice in Figure 19.4 that we have drawn the utility possibilities schedule with distortionary taxation as backward-bending.[7] There is a maximum amount of revenue that we can extract from the higher-income individuals (without direct compulsion). Assume, for instance, that we imposed simply a proportional tax on those with high incomes. Although we observed earlier that the effect of increasing the tax (lowering the wage) was in general ambiguous, beyond some point the tax will lead the individual to work less. (More accurately, the individual will engage in fewer transactions through the market: he may be working just as hard, but not for cash. He will be induced to bake his own bread, paint his own house, etc.) There is thus a maximum revenue that can be raised. (If the government attempts to raise this revenue through a progressive flat-rate tax, the maximum that the government can raise from the rich is even lower.) This means that there is a maximum amount that the government can redistribute to the poor. This is the point at which the utility possibilities schedule turns back. Further increases in the tax rate mean that to finance the given level of public goods the exemption level must be decreased. We have marked this point on Figure 19.4 with R, after John Rawls,[8] who argued that society should choose the tax rate that maximizes the welfare of the worst-off individual.

Notice that there is a maximum tax rate consistent with the Rawlsian position. Society can have too high a tax rate. Such tax rates are Pareto inferior—

---

[7] Since the definition of the utility possibilities schedule is the maximum level of utility that Individual 1 can obtain given the level of utility obtained by Individual 2, formally the utility possibilities schedule is only the portion AR of the black curve depicted in Figure 19.4.

[8] John Rawls, *A Theory of Justice* (New York: Oxford University Press, 1973).

i.e., by lowering the tax rate, everyone could be made better off. There are those who believe that many Western European countries have reached tax rates that, if not exceeding this point, are close to it. In the United States, this view was popularized through what has come to be called the **Laffer curve,** which, as we described in Chapter 5, is simply the curve relating revenues to the tax rates, showing that beyond some point further increases in the tax rate actually lead to a lowering of tax revenues. As part of President Reagan's economic program, it was argued that a lowering of the tax rate would lead to such a large increase in national output that tax revenues would actually increase. The administration's belief, in other words, was that we were beyond the point at which the maximum tax revenue was raised. There was scanty empirical evidence in support of this view, and considerable evidence against it.[9] As it turned out, the short-run supply responses were far less than the advocates of the tax cut had predicted; but these short-run responses may have been dominated by other factors, such as the high rates of interest, which occurred simultaneously. And the long-run responses may be much greater. Still, the consensus among most economists is that we are not near the point of maximum government revenue. It still may be the case that at current tax rates, the decrease in inequality may be small relative to the deadweight loss imposed by the tax structure; that is, we may be sufficiently close to the point R that to increase the welfare of those with lower incomes requires an inordinate sacrifice in the welfare of those with higher incomes. On this question there is no consensus among economists.

Relationship between Progressivity and Government Expenditures

Several points are, however, clear. First, if governments did not have to raise revenue at all to finance public expenditures, it would with a utilitarian social welfare function (or any social welfare function that values equality) still be desirable to redistribute income through a progressive tax structure. There is a negligible deadweight loss from a small tax, but a finite gain in redistribution. Those whose income fell below some critical level would receive some income from the government.

Second, if the government wishes to raise a great deal of revenue for public expenditures, more than the maximum amount that can be attained through a proportional income tax, it may need to impose a lump sum tax on all individuals *plus* a proportional rate on all income. More generally, the greater the government's expenditure on pure public goods (e.g., military expenditures), the lower, in general, will be the funds that are available for redistribution, and the less progressive will be the optimal tax structure.

A numerical calculation of the optimal flat-tax rate. Nick Stern, of Warwick University, calculated the optimal linear flat-rate tax using what he thought were reseasonable estimates of the labor supply elasticity and the distribution of individuals' productivity in the economy.[10] He found, assum-

---

[9] See, for instance, Don Fullerton, "On the Possibility of An Inverse Relationship between Tax Rates and Government Revenues," *Journal of Public Economics* 19 (1982): 3–23.

[10] Nicholas H. Stern, "On the Specification of Models of Optimum Income Taxation," *Journal of Public Economics* 6 (1976): 123–62. The results of the calculations are very sensitive to all the assumptions made

ing that government expenditures on public goods amounted to 20 percent of national income, that while with a utilitarian social welfare function the optimal flat rate tax was 19 percent, with a Rawlsian social welfare function—where its only concern was with the poorest individual—it was around 80 percent.

THE OPTIMAL STRUCTURE OF INCOME TAXES

The United States—and most other Western countries—does not employ a progressive flat-rate tax. Rather, marginal tax rates increase with income. The issue of whether this is desirable has recently been the subject of considerable debate in the United States. The Reagan tax reform proposals were based on the premise that marginal tax rates for the rich were too high; while the maximum marginal tax rate was lowered from 70 to 50 percent in 1981, Reagan proposed to lower it further to 35 percent. Here, we attempt to identify the trade-offs between deadweight loss and redistribution that result from having a tax structure with varying marginal tax rates.

The distortion (the deadweight loss) associated with a tax system is related to the magnitude of the marginal tax rate. By raising the marginal tax rate at one income level—say, between $15,000 and $20,000—the government can raise the *average* tax rate at higher income levels without altering the marginal tax rate at these higher income levels. Consider what happens to an individual making $25,000. His average tax has gone up, because he has to pay more on his income between $15,000 and $20,000. But his marginal rate—the tax on the 25,000th dollar—remains the same. The extra distortion introduced by the higher taxes is measured only through its effect on individuals making $15,000 to $20,000, those whose marginal rate has increased. There is a trade-off between a greater deadweight loss at the lower-income level and greater revenue for the same deadweight loss at upper-income levels.

Some elementary considerations determine whether increasing the rate on one income bracket is likely to be welfare-enhancing. If for instance there are relatively few individuals in the group whose marginal tax rate has been increased, the welfare loss (from the deadweight loss) will be small.

The fact that by raising marginal tax rates on middle-income individuals one can obtain greater revenue from the rich, with the same deadweight loss, suggests that it may be desirable for middle-income individuals to have higher marginal tax rates than upper-income individuals. However, the fact that there are many middle-income individuals, so that the deadweight loss from increasing marginal tax rates on middle-income individuals is very large, suggests that they should face lower marginal tax rates. In the examples investigated in detail by James Mirrlees, of Oxford University, these two effects offset each other, and the optimal tax schedule was close to the progressive flat tax.[11]

---

and therefore need to be considered with a great deal of caution. The numbers presented here reflect an assumed elasticity of substitution between leisure and consumption of 0.6. As we noted in Chapter 18, there is considerable controversy concerning the magnitude of this elasticity.

[11] J. Mirrlees, "An Exploration in the Theory of Optimum Income Taxation," *Review of Economic Studies* 38 (1971): 175–208.

Labor Supply Elasticities and Tax Rates

If the labor supply response of different groups (individuals with different incomes) differs systematically, the tax rates they should face should differ.

Assume that the government could impose, for instance, one tax rate on unskilled workers and another on skilled workers. It wishes to do so to maximize the sum of utilities (a utilitarian social welfare function). Assume it has to raise a fixed amount of revenue between two groups. Clearly, it will set the tax rates so that the loss in utility from an increase in revenues by a dollar (resulting from an increase in tax rates) on one group is exactly equal to the loss in utility from an increase in revenues by a dollar on the other group.

Increasing the tax rate on some group is equivalent to reducing the wage paid that group. We plot utility as a function of tax rate in Panel A of Figure 19.5. The loss in utility from an increase in the tax rate is proportional to the labor supply of the group (the larger the labor supply, the greater the reduction in income) and its marginal utility of income.[12]

The increase in tax revenue from an increase in the tax rate increases with the amount of labor supplied. But there is an indirect effect: the higher tax rate may reduce (or increase) the labor supplied. The tax revenue from tax rate t is twL, where w is the wage rate and L is the labor supplied. As t increases, tax revenue will not increase as much if L decreases as it would if L remained unchanged. In fact, if L decreases enough, total tax revenue could actually decline as t increases, as depicted in Panel B of Figure 19.5. The magnitude of the decrease in the labor supply is measured by the elasticity of labor supply. The greater the elasticity of labor supply, the smaller the increase in government revenue from an increase in the tax rate.[13]

The optimal tax rates must be such that loss in utility from increasing the revenue raised by a dollar from each group is the same. The change in utility per unit change in revenue for two different groups is plotted in Panel C of the figure.

Thus a group with a lower income is likely to have a higher marginal utility of income, and this effect in itself suggests that it should have a lower tax rate. But if it reduces its labor supply less than some other group (other things being equal), its tax rate should be higher.

If the elasticity of labor supply among those in managerial, executive, and professional positions is lower than the labor supply elasticity of other workers, this effect (by itself) suggests that the former group should be taxed more heavily than the latter one.

In Chapter 16 we showed how a utilitarian would impose much higher tax rates on high-income individuals than on low-income individuals; the taxes would be set so that the marginal utility of income would be equated. But

---

[12] For those familiar with calculus, this result can be shown simply by using the indirect utility function V (w,p,I), which gives the level of utility as a function of wages, prices, and other sources of income. It is possible to show that

$$\frac{dV}{dw} = L\frac{dV}{dI}.$$

dV / dI is just the marginal utility of income.

[13]

$$\frac{dR}{dt} = wL + wt\frac{dL}{dt} = wL\left(1 - t\frac{w}{L}\frac{\partial L}{\partial w}\right), \quad \text{where} \quad \frac{w}{L}\frac{\partial L}{\partial w} = \text{elasticity of labor supply.}$$

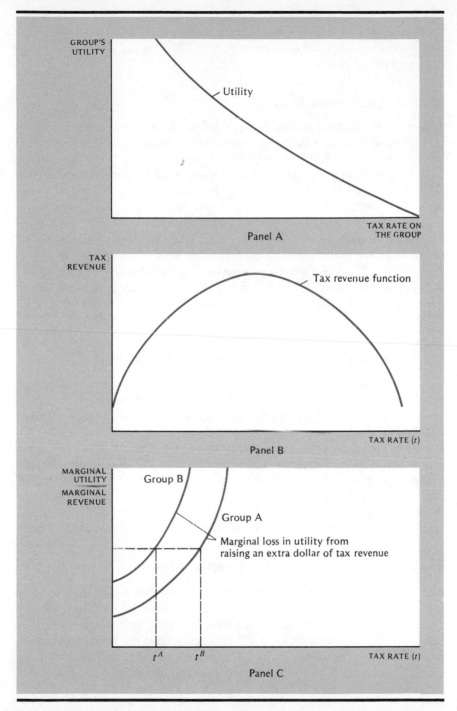

19.5   OPTIMAL TAXATION WITH DIFFERENT GROUPS If different tax rates can be imposed on different groups, maximizing the sum of utilities implies that the loss in utility per extra dollar raised is the same for all groups. This can be constructed as follows: in Panel A we plot the utility level as a function of the tax rate. In Panel B we plot the revenue raised as a function of the tax rate. At each level of t, we calculate the loss in utility from a further increment in the tax rate and the increase in revenue; dividing one by the other, we obtain Panel C.

that analysis assumed that labor supply was inelastic—the individual's before-tax income was not affected by the taxes imposed. The fact that individuals will respond to high tax rates by reducing labor supply limits the optimal degree of progressivity.

General Equilibrium Effects

So far we have assumed that the income tax has no effect on before-tax incomes, that there is, in other words, no *shifting* of the income tax. There are some economists, however, who believe that there may be considerable shifting.

There are several arguments that suggest, in particular, that the income tax system has increased the degree of before-tax inequality. First, there are some who believe that the wages and fees of managers and professionals adjust to the taxes, leaving their after-tax income relatively unchanged. Moreover, if as a result of the income tax, skilled workers supply less labor, and investment is discouraged, unskilled laborers' productivity, and hence their wage, will decline. At the present time, unfortunately, we do not know the quantitative significance of these effects. If they are important, it suggests that the benefits of progressivity are less than they seem when these effects are ignored.[14]

REDISTRIBUTION THROUGH COMMODITY TAXES

In the previous section we argued that the primary reason for resorting to distortionary taxation was to enable the government to redistribute income more effectively, to achieve a more egalitarian society than could be obtained with *uniform* lump sum taxes.

Should government use commodity taxes in addition to income taxes to raise revenue and redistribute income? That is, if we supplement well-designed income tax (as described in the previous paragraphs) with taxes on, say, perfume and luxury cars, can we raise the same revenue, achieve the same distribution goals, at less loss in efficiency? Is a tax system that uses both commodity taxes and income taxes more efficient than just an income tax?

The Inefficiency of Commodity Taxation

The question has been one of continuing debate among economists. In Chapter 17 we noted that taxing commodities at the same rate was equivalent to an income tax; hence we are concerned here only with the imposition of taxes on different commodities at different rates, what are sometimes referred to as *differential commodity taxes*. One often-quoted argument, that taxing commodities at different rates introduces additional distortions, has already been shown to be fallacious: one simply cannot count the number of distortions.

---

[14]The importance of these general equilibrium effects in the design of optimal taxes was noted by Martin Feldstein, "On the Optimal Progressivity of the Income Tax," *Journal of Public Economics* 2 (1973): 357–76, using a simulation model. His results were corroborated and extended in subsequent theoretical work by N. Stern, "Optimum Taxation with Errors in Administration," *Journal of Public Economics* 17 (1982): 181–211; F. Allen, "Optimal Linear Income Taxation with General Equilibrium Effects on Wages," *Journal of Public Economics* 17 (1982): 135–43; J. E. Stiglitz, "Self-Selection and Pareto-Efficient Taxation."

It has been shown that if one has a well-designed income tax, adding differential commodity taxation is likely to add little, if anything, to the ability to redistribute income.[15] The caveat that there be a well-designed income tax is important: in many countries income tax evasion is sufficiently prevalent that virtually the only way effective redistribution may occur is through the taxation of commodities consumed by the rich.

Further Arguments against Differential Commodity Taxation

There are two further arguments against taxing different commodities at different rates. The first is that such differential taxation is administratively complex; there are always some commodities that might fall into either the high-tax or low-tax categories, and there are thus administrative problems (and inequities) associated with drawing these distinctions.

Second, differential taxation might well be used to serve other purposes; it opens up the possibility of some groups using the tax system to discriminate against others. For instance, in the United Kingdom, scotch is the prevalent drink in Scotland, while beer is more popular in England. It would not, of course, be acceptable to impose a tax on those citizens of the United Kingdom who happened to live in Scotland that would be different from that imposed on those who live in England. But much the same affect could be obtained by taxing beer and Scotch at different rates.

In the United States prior to the passage of the Sixteenth Amendment, which made income taxes legal, the federal government had to rely on commodity taxes. Different patterns of taxation had important differential effects on different regions. A tariff on industrial products benefited the Northeast at the expense of the South. In many countries today, the crops grown and the products produced and consumed in different areas may differ markedly. Differential taxation opens up the way for those in one region to use the tax structure to exploit those in another.

Ramsey Taxes

More than fifty years ago the great Cambridge economist Frank Ramsey asked: What taxes should be imposed on different commodities, assuming the government could not impose lump sum taxes?[16] He was not concerned with redistribution but simply with identifying what we today would call the Pareto-efficient set of taxes under the assumption that lump sum taxes are infeasible. In other words, he asked what tax structure would minimize the deadweight loss associated with raising a given amount of government revenue. Thus, in his analysis, Ramsey assumed all individuals were identical.

---

[15] A. B. Atkinson and J. E. Stiglitz, *Lectures on Public Economics*. One intuitive way of seeing their result is to observe that, to increase society's ability to redistribute, one must tax commodities that are income-elastic more heavily than those that are income-inelastic—e.g., perfume should be taxed more heavily than bread. But many of the income-elastic commodities are also price-elastic, and hence the distortions associated with taxing them are greater. The optimal tax balances off the two effects; and in the balance, there is little gain from taxing different commodities at different rates. See footnote 6 for a discussion of the conditions under which no commodity taxation is desirable.

[16] F. Ramsey, "A Contribution to the Theory of Taxation," *Economic Journal* 37 (1927): 47–61. The question had been posed to him by his teacher, A. C. Pigou. See A. C. Pigou, *A Study in Public Finance* (London: Macmillan, 3rd ed., 1947).

The set of commodity taxes that minimize the deadweight loss are called **Ramsey taxes** and have a remarkably simple form. Under certain simplifying conditions, Ramsey taxes are proportional to the sum of the reciprocal of the elasticity of demand and supply:

$$\frac{t}{p} = k(^1/\eta_u^d + ^1/\eta^s),$$

where k is a proportionality factor that depends on the total amount of revenue the government is attempting to raise, t is the tax rate, p is the (after-tax) price, η_u^d is the (compensated) elasticity of demand, and η^s is the elasticity of supply. If the elasticity of supply is infinite (a horizontal supply schedule), the tax should be simply inversely proportional to the (compensated) elasticity of demand. Ramsey's result should not come as a surprise. In Chapter 18 we showed that the deadweight loss from a tax increased with the elasticity of demand and the elasticity of supply.

Figure 19.6 shows the solution to the optimal commodity tax problem. Panel A depicts the deadweight loss as a function of the tax rate imposed on commodity i. Panel B shows the revenue raised as a function of the tax rate imposed on commodity i. From these two diagrams we can calculate, at each tax rate, the ratio of the increase in deadweight loss to the ratio of the increase in tax revenues from increasing the tax a little bit. A similar curve can be derived for commodity j, as shown in Panel C. The tax rates should be set so that the increase in deadweight loss per extra dollar raised is the same for each commodity. If the increase in excess burden per extra dollar raised were greater for one commodity than for another, by adjusting tax rates so that one less dollar was raised on the first commodity and one more dollar was raised on the second commodity, total excess burden would be reduced. Notice that we have drawn the curves not only so that excess burden increases as the revenue raised increases, but also so that each increment in revenue increases the excess burden more. This follows from the fact that the deadweight loss increases with the square of the tax rate.

Optimal Commodity Taxation with Interdependent Demands

The result we have just given requires that the compensated demand curves of each commodity are independent; that is, the demand for one commodity does not depend on the price of another. Another interpretation of Ramsey's result holds when supply curves are infinitely elastic, whether or not demand curves are interdependent: *the optimal tax structure is such that the percentage reduction in the demand for each commodity is the same.*[17]

Alternative Interpretation: Optimal Commodity Tax Structure with Interdependent Demands

We showed in Chapter 17 that a uniform tax on commodities is equivalent to a tax on labor (income). An income tax is distortionary because it induces

---

[17] Note that if $\eta^s = \infty$, $t/p = k/\eta^d$: the percentage tax is inversely proportional to the demand elasticity. The percentage change in output is equal to the percentage increase in price $\times$ percent of change in demand from a percent of change in price $= k/\eta^d \times \eta^d = k$—i.e., it is the same for all commodities. (These results are approximate; the exact characterization requires the use of compensated demand curves.)

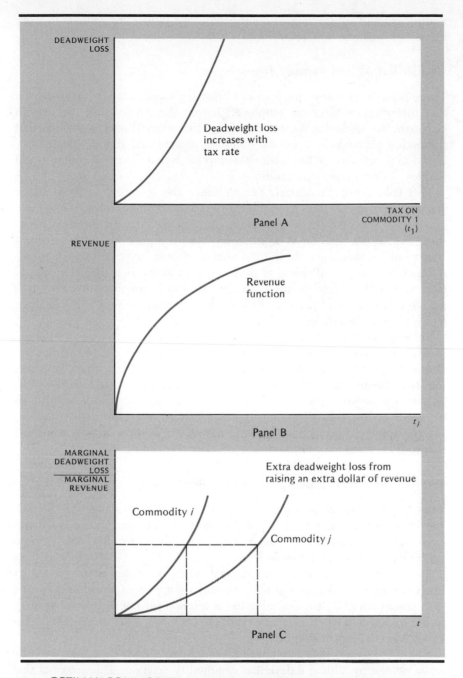

19.6 OPTIMAL COMMODITY TAXATION Optimal commodity taxes entail that marginal excess burden per marginal dollar raised be the same for all commodities.

individuals to make incorrect decisions concerning the amount of labor they wish to supply. Commodity taxation may help correct that distortion. If we tax commodities that are complements for leisure and subsidize commodities that are complements for work, we encourage individuals to work, and thus reduce the distortion caused by a uniform tax. For instance, by taxing ski equipment and subsidizing commuter costs we induce individuals to work more and consume less leisure.[18]

Redistribution and Ramsey Taxes

There is one very disturbing feature of Ramsey's analysis. The major reason that distortionary taxes are employed is that the government has certain redistributive goals that it cannot achieve otherwise. Thus it is peculiar that the earlier discussions of optimal taxation assumed that all individuals were identical (in which case the natural assumption is that the government would employ uniform lump sum taxation).

This failure was particularly vexing, since the results described earlier suggest that high tax rates should be imposed on commodities with low price elasticities, such as food. These commodities often have low income elasticities, so that if a high tax is imposed on them the poor will have to bear a larger burden than the rich. But the original reason for employing commodity taxation was to shift more of the burden onto the rich than they would face, say, with a uniform lump sum or uniform commodity tax. Ramsey's analysis thus seemed to provide little guidance for any serious policy analysis and was, accordingly, largely dismissed.

Subsequent research has extended Ramsey's original analysis to include redistributive goals.[19] Not surprisingly, whether one wishes to tax income-elastic and price-elastic commodities, such as perfume, at a higher or lower rate than income-inelastic and price-inelastic commodities like food depends, in part, on the strength of one's concern for income redistribution. But, as we noted earlier, regardless of one's attitudes toward income redistribution, with a well-designed income tax there appears little to be gained by adding differential commodity taxation.

Interest Income Taxation and Commodity Taxation

In our earlier discussion we showed how a tax on interest income changed the slope of the budget constraint (between current and future consumption). It discourages future consumption. It has the same effect that a tax on future consumption only would have.

Thus an income tax that taxes interest, such as a differential commodity tax, taxes future consumption more heavily than current consumption. The question of whether it is desirable to tax interest income is then equivalent to the question of whether it is desirable to tax future consumption at higher rates than current consumption.

We noted earlier that with a well-designed income tax there may be little to be gained by adding differential commodity taxation. This suggests that in designing the income tax, interest income should be exempt from taxation. An income tax that exempts interest income is, of course, equivalent

---

[18] This interpretation was noted in W. J. Corlett and D. C. Hague, "Complementarity and the Excess Burden of Taxation," *Review of Economic Studies* 21 (1953): 21–30.

[19] See, in particular, P. Diamond and J. Mirrlees, "Optimal Taxation and Public Production, I: Production Efficiency and II: Tax Rules," *American Economic Review* 61 (1971): 8–27 and 261–78; P. Diamond, "A Many-Person Ramsay Tax Rule," *Journal of Public Economics* 4 (1975): 335–42; A. B. Atkinson and J. E. Stiglitz, "The Structure of Indirect Taxation and Economic Efficiency," *Journal of Public Economics* 1 (1972): 97–119; A. B. Atkinson and J. E. Stiglitz, "The Design of Tax Structure: Direct versus Indirect Taxation," *Journal of Public Economics* 6 (1976): 55–75.

to a wage tax, and we showed in Chapter 17 that a wage tax was equivalent to a consumption tax. This suggests that it may be optimal to have a consumption tax. We discuss this further in Chapter 25.

OPTIMAL TAXATION AND PRODUCTION EFFICIENCY

Consumption taxes have the effect of putting a wedge between the individual's marginal rate of substitution and the marginal rate of transformation. Figure 19.7 depicts the loss in welfare from distortionary taxation. The economy is still on its production possibilities schedule, but the representative individual's indifference curve is no longer tangent to the production possibilities schedule. As a result, the individual is worse off. (E_1 is on a lower indifference curve than E_2.) This is the cost associated with the distortion.

Many of our taxes also affect the production efficiency of the economy, which is to say that they result in the economy not being on its production possibilities schedule. Production efficiency requires that the marginal rate of substitution between any two inputs be the same in all firms, and the marginal rate of transformation between any two outputs (or between an input and an output) be the same in all firms. Thus, any tax on an input that is not uniform across all firms, or any tax on an output that is not uniform across all firms, results in the economy not being productively efficient. For instance, the corporation profits tax is widely viewed to tax the input of capital on incorporated firms and to result in the after-tax cost of capital that

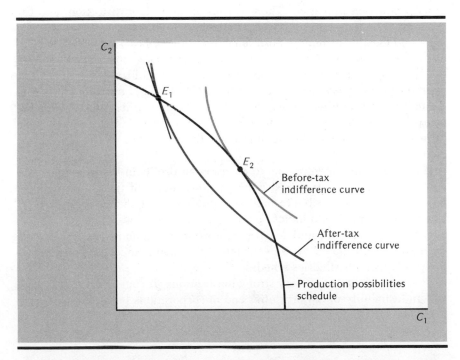

19.7 GENERAL EQUILIBRIUM EFFECTS OF COMMODITY TAXATION With differential commodity taxes, the economy is still producing along its production possibilities schedule, but the marginal rate of substitution (the slope of the indifference curve) is not equal to the marginal rate of transformation (the slope of the production possibilities schedule).

such firms face differing from that in unincorporated industries. Also, while gasoline that is used for most business purposes is taxed, gasoline used for farming is not. But these are only the most obvious examples.

Many production activities are performed both in the market and non-market sectors. Only those performed in the market sector are taxed. Thus an individual driving himself to work is performing the same service that a taxi cab driver who drives the individual to work performs. Yet, there is a tax on the latter and not on the former. A person who bakes a loaf of bread at home is performing a service similar to that of a baker but is not taxed in the same way that the baker is taxed. There is thus a distortion between the marketed and nonmarketed sectors, and the economy is not productively efficient.

Whenever a commodity is used both by businesses and consumers and the tax is imposed on both (businesses are not exempted), there is a loss in productive efficiency. Thus import duties and sales taxes create a production distortion.

To see this most clearly, consider a firm that produces and uses computers in its own production plants; the cost of the computer is simply the cost of the factors of production (including the return to capital employed in the production). In a competitive economy this firm would be forced to sell the computers at its costs of production, so that the cost of any other firm using a computer would be the same as the cost of the manufacturing firm in using it. But now, when a sales tax is imposed, the cost to the firm manufacturing the computer using it is less than the cost of another firm using the computer in its production processes. There is thus an important distortion, and the economy is no longer productively efficient.

Should the government impose such distortionary taxes if it wishes to minimize the deadweight loss of the tax system? One naïve answer to this question is to say, of course not. The government should not introduce any additional distortions that it does not need to. This kind of argument is similar to the arguments we discussed earlier concerning differential commodity taxes. It makes no sense simply to count the number of distortions. Yet it turns out that under some circumstances, the conclusion of the naïve argument is correct.

If the government were able to tax away all profits in the private sector, and if there are no other restrictions in the ability of the government to impose taxes, it is possible to show that productive efficiency is desirable.[20] The government should impose no distortionary taxes on businesses. Whatever the government could do with a distortionary tax on producers, it could do better with a direct tax on consumers that maintained the economy on the production possibilities schedule.[21]

This analysis has some very strong implications. It suggests, in particular, the undesirability of import duties and of corporations being taxed at a different rate than unincorporated businesses.

---

[20] The sole restriction is that the government cannot impose lump sum taxes.

[21] This result was originally established in the important paper by Diamond and Mirrlees, "Optimal Taxation and Public Production, I: Production Efficiency," *American Economic Review* 61 (1971): 8–27.

There are many instances, however, when the government cannot make distinctions it would like to make. For instance, it cannot distinguish between final consumer use of a commodity and the use of the commodity by a business. It cannot distinguish between capital and wage income in the unincorporated sector, and hence an unincorporated profits tax is not feasible. It cannot distinguish between pure profits and return to entrepreneurship. Whenever the government is not able to identify and tax away all pure profits in the private sector and whenever there are other restrictions on the ability of the government to impose taxes, it may be desirable to impose distortionary taxes on producers.[22]

The arguments in favor of the productive efficiency of the economy also have some important implications for the choice of projects in the public sector. The government, in its role as a producer, can be viewed as just like any other producer; thus if the economy is to be productively efficient, the marginal rates of substitution among inputs in the public sector must be the same as in the private sector, and marginal rates of transformation between any two outputs must be the same. If the government is considering the construction of an electric power plant, it should use in its project evaluation exactly the same prices as a private firm would use; for instance, in evaluating outputs in different dates, it should use the rate of interest facing private producers.

One must be careful, however, not to push this argument too far. As we argued in Chapter 5, many public projects are concerned explicitly with distributional objectives that cannot be obtained in other ways. The distributional implications of labor training programs should probably not be ignored, for instance, in evaluating such programs.[23]

THE DEPENDENCE OF OPTIMAL TAX STRUCTURE ON THE SET OF AVAILABLE TAXES

Throughout this chapter, we have noticed the dependence of the optimal tax results on the assumptions made concerning the set of available taxes. This was particularly noticeable for commodity taxation; whether there should be differential commodity taxation, and, if so, what determines the differences in tax rates, depends on whether there is an income tax or not, and if there is an income tax, whether it is a flat-rate tax or not. Ramsey showed that in the absence of any income tax, different commodities should be taxed at different rates, depending only on the elasticities of demand and supply. With 100 percent taxes on profits, the optimal tax depends only on the demand elasticities, not on supply elasticities.[24] When there is an optimally chosen

[22]This result was established in J. E. Stiglitz and P. Dasgupta, "Differential Taxation, Public Goods and Economic Efficiency," *Review of Economic Studies* 39 (1971): 151–74.

[23]J. E. Stiglitz, "The Rate of Discount for Benefit-Cost Analysis and the Theory of the Second Best," in *Discounting for Time and Risk in Energy Policy*, ed. F. R. Ruskin (Baltimore, MD: Johns Hopkins University Press, 1982), pp. 151–204.

[24]More generally, Stiglitz and Dasgupta establish that if there is a tax of profits at the rate τ, the optimal tax structure is of the form

$$\frac{t}{p} = k\left(\frac{1}{\eta^d} + \frac{1-\tau}{\eta^s}\right),$$

where τ is the tax rate on profits.

income tax, it may be optimal to have no differential commodity tax; and when differential commodity taxes are desirable, they do not depend simply on the elasticities of demand.

There should be uniform taxes in the case where 1) the government is restricted to using a flat-rate income tax but has chosen the rate optimally, using, say, a utilitarian social welfare function; 2) the only sources of differences in income are differences in ability (giving rise to differences in wage rates); 3) the demand for each commodity depends on its own price; and 4) the price elasticities of demand are constant.[25] Differences in optimal tax rates will have to depend in part at least on the rate of change of the elasticity of demand, a parameter about which economists have little knowledge.

It should be emphasized, however, that the set of taxes that is feasible should itself be a subject for analysis: it depends, in particular, on what variables are easily observable and verifiable. In many developing economies, in which there are many barter transactions (trade not for cash) and in which the level of record keeping is much lower than elsewhere, it is difficult to enforce an income tax; commodity taxes must be relied on to redistribute income and to ensure that the burden of taxation is equitably borne. But in the United States the case for the use of redistributive commodity taxation is much weaker.

SUMMARY

1. Pareto-efficient tax structures ensure that the economy operates on its utility possibilities schedule. The nature of the Pareto-efficient tax structure, in turn, depends on the information available to the government.

2. There are important trade-offs in the design of tax structures between distributional goals and efficiency. The optimal tax structure balances the gains from additional redistribution with the costs in terms of loss in efficiency.

3. The deadweight loss associated with the magnitude of the substitution effect suggests that it is desirable to have low marginal rates in those parts of the income distribution where there are a large number of individuals, which is to say in the middle-income ranges. On the other hand, high marginal rates in such ranges enable the government to impose a higher average rate with a lower marginal rate on the upper-income individuals and thus reduce the deadweight loss per dollar of revenue raised resulting from the tax on upper-income individuals. The net consequences of the two effects together is that it may be desirable to have a flat-rate tax.

4. If the government can impose a redistributive income tax, there appears to be little scope for additional redistribution through commodity taxation.

5. Ramsey taxes minimize the deadweight loss associated with raising a given revenue through commodity taxes alone. In the simple case of independent demand and supply curves, tax rates are lower the higher are demand and supply elasticities.

---

[25] Under the first three assumptions the tax is proportional to ϕ_k / η_k^{ℓ}, where ϕ_k is a "distributional" characteristic of the good. Goods that (other things being equal) are consumed proportionately by the rich should be taxed more heavily. Unfortunately, such luxury goods also tend to have high demand elasticities. Under the third and fourth assumptions, ϕ_k is (approximately) proportional to η^d. Hence ϕ_k / η^d is approximately the same for all consumers.

6. If there are no profits in the private sector (or the government can impose 100 percent profits taxes) and there are not other restrictions on the ability of the government to impose taxes, then the government should not impose any taxes that interfere with the productive efficiency of the economy. When these stringent assumptions are removed, it may be desirable to introduce taxes that interfere with productive efficiency and to take into account distributional considerations in the evaluation of public projects.

KEY CONCEPTS

Second best	Progressive tax
Pareto-efficient taxes	Regressive tax
Optimal tax	Ramsey tax

QUESTIONS AND PROBLEMS

1. "If there are groups in the population who differ in their labor supply elasticity, they should be taxed at different rates." Justify this in terms of the theory of optimal taxation, and discuss its implications for the taxation of working spouses.

2. Earlier, we noted that consumption at different dates could be interpreted just like consumption of different commodities (at the same date). What do the results on optimal taxation imply about the desirability of taxing interest income? (Hint: recall that the price of consumption tomorrow relative to the consumption today is just $1/1+r$, where r is the rate of interest.)

3. Explain why it might be desirable to have a regressive tax structure, even if the social welfare function is utilitarian, when general equilibrium effects of taxes are taken into account. Would it ever be desirable to impose a negative marginal tax rate on very high-income individuals?

4. If you believed that those who were more productive in earning income also had a higher marginal utility of income (they were more efficient in consumption), what would that imply for the design of tax structures? Discuss the reasonableness of alternative assumptions.

5. Under what circumstances will an increase in progressivity reduce the degree of before-tax inequality?

6. To what extent do you think that differences in views concerning how progressive our tax structure should be reflect differences in values, and to what extent do they reflect differences in judgments concerning the economic consequences of progressivity (deadweight loss, shifting)?

7. One argument sometimes made in favor of the use of commodity taxation rather than income taxation is that people do not accurately perceive the amount they pay in commodity taxes. They will object less to a 20 percent income tax supplemented by a 10 percent sales tax than to a 30 percent income tax. Do you think this is true? If it is, what do you think it implies about the design of tax policy?

PART FIVE

TAXATION IN THE UNITED STATES

Here we apply the general principles of taxation developed in Part IV to the analysis of taxation in the United States. After first discussing the two major taxes, the income tax and the corporation tax, we discuss the wide range of taxes that affect households and capital. The past decade has seen an increasing concern with tax avoidance and numerous proposals for reform of the tax code to reduce tax avoidance and to reduce the other inequities and inefficiencies of our present tax system, culminating in a major initiative by President Reagan. After explaining the basic principles of tax avoidance, we evaluate four of the major proposals for tax reform.

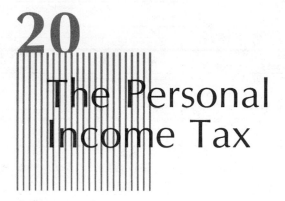

20

The Personal Income Tax

The personal income tax is the single most important source of revenue for the federal government. It is also the tax that impinges on our lives more than any other. Discussions of income taxes—how they are unfair, how to avoid them or (even) evade them—occupy much of the dinnertime conversations of upper-middle-income Americans. Billions of dollars are spent every year for tax lawyers and tax accountants in an attempt to reduce taxes. Tax avoidance has almost become a national sport, with the government trying to close the loopholes as fast as smart tax lawyers and accountants find them in each new set of laws. Tax evasion has also grown. It is estimated, for instance, that less than 60 percent of capital gains are reported. There are now many who believe that the income tax has become grossly unfair, and there is widespread feeling that there ought to be a complete overhaul of the personal income tax system. This was the position taken by President Reagan in his tax reform proposals in 1984.

To understand why the income tax system has become such a subject of controversy, we begin by examining how the government determines each individual's tax liability. We shall examine the rationale for—and the consequences of—each of the major provisions. We then discuss in some detail the equity and efficiency consequences of some of the central provisions.

AN OUTLINE OF THE UNITED STATES INCOME TAX

On the following two pages we show the basic 1040 tax form, the most commonly used document for reporting personal income for individuals and fam-

Form **1040** Department of the Treasury—Internal Revenue Service **U.S. Individual Income Tax Return** **1985** (O)

| For the year January 1-December 31, 1985, or other tax year beginning | , 1985, ending | , 19 | OMB No. 1545-0074 |

Use IRS label. Otherwise, please print or type.	Your first name and initial (if joint return, also give spouse's name and initial)	Last name	Your social security number
	Present home address (number and street, including apartment number, or rural route)		Spouse's social security number
	City, town or post office, state, and ZIP code	Your occupation	
		Spouse's occupation	

Presidential Election Campaign ▶ Do you want $1 to go to this fund? . . . . Yes ☐ No ☐ **Note:** *Checking "Yes" will not change your tax or reduce your refund.*
If joint return, does your spouse want $1 to go to this fund?. . Yes ☐ No ☐

Filing Status

Check only one box.

1 ☐ Single
2 ☐ Married filing joint return (even if only one had income)
3 ☐ Married filing separate return. Enter spouse's social security no. above and full name here. _____
4 ☐ Head of household (with qualifying person). (See page 5 of Instructions.) If the qualifying person is your unmarried child but not your dependent, write child's name here. _____
5 ☐ Qualifying widow(er) with dependent child (year spouse died ▶ 19). (See page 6 of Instructions.)

For Privacy Act and Paperwork Reduction Act Notice, see Instructions.

Exemptions

Always check the box labeled Yourself. Check other boxes if they apply.

6a ☐ Yourself ☐ 65 or over ☐ Blind
b ☐ Spouse ☐ 65 or over ☐ Blind

Enter number of boxes checked on 6a and b ▶ ☐

c First names of your dependent children who lived with you _____

Enter number of children listed on 6c ▶ ☐

d First names of your dependent children who did not live with you (see page 6). _____
(If pre-1985 agreement, check here ▶ ☐ .)

Enter number of children listed on 6d ▶ ☐

e Other dependents:		(3) Number of months lived in your home	(4) Did dependent have income of $1,040 or more?	(5) Did you provide more than one-half of dependent's support?
(1) Name	(2) Relationship			

Enter number of other dependents ▶ ☐

f Total number of exemptions claimed (also complete line 36). . . . .

Add numbers entered in boxes above ▶ ☐

Income

Please attach Copy B of your Forms W-2, W-2G, and W-2P here.

If you do not have a W-2, see page 4 of Instructions.

7	Wages, salaries, tips, etc. (Attach Form(s) W-2.)	7	
8	Interest income (also attach Schedule B if over $400)	8	
9a	Dividends (also attach Schedule B if over $400) _____ , 9b Exclusion _____		
c	Subtract line 9b from line 9a and enter the result	9c	
10	Taxable refunds of state and local income taxes, if any, from the worksheet on page 9 of Instructions.	10	
11	Alimony received	11	
12	Business income or (loss) (attach Schedule C)	12	
13	Capital gain or (loss) (attach Schedule D)	13	
14	40% of capital gain distributions not reported on line 13 (see page 9 of Instructions)	14	
15	Other gains or (losses) (attach Form 4797)	15	
16	Fully taxable pensions, IRA distributions, and annuities not reported on line 17 (see page 9). .	16	
17a	Other pensions and annuities, including rollovers. Total received 17a		
b	Taxable amount, if any, from the worksheet on page 10 of Instructions	17b	
18	Rents, royalties, partnerships, estates, trusts, etc. (attach Schedule E)	18	
19	Farm income or (loss) (attach Schedule F)	19	
20a	Unemployment compensation (insurance). Total received . . 20a		
b	Taxable amount, if any, from the worksheet on page 10 of Instructions	20b	
21a	Social security benefits (see page 10). Total received. . . . 21a		
b	Taxable amount, if any, from worksheet on page 11. { Tax-exempt interest _____ }	21b	
22	Other income (list type and amount—see page 11 of Instructions) _____		
		22	
23	Add lines 7 through 22. This is your **total income** . . . . ▶	23	

Please attach check or money order here.

Adjustments to Income

(See Instructions on page 11.)

24	Moving expense (attach Form 3903 or 3903F)	24	
25	Employee business expenses (attach Form 2106).	25	
26	IRA deduction, from the worksheet on page 12	26	
27	Keogh retirement plan deduction	27	
28	Penalty on early withdrawal of savings	28	
29	Alimony paid (recipient's last name _____ and social security no. _____)	29	
30	Deduction for a married couple when both work (attach Schedule W)	30	
31	Add lines 24 through 30. These are your **total adjustments** . . . . ▶	31	

Adjusted Gross Income

| 32 | Subtract line 31 from line 23. This is your **adjusted gross income.** If this line is less than $11,000 and a child lived with you, see "Earned Income Credit" (line 59) on page 16 of Instructions. If you want IRS to figure your tax, see page 13 of Instructions . . . . . ▶ | 32 | |

Tax Compu- tation (See Instructions on page 13.)	**33** Amount from line 32 (adjusted gross income)	**33**
	34a If you itemize, attach Schedule A (Form 1040) and enter the amount from Schedule A, line 26 . .	**34a**
	Caution: If you have unearned income and can be claimed as a dependent on your parents' return, check here ▶ ☐ and see page 13 of Instructions. Also see page 13 if you are married filing a separate return and your spouse itemizes deductions, or you are a dual-status alien.	
	b If you do not itemize but you made charitable contributions, enter your cash contributions here. (If you gave $3,000 or more to any one organization, see page 14.) **34b**	
	c Enter your noncash contributions (you must attach Form 8283 if over $500) **34c**	
	d Add lines 34b and 34c. Enter the total **34d**	
	e Divide the amount on line 34d by 2. Enter the result here	**34e**
	35 Subtract line 34a or line 34e, whichever applies, from line 33	**35**
	36 Multiply $1,040 by the total number of exemptions claimed on line 6f (see page 14) . . .	**36**
	37 Taxable income. Subtract line 36 from line 35. Enter the result (but not less than zero)	**37**
	38 Enter tax here. Check if from ☐ Tax Table, ☐ Tax Rate Schedule X, Y, or Z, or ☐ Schedule G	**38**
	39 Additional taxes. (See page 14 of Instructions.) Enter here and check if from ☐ Form 4970, ☐ Form 4972, or ☐ Form 5544	**39**
	40 Add lines 38 and 39. Enter the total . . . . ▶	**40**
Credits (See Instructions on page 14.)	**41** Credit for child and dependent care expenses (attach Form 2441) **41**	
	42 Credit for the elderly and the permanently and totally disabled (attach Schedule R) **42**	
	43 Residential energy credit (attach Form 5695) **43**	
	44 Partial credit for political contributions for which you have receipts **44**	
	45 Add lines 41 through 44. These are your total personal credits	**45**
	46 Subtract line 45 from line 40. Enter the result (but not less than zero)	**46**
	47 Foreign tax credit (attach Form 1116) **47**	
	48 General business credit. Check if from ☐ Form 3800, ☐ Form 3468, ☐ Form 5884, ☐ Form 6478 . . . . . **48**	
	49 Add lines 47 and 48. These are your total business and other credits	**49**
	50 Subtract line 49 from line 46. Enter the result (but not less than zero) . . . . ▶	**50**
Other Taxes (Including Advance EIC Payments)	**51** Self-employment tax (attach Schedule SE)	**51**
	52 Alternative minimum tax (attach Form 6251)	**52**
	53 Tax from recapture of investment credit (attach Form 4255)	**53**
	54 Social security tax on tip income not reported to employer (attach Form 4137) . . .	**54**
	55 Tax on an IRA (attach Form 5329)	**55**
	56 Add lines 50 through 55. This is your **total tax** . . . . ▶	**56**
Payments Attach Forms W-2, W-2G, and W-2P to front.	**57** Federal income tax withheld **57**	
	58 1985 estimated tax payments and amount applied from 1984 return **58**	
	59 Earned income credit (see page 16) **59**	
	60 Amount paid with Form 4868 . . . . **60**	
	61 Excess social security tax and RRTA tax withheld (two or more employers) **61**	
	62 Credit for Federal tax on gasoline and special fuels (attach Form 4136) **62**	
	63 Regulated Investment Company credit (attach Form 2439) . . . **63**	
	64 Add lines 57 through 63. These are your **total payments** . . . . ▶	**64**
Refund or Amount You Owe	**65** If line 64 is larger than line 56, enter amount **OVERPAID** . . . . ▶	**65**
	66 Amount of line 65 to be **REFUNDED TO YOU** . . . . ▶	**66**
	67 Amount of line 65 to be applied to your 1986 estimated tax . . . ▶	**67**
	68 If line 56 is larger than line 64, enter **AMOUNT YOU OWE.** Attach check or money order for full amount payable to "Internal Revenue Service." Write your social security number and "1985 Form 1040" on it . . ▶	**68**
	Check ▶ ☐ if Form 2210 (2210F) is attached. See page 17. **Penalty: $**	
Please Sign Here	▶ Under penalties of perjury, I declare that I have examined this return and accompanying schedules and statements, and to the best of my knowledge and belief, they are true, correct, and complete. Declaration of preparer (other than taxpayer) is based on all information of which preparer has any knowledge.	
	Your signature　　　　　　　Date　　　　　　　Spouse's signature (if filing jointly, BOTH must sign)	
Paid Preparer's Use Only	Preparer's signature ▶　　　　　　Date　　　Check if self-employed ☐　　Preparer's social security no.	
	Firm's name (or yours, if self-employed) and address ▶　　　　　　　E.I. No.　　　ZIP code	

ilies. People with lower income who do not itemize their deductions use a simplified version of the 1040.

On lines 7–23 of Form 1040 one calculates the *adjusted gross income.* First one simply adds up the total of wages and salaries, dividends and interest received, net income from one's business, net rent (after expenses) from rental properties, and the gains and losses one has incurred on the sale of assets. Long-term capital gains are only partially taxable (60 percent of long-term capital gains are excludable from income). Pensions and unemployment insurance are also only partially taxable (pensions are taxable to the extent that receipts exceed contributions upon which tax has already been paid). Alimony is also included in income. While prizes are, in general, taxable, rewards for achievement, such as the Nobel Prize, are not. Gambling earnings are (though gambling losses are not deductible). Welfare benefits are not included as income, illegal earnings (such as from prostitution) are taxable but not generally reported, interest on state and local bonds is not.

The second step on Form 1040 is to subtract from the gross income certain expenses associated with earning income on lines 24–31. Some examples are moving expenses (if the change of residence was job-related) and employee business expenses. One also subtracts certain tax-exempt savings plans, such as individual retirement accounts (IRAs) or Keogh accounts (retirement accounts for the self-employed) and alimony paid. After subtracting these from total income, one obtains what is called **adjusted gross income** on line 32.

At line 34 there are two alternatives. One can take what is referred to as the **standard deduction,** a subtraction of $3,400 for a married couple or $2,300 for a single individual. This standard deduction is built into the tax table and is referred to as the zero-bracket amount. Alternatively, the individual can itemize his deductions, listing on a supplementary schedule (Schedule A) all medical expenses, interest, state and local taxes, charity, and casualty losses.[1] Most homeowners use Schedule A because mortgage interest expenses usually exceed the standard deduction.

On line 36 the taxpayer deducts $1,000 for each of what are referred to as personal "exemptions." For most families this simply means a deduction for each member of the family, but problems arise when there are individuals who are supported in part by more than one individual (or earn part of their support themselves).

The exemptions do not, of course, represent the additional costs of support for an additional person: these typically are far greater than $1,000. Rather, the exemptions, combined with the standard deduction, are intended to ensure that no taxes are imposed on the very poor. As we noted in Chapter 16, changes in this minimum income, below which no tax is imposed, have until recent years very roughly followed what is called the poverty level.

One can then calculate one's basic tax liability. The tax will depend on whether the individual is single, married filing jointly with a spouse, married filing separately, or a head of a household (this information is provided on lines 1–5).

Finally, one is allowed to subtract certain **tax credits.** For instance, in families in which both parents work, a credit of up to 20 percent of expen-

---

[1] Even if you do not itemize, some charitable contributions are now deductible (line 34b).

ditures for child care up to $4,800 is allowed. Thus a family with two children
spending the full $4,800 that qualifies for the full 20 percent credit would
have its tax liability reduced by

$$.20 \times \$4,800 = \$960.00.$$

Similarly, credits are provided for new investment, for taxes paid to foreign
governments, and for certain categories of expenditures.

The difference between a tax credit and a tax deduction is that the deduction is a subtraction from income; the reduction in taxes resulting from a
deduction depends on the individual's marginal tax bracket. Thus if child
care expenses were deductible, the reduction in the tax from $100 of child
care expenses would be $50 for someone in the 50 percent bracket (someone
who pays a marginal tax rate of 50 percent), $20 for someone in the 20 per-
cent bracket. With a credit, the amount of tax due is reduced; the tax savings
thus do not depend on the individual's income. A simple 20 percent child
care credit reduces the taxes of anyone with $100 of child care expenses by
$20, regardless of income (so long as their total tax liability exceeds $20).[2]

To determine the amount owed the government, one simply subtracts on
line 50 the tax credits from the tax liability calculated earlier to obtain what
we can refer to as the net tax liability.

Next, on lines 65–68, one calculates the amount that one has already paid
to the government (withheld from wage income). If the amount withheld
exceeds the taxes due, one receives a refund; if it is less, one sends the IRS
a check.

Additional Forms

Supplementing the basic 1040 schedule are a number of attachments providing part of the documentation behind the entries. Schedule A, for instance,
shows the itemized deductions, and Schedule C shows net business income
(gross income minus expenses). Several of the schedules are concerned with
reporting income on capital: B with interest and dividends, D with capital
gains, and E with income from rental property.

PRINCIPLES BEHIND THE UNITED STATES INCOME TAX

The basic principles underlying the tax system are worth reviewing, even
though the long political process from which they evolved has produced
results that may not be consistent with these "basic principles."

The Income-Based Principle

The current United States tax code rests on the premise that the appropriate
basis for assessing tax liability is the individual's income (net of expenses
personally incurred on the job).

For the most part, economists have argued that a *comprehensive* definition of income be used that includes not only cash income but capital gains
(whether the gain is realized or simply accrued). A number of other adjust-

[2]The provisions for child care in the current tax law are slightly more complicated than this simple case.

ments have to be made to convert your "cash" income into the "comprehensive" income that, in principle, should form the basis of taxation. This comprehensive definition of income is referred to as the Haig-Simons concept, after two early twentieth-century economists who advocated its use. They believed that such a comprehensive income measure most accurately reflects "ability to pay."

We describe below the major differences between how our tax system measures income and the Haig-Simons concept of "comprehensive" income.

1. Cash Basis. For the most part, only **cash-basis** market transactions are taxed. The tax is thus levied on a notion of income that is somewhat narrower than that which most economists would ideally like to see employed. Certain nonmarketed (noncash) economic activities are excluded, though activities that appear to be identical and are marketed are subject to taxation. For instance, services provided in the household sector are not taxed, while identical services, when purchased, are subject to taxation. A maid who cleans house has her compensation taxed, while a spouse who performs exactly the same services in her or his home (and whose support by the spouse working outside the home can be thought of, at least partially, as compensation for the services performed) is not taxed. If an individual owns a house and rents it out, the net rental income is subject to taxation; if the individual lives in the house himself, no tax is due. The primary reason for this is the difficulty of determining appropriate values in the absence of market transactions; when there is a market transaction, there is an observable variable, the transaction price, which we can (and do) use to value the service.

Some noncash transactions are listed in the tax code but are difficult to enforce. Barter arrangements (Sally Housepainter paints Joe Carpenter's house in return for his building her a new garage) are subject to tax. Also, when employers provide in-kind payments to their employees (such as making an automobile available for personal use), then, in principle, the individual is required to assess the value of these payments and report them on his 1040 form. In fact, noncash payments are seldom reported.

Also, it should be noted that while no country has attempted to tax the *imputed* value of services of spouses, some countries (such as Sweden) have attempted to tax the "rent" on owner-occupied houses, as if the individual rented the house to himself. The difficulty of assessing the implicit rent on an owner-occupied house is not much different from the difficulty of assessing property values.

The other major category of what economists view as income that is not included in the income tax bases is *unrealized capital gains.* Capital gains (the increase in the value of an asset) are taxed only when the asset is sold. Capital gains are taxed, in other words, only upon *realization,* rather than on an *accrual* basis (that is, as they actually occur from year to year).

To see why economists have argued that income should include capital gains, consider two individuals: one puts his $100 savings in a bank and earns 10 percent interest. His income is $10. The other buys $100 worth of gold. During the course of the year, the price of gold rises by 10 percent. At the end of the year, he could sell his gold for $110. The capital gain increases the wealth of the individual just as the interest payments do; from an economic point of view, the two appear to be identical. The tax liabilities of the two individuals will differ: the individual who purchases gold only has to pay a tax on his capital gain *when* he sells the asset. One of the reasons for this is that in the absence of the sale, the government would have to make an inference about the magnitude of capital gains, and such inferences are always subject to dispute. Capital gains are not, in other words, an easily observable variable. This is not always true: for instance, the market value of most securities is printed daily in the newspaper. Since 1981, in fact, individuals trading in futures markets (where, for instance, promises to deliver corn or wheat in three or six months' time are bought and sold) have been taxed on the basis of the actual market value of their holding at the end of the year, whether or not gains or losses are realized.

2. *Equity-Based Adjustments.* Individuals who have large medical expenses or casualty losses are allowed to deduct a portion of those expenses from their income, presumably on the grounds that they are not in as good a position for paying taxes as someone with the same income without those expenses.

3. *Incentive-Based Adjustments.* The tax code is used to encourage certain activities by allowing tax credits or deductions for those expenditures. Incentives are provided for energy conservation, for investment, and for charitable contributions.

4. *Special Treatment of Capital Income.* The tax laws treat capital and wage income differently. There are a variety of explanations for this: the difficulty of assessing the magnitude of the returns to capital plays some role, while attempts to encourage savings as a source of national economic growth were prominent in the discussions on the tax bill of 1981 when several of the special provisions were introduced.

The Progressivity Principle

Our tax structure is based on the premise that those with higher incomes not only should pay more but should pay a larger fraction of their income in taxes. Progressivity is reflected in an increase not only in average rates but in marginal rates. These increase from 11 percent for a single individual with an income of $2,300 to 50 percent for an individual with an income over $55,300. The effect of the adjustments to income we described earlier (as well as a number of other loopholes we shall discuss later) is to reduce significantly the effective degree of progressivity. To limit the extent to which individuals can avail themselves of these loopholes, Congress has passed a *minimum tax*, the intent of which is to ensure that upper income individuals pay a tax at least equal to 20 percent of their income (in excess of a basic exemption level).

The net consequence of the special provisions is that **effective tax rates**, the ratio of tax payments to a measure of full income, increase to a maximum of 26.4 percent and actually decline for those with incomes in excess of $1 million, as Table 20.1 demonstrates.[3] Total taxes paid rises rapidly with income:

[3] In the table, reported adjusted gross income is increased to take account of income in tax-exempt forms. There is some controversy about some of the adjustments; in particular, the inclusion of tax-exempt interest. The rates of return on these assets are somewhat lower than on taxable bonds; the difference can be thought of as a tax payment (made to state and local governments). Nonetheless, the basic picture presented by Table 20.1 appears to be accurate.

Table 20.1 EFFECTIVE TAX RATES UNDER PRESENT LAW, BY INCOME CLASS, 1984 (income classes in thousands of dollars; rates in percent)

Expanded Adjusted Gross Income Class*	Present Law
0–5,000	0.7
5,000–10,000	4.0
10,000–15,000	6.0
15,000–20,000	7.7
20,000–25,000	9.1
25,000–35,000	10.0
35,000–50,000	11.4
50,000–100,000	15.5
100,000–500,000	23.0
500,000–1,000,000	26.4
1,000,000–and over	23.1
All classes	12.0

Source: J. A. Pechman and J. K. Scholz, "Comprehensive Income Taxation and Rate Reduction," *Tax Notes* 17 (1982; Washington, D.C.: Brookings Institution, Brookings Reprint 390).
*Adjusted gross income plus sick pay, excluded capital gains and dividends, interest on life insurance and state and local bond interest, all unemployment benefits, 50 percent of social security benefits, workmen's compensation, veterans' benefits, tax preferences reported for purposes of the minimum tax, one-third of employer-provided health insurance, employer-provided life insurance, and IRA deductions by those covered under private pension plans.

the effective tax *rate* paid by someone at $25,000 income is two and one-half times that paid by someone at $5,000 income, and at $50,000, one and one-half times that paid by someone at $25,000. Table 20.2 shows both the number of taxpayers and the amount of tax they pay, by income categories. The lowest 37 percent of returns filed paid only 2.7 percent of the total taxes. Those with tax liabilities between $25,000 and $50,000, while constituting only one-fifth of the returns, paid two-fifths of the total tax.

Table 20.2 DISTRIBUTION OF FEDERAL INDIVIDUAL INCOME TAX RETURNS AND TAX LIABILITIES, 1982

Adjusted Gross Income Class (dollars)	Returns Filed		Tax Liabilities*	
	Number (thousands)	Percent of Total	Amount (millions of dollars)	Percent of Total
Under 5,000†	18,056	18.9	901	0.3
5,000–10,000	17,086	17.9	6,975	2.4
10,000–25,000	33,511	35.2	60,539	21.4
25,000–50,000	22,091	23.2	114,536	40.4
50,000–100,000	3,804	4.0	51,464	18.2
100,000–200,000	574	0.6	22,200	7.8
200,000–500,000	142	0.15	14,340	5.1
500,000–1,000,000	22	‡	5,584	2.0
1,000,000 and over	8	‡	6,921	2.4
Total	95,297	100.0	283,465	100

Source: Statistics of Income, Individual Income Tax Returns. Figures are rounded. From J. Pechman, "Federal Tax Policy," p. 358.
*Income tax after credits.
†Includes returns with no adjusted gross income.
‡Less than 0.05 percent.

The Family-Based Principle

The basic unit of taxation in the United States is not the individual but the family. Two individuals who decide to get married (and thus change their family status) will find that their tax liabilities are altered. The tax code attempts to make some limited adjustments for families in different circumstances. Families in which there is only one adult face a rate that is halfway between those of an individual and a two-adult family. Families with children are allowed exemptions for each child, as mentioned earlier. Families in which both parents work are allowed a credit for child care, and (since 1983) a deduction of 10 percent of the lower income earner's income (up to a maximum deduction of $3,000). Whether these are "fair" or "appropriate" is a question we shall discuss later.

Although the tax system is basically family based, it is not completely so: income of children is not included in family income. This opens up certain possibilities for families to reduce their income tax liabilities by shifting income among family members.

The United States is now one of the few countries still employing a family-based tax system; other countries, such as Canada, have an individual-based system, where each individual is taxed on his own income.

Divorce presents problems for a family-based tax system. Under present provisions, alimony (but not child support) is deductible by the party paying it and taxable for the party receiving it.[4]

The Annual Measure of Income Principle

The United States income tax is based on annual income, not lifetime income. To see the implications of this, consider two individuals with the same lifetime income. One individual's income fluctuates greatly from year to year; the other individual's income remains constant. Because of the progressive nature of our tax system, the individual with the fluctuating income will have to pay more taxes over his lifetime than the individual with a steady income.[5] To see this, consider an individual who has a zero income one year and a $100,000 income the next year. His tax liabilities in the first year are zero; in the second, $39,473. His average tax is $19,736.50. In contrast, an individual with a steady $50,000 income pays $14,735 every year, or 25 percent less.

The government recognized that this introduces a distortion (discouraging individuals from entering occupations with fluctuating income) and made some provisions for income averaging, so that the individual with a fluctuating income is taxed at slightly lower rates, but the provisions are far from adequate; there is still a significant inequity.

The annual basis of taxation has other effects: an individual who has the option of paying some deductible expense on December 31 or on January 1 has a strong incentive to do so on December 31. An individual who has an

---

[4]Thus with the progressive tax structure, if the husband and wife are in very different tax brackets, it pays to label payments that are really child support as alimony. Like everything else in modern life, it requires care and thought to get divorced in a manner that minimizes tax liabilities.

[5]At least in present-value terms.

option of being paid on December 31 or on January 1 has a strong incentive to ask for a postponement of his check until January 1.[6]

DETERMINING INCOME

For most wage earners, determining income for tax purposes is a simple matter. They simply add up their paychecks, interest, dividends, etc. But for those who run their own business it is not. There are two central problems. The first is concerned with determining depreciation and adjusting the cost of inventories for inflation. These are sufficiently difficult and complex questions that we postpone them for the next two chapters. The second problem is differentiating between consumption expenditures and legitimate business expenses.

The tax code recognizes that legitimate expenses required in order to earn a living ought to be deducted from an individual's income. The principle seems clear. Surely, a store owner who sells candy should not be taxed on the total value of his sales; his expenses—the rent to his store, the purchase of candy from the candy manufacturer, the salaries he pays his employees—should all be deducted from sales to calculate his gross income. But what about the candy he consumes while he is working? He may claim that his consumption of candy is a form of advertising; when customers see him chewing candy, they increase their purchases. But what of the candy that he consumes when no one is around? He may claim he is "testing" various samples, to ensure the quality of the candy he sells. One might suspect that the real motive lying behind the candy store owner eating his candy is neither of these expressed explanations: he simply likes candy.

This example illustrates the two central problems:

a) In many instances it is impossible to ascertain what are and are not legitimate business expenses.

b) Even when the distinctions between legitimate and illegitimate business expenses are conceptually clear, it is often impossible to perform the required monitoring. It is difficult to imagine the kinds of records that would be required to isolate the owner's consumption of candy (if we recognized that consumption is not a legitimate business expense).

Hence the government can either allow a fairly generous treatment of expenses—for instance, travel, in which case the individual who is doing it really for recreation purposes is unfairly receiving the tax benefit—or the government can be fairly restrictive—for instance, by not allowing first-class travel, not allowing meal deductions above a certain amount, in which case the individual who has no recreational motive may be unfairly burdened. There is no way the tax code can be fair to both of these individuals.

Similarly, in many businesses there is very little difference between advertising and entertainment expenses. Taking a client out to dinner is a method of persuasion to buy your product, just as putting an advertisement in the newspaper is an attempt to persuade customers to buy your product. On the other hand, there are other instances where "business" entertainment is purely a matter of having a good dinner at Uncle Sam's expense.

---

[6]Both statements are made on the assumption that the individual is in the same marginal tax bracket both years.

The essential point is that it is impossible to devise a system of distinguishing between legitimate and illegitimate expenditures in a way most of us would consider to be fair; someone always either is unfairly burdened or benefits unfairly, no matter what rule is devised.

Moreover, any rule induces economic distortions. If deductions for travel expenses are restricted, businesses requiring travel will be discouraged; if travel expenses are not restricted, businesses requiring travel may be encouraged. They are a form of tax-exempt income. Furthermore, if travel expenses are restricted, business may substitute less efficient communication methods for travel.

In Figure 20.1, Panel A, we consider a self-employed individual who is able to claim business entertainment as a deduction. The deductibility of these expenses shifts his budget constraint, the alternative combinations of "entertainment" and "other consumption goods" the individual can purchase. Entertainment becomes relatively less expensive; if the individual is in the 50 percent tax bracket, he has to give up only 50 cents' worth of other goods to get a dollar's worth of entertainment. His consumption decisions are clearly distorted.

Panel B shows what happens if travel expenses are not deductible. Isocost curves, which give those combinations of inputs that cost the firm the same amount, are drawn with and without the tax deductibility of travel. The firm can have more trips and fewer telephone calls on the same communication budget. Not allowing tax-deductible travel expenses (or putting a limit on these expenses) shifts the isocost curve. Now every dollar of telephone expenses costs the firm 50 cents, if the firm is in the 50 percent tax bracket, but every dollar of travel costs the firm a dollar. Travel has become effectively twice as expensive. Thus firms will be induced to use more telephones, even though telephones may be a less effective way of communicating.

Many (but by no means all) of the provisions of the tax code that seem unfair and distortionary are not the result of malevolent and stupid politicians. There is no ideal income tax. In the design of the tax code, one must weigh one inequity against another, one distortion against another. The objective of our discussion is to clarify these trade-offs, to avoid the all-too-frequent situation where, in the process of correcting one inequity or distortion, the authorities discover that they have created a new one, worse than the first.

What Constitutes a Business?

Not only is it difficult to determine what are legitimate business expenses, in some cases it is even difficult to determine what is a business. For instance, individuals who raise horses could be raising horses as a business, to sell them at a capital gain. On the other hand, they could be keeping the horses simply for their own pleasure. If they buy a horse, keep it for several years, sell it, and make a loss, the loss is really not on a business activity or on an asset but on an ordinary pleasurable activity. One could argue that there is no reason that their capital loss should be deducted from the individual's income tax. On the other hand, there are individuals who do raise horses for

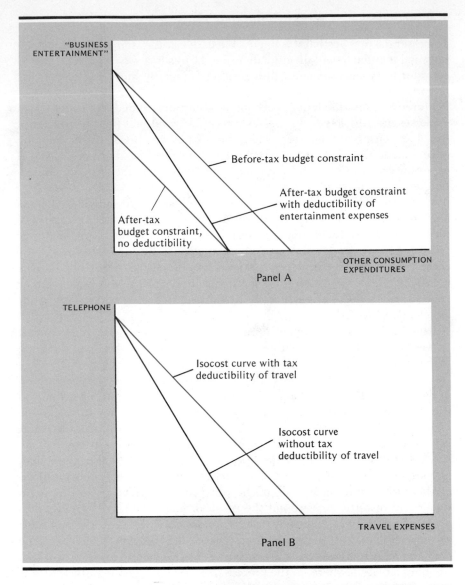

"BUSINESS ENTERTAINMENT"

Before-tax budget constraint

After-tax budget constraint
with deductibility of
entertainment expenses

After-tax
budget constraint,
no deductibility

OTHER CONSUMPTION
EXPENDITURES

Panel A

TELEPHONE

Isocost curve with tax
deductibility of travel

Isocost curve
without tax
deductibility of travel

TRAVEL EXPENSES

Panel B

20.1 DILEMMAS OF TAX DEDUCTIBILITY OF ENTERTAINMENT, TRAVEL, AND RELATED EXPENDITURES (A) For a self-employed individual who can claim a deduction for "business entertainment," the tax system reduces the cost of this form of consumption relative to other forms of consumption. There is a distortion (and hence a deadweight loss). (B) If firms were denied the right to deduct travel expenses from income as a legitimate business expense, travel would become a relatively more expensive way of communicating than other forms of communication, such as telephone; thus production decisions would be distorted.

purposes of capital gains—buying them at a lower price, feeding them, and then selling them at a higher price. Not to allow these individuals who are in the business of raising horses for profit to deduct their losses would seem to be grossly unfair. The difficulty is that it is virtually impossible to distinguish between the two situations.

The government attempts to combat this kind of tax avoidance by insisting that serious businesses make a profit. The rule of thumb is that an individual must make a profit at least one year out of three. Rules such as this obviously do succeed in reducing the amount of tax avoidance. At the same time, of course, there are individuals who are seriously in business who make losses year after year for a period in excess of three or four years. Setting up businesses often takes three or four years in order to establish a reputation—and a profit.

Employee Business Deductions

In principle, the "necessary costs" of working should be deductible. The difficulty is ascertaining what are necessary costs. Because of the impossibility of doing this on a case-by-case basis, the government has set up certain basic rules: some educational expenses are deductible, others are not. Moving expenses are deductible, commuting expenses are not.

SCHEDULE A: DEDUCTIONS

There are five important kinds of expenditure for which deductions are allowed: medical expenses, interest, state and local taxes, charities, and casualties. The deductions are itemized on Schedule A and their sum is used on Form 1040, line 34.

Medical Expenses

The motivation for allowing medical expenditures to be deducted from income seems perfectly obvious: health problems lead to costly medical bills and often reduce the individual's earnings as well. An individual who is spending all of his income on doctor bills simply to stay alive has a lower ability to pay than an individual with the same income but no medical expenses. Ability to pay is measured best not by total income but by discretionary income, the amount in excess of the amount required to survive.

This argument has been criticized on two grounds. First, there are other categories of expenditures (such as food) that, at least at some level, are equally necessary. But differences on the necessary amount of food are likely to be smaller than differences in the necessary amount of medical expenditures, and in any case, the differences are virtually impossible to measure. Second, a significant fraction of medical expenses are discretionary (e.g., staying in a private room rather than in a semi-private room, having a television set in one's room, plastic surgery to stay young-looking, etc.), and the law makes no distinction between "necessary" and "discretionary" expenditures. Again, however, this is understandable, since the distinction, though clear in principle, is virtually impossible to make in practice. The tax rules now allow deductions of medical expenses only to the extent that they exceed 5 percent of gross income (for drugs, expenditures need only exceed 1 percent of gross income). This corresponds approximately to the level of expenditures of the median family—which seems to reflect the judgment that significant inequities in ability to pay only arise with significant medical costs, and that these large medical costs are likely (but not always) to be nondiscretionary.

To the extent that medical expenditures are discretionary, the provisions for deducting them effectively reduce the price of medical services. For someone in the 50 percent marginal tax bracket whose medical expenses exceed the 5 percent minimum, the private cost of an extra $100 of medical services is only $50. The distortions this introduces are obvious: the individual has an incentive to spend too much on medical services (relative to other commodities).

Note that the amount by which the effective price of medical services is reduced depends on the marginal tax bracket of the individual. For an individual in the 14 percent bracket, an extra $100 of medical services costs $86; for someone in the 25 percent bracket, an extra $100 of medical services costs only $75. Whenever individuals face different prices for the same commodity, there is inefficiency.

Along with the inefficiencies introduced by the provisions for the deductibility of medical expenses, the provision for deductibility of medical expenses has also been objected to on grounds that it is unfair. First, as a result of this provision, individuals with the same income but different medical expenses pay different taxes. Second, the reduction in the tax liability of an individual at a higher income level is greater than that of an individual at a lower income level. Thus if an individual in the 50 percent bracket incurs a $1,000 medical expense (ignoring for the moment the provision limiting the amount that can be deducted), his tax liability is reduced by $500. On the other hand, an individual in the 25 percent bracket would have his tax liability reduced by only $250. The *value* of the provisions for deductibility of expenses is thus much greater for the individual in the higher bracket.

The efficiency and equity arguments against deducting medical expenses (which apply to other categories of deductions as well) have led many economists to conclude that credits are preferable to deductions. But these arguments are not completely persuasive. Recall that the motivation for allowing the deduction was that we wished to base taxes on some measure of ability to pay. It was believed that medical expenses reduce the individual's ability to pay. If this is true, the equitable procedure is to allow a deduction for medical expenses. Thus the arguments that the medical deduction is not equitable because it provides a greater subsidy to those who are in a high marginal bracket than to those in the lower marginal bracket misses the point: in both cases, gross income incorrectly measures the individual's ability to pay. It is, of course, true that the provision introduces strong distortions, particularly for individuals in high marginal brackets. As we discussed earlier, there is an important equity / efficiency trade-off, and as a result, one might argue that full deductibility, particularly for individuals at the higher marginal rates, is not desirable. The fraction of medical expenses that should be tax-deductible would presumably depend on the elasticity of demand for medical services; as we noted earlier, if the elasticity is low, the distortion is low, and there will be little gain in efficiency from making medical expenditures only partially deductible. On the other hand, if the elasticity of demand for medical expenditures is large, there are potentially great gains in efficiency, and then we may wish to have only a fraction of medical expenses deductible.

Interest

The motivation for the tax deductibility of interest is simple: income (as usually defined) includes wages plus net interest receipts—i.e., the difference between interest paid and interest received. If we believe that an individual who has positive net interest receipts has a higher ability to pay than someone with no interest receipts and an individual with negative net interest receipts has a lower ability to pay, interest paid should be tax-deductible.

Those who believe that consumption provides the appropriate basis of taxation argue that interest should not be taxed and that interest payments should not be tax-deductible. Even those who believe that income is the appropriate tax base have, however, been concerned with the inequities and inefficiencies to which interest deductibility gives rise. First, since some types of capital income receive favorable tax treatment, borrowing to finance favored types of investments provides one of the major classes of tax avoidance devices. Second, the present system encourages borrowing, and thus discourages saving. Present tax regulations limit the extent of interest deductibility. Whether these are sufficient or effective is debatable.[7] For instance, President Reagan has proposed to limit the deductibility of interest to mortgages on one's principal residence.

State and Local Taxes

State and local taxes are deductible. The primary motivation for this provision is the concern that without such a provision, the imposition of federal taxation would seriously impair the ability of the states to raise revenues. Indeed, without such a provision, during World War II, when federal marginal tax rates reached as high as 94 percent, some individuals would have faced total marginal tax rates (combining federal and state taxes) in excess of 100 percent. Some individuals also have expressed a concern that without such a provision, there is effectively double taxation of the same income. Whether such double taxation is inequitable is, however, another question. If the taxes are thought of as being associated with the benefits of living in a particular locale, it is not obvious that these expenditures should be treated any differently from expenditures on other goods and services. This is the view taken by President Reagan who proposed to eliminate this deduction.

Indeed, the deductibility of local taxes may give rise to an important source of distortions and inequities. Many of the services provided by local communities—garbage collection, sewage disposal, education—differ little from similar commodities that can be purchased privately. Such services provided by local communities are known as "local public goods"—though all members of the community benefit from these goods, those outside the community do not. Thus the deductibility of local taxes encourages the public provision of these goods and services (regardless of whether the services might be more efficiently provided privately) and encourages the consumption of those goods and services that can be provided through local communities.

---

[7]These provisions limit the amount of interest other than mortgage interest that is deductible. The main effect of the provisions may be to encourage individuals to take out larger mortgages than they otherwise would, and to encourage investment in real estate.

To see this, consider a small community consisting of wealthy homeowners. They face a choice of having a token public school system and sending their children to private school or having a first-rate public school system. For simplicity, we ignore the costs of a token public school system (in fact, state laws may require a high level of expenditure on public schools, and the first option may not really be available; individuals in some rich communities where many of the children go to private school do, however, seem to spend less on their schools than do those in less well-to-do communities). With a private school system, the residents pay an average of, say, $E per family. If they now switch to the public school system, and again pay an average of $E per family, raised by means of taxes, the cost is only $(1 − t)E, where t is the marginal federal income tax rate, since the taxes are deductible from the federal income tax. All communities will have an incentive to spend an excessive amount on education, but the amount of the subsidy is greater the wealthier the community.

The same argument applies, of course, to garbage collection or any other publicly provided service. Note that communities that do not provide public sewage collection (individuals have to use septic tanks) are thus disadvantaged relative to communities with public sewage collection. And there will be instances where, on efficiency grounds, septic tanks would be preferable to public sewage collection, but given the subsidy of public sewage collection, the latter will be employed.

The ability of communities to issue tax-exempt bonds (bonds, the interest on which is not taxable) provides further distortions.

Charity

Gifts for charitable purposes, for education, religion, health, and welfare are one of the more controversial provisions of the tax code. The motivation for allowing these expenditures to be deductible is clear. As we discussed at greater length in Chapter 5, there are insufficient private incentives for spending money on goods that generate benefits to others. Money spent to develop a polio vaccine may yield little direct benefit to the giver but may provide great benefits for mankind. Similarly, gifts to educational and other cultural institutions may contribute much to the welfare of society, but relatively few of the benefits accrue directly to the benefactors. Opponents of the deduction for charity argue that:

a) many of the expenditures are not really for public goods;

b) the public—i.e., the government—should determine directly how expenditures on public goods should be allocated;

c) the provision for deductibility of charitable gifts mainly benefits the rich and thus reduces the redistributive impact of our tax system; and

d) eliminating the provision for the deductibility of charitable gifts would have little effect on charitable giving.

It is difficult to assess the validity of these various claims. Many of the most important advances in medicine have been the outcome of research supported by private foundations. For example, the Rockefeller Foundation's development of "miracle seeds" brought on a Green Revolution in developing countries that has greatly increased the availability of food in these countries.

There is some evidence that elimination of the deductibility of charitable donations would have a substantial effect on gift giving.[8]

Whether the deductibility provisions result in the tax system being unfair is also not clear. Clearly, to the extent that wealthy individuals create foundations that pay high salaries to their officers but spend little on true public goods, the provisions for charitable donations may well be thought to be inequitable. But to the extent that the expenditures are really for public goods, the giver gets no more enjoyment out of the expenditure than do many other members of society. There is no more reason to include these expenditures in his income than in that of any other individual (who benefits equally by it).

If the appropriate basis of taxation is "income available for spending on private goods," the appropriate tax treatment is allowing a full deduction (just as we argued earlier that the appropriate tax treatment of medical expenses was a deduction, not a credit). But the consequence of this is that the marginal cost of charity is less for those in high tax brackets than for those in low ones.

There are, of course, abuses of the provisions for charitable deductions. Most of these are associated with the difficulties of valuing capital assets that are donated to charities. Assume an individual has a painting he purchased for $100,000; if he were to sell it, he would currently get, let us say, $1.1 million. He would have to pay a capital gains tax of, say, 20 percent on the capital gain, so after tax he would have $900,000. He can, instead, donate the painting to his favorite charity and deduct the full $1.1 million from his income tax (provided his income is in excess of $5.5 million—there is a maximum charitable deduction of 20 percent of income). His income tax would have been reduced by $550,000 (assuming he is in the 50 percent bracket). The cost of giving away $1.1 million is only a reduction in consumption of $350,000.

But there is often considerable arbitrariness in determining the fair market value of a painting. Assume he claims he could have sold it for $1,800,000, a claim he may find an appraiser to substantiate. (Indeed, to realize $1.1 million on a sale, after paying selling agent commissions, he may have had to sell it for almost that amount.) Then he would actually be as well off giving his painting away as he would be selling it (see Table 20.3).

Assume that, rather than giving it away, he lends it for a period of twenty years. He may attempt to claim that the value today of the painting being returned to him in twenty years is small, and hence the "gift" of the loan is worth, in fact, close to $1 million. He can thus get a tax deduction of $500,000 and in twenty years have his painting back: he apparently can have his cake and eat it, too.

As with other stories of abuse in the public sector, the story of our charitable art collector clouds a more basic question concerning the manner in

[8] Martin Feldstein ("The Income Tax and Charitable Contributors, Part II: The Impact of Religious Education and Other Organizations," *National Tax Journal*, June 1975, p. 217) estimated that eliminating tax deductibility for someone in the 50 percent tax bracket would reduce charitable contributions to educational institutions by three-quarters; the loss to the charities would be one and one-half times the gain to the federal government. (Someone who had been giving $1,000 would now give $250; treasury revenues would thus increase by $500, but charitable contributions would decrease by $750.) Hospitals would similarly be hard hit. The least sensitive were contributions to religious organizations. See also C. T. Clotfelter and E. Steuerle, "Charitable Contributions," in *How Taxes Affect Economic Behavior*, H. J. Aaron and J. A. Pechman, eds. (Washington, D.C.: Brookings Institution, 1981).

Table 20.3 THE ADVANTAGES OF GIVING TO CHARITY

Direct Sale

True value of painting	$1.1 mil
less tax (20 percent of capital gain)	.2 mil
Net proceeds	.9 mil

Direct Gift—honest evaluation
Tax deduction = .5 × $1.1 = .55 million
Net cost of gift $.35 million

Direct Gift—dishonest evaluation
Claimed value of painting $1.8 million
Tax deductions = .5 × $1.8 mil = .9 million
Net cost of gift   0

Loan of Painting—Having Your Cake and Eating It, Too

Value of gift	$1.1 million
less value of returned painting in 20 years' time	.1 million
Net value of gift	$1.0 million
Tax deduction	$ .5 million

which decisions regarding the supply of public goods should be made. Those who argue that these decisions should be made publicly point out that for someone in the 50 percent bracket, the government foregoes $50 for each $100 of charity, while the individual only foregoes $50. On the other hand, the political processes do not provide a very efficient mechanism for registering individuals' attitudes toward different public goods. Individuals vote for representatives and have little opportunity for expressing their views on the relative allocation, say, of educational and health expenditures.

The provisions for charitable deductions have encouraged a system in which public goods are provided by a variety of institutions. Individuals can express their views about the importance of different categories of public goods in a variety of ways. If the government were the only source of funds for, say, health research, the views of that bureaucracy would exclusively determine the direction of health research; as it is, these decisions can be made independently in a variety of institutions. The arguments for the decentralization of decision making for public goods are closely parallel to those for the decentralization of decision making in other areas: having competing (or at least alternative) organizations providing similar services leads to greater efficiency, and it allows for diversification, so that the consequences of mistakes will be smaller.[9]

Casualty

Individuals are allowed to deduct losses from thefts, fire, accident, and other casualties that exceed 10 percent of the individual's income. The motivation

[9]The provisions for the deductibility of expenditures on religious charities has another motivation: some argue that the constitutional prohibition against legislation interfering with the free exercise of religion prohibits taxation on religious organizations. Although this may provide a justification of exempting religious institutions directly from taxation, it does not seem to provide justification for deducting gifts to churches for purposes of the income tax.

for these provisions is again clear. These losses reduce the individual's ability to pay; they represent "expenditures" that were not voluntary and from which the individual presumably got no enjoyment.

This provision has, however, some important consequences. In particular, it means that the government effectively provides a kind of insurance against these casualties. The magnitude of the insurance depends (as we noted in our discussion of the medical deduction) on the individual's marginal tax bracket. Individuals are obviously much better off than if the government did not provide this kind of insurance. On the other hand, these provisions in turn may seriously distort individuals' behavior. Insurance, in general, reduces individuals' incentives to avoid the losses in question. Thus if the government pays 50 percent of the loss, the individual may not take as much effort to avoid being robbed. There may be significant amounts of social waste as a result.[10]

UNIT OF TAXATION

The final stage in determining tax liabilities entails looking up in the tax tables the tax due, which depends both on the income and the filing status—i.e., whether single, married, or head of household. Our present tax system, as we noted earlier, is based on the family as the unit of taxation; because of some inequities that result, two important modifications are made, for child care expenses and for families with two earners. To see the consequences, both for efficiency and equity, of our present tax structure, we first examine the tax structure in the absence of these provisions. Without them, the tax structure would penalize marriages between partners with equal incomes and encourage marriages between partners with very unequal incomes.

To see this, we discuss the tax liabilities of Abigail and Billy, presently living together but not married. They have the same income ($25,000 per year each), and when they get married, their incomes are effectively added together, thus subjecting them to much higher marginal tax rates. Before getting married, they each pay $4,517 in taxes, for a total of $9,034. After getting married, their tax bill will rise to $11,224. (These calculations are based on the 1983 tax rates.) The marriage tax is $2,190. If they anticipate remaining married for, say, fifty years, and did not anticipate any change in their salaries (after adjusting for inflation) over that period, the total cost of getting married would exceed (with a 5 percent real interest rate) $40,000. If Abigail and Billy have some doubts about whether to get married, this calculation might well resolve those doubts.

Consider, on the other hand, Amy, a low-paid ($7,000-per-year) secretary, who is living with her boyfriend, Bradford, a high-paid ($43,000 per year) stock executive. If they were to get married, their tax liability would be reduced. Before marriage, he pays $11,149 in taxes, while she pays $495 in taxes, for a total of $11,644. After marriage, their tax liability is reduced to $11,224, a marriage bonus of $422.

The 1981 law, which allows the deduction of 10 percent of the income of

---

[10]The force of these arguments was much stronger when all casualty losses in excess of $100 were deductible (before 1983).

the spouse with the lower income, up to $3,000 (that is, a maximum deduction of $3,000), reduces the size of the marriage penalty but does not eliminate it. Consider again Abigail and Billy. They can deduct $2,500 from their taxable income, so that their tax liability is now $10,238: their marriage tax is still over $1,000. The act of getting married increases their tax liabilities by more than 10 percent.

Amy and Bradford benefit by this provision as well: their taxes are $10,944. But now Abigail and Billy are better off than Amy and Bradford, paying $700 less on the same combined income.

Was it the intent of Congress, in enacting the tax code, to encourage marriages between individuals with very different incomes and discourage marriages such as that between Abigail and Billy? Probably not.

But consider now what happens if we change the tax code to have all individuals pay on the basis of their own income. For simplicity, in making these comparisons, we use 1983's single taxpayers' tax schedule. Now, Abigail and Billy neither benefit nor are penalized by marriage. This provision does eliminate the discrimination against those who choose to live together under the bonds of matrimony.

Consider Amy and Bradford. They have the same family income as Abigail and Billy. But now, their total tax liability is $11,149, as opposed to that of Abigail and Billy, whose tax bill is only $9,034. Not surprisingly, Bradford and Amy think this unfair; the small discrepancy ($700) that we noted under the present tax system, where 10 percent of Abigail's salary was deducted, has now increased to more than $2,100. There is no tax arrangement that appears to be "fair" in all circumstances.

Do the general theories of fairness we discussed in Chapter 16 provide any guidance? The ability-to-pay approach suggests that two families (with the same number of children) with the same income ought to pay the same taxes. Since the costs of two individuals living together are much lower than twice the costs of two individuals living singly, the ability-to-pay approach would suggest that whenever two individuals cohabit, they should be subjected to higher taxation than if they live singly. Unfortunately, the tax authorities cannot easily monitor cohabitation; so long as the vast majority of cohabitors are married, marriage is a good surrogate. Thus, provided the distortionary effects of the marriage tax are not too large (and there is little evidence to suggest that many individuals' decisions are strongly affected), the present tax structure may not be unreasonable.

The utilitarian view attempts to ascertain how the family circumstances in which individuals find themselves affect their marginal utility of income.

In both the utilitarian and ability-to-pay approaches, one might want to distinguish between the family with two workers and that with one worker. Assume the families have the same total income. The current tax system treats the two alike. Yet the family with both individuals working has to purchase many services that the nonworking spouse provides free. Both those who believe in ability to pay and in utilitarianism might well argue that the family with two working individuals should pay a lower tax than the family with one worker.

These problems are exacerbated by the presence of children. The tax credit for child care is designed to reduce the inequities and inefficiencies that arise when both individuals work and someone must be hired to take care of the children.

Present tax law allows a credit on up to $2,400 of child care expenses if there is one child, or $4,800 if there are two or more children, for households in which both parents work. If a woman with a child goes to work and has to pay someone to take care of her child, her *net* income, measuring her ability to pay, is just the difference between what she receives and what she must pay out. If she receives $15,000 and must pay out $5,000 in child care expenses, her net income is only $10,000. Not allowing the deduction of these expenses creates strong distortions. Assume the woman is married, and as a result of her husband's income is in the 50 percent bracket. If she makes $15,000, her after-tax income is $7,500. If she pays $5,000 for child care, her total increase in spending income (after taxes) is only $2,500. Not only is she thereby discouraged from undertaking the job, it seems a grossly unfair reward for working. Allowing a credit of $800 goes only a little way toward fully alleviating the distortions or correcting the inequities.

The problems—both the inequities and the distortions—arise from the inability to measure (and therefore to tax) the household services provided within the family. Here, the failure to tax the "imputed" services of wives (spouses) discriminates in favor of wives providing household services and against the purchase of those services in the market.

In designing the child care tax credit, the government was apparently more concerned about equity considerations than about efficiency. A deduction for child care expenses would have benefited upper-income individuals more than lower income individuals. But the distortion—in deciding whether to enter the labor force or not—is higher among individuals who face higher tax brackets; the present tax system leaves a significant distortion for families in tax brackets exceeding 20 percent.

Income Shifting

Although our tax structure fundamentally rests on the family unit, we have not gone all the way: children's income is not added to that of their parents (although in the 1984 Treasury Tax Reform Study it was proposed that income of all children under fourteen be added to their parents'). This opens up a major loophole for those with capital and business income. They can transfer income to their children, who are taxed at lower marginal rates.

Consider Horatio A., who, after poor beginnings, is now making $1 million (including return on capital) a year. He has a wife and two children. He pays $482,002 in taxes. He now goes to a good tax lawyer, who advises him to shift some of his income to his children (by shifting some of his assets, which he was planning to do anyway). He shifts enough so that each of his children now have a modest $109,400 in income. By doing this, he is able to reduce total family tax liability by $32,000—less than 10 percent of his total taxes, but certainly enough to pay his tax lawyer's fees.[11]

The Advantages of a Flat-Rate Tax Schedule

There is one—and only one—way of avoiding all the inequities surrounding the choice of unit of taxation. That is to impose a *flat-rate tax schedule*. If all individuals pay a proportional tax on income in excess of a basic exemption level (and those with an income below this exemption level receive a "credit" from the government), there is no incentive for income shifting; there is no penalty and no reward for marriage.

EFFECTIVE TAX RATES: A CLOSER LOOK

The net impact of the variety of special provisions we have discussed in this chapter is that effective tax rates (the ratio of tax payments to income) are much less than those legislated, and the degree of progressivity is less. Table 20.4 shows how the average nominal tax rate of 30.1 percent (assuming married individuals had to file separate returns) became an effective tax rate of 11.5 percent. The two most important reductions are from deductions (7.6 percentage points) and income splitting (3.6 percentage points). Of the deductions, the two most important are interest and local and state taxes. Together, they comprise almost three-fourths of all deductions. In Figure 20.2 we show how the actual (effective) tax rates for different income classes differ from the nominal rates. Those with incomes in excess of $1 million benefit particularly from the special provisions for the taxation of capital, so much so that their effective tax rate is no higher than someone in the $50,000–$200,000 category.

It is important to realize, however, that though the average (or effective) tax rate may be much lower than the nominal rate, the **marginal rate** may not be that much different (and in some cases may be higher). To see how this could happen, consider an individual who earns $25,999, has two chil-

Table 20.4 INFLUENCE OF VARIOUS PROVISIONS IN EFFECTIVE RATES OF FEDERAL INDIVIDUAL INCOME TAX, 1985

Nominal tax rate		30.1
Less Personal exemptions	3.3	
Transfer payments	2.1	
Income splitting	3.6	
Tax preferences for capital (capital gains, IRA, Keogh, etc.)	1.5	
Deductions	7.6	
Credits	.5	
Actual Tax Rate		11.5

Source: J. Pechman, *Federal Tax Policies* (Washington, D.C.: Brookings Institution, 1983), p. 361.

---

[11] In Chapter 24 we shall show how, had he gotten a somewhat better tax lawyer, he could have reduced his tax liabilities even further. He could, for instance, have set up a series of trust funds for his two children. A trust fund holds money, for the benefit of a particular individual (or group of individuals). It is a legal entity and is treated as a separate taxpayer, though subject to rates that are even higher than those for a single individual. By setting up these trusts, he may have been able to avoid more than $100,000 additionally in taxes.

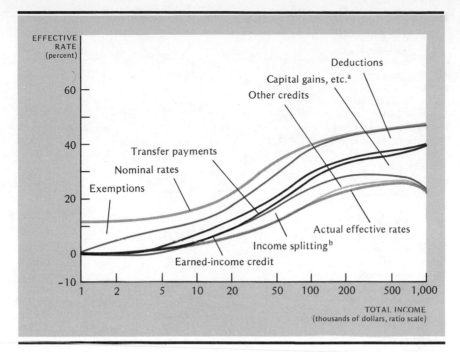

20.2 INFLUENCES OF VARIOUS PROVISIONS ON EFFECTIVE RATES OF FEDERAL INDIVIDUAL INCOME TAX, 1985 Special provisions of the U.S. income tax reduce the degree of progressivity of the income tax. SOURCE: J. A. Pechman, *Federal Tax Policy* (New York: McGraw-Hill, 1983).

dren, and pays $4,800 in child care expenses, $1,000 in interest payments, $500 in drug expenses, and $4,000 in other medical expenses. When his income rises by $2,001, the amount he is allowed to deduct for medicine is reduced and his child care allowances are reduced. The net effect is that while with his taxable income (income after allowing for deductions, exemptions, etc.) of $18,058, he should be paying a marginal tax rate of 19 percent, his actual marginal tax rate is almost 25 percent (see Table 20.5). (This excludes state taxes and social security, which may make his marginal tax rate even higher.) The distortions in any tax system are associated with the marginal tax rates; we have evolved toward a system in which there are high marginal tax rates and low average tax rates. This has become a major cause of concern, one that we discuss further in Chapter 25.

SUMMARY

1. The United States income tax system is based on the principle that taxes should be related progressively to the family's cash (marketed) annual income. The tax code discriminates in favor of nonmarket transactions; against single individuals; and against those with fluctuating income.

2. A principal difficulty encountered in defining income is distinguishing activities that are motivated by business considerations from ordinary consumption activities.

Table 20.5 TAX LAWS MAKE AVERAGE TAX RATES LOW, WHILE MARGINAL TAX RATES ARE HIGH

Calculation of Taxes		Initially		After $2,001 Pay Raise
Adjusted gross income		25,999		28,000
Drugs	500		500	
less 1% of adjusted gross income	259		280	
Equals deduction for drugs		241		220
Other medical expenses	4,000		4,000	
less 5% of adjusted gross income	1,300		1,400	
Equals deduction for medical expenses		2,700		2,600
Interest		1,000		1,000
Total deduction		3,941		3,820
Less exemptions		4,000		4,000
Taxable income		18,058		20,180
Tax		2,240		2,639
Child care tax credit				
22 percent of $4,800		1,056		
20 percent of $4,800				960
Net tax liability		1,184		1,679
Average tax rate		4.6%		6%
Change in tax liability				$495
Ratio of change in tax liability to change in income				24.7%
Legislated Marginal Tax Rate				19.0%

3. The tax code makes a number of adjustments to income, motivated both by equity and by incentive considerations. But regardless of their motivations, the deductions have both incentive and equity effects that need to be taken into account. For instance, the medical deduction effectively lowers the price of medical care; and it lowers it more for high-income individuals.

4. The tax system makes a number of adjustments that are intended to ensure that those in different family situations face equitable taxes. There is a limited tax credit for child care expenses and a limited deduction for earnings of the spouse with the lower income. Still, the current system imposes a marriage penalty on individuals with similar incomes and a marriage subsidy on individuals with very dissimilar incomes.

5. Many of the problems associated with the tax system arise from the unobservability (or the costs of observing) the essential variables.

6. One of the consequences of the special provisions is that while we have low average tax rates (ratio of taxes paid to income), we have high effective marginal tax rates.

KEY CONCEPTS

Adjusted gross income	Cash basis	Marriage tax
Standard deduction	Effective tax rate	Child care allowance
Tax credits	Capital gains	Income shifting
Haig-Simons income concept	Realization versus accrual	Marginal tax rate
		Minimum tax

1. For each of the provisions of the tax code listed below, which provides the best explanation: incentives; horizontal equity; vertical equity; administrative reasons; or special-interest groups?
   a) Deductibility of interest
   b) Deductibility of casualty losses
   c) Deductibility of medical expenses
   d) Deductibility of charitable contributions
   e) Child care tax credit
   f) IRA accounts
   g) Credit on taxes paid to foreign governments

2. Discuss the arguments for and against using a tax credit rather than a deduction for: medical expenses; charitable contributions; and child care expenses.

3. If you were asked to write the regulations concerning the deductibility of business expenses, how would you treat the following items, and why? Discuss the inequities and inefficiencies associated with alternative possible rules:
   a) Educational expenses required to maintain one's current job
   b) Educational expenses incurred to obtain a better job
   c) Moving expenses arising from a reassignment by one's present employer
   d) Moving expenses incurred in obtaining a new job
   e) Business suit worn by an individual who does not wear suits except for business
   f) Business lunches costing more than $25
   g) Cars costing more than $16,000
   h) Commuting costs
   i) Car expenses of a traveling salesman
   j) Subsidized cafeteria lunches

4. Money that scientists receive from winning the Nobel Prize (or similar prizes) is not taxable. On the other hand, money received by lottery winners (as well as gambling receipts) is taxable. Can you justify this difference in treatment? While the receipts from gambling are taxable, losses are not deductible. Is this fair? What distortions does this introduce?

5. Do you think that the current tax treatment of children is fair? (There is a $1,000 exemption for each child. Thus individuals in higher tax brackets have their taxes reduced more by having an additional child than do individuals in lower tax brackets.) Should the exemptions be related to the cost of rearing a child, which will depend on the income of the parent? Does your answer depend on whether you think the appropriate basis of taxation is ability to pay? On whether you are a utilitarian? On whether you think that the current population of the United States is too small? Too large?

6. Discuss the efficiency and equity consequences of:
   a) not allowing the deduction of expenses on summer vacation homes for the ten months a year when the owner puts the house up for rent. Is this a "legitimate" business?
   b) not allowing the deduction of commuting expenses
   c) not allowing the deduction of certain educational expenses
      In each case, consider what would happen if the current rules were modified. Can you suggest modifications that would make the rules seem "fairer" or more efficient?

21

The Corporation Income Tax

Early in 1983, in an offhand remark, President Reagan suggested that we should abolish our corporation income tax. The remark caused quite a stir: it was widely interpreted to reflect his probusiness orientation, to further shift the burden of taxation away from the well off and onto the poor. What was not widely recognized at the time was that, two years earlier, the tax had been almost abolished: the special provisions that were written into the 1981 tax bill concerning depreciation meant that the revenue derived from the corporate tax was rapidly dwindling. While in 1952 a third of federal revenue came from the corporation income tax, and in 1980 12½ percent, by 1983 it was down to just over 6 percent. (By 1984, it had recovered slightly to 8.5 percent.) During the same period, the percentage of business income originating in the corporate sector increased from approximately 60 percent to 75 percent.

Though President Reagan's 1985 tax proposals included provisions that would increase the effective rate of taxation on corporations, this was motivated more by political considerations than by a change in his basic position concerning the undesirability of the corporation tax. To get the reforms in the individual income tax that he thought were so important accepted, tax rates had to come down. Revenues from other sources had to be increased. The corporation tax was the obvious target, particularly since the 1981 Act had introduced some important distortions in how investment was allocated. The elimination of these distortions would enable the government to lower corporation tax rates and increase revenues raised.

We shall see in this chapter how a tax that raises little revenue can still cause large distortions and inequities.

The corporate income tax is imposed on the profits of an *incorporated* business. The essential difference between incorporated businesses and unincorporated businesses is the liability of investors. Corporations have limited liability; that is, investors in corporations can lose only the amount of money they have paid to the firm. (In contrast, if an unincorporated business has debts it cannot pay, the creditors can attempt to recover their losses from the owners.) Because of the protection provided by limited liability to investors, almost all large firms in the United States are incorporated.

The corporation income tax is imposed on the net income of the corporation. The net income is defined as revenues net of costs: wages and other inputs, interest payments, and *depreciation allowances*.[1] Depreciation allowances are adjustments to income to reflect the fact that the value of the firm's plant and equipment decreases as they are used and age. As with the individual income tax, there is a progressive rate structure, with a tax rate of 15 percent on incomes below $25,000. The rate is 46 percent for incomes in excess of $100,000 (see Table 21.1). Because most production in the United States occurs in large firms paying the maximum rate, for the rest of the discussion we shall focus on these firms.

As with the individual income tax, after the tax liability is calculated, firms' taxes are reduced by tax credits. The most important tax credit is for new investment. The investment tax credit is 6 percent of short-lived machines and 10 percent of long-lived machines. Short-lived machines are machines that are eligible to be depreciated over a three-year period and include automobiles and home computers. The tax law specifies which kinds of investment are subject to which rates.

Table 21.1   CORPORATE TAX RATES

First $25,000	15%
25,000–50,000	18
50,000–75,000	30
50,000–	40
100,000	46
over 100,000	

JUSTIFICATION FOR THE CORPORATION INCOME TAX

The rationale for the corporation income tax has never been completely clear. Some believe that corporations, like individuals, ought to pay taxes. But most economists find this argument unpersuasive; it is not the corporation that pays the tax, but people: those who work for the corporation, those who supply capital to it, and those who buy the goods produced by it. The tax can be viewed as a tax on the corporate form of organization (on limited

[1] There are several other detailed provisions that we shall ignore in our discussion: dividends received are taxed at only 15 percent; capital gains are subject to special treatment. If a firm is "closely held" (most of the shares are owned by a few individuals and their relatives), it is subject to special rules concerning the distribution of earnings. Other important tax credits include a 25 percent credit for incremental expenditures on research and development; firms that have paid taxes abroad receive some credit for these foreign taxes (as do individuals).

liability): is there any reason that the government should wish to discourage this form of organization, or to penalize those who derive income from this form of organization?[2] Most economists cannot see any strong argument for differential treatment. Indeed, while politicians often justify it in terms of its progressive effects, it is even possible that it has no significant redistributive effect. This is hard to determine because of the difficulties of ascertaining who really bears the corporate tax burden, as we noted in Chapter 17.

There are perhaps two main arguments in favor of the corporate income tax. In the first, the corporation tax is viewed as a withholding tax on those who receive capital income from the corporation (like the withholding tax that is imposed on wage earners). Without such a tax, it is feared that many wealthy individuals might escape taxation. But there are two criticisms of this view. First, if it were viewed as a withholding tax, the eventual beneficiaries of corporate income should be credited with having paid taxes on this income; though there have been proposals to do that, at present it is not done. Secondly, there is no persuasive reason that interest payments should be exempt from the withholding tax but dividend payments not be exempt.

The second argument in favor of the tax is political: politicians like it precisely because it is not clear who pays the tax. Under the present provisions, for instance, while there is widespread belief that corporations are paying 46 percent of their income to the government and thus contributing a fair share, corporations are not too unhappy about the tax, because they know that it is not costing them very much. The politician can curry the popular favor without antagonizing the businessman. But most economists would argue that the difficulties in ascertaining who bears the burden of the tax is actually an argument against the tax.[3] The corporation income tax does not do well on the criterion of "political responsiveness" that we presented in Chapter 16.

THE INCIDENCE OF THE CORPORATION INCOME TAX AND ITS EFFECTS ON ECONOMIC EFFICIENCY

The first problem in ascertaining who bears the burden of the tax is to determine what the tax is a tax on. Is it a tax on the return of capital in the corporate sector? Is it a tax on profits and rents in the corporate sector? (Profits and rents are what is left over after subtracting wages and return to capital from the firm's revenues.) And if it is a tax on profits and rents, what gives rise to those profits and rents?

Taxing Pure Profits of the Corporate Sector

Assume, for instance, that the government allowed firms to deduct all of their investment expenditures in the year in which they occurred but did not allow any deduction for interest payments. All of the inputs in produc-

---

[2]The special provisions of the tax code may, in fact, result in favorable treatment for the corporate form of organization. The question remains the same: is there any reason that the government wishes to encourage this form of organization, or to reward those who derive income from this form of organization?

[3]A third argument is that one might like to tax income to capital more heavily than wage income. One cannot easily differentiate wage and capital income in the unincorporated sector. One can in the corporate sector. But this view is not consistent with the deductibility of interest payments from the corporation income tax. (Besides, it is not clear that the return to capital should be taxed at all, let alone more heavily than wage income.)

tion would then be tax-deductible. The tax would then be a pure profits tax.
A pure profits tax is not distortionary. It does not affect the supply or the demand curve. It does not affect the equilibrium output or price. All that happens is a fraction of the profits go to the government rather than to the shareholders.

To see that such a tax would be nondistortionary, consider the investment decision of the firm in the absence of taxation. It would compare the returns to the investment with the costs; if the returns exceed the costs, it would undertake the project.[4] Now, assume that a 50 percent tax is imposed; the return is reduced by 50 percent. But since the total investment is tax-deductible, the effective cost to the firm is reduced by 50 percent. Any project that was desirable before is still desirable; any project that was not before is still not.

But the United States corporation income tax is not a pure profits tax. Firms cannot deduct the entire value of their investment in the year in which this occurs, and they can deduct interest payments.

Taxing Income from Capital in the Corporate Sector

Let us now consider another hypothetical tax, a tax on the income to capital in the corporate sector. Such a tax would not allow deductibility of interest and would have depreciation allowances that corresponded to the true decrease in the market value of the plant and equipment. The United States corporation income tax is not a *pure* tax on income from capital. But most of the economics literature has focused on this case, and it is necessary to understand it before considering our impure system.

In discussing tax incidence, we pointed out that a tax could be shifted forward (onto consumers) or backward (onto workers). Even if the tax is not shifted onto consumers or workers, it will not be borne solely by owners of firms in the corporate sector if it can have its effects spread to owners of capital everywhere. Our earlier discussion identified three critical determinants of the incidence of any tax: a) the elasticity of demand; b) the elasticity of supply; and c) whether the market was competitive or not. Because long-run elasticities of supply might be much larger than short-run elasticities, the incidence of a tax in the long run might be markedly different from the short-run incidence.

In the short run, the supply of capital to the corporate sector is relatively fixed. The tax on income from capital in the corporate sector should in the very short run thus be borne by capital.[5] But the capital of the sector is not fixed for long: every year a significant fraction of it wears out and has to be replaced. If the return to this capital is below the return yielded elsewhere, firms will not invest. Capital will flow out of the sector.

---

[4]More formally, the firm would calculate the present discounted value of the marginal returns from an increase in investment. See Chapter 10 for a discussion of the concept of present discounted value.

[5]This would be true both in perfectly competitive markets and in markets with a single monopolist. In oligopolies (markets in which there is more than one firm but not a large number of firms) the increase in taxes may serve as the basis of a coordinated price increase, shifting the burden onto consumers. Even in fairly competitive markets, however, the short-run response may entail some price increase; firms frequently set prices by certain rules of thumb, which entail a given mark-up over variable costs. The long-run equilibrium in these industries has the mark-up adjust to the competitive level. In the short run, the market may be out of equilibrium.

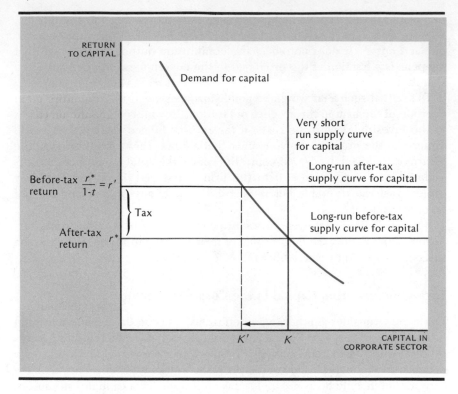

21.1 THE LONG-RUN SUPPLY SCHEDULE OF CAPITAL If the long-run supply of capital is very elastic, the after-tax return to capital is unaffected by the tax. In the short run, the tax will be borne by capital.

Infinite Elasticity Long-Run Supply Responses. One hypothesis is that, at least at present, the long-run supply schedule of capital to the corporate sector is close to horizontal, as shown in Figure 21.1. There are two reasons for this. The first is that today there is a well-functioning international capital market; rates of return in the United States are closely linked to those in Europe, Japan, and other countries. A small country like Switzerland faces a horizontal supply schedule for capital. The amount that it borrows or lends has virtually no effect on the rate of interest prevailing in the international market. Investment in the corporate sector in the United States is obviously larger than that of Switzerland; but corporate bonds and equity still represent less than 10 percent of the assets of individuals in the United States. Thus the hypothesis that the interest rate is not changed significantly by a change in investment in the corporate sector is not implausible.

Alternatively, some economists have suggested that even in a closed economy (an economy in which there are no flows of capital, either into it from abroad or out of it), the long-run supply curve is close to horizontal, because the long-run response of savings to the return to capital is very elastic.[6]

[6]This is implicit in many of the formal models economists have employed, where, for instance, savings are determined by individuals maximizing the discounted sum of their utility (over an indefinite future) with a constant discount rate. For a discussion of the use of these models, see R. Hall, "Consumption Taxes versus Income Taxes: Implications for Economic Growth," *Proceedings of the 61st National Tax Conference*, National

If there is a horizontal long-run supply schedule of capital, the effect of the tax is to raise the before-tax rate of return so that the after-tax return is unchanged (Figure 21.1). Thus, if before the tax the rate of return on capital was r^*, the tax raises the rate of return to r', where $r'(1-t) = r^*$, or $r' = r^*/(1-t)$.

If a tax on capital income were imposed uniformly over the entire economy, the consequences of this would be simple: the amount of capital employed in the economy would decrease from K to K'. Since the amount of capital would be reduced, the income per capita would be smaller.

We are discussing here, however, a tax that is imposed on only part of the economy, on capital income in the incorporated sector. This tax has two effects: it discourages the use of capital in the corporate sector, and because it increases the cost of capital in the corporate sector relative to the unincorporated sector, it discourages production in the corporate sector relative to the unincorporated sector.

In the long run, with an elastic supply of capital, a tax on capital income in the corporate sector is not borne by capital; it is borne by consumers of the goods produced by the corporate sector.[7]

The Effects of the Tax in the "Intermediate Run." There is a peculiar case between the short run and the long run upon which economists have focused considerable attention. This is a situation in which the aggregate supply of capital is fixed, but capital can shift between sectors.[8] In that case, the supply schedule of capital to the corporate sector is not horizontal. Then, the magnitude of shifting depends on the elasticity of the demand and supply for corporate capital. These are both *derived* functions—that is, the demand for capital in the corporate sector is equal to the demand for capital per unit output times the demand for the output of the corporate sector. As the interest rate rises, less capital is used for each unit of output. Moreover, the price of the output increases, since the marginal cost of production increases when the cost of any input increases, and this reduces the demand for the product. Thus an increase in the cost of capital to the corporate sector reduces the demand for capital on both accounts. The demand for capital will be elastic if the elasticity of demand for output is large (so that the demand decreases a great deal from a small increase in price) and if a slight increase in the cost of capital relative to the wage induces firms to substitute a lot of labor for capital (so we say that the elasticity of substitution is large). The elasticity of the supply of capital to the corporate sector depends on the elasticity of substitution in the unincorporated sector and the elasticity of demand in that sector.

Tax Association, Columbus, Ohio, and R. Barro, "Are Bonds Wealth?" *Journal of Political Economy* 82 (1974): 1095–1117.

[7]Workers and owners of capital are both worse off, to the extent that they consume the products of the corporate sector.

[8]We call this case peculiar because the time involved for shifting capital between sectors is, with a few exceptions, the same as the time involved for the investment decision—i.e. the time for a change in the aggregate supply of capital. Some kinds of machines (cars) and some structures are readily shiftable, but most shifting of capital occurs by firms not deciding to reinvest their capital in the corporate sector, in response to lowered returns.

This model was first investigated in detail by Chicago economist Arnold Harberger and is often referred to as the "Harberger" model. See A. C. Harberger, "The Incidence of the Corporation Income Tax," *Journal of Political Economy* 70 (1962): 215–40.

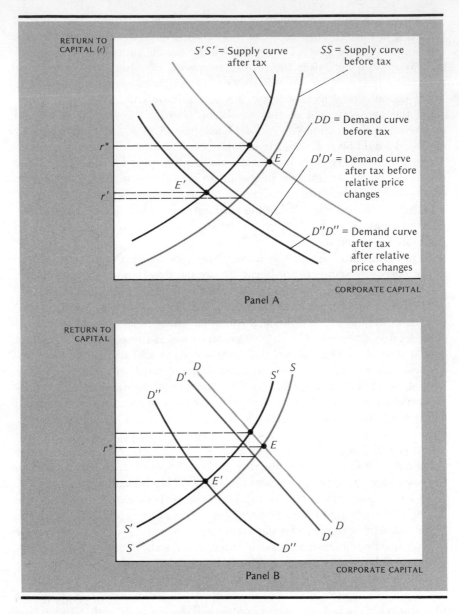

21.2 SHIFTING OF THE CORPORATE INCOME TAX IN INTERMEDIATE CASE The decrease in after-tax return may exceed the tax.

The effects of the tax can be divided into two stages, as we see in Figure 21.2. First, at fixed relative prices, the tax shifts the demand curve for capital down, from DD to $D'D'$. (The market rate of interest is r. To pay investors an after-tax return of r, the investment must yield a before-tax return greater than r; there will thus be less demand for capital.) Secondly, as prices adjust to reflect the changed costs of production, there is a shift of demand toward the unincorporated sector; thus the demand curve shifts from $D'D'$ to $D''D''$

and the supply curve shifts from SS to S'S'. If the corporate sector is relatively capital-intensive (that is, the ratio of capital to labor exceeds that in the unincorporated sector), the net effect of this is to decrease the demand for, and hence the return to, capital. Thus it is possible for the after-tax return to decrease by more than the tax, as in Panel B. This may happen with reasonable values of the parameters (plausible values for the capital labor ratios in both sections, demand elasticities, etc.)

Since the before-tax rate of interest falls, some of the burden of the tax is shifted onto capital owners as a whole. If the after-tax cost of capital has increased, some part of the tax is shifted onto consumers.

Distortions with a Capital Tax. In our discussion attempting to ascertain the incidence of a tax on capital in the corporate sector, we have identified two distortions associated with the tax. First, there is a production distortion. Production efficiency requires that the marginal rate of substitution between any two factors be the same in all uses.[9] Cost-minimizing firms will equate the marginal rate of substitution with the relative factor prices. To see this, we have depicted isocost curves in Figure 21.3A, giving those combinations of capital and labor that cost the firm the same amount. The slope of the isocost curve is the ratio of the cost of capital to the cost of labor; that is, if one worker costs $20,000 a year, and a machine cost $40,000 a year to rent, the firm can decrease its purchases of machines by one and increase its hiring of labor by two and have total costs remain unchanged. Figure 21.3A also shows the isoquant curve, which gives the amounts of labor and capital needed to produce the desired quantity of output. The cost-minimizing firm wishes to get to the lowest isocost curve possible, consistent with producing its given output; this is the tangency between the isocost curve and the isoquant. Since the slope of the isoquant is the marginal rate of substitution, cost minimization entails setting the marginal rate of substitution equal to the *after-tax* relative factor prices. If all firms have the same relative factor prices, all will have the same marginal rate of substitution, and the economy will be productively efficient.

By the same token, if the relative factor prices in the corporate sector differ from those in the unincorporated sector, their marginal rates of substitution will differ, and the economy will not be operating on the production possibility schedule. Only in the extreme case, where firms cannot substitute capital for labor (Figure 21.3B) will there be no production distortion.

The second distortion has to do with the level of output of goods in the corporate sector: if there were no production distortion (because the elasticity of substitution between capital and labor was zero) then the tax is equivalent to an excise tax on the output of the corporate sector; in Chapter 19 we showed why such a tax was inefficient, and indeed, related the magnitude of the *excess burden* to the elasticity of demand and supply.

---

[9] Recall the definition of the marginal rate of substitution: it is the amount by which capital may be reduced, if we increase labor input by a unit, to keep output constant. Assume that the marginal rate of substitution of capital for labor in the corporate sector were 3 and in the noncorporate sector, 1. If we shifted one unit of labor from the noncorporate sector to the corporate sector, we could keep output the same in the corporate sector if we reduced the capital input by 3 units. To keep output in the noncorporate sector unchanged, we need to transfer one of these units to that sector. We still have 2 units of capital left over, which we can use to increase output in both sectors.

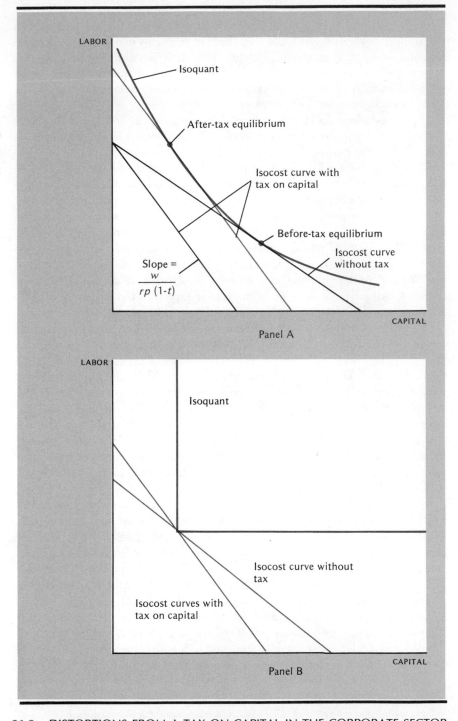

LABOR

Isoquant

After-tax equilibrium

Isocost curve with
tax on capital

Before-tax equilibrium

Isocost curve
without tax

Slope =
$\dfrac{w}{rp\,(1\text{-}t)}$

CAPITAL

Panel A

LABOR

Isoquant

Isocost curve without
tax

Isocost curves with
tax on capital

CAPITAL

Panel B

21.3   DISTORTIONS FROM A TAX ON CAPITAL IN THE CORPORATE SECTOR
(A) Capital and labor are substitutes. Tax on capital induces firms to substitute labor for capital.
(B) Isoquant when capital and labor are required in fixed proportion. In this case a tax on capital
in the corporate sector induces no production inefficiencies.

In our discussion in Chapter 17, we showed how with monopoly, the price may rise by more or less than the increase in the marginal cost of production; it depended not only on the shape of the marginal cost schedule but on the shape of the demand schedule. With constant elasticity demand curves and horizontal marginal cost schedules, prices increased by more than the tax.

On the other hand, when there are monopolies, there are monopoly profits. A corporate income tax can then be viewed as a tax on the return to capital in the corporate sector plus a tax on pure (monopoly) profits. (With competition, and with constant returns to scale, there are no pure profits.) That part of the tax corresponding to a tax on monopoly profits has no distortion.

Whether the distortionary effects of the corporation income tax would be greater (per dollar raised) with monopoly or competition is ambiguous. On the one hand, to the extent that the tax is partly a pure profits tax, it is nondistortionary; on the other hand, to the extent that it acts as an excise tax, and production of the sector is already lower than the socially optimal level, it causes a greater distortion.[10]

The Corporation Income Tax as a Tax on Entrepreneurship

In the preceding analysis we assumed that the corporation income tax was a tax on the return to capital (and on pure profits, if they exist) in the corporate sector. This would be true if the depreciation allowances were correct (which they are not), if there were no investment tax credit (but there is), and if there were no deduction for interest paid (but there is). These provisions have an enormous effect on the impact of the tax; they are not just minor wrinkles in the tax code. To see their implications, let us continue with our assumptions that there is no investment tax credit and that depreciation allowances correctly reflect the decrease in the value of aging plant and equipment. What happens if (as in our tax code) interest payments are tax-deductible? A firm that raised all of its capital by borrowing would find that it faced little tax. The returns to capital would be distributed to the bond holder and thus not be subjected to the corporation tax. Since debt is treated preferentially to equity, the financial structure of the firm will be "biased" toward debt. Since firms always have the option of financing an additional unit of investment at the margin by borrowing, and since the corporation tax is not levied on the return to bond holders, the corporation tax may have little effect, at the margin, on the investment decisions of the firm.

In deciding how much to invest, the firm wishes to know what the extra—i.e., marginal—return to the firm will be. What the firm is concerned with is the after-tax returns. It takes into account the extra taxes it pays, as a result of its extra income; but it also takes into account the reduction in its tax

---

[10] We noted earlier that the deadweight loss increases with the square of the tax. The effect of a monopoly is similar to that of a tax. Indeed, if the elasticity of demand is, say, 2, the effect is analogous to a 50 percent tax being imposed on a competitive industry. Imposing a 10 percent tax on the output of the monopoly has the incremental deadweight loss associated with increasing the tax on a competitive industry from 50 percent to 60 percent (which is an order of magnitude larger than the incremental deadweight loss from increasing the tax from 0 percent to 10 percent.)

liabilities, as a result of the additional depreciation allowances, or the tax-deductibility of interest payments. If the firm borrows funds, in the absence of tax, the marginal cost of capital is simply the interest rate it has to pay on an additional loan to finance the additional investment. If the interest is tax-deductible, the after-tax marginal cost is $r(1-t)$, where r is the rate of interest and t is the tax rate. If the interest rate is 10 percent and the tax rate is 50 percent, the after-tax cost is only 5 percent.

The firm's returns are reduced by $1-t$, but so is the cost of acquiring capital: hence if the net return was positive before the imposition of the tax, it still is; if the net return was negative, it still is. Investment decisions are unaffected.

This assumes that the firm had the option of financing its *marginal* investment project by borrowing; in other words, the firm, at the margin, asks itself, Is it worth borrowing a little bit more to invest a little bit more?[11]

If the tax is not a tax on the return to capital, at least at the margin, what is it a tax on? Capital is provided to firms in two forms: in the form of debt, in which the supplier of capital is guaranteed a given return, provided that the firm does not go bankrupt (in which case he gets whatever is left), or in the form of equity. Those who invest in equity (buy shares) do not get any guaranteed return, but if the firm does well, they share in the profits and capital gains.

Newly established firms sell shares to raise capital; it is often the only source of capital they can obtain—banks find long-term loans too risky, and these firms are too small to issue long-term bonds. The original entrepreneur usually takes his return largely in the form of stock ownership (rather than wage payments). Thus *the corporation income tax, which exempts interest payments, can be viewed effectively as a tax on entrepreneurship; it has an effect on the investment of new firms that cannot raise funds by borrowing additional amounts.*

If this view is correct, the long-run effects of the tax are not so much those associated with the intersectoral allocation of resources; rather they have to do with the degree of innovativeness of the corporate sector, the rate of technical progress. And the magnitude of the effects depends on the elasticity of supply of entrepreneurship and risk taking, something about which economists have little knowledge.[12]

The Corporation Tax and Established Firms

The view that the corporation tax is nondistortionary for established firms is, however, somewhat controversial. Critics of this view argue that it ignores the fact that firms, at the margin, do finance a significant fraction of their

---

[11] Equivalently, a firm with outstanding debt that is not currently borrowing from the market but that is doing some investment can ask itself, Is it worth investing a little bit less, and using the extra funds to repay some of its outstanding debt obligations?

This view of the corporation income tax was put forward in J. E. Stiglitz, "Taxation, Corporate Financial Policy and the Cost of Capital," *Journal of Public Economics*, February 1973, pp. 1–34 and J. E. Stiglitz, "The Corporation Income Tax," *Journal of Public Economics*, April–May 1976, pp. 303–11.

[12] Some of the negative effects are mitigated by the specially favorable treatment of capital gains and depreciation, which we discuss below.

investment by means other than borrowing. As we have noted, the argument presented above does not actually require that the firm borrow; it only requires that the firm can change its level of indebtedness in response to an increase in investment. If the firm would otherwise have used some of its funds to retire some of its debt but chooses instead to increase its level of investment, the effects are precisely the same as those we have just described.

If a firm has the option of financing its marginal investment by borrowing but chooses not to do so, the after-tax cost of the alternative financial arrangements must be even less than that of debt; since taxes reduce the after-tax cost of borrowing by the same amount they reduce the after-tax return, this implies that taxes can only have a positive effect on investment.

For a variety of reasons, however, firms may not be able to borrow (or they may have to pay much higher interest rates to borrow additional funds). Then the cost of inside funds (funds inside the firm) and outside funds (funds raised by issuing new equities or bonds or borrowing from the bank) may be markedly different.[13] There may be many projects worth undertaking, at the marginal cost of inside funds but not at the marginal cost of outside funds. The corporation income tax reduces the supply of inside funds and thus has a direct effect in reducing investment.

Many empirical studies of the effects of the corporation income tax simply assume that it increases the marginal cost of capital to the firm—the amount it would cost the firm to invest an additional dollar—by an amount equal to the average tax payments per unit of capital. That is, they assume that the marginal and average costs of capital are the same. Regardless of whether one holds the view that the marginal cost of capital is equal to (or less than) the marginal cost of funds raised by borrowing, there is no justification for the hypothesis that marginal and average costs of capital are the same.

DEPRECIATION AND INVESTMENT TAX CREDITS

So far, we have assumed that the depreciation allowances accurately reflect the change in the market value of machines. In fact, the current depreciation system is excessively generous—that is, the government usually allows firms to deduct in the early years of the life of an asset more than its decline in value. This amounts to an effective subsidy on capital goods.

To see this, consider a simple example of a machine that lasts for two years, costs $210, yields a return of $110 both in the year in which it is installed and in the following year, and is then worthless. The interest rate is 10 percent. The present discounted value of the revenues from the machine before taxes is First-Year Income + Second-Year Income / Discount Factor =

$$110 + \frac{110}{1+r} = 110 + \frac{110}{1.1} = 210.$$

The machine is just worth investing in.

Now assume that a 50 percent tax is levied on income after depreciation. At the end of the first year, the machine is worth $110. (It will yield $110

---

[13] Recent theoretical explanations of this fact have focused on the role of imperfect information.

that year, after which it will be worthless. Hence, in a competitive market, the machine will sell for $110.) Thus the depreciation during the first year is $100, the net income is $10 ($110 − depreciation), and the tax due is $5. The second year the net income is zero; since the machine is worthless at the end of the year, the depreciation is equal to the return. There is no tax due. Because of the 50 percent tax on the return to capital, we have to discount at 5 percent, not 10 percent (5 percent is the after-tax interest rate.) The present discounted value of the machine is First-Year After-Tax Income + Second-Year After-Tax Income / After-Tax Discount Factor =

$$105 + \frac{110}{1 + r(1 - t)} = 105 + \frac{110}{1.05} = 210.^{14}$$

The machine is still just worth undertaking. This is a general result. With **true economic depreciation**—depreciation allowances that accurately reflect the change in the value of an asset—if investments are valued at the after-tax rate of interest, there is no distortion.[15] But now, if we allow more generous depreciation allowances ("accelerated depreciation"), the net return to the investment can become very positive: projects that were previously not profitable will be undertaken. Assume, for instance, that we allowed the entire investment to be depreciated in the first year. Then the present discounted value of the investment can be calculated as follows:

Income first year	$110
Depreciation allowance	210
Net income	−100

The firm receives a check from the government of $50 (its tax liability on other income is reduced by $50). The second year it has a large tax liability.

Income second year	$110
Depreciation allowances	0
Net income before taxes	110
Taxes	55
Net income after taxes	50

The present discounted value of the project is:

Income first year	110
Tax rebate	50
Net income after taxes second year	52.40
55 × 1 / 1.05	
Total	212.40

The distortion for short-lived assets (two years) is not large; but for longer-lived assets, there are very large distortions associated with our current system of depreciation allowances. These are exacerbated by the investment

---

[14] In these calculations, we have ignored the distinction of whether returns accrue at the beginning of the period or the end, and all our calculations are approximate. (Thus 110 / 1.05 = 104.76.) But the result—that, with true economic depreciation, the value of a machine will be unaffected—is general.

[15] This result was first noted by Paul Samuelson. See P. A. Samuelson, "Tax Deductibility of Economic Depreciation to Insure Invariant Valuations," *Journal of Political Economy* 72 (1964): 604–6.

tax credit. A 10 percent tax credit effectively reduces the cost of the machine by 10 percent. In the above example, a 10 percent tax credit would have reduced the cost of the machine from $210 to $189. The net return of the machine, which was initially just 0, is $23.40.

As a result of the investment tax credit and accelerated depreciation, it appears as if the current corporate income tax, at the margin, represents a subsidy to capital. Firms take advantage of this subsidy. These generous depreciation allowances also provide the explanation for the decline in revenues from the tax.

Depreciation Allowances since 1981

Prior to 1981, depreciation allowances were designed to reflect accurately the true decrease in the value of machines or buildings. An estimate of the life of the machine was made; if it was 10 years, the depreciation allowance was $\frac{1}{10}$ the value of the machine; if 5 years, the depreciation allowance was $\frac{1}{5}$ the value of the machine. This method of depreciation is called straight-line depreciation.[16] In 1981 this basic principle was abandoned. The depreciation rates now have little to do with the life of the asset. Assets are divided into three categories: 3-year property, 5-year property, and real estate. The fractions of the initial value of the asset that can be deducted in each year are set forth in Table 21.2.

Even the government realized that the net effect of the depreciation allowances plus the investment tax credit was overly generous, resulting in an effective rate of taxation on some categories of assets that was negative.

Table 21.2   DEPRECIATION ALLOWANCES (in percentages)

Year	3-Year Asset	5-Year Asset	Real Estate
1	25	15	10
2	38	22	9
3	37	21	8
4		21	7
5		21	6
6			0
7			5
8			5
9			5
10			5
11			5
12			5
13			4
14			4
15			4
16			4
17			4
18			4

---

[16]As always, the tax code is more complicated than any simple exposition allows. There are a few assets that can be depreciated over 10 years. There are special provisions relating to the depreciation of utilities and certain categories of structures. Also, since a 10-year machine typically does not lose $\frac{1}{10}$ of its value each year, even straight-line depreciation does not correspond exactly to "true" economic depreciation.

In 1982 the law was slightly modified, so that if a firm takes an investment tax credit, the total amount of depreciation allowances is reduced by half the amount of the tax credit. (The tax credit is 10 percent on 5-year assets, 6 percent on 3-year assets.) The tax law was changed again in 1984, so that real estate now has an 18-year lifetime instead of the 15-year lifetime under the 1981 law.

To see the net impact of the current tax system, consider an asset that lives for 5 years and costs $100 but that the government allows to be depreciated in 3 years. The asset is assumed to yield a constant amount each year ($24) and to have no salvage value rate after 5 years. The interest rate is assumed to be 10 percent. In the first column of Table 21.3 we show the

Table 21.3 COMPARISON OF TRUE ECONOMIC DEPRECIATION, STRAIGHT-LINE DEPRECIATION, AND DEPRECIATION UNDER THE CURRENT TAX LAW

Year	Discount Factor (10% interest rate)	1 True Economic Depreciation	2 Present Value	3 Straight Line	4 Present Value	5 Current System	6 Present Value
1	1	16	16	20	20	25	25
2	$1/(1.10) = .909$	18	16.36	20	18.18	38	34.54
3	$1/(1.10)^2 = .826$	20	16.52	20	16.52	37	30.56
4	$1/(1.10)^3 = .751$	22	16.52	20	15.02		
5	$1/(1.10)^4 = .683$	24	16.39	20	13.65		
			81.79		83.37		90.10

true economic depreciation rate, in the second the present discounted value of these depreciation allowances (as viewed at the time of purchase). The third and fourth columns show depreciation with straight line, and the fifth and sixth columns show depreciation under the current system. It is clear that there is a very large subsidy.

Far more disturbing, however, is the fact that the magnitude of the subsidy varies greatly from one asset to another. For some assets the current system is only slightly favorable; but for long-lived assets it provides a major subsidy. As a result, some industries, such as transportation and mining, actually face a negative effective tax rate (of 2.9 percent and 3.4 percent, respectively), while others faces a positive effective industry. The varied effective rates distort the pattern of investment, both within and across industries.

To achieve neutrality in the choice of investment projects, the government has two options. One we have already described: it could allow true economic depreciation allowances (or at least attempt to devise rules that more closely approximate true economic depreciation).

The second method entails the government allowing a 100 percent deduction for the cost of the investment. Then the government is reducing the costs of the project by exactly the same amount that it is reducing the benefits (the returns that the firm receives). The government is, in effect, entering as a silent partner into the enterprise. A project for which the present discounted value of returns exceeds the cost—which therefore would have been undertaken in the absence of the tax—will still be undertaken.

While the first method corresponds to a nondistortionary interest income tax, the second method corresponds to a nondistortionary pure profits tax: the difference between the present discounted value of the returns to an investment project and its costs can be thought of as pure profits.[17]

455 Estimates of the Shifting of the Corporation Income Tax

EMPIRICAL ESTIMATES OF THE SHIFTING OF THE CORPORATION INCOME TAX AND ITS DEADWEIGHT LOSS

There have been several attempts to estimate the extent of shifting of the corporation income tax.

Two-Sector Models. One set of studies assumes that the tax is a tax on the return to capital in the corporate sector; that the corporate sector is competitive (and has constant returns to scale); and that the total available supply of capital is fixed but that the capital can shift between sectors (what we identified as the "intermediate" run model above).

John Shoven of Stanford University has solved explicitly for the general equilibrium of the economy, comparing the present equilibrium with what it would have been in the absence of the distortionary corporate tax. Shoven found that the extent of shifting depends critically on assumptions one makes about how easy it is to substitute capital for labor in each of the two sectors, as well as the consumer demand elasticities. In Table 21.4 we present the results for a number of different cases.

Table 21.4   CAPITAL SHARE OF THE TAX BURDEN (in percentages)

Elasticity of Substitution		Consumer Demand Elasticities	
Corporate Sector	Unincorporated Sector	1.	.5
1	1	100	118
1	.25	128	162
.25	.25	33	52

Source: John Shoven, "The Incidence and Efficiency Effects of Taxes on Income from Capital," *Journal of Political Economy* 84 (1976): 1261–84.

In the table, the elasticity of substitution measures the ease with which capital can be substituted for labor. A high value implies that it is easy to substitute capital for labor. There is no agreement among economists about what is the best estimate of this parameter, so we have presented two alternative cases.

The share of the burden is measured by the change in the income of capital divided by the revenue. When the burden exceeds 100 percent, it implies that the income of capital is reduced by more than the tax. The corporate sector is relatively capital-intensive (that is, there is a lot more capital used for each worker than in the unincorporated sector). Hence a shift in demand toward the unincorporated sector indirectly reduces the demand for capital, and thus the returns to capital. The smaller the elasticity of substitution in

---

[17]It may, in fact, be a tax on entrepreneurship, not on pure profits, as we noted earlier.

the unincorporated sector, the greater the extent to which the return to capital must be lowered to absorb all the capital that is released as a result of the change in the composition of demand. This explains why we see in the table capital bearing 162 percent of the burden of the tax in the case where the elasticity of substitution in the unincorporated sector is very low and the demand elasticity is low.

Note that without knowing precisely the value of the demand elasticities and elasticities of substitution, we cannot even tell whether capital bears more or less than 100 percent of the burden. No wonder, then, that there is no agreement about whether the corporation tax is, effectively, a tax on capital or a tax on consumers!

Time-Series Analysis. A second set of empirical studies attempts to use time-series data (that is, data on profits, tax rates, capital, etc., extending over a large number of years) to make inferences about the extent of shifting of the tax. Over the past fifty years there have been numerous changes in the level of the corporate tax; and at the same time, there have been some changes in the after-tax rate of return on capital. Some of the changes in the after-tax rate of return on capital result from changes in the capital stock, some result from productivity changes (technological improvements), and some result from variations in aggregate demand over the business cycle. These studies attempted to ascertain how much of the change in the after-tax rate of return can be accounted for by the changes in the corporation tax rather than by these other variables.

The studies faced a critical problem: It is often difficult to distinguish the effects of these other variables from the effects of the changes in the tax rate. Both the tax rate and the level of capital stock have increased over the past fifty years. When two variables move together like this, it is often difficult to disentangle their effects. Moreover, some of the adjustments to changes in the tax rate may take several years, and by then the tax rate may have changed again. If the tax changes were not anticipated, the full effects may not show up until several years after the tax change occurred. On the other hand, if the tax change was anticipated, some of the effects will start to become apparent even before the tax change goes into effect. To identify accurately the effects of the tax change one has to know (or be able to ascertain from the data) the extent to which the tax change was anticipated. Given these difficulties, it is not surprising that the results of the studies are inconclusive.[18]

Differential Tax Treatment of Assets. The studies mentioned so far focused on the distortionary effects of the corporation income tax in shifting capital

---

[18] Musgrave and Krzyaniak, who did the first of the studies, found that there was more than 100 percent shifting (that is, an increase in tax liabilities by $1 per unit of capital raised before-tax profits by $1.35). Their study was criticized by Cragg, Harberger, and Mieszkowski, who found that the extent of shifting was much smaller (60 percent). Goode estimated that the extent of shifting varied significantly from industry to industry, being negative for some and close to 100 percent for others (rubber and chemical). His studies have been criticized for providing estimates that are biased toward zero and for employing a number of ad hoc assumptions. M. Krzyaniak and R. A. Musgrave, *The Shifting of the Corporation Income Tax* (Baltimore, MD: Johns Hopkins University Press, 1963). R. Goode, *The Individual Income Tax* (Washington, D.C.: Brookings Institution, 1964; 2nd ed., 1976). P. M. Mieszkowski, "Tax Incidence Theory: The Effects of Taxes on the Distribution of Income," *Journal of Economic Literature* 4 (1969): 1103–24. J. G. Cragg, A. C. Harberger, and P. Mieszkowski "Empirical Evidence on the Incidence of the Corporation Income Tax," *Journal of Political Economy* 75 (1967): 811–21.

457
Integration of
the Personal
Income Tax
and the Cor-
porate Tax

from one sector to another. We emphasized earlier, however, the importance of the distortions arising from the differential tax treatment of different
categories of assets. Alan Auerbach of the University of Pennsylvania has
estimated that the welfare losses from these within industry distortions are
five times as large (under the current tax law) as the distortions between
industries. (He estimates the total deadweight loss in 1981 to be approximately 10 percent of the revenue collected.)[19]

INTEGRATION OF THE PERSONAL INCOME TAX AND THE CORPORATE TAX

We have discussed the effects of the corporation income tax, ignoring the
consequences of the interaction between the corporation income tax and the
individual income tax. The interaction is important.

The standard view has been that the corporation tax represents double
taxation of the return to capital in the corporate sector. The return is first
taxed at the corporate level, and what remains is taxed again at the individual
level. Thus $1,000,000 earned in the corporate sector is first taxed at 46
percent; and if the remaining $640,000 is distributed as dividends to one
individual, and the individual is in the 50 percent marginal tax bracket, the
individual has only $320,000 after tax: he has paid an effective tax rate of 68
percent. Prior to 1981 a wealthy individual would have had to pay 70 percent
of his dividends as taxes, so he would have after taxes only $192,000, an
effective tax rate of 81.8 percent. This "double taxation" seems both inequitable and inefficient, discouraging investment in the corporate sector.

More recent studies have questioned this view. They have recognized that
corporations have certain advantages. After-tax income need not be distributed as dividends, it may be retained and invested; as a result, the value of
the firm increases, but the increases in firm value are taxed at the favorable
capital gains tax rates.[20] Moreover, firms can provide certain pension and
other fringe benefits, which also receive favorable tax treatment. While before
1981, when the maximum individual income tax rate was 70 percent, these
advantages probably outweighed the disadvantages, now the differences are
not so large.[21]

The Advantages of Retained Earnings

To see the advantages that retained earnings affords under our present tax
system, consider a firm that has $100,000 to distribute to shareholders. To
see the combined effects of the corporate and individual income taxes, it is
useful to think of a firm that is owned by a single shareholder. However, the

---

[19] A. J. Auerbach, "Corporation Taxation in the United States," *Brookings Papers on Economic Activity*, 2
(Washington, D.C.: Brookings Institution, 1983), pp. 451–513.

[20] Moreover, if the firm invests in shares in other firms, any dividends it receives from these other firms
are taxed at only 15 percent. There are restrictions on the extent to which closely held corporations can invest
in other firms without encountering special tax penalties.

[21] In 1984 the advantages of corporations were further reduced by restrictions imposed on the kinds of
fringe benefits they could provide to their employees.

For small corporations, which had to pay only a 15 percent tax rate, there were still distinct advantages
arising out of the ability to postpone taxes; these advantages have to be offset against stricter bookkeeping
requirements.

analysis can easily be extended to the more general case of firms owned by many shareholders. Assume the stockholder expects to live for just one more year and leave his entire wealth to his children. He wants to maximize what he can leave to his children after paying taxes. Assume the firm retained its earnings, using the proceeds to retire $100,000 of the firm's debt. If the interest rate is 10 percent, the firm's gross income next period will be increased by $10,000. The firm is assumed to be at the 50 percent tax bracket.[22] Thus its after-tax income is increased by $5,000 (since interest is tax-deductible). When the individual goes to sell his shares, his firm is worth $105,000 more than in the previous case (the $5,000 in net interest savings (after tax) plus the $100,000 from the smaller level of indebtedness). Under the current tax system he will, at most, pay a 20 percent capital gains tax, if he sells his shares before he dies, or nothing, if his estate sells his shares after his death. It is clear that he may strongly prefer his firm to retain its earnings.

The strategy of investing retained earnings may be preferable to that of distributing earnings and financing investments by borrowing, because he may be able to take advantage of the favorable treatment of capital gains (obtaining the returns from his investment in the form of an increase in the value of his shares, rather than as dividends).

Thus our tax system makes it advantageous for firms to finance much of their investment through retained earnings. Investments in excess of those that can be financed out of retained earnings should be financed by borrowing (because of the tax-deductibility of interest).

The Dividend Paradox

There is a further implication of the special treatment of capital gains. As much as possible, firms should distribute their returns to shareholders in the form of capital gains rather than dividends. If the firm announced that it was buying back 5 percent of the shares of each shareholder, what the individual receives from the company would be considered a capital gain (or return of the original investment) and thus would receive more favorable tax treatment than if the individual received the same amount as a dividend. But the economic consequences (other than the tax treatment) would be the same. An individual who owned 1 percent of the shares of the firm would still own 1 percent of the shares of the firm. The number of shares would have changed, but what is relevant for an individual's income is not the total number of shares he owns but his *proportion* of the shares (his "share" in the company).

Obviously, the magnitude of the tax savings depends on the tax bracket of the individual, though it is significant for all taxpayers (i.e., for all shareholders except tax-exempt institutions), since the tax on long-term capital gains is only 40 percent of the tax on dividends.

There are other methods by which a firm can effectively distribute its profits in the form of capital gains. Consider what would happen if you owned two companies, Company A and Company B. Assume Company A had a lot of cash on hand that it would like to distribute to you. It could issue a dividend, and you would have to pay ordinary income taxes on your receipt.

---

[22]Throughout the remainder of the chapter, to simplify the calculations we assume a 50 percent corporate tax rate rather than 46 percent.

Alternatively, you could ask Company A to buy Company B (since you own both companies, this purchase of one company by another has no consequences, other than for purposes of taxation). As part of the deal, Company A pays the owner of the shares of Company B a certain amount of money for his shares. The difference between what the Company B stockholder receives and what he originally paid for Company B is the only part of what he receives that is taxable, and then it is taxable only at capital gains rates, even though the cash goes to the owner just as in the first case. It is obvious that there are great tax advantages to this "paper" charade. It is easy to see through the charade when the same person owns both companies. But essentially the same principles apply when two different people own the companies. Some economists believe that this has provided one of the major motivations for mergers and takeovers in recent years.

Another example may help illustrate what is at issue. Consider M Publishing Company and D Software Company. M Publishing Company has $100,000 cash on hand and has $900,000 of plant and equipment. The publishing business is not doing well, and its owner does not want to invest further in it. He would like to distribute the $100,000 so that he can invest in a more dynamic industry, such as computer software. But he knows that if the funds are distributed as dividends, he will only get $50,000 after tax (since he is in the 50 percent tax bracket). Across the street is D Software Company. It was founded ten years ago by David D (with almost no investment other than his time) and is now worth $600,000. David D would like to cash in on his good fortune. Consider now what happens if M Publishing Company and D Software Company merge. The terms of the merger provide that David D gets a one-third ownership in the new company, M&D Enterprises (which is worth $1.5 million) and that David D gets a $100,000 cash payment. The IRS rules that the exchange of shares is not taxable but that the $100,000 cash payment to David D is subject to the capital gains tax. Since David D is in the 50 percent tax bracket, he pays $20,000 tax. (Capital gains are taxed at 40 percent of ordinary rates.) Total tax liabilities have been reduced by $30,000 by this method.

The Basic Principles

The fact that our tax code does not tax all transactions at the same rate has two basic implications for the relationship between corporations and individuals.

1. Avoid transferring income from the corporate to the household sector whenever possible.

2. When income must be transferred, do it in a form so that it is eligible for capital gains treatment.

In Figure 21.4 we have drawn a schematic picture of the relationship between the corporate and the household sector. Funds flow from the corporate sector to the household sector in the form of dividends, interest, and share repurchases. Funds flow from the household sector to the corporate sector in the form of new bonds and new equities. Funds flow within the household sector as individuals purchase shares and bonds from each other. And funds flow within the corporate sector as corporations purchase one

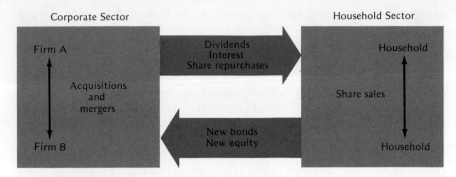

21.4 FLOW OF FUNDS BETWEEN AND WITHIN HOUSEHOLD AND CORPO-
RATE SECTORS Funds flow from the corporate sector to the household sector, from the
household sector to the corporate sector, and within each of the two sectors.

another and are merged. The tax authorities (for reasons that are not well
understood) impose a heavier set of taxes on one set of these transactions—
on dividends and interest—than on the others. Thus the kind of transaction
where a firm distributes dividends that are then reinvested is a particularly
foolish transaction: if the funds had remained in the corporate sector, the tax
might have been avoided.

There are easy means by which the corporate sector collectively, and each
firm individually, could reduce its tax liabilities by taking advantage of these
basic principles. The fact that they fail to do so is referred to as the **dividend
paradox.**[23] A number of possible explanations have been put forward, most
of which are not very convincing. One is that dividends serve as a "signal"
concerning the firms' net worth. Though this may be true, buying back shares
should be an equally effective signal.

Though many owners of stock are tax-exempt (and thus indifferent to
whether the firm issues dividends or buys back shares), individual shareholders who pay taxes should prefer share buy-backs. Dividends do receive
favorable treatment under the corporate income tax (subject only to 15 percent tax); but in a well-functioning capital market it is hard to explain why
one firm would retain shares in another, thus subjecting the returns to double taxation (the 15 percent tax, plus the additional tax when the proceeds
are eventually distributed to shareholders).

Other Tax Paradoxes

Firms' dividend policy is not the only inexplicable aspect of corporate behavior toward taxation. When accelerated depreciation was first introduced, many
firms did not take advantage of it.

Firms have a choice of how to treat their inventories. Assume a firm that
is selling steel beams bought some steel at $40 a ton and some at $100 a ton,

---

[23]The dividend paradox was discussed in J. E. Stiglitz, "Taxation, Corporate Financial Policy, and the Cost
of Capital," *Journal of Public Economics* 12 (1973): 1–34. Subsequent studies include J. Poterba and L. H.
Summers, "Dividend Taxes, Corporate Investment, and 'Q'," *Journal of Public Economics*, 1983, pp. 135–
67; A. Auerbach, "Wealth Maximization and the Cost of Capital," *Quarterly Journal of Economics*, August
1979, pp. 433–66; D. Bradford, "The Incidence and Allocation Effect of a Tax on Corporate Distributions,"
Journal of Public Economics 15 (1981): 1–22; and M. King, *Public Policy and the Corporation* (London:
Chapman and Hall, 1977).

a few months later, as a result of rapid inflation in the industry. Both steel beams are in its inventory. When it sells some for, say, $110 a ton of steel beams does it say its cost of purchase was $40 or $100? The Internal Revenue Service allows the firm to choose what to say, so long as it does so in a consistent manner. It can either say that it is always selling the item most recently acquired (this is called the last in, first out system, or LIFO) or that it is selling the first item acquired (first in, first out, or FIFO). In inflationary periods LIFO has a decided advantage over FIFO. Current tax liabilities are lower (though future tax liabilities are increased by the same amount). But the general principle that a dollar today is worth more than a dollar tomorrow implies that firms are better off with lower current tax liabilities. Yet, amazingly, firms were very slow to switch to LIFO, and even today, many firms continue to use FIFO.

Two explanations are offered for such seeming irrationalities. One is that managers of the firm are not profit maximizing and that the discipline afforded by a competitive marketplace, which is supposed to ensure efficiency, works only weakly. The second is that firms are rational but that shareholders are irrational. Shareholders do not understand how the tax system works. It is unlikely that they would notice a firm switch to the LIFO system, but they do see the firm's current reported profits decline, and they believe that the firm is not doing as well as it was. As a result, the price of the firm's shares declines. Consider what might happen if a firm failed to pay a dividend but instead distributed the same amount it previously had distributed as dividends in the form of capital gains (buying back shares). Consumers might get confused and value the firm less than they otherwise would. Managers, whose compensation often depends partly on the market value of the firm, thus prefer to keep shareholders "happy" by engaging in policies that do not minimize the firms' tax liabilities. Both explanations are probably partially correct.

The Corporate Veil

Our analysis of the dividend paradox is predicated on the assumption that individuals can understand what is going on inside the firm: that they are indifferent, for instance, when choosing between owning 10 shares in a firm with 1,000 shares or 9 shares in the same firm out of 900 shares; that if the firm reduces its debt obligations by $1,000, the market will see that the net worth of the firm is now $1,000 greater, and its share prices will correspondingly increase; that if the firm invested $1 million of retained earnings, and a shareholder owns 1 percent, it is *as if* the shareholder himself had invested $10,000 directly. We assume, in other words, that individuals can see through the **corporate veil** to what is really going on; as we have noted, there are several puzzling aspects of corporate behavior that seem inconsistent with the hypothesis that individuals do see through the corporate veil.

EFFECTIVE MARGINAL TAX RATES

We have noted that the total tax (corporate plus individual) paid on the return to an investment will depend on how the investment is financed and how the return is distributed to shareholders. If the marginal investment were financed by borrowing, and if there were no investment tax credit (as there is), and depreciation allowances accurately reflected decreases in the value of assets (as they do not), then the effective marginal tax rate would be zero: the return to capital and the cost of capital would be reduced proportionately. But there is accelerated depreciation (so that the present discounted value of the depreciated allowances exceeds the present discounted value of "true economic depreciation"); and there is a significant investment tax credit. These imply that the effective marginal tax rate is negative. On the other hand, firms may finance some of their marginal investments with equity (retained earnings or new shares). Calculating the effective marginal tax rate is more complicated then. If the extra return is distributed as dividends, the total taxes paid are much larger than if the extra return is distributed via capital gains; and if it is distributed via capital gains, the effective rate depends on how long it is before the owner of the firm (or of its shares) realizes the capital gain, or whether realization is postponed until death. Though there are numerous studies calculating the effective marginal tax rate, assuming that the marginal investment is financed by the same mixture of debt and equity that the firm employs as a whole, and that it distributes a fixed fraction of its earnings as dividends (the remainder being retained, increasing the value of the firm) there is little justification for these assumptions. Under these assumptions, it is still true that there are large differences in effective marginal tax rates among different firms and forms of investment, but now some firms face positive effective marginal tax rates.

Leasing and the Investment Tax Credit

The investment tax credit has the effect of the government paying a fraction of the costs of machines purchased with it. The government presently pays 6 percent of the cost of machines that are allowed a 3-year lifetime and 10 percent of the cost of machines that are allowed a 5-year lifetime. The government does not actually pay the cost directly. But it pays it by allowing the individual to deduct from the amount that he would pay the government in taxes 10 percent of his expenditures on investment. It is a form of tax expenditure, here used to encourage investment. The government could just as well have required individuals to pay their full taxes and then separately apply for an investment subsidy. This approach would have brought out into the open the magnitude of the government subsidies to investment. The government budget would thereby have been increased, but nothing *real* would have occurred. This again illustrates how careful one must be in interpreting data concerning the size and rate of growth of the public sector.

The present system has tremendous administrative advantages but at the same time results in a major problem: some firms do not have any income, and so no income tax liability, against which they can take their investment tax credit. Effectively, this means that the cost of investment to companies that are doing poorly is much greater than the cost of investment to companies that are doing well. Consider a company that is currently doing poorly and will be doing poorly when the returns to the investment occur. Then since the returns will not be taxed—there will be losses in other parts of the firm to offset the returns on this productive investment—the tax system may cause no distortion. But most firms that are doing badly anticipate doing better in the future; this implies that while the firm is not able to take advantage today of the investment credit, it will have to pay taxes on the returns to that investment just like any other firm. Thus the system of tax credits causes a strong distortion against investment in firms that are currently not doing well and helps to perpetuate their current position.[24]

The market always attempts to find ways of dealing with such inefficiencies created by the tax system. One way is for the firm with losses to merge with a firm with profits. These are referred to as tax-induced mergers. There are many economists who are concerned with the long-run consequences of these mergers. Such mergers may limit competition in the economy. Moreover, it is believed that the vitality of a capitalist economy depends on having a large variety of firms; each firm has its own strengths and is thus in a position to take advantage of different situations. Some have made the analogy between firms and species of animals. Just as it may be advantageous to preserve a rich genetic pool, to be drawn upon in a variety of circumstances, so too may it be desirable to have a diversity of firms in the economy. The provisions of the tax code that encourage mergers (mergers that, in terms of more narrowly defined economic criteria, might not be desirable) should, in this view, be altered.

A second method of counteracting inefficiencies in the tax system is called *leasing*. Assume that a firm such as Chrysler has large losses and so cannot take advantage of tax credits on its investment. To modernize its plants it would like to invest $1 billion. (Were General Motors to invest $1 billion, the government would, effectively, finance 10 percent of that investment.) Chrysler approaches a firm that has large profits (Exxon). This firm buys the machines, and Chrysler rents the machines from it. Since this other firm has profits against which it can take an investment credit, the terms on which it is willing to lease the machines are very favorable. Moreover, the nominal owner (Exxon) is also allowed to take the depreciation allowance. Apart from the transactions costs, it is *as if* the government gave the tax benefits of the investment credit and depreciation allowances directly to Chrysler. But rather than engage in such a direct transfer, the government prefers a more roundabout approach. Exxon, from whom Chrysler leased its machines, could just as well have paid its full taxes, and then the government could have granted the investment subsidy to Chrysler. Instead, Exxon pays the subsidy directly to Chrysler.

Exxon presumably must be compensated for performing this service: some of the benefits accrue to it. It appears that on average, more than 80 percent of the benefits accrue to the firms, such as Chrysler, who are leasing the machines. The fraction is determined by market competition: if there are relatively few firms like Chrysler who cannot take advantage of their investment tax credits, and many firms like Exxon who would like to have their tax liabilities reduced, the fraction of the benefits that accrue to the leasing firms (such as Chrysler) will be large.

---

[24]This is only partly offset by provisions allowing for carrying these tax credits forward. (Future tax savings are worth less than current tax savings.)

These leasing arrangements had been employed for years, but there were a number of restrictions that made them unattractive for many firms. The intent of the restrictions was to ensure that the lease was not done *simply* for tax reasons. Thus the nominal owner of the asset had to bear certain risks, much as he would if he were buying the asset for himself.

The Tax Bill of 1981 changed all that. It created what were called Safe-Harbor leases, the effect of which was to allow leases, the sole purpose of which was to take advantage of the investment tax credits and depreciation allowances. Effectively, it allowed one firm to buy another firm's tax credits.

Though the Treasury had forecast fairly accurately the extent to which firms would take advantage of this provision, Congress and the public seem to have been taken by surprise: more than $20 billion of tax benefits were taken in the first year alone. This gave rise to a clamor against this giveaway to firms, and the Tax Bill of 1982 reduced the benefits considerably. But in the clamor the basic issue became lost. The issue was simply whether firms that were doing poorly should receive the same subsidies to their investment that firms doing well should receive. The government may or may not wish to subsidize investment; there are good arguments that could be made either way. But it seems unlikely that as a matter of public policy those subsidies should be restricted to firms that are doing well.

Toward the Elimination of the Corporation Income Tax

In spite of the fury to which President Reagan's proposal to abolish the corporation income tax gave rise, most economists would agree that major reform is needed. One set of reforms is to change the current system of depreciation allowances. A major fundamental reform is to integrate the corporation income tax with the individual income tax. The distortions associated with discouraging the flow of funds from the corporate to the household sector, in the decisions firms make in how to finance their investments (at least partially) and the encouragement of mergers and acquisitions, seem not to be justified by any compensating arguments, for instance, in terms of equity. Several countries have in fact integrated the two. There are a variety of ways in which such integration might work. One simple way is the following. There would be some reckoning of the taxes the corporation has paid on behalf of its shareholders, and some reckoning of the income of the corporation that can be attributed to the shareholder; the income would be added to the individual's tax base, the tax to what has been withheld on his wage income. Such an integration, its advocates claim, would not only be fair but would eliminate some of the important distortions we discussed in the preceding sections.

How would such a scheme work? Assume that a firm had profits of $10,000 on which is paid a tax of 50 percent, or $5,000, and there were 10 outstanding shares. At the end of the year, each shareholder would receive a statement from the corporation saying that he had earned $1,000 per share and that $500 in taxes had been withheld on each share. A shareholder who owned one share would thus add $1,000 to his income and add $500 to the amount he had already paid to the government (the amount that had been withheld on this wage income). For an individual in the 50 percent tax bracket there would be no additional tax; and an individual in a tax bracket lower than 50 percent would have his tax liability effectively reduced. If he were in the 30 percent tax bracket he would owe an extra $300, but he would be credited with having paid $500: his net tax liability would be reduced by $200.

In this scheme, dividends would not be included in income separately. To do so would be double counting, since earnings—which include retained earnings and dividends—would already be included in income. Retained earnings cause a slight problem: in the absence of taxation, we could have imagined the firm paying out all of the earnings to the shareholders, and then the shareholders investing a part of what they receive back to the firm. Retained earnings are equivalent to a reinvestment by the individual in his firm. If there is a capital gains tax, account of this must be taken in determining what tax is due. Effectively, an individual's "share" of the retained earnings ought to be included in his "cost" of acquiring the shares. Assume an individual bought a share for $1,000. The next year the firm had a profit of $1,000 per share, paid $500 in taxes, and then distributed $200 in dividends and retained the remaining $300. (All of these numbers are calculated on a per-share basis). The next year the individual sells his share for $1,400. What is his capital gain? His total investment in the share is his original expenditure of $1,000, *plus* the $300 of retained earnings, for a total of $1,300. Thus his capital gain is only $100.[25]

The tax treatment we have described for corporations is essentially the treatment that partnerships presently receive. At the end of a year, the income of the partnership is allocated to each of the partners. The only difference is that there is no "withholding tax" on partnerships.

The system just described represents a partial withholding tax on income to capital earned in the corporate sector. One could either extend the degree of withholding (making interest payments also subject to withholding) or decrease the degree of withholding (putting all the responsibility for payment on the individual). Prior to computerization, a strong argument could be made for withholding, since there was a fairly low degree of tax compliance among those who receive dividends and interests. Now, all firms report dividend and interest payments to the IRS, and compliance is not a significant problem. In 1983 Congress passed a law extending withholding of interest, but after powerful lobbying by banks and other institutions who claimed that it would impose high administrative costs on them, the bill was rescinded. How significant these administrative costs are (given the computerization almost universally employed) is a moot question. The major disadvantage of making the corporations withhold the tax is that it may reduce the amount of funds available for reinvestment; firms must raise more funds from the outside. The costs of raising funds may be significant. On the other hand,

---

[25] Some economists, such as Joseph Pechman of the Brookings Institution, believe that the administrative problems associated with full integration make this infeasible. These problems are particularly severe, as we have noted, if there is a capital gains tax; individuals would have to keep a running account of the funds invested on their behalf by the firm through retained earnings. With modern computer technology, this problem is not as formidable as it would previously have seemed.

forcing firms to justify their additional capital requirements to suppliers of capital may have certain advantages.[26]

The recent Treasury proposal that 10 percent of dividends be deductible from the corporations' income (for determining its tax liability) is viewed by some as a first step toward the full integration of the personal and corporation income taxes. To others, it represents a minor redressing of the imbalance between the treatment of interest and dividends.

SUMMARY

1. If the supply of capital is perfectly elastic in the long run and the economy is competitive, a tax on the return to corporate capital is borne by consumers. The after-tax return to capital is unchanged. The tax causes two distortions, in the production efficiency of the economy (the economy no longer operates along its production possibilities schedule) and in the output mix (production is shifted toward the noncorporate sector).

2. If the supply of capital in the economy is fixed and the economy is competitive, the effect of the tax is to shift capital out of the corporate sector into the noncorporate sector, because after-tax returns in both must be the same. The after-tax return will normally be lower than prior to the imposition of the tax. In this case, some of the burden of the tax lies on owners of capital. After-tax returns to capital may be lowered by more than the tax.

3. If the corporate sector is noncompetitive, the increase in price may exceed the increase in the costs of production resulting from the tax. There may appear to be more (in this sense) than 100 percent shifting.

4. Under our present tax system, interest payments are tax-deductible; this implies that if marginal investment can be thought of as being financed through debt, the corporation tax causes no distortion in the investment of the firm. The tax is best viewed as a tax on entrepreneurship.

5. The corporation income tax has an effect on how firms raise capital. There is no reason to believe that they finance new investments in the same way as they financed their previous investments, and there is thus no reason for the marginal cost of capital to be affected in the same way that their average cost of capital is increased.

6. In assessing the impact of the corporation income tax, one needs to consider the effect of the corporation tax simultaneously with the effects of the individual income tax and, in particular, with the special treatment of capital gains. Such an integrated view yields two principles: firms should avoid distributing income to the household sector; and whenever they distribute income to the household sector they should do it in such a way as to make it subject to capital gains taxation.

7. The fact that firms pay dividends, which impose a tax burden on the shareholders, when there are other ways of distributing income to shareholders, is called the dividend paradox.

8. Leasing provides one method by which firms without profits can take advantage of the investment tax credit. A system of refundable tax credits or direct investment grants would make the cost of the investment tax credit program more apparent and would eliminate the bias against firms that are currently doing badly.

---

[26]This becomes particularly important when many shareholders are less informed than the firm's managers about the firm's prospects; under these conditions of imperfect information, there is an important distinction between inside funds and outside funds, and shareholders may not see perfectly through the corporate veil.

9. The current corporation income tax introduces several distortions, fails to raise significant amounts of revenue, and demonstrates little evidence that it has a significant (positive) redistributive effect. Many economists believe that the corporation income tax should be fully integrated with the individual income tax.

KEY CONCEPTS

Depreciation allowances	Distortions
Debt	Integration of corporate and individual income tax
Equity	Profits
Retained earnings	Corporate veil

QUESTIONS AND PROBLEMS

1. Discuss some of the controversies concerning who bears the burden of the corporation income tax. To what extent are differences in views accounted for by:
   a) differences in assumptions concerning the nature of the tax;
   b) differences in assumptions concerning the nature of the economy; and
   c) differences in interpretation of the data?

2. Is it possible for: a) the price of output of the corporate sector to rise by more than the tax revenues collected (per unit of output); b) the after-tax rate of return in the corporate sector to increase, after the imposition of the corporate income tax? Give conditions under which either of these may occur.

3. As a result of the provisions of leasing, several firms that had high profits paid no taxes. Discuss the equity and efficiency implications of this.

4. It is difficult to ascertain precisely the decline in the value of most assets as they grow older. An exception is automobiles. Assume a new car costs $5,000, that its value at the end of one year is $4,000, at the end of two years $3,000, at the end of three years $2,000, and that it loses $250 in value for each of the following eight years. What is the true economic depreciation? What is the present discounted value of this, assuming a 5 percent after-tax interest rate? What will be the depreciation allowances under the current system? What is the present discounted value of these depreciation allowances?

5. The Treasury's proposal for allowing 10 percent of dividends to be deductible by the corporation has encountered some opposition from corporations who say that they will be "forced" to pay higher dividends as a result. Discuss the consequences of the Treasury's proposal. What does this kind of opposition suggest about the corporate veil?

6. Supporters of the 1981 depreciation system acknowledge that it favors heavy industry ("Smokestack America") but argue that this is desirable. Why do economists tend to look askance at such arguments? Can you identify any major market failures? If it were decided to subsidize these industries, in what other ways might it be done?

22

The Taxation of Capital

The United States, like most other countries, imposes a wide variety of taxes on the return to savings, on the interest individuals receive on their bank accounts, on the dividends they receive on their stocks, and on the capital gains they receive from their assets. States and communities often impose taxes on property. When rich individuals die, what they leave to their descendants is taxed. The income of corporations, partly a return on the capital that is invested in the corporation, is taxed. We refer to all of these taxes as *taxes on capital*.

Prior to the 1981 tax bill there were those who attributed much of the slowdown of growth in the United States to the oppressive effects of the taxation of capital, because such taxes have discouraged savings, investment, and risk taking. Furthermore, these taxes have a number of elaborate provisions that enable those who can afford good tax lawyers and accountants to avoid not only most of their taxes on capital but much of the taxes they otherwise would have faced on their wage income. Many economists believe that the inequities and inefficiencies that we associate with capital taxation are for the most part the consequence of these special provisions. Others believe that it is impossible to design a capital tax that is both fair and nondistortionary. Some of these economists argue for the abolition of the taxation of capital.

THE TAXES ON CAPITAL

There are four major taxes on capital: the individual income tax; the corporation income tax; the property tax; and the estate and gift tax. The estate tax is a tax on the transfer of capital, the corporate and individual income taxes tax the return to capital, and the property tax is a tax on the value of (particular categories of) capital.[1] There have been proposals for a net worth tax, a tax on the total (net) value of each individual's capital.

After reviewing the provisions of the individual income tax that relate to the taxation of capital, we suggest some reasons why it is so difficult to design a simple, nondistortionary, equitable tax on capital. We then discuss what would be the consequences of a simple, uniform capital tax and show some of the distortions associated with the special provisions of the tax code. We conclude with a brief description and analysis of the estate and gift tax.

Treatment of Capital by the Individual Income Tax

Within the individual income tax, there are a number of important ways that capital is treated differently from wage income. Most of these currently result in a favorable treatment of the return to savings.

1. *Dividend Exclusion.* The first $200 of dividends are exempt from taxation ($400 for a married couple). The motivation for this is not clear. The justification sometimes put forward, that corporation income has already been taxed,[2] and therefore taxing dividends constitutes double taxation, has some validity. But it is just as valid for dividends in excess of $200 as it is for those less than $200.

2. *Deferred Taxation of Savings.* There are a number of provisions that allow taxes on savings to be deferred. Contributions to pension funds, for instance, are not treated as income at the time the contributions are made; they are taxed only when the individual receives the pension. There are now a number of programs for self-employed individuals, and supplementary programs for employed individuals, which allow the individual's savings to be tax-deferred. These are referred to as Keogh Plans, Individual Retirement Accounts (IRAs), and Supplementary Retirement Accounts (SRAs).

The way these provisions work is simple. Consider an IRA. The individual can put into this account $2,000 every year. He simply subtracts the amount he contributes to this account from his income tax (on line 26 of Form 1040). So long as the money remains in the IRA account, the individual does not have to pay any tax on the interest that accumulates. The individual is allowed to take money out of the IRA account when he turns fifty-nine. He is then taxed on the money he takes out (as ordinary income). There is a penalty for taking money out prior to age fifty-nine. *The consequence of these programs is to make interest (on these deposits) exempt from the income tax and to allow individuals to defer their tax until they are at a lower tax bracket.* To see this, consider the tax liability of an individual who saves $100 in one of these programs and then retires in two years. For simplicity, we assume his marginal tax rate both now and at retirement is 50 percent. His IRA account earns, say, 10 percent per year, so that at the end of the first year he has

---

[1] In the previous chapter we showed that there was, in fact, some controversy about whether, or the extent to which, the corporation tax was a tax on capital.

[2] We noted in the previous chapter that interest paid out to bondholders was deductible from the corporation income tax but dividends paid to shareholders were not.

$110, and at the end of the second year $121. He then pays a 50 percent tax. His total after-tax income is $60.50.

Now consider what would have happened if the government had simply exempted interest income. The $100 would have been taxed at the time he received it at 50 percent, leaving $50, which would have been invested. At the end of the first year he would have had $55. Since interest income is exempt, he would be able to reinvest the entire $55, yielding, at the end of the second year, $60.50.

On the other hand, many individuals have a lower income when they retire than when they worked and thus are subject to much lower tax rates. The current system allows income that is used in retirement to be taxed at the lower marginal rates prevalent then.

Our present tax structure allows, in most cases, preferential treatment only on savings for retirement. Not all savings are tax-deferred. On the other hand, the penalties are sufficiently low (at current interest rates of 10 percent or more) that it pays most individuals to save through these methods provided they plan to hold their savings for at least two years. (The penalty on early withdrawal is only 10 percent.)

3. *Housing*. The most important investment for the majority of individuals is a house. The return to this asset—the housing service it provides—is not taxed in the United States. And the capital gains on owner-occupied dwellings are tax exempt if:

a) the individual repurchases a house at least equal in value (called a rollover provision), or

b) the individual is over fifty-five and the capital gain is less than $125,000.

As a result of these provisions, a capital gains liability is incurred on only a small fraction of house sales. Moreover, since house sales are not reported directly to the IRS, there is a suspicion that even when there is a tax liability, it is often not paid.

4. *Interest on State and Municipal Bonds (and Certain Other Bonds)*. Interest on state and municipal bonds is tax-exempt. These may include bonds used by municipalities to finance schools and by states to finance roads; industrial revenue bonds, which raise funds that are re-lent to businesses located in the town; and community-issued bonds that raise funds to be re-lent for mortgages for lower- and middle-income individuals. Some states have set up special agencies to borrow funds to finance dormitories at private as well as state universities, to build sports complexes, and to construct hospitals.

5. *Tax Deduction of Interest*. Interest payments are deductible. There is a limitation on the deductibility of nonmortgage interest payments. If these exceed investment income (the precise definition of which is fairly complicated) by more than $10,000, the excess is not tax-deductible.

6. *Capital Gains*. Capital gains are the increases in the value of an asset (capital losses are, similarly, decreases in the value of an asset). Assets include land, buildings, machines (including cars), securities (stocks and bonds)— almost anything that is bought at one date and sold at another.[3] There are a

---

[3] No definition is perfect. There have been controversies over whether certain transactions (for instance, the purchase or sale of contracts on the futures market) should be treated as eligible for capital gains treat-

number of important provisions of the tax code affecting the treatment of capital gains.

First, capital gains are taxed not as they *accrue* (that is, as they actually occur) but only upon *realization*—that is, when the individual actually sells his asset. Thus if you buy a stock and it goes up in value, you do not pay the tax on your increased wealth until you sell the stock. Losses are treated the same way. You cannot deduct a decline in the stock's value unless and until you sell it.[4]

Second, there is an important distinction between long-term capital gains and losses and short-term capital gains and losses—i.e., between the gains and losses on assets one has held for a long time and those one has held for a short time. Long-term capital gains are taxed at only 40 percent of the rate at which other forms of income are taxed, and 50 percent of long-term capital *losses* are deductible. The length of the period for which one must hold an asset in order for it to be eligible for long-term treatment has varied markedly over time and may differ from one kind of asset to another. Since 1984, assets have to be held only for six months to be eligible for long-term treatment. Prior to 1984, while most assets had to be held for more than a year to be eligible for long-term treatment, those trading in commodities markets (the markets in which wheat, corn, and other agricultural products, as well as certain metals and other commodities, are traded) became eligible for long-term treatment after only six months.

Third, there is a limit to the net amount of losses ($3,000) an individual can subtract from his otherwise taxable income; but losses not taken in one year can be carried over to subsequent years.

When capital assets are passed on to one's heirs, the accrued capital gain escapes taxation. The children inherit the assets but are allowed to take as their cost of acquisition (for the purposes of calculating their capital gains tax) the value of the assets at the time they—not their parents—acquired the asset. This is not true if a parent gives an asset as a gift to his child.

Consequences of Special Provisions for Taxation of Capital Income

The net effect of all of these provisions is to make a substantial fraction of the return to capital in the United States exempt from taxation. Table 22.1 lists the major categories of assets and liabilities in the United States and the value of the special tax provisions. If long-term gains were fully taxed, tax revenues would be almost $18 billion higher. (The table also uncovers the sizable benefits accruing to some industries—the capital gain treatment afforded timber is, by itself, worth more than a half-billion dollars.)

So important are the exemptions that the amount shown for interest deductions on individual income taxes actually exceeds the amount shown for interest received.

---

ment. For example, though when an individual sells a car for more than he paid he should, in principle, pay a capital gains tax on the increase in value, few individuals report capital gains received on such durables.

[4] Important exemptions are trades on futures markets.

Table 22.1 SOME SPECIAL PROVISIONS FOR THE TREATMENT OF CAPITAL

	Estimated Tax Expenditure (in millions)	
	Corporations	Individuals
General Science, Space, and Technology		
Expensing of R & D expenditures	$ 710	$ 50
Credit for increasing research activities	655	25
Energy, Natural Resources, and Environment		
Expensing of exploration and development expenditures	1,075	1,135
Excess of percentage over cost depletion	985	835
Capital gains treatment of royalties on coal	40	155
Exclusion of interest on state and local industrial development bonds for certain energy facilities	155	40
Exclusion of interest on state and local bonds for pollution control and sewage and waste disposal facilities	1,105	295
Capital gains treatment of certain timber income	430	155
Agriculture		
Expensing of certain capital outlays	95	510
Capital gains treatment of certain income	35	575
Housing		
Deductibility of property tax on owner-occupied homes	—	9,640
Exclusion of interest on state and local housing bonds for owner-occupied housing	1,160	320
Exclusion of interest on state and local debt for rental housing	660	420
Accelerated depreciation of buildings other than rental housing	215	185
Deductibility of mortgage interest on owner-occupied homes	—	25,130
Deferral of capital gains on home sales	—	1,800
Exclusion of capital gains on home sales for persons age fifty-five and over	—	805

Source: *Special Analysis, Budget of the United States Government, Fiscal Year 1985.*

SOME EXPLANATION FOR THE COMPLEXITY OF CAPITAL TAXATION

Why is the taxation of capital so complicated? Part of the complexity stems from attempts to design an equitable and efficient tax structure, and part of it arises from the political processes by which the tax structure is determined.

Observability and Administrative Costs

Much of the return to capital is not taxed or is taxed in a favorable way, because of the costs of ascertaining what the returns are or to whom they accrue.

	Estimated Tax Expenditure (in millions)	
	Corporations	Individuals
Capital Gains		
Capital gains (other than agriculture, timber, iron ore, and coal)	2,130	15,720
Carryover basis of capital gains at death	—	4,355
Other Savings Incentives		
Deductibility of interest on consumer credit		10,845
Exclusion of interest on life insurance savings		5,180
Safe-harbor leasing rules	2,340	—
Dividend exclusion		460
Investment Incentives		
Investment credit (other than listed elsewhere)	26,495	3,190
Accelerated depreciation of machinery and equipment	23,650	2,335
Exclusion of interest on small-issue industrial development bonds	1,085	960
Community and Regional Development		
Investment credit for rehabilitation of structures	185	160
Tax incentives for preservation of historical structures	182	250
Exclusion of interest on Industrial Development Bonds for airports, docks, and sports convention facilities	400	100
Retirement		
Net exclusion of pension contributions and earnings:		
Employer plans		56,340
Individual Retirement Accounts		9,840
Keogh Plans		1,530
General-Purpose Fiscal Assistance		
Exclusion of interest on public-purpose state and local debt	7,715	2,675
Interest		
Deferral of interest on savings bonds		771

The reason that the services of owner-occupied houses—the imputed rents—are not taxed is partly the difficulty of assessing what those imputed rents are; the reason that capital gains are taxed upon realization rather than accrual is partly that it is difficult to ascertain the magnitude of accrued gains.

Many corporations used to have what are called unfunded pension schemes; that is, the corporation did not set aside a particular amount of money to fund the pensions of its employees but financed them out of current revenues at the time they were paid out. Many firms have what are called defined benefit plans, where there are specific benefits related to the length of service and salary of the employees. In either of these cases, it would be almost impossible administratively to include the value of the individual's increased pension in his current income for tax purposes. Only in those cases where the employer had provided what is called a defined contribution plan, where he set aside a particular amount in the name of a particular individual for his retirement, would it be easy to ascertain the appropriate amount to be taxed.

Horizontal Equality and Efficiency

In each of these examples there are closely related categories of assets for which the returns are observable; there are similar situations where taxes could be imposed with relatively low administrative costs. But to do so would introduce horizontal inequities and distortions.

Thus it would be possible to tax defined contribution pension plans. But to tax these pensions schemes and not others seems inequitable and would be distortionary; firms simply would not employ defined contribution plans were they the only kinds of pensions that were taxed.

But then equitable treatment of those who are self-employed, in comparison with those who are employed by firms with pensions, requires that the self-employed be able to provide tax-deferred pensions for themselves. Keogh plans allow for this. But what, then, of the individual who works for a firm that does not have a pension plan? And what of the individual's spouse? She or he could be thought of as being employed by the individual, and was it not equally important for her or him to put aside money for old age?[5] Thus, the IRA was born.

Similarly, though it is virtually impossible to tax the gains on many assets as they accrue, there are some assets for which it is possible to do so (marketable securities). But to tax these assets and not nonmarketed assets seems to introduce an inequity and a distortion.

Other Equity Considerations

Views of equity play a part in some other aspects of the special treatment of capital income. The lower tax rate on long-term gains is motivated in part by equity considerations. A large part of the long-term capital gains in recent years has arisen from inflation; such gains are really illusory. The real value of the asset, taking into account the effects of inflation, may actually have decreased. In such circumstances, it appears inequitable to impose a tax on purely nominal capital gains. This argument is persuasive, but it is obviously only part of the explanation of the special treatment of capital gains—were it the only reason, there would be more direct and more equitable ways of taking into account the effect of inflation.

Some of the provisions are justified by concerns of vertical equity, but these arguments are also not very persuasive. For instance, the exemption of the first $200 of dividend income is motivated partly by a concern for poor widows who may be largely dependent on these dividends and interest to live; but whether these individuals are the primary beneficiaries of the provision is debatable. And whether the tax law should discriminate among those with low income in favor of those with dividend income is questionable.[6]

---

[5]This inequity in not allowing housewives to set aside money for their retirement in tax-free accounts is perhaps more apparent than real: housewives are also not taxed on their imputed income (the income that they would receive were they performing similar services in the marketplace).

[6]This exclusion may also be partly motivated by administrative convenience: it saves those with limited amounts of dividends the trouble of keeping detailed records of their dividends.

Political Pressures

475
**Equity and
Efficiency
Considera-
tions in the
Taxation of
Capital**

Some of the provisions are motivated by the political pressures of particular interest groups. The All-Saver Certificates (which effectively allowed limited tax exemption on certain bank deposits) were introduced primarily to aid savings institutions that were facing a difficult period in the early 1980s. Banking regulations restricted the interest rate that these institutions could pay on their deposits, keeping them well below the rates paid by money market funds. As a result, these institutions faced massive withdrawals of funds. Moreover, their major asset was long-term mortgages. When interest rates rose in the early 1980s, the value of these assets declined, putting many banks and savings institutions in a precarious financial position. They lobbied for some kind of assistance and were successful: Congress allowed them to issue tax-exempt certificates.

In the same year that Congress enacted the All-Saver Certificates, it also passed a provision exempting $1,000 of dividends on securities of electric utilities (provided they were reinvested in the utilities), again a result of the lobbying of a special-interest group.

Incentive Effects

Finally, some of the special provisions are justified on their beneficial incentive effects: the special treatment of capital gains has been justified on the grounds that it encourages risk taking. Although capital gains are one of the important forms of return to risky investment, the return to risky investments can take other forms as well; and relatively nonrisky investments can earn their returns in the form of capital gains. As we shall see, the differential treatment of capital gains gives rise to a number of important problems.

More generally, the special treatment of savings was introduced to encourage savings. Even if one believes that that was a desirable objective, it turns out that the way this has been done (through IRA, Keogh, and other similar accounts) is probably not very effective.

EQUITY AND EFFICIENCY CONSIDERATIONS IN THE TAXATION OF CAPITAL

Should we have any taxation of capital? Does the taxation of capital represent double taxation (the individual is taxed once when he earns the income and again on the interest he earns on his savings)? The general framework we established in Chapters 16 to 19 provides some insights into this question.

First, we noted that on philosophical grounds arguments could be made both for an income tax and a consumption tax, a tax that exempted interest income. If we had a redistributive consumption or wage tax, under certain conditions no tax on interest should be imposed. A tax on interest is equivalent to taxing consumption at later dates at a higher rate than current consumption. Differential treatment of consumption of different commodities (consumption at different dates) might simply add to the deadweight loss associated with the tax without increasing equity. Though the conditions under which this result holds are somewhat restrictive, under other conditions it is as likely that where there should be an interest income subsidy there should be an interest income tax.

A critical assumption of that analysis, however, was that we could clearly distinguish between wage and capital income, and that individuals differed only in their ability to work, not in their ability to invest capital. When some individuals are better investors than others, there is an important equity-efficiency trade-off. If we do not tax interest income, those who have the ability to earn higher returns on their capital will not pay the higher taxes that most people feel they should.

On the other hand, taxing the return to capital reduces incentives for finding more profitable investment opportunities.[7] Moreover, the productive efficiency of the economy requires that capital be managed by those best able to do so; *if* the ability to invest well is correlated over time—those who earned a high return in one year, on average, will earn a high return in succeeding years—then taking money away from those who have earned a high return reduces the amount of capital that they control (and can allocate) and hence reduces the efficiency of the economy.

Equity Consequences of Changes in Tax Rates

Changes in the tax rates imposed on capital goods can cause serious equity problems. Assume that a tax is imposed on the return to land. This has the immediate effect of reducing the market value of the land. The tax is borne not by those who, in the future, will own the land. The tax is borne by the landowner at the time it is imposed, because the tax is *capitalized* in the market value of the asset.

These equity concerns are of particular importance when a tax change affects only one class of assets. There is seldom a good reason why the individuals who happen to be the owners of the asset at the time of the tax change should bear the burden of the tax. Thus the elimination of the interest deduction for home mortgages would have a short-run effect of lowering the demand for (owner-occupied) housing, causing an immediate reduction in the price of houses and land. In the long run, of course, the price of housing will reflect the costs of construction; at the lower price, it will not pay to construct as many houses. As the supply of housing is reduced the price will increase until it rises to the point where construction of new houses again becomes viable.

EFFECTS OF UNIFORM CAPITAL TAXES

One of the consequences of the complexity of our tax on capital income is that it may be possible for an individual to greatly reduce, or effectively eliminate, the taxes he pays on capital (or even on wages). To do so, however, may require distortions in his pattern of savings and investment. In any case, the consequence of these provisions is that it is difficult to assess what the effective tax rate on capital is.

---

[7]In the sense that the allocation of effort increases the return to capital, some part of the incremental return should be thought of as a return to labor; there is no operational way, however, of identifying the part of the return to capital that is the result of the investor's efforts at finding a good investment.

In this and the next section we shall ignore these complexities and focus our attention on two of the consequences of a simple tax on capital income.

Effect of Capital Taxation on Savings

From Chapter 18 we know that we can decompose the effects of interest income tax into an income effect and a substitution effect. The substitution effect always leads to increased current-period consumption (reduced savings). Whether the income effect is positive or negative depends on whether the individual is a borrower or a lender. The tax deductibility of interest implies that borrowers are better off; their income effect is positive; they increase their current-period consumption. Hence for borrowers, income and substitution effects both work to increase current consumption and to decrease savings. Lenders (net suppliers of capital) are worse off: they decrease current consumption. Hence substitution and income effects work in opposite directions.

Most of the empirical evidence on whether aggregate savings increase or decrease with a raising of the after-tax return indicates that there is a slight negative effect.[8]

Corporate and Household Savings: The Corporate Veil. Much of savings is done not directly by households but by corporations, through their retained earnings. As we saw in Chapter 21, the provisions of the corporate tax greatly affect the incentives for savings to be done in this form. There is considerable controversy about the implications of this for household savings. There are those who believe that individuals see through the *corporate veil,* that they treat $1,000 saved by the corporation in which they own a 1 percent interest as if they had saved $10.[9]

It is important to realize that not all investors need to be well informed to see through the corporate veil. All that is required is that enough investors realize that a firm that has invested $1 million should have a market value $1 million larger than it was before to raise the market price by the requisite amount. Uninformed shareholders may not know why the firm's shares have increased in value. All they know is that they have. And the increase in wealth leads to increased current consumption (decreased savings).

In this view, then, the division of savings between household savings and corporate savings is purely an artifact of our current tax laws. It is *as if* the corporation distributed all of its profits to its shareholders, and then they decided how much to save.

---

[8] Michael Boskin of Stanford University has obtained perhaps the strongest negative response, arguing that an increase in the return to savings by one percentage point, say, from 4 percent to 5 percent, reduces savings by one percentage point. Howrey and Hymans of the University of Michigan claim that they have been unable to isolate a significant interest rate effect. See M. Boskin, "Taxation, Savings, and the Rate of Interest,"*Journal of Political Economy* 86 (1978): S3–S27 and E. Philip Howrey and Saul H. Hymans, in *What Should Be Taxed: Income or Expenditures,* ed. J. A. Pechman (Washington, D.C.: Brookings Institution, 1980).

[9] In this view, then, in the absence of taxation, whether firms paid dividends or retained earnings would make no difference. This view has been put forward by F. Modigliani and M. H. Miller, "The Cost of Capital, Corporation Finance, and the Theory of Investment," *American Economic Review* 48 (1958): 261–97, and by J. E. Stiglitz, "On the Irrelevance of Corporation Financial Policy," *American Economic Review* 64(1974): 851–66.

Many economists believe, however, that individuals do not have enough information or are not so rational as to fully integrate corporate savings into their household accounts. Individuals cannot, in this view, fully see through the corporate veil. Exponents of this view point out, for instance, that individual shareholders seldom read the annual accounts of the firm, and that even were they to do so, they would find it difficult to ascertain the magnitude of savings that had been done on their behalf by the firm. If one believed that the stock market values accurately reflected the true capital value of the firm, they could infer how much had been saved. But those who believe in the corporate veil tend also to believe that the stock market reflects true capital values only imperfectly and that households do not pay much attention to the day-to-day variations in the market value of their securities. In this view, then, one can (at least for short-term purposes) analyze separately the effect of capital taxation on corporation savings and on household savings.

Both sides agree that in the long run any policy that led systematically to increased corporate savings would *eventually* have an impact on household savings, if only because such a policy would have a systematic effect on the value of corporations and, through this, on the individuals' views of their net worth.[10]

The Consequences of a Reduction in Savings. While there is some controversy about the magnitude, and possibly even the sign, of the change in savings resulting from an interest income tax, the general view is that there is probably a slight negative effect. The next question is: What are the consequences of this? Should it be a matter of concern? The reduction in savings will normally lead to a reduction in capital accumulation and, in the long run, to a reduction in output per capita.

These effects may, however, be offset, in four different ways. First, the government can attempt to encourage savings in some other way: if, for instance, it reduces social security benefits, individuals may be induced to save more for their retirement. Second, it can attempt to reduce the fraction of savings that go into government bonds, thus increasing the fraction of savings that can go into real investment. (It can do this by reducing the government's indebtedness.) Third, a decreasing amount of capital affects the market value of other assets and, in particular, land. If land and capital are complementary, the decrease in capital reduces the return to land and hence reduces the market value of land. The decrease in capital is thus smaller than the decrease in savings.[11] (That is, some of the decreased savings takes the form of smaller holdings of land.)

Fourth, it can encourage investment, by providing an investment tax credit or accelerated depreciation. The effect of this is seen in Figure 22.1, where,

---

[10]It is important to note, however, that there have been marked variations in the ratio of stock market values to the estimated value of the firms' capital stock. Most observers attribute it to the fact that the stock market only imperfectly reflects capital asset values.

[11]The market value of land before taxes (in long-run equilibrium) is just the present discounted value of rentals, or R/r, where R is the rental flow and r is the rate of interest. In the short run, with a fixed supply of capital, a tax on the return to land and capital leaves the value of land unchanged at $(1-t)R/(1-t)r = R/r$. But as capital decreases, the real rate of interest increases and (if capital and land are complements) R decreases. Both effects lead to a decrease in the value of land. (Note that it is possible that, if land and capital are substitutes, the decrease in capital will actually increase the market value of land, thus exacerbating the decline in capital stock.)

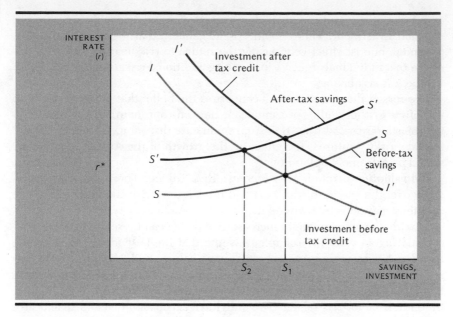

22.1 ENCOURAGING INVESTMENT THROUGH THE INVESTMENT TAX CREDIT
The effects of the reduction in savings can be offset by an investment tax credit.

for simplicity, we assume all savings are invested in capital (we ignore, in other words, savings in government bonds or land). The interest income tax decreases the supply of savings at each interest rate, so the market equilibrium level of savings (investment) decreases from S_1 to S_2. An investment tax credit shifts the investment schedule so that at each r, the demand for investment is increased. This is the movement from II to $I'I'$; a sufficiently large investment credit shifts it enough to restore investment to its original level, S_1. The after-tax return has been restored to its original level. The question arises: would it not have been simpler and probably less distortionary to exempt savings from taxation and not to have provided the investment tax credit?[12]

Effect of Capital Taxes on Risk Taking

There has long been a concern that the taxation of capital leads to a reduction in risk taking. We shall see that it is possible for an appropriately designed tax on capital income actually to lead to an increase in risk taking, but some of the features of our tax system do serve to discourage risk taking.

Although some individuals enjoy taking risks on a regular basis, and almost all individuals enjoy taking small risks occasionally (as evidenced by the popularity of state lotteries and the gambling casinos of Atlantic City and Las Vegas), most individuals take a more conservative position when it comes to managing their wealth. They are willing to take risks, but only if they receive,

---

[12]The investment tax credit affects only new investment, while a reduction in the tax on the return to capital affects old investments as well. Thus there may be large redistributive consequences to a change from one policy to the other.

as compensation, a sufficiently high return over what they could have obtained in a safe investment. There is widespread concern that, by taxing the return to capital, one is, effectively, taxing the return to risk bearing, the risk premium that individuals receive for bearing additional risks. As a result, there will be less risk taking.

The reason that this is of such concern is the belief that entrepreneurship is central to the vitality of capitalism, and entrepreneurship involves risk taking in an essential way. If entrepreneurs are discouraged from undertaking new risky ventures, the effect on the growth of the American economy would be extremely deleterious.

Why Capital Taxation May Increase Risk Taking. There is some controversy over the extent to which current taxes reduce risk taking. It is possible that they may actually increase it.

That the income tax might increase risk taking can be seen most easily by considering an extreme example. Assume that the individual has to decide between two assets: a safe asset yielding no return, and a risky asset that has a 50 percent chance of yielding a very large return and a 50 percent chance of yielding a negative return. The average return is positive, to compensate the individual for risk taking. The individual is conservative and so allocates a fraction of his wealth to the safe asset and the remaining to the risky asset. We now impose a tax on the return to capital, but we allow a full deduction against other income for losses. The safe asset is unaffected. The risky asset has its return reduced by half, but the losses are also reduced by half. How does the individual respond to this? If he doubles the amount he previously invested in the risky asset, his after-tax income when the return is positive is the same, and his after-tax income when the return is negative is also the same. The tax has left him completely unaffected. Effectively, the government is sharing in the risks of the individual. By its willingness to share the risks—the losses as well as the gains—it is acting as a silent partner. And because the government is willing to share the risk, the individual is willing to increase his risk taking.[13]

This situation has one other interesting property: the tax yields on average a return to the government but has no effect on the welfare of the individual. The individual is unaffected, because his after-tax position is the same as it was in the before-tax situation (whether the risky asset has a positive or negative return).

This tax seems to do what no other tax seems capable of doing: it raises revenue without lowering welfare. Before becoming too excited about this prospect, one must keep several caveats in mind.

Why Capital Taxation May Reduce Net Risk Taking. First, with a progressive tax structure, returns to a successful investment are taxed more heavily than losses from unsuccessful investments are subsidized. There is thus a bias against risk taking.

Second, there are limitations on the magnitudes of the losses that can be

---

[13] For an early discussion of the effect of taxation on risk taking, see E. D. Domar and R. A. Musgrave, "Proportional Income Taxation and Risk-Taking," *Quarterly Journal of Economics* 58 (1944): 388–422. The standard current view is presented in J. E. Stiglitz "The Effects of Income, Wealth and Capital Gains Taxation on Risk Taking," *Quarterly Journal of Economics* 83 (1969): 262–83. See also A. B. Atkinson and J. E. Stiglitz, *Lectures on Public Economics* (New York: McGraw-Hill, 1980), Ch. 4.

offset. For an individual, net losses are limited to $3,000. Thus the government, while sharing in the gains, shares only in some of the losses. Again, there is a bias against risk taking.

The importance of having the government share in the risk taking depends on how well the private market does. For securities that are actively traded on the stock market, the risks are widely spread throughout the economy, and there is no reason to believe that the government can significantly increase the degree of risk sharing. For smaller firms the government may, however, be able to provide risk sharing opportunities that the market cannot provide.

A final objection is that we have assumed that the safe rate of return is zero.[14] If there is a significant positive return on safe assets, and it is taxed, there will be significant wealth effect associated with the capital tax. This wealth effect may lead to the reduction in the demand for risky assets.

In short, a proportional tax on the return to capital would probably encourage risk taking, but this positive effect may well be more than offset by the negative effects we have just described. Probably the single provision that has the most deleterious effect on risk taking is the limitation on loss deductibility.[15]

As in the case of savings, the apparent effects of a proportional income tax on risk taking might not be too large. The distortions associated with our current tax system arise more from the variety of special provisions; these special provisions reduce the revenue and increase the inefficiencies induced by the tax, as we shall now see.

CAPITAL GAINS TAXATION

Perhaps the largest set of distortions arises from the special treatment of capital gains. The capital gains tax provides methods of tax *arbitrage:* individuals can engage in a set of financial transactions, which have no real effects on the economy but which do reduce their tax liabilities. In Chapter 24 we describe several of the ways in which this can be done. Here we wish to focus on the distortionary effects of the tax.

The Locked-In Effect

One important distortion associated with the taxation of capital gains is the **locked-in effect.** It arises from the fact that capital gains are taxed only upon realization. Thus an individual who owns a security that has increased in value may be reluctant to sell it, since he knows that if he sells it he will have to pay a tax. If he continues to hold the asset, he can postpone the tax until some later date. As we noted earlier, a dollar today is worth more than a dollar tomorrow (since one could invest the dollar today and obtain $1 + r$ dollars tomorrow, where r is the rate of return on capital). By the same

---

[14]The real rate of return on government securities during the past half-century has, indeed, been close to zero (averaging about 1 percent). On the other hand, it should be noted that for our analysis, government securities are only safe, in real terms, if there is no uncertainty about the rate of inflation.

[15]This limitation serves some important positive functions, within our present tax structure. As we shall show, in the absence of this provision it would be even easier than it is at present for individuals to eliminate all of their tax liabilities or, in any case, to significantly reduce them.

token, an individual would prefer paying a tax tomorrow over paying a tax today. The present discounted value of his tax liabilities is reduced by the postponement of the tax.[16] The individual is thus induced to hold on to his securities rather than to sell them. This is referred to as the locked-in effect.

The consequences of this may easily be seen. Assume that an individual had bought a security at $1, and that it suddenly rose to $101. He now expects that it will earn a return lower than the return he could obtain elsewhere. Assume, for instance, that he believes that there is another investment opportunity that could earn a return of 10 percent. In the absence of taxation, he would simply sell his security and buy the new investment.

Consider now what happens if he sells his stock. He must immediately pay a capital gains tax. If he were initially in the 50 percent tax bracket, since long-term capital gains are taxed at 40 percent of ordinary rates he would have to pay a tax of $20 (40 percent of 50 percent is 20 percent, times the capital gain of one hundred dollars). He would thus have only $81 to reinvest.

Assume he believes he will need the money in one year's time. His after-tax yield is 0.50×10 percent $= 5$ percent. Then, in one year's time he will have

$$\$81 \times 1.05 = \$85.05.$$

On the other hand, if the present investment increases in value at only 8 percent he will have

$$\$101 \times 1.08 = \$109.08.$$

He must pay a capital gains tax of 20 percent on his gain, so after tax he obtains $87.46. Thus he is better off, even though his asset presently yields a lower return than others available.

Consequences and Importance of Locked-In Effect

There is considerable debate about the consequences and importance of this locked-in effect. Martin Feldstein has claimed that the effect is so large that reducing the capital gains tax would actually lead individuals to sell securities that they previously had refused to sell, to such an extent that government revenues would actually increase.[17]

Critics of this view, while questioning the statistical studies upon which Feldstein reached his conclusions, point out that this is only a short-run revenue gain; the taxes that individuals pay now will not be paid later. There may be a short-run gain, and little or no change in government revenues in the long run. Moreover, because the reduction in the tax makes individuals better off, the tax may lead to an increase in current consumption at the same time that current government revenues are increased.

---

[16] Recall from Chapter 10 the definition of present discounted value. The present discounted value of a dollar tomorrow is $\$1/1 + r$; that is, a dollar tomorrow is worth (is equivalent to) $\$1/1 + r$ today.

[17] M. S. Feldstein, J. Slemrod, and S. Yitzhaki, "The Effects of Taxing on Selling and Switching of Common Stock and the Realization of Capital Gains," *Quarterly Journal of Economics* 94 (1980): 777–91.

There are further debates about the welfare consequences of the locked-in effect. Much of the discussion has focused on individuals' purchases of securities. Economic efficiency requires that each security be held by the individual who values it the most, who thinks that it will yield the highest return.[18] The locked-in effect means that an individual may retain a security, even though there is someone else who values it more. This results in what is referred to as *exchange inefficiency*. There are some economists, however, who believe that the economic consequences of this should not be taken too seriously. They argue that the stock market is essentially a rich man's gambling casino and that though the locked-in effect may impair the efficiency of this gambling casino, it has few further repercussions for the economy. There is not, in this view, a very direct or strong relationship between the effect of the capital gains tax on the performance of the stock market and the decisions made by the managers and owners of firms concerning, for instance, their investment and production.

The one area in which the capital gains tax may have a significant effect on the production efficiency of the economy is in smaller, owner-managed firms. There comes a point in the life cycle of such firms where the original owner-manager's skills and talents become less appropriate for the development of the firm. In the absence of capital gains taxation, the original owner-manager might like to sell his firm to some other entrepreneur; but he is discouraged from doing so because of the high cost imposed by the capital gains tax.

THE CONSEQUENCES OF OTHER SPECIAL PROVISIONS FOR THE TREATMENT OF THE RETURN TO CAPITAL

In Chapter 21 we noted how the system of depreciation allowances results in markedly different effective rates of taxation on different kinds of capital. The tax system, in trying to encourage investment, thus distorts the pattern of investment, encouraging investment in certain categories of assets. Similarly, the fact that the return to owner-occupied homes is subject to such favorable treatment (with interest payments being, at the same time, tax-deductible) implies that investment is diverted from the manufacturing sector to housing. Again, there is an inefficiency. Other special provisions introduce important inequities.

IRA Accounts: A Case Study

The attempt to encourage savings by allowing individuals to open up tax-deferred savings accounts provides an excellent example of a badly designed economic policy: it fails to accomplish its objectives and has strong distributional consequences.

Effectively, IRA accounts represent a lump sum transfer to those with access to credit, for those with any liquid assets, or for those saving more

---

[18] We define economic efficiency in the usual sense of Pareto efficiency. In the presence of risk, however, there is some question about the appropriate way of measuring the welfare of each individual. The sense in which we use the term here is in terms of the individual's own expectations concerning the outcome, regardless of the objective reality of those expectations.

than $2,000 a year. Only for those who are sufficiently poor not to fall within one of these three categories is there a substitution effect.

Those with access to credit can simply borrow $2,000 (though they may have to give another reason for borrowing, such as to take a vacation) and put it into the IRA account. Assume the IRA account pays 10 percent interest, and the individual is in the 30 percent bracket. If he could borrow at 10 percent interest, the tax deduction would be worth 10 percent × $2,000 × .3 = $6.0.[19] There has been no increase in *net* savings (the individual's indebtedness just offsets his savings).[20] Similarly, any individual with a liquid asset (such as a savings account) simply transfers $2,000 from his savings account to his IRA account; nothing really has changed, except his tax liabilities.

For individuals without access to credit, and without other assets, the budget constraint is shifted. In Figure 22.2 we have drawn the before-tax budget constraint. We have assumed that the individual is saving for retirement. By consuming less today, he can consume more in his retirement. The slope of the budget constraint is $1 + r$, where r is the return on his savings. With an income tax, the after-tax return is lowered, and the budget constraint shifts down. Now, with IRA accounts, if the individual saves only a limited amount, his budget constraint is the same as it was prior to the imposition of the tax. For large savings, the after-tax return is the same as it was prior to the provision of IRAs. Thus for individuals who save a little there is a substitution effect as well as an income effect: savings may be increased. But for individuals who are saving more than $2,000 a year there is an income effect but no substitution effect. For these individuals, the IRAs have unambiguously increased current consumption (reduced savings), relative to what they would be with an income tax but without IRAs.

Owner-Occupied Housing: Another Case Study

An illustration of both the complexity of the tax law and the difficulty of ascertaining the nature of its biases is found in owner-occupied housing. There is concern that housing is favored over other forms of investment and that owner-occupied housing is favored over rental housing (which has both distributional and efficiency consequences).

The tax advantages of owner-occupied housing are: a) the return is not taxed (in contrast to rental housing, where the landlord pays a tax on his income, and the renter cannot deduct his rent); b) interest payments and property taxes are deductible; and c) capital gains enjoy particularly favorable treatment. On the other hand, the owner of a rental property can depreciate his property, can deduct maintenance expenses (and may even be able to deduct some capital expenditures under the guise of maintenance expenditures), and, like the owner-occupier, can deduct both interest pay-

---

[19] Recall from our earlier discussion that the effect of tax deferral on IRA accounts is equivalent to the exemption of interest.

[20] The individual may not even be aware that he is engaging in what we call "tax arbitrage." On January 1 he is persuaded by the newspaper ads that putting money into an IRA account is a good deal. On June 1 he decides to take a vacation and realizes he doesn't have enough cash on hand, so he borrows to finance his vacation. It is as if he borrowed directly to put funds into the IRA account.

485
The Conse-
quences of
Other Special
Provisions for
the Treatment
of the Return
to Capital

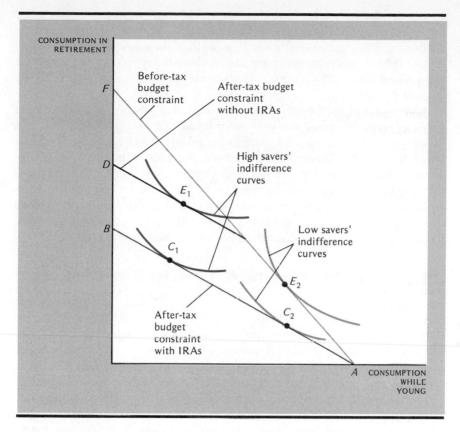

22.2 THE EFFECT OF IRA ACCOUNTS For individuals who save little, there are offsetting substitution and income effects, savings may be increased. But for individuals who are saving more than $2,000 a year, IRAs have unambiguously increased current consumption (reduced savings).

ments and property taxes.[21] In recent years, the allowances for depreciation have far exceeded true economic depreciation. The value of these deductions depends on the tax bracket of the individual. In a competitive market, the tax savings of the marginal investor (the investor who is just indifferent when choosing between investing in real estate and investing somewhere else) are passed along to the renter. If the marginal investor were in the 50 percent tax bracket, any advantages granted to rental housing would be received by renters as if they were in the 50 percent tax bracket.

Who is favored by our present tax code? It used to be thought that owners were favored, since they were allowed to deduct mortgage interest but did not have to pay taxes on "imputed income."[22] But this ignored the favorable

---

[21] There are further problems associated with ascertaining who bears the property tax. In the work described below, it is assumed that the tax is borne by the person paying the tax; but in fact, insofar as the tax is a tax on land, it may simply change property values; it affects owners of property at the time the tax is imposed, but not current owners.

[22] See F. deLeeuw al Ozanne, "Housing," in *How Taxes Affect Economic Behavior*, H. J. Aaron and J. A. Pechman, eds. (Washington, D.C.: Brookings Institution, 1981).

treatment afforded rental housing. One study, using estimates of the actual tax brackets of those who invested in each type, showed that debt-financed rental housing is subsidized more heavily than owner-occupied housing; if the subsidies to rental housing are passed along to renters (as they would be in a competitive market), renters are favored over those who own their own homes.[23]

It also used to be thought that owner-occupied housing was favored not only over rental housing but over other forms of investment, and that as a result there was excessive investment in housing relative to, say, manufacturing. One study estimated that eliminating the interest deduction for owner-occupied housing alone would reduce the long-run equilibrium housing stock by 8 percent. The generous depreciation allowances for many forms of capital combined with the investment tax credit since 1981 have, however, revised this presumption. Future changes in depreciation allowances may again easily change the patterns of distortions associated with capital taxation.

THE TAX TREATMENT OF THE RETURNS TO CAPITAL UNDER INFLATION

In the later 1970s and early 1980s, the United States went through a period of high inflation, with rates of price increases exceeding 10 percent. (This was low by standards in other countries, where inflation rates have exceeded 100 percent per month.) It became clear that when inflation rates were high, our tax system did not treat tax returns to capital in a fair or efficient manner.

The tax system taxes nominal returns, not real returns. Thus the first consequence of the presence of inflation is that individuals who find themselves with a small positive before-tax real return on capital find that they have a large negative after-tax real return.

Consider an individual in the 50 percent tax bracket, receiving a 12 percent return (say, in the form of interest) with an inflation rate of 10 percent. Most of the return in periods of high inflation is just an adjustment for the decreased purchasing power of money. His real return is only 2 percent. (The real rate of return on an asset is just the nominal return minus the rate of inflation.) But the present tax laws do not take account of this. This individual would have to pay 50 percent of the return to the government (ignoring state and local income taxes), leaving him a net after-tax return of 6 percent. With inflation, his real return is 6 percent − 10 percent = −4 percent. He loses 4 percent of his ability to consume simply by postponing consumption by one year. One would expect that this would serve as a strong discouragement to savings.

Much of the capital gains derived from the stock market between 1974 and 1982 were nominal capital gains: the price of shares was doing little more than keeping up with inflation (and in many cases not even doing that). But since the price level doubled, individuals found themselves paying a large capital gains tax if they sold their shares. Again, this seemed unfair. The attempt to correct for this by providing a lower tax rate on capital gains

---

[23] See M. King and D. Fullerton, *The Taxation of Income from Capital* (Chicago: University of Chicago Press, 1984), p. 256.

seemed a particularly rough adjustment. It would be no more difficult to have only real capital gains taxed: increases in prices in excess of the rate of inflation would be taxed.

On the other hand, the fact that the interest payments that are tax-deductible are nominal interest payments (the dollars one pays back are worth less than the dollars one borrowed, when there is inflation, and hence the nominal interest payments exceed the real cost of capital) creates a bias in favor of borrowing. This, combined with the special treatment of capital gains, creates in some cases effective negative rates of taxation on capital, and distorts the allocation of capital.

Inflation not only means that nominal capital gains are greater than real capital gains and nominal interest payments exceed the real cost of borrowing but also that depreciation allowances do not correspond to the real decrease in the value of aging assets.

It is apparent that our current tax system is not inflation-neutral; that as a result of inflation, in some circumstances, assets with a positive before-tax return have a negative after-tax return, discouraging investment, while in other cases, the tax system encourages investment.

What is required is full indexation. Partial indexation (such as indexing capital gains but not debt) may exacerbate some of the distortions and will not eliminate others.

ESTATE AND GIFT TAXES

Estate and gift taxes tax the transfer of wealth from one individual to another.[24] The objective of the tax is partly to limit accumulations of wealth (though if that were its sole objective, the appropriate basis of taxation would be the individual receiving the bequest rather than the individual giving it).

With the Tax Bill of 1981, the minimum size estate that is subject to taxation is $600,000. The maximum rate has been reduced in recent years from 77 percent to 50 percent. There are special provisions for the transfer of assets from an individual to his or her spouse.

The tax can be thought of as a tax imposed on a particular category of expenditures: on bequests and gifts. Like any tax, it has an income effect and a substitution effect: because bequests are "more expensive"—the individual has to give up more of his current consumption to give a unit of consumption to his heirs—he increases his current consumption; because individuals are worse off, they consume less. Thus the net effect on consumption is ambiguous. On the other hand, there is a strong presumption that at the confiscatory tax rates imposed by some governments (exceeding 90 percent of the estate), the substitution effect probably outweighs the income effect, and savings are reduced.

The significance of this is controversial. There are at least two primary motivations for savings: to provide for retirement (this is called life-cycle savings) and to provide for one's heirs. It used to be thought that most savings were motivated by life-cycle considerations, so that even if the estate

---

[24] We shall limit ourselves to the federal estate and gift tax. These two are now integrated.

tax discouraged inheritances, it would have an insignificant effect on aggregate savings. More recent studies have suggested that inheritance may play a more important role: not only is it difficult to account for the aggregate level of savings with a life-cycle model, but the distribution of wealth ownership (which is very skewed—that is, a small percentage of the population has a fairly large percentage of the wealth, a much larger percentage of wealth than of income) implies that inheritances play an important role.[25]

THE EFFECTIVE TAX ON CAPITAL

To assess the effect of the tax system on capital, one has to take into account all of the taxes on capital, with all of their myriad provisions. If an individual invests a dollar more, on an asset that yields a before-tax return of, say, 10 percent, what will his after-tax return be, after paying property taxes, capital gains taxes, corporation taxes, taxes on dividends, interest, etc.? Alternatively, what before-tax rate of return is required if the individual is to obtain, say, an after-tax return of 10 percent?

We noted in our discussion of the individual income tax that there may be a marked difference between the effective *average* tax rate and the effective *marginal* tax rate. There we observed that marginal tax rates may be higher than average tax rates. For many kinds of capital, just the opposite occurs because of the favorable depreciation allowances since 1981. While the average tax rate remains positive, for some kinds of investment the marginal tax rate may be negative, although for others it may be very positive.

One study conducted at the Treasury Department suggested that of the total income from capital in the United States, 80 percent received some kind of preferential treatment. Indeed, less than one-third was even subject to income taxation.[26]

Particularly interesting are interest payments. Of the $491.1 billion of interest paid directly or indirectly to domestic recipients in 1981, almost half was untaxed. Interest payments are deductible; still, the receipts should exceed the deductions because government and foreign interest payments are not taken as tax deductions on anyone's returns. Nevertheless, the net taxes paid on interest income in 1981 was a *negative $29 billion*. Those who deducted interest were at a higher tax bracket than those who paid interest.[27]

The total tax on capital consists, of course, not only of the federal income tax but of property taxes and state and local taxes. What is relevant, of course, for resource allocation is the *marginal* tax rate. Calculating effective marginal tax rates is not an easy matter. Consider a $100,000 investment yielding a return over ten years. We calculate the after-tax rate of return by first sub-

[25] A recent study by Laurence Kotlikoff of Boston University and Lawrence Summers of Harvard suggests that as much as two-thirds of capital accumulation is due to inheritances. See L. Kotlikoff and L. Summers, "The Role of Intergenerational Transfers in Aggregate Capital Accumulation," *Journal of Political Economy* 89 (1981): 706–32. See also J. S. Fleming, "The Effects of Earnings Inequality, Imperfect Capital Markets, and Dynastic Altruism on the Distribution of Wealth in Life Cycle Models," *Economica* 46 (1979): 363–80.

[26] E. Steuerle, "Is Income from Capital Subject to Individual Income Taxation?" *Public Finance Quarterly*, July 1982, pp. 283–303.

[27] E. Steuerle, "Tax Arbitrage, Inflation, and the Taxation of Interest Payments and Receipts," *Wayne State Law Review*, 1984.

tracting the investment tax credit (this lowers the effective cost of the machine). The return stream is lowered by the corporate taxes associated with marginal investment. The tax payments may be negative, because of depreciation allowances and deductions for interest payments on any loans to finance the investment. The return stream is also lowered by any property taxes that the firm must pay on its machine. But this is not the end of the story: the profits have to go somewhere (and the losses have to come from somewhere). If the profits are retained, the value of the firm will increase, and eventually shareholders will have to pay a capital gains tax; if the profits are distributed in the form of dividends, the net receipts of the investor—after tax—are reduced by the amount of tax he has to pay. A full calculation of the effective marginal tax rate takes into account all of the marginal taxes—property, corporate, personal—that are paid as a result of the investment.

Table 22.2 EFFECTIVE MARGINAL TAX RATES: DEBT-FINANCED INVESTMENTS

	Corporate	Noncorporate
Equipment	−2.082	−.528
Structures	−.464	.082
Public Utilities	−.561	.026
Inventories	−.890	.088
Land	−.665	.144
	Owner-occupied	Noncorporate
Residential structures	.203	.155

Source: D. Fullerton and Y. K. Henderson, "Incentive Effects of Taxes on Income from Capital: Alternative Policies in the 1980s," in C. R. Hulten and I. V. Sawhill, eds., *The Legacy of Reaganomics: Prospects for Long-Term Growth* (Washington, D.C.: The Urban Institute Press, 1984).

Perhaps the most thorough recent study of effective marginal tax rates is that of Don Fullerton and Y. K. Henderson. Table 22.2 shows their calculations for a debt-financed investment. The effect of the 1982 law was to make effective marginal tax rates in the corporate sector (for equipment, structures, public utilities, inventories, and land) negative. A negative tax rate means that the government is effectively subsidizing the investment; a tax rate of −200.2 percent (corporate equipment) means that if the after-tax return is 10 percent, the before-tax return is less than −10 percent (the subsidy is 200 percent of the after-tax return). Thus investments that yield a negative return are still profitable, so long as the return is not too negative.[28]

These calculations assume that the marginal investment is financed by debt. If the marginal investment were financed in the same way that the average investment was financed (the same ratio of debt to equity),[29] the effective marginal tax rates would be larger; but there would still be many categories of investment with negative effective marginal tax rates, and the

---

[28] From M. King and D. Fullerton, *The Taxation of Income from Capital* (Chicago: University of Chicago Press, 1984), p. 256. They also provide comparisons of effective marginal tax rates between the United States and several other countries.

[29] But there is no reason for the marginal debt equity ratio to be the same as the average.

differences in effective marginal tax rates among categories of assets would remain large. The effective marginal tax rates, as we have already noted, depend on the rate of inflation. If the rate of inflation were to increase, the effective marginal tax rate for many kinds of debt-financed investment would become even more negative.

The overall effective marginal tax rate in the noncorporate sector of 11.6 percent was low—lower than on most wage income. Note too that residential structures faced *higher* effective marginal tax rates than other categories of investment and that owner-occupied housing was taxed even more than residential structures.

SUMMARY

1. The complexities in the provisions governing the taxation of capital arise partly out of concern for equity, partly for administrative reasons, partly because the government is using the tax system to encourage certain kinds of economic activities, and partly because the special-interest groups have been successful in obtaining favorable treatment for themselves.

2. In the analysis of the effects of capital taxation, we differentiated between the effects of a general (uniform) tax on the return to capital and *selective* taxes.

3. The equilibrium level of investment is determined by three factors: the supply of savings, the demand for investment, and government policies that affect the supply of (and demand for) government securities and money.

4. On theoretical grounds it is possible for a general tax on the return to savings either to increase or to decrease savings. Some empirical evidence suggests that lowering the after-tax return may reduce savings slightly. Since much of savings is done through institutional mechanisms, the long-run response to changes in the after-tax return may be considerably greater than the short-run response.

5. The demand for investment is affected both by depreciation allowances and by the investment tax credit.

6. Though a proportional tax on the return to capital might induce an increase in risk taking, a progressive tax, with limited loss offsets (such as in the United States), may discourage risk taking. An evaluation of the effect depends partly on one's views concerning the market's abilities to share risks.

7. Long-term gains are taxed at much lower rates than other forms of income and are taxed only upon realization. As a result, there is a locked-in effect. There is some controversy over the magnitude and economic significance of the locked-in effect.

8. The special treatment for savings for retirement (IRA accounts, Keogh accounts, etc.) leaves incentives for savings unchanged for most well-off individuals; since they have only an income effect, and no substitution effect, they may reduce savings. In addition, they have a regressive distributive effect.

9. The special provisions for the treatment of owner-occupied housing, the use of depreciation rates that differ from true economic depreciation, and the ease with which different kinds of investments can take advantage of the special provisions for capital gains all result in significant distortions in the pattern of investment allocation; the effective marginal tax rates on many forms of capital in the corporate sector are now negative.

Investment tax credit
Locked-in effect
Capitalization

QUESTIONS AND PROBLEMS

1. Discuss the equity and efficiency consequences of changing the rules for IRA accounts so that only amounts in excess of $2,000 per year are afforded special tax treatment.

2. Contrast the effects of a single community raising its property tax rates with a uniform increase in property tax rates by all communities.

3. Do policies that encourage savings automatically lead to more investment? If you wanted to encourage investment in manufacturing, what policies might you advocate? How do current policies encourage, or discourage, investment in manufacturing? To what extent do your answers depend on alternative theories concerning the economy—e.g., how savings and investment are determined?

4. Contrast the effects of investing $1000 at 10 percent in a bank account for two years with (a) the effects of an IRA account with and without a 10 percent penalty for early withdrawal and (b) the effects of exempting interest from taxation.

5. Who benefits from the provisions allowing for the tax exemption of interest income on municipal bonds? What do you think might happen to the interest rates these bonds pay if individuals were allowed to borrow to buy these bonds, deducting the interest on their loans?

23

Taxation and Labor Supply

The effects of taxation on the supply of labor have been a central concern of economists: many believe that our tax system has had a negative effect on both quantity and quality of labor supplied.

EFFECTS OF TAXATION ON THE QUANTITY OF LABOR SUPPLIED

Unfortunately, it is difficult to measure quality or effort, and, accordingly, it is difficult to estimate the magnitude of the effect of taxation. Economists have focused their attention on the effect on quantity. Three aspects of this have been studied: a) hours supplied by men; b) participation rates of women; and c) retirement decisions.

Taxes and Hours Worked

Has the tax system led individuals to work more or fewer hours than they otherwise would have worked?

Many students' (and a few economists') first reaction to this question is that taxes have little to do with the number of hours worked; most jobs specify the number of hours to work; the individual has little discretion. The number of hours specified by the job, in turn, is a consequence of technological or institutional considerations, union and government regulations. These institutional considerations do mean that, in the short run, individuals may have less choice about the number of hours that they work than they otherwise would. But institutions do change. The standard work week has been drastically shortened in the past eighty-five years; in manufacturing, for instance, it declined from fifty-five hours in 1900 to fewer than forty today.

493
**Effects of Tax-
ation on the
Quantity of
Labor Sup-
plied**

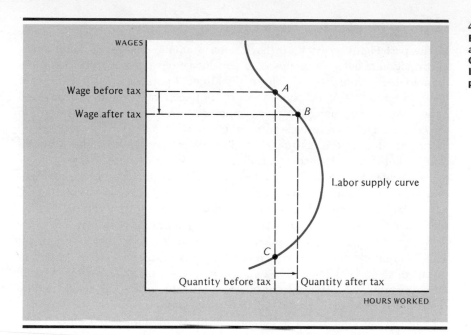

23.1 LABOR SUPPLY CURVE With a backward-bending supply curve, an increase in a tax on wages—equivalent to a decrease in wages—increases labor supply.

Most economists would argue that this marked change in hours worked is at least partly in response to economic forces; though each individual may not have full discretion over the number of hours he works, the contracts firms offer and the bargains unions make reflect the preferences of the workers. As their wages have risen, they have chosen to take some of their gains in the form of increased leisure. The increased wages have two effects. The income effect leads individuals to work less; the substitution effect leads individuals to work more. The fact that as wages have risen hours have declined implies that the income effect has dominated the substitution effect. This implies that the labor supply schedule is backward-bending, as shown in Figure 23.1.[1]

The imposition of a *proportional* tax is equivalent to a reduction in wages; thus with a backward-bending schedule a proportional income tax leads to an increase in total work (from what it otherwise would have been), moving from point A to point B in Figure 23.1. With a progressive income tax, the substitution effect is larger (the marginal rate exceeds the average rate), and hence it is possible that the total effect is negative (moving from B to C in Figure 23.1).[2]

---

[1]One has to be careful of using time-series data to predict what would happen were the wage today to be (permanently) decreased. There have been many changes (such as the prices of different goods, including those that might affect the demand for leisure). But the "suggestion" from time-series data is corroborated by other data discussed below.

[2]Consider the simplest progressive tax, a progressive flat rate tax with a positive exemption level. As the exemption level is increased, at a fixed tax rate, all individuals will work less; there is only an income effect. This effect may be large enough so that while a proportional tax would increase labor supply, a progressive tax reduces it.

Taxes and Female Labor Force Participation

In the past eighty years there have been dramatic changes in **labor force participation** of different groups. The percentage of women working has more than doubled, from 20.4 percent in 1900 to 46.4 percent in 1980. There are many factors affecting decisions to work, but economic considerations—and hence taxes—are among the more important. The labor force participation of women might have increased even more were it not for the discouragement provided by the tax structure. The effect may be particularly significant for both very low-income families and high-income families.

To see how the tax-welfare system may discourage labor force participation for a low-income woman, turn to Figure 23.2, where we depict a case where the government has accompanied a high level of minimum guaranteed income with a high (here 100 percent) marginal tax rate. In this situation, the increase in consumption from foregoing leisure may be minimal. This is precisely the case with several aspects of our welfare system. For instance, since 1981 the Aid to Families with Dependent Children (AFDC) program provided a 100 percent effective tax rate on any income earned by the mother; that is, for each dollar that she earned (or that she reported earning) she lost one dollar of benefits. Figure 23.2 depicts her budget constraint. The indifference curve with zero labor supply, and the full AFDC grant, is marked A. In this example, it is clear that her optimal decision will be not to work. It is also clear that letting her keep 50 cents on the dollar will lead her to work more, will reduce government outlays, and will make her better off. (The new equilibrium is marked E'.)

The reason that women in high-income families are discouraged from working is rather different. There are theoretical reasons to expect that taxation may have different effects on the head of the household (usually men) than on secondary workers (usually married women). Because most families file joint returns, the marginal tax rate on the secondary worker's first dollar earned is likely to be quite high. Thus the substitution effect is large and the reduction in labor supply and the deadweight loss are likely to be much higher than for the primary worker. The empirical findings that we describe below are consistent with this view.

(Of course, the total effect of taxes on female labor supply are, on theoretical grounds, ambiguous. While the income effect—including the reduction in the husband's after-tax income—leads to an increase in labor supply, the substitution effect leads to a reduction.)

There are, however, some grounds for expecting females to be quite sensitive to changes in after-tax wage. When the married woman does not work outside of the home, she is still being productive; it is only that her services are not monetized, and therefore not taxed. Frequently, when she goes to work, the family will have to replace those services in one way or another. It may hire someone to do the cleaning or cooking; it may rely more on frozen dinners or eat out more often (effectively purchasing the cooking services that the wife previously supplied). Thus the net gain to the family is much less than the gross income of the wife. Assume, for instance, that the wife earns $10,000 a year but the family spends an extra $7,000 to purchase services to replace those she had previously performed. The net gain to the

495
**Effects of Tax-
ation on the
Quantity of
Labor Sup-
plied**

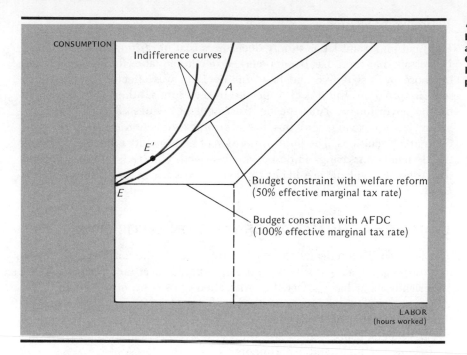

23.2 EFFECT OF *AFDC* ON BUDGET CONSTRAINTS AND LABOR SUPPLY With *AFDC* there is a 100 percent tax rate. This discourages labor force participation. A reduction of the effective marginal tax rate to 50 percent will increase labor supply, make individuals better off, and reduce costs.

family is only $3,000. From the point of view of economic efficiency, the woman should choose to work. Her productivity in the workplace exceeds her productivity at home. Now consider what happens if, as a result of her husband's income, she is in the 40 percent tax bracket. Her after-tax income is only $6,000, but she has to pay out $7,000 to replace the services she previously had performed. The family is worse off. Now, to the extent her decision to work is based on economic considerations, she will be discouraged from working. The tax, though only 40 percent of her income, represents more than 100 percent of the surplus of her income over the costs of replacing her services. It is thus not surprising to find that women are very sensitive to the wage rate they face.

Institutional factors, which limit the availability of part-time jobs, may further exacerbate the negative effect of the income tax / welfare system on labor force participation. Individuals face a discrete choice of either working, say, forty hours, or not working at all. If she could, she might prefer to work twenty hours, but of the two extremes, she prefers not to work than to work full time, given the marked reduction in returns from working resulting from the income tax.[3]

---

[3] Although it is often "feasible" to work part time, pay for part-time work is often much lower than pay for the equivalent full-time work.

Retirement Decision

The final important labor supply decision is that of retirement. In Chapter 13 we saw that there has been a marked decline in labor force participation by those over sixty-five and how this decision was affected by the social security program. But it is also affected by a variety of other measures taken by the government. Thus the tax treatment of savings affects individuals' incentives for saving, and this has a strong interaction with individuals' retirement decisions. The public provision of high-quality education reduces the demands on savings imposed on those with children; and this implies that these individuals are likely to have more savings available for retirement.

EVALUATING THE EFFECTS OF TAXES ON LABOR SUPPLIED

The fact that theoretically the effect of an income tax on labor supply is indeterminate makes it all the more important to attempt to determine empirically what has, in fact, been its effects. In spite of the determined attempts of economists to estimate the effects of taxation on labor supply, there is no consensus concerning the magnitude of the effects. Three methods have been employed to study these questions: surveys, cross-section econometric models, and experiments.

Surveys

The first involves surveying individuals, asking them whether they were led to work more or less than they otherwise would as a result of taxation. Not surprisingly, the responses obtained were mixed; some claimed, in effect, that they worked harder because they needed to make up for what the government had taken away (for them, evidently, the income effect exceeded the substitution effect), while others claimed just the opposite (implicitly, the substitution effect dominated the income effect).[4] Although the studies do confirm the theorists' belief that the effects of taxation on labor supply are indeterminate, they are of limited use: they do not provide a very accurate quantitative indication of the magnitude of the effects.[5]

Statistical Techniques Using Market Data

The second method entails using statistical techniques to analyze how individuals in the past have responded to changes in their after-tax wages. In general, we do not have data on how particular individuals responded to changes in wages. Rather, we have data on how many hours individuals who

---

[4] Among the most famous of these studies are those by Dan Holland of M.I.T. (D. M. Holland, "The Effect of Taxation on Effort: Some Results for Business Executives," *National Tax Association Proceedings of the Sixty-Second Annual Conference*, September 29–October 3, 1969) and George Break, of the University of California (G. Break, "Income Taxes and Incentives to Work: An Empirical Study," *American Economic Review* 47 [1957]: 529–49).

[5] Moreover, surveys have, in other contexts, proven an unreliable indicator of how individuals behave: they reflect how individuals perceive their behavior to be affected, but there are often marked discrepancies between individuals' perception of their behavior and the behavior itself.

have different wages work. Those who have higher wages seem to work more hours. We can calculate from this the "average" effect of wages on hours worked.

497
Evaluating the
Effects of
Taxes on
Labor Sup-
plied

To this point, we have simply described a correlation, an observed relationship between two economic variables. We now wish to use this to make an *inference*, a prediction or a statement about the effect of lowering wages resulting from, say, the imposition of a tax. To make such an inference, we must make an assumption: that the reason individuals who receive higher wages are observed to work more is that they choose to work more because of the higher wage; in other words, an individual who receives a higher wage is essentially like the one who receives a lower wage; the only important difference is the difference in pay, and it is this difference that leads to a difference in the number of hours worked. There are, of course, other important differences, and more sophisticated statistical analyses attempt to take as many of these differences (say, age or occupation or sex) into account; they attempt to see, of individuals of the same age, occupation, or sex (or who have other characteristics in common), whether those who receive higher wages work more.

There are two consistent findings across these studies of the effect of wage changes on labor supply: the total effect on labor supply of men is small, but the effect on female labor supply may be substantial. Recall that the deadweight loss associated with a tax is related to the substitution effect; though the total effect of a tax may be negligible, with the income effect offsetting the substitution effect, it is possible that there is a substantial substitution effect; and hence a substantial deadweight loss. There is not a consensus concerning whether the deadweight loss is large or small.

One of the more sophisticated studies of labor supply is that of Jerry Hausman of M.I.T. In his statistical analysis he attempted to take into account both the fact that individuals differed in their tastes for goods versus leisure and relevant details of our tax structure and welfare program. His major findings include the following:

a) Federal taxes cause an average male in the $8,000–$12,000 bracket (1975) to work 8 percent less than he would have chosen to work in the absence of taxation. The substitution effect is large, leading to a large deadweight loss. (Recall the discussion of Chapter 18 on the measurement of deadweight loss.) For an "average person" this amounted to $235, or 2.4 percent of his net income and a striking 21.8 percent of the tax revenues collected from him; for an individual earning $10 an hour (at a time when the average wage was $6.18 an hour), the deadweight loss amounted to $1,883 per year, or 11.7 percent of net income, or 54.2 percent of tax revenues (see Table 23.1).

b) While the (uncompensated) wage elasticity (the percentage change in labor supply resulting from a 1 percent change in the wage rate) for males was close to zero, that for females is approximately .9. This means that lowering the after-tax wage for women by 20 percent lowers the average number of hours by approximately 18 percent.

Our theoretical expectations of a high substitution effect were confirmed. The deadweight loss for a wife working full time, earning $4 an hour, with a husband earning $10,000 (so they faced a marginal tax rate of 28 percent) was $1,208, or 58.1 percent of tax revenues. If she were taxed as a single

Table 23.1 DEADWEIGHT LOSS CALCULATION FOR THE AVERAGE INDIVIDUAL

Dollars unless otherwise specified

Average Wage (dollars)	Before-Tax Income	Tax Paid	Dead-weight Loss	Dead-weight Loss as Percent of Net Income	Dead-weight Loss as Percent of Taxes	Dead-weight Loss with Proportional Tax
6.18 an hour	10,976	1,078	235	2.4	21.8	129
10.00 an hour	19,662	3,474	1,883	11.7	54.2	885

Source: J. Hausman, "Labor Supply," in How Taxes Affect Economic Behavior, H. J. Aaron and J. Pechman, eds., (Washington, D.C.: Brookings Institution, 1981), pp. 27–72.

individual, the deadweight loss, though still significant ($731), was substantially smaller.

c) The magnitude of the labor responses for female-headed households lies between that of men and married women.

It should be noted, however, that other studies of male labor supply elasticities have not yielded results that indicate that the distortions are as large as those estimated by Hausman. Thus there is not universal consensus among economists that the gains in efficiency from lowering the marginal tax rate would be anywhere near as large as those claimed by Hausman.

Negative Income Tax Experiments

The third approach to obtaining a quantitative estimate of the magnitude of the labor supply responses to tax changes is an experimental approach. The question we are interested in is: What would happen to the labor supply if we raised or lowered tax rates (or changed the tax structure in some other way)? One approach is to say, "Let's change the tax structure and see what happens." This could be an expensive approach: the change might have a very negative effect on labor supply, but before the effects are recognized and the tax structure changed again, considerable damage (welfare loss) could have occurred.

But we can learn something by changing the tax structure for just a small portion of the population. Just as opinion polls can give fairly accurate estimates of how voters will vote in an election, simply by asking a small sample of the population (often fewer than 1,000 individuals), so too the response of a small sample may give a fairly reliable indication of how other, similar individuals would respond were they to face the alternative tax structure. Opinion polls are careful to obtain a representative sample of views; that is, they make sure that views of young and old, of the rich and poor, of skilled and unskilled workers, of married and unmarried individuals, etc., are all represented, and in forming their estimate of how the population as a whole will vote, they assign weights corresponding to the relative importance of the various groups in the population (when they are attempting to predict the outcome of elections, they assign weights corresponding to the known likelihood that members of different groups vote).

In the late 1960s and early 1970s there was a series of such experiments, attempting to ascertain in particular the effects of changes in the tax structure and welfare system on the labor supplied by poorer individuals. Different individuals were confronted with different tax structures, making it possible, in principle, not only to estimate the overall effect of tax changes but to separate out the income effects from the substitution effects.

For instance, while our current welfare system has a fairly high effective marginal tax rate, with a negative income tax the government might reduce an individual's benefits by less as his income rose. Since the negative income tax experiments focused on lower-income individuals, they were mainly concerned with the effect of alternative subsidy systems on labor supply. The government attempted to assess the effects of different levels of guaranteed income and different tax rates. Similar individuals were confronted with different support levels but the same tax rate, or different tax rates with the same support levels. In principle, therefore, the experiments enable the identification of income and substitution effects.

The results were consistent with the view that the overall effect of taxes on labor supply is relatively small. The report on the first such experiment, conducted in New Jersey, described it as presenting "a picture of generally small absolute labor supply differentials between" those who were confronted with the alternative tax / welfare structures and those who faced the existing tax / welfare structure. "Only among wives, whose mean labor supply is quite small to begin with, are the differentials large in relative terms."[6]

The experiments yielded some further results concerning the possible effects of changes in the welfare / tax system. Providing more income to the poor resulted in their searching longer for a job when they became unemployed.

While the early experiments focused on the effect of alternative tax-subsidy schemes on labor supply (and related variables, like job search), later studies attempted to ascertain whether there were other effects as well. For instance, an experiment in Gary, Indiana, found a higher birth weight of babies—an indication of health of the child—in families whose income had been increased. An experiment conducted in Seattle, Washington, found that providing women with a guaranteed income, as the negative income tax does, might contribute to the break-up of families. Economic necessity may be forcing many families to stay together.

The experiments represent an important advance in the tools that are available to social scientists. At the same time, there are some important limitations to the experimental approach in general—and to the above-mentioned experiments in particular—that have to be borne in mind in evaluating the results.

First, there is a well-known phenomenon called the **Hawthorne effect,** which plagues all experimental work with individuals: when an individual is included in an experiment, and he knows his behavior is being examined, his behavior is often altered.

Second, there are problems associated with ensuring that one obtains a representative sample. Since participation in the experiment is voluntary, there may be systematic biases associated with the kinds of individuals who refuse to participate.

---

[6] U.S. Department of Health, Education and Welfare, *Summary Report: New Jersey Graduated Work Incentive Experiments* (Washington, D.C.: Government Printing Office, 1973).

Third, the response of individuals to short-run changes may be different from their responses to long-run changes. On the one hand, a temporary change in the tax structure that leads them to be better off has a smaller effect on lifetime income than a permanent change in the tax structure; hence the income effect may be understated. On the other hand, since the experiment often involved individuals facing a higher marginal tax rate during the course of the experiment, the after-tax wage was temporarily reduced; a temporary reduction in the wage may have different effects than a permanent reduction. In the absence of costs of adjustment there is a presumption that individuals will reduce their work (increase their leisure) more than they would with a permanent wage reduction. Thus an individual who was planning to take some time off from work (a woman who was thinking of having children at some time in the not too distant future) might have taken advantage of the temporary availability of the subsidy. If this is true, the experiments overstated the substitution effect. On the other hand, costs of adjustment may be very high; an individual might be reluctant to quit his current job, knowing that he will want it back in three years' time (when the experiment is over), because he believes it will be difficult to get it back then. If these effects are important, the experiment may have understated not only the income effects but the substitution effects. Some of the more recent experiments have attempted to ascertain the magnitude of the biases in the estimates resulting from the fact that the change in tax structure / welfare payments was only temporary by guaranteeing to the individual the same tax structure / welfare structure over a more extended period (up to twenty years).

A final important qualification on interpreting whether the experiments provide an accurate statement of the extent to which labor supply would be affected by changes in tax laws or welfare programs relates to the role of institutions in determining the length of the work week. We commented earlier that while in the short run institutional practices play an important role in restricting individuals' choices over the number of hours worked, these institutional practices themselves change, partly in response to changes in the economic environment. Thus many of the individuals in the experiment may have had only limited discretion over the number of hours they worked; but if everyone in society were confronted with the new tax / welfare payments structure, pressures might develop to alter these institutional practices to bring them more into conformity with individuals' preferences.

IMPLICATIONS OF LABOR SUPPLY ELASTICITY ESTIMATES

If the compensated labor supply elasticity is large, there will be a large dead-weight loss associated with the tax system. In that case significant gains in efficiency, with possibly limited effects on distribution, can be achieved by lowering the degree of progressivity. That was the finding of Jerry Hausman. Hausman calculated the flat-rate taxes associated with different exemption levels required to raise the same amount of revenue that our present tax system does and compared the hours worked and the deadweight loss under the present system with the alternatives. As the exemption increases, of course, the required tax rate increases. The results are presented in

Exemption Level (dollars)	Tax Rate (percent)	Effect on Desired Annual Hours of Work	Deadweight Loss as a Percent of Taxes	Tax Rate on Annual Income of			
				$4,000	$8,000	$16,000	$24,000
0	14.6	−27.5	7.1	0.146	0.146	0.146	0.146
1,000	15.4	−28.2	8.3	0.116	0.135	0.144	0.148
2,000	16.9	−29.9	9.8	0.085	0.127	0.148	0.155
4,000	20.7	−34.5	14.5	0.000	0.104	0.155	0.172
Current tax system	Internal revenue code	−197.5	28.7	0.119	0.147	0.173	0.188

Source: J. Hausman, "Labor Supply," p. 64.

Table 23.2. Three results should be noted. First, these alternative tax structures depress labor supply much less than does the current system. Second,
while he estimates the dead weight loss as a percent of taxes raised to be
28.7 percent for the current system, with a progressive flat-rate tax system,
even with a $4,000 exemption level, this is reduced by half, to 14.5 percent.
If the exemption level is set at zero (a strictly proportional tax), the deadweight loss is only 7 percent of total revenue raised. Third, because of the
large increase in labor supply, for most individuals tax rates can be reduced
without loss of revenue. An individual with an income of $4,000 would face
an average tax that is lower with a flat-rate tax and a $1,000 exemption than
he does under the current progressive tax system, and even more marked
reductions in the average taxes paid by an individual earning higher incomes
should be noted. The present tax system may be "inefficient": it may be
possible, by redesigning the tax structure, to make almost everyone better
off.

OTHER DIMENSIONS TO LABOR SUPPLY

The preceding discussion focused on how the current tax rate may affect the
individual's decision concerning whether to participate in the labor force
and, if so, how many hours he should work. Such a discussion oversimplifies
the analysis of the effect of taxation in several important respects.

Effort

First, it ignores the many important decisions of the individual that affect
the quality of labor supplied in the market. Individuals have considerable
discretion about the effort they put into a job; one of the important returns
to putting in more effort is the financial return obtained from the higher pay
one is likely to receive, either directly or indirectly, as a result of promo-
tions. Pay, of course, is only one of the reasons that individuals work hard.
They also work hard for status, recognition from their peers, etc. Without
denying the importance of these factors—though they tend to be more
important in more skilled, professional, and managerial occupations than in
unskilled jobs—all that our analysis requires is that individuals are partially
motivated by financial returns; for most individuals, working in most jobs,
this is clearly apparent.

Job Choice

The tax structure affects the choice of jobs. Individuals of equal ability do not, in general, receive the same wage in all jobs. Some jobs are particularly unpleasant, and individuals have to be compensated to undertake them; examples of this may include work as a sanitary engineer or at a job with long or inconvenient hours.

Other jobs are viewed to be particularly pleasant; individuals are willing to take them even when they pay less than other jobs for individuals of comparable skills. Teachers, for instance, work fewer hours per year than others. Ski instructors get to spend part of every day skiing. Other jobs confer status or provide other "perks." We refer to these benefits generally as **nonpecuniary benefits.** The tax system penalizes occupations with negative nonpecuniary benefits; they are taxed on all of their monetary compensation, part of which is intended to compensate them for these negative nonpecuniary attributes of the job. Meanwhile, those with large nonpecuniary benefits receive favorable treatment. There is thus a distortion in the pattern of allocation of labor.

Education

We discussed earlier how a variety of government programs affect individuals' decisions concerning when to leave the labor force (that is, the date of retirement). Similarly, a variety of government programs affect the decision of when to enter the labor force (that is, how long to remain in school). Subsidized colleges and universities and subsidized loan programs encourage students to remain in school, while not allowing tuition expenditures to be deductible discourages educational expenditures (while investments in education are not tax-deductible, the returns are taxed).

Labor Supply and Other Household Decisions

The decisions we have described concerning labor supply both affect and are affected by a variety of other decisions made within the household, decisions that themselves are affected by a variety of government policies. Both marriage and divorce are affected by tax policy (see Chapter 20 for a discussion of the marriage tax and the tax treatment of alimony). Social security rules penalize short marriages that end in divorce: the ex-wife is entitled to benefits only if the couple remain married for ten years. Current tax policy, to the extent that it discourages labor force participation by wives, simultaneously encourages children: a major part of the cost of a child is the opportunity cost of the mother's time, her lost wages. In some countries, where there has been concern about a declining population, government has enacted policies (such as child subsidies, more favorable income tax treatment for larger families, provision of child care facilities) to encourage reproduction. Other countries, such as China, where there is a concern about the economic consequences of rapid population growth, have enacted policies designed to reduce dramatically the birth rate.

We have already noted the importance of savings for the retirement decision. Savings, in turn, are affected by tax policy (the special treatment of
pensions, IRA accounts, etc.), and by government expenditure programs.
The provision of medical insurance (encouraged by current tax policy) and
medicare make precautionary savings (savings for medical expenses) less
important; student loan programs make savings for children's education less
important.

The important point to remember is that though we study the effects of
each policy (tax, expenditure) on each decision (savings, labor supply) alone,
in fact all the decisions are interconnected, and virtually all government
policies have some effects, direct or indirect, on each of the decisions.

Form of Compensation

Finally, the tax structure affects the form in which individuals receive their
pay. It encourages firms to compensate their employees in forms that are
not taxable. This provides one of the explanations of the rapid growth of
fringe benefits (of, for instance, employer-sponsored health programs) during the past three decades. Expense accounts, training programs held in
attractive resorts, and subsidized meals are all forms of nontaxable compensation. Perhaps the most important effect of the tax structure on the form of
pay is the encouragement that it provides for "deferred compensation"—
pensions and stock options.

SUMMARY

1. On theoretical grounds, the effect of taxation on labor supply is ambiguous. There
   is an income effect and a substitution effect working in opposite directions.
2. Empirical evidence suggests that for males the substitution and income effects
   cancel; the total effect on labor supply is probably not large; while for females,
   there may be a marked effect on labor force participation. On the other hand,
   even though the total effect may be small for males, the substitution effect, and
   hence the deadweight loss associated with the tax, may be very large.
3. Reforms—such as substituting a progressive flat-rate tax for our current system—
   may be able to increase the welfare of most individuals, increase labor supply, and
   reduce the deadweight loss.
4. The tax system encourages jobs with large nonpecuniary benefits and encourages
   compensation in forms that are not taxed or receive preferential treatment..

KEY CONCEPTS

Labor force participation
Hawthorne effect
Nonpecuniary benefits

QUESTIONS AND PROBLEMS

1. Prior to 1981, the government imposed only a 67 percent marginal tax rate on
   AFDC. Draw the budget constraint. Draw the indifference curve of someone who
   still prefers to remain out of the labor force. Draw the indifference curve of some-

one who now prefers to work rather than to remain out of the labor force. Show how, for this person, lowering the tax rate will increase welfare, reduce costs, and increase labor supply. What can you say about government policy if there are some individuals of the first type and some of the second type?

2. Consider the consequences of a switch to a progressive flat-rate tax. This implies that high-income individuals will face lower marginal tax rates than at present. What do you expect the effect on their labor supply will be if: a) their average rate is increased; or b) their average rate is decreased? Some middle-income individuals may find they face the same marginal tax rate. What do you expect the effect on their labor supply will be if their average rate is increased? decreased? Finally, some poorer individuals may find their marginal rate increased. What will be the effect on their labor supply if their average rate is increased? decreased? On theoretical grounds, what can you say about the total impact?

3. What will be the effect of a switch to taxing individuals on the basis of their own income (rather than family income) on labor force participation of wives?

4. Taxes and government expenditure programs affect a variety of other aspects of household behavior. Some economists, for instance, argue that they affect birth rates. What provisions of the tax system might affect the decision to have a child? What government expenditure programs?

24

A Student's Guide to Tax Avoidance

There is widespread belief that the rich are able to avoid much of the taxes that they otherwise would pay by taking advantage of loopholes within the tax law. Most of these loopholes arise from the special provisions that govern the rates at which different kinds of capital income are taxed. The incentive to find loopholes to reduce tax liabilities is greatly enhanced by the high marginal tax rates of our progressive tax structure.

Although tax laws change, there is a constant duel between the tax authorities and the tax lawyers, with the tax lawyers developing new loopholes almost as fast as the tax authorities close old ones. If you understand the basic principles of tax avoidance, you will be able to adapt to these changes in the tax law.

From the public policy point of view, it is imperative to understand the nature of tax loopholes for two reasons. The total impact of the tax law depends as much on these special provisions as it does on the overall design. It may make little difference that we have enacted a progressive tax structure if the loopholes provide a method by which the rich can avoid paying high tax rates. Secondly, distortions in the patterns of investment and savings caused by these special provisions may be more significant than the distortions in the level of savings and investment caused by uniform capital taxation.

It is important to emphasize that what we are concerned with here is **tax avoidance,** as opposed to **tax evasion.** Tax evasion is illegal. Tax avoidance entails taking full advantage of the provisions of the tax code to reduce one's tax obligations.

*"Now, this over here, this is why you're going
to have to go to jail."*

Drawing by Mankoff; © 1982 *The New Yorker Magazine, Inc.*

There are three basic principles involved in tax avoidance: income splitting, postponement of taxes, and arbitrage among the different rates at which
the returns of capital are taxed.

The next three sections discuss each of these in turn.

INCOME SPLITTING

The first principle is quite simple. Under a tax structure with increasing
marginal rates, such as that found in the United States, the tax on a single
person with a $30,000 income is three times the tax on an individual with a
$15,000 income. In 1984 a single person with a $30,000 income would pay
$7,873, while a single person with a $15,000 income would pay $2,580. Thus
it pays an individual to split his income into as many taxable entities as possible. For instance, if an individual with capital gave some of his assets to his
children, the income from those assets would be taxed at the children's rate.
The government attempts to ensure that he really has given the money away,
and thus looks askance if the individual who gives the money serves as the
custodian of the funds.

But the taxpayer who is determined to avoid paying taxes can do better.
He can establish a set of trust funds for his children. A trust is a legal entity
(just as a corporation is a legal entity). It has certain powers, given to it by
the legal document setting up the trust: it can invest funds and it may be
able to borrow or to lend. The document setting up the trust names an
individual or a bank (or some other institution) as the trustee (manager of
the trust). The income of the trust is used for the benefit of the beneficiaries
who are named in the trust.

The funds cannot, however, be used for purposes that are the legal obligations of the parent. The parent cannot charge his children for room and
board and draw payment from the trust to cover such household expenses.

Legal obligations of the parents vary from state to state. In most states, the
funds can be used to pay for college education, and even summer camp.

The trust is taxed as if it were a separate individual (though the tax rate is
slightly higher than on single individuals). If an individual has four children
and he sets up two trusts for each child, he can effectively split the part of
his capital income that he wishes to turn over to his children eight ways.[1]
The consequence is that a parent who wishes to give a portion of his income
to his children may do so and have that income taxed at low rates. An important class called *Clifford trusts* even enable the individual to get back his
original principal at the termination of the trust.[2] While the children get the
income, the parent does not really give up the asset.

There are three important points to note about income splitting. First, it
requires the transfer of an asset such as stocks, bonds, real estate, or a share
in the parents' business.

Secondly, income splitting works simply because of the fact that marginal
tax rates increase with income. With a flat-rate tax structure, in which the
marginal rate is constant (the individual is taxed on the excess of his income
over some exemption level at a fixed rate), there is no incentive for income
splitting, provided that the exemption level for a family is proportional to
the number of individuals in the family.

Thirdly, even with several trusts, there is only a limited reduction in the
tax liability an individual can achieve through income splitting. If a married
couple splits its income with a child (but did not set up any trusts), the
maximum savings in taxes that they could obtain is $8,377.[3] If a wealthy,
married couple with four children sets up eight trusts, their maximum total
tax savings is $90,700. The minimum income required to achieve this tax
savings is $745,400. Somebody with this income has his effective tax rate
reduced from 47.9 percent to 35.7 percent.

Under Reagan's 1985 tax reform proposal, opportunities for income splitting would be curtailed, but not eliminated. It would be harder to use trusts,
and income from capital given to a child by his or her parents would be
included in the parent's income, until the child is fourteen.

POSTPONEMENT OF TAXES

A dollar today is worth more than a dollar next year. Accordingly, if one has
a choice, it is always better to postpone one's taxes. (More formally, we say
that the present discounted value of an individual's tax liabilities can be reduced
in this way.)

There are several major methods of postponing taxes.

[1] The trusts cannot be identical; that is, they must differ substantively so that they serve a purpose other
than simple income splitting. Thus one trust may be a Clifford trust (defined below) and another one an
ordinary trust.

[2] The major restriction on these is that they must be at least ten-year trusts.

[3] This is calculated in the following way. In 1983 a single individual reached a maximum marginal tax rate
of 50 percent at an income of $38,702, while a married couple reached the maximum tax rate of 50 percent
at an income of $53,000. Thus if a parent who was in the 50 percent bracket transferred more than $38,702
to a child, both he and his child would be in the same marginal tax bracket; additional transfers would not
reduce aggregate family taxes. The taxes that a very rich family would have paid on $53,000 transferred to
the child are $26,500. The tax that the single individual pays on this amount is $17,123. The tax saving is
thus $8,377. The maximum tax saving from a trust is calculated in a similar manner.

IRA Accounts, Keogh Accounts, and Pensions

These savings programs (allegedly for retirement purposes) provide the most widely known method of tax deferral. When individuals put income into these accounts (or a firm puts money into a pension plan), the payment is not subject to taxation; only when the income is eventually received is there a tax liability. The tax advantage of these programs can be viewed as arising from the deferral of the tax.[4] Though allegedly for retirement, we noted in Chapter 22 that the penalties on early withdrawal cease to be significant if the taxpayer keeps the funds in the account for several years.

Capital Gains and the Postponement of Taxes

Capital gains, as we have observed, are taxed only upon realization. If one buys a capital asset and it goes up in value, one can postpone paying the tax simply by not selling the asset. If one would like to sell part of the asset, in order to buy, say, some consumer goods, it is better to borrow, using the asset as collateral. This method has a further advantage: if one postpones the tax until death, no capital gains tax is due.

Avoiding the Risks Associated with Postponing Capital Gains Taxes

Keeping the asset in one's portfolio may impose a risk on an individual that he does not wish to bear. There may be ways he can effectively eliminate this risk. If there is an asset with a return that is highly *negatively correlated* with the given security (that is, it has a high return when the original security has a low return, and, conversely, it has a low return when the original security has a high return), then by buying that asset, the fluctuations in the price of the two assets effectively cancel each other, one going up when the other goes down; and so the individual will not bear any risk.

Alternatively, if there is security that is highly *positively correlated* with the given asset, the individual sells *short* the security. Selling short a security is, in principle, like borrowing money, except the amount that you have to repay at the end of, say, a year depends on the price of the stock. If the price goes up, you have to pay back more and are worse off; if the price goes down, you have to pay back less and are better off. Assume, for instance, that 100 shares of the Super Ice Cream Company are presently selling for $1,000. Someone might lend $1,000 in return for a promise to repay the value of 100 shares of the Super Ice Cream Company a year from now. If the price of a share rises from $10 to $11, you have to pay back $1,100; if it falls from $10 to $9, you only have to pay back $900. What is important about a short sale is that since you are better off when the price of the stock goes down, this risk cancels the risk associated with owning a share of the security.

More generally, in a perfect capital market we can always find a set of transactions that allows one to offset the risks associated with holding on to an asset on which one has made a capital gain.[5]

---

[4] Recall, however, our discussion of Chapter 22 where we showed that these programs could also be viewed as exempting from taxation the return on savings in these accounts.

[5] In practice, for those with very limited capital, the costs of engaging in these transactions to offset the risks may be significant.

Assume now that an individual bought security A and then bought another security B, which was highly negatively correlated with the first security. The individual would be bearing little risk. What he gained on one he would lose on the other. When A's price was up he would be better off on that account, but he would be worse off on B's account. Why would anyone do something like that? If done properly, there are distinct tax advantages.

On December 31, if stock A has gone up in price he sells security B (which has gone down), realizing a capital loss. If stock A has gone down in price he sells it, again realizing a capital loss. For the current year, he shows a loss on his books, which reduces his tax liability.

On January 1 he closes out the rest of his position; that is, if the price of A was up on December 31, so that he sold security B on December 31, on January 1 he sells his stock in A, or vice versa.

He has, by this means, reduced his tax liability this year and increased his tax liability next year. But next year he can do the same, postponing his taxes for still another year.

Straddles

The use of **straddles** for postponing taxes was particularly prevalent in commodities markets until 1981. Traders in commodities had been buying, for instance, wheat for delivery in two months and selling wheat for delivery in three months,[6] even before the tax advantages became apparent. When an individual does this, he is said to be engaging in a straddle. The price of a contract for delivery of wheat in two months and the price of a contract for delivery of wheat in three months are highly correlated; they tend to move together. If it becomes apparent that there is a crop failure in Russia, the price of both contracts goes up; if it becomes apparent that there is a bumper crop, the price of both contracts goes down. The two contracts are not, however, *perfectly correlated*. (Perfect correlation would entail that a 1 percent change in one contract always be accompanied by a 1 percent change in the other). If most harvests occur in the fall, wheat for delivery in February will have a higher price than wheat for delivery in January, since it will have to be stored a month longer. If the cost of storage goes up, the price of "February wheat" may increase relative to the price of "January wheat." One of the more important costs associated with storage are interest costs; and if the interest rate rises a great deal, the two prices may move quite differently. Thus an individual who buys January wheat and sells February wheat is largely speculating on what will happen to the cost of storage. There may be an economic reason for traders in commodities wanting to speculate on this; there are real economic risks involved. At the same time, in periods during which interest rates are very stable, the risks are very low. The prices of the January and February contracts are very highly correlated.

---

[6]That is, selling a promise to deliver wheat in three months' time. Most individuals who buy and sell promises to deliver wheat neither own the wheat nor intend to take delivery of the wheat. The contract (the "promise") has a market price. If they buy it on one day at a given price, they hope to sell it later at a higher price. If they sell a contract to deliver wheat at some date, prior to the delivery date they buy the contract back, at whatever the market price for the contract is at that date.

Closing the Straddle Loophole

Prior to 1981 these straddles were a major method by which investors postponed taxes. The government has long taken the position that transactions taken solely for the purpose of tax avoidance need not be granted the favorable tax treatment sought. The government could attempt to refuse to allow the individual to take the losses that he had realized in the part of the transactions that he closed out in December. What was at issue was whether there was a real economic risk involved in the straddle position, or whether the straddle was undertaken solely as a method of postponing taxes. The volatility of interest rates in the early 1980s made it abundantly clear that there was some risk associated with these straddles; the difficulty facing the Internal Revenue Service in ascertaining the *motive* for the transactions would seem almost insurmountable. Occasionally, however, the motive is clear.

In a famous case involving two individuals trading through the brokerage firm Merrill Lynch, the court ruled that there was evidence the parties had engaged in the straddles for reasons of tax avoidance; at the same time, it made clear that there was no presumption that those engaged in straddles were doing so primarily or solely for tax avoidance reasons.

While the Merrill Lynch case was in the courts, Congress acted to close this loophole, requiring those trading in commodities to report their gains and losses as if they had been realized on December 31, whether or not they had closed out their position. A special tax rate of 32 percent was applied to these gains and losses.

But while Congress thus closed one loophole, it left others standing; for instance, trading in the options markets for securities was explicitly exempted from the provisions of the act. An option on the stock market entails the individual promising to deliver in, say, three months' time, 100 shares of, say GM stock at a price of $25. To postpone taxes the individual thus buys an option for delivery in three months and sells a contract for delivery in four months. Again, the two options are highly correlated. (The transactions costs are perhaps slightly higher in the options market than on the commodities market, making it more expensive for individuals to postpone their taxes this way, but not impossible.)

In drafting the legislation affecting straddles, Congress was quite aware of the central feature that enables individuals to postpone taxes without bearing risk. The individual buys and sells two highly correlated securities. But distinguishing those cases where the transaction is undertaken for other reasons is virtually impossible; there is no criterion that economists would find acceptable, and even were it possible to make a meaningful distinction, finding the appropriate legal language to make the distinction enforceable is equally difficult. Congress, in acting to deny the beneficial tax consequences of tax straddles, defined straddles as portfolio positions, the risk of which was less than the risk associated with each of the parts. But this is precisely the purpose of portfolio diversification, and taken literally, the language suggests that anyone who is attempting to diversify his portfolio is engaged in a straddle. This is an example of the kind of language that almost unavoidably gives rise to litigation.

The two principles of tax avoidance described so far, income splitting and tax postponement, are quantitatively probably much less significant than **tax arbitrage,** which involves taking advantage of the different rates of taxation imposed on the return to various assets and on different people. With tax arbitrage an individual can engage in a set of financial transactions to reduce the present discounted value of his tax liabilities without encountering any significant increase in risk.[7]

Strictly speaking, the term *arbitrage* refers to situations where there is a sure gain—i.e., there is no risk assumed. Though in theory the tax code provides many opportunities for riskless tax arbitrage, in practice most tax avoidance activities involve the assumption of some risk. This is partly because of the general provision in the tax code that asserts that a set of transactions undertaken solely to avoid taxes will not be granted the favorable tax treatment. There are many situations where individuals must show that they are "at risk" to obtain the deferred tax treatment. But the risks that have to be borne are minimal.

The term is also applied to situations where different individuals face different tax rates, and a set of riskless transactions can be so designed so that both are better off as a result of the reduction in their joint tax liabilities.

Borrowing to Buy Capital Assets: Taking Advantage of Capital Gains

As we noted in the previous chapter, long-term capital gains are taxed at 40 percent of the rate of short-term captial gains. This opens up a large number of avenues for reducing one's tax liabilities. The most prevalant of these entails borrowing to buy an asset on which a long-term capital gain is expected to accrue.

From an economic point of view, it makes no difference whether an asset earns a return in the form of capital gains or in the form of dividends and interest. It is the total return, capital gain plus dividends (or interest, or rental payment), with which the individual is concerned. The tax authorities, however, make a significant distinction in the way these different kinds of returns are taxed and thus provide an incentive to ensure that the return accrues in the form of capital gains.

The consequences of this—and the possibilities it opens up for tax avoidance—may be seen most clearly in the case of real estate. Consider a piece of land that in the absence of taxation would have been held for speculative purposes. The potential buyer anticipates that in seven years' time there will be a large demand for a vacant lot in the center of the city and that, accordingly, the price of land will rise between now and then by an average rate of approximately 10 percent, just equal to the rate of interest, so that in seven years' time its value will double. The land now costs $1,000.

---

[7]Note that under our definition of tax arbitrage (where what is reduced is the present discounted value of tax liabilities, not tax liabilities at every date) many of the schemes for tax deferral fit, such as borrowing to put money into IRA accounts.

Assume the individual borrows the $1,000 and makes an arrangement with the bank that no interest is due for seven years. In seven years the value of the land will have doubled. He will receive $2,000 for selling the land. But he will owe the bank, with compound interest, $2,000. He just breaks even.

Consider now what happens under our present tax system. All of the interest is tax-deductible. When the individual goes to pay back the bank, the $1,000 of cumulative interest is tax-deductible, costing him net $500 (assuming he is in the 50 percent marginal tax bracket). On the other hand, the $1,000 in capital gains is subject to long-term capital gains treatment. He only pays a 20 percent tax on it, so after selling his property, he has $1,800; after paying back the bank, plus interest (after tax), he has $300.[8]

Notice that in doing this he has not had to put out any funds of his own. He has simply engaged in tax arbitrage, taking advantage of the difference between the capital gains tax rate and the rate at which interest is deductible.

Indeed, in principle, he can engage in this to the point where he has no tax liability at all. He can use this to offset not only his tax liability on his capital income but his tax liability on his wage income.

This is a loophole the Internal Revenue Service has seemed to recognize, and it imposes restrictions on the maximum amount of interest deductions one can take that are not matched by returns on investment, other than for mortgages. But the restrictions still leave considerable scope for tax avoidance and do not appear to be very effective. Relatively few individuals appear to be constrained by this restriction.[9]

Capital Gains and Depreciation

We consider now a second example to see how the interaction between the provisions for capital gains and depreciation provide further opportunities for tax avoidance. We saw in Chapter 21 that depreciation allowances under present law exceed true economic depreciation. We argued that if true economic depreciation allowances were provided, the capital tax would have no distortionary effect; in particular, that if the present discounted value of an asset just equaled its cost in the absence of taxation, it would also just equal its cost under taxation. But with accelerated depreciation, the present discounted value of the returns after tax will exceed the costs. While earlier an individual who borrowed to buy the investment would have just broken even, now he makes a positive return, but the return is just the tax savings from accelerated depreciation.

In discussing this, we failed to note that when the individual sells the asset, since the value of the asset will exceed the "depreciated value" (i.e., the original price minus what the individual has subtracted for depreciation allowances), he will be subjected to taxation on the difference. If he were subjected to tax at the ordinary rate, the effect of the accelerated depreciation would simply be a postponement of taxes—though it still would have

[8]We ignore some details concerning the timing of the interest deductions.
[9]See D. Feenberg, "Does the Investment Interest Limitation Explain the Existence of Dividends?" *Journal of Financial Economics* 9(1981): 265–69.

considerable economic value. But the difference may be subjected to capital gains taxes, in which case he is still better off.

Make the extreme assumption, for instance, that an individual is contemplating buying a building that will last forever, that there is no inflation, and that the real rate of interest is 2 percent.[10] The building yields a rent of $2,000 a year and thus, in the absence of taxes, would sell for $100,000. An individual could borrow the $100,000 and just cover his interest costs. Now the government allows the individual to deduct his interest payments, taxes his rentals, allows a depreciation assuming a fifteen-year lifetime, and taxes the difference between what he sells the asset for and its depreciation value.[11] Now assume the individual holds onto the building for only one year (just long enough for it to be eligible for long-term capital gains treatment). Then, on a straight-line depreciation, the individual deducts ⅟₁₅th of the purchase price—i.e., 6⅔ percent—for depreciation. His interest payment is deductible and just cancels his rental payment, which is taxable. Thus if he is in the 50 percent tax bracket, he has a current reduction in his tax liabilities of $3,333. Next year, when he sells the asset, he will sell it for the original price, $100,000 (since the building does not deteriorate, and there is no inflation). He will have to report a capital gain of $6,667 (since he had previously "depreciated" the buildings by that amount). Thus next year his tax liability has increased by 20 percent times $6,667, or $1,333; he has gained because capital gains are taxed at 40 percent of ordinary rates. If he had held on to the asset longer he would have gained from the postponment of the tax, which is payable only upon realization of the gain. (If the capital gains were taxed at full rates, he would still be better off because of this.)

The Effect of Inflation. He does even better in periods of inflation. Assume, to use numbers that are somewhat more realistic, that the interest rate was 12 percent and the rate of inflation was 10 percent, so the real rate of interest remains at 2 percent. If the rent the first year is $2,000 and is rising at 10 percent, the price initially was $100,000, and the value of the building will be rising at 10 percent; the individual will again be indifferent when choosing between purchasing and not purchasing the building. In the absence of taxation, he could have purchased the building by borrowing. At the end of the year he would have to repay the bank $112,000 ($100,000 plus 12 percent interest). He could sell the building for $110,000 ($100,000 plus 10 percent for inflation), and he would have received $2,000 rent.

Again, his (now higher) interest is tax-deductible, while his rent remains taxed. His depreciation allowance is unaffected. It is still $6,667 ($100,000/15). His current tax liabilities are reduced by $3,333 ($6,666 × .5; from the depreciation) plus $5,000 (by the interest in excess of rental receipts). Next year, when he sells the building, he will have a capital gain of $16,667 ($10,000 from inflation, plus $6,667 from the depreciation allowance). If he were taxed on this at full rates, the tax would be $8,333, just offsetting the $8,333 of tax

---

[10] The calculations for assessing the value of a very long-lived building and an "infinitely" lived building are not much different.

[11] This was the lifetime used for buildings from 1981 until 1984. In 1984 Congress lengthened the lifetime to eighteen years. Throughout we assume, for simplicity, straight line depreciation.

reductions that he received in the first year. But if the $16,667 capital gain is taxed at 20 percent, his total tax liability is only $3,333. Thus, even ignoring the advantages of postponement, his tax liability is reduced by $5,000. Again, note that in this example the individual was not required to put up any capital.

Maintenance Expenditures and Capital Gains

We turn now to a third example, which shows still another way in which individuals can take advantage of the special treatment of capital gains. This time we focus on maintenance expenditures, which are deductible against current income. The Internal Revenue Service makes a distinction between maintenance expenditures and capital improvements (which cannot be deducted against current income). In practice, the distinction is a fine one, and except for certain obvious expenditures (a completely new roof, a new furnace, etc.), the individual is allowed to make deductions against current income. In this case we shall see that there may be an important economic distortion associated with the tax system, in encouraging excessive expenditures on maintenance of capital structures.

Consider an investor contemplating purchasing a building. It costs $100,000. The building will last for thirty years (without any maintenance), at the end of which time it will be worthless; it will be torn down (at negligible costs) and a new building constructed on the site. With maintenance expenditures of $2,500 annually in real terms (the costs rise with inflation), the building can be maintained in its present state indefinitely, so that if the rate of inflation is 10 percent, in thirty years it will sell for 20 times its present price (10 percent compounded continuously over thirty years). The present discounted value of the expenditures (assuming an interest rate of 12 percent) on maintenance over thirty years is $56,400; the return is the value of the building: without maintenance expenditures, the building was worthless; now it can be sold for $2,000,000.[12] The present discounted value of $2,000,000 is $54,648. It does not pay to maintain the building. It is better to let it decay and be replaced by a new one in thirty years' time.

To see how the tax law distorts decisions and provides easy vehicles for tax avoidance, assume that the individual borrows to buy the building. We assume that in the initial situation the present discounted value of rentals from the building over thirty years equals the cost. This implies that if he borrows, the present discounted value of his rental receipts will just enable him to repay the loan with interest. He would, in the absence of taxes, be indifferent to undertaking the investment project. Now, consider what happens with our tax structure. It taxes his rental receipts but allows him to depreciate the building and deduct the maintenance costs. As a result of accelerated depreciation combined with the tax-deductibility of interest and maintenance expenditures, the present discounted value of his net tax lia-

---

[12]The number may seem large, but the "magic" of compound interest does this. Throughout we assume continuous (daily) compounding. Thus with continuous compounding at an interest rate of 10 percent, a dollar today will be $1 \times e^{.1 \times 30} = \$20$ in 30 years. With annual compounding a dollar today will be worth $1 \times (1.1)^{30} = 17.45$ in 30 years.

bilities is negative. Even if when he sells the building, in thirty years' time, he had to pay taxes at ordinary rates on his capital gain (over the depreciated value of the asset), he would have gained, through the postponement effect. But he also gains from the fact that his return is taxed at the favorable long-term capital gains rates, while his interest and maintenance expenditures are deductible at ordinary rates.

The government thus subsidizes the investment twice; once through the accelerated depreciation and secondly through the special provisions for capital gains. Notice that the individual again did not need any capital to make the investment; the return is completely in terms of the reduction in his tax liabilities (recall that the real return of the investment in maintenance expenditures in the absence of taxes was just slightly negative.)

Borrowing to Buy State and Local (Tax-Exempt) Bonds

Interest on state and local bonds is not taxable. Assume that state and local bonds yield 10 percent, and the individual can borrow money from the bank at 12 percent. If the individual is in the 50 percent marginal tax bracket, it pays for him to borrow, say, $10,000 to buy a tax-exempt bond. Every year he will have to pay the bank $1,200 in interest, but the after-tax cost of this is only $600. On the other hand, his tax-exempt bond yields him $1,000. He makes a clear profit (after taxes) of $400. The government, not surprisingly, does not allow this: it does not allow you to deduct interest on loans used to buy tax-exempt bonds. But funds are fungible: it may be impossible for the government to know whether you borrowed more than was needed when you constructed your house, so that you had more money left over to buy tax-exempt bonds. This problem is sufficiently prevalent that there are precise rules specifying the conditions under which a loan will be treated as if it were made for the purposes of buying a tax-exempt bond.

Tax Arbitrage Involving Institutions and Individuals Facing Different Tax Rates

The examples of tax arbitrage described so far entail taking advantage of the fact that different forms of capital income receive different treatment and are fixed at different rates. Tax arbitrage opportunities are also opened up when different individuals and institutions face different tax rates. The financial arrangements of leasing, in which investment tax credits and depreciation allowances are tranferred from firms without sufficient net income to take advantage of them to those who are, provide one example, as we saw in Chapter 21.

Another example is provided by state and local bonds. Because of the tax exemption of these bonds, the interest rates they pay are lower than on comparable taxable bonds. It thus is worth it for a community to borrow and relend the money. Today many communities are engaged in this form of tax arbitrage.

COMMON TAX SHELTERS

Investment schemes devised primarily to reduce one's tax liabilities are called **tax shelters.** As we have noted before, for a tax shelter to be valid there has to be an economic motive involved other than the avoidance of taxation.

The most common tax shelters have been in oil and gas and in real estate. The choice of an appropriate tax shelter for a particular individual is a complicated matter, and there are a number of detailed provisions of the tax code that need to be taken into account. Among these are the following:

One way that the goverment attempts to ensure that there is an economic motive for undertaking a transaction is that the individual has to have something at risk. Assume an individual borrows money to buy a machine; the revenue from the machine is supposed to pay back the loan. The machine turns out to be a dud. If the lender cannot go back to the borrower to obtain repayment of the loan, the borrower is not at risk for the amount of the loan. Real-estate tax shelters are exempt from the at-risk requirements, which makes them particularly attractive for individuals of limited wealth who cannot afford the risks associated with a typical equipment-leasing tax shelter.

As part of the individual income tax, the government imposes a 20 percent *minimum tax* on total income (above a certain theshhold). Total income is calculated by taking the individual's taxable income and adding back into it certain *tax preference* items. These include the 60 percent of long-term capital gains that is ordinarily excluded and the value of accelerated depreciation.

Since many tax shelters work through large interest deductions, the limitations on interest deductibility turn out to be important for some individuals (whose interest and dividend income from other sources is limited).

The value of the accelerated depreciation is subject to ordinary income taxation when an asset is sold (we say that the accelerated depreciation is "recaptured"). As we have noted, there is still a gain to the taxpayer, through the postponement of taxes.

In Table 24.1 we present a summary of the various tax shelters, with their advantages and disadvantages.

WHO GAINS FROM LOOPHOLES?

We have not attempted in this chapter to provide an exhaustive list of loopholes, tax avoidance devices, and tax shelters. These change rapidly; at a given moment, some of the loopholes will have been closed and others opened up. The principles involved, however, remain the same.

Different industries have very strong incentives to attempt to garner for themselves special treatment. There is often some small justification for the special treatment. This special treatment opens up a loophole, which can usually be put into one of the categories that we have described in this chapter. It is important to note, however, to whom the benefits of these tax shelters accrue. They usually do not accrue to the investor attempting to take advantage of them. The competitive market takes care of that: different investors compete sufficiently vigorously to take advantage of the special tax

Table 24.1 SOME COMMON TAX SHELTERS*

Types of Shelter	Tax Benefits	Problems
Oil and gas	Deduct intangible drilling costs†	Risky
	Depletion allowances (reduced to 15 percent by 1984)	Not very liquid
Real Estate	Can borrow a large fraction of investment, deducting interest payments	Recapture of accelerated depreciation
	At-risk rules‡ not applicable	Not liquid
	Capital gains potential	Often risky
	Special benefits for special categories of real estate (e.g., rehabilitation)	Often high transaction costs
	Accelerated depreciation	
Equipment leasing	Accelerated depreciation	At-risk provisions
	Investment tax credit	Depreciation recapture
	May be able to borrow to finance investment	Not liquid
		Risk associated with value of equipment at end of lease
Cattle and other agriculture	Deduct supplies as consumed	At-risk provisions

*Adapted from the *New York Times*, March 4, 1984.

†Intangible drilling costs are costs other than the direct costs of machinery used. Intangible drilling costs include, for instance, overhead.

‡See p. 516 for what is meant by being "at risk."

advantages that the after-tax return—which, after all, is what the individual is really concerned with—is driven down to the after-tax return on other, less advantaged investments. The consequences of the special treatment, then, are twofold. First, it diverts resources into the industry that is receiving the special treatment. This may be the intention of the legislation, but it usually is not. Secondly, the major beneficiaries are the owners of the assets in the industry at the time that the loophole is opened up. It usually takes some time before real resources get diverted into the industry. In the meanwhile the original owners enjoy a windfall capital gain. The tax advantages are capitalized in the value of their assets; that is, if they sell their assets, they will receive a higher price for them; the individual buying the asset will pay a sufficiently high price that *his* after-tax return is the same as it would be on any other asset.

Just as the imposition of such a tax benefit causes an inequity, a windfall gain for the current owners, the removal of the tax benefit causes an inequity, a windfall capital loss on the current owners. If the assets in the industry are owned by the same individuals when the benefit is granted as when it is withdrawn, the two cancel each other. But frequently, the removal of the special treatment occurs several years later, and it is important to recognize that it is different individuals who will be affected by the removal of the special treatment. Closing the loophole is likely to be inequitable.

Two industries for which tax shelters have been widely discussed are cattle and oil and gas.

Cattle

Firms typically buy a young calf, feed it, and later sell it. The question is, is the gain on the sale of cattle ordinary income or capital gain? The cattle industry succeeded in getting it to be treated as a capital gain. At the same time, the expenses involved in feeding cattle (and the interest on the funds borrowed to finance the purchase of the cattle) are tax-deductible, at full rates. This tax avoidance device is thus similar to that involved in real estate, where maintenance expenditures (like the food) are deductible against ordinary income but the gain is taxable at capital gains rates.

Who benefits from this loophole? Not even cattle owners necessarily benefit, since the higher after-tax returns attract others to enter the industry; this forces the price of cattle down, to the point where the after-tax return is approximately the same as it is in any other industry. The reason for this is that the supply of cattle is relatively elastic. In Chapter 6 we saw that a tax on an industry with an elastic supply function was reflected completely in the price consumers paid: producers were unaffected. Exactly the same applies for a subsidy as it does for a tax.

The return to any perfectly mobile factors—such as capital—will be unaffected by such a subsidy. All the benefits accrue to the owners of factors that are specific to the industry, such as land that cannot be used for other purposes. If all factors are "mobile"—land that is used in cattle raising can be used for other purposes almost as well—most of the benefits accrue to customers.

Gas and Oil

Exploration of gas and oil represent perhaps the most notorious tax shelter (other than real estate). There are a number of provisions providing beneficial treatment to gas and oil. Earlier we discussed depreciation allowances. These are provided to take account of the fact that as a machine is used, it becomes less valuable (it wears out and becomes obsolete). Similarly, as oil is extracted from a well the well becomes less valuable. To compensate for this, the government provides depletion allowances. These are related not directly to the changes in the value of the asset but to the value of the oil extracted. Their level has varied over time, at one time reaching 22 percent of the value of the oil sold. The correspondence between depletion allowance and the change in the value of the well is even weaker than that between depreciation allowance for a machine and "true economic depreciation". Over the life of the well, the depletion allowance may, for instance, exceed the purchase price of the asset, and when an oil well (or lease) is sold, a capital loss can be taken against the original purchase price without accounting for the depletion allowances taken in the interim. It is as if the government is allowing two tax deductions for the decrease in the value of the asset.

Even worse, much of the expenditure on oil exploration is deductible as a current expense rather than as a capital expenditure. Only about one well in ten turns out to have a sufficient amount of oil to extract. The question is, should all the expenditures, on successful or unsuccessful wells, be lumped together and considered the capital cost associated with obtaining oil? From an economic point of view this would seem reasonable. But consider the consequence of doing this. It would provide an incentive for each well to be drilled by a separate company or partnership (it is easy to establish separate companies).[13] This would make it impossible to lump the unsuccessful wells with the good wells. A company that failed would report a loss and go out of business. Thus, as unreasonable as it may seem to treat exploration expenditures as current, rather than capital, expenditures, there may be no easy alternative.

But again we need to ask who gains by these tax loopholes. Industry experts claim that the return to capital in the oil industry, after tax, is no higher than elsewhere. But this is exactly what theory would predict: the benefits of the tax loopholes accrue to the owners of the inelastic factors, the land under which there is oil, not "mobile" factors, like capital and labor.[14]

SUMMARY

1. There are three major principles underlying most of the devices by which individuals can legally attempt to reduce their tax liabilities: income splitting, tax deferral, and tax arbitrage.

2. Income splitting occurs under progressive taxes, where a family, by transferring assets to children and to trusts, reduces its total family tax liability.

3. Tax deferral is based on the concept that a dollar today is worth more than a dollar tomorrow, so taxes paid in the future are less costly than those paid today.

4. Tax arbitrage takes advantage of the different rates at which various forms of capital income are taxed. Most of the tax arbitrage devices take advantage of the special treatment of capital gains.

5. Tax loopholes have distortionary effects, and the benefits often do not accrue to those that they seem to be benefiting. The tax benefits of industry-specific loopholes (such as those relating to oil and gas) accrue to the owners of the inelastic factors in the industry (the land under which the hydrocarbon deposits lie), not to elastic factors (labor and capital).

KEY CONCEPTS

Tax avoidance	Income splitting
Tax evasion	Straddles
Tax shelters	Tax arbitrage

QUESTIONS AND PROBLEMS

1. In the text, we showed how straddles could be used to *postpone* taxes. Prior to 1981, positions in the commodity market (that is, promises to buy or sell at some future date) that were held for more than six months received the favorable long-term capital gains treatment. Explain how an individual engaging in a straddle—

---

[13] If wells are drilled by separate companies, one would want to ensure that each one had enough profits to take advantage of the tax deductibility of losses.

[14] Thus if there were only inelastic factors involved, this tax loophole would have equity consequences but no distortionary consequences.

closing out (that is, selling) one part of his position just before six months and the other just after six months—could make a tax arbitrage return.

2. A common method of income splitting prior to 1984 was the granting of interest-free loans within a family. (These are referred to as Crown loans.) What would be the tax savings of an individual in the 50 percent marginal tax bracket from a $20,000 loan made to a child who had no other income, if the interest rate is 10 percent?

3. Describe the tax savings for someone in the 50 percent marginal tax rate who owns a business with $10,000 in "profits" if he incorporates, giving his children a 50 percent interest in the business. Assume his children have no other income.

4. Use a demand and supply curve diagram to contrast the effects of the special treatment to cattle (assuming a horizontal supply schedule) and to oil (assuming a vertical supply schedule.)

25

Reform of the Tax System

On May 29, 1985, President Reagan transmitted to Congress a proposal for a major tax reform. In his message to Congress, he wrote:

> We face an historic challenge: to change our present tax system into a model of fairness, simplicity, efficiency, and compassion, to remove the obstacles to growth and unlock the door to a future of unparalleled innovation and achievement.
>
> For too long our tax code has been a source of ridicule and resentment, violating our Nation's most fundamental principles of justice and fair play. While most Americans labor under excessively high tax rates that discourage work and cut drastically into savings, many are able to exploit the tangled mass of loopholes that has grown up around our tax code to avoid paying their fair share—and sometimes paying any taxes at all. . . .

His sentiments reflected the feelings of the majority of Americans. One recent poll, for instance, reported that 69 percent of those asked said that they believe that people with more money paid too little in taxes.[1] Though there is a consensus that reform is needed, there is not consensus on how best to reform the system. The beneficiaries of each of the special provisions that the Reagan proposal would do away with have tried to argue for the preservation of their special treatment.

Any reform will hurt a large number of special-interest groups; but most economists believe that there would be an enormous overall gain. If all groups could simultaneously be persuaded to give up their special treatment, a fairer and more efficient tax structure could be devised. Though some individuals

---

[1] The New York Times / CBS News Poll, reported in *The New York Times*, January 24, 1985, p. D1.

may be disadvantaged in the short run, the long-run stimulus that such a reform would provide for the economy would ensure that almost everyone would, eventually, be better off. The disadvantaged groups see their certain losses in the short run and are unsure about the long-run gains. Individuals find it difficult to balance their gains and their losses; a general paranoia results in most believing that they will be among the disadvantaged. The result is that it has been difficult to enact a meaningful tax reform. The political processes that make tax reform so difficult also make it, in many economists' judgment, imperative to adopt a simple tax system that does not give the special-interest groups any scope. As this book goes to press, the fortune of Reagan's proposals remains up in the air. Will the bill that is eventually passed be a major reform, as the president hoped, or will it be another in the long line of bills that, while closing some loopholes, opens up others, and while simplifying some provisions, makes others more complex? This chapter is not concerned with a detailed evaluation of Reagan's proposals but rather with describing and evaluating four major tax reform proposals that have been the subject of discussion, both here and abroad, over the past decade: the comprehensive income tax, the flat-rate tax, the consumption tax, and the value-added tax.

THE IMPETUS FOR REFORM

The impetus for a major reform in our tax system comes from the widespread belief that it has high administrative costs, that even with these high administrative costs compliance is decreasing, that it is riddled with inequities, and that the high marginal tax rates and the myriad special provisions give rise to significant inefficiencies and are perhaps an important contributor to the marked slowdown in the increase in productivity of the United States economy in recent years.

Administrative Costs

The brunt of the administrative costs of the United States income tax is borne by the taxpayers; and the costs are not only the direct costs of filling out the tax returns but the indirect costs of record keeping required to comply with the tax laws. No estimate of these indirect costs has been made, but the government has made an estimate of the direct costs of reporting in 1977. The public spent about 613 million hours filling out tax forms.

The tax laws are so complex that nearly half of all taxpayers use tax preparers. Joel Slemrod, of the University of Minnesota, estimated that in 1982 taxpayers spent between $17 and $27 billion on compliance costs (the value of their time plus what they paid to tax preparers), or from 5 percent to 7 percent of the revenue raised by the federal and state income tax systems combined. This included between 1.8 and 2.1 billion hours spent filling out tax returns, and between $3.0 and $3.4 billion was spent on professional tax assistance.[2]

---

[2] His estimates were based on a survey of Minnesota taxpayers. See J. Slemrod and N. Sorum, "The Compliance Cost of the U.S. Individual Income Tax System," February 1984, University of Minnesota (mimeographed).

Complexity

The complexity of the tax code contributes to the high administrative costs, to the low level of compliance, and to the widespread sense of inequity. There are many indicators of this complexity. We have already noted that almost half of all taxpayers resort to professional assistance to complete their tax returns. There are more than 250 different forms. As one book on the tax system notes,

> The entire Code of Federal Regulations, all general and permanent laws in force in the United States, has 50 different titles filling more than 180 volumes. Title 26, the Internal Revenue code, is responsible for 14 of these volumes, of which 8 are just for the income tax. Title 26 occupies 14 inches of library shelf space. The eight volumes for the income tax fill 5,105 pages, cost $65.00 per set, and weigh 12 pounds 2 ounces. The 1981 Economic Recovery Act amended some 89 separate sections of the tax code. To explain these changes, the staff of the Joint Committee on Taxation published a 411-page booklet. . . .[3]

The complexity is reflected in the difficulties that even the Internal Revenue Service has in accurately assessing tax liabilities. Ralph Nader's Tax Reform Research Group created a tax schedule for a fictional couple that they sent to 22 IRS offices. The tax liabilities assessed by the different offices differed markedly, from a high refund of $811.96 to a tax underpayment of $52.14. IRS studies have shown error rates for commercial firms working on tax returns of 82 percent of individuals with low incomes. And people trained and employed by the IRS computed the wrong tax 72 percent of the time handling relatively simple tax problems.[4]

Another indication of the complexity of the code—the difficulty that individuals have of knowing whether they are or are not complying with the law—is provided by the fact that, when individuals go to court to challenge the IRS, they generally win: the IRS recovers only about one-third of what it claims.[5] Instances where one court has ruled one way and another a different way on the same issue make the plight of the taxpayer even more difficult. For example, as we noted in Chapter 20, commuting costs are not, in general, deductible. A Federal Appeals Court in New York ruled, however, that airplane pilots could deduct the costs of using their automobiles to transport their heavy paraphernalia (and themselves) between their homes and the airport. But a tax court in Florida, not bound by a decision in New York, ruled the other way.[6]

Compliance

To collect its taxes, the federal government relies on a combination of voluntary compliance coupled with the threat of prosecution for outright fraud. To assist individuals whose sense of moral responsibility might be too weak

---

[3] R. Hall and A. Rabushka, *Low Tax, Flat Tax, Simple Tax* (New York: McGraw-Hill, 1983).
[4] *Consumer Reports*, March 1976.
[5] *Business Week*, April 16, 1984, p. 87.
[6] Ibid.

to induce them to report all of their income, the government requires employers to report what wages they pay to their workers and firms to report what dividends and interest they pay to shareholders and bondholders. The government has only limited facilities, however, for checking on cash transactions, and the ability to avoid taxes by using cash has encouraged the growth of what is called the underground economy. Though precise estimates of the size of the underground economy are hard to come by, some observers believe that it may involve up to one-quarter of the work force and 15 percent of the GNP. It includes unreported income not only of drug dealers, babysitters, and domestic help but of carpenters, gardeners, and those who sell merchandise on the street.[7]

The Internal Revenue Service estimates that of the $750 billion that individuals were supposed to pay in taxes in 1982, $100 billion were not paid. (This does not include those who reduce their tax liabilities by taking advantage of the loopholes; the $100 billion represents those who do not report all of their income.) The extent of noncompliance has been growing more rapidly than tax revenues, from $29 billion a decade ago to an estimated $180 billion by 1985.

The most important sources of noncompliance are shown in Table 25.1.[8] Some observers believe even these estimates are conservative. The decrease in compliance may be partly a result of the increasing complexity of the tax code and the sense that it is inequitable; it may be partly attributed to the fact that the increased marginal tax rates make compliance more expensive; and it may be partly a consequence of the decreased likelihood of being caught. While the government audited 2.59 percent of the tax returns in 1976, in 1981 it audited only 1.55 percent of all returns, and by 1984 the percentage was down to just over 1.3 percent.

Finally, many individuals, even after reporting their income, do not pay their taxes. Presently, the IRS claims that taxpayers owe more than $27 billion in back taxes, a threefold increase from the $8.3 billion in 1977.

Tax Avoidance

Tax avoidance—taking advantage of all the loopholes in the tax structure—results in a significant erosion of the tax base and has increased rapidly in recent years. In the previous chapter we discussed the principles of tax avoidance as well as some of the more important tax shelters.

There is a market for tax avoidance activities, just as there are markets for conventional commodities. The demand for tax avoidance activities depends on how much one can save. This, in turn, depends on several factors, the most important of which is probably the marginal tax rate. Since the bound-

---

[7] By its nature, it is difficult to obtain accurate measures of the underground economy. One recent survey of studies provided a range (as a percentage of GNP) from 3.5 percent to 33 percent for the United States. See Bruno S. Frey and Werner W. Pommerehne, "Measuring the Hidden Ecomomy: Though This Be Madness, There Is Method in It," in V. Tanzi, *The Underground Economy in the United States and Abroad* (Lexington, MA: Lexington Books, 1982).

[8] Unreported illegal income, though not so important as some of the sources of tax evasion given in the first part of Table 25.1, is still an important source of tax evasion. (Al Capone, the 1920s mobster, was convicted for failing to report his illegal income when other charges would not stick.) Illegal income in the United States has increased almost fourfold in the eight years between 1973 and 1981.

Table 25.1 INCOME THAT ESCAPES THE TAX NET

	Shown on Tax Returns	Should Have Been Shown	Percent Unreported
	(in billions of dollars; 1981 estimates)		
Legal Income			
Wages and salaries	$1,455.2	$1,549.7	6.1%
Pensions and annuities	58.5	67.3	13.1
Interest	129.1	149.6	13.7
Dividends	44.9	53.7	16.4
Estate and trust	3.9	5.2	25.8
State income tax refunds, alimony, and other income	11.7	18.9	38.0
Royalties	4.4	7.1	38.8
Capital gains	25.9	43.7	40.7
Nonfarm proprietor	53.5	106.5	49.7
Partnership and small business corporation	14.9	31.6	52.9
Rents	2.5	6.9	62.8
Off-the-book services	4.5	21.5	79.1
Farm proprietor	−2.0	11.1	NA
Total Income	$1,807.0	$2,072.8	12.8%
The Illegal Sector			
Drugs*			6.1
Gambling			.9
Prostitution†			1.9
Total‡			9.0%

NA = not applicable (total farm income reported was negative).
*The drugs included were limited to heroin, cocaine, and marijuana.
†Female prostitution only.
‡Sum of components may not add to totals, due to rounding.
Source: *Business Week*, April 16, 1984, p. 9. Internal Revenue Service, *Income Tax Compliance Research, Estimates for 1973–1981*, July 1983.

ary between tax avoidance and tax evasion is often blurred, IRS auditing policy (and the penalties imposed on those who use shelters that are disallowed) is another important determinant of the demand for tax shelters. The supply of tax shelters, on the other hand, depends on the loopholes that are built into the tax law.

It might have been thought that the Economic Recovery Tax Act of 1981, which reduced the maximum tax bracket from 70 percent to 50 percent, would have decreased the demand for tax shelters; but at the same time its generous provisions for depreciation, leasing, and research and development expenditures increased the benefits of certain categories of tax shelters, and this "supply effect" more than offset the effect of the reduction in the marginal tax rates. The consequences were predictable: a large growth in R&D, equipment leasing, and, in particular, real estate tax shelters. One tax shelter expert, Robert Stanger, suggested that the Economic Recovery Tax Act of 1981 might more aptly be called "the Real Estate Benefit Act."[9]

The line between tax avoidance and evasion, as we have noted, is not

[9] Quoted in *Newsweek*, April 16, 1984, p. 58.

always easily defined. Thus in 1983 IRS agents audited 96,000 returns with tax shelters, obtaining an additional $1.8 billion in returns.

Whether as a result of tax avoidance or tax evasion, the net effect is that certain industries—such as real estate—are effectively exempt from taxation. Thus in real estate and insurance reported *losses* in partnerships (the form tax shelters usually take) more than doubled from 1980 to 1981, from $3.6 billion to $7.6 billion in 1981. Indeed, the two industries combined (including partnerships plus sole proprietorships) showed an overall loss of $50 million in 1981.[10]

Is There a Crisis?

Though there has been growing dissatisfaction with our income tax system, reaching what many believe to be a crisis situation, Brookings Institution economist Joseph Pechman has argued that the popular discussions have magnified the problem out of proportion. He points out that the ratio of income reported on tax returns to personal income (as calculated by the Department of Commerce) has not changed dramatically in recent years, actually increasing from less than 40 percent in 1950 to almost 50 percent today (see Figure 25.1).

While Pechman believes strongly in tax reform—in particular in eliminating many of the loopholes—he does not believe that the current problems are significant enough to necessitate changing the tax base (taxing consumption rather than income) or reducing the progressive nature of our tax system.

PRINCIPLES OF TAX REFORM

Our discussion provides several guidelines for the reform of the tax system.

First, the magnitude of the distortions is associated with the magnitude of the marginal tax rate. Thus one should attempt to design tax systems with low marginal rates. We have encountered numerous instances in which our tax code seems to be perverse: wealthy individuals face high marginal rates but low average rates. Because of the numerous special provisions of the individual income tax code, to obtain the requisite revenue, relatively high tax rates have to be imposed on the remaining fraction of taxable income. Because of the generous provisions for accelerated depreciation and the investment tax credit, the net revenue raised by the corporate income tax may be relatively low, but high tax rates (at the margin) may still have large distortionary effects.

Second, tax avoidance schemes are primarily associated with the progressivity of the tax schedule and with the taxation of capital—in particular, the taxation of different kinds of capital income at different rates. Reducing the level of marginal tax rates would reduce incentives to engage in tax evasion and tax avoidance. Reducing (or eliminating) the differential treatment of income would reduce the incentive, and ability, to engage in tax arbitrage.

---

[10]Indeed, all partnerships in the country, regardless of industry, showed an aggregate loss of $2.7 billion in 1981. Source: R. A. Wilson, "Unincorporated Business Activity," in *Statistics of Income* (Washington, D.C.: Internal Revenue Service, Summer 1983), pp. 63–72.

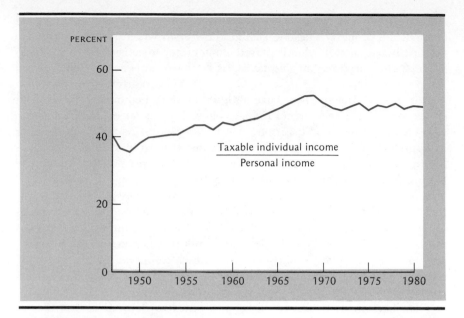

25.1 RATIO OF TAXABLE INDIVIDUAL INCOME TO PERSONAL INCOME, 1947−81. The ratio of income reported on tax returns to personal income as calculated by the Department of Commerce has not changed radically in recent years. SOURCE: J. A. Pechman, *Federal Tax Policy* (New York: McGraw-Hill, 1983), p. 63.

Third, the complexity of the tax code arises from many of the same sources that give rise to tax avoidance. For instance, whenever different categories of income are taxed differently, individuals will attempt to ensure that their income receives the favorable treatment. It seems a general rule that defining clear distinctions in law is much harder than in theory. We noted, for instance, that the distinction between a capital gain and interest is less clear than it might seem. A promise to pay $100 in ten years' time is clearly a bond; but if the bond is issued with no interest payments, its current price will be low (approximately $50 at an interest rate of 7 percent). Is the increase in price over the next seven years (from $50 to $100) a capital gain or is it disguised interest? Though Congress has enacted legislation to deny individuals the opportunity to take advantage of this particular ruse, clever tax lawyers and accountants are always in search for more subtle ways of converting ordinary income into capital gains; even when the IRS is successful in stopping a particular practice, it is at the cost of an ever-increasing complexity in the tax code.

Tax avoidance and tax evasion, besides making the tax system less progressive (and less equitable, since some individuals are in a better position to take advantage of these tax avoidance schemes and to evade taxes than others) than it otherwise would be, introduce important inefficiencies. Not only should the costs of designing and implementing these schemes (the accountants' and tax lawyers' fees) be treated as a deadweight loss, but there are further deadweight losses resulting from the resource allocation distortions to which they give rise. For instance, the tax shelter provided by cattle may have led to excessive investment in cattle.

A quite different argument in favor of simple, direct taxes is that a "good tax" has the property that one should know upon whom it falls, who bears the tax. Because its burden is passed along either to consumers or to stockholders, the corporate income tax is, as we have noted, a particularly bad tax in this respect.

The general principles we have outlined often run counter to other principles, or other objectives, of public policy. For instance, there are those who believe that a good tax is one that is not painful. As a finance minister to Louis XIV wrote: "The art of taxation consists in so plucking the goose as to obtain the largest amount of feathers with the least possible amount of hissing."[11] The corporate income tax may be a good tax in this respect.

Similarly, we noted in our earlier discussions that many of the distinctions that make the tax code complex, possibly unfair, and undoubtedly distortionary were introduced at least partly to make the tax system reflect our view more accurately of equity (the sick should not pay so much as the healthy), and partly to improve the efficiency with which resources are allocated (the energy conservation credits were introduced because it was believed that private incentives to conserve energy were insufficient).

What has emerged clearly during the past two decades is that the tax system cannot do everything. If we ask it to do too much, it may not do well in any of its objectives. The basic questions facing tax reform are thus:

1) Are there ways of simplifying the tax system that do not sacrifice "too much" of the distributive objectives, while gaining significantly in economic efficiency?

2) Though society as a whole may be better off as a result of tax reforms, the reforms are seldom "Pareto improvements." Are there ways of designing the transition from the old system to the new system in which relatively few individuals are significantly disadvantaged? This is important, in part to make the reforms politically acceptable.

3) The tax system has been viewed as a relatively efficient way by which the government can pursue certain of its objectives. For the government to have designed a direct grant system for encouraging energy conservation would have been extremely difficult. Encouraging energy conservation through the tax system seemed a particularly effective (and administratively inexpensive way) by which this national objective could be pursued. Indeed, there has been a long tradition in economics advocating the use of "corrective taxes" to alleviate the inefficiencies arising from externalities (Chapter 8). If a simplification of the tax system entails an abandonment of the use of (broadly construed) corrective (incentive) taxes, are there other ways by which these objectives could be attained, with at least the same degree of effectiveness that they are achieved at present?

Some Recent Proposals for the Reform of the United States Income Tax

Recent proposals to reform the tax system have focused on three issues:

1) Broadening the tax base by reducing or eliminating special deductions

---

[11] Quoted in *Newsweek*, April 16, 1984, p. 69.

and credits. A tax in which there are no special deductions and credits is called a **comprehensive income tax.**

2) Reducing the extent of differences in the marginal rates different individuals pay; the most extreme form the proposals take is the **flat-rate tax**, in which all individuals would be subjected to the same marginal tax rate (the tax would still be progressive, since only income above a certain exemption level would be subject to taxation).

3) Changing the *base* of the tax system from income to consumption.

There are specific proposals, combining various ingredients of the reform package. Some, for instance, call for a change in the base to consumption *and* a reduction in the degree of progressivity; many call for reducing most (but not all) of the special deductions (they are not fully comprehensive) and reducing but not eliminating differences in marginal rates (they are not flat-rate taxes). Some proposals call for **supplementing** the current income tax system rather than replacing it. In this chapter we shall assess the extent to which four "pure" proposals satisfy the general principles of reform outlined earlier, and the extent to which they are likely to alleviate the criticisms leveled against the current system.

THE COMPREHENSIVE INCOME TAX

The central issue in evaluating the comprehensive income tax is the extent to which the various special provisions reflect society's attempt to devise an equitable tax structure that encourages particularly desirable economic activities; and the extent to which the various special provisions reflect the success of special-interest groups in promoting their own interests at public expense. A related issue is the political feasibility of eliminating some of the more important special provisions, and therefore the feasibility of obtaining a tax base that is substantially more comprehensive than the current one.

Table 25.2 gives an idea of the relationship between the tax base and national income. The tax base (in excess of the zero bracket amount, the amount below which no tax is imposed)—$1,170.1 billion—was just under half of personal income.[12] There are several major "leakages" in going from personal income to adjusted gross income. The largest arises from the exemption of transfer payments (such as social security), imputed income (the return on owner-occupied houses), and investment income in life insurance companies, pension funds, and other tax-exempt forms.

Still further "leakages" arise in going from adjusted gross income to taxable income: deductions alone—$149.3 billion—amount to almost 10 percent of adjusted gross income.

But even personal income (as defined in the National Income Accounts) underestimates what a truly comprehensive income tax base should include. It does not include, for instance, capital gains or many nontaxable fringe benefits (such as health insurance) paid by the employer.[13]

With the shrunken tax base, the tax rates necessary to raise the required revenue must be high, particularly if some degree of progressivity is to be

---

[12] Personal income is the measure of income accruing to individuals in the official National Income Accounts.

[13] At the same time, it does include several items that are not likely to be included in any comprehensive income tax in the United States—in particular, imputed rents to owner-occupied houses.

Table 25.2 DERIVATION OF TAX BASE, 1981

Income and Adjustment Items		Amount (in billions of dollars)
1. Personal income		$2,435.0
2. Portion of personal income not included in adjusted gross income		663.9
a. Transfer payments (except taxable military pay and taxable government pensions)	297.2	
b. Other labor income (except fees)	141.5	
c. Imputed income	60.6	
d. Investment income received by nonprofit institutions or retained by fiduciaries	24.4	
e. Investment income retained by life insurance carriers and noninsured pension funds	55.3	
f. Differences in accounting treatment	30.5	
g. Other excluded or exempt income	54.4	
3. Portion of adjusted gross income not included in personal income		181.9
a. Personal contributions for social insurance	104.6	
b. Net gain from sale of assets	29.6	
c. Taxable private pensions	35.6	
d. Small business corporation income	−0.4	
e. Other	12.6	
4. Total adjustments for conceptual differences (line 2 minus line 3)		482.0
5. Estimated adjusted gross income of taxable and nontaxable individuals		
(line 1 minus line 4)		1,953.0
6. Less amount not reported		180.4
Less amount reported on nontaxable returns		51.4
Equals adjusted gross income on taxable returns		1,721.2
Less exemptions on taxable returns		188.2
Less deductions on taxable return		149.3
Equals taxable income on taxable returns		1,383.7
Add taxable income on nontaxable returns		27.2
Equals taxable income of individuals		1,410.9
Deduct zero-bracket amount		240.8
Taxable income in excess of zero-bracket amount		1,170.1

Source: Derived from J. A. Pechman, *Federal Tax Policy* (Washington, D.C.: Brookings Institution, 1984).

introduced. The intent of the comprehensive income tax is to broaden the tax base and thus allow a reduction in the tax rates. Reviewing the major personal income tax deductions, a fully comprehensive tax would eliminate the following, among others: the deduction of interest for mortgage and other purposes; the deduction for medical expenses; the nontaxability of employer-financed health insurance; the deduction of state and local taxes and the tax exemption of interest on state and local bonds; the deduction of charitable contributions; and special provisions relating to the taxation of capital.

The elimination of the deductibility of mortgage interest is probably the largest single stumbling block in the adoption of a comprehensive tax. Many individuals perceive that their interests would be adversely affected by the elimination of this provision, which is why several of the proposals for the reform of the tax system attempt to compromise on this issue. One proposal, for instance, allows partial deductibility, while others put an unindexed cap on the amount that can be deducted (with the view that, with inflation, the value of the deduction will gradually be eliminated). Purists maintain that the only meaningful reform is a "clean" reform: once the principle of no deductions is breached, it will be impossible to draw the line.

There are other ways that the tax base could be broadened; the government could tighten up standards for business deductions, for travel and entertainment expenses, etc. How much revenue could be gained thereby, and the extent to which such changes would be inequitable (taxing legitimate business expenses) or ineffective (firms might find alternative ways of providing equivalent compensation in a tax-deductible manner), are debatable. Some claim that such tax treatment would have a deleterious effect on the efficiency of American enterprises, while others claim that the current tax system encourages certain categories of wasteful expenditures.

THE FLAT-RATE TAX

A second major proposal for the reform of our tax system is the flat-rate tax. Its advocates believe that the major problems in our current tax system arise from the steep progressivity of the tax rates.

They believe that the tax structure would be simplified by having a single tax rate. The difference between the individual's income and a given exemption level would be subject to a flat-tax rate. All individuals would thus face the same marginal tax rate.

Advantages of the Flat-Rate Tax: Reduced Tax Avoidance

The elimination of the nominally high tax rates on the very rich would eliminate the incentives of the rich to take advantage of the inevitable loopholes that creep into any tax system. For an individual in the 50 percent marginal tax bracket, the return to spending his resources, time, and energy to reduce his tax bill may be much higher than the return to spending his time and energy on more socially productive uses. The transaction costs associated with many tax-avoidance schemes are very large; an individual may spend 95 cents to avoid $1's worth of taxes, and he is still better off. Reducing the marginal tax rate would make many of the popular tax-avoidance schemes financially unviable. The *uniformity* of the tax rate would also eliminate many of the tax-avoidance schemes. The head of the family, the children, and the trusts would all face the same marginal tax rate.

Similarly, it may pay an individual at a high marginal tax rate to borrow money from an individual at a low marginal tax rate under the current tax code, since the tax savings in the interest deduction to the former exceeds the tax liability on the latter. Again, these noneconomic motives for lending would be eliminated if everyone were at the same marginal tax rate.[14]

---

[14]It should also be noted that some inequities and inefficiencies associated with the tax exemption of interest on state and local bonds arise from the fact that marginal tax rates increase with income. Presumably, if all individuals had the same marginal tax rate, returns on these bonds would adjust so that all individuals would have the same after-tax return, whether on tax-exempt or taxable bonds. The distortion associated with excessive expenditures on local public goods (and in particular, on local capital goods) would, of course, remain.

Administrative Advantages of the Flat-Rate Tax

The uniformity of marginal tax rates—with its implication that it does not make any difference to whom one assigns a given income—has some administrative advantages as well. It means that income can be taxed at source; taxing income at source will reduce compliance costs and increase compliance rates. It would also be easy to impose a tax on fringe benefits (such as hospital insurance or employee cafeterias); since the tax paid would be the same, no matter who receives the tax, the government does not need to ascertain who benefited from a particular fringe-benefit program.

In fact, since all wages are taxed at the same rate, the government could impose a (value-added) tax on net revenues of the firm, providing a fixed lump-sum grant to each individual. Advocates of the flat-rate tax also point to the marked administrative advantages that could result from the integration of the corporation income tax and a flat-rate individual income tax. We noted, for instance, the problem that arises in disallowing interest deductions by individuals who can claim to be borrowing for business purposes. Since every interest payment gives rise to a deduction as well as a tax, when all individuals are at the same rate, the two exactly net out. Since again everyone is taxed at the same rate, one might as well tax businesses on their net income (at the same flat rate). Individuals would be taxed only on their wage incomes. Individuals would, effectively, be paying tax on all of their capital income, not just on that part distributed to them in the form of interest and dividends; but the tax would be collected at the level of the firm.

Redistribution and the Flat-Rate Tax

Redistributive objectives could still be attained with a flat-rate tax. The higher the level of exemption, the greater the proportion of the tax burden that will have to be borne by higher-income individuals. In Chapter 23 we discussed the study of Hausman, who claims that it may be possible, by introducing a flat-rate tax, to lower the tax rate facing almost all income groups; the reduction in the distortions generates a large increase in labor supply.

These results are, however, controversial. Those who believe that the labor supply is relatively inelastic are concerned that to provide a reasonable level of exemption would require imposing a high marginal tax rate on those with incomes over the exemption level.

Modified Flat-Rate Proposals

Many critics of the flat-rate tax agree, however, that there would be great advantages in reducing the degree of progressivity. Some suggest, for instance, that there should be only two or three rates, with the maximum rate lower than the current maximum rate of 50 percent. By narrowing the spread of rates and lowering the maximum rate (with, say, incomes slightly above the exemption level being taxed at a marginal rate of 15 percent and the maximum rate at 35 percent), much of the incentive for tax avoidance would be reduced, while redistributive objectives could be attained more easily than they could with a single flat-rate tax. Alternative versions of these modified flat-rate proposals have been introduced by Senators Bradley of New Jersey, Gephardt of Missouri, and Roth of Delaware and by Representative Kemp of New York.

Both of these "flat-rate proposals" entail an extensive broadening of the tax base as well, though they attempt to make political compromises where they feel they must. For instance, the Bradley-Gephardt proposal, though not eliminating the home mortgage deduction, restricts it to the lowest tax bracket.

Purists claim that any deviation from a strict flat rate will substantially increase the administrative complexity of the system, and if it is done in a way to raise any significant amount of revenue, of necessity must provide correspondingly significant incentives for engaging in the kinds of tax-avoidance schemes described earlier.

THE CONSUMPTION TAX

One version of the flat-rate tax that has been extensively discussed combines the use of a flat-rate tax with a change to consumption as the tax base. To see the advantages of this proposal, we must first discuss the general issue of a consumption tax.

The question of whether consumption or income provides a better basis for taxation has been debated for more than fifty years. Sixty years ago Irving Fisher, of Yale, argued that it was more appropriate to tax individuals on the basis of what they take out of society (consumption) rather than what they contribute to society (which was measured by their income). To tax consumption, one does not need actually to monitor an individual's purchases of goods. Rather, all one needs to observe is an individual's cash flow. Since

$$\text{Income} = \text{Consumption} + \text{Savings},$$

if one can measure income (total receipts) and savings, one can infer what the level of consumption is. The measurement of income involves problems of the kind we have encountered in our analysis of the income tax (distinguishing between legitimate business expenditures and consumption expenditures). The consumption tax does not solve these problems, but neither does it make them any worse. The problem of measuring an individual's savings is also not particularly difficult: one simple method calculates the total value of sales of securities during a year, less the total value of purchases during the same period. The difference plus the individual's wage income is his cash flow and is equal to his consumption.

Equivalence between Wage Tax and a Consumption Tax

In Chapter 17 we showed that a proportional consumption tax is equivalent to a proportional wage tax. Taxing consumption alone is equivalent to exempting income from capital. Those who believe that the major problems with our present tax system arise from the taxation of income from capital thus believe that a consumption tax will eliminate most of our current tax problems. Those who believe that exempting interest income is inequitable believe that a consumption tax is unfair. (A proposal for a tax on wages only would be politically much less popular than a proposal for a tax on consumption, though the two are in fact equivalent.)

The fact that a wage tax and a consumption tax are equivalent provides two alternative ways of levying the tax. We have described one way: the cash flow approach. The alternative way is simply to tax wage income. The cash flow approach has a major problem with the treatment of consumer durables, such as housing; the individual spends a large amount of money at one particular moment and would thus have a large tax liability. To avoid the problems to which this gives rise, the Treasury Department proposed in 1977 a mixture of the two approaches, which we describe briefly below (p. 536).

Though the two approaches are theoretically equivalent, they differ in the pattern of cash flow to the government and the problems that arise in the process of going from our present income tax system to the new tax basis. If individuals are, on average, saving, wage income, on average, exceeds consumption. Thus, though the *present discounted value* of tax revenues from a wage tax and a consumption tax would be the same, in the switch to a consumption tax, there would be a delay in the receipt of revenues; the government would have to finance its expenditures in the intervening period by an increase in debt.

Since, if bequests are included, consumption and income are equivalent (in present value terms), a consumption tax can also be viewed as a *lifetime income tax*. Most ecomomists would argue that lifetime income is a better basis for levying taxes than annual income. In this view, then, there is little disagreement between advocates of a consumption tax and advocates of an income tax.

Arguments for the Consumption Tax

Recent arguments for the consumption tax are based on its advantages in terms of administrative simplicity and stand in marked contrast to the traditional arguments in favor of the consumption tax, which we have presented in previous chapters. The most important traditional arguments are: a) consumption is a "fairer basis of taxation": it seems fairer to tax individuals on the basis of what they take out of society (consumption) than what they contribute (income); and b) consumption is a less distortionary basis of taxation.

The traditional form in which the efficiency argument was cast, that there were fewer distortions with a consumption tax than with an income tax, was shown to be incorrect. In one central case, where the only difference in individuals' incomes arose from differences in abilities, where relative wages were fixed, and where individuals' marginal rates of substitution between consumption early in life and later in life did not depend on how much they worked, a consumption tax was shown to be the (Pareto-) efficient form of taxation: no tax should be imposed on interest income. When these assumptions were not satisfied, in some cases it was desirable to impose an interest income *subsidy*, not an interest income tax. There are two circumstances under which a persuasive case for an interest income tax (in addition to a consumption tax) can be made: a) if such a tax changes the *before-tax* distribution in a desirable way; that is, if decreasing the after-tax return to capital discourages savings, and if unskilled labor and capital are substitutes, the lower capital supply will increase the relative wages of the unskilled; since there is a deadweight loss in redistributing income, it is always desirable to incur some deadweight loss to change the before-tax distribution of income; and b) if individuals differ in their ability to invest, with some individuals obtaining a much higher return to their investments than others; then a wage tax alone (or, equivalently, a consumption tax) will not be able to redistribute income efficiently.

The recent resurgence of interest in the consumption tax has been motivated not so much by the traditional issues of equity (double taxation, whether consumption is a fairer basis of judging ability to pay than income, etc.) or efficiency (whether it is distortionary to tax interest income), which we have just discussed. Rather, it has been motivated by two concerns. We noted in Chapter 22 that many of the distortions in our tax system arise from the myriad of special provisions relating to the treatment of capital. Under the current tax system, a significant fraction of the return to capital is tax exempt (owner-occupied housing pensions, IRAs, etc.) or taxed at preferential rates (capital gains). We thus have a system that is partly a consumption tax, partly an income tax. This hybrid may be less equitable, more distortionary, and more administratively complex than either a true income tax or a true consumption tax.

Concern with the administrative complexity of our tax laws, and the belief that much of this complexity arises from the taxation of capital, provides a second major motivation for interest in a consumption tax. In the previous chapter we noted too that most of the tax-avoidance schemes were related to the taxation of capital. Income splitting typically requires the transfer (or loan) of an asset. Most forms of tax deferral are attempts to avoid the taxation of interest. And a major source of tax arbitrage is the capital gains tax. Even without the special rates presently afforded, individuals could take advantage of the fact that capital gains are taxed on the basis of realization.

Moreover, the complexity and distortions that arise from the interaction of our individual income tax and corporate income tax systems could be reduced with a switch to a consumption tax, particularly one based on the cash flow approach. Receipts from the corporate sector would be added to the cash flow (subject to tax), while payments to the corporate sector would be subtracted. All the complexity of the corporation tax, including the distortionary provisions for depreciation, could simply be eliminated, without fear that the corporations would be used as a vehicle for tax avoidance.

The consumption tax would not eliminate all administrative problems. As we have noted, there would remain a problem in identifying legitimate business expenses. This problem would be no more severe—and no less severe—than under the current income tax system.

Critics of the consumption tax are not persuaded by the arguments for it based on its administrative advantages. First, they point out that the administrative problems with any tax can be eliminated simply by eliminating the tax. The fact that there are administrative problems with a tax on the income from capital is an argument for its abolition only if it can be shown that it is impossible to design a "reasonably" nondistortionary and "reasonably" equitable tax. Advocates of a broadly based *income* tax believe that such a tax can be designed eliminating, for instance, the special provisions for capital gains. Though the imputed return to housing will escape taxation, and pension schemes will allow the effective avoidance of taxation on interest on savings for retirement, it is still possible (they believe) to tax a significant fraction of the return to capital; and they believe that the distortions arising from taxing some of the returns to capital and not others are worth the gains in equity from the tax.

Moreover, critics of the consumption tax fear that while we know the problems with our current system, we will only gradually find out those associated with running a consumption tax. These, they suspect, are no less severe than those of our current system.

Some Aspects of the Design of a Consumption Tax

During President Ford's administration, the Office of Tax Analysis of the Treasury Department, headed by economist David Bradford of Princeton, gave careful consideration to how one might design a consumption tax in practice. They became convinced that the administrative problems were, overall, much less severe than under the present system. In the following paragraphs we discuss three of the difficulties encountered.

1. *Housing under the Consumption Tax.* Housing presents a problem for the consumption tax, just as it does for the income tax. We argued in our discussion of the income tax that the theoretically appropriate way of dealing with housing was to *impute* to income an amount corresponding to the services yielded by the house—i.e., to impute a rental value. Similarly, with the cash flow approach to the consumption tax, the purchase of a house represents an investment, and the expenditures to purchase a house should be subtracted from income to determine the tax base. Later, however, the services yielded by the house should be included as "consumption" and added to the tax base. But given the difficulties of imputing the services yielded by the house, an alternative procedure has certain advantages whereby the expenditures on the purchase of a house are not subtracted from income, and the services yielded by the assets are not added back.

The major disadvantage arises when the tax rates on consumption are progressive. Then, an individual who sells some of his securities to buy a house would appear to be dissaving (the reduction in his ownership of his securities is viewed as dissaving), and the value of this dissaving would be added to his income to form an estimate of his consumption. In fact, of course, the individual is simply changing the *form* in which he holds his assets; that is, he is substituting one set of assets (securities) for another (housing).[15] Thus any system of consumption taxation must make some special provisions for housing.

2. *Bequests.* The second problem has to do with bequests and inheri-

---

[15] With a flat-rate consumption tax, this makes no difference; his tax liability would be increased at one date and decreased at another. With a system of lifetime effective averaging described below, the increased tax this period (with a reduced tax liability at some date in the future) again would cause no problems provided the individual had the liquidity to pay the tax.

Modern computer technology makes it feasible to design taxes based on lifetime consumption. A running account is kept of each individual's consumption (appropriately discounted over time) and tax payments. Individuals would be allowed to prepay or to defer taxes under stipulated conditions.

tances. Should these be treated as consumption by the donor and as income by the receiver? One view treats the individual and his descendants as a single extended family. In this view, transfers between a parent and his child should not be taxed. Each consumption unit should be taxed only once. If a parent gives an asset to a child and the child sells the asset to buy consumption goods, a tax will be levied on the child. The other view says that giving money to a child is no different from spending money in any other way. The parent does it presumably because he receives pleasure from it. From this point of view, it is a "consumption" expenditure. Thus bequests ought to be taxed as if they were consumption expenditures. At the same time, bequests ought to be treated as income to the child; if the child sells the asset to purchase consumption goods, the child will be liable to pay the consumption tax.

The different approaches obviously may have different consequences for bequests. Some critics of the consumption tax are concerned that exempting bequests totally from taxation may lead to excessive concentration of wealth. Defenders of the consumption tax claim that if one is concerned about the concentration of wealth, one ought to attack that problem directly; for instance, by imposing a progressive wealth tax. Critics of the consumption tax claim that wealthy individuals will find ways of avoiding such a tax, and the way to increase the likelihood that they pay their fair share is to tax both capital income and bequests.

3. *Problems of Transition.* Some economists have been concerned with the transition from the income tax to the consumption tax. One problem we have already discussed: the cash flow to the government might be reduced in the interim, requiring further government borrowing.[16]

A second problem is the treatment of previously accumulated capital. Should individuals be taxed when they sell their previously purchased assets to buy consumption goods? Assume the individual had been saving out of his wage income; he has already paid an income tax. To tax him again when he consumes seems unfair. It seems to be an unjust tax on the thrifty. (Notice that what we are talking about here is a tax not only on interest income but on the whole value of the asset when he sells it.) Such a tax is called a *capital levy.* If it is not anticipated, and if individuals do not believe that it will be imposed again, it is not distortionary. But if individuals believe that it may be imposed again, it can have a very discouraging effect on savings.

On the other hand, much of current savings is from income that escaped income taxation. When an individual leaves an asset that has increased in value to his child, the capital gain effectively escapes taxation. Not to tax this saving also seems unfair. The problem is, we cannot distinguish between these two types of savings. The transition rules from an income tax to a consumption tax that one thinks are appropriate are determined by how one thinks one should deal with previously accumulated savings.

If one thinks that previous savings should not be taxed, there is no problem: individuals would be allowed to consume by selling assets they currently own without paying any tax. If one thinks that previous savings should

[16] This increased deficit should not, however, have a significant deleterious effect on the economy; since individuals should anticipate their future tax liability, they would increase their savings in a corresponding amount.

be taxed, all individuals would have to be required to register their current assets. When these assets were sold, the cash flow would be recorded and a tax imposed. There is some concern that individuals might underreport their present assets and that their true consumption would thus exceed their reported consumption. How serious this problem would be in the United States is not clear: it would not appear to be a problem at least for stocks and bonds.

There is a second transition problem: there are marked differences in the ratio of consumption to income for individuals in different stages of their life. Thus for retired individuals, who are dissaving, consumption typically exceeds income; for some younger individuals, income exceeds consumption. Unless previously accumulated capital was exempt from taxation, older individuals at the time of the transition would be disadvantaged.

Since in the popular view, older individuals are poorer, this seems inequitable. But several points need to be kept in mind: those older individuals who will be particularly disadvantaged are not the poor (who have little capital to dissave) but the wealthier older individuals. Moreover, a consumption tax can be progressive (see below), so that poorer older individuals might actually pay a lower tax than under the present system. More importantly, one needs to ask: once one has agreed upon what an appropriate basis of taxation should be (e.g., whether income or consumption provides a fairer basis of taxation, a better measure of ability to pay), is there any reason that an older individual with the same income or consumption as a younger person should be treated differently from a younger person (particularly if his or her medical expenses are being taken care of by another government program, and consumption of medical services, at least when paid by third parties, is not taxed)? Note that this transitional problem is important only if a tax is imposed on consumption out of current capital. If it is exempt, the elderly are probably advantaged. (To the extent that they dissave from IRA and other forms of savings that are currently tax-deferred, the appropriate treatment would be to impose a tax on their consumption.)

Is a Consumption Tax Inequalitarian?

There is a widespread view that a consumption tax would be less equalitarian than an income tax, that it would hurt the poor relative to the rich. This view is based on several misconceptions. First, there is a confusion between a sales tax and a consumption tax. The two are clearly similar. But sales taxes, as imposed in most states, are levied only on certain commodities. Since vacations abroad, luxury homes, and diamonds purchased out of state typically escape such taxes, the fraction of a rich person's income spent on goods on which he has to pay a sales tax is typically smaller than the fraction of a poor person's income. Thus sales taxes are usually viewed to be regressive. But a consumption tax is levied on all consumption. Moreover, sales taxes are usually levied as a fixed percentage of the amount spent. But a consumption tax can be highly progressive; that is, one could design a consumption tax where, for instance, the first $4,000 of consumption is tax-exempt, the next $10,000 is taxed at 20 percent, the next $10,000 at 30 percent, and consumption beyond $24,000 is taxed at 40 percent. Finally, there is some confusion about the appropriate way of measuring the degree of progressivity of the tax system. If one believes that consumption is a fairer tax base than income, the correct way of measuring progressivity relates tax payments to consumption; the fact that the ratio of consumption to income declines with income, so that the ratio of tax payments to income does not increase as rapidly as the ratio of tax payments to consumption, is irrelevant.

A FLAT-RATE CONSUMPTION TAX

Though the consumption tax can thus be made highly progressive, with marginal tax rates increasing with the level of consumption, some economists have advocated a flat-rate consumption tax. The marginal rate on all consumption would be the same. The tax would still be progressive, because there would be an exemption level (only consumption over the exemption level would be taxed).

Earlier, we noted that there were significant administrative advantages in a flat-rate income tax. The advantages of a flat-rate consumption tax are similar. Taxes can be imposed completely at source: there would be a flat percentage withholding of all expenditures on personnel (wages and fringe benefits). The individual's entire tax form could be put onto a postcard. A flat-rate consumption tax has been proposed by Stanford political economists Robert Hall and Alvin Rabushka. They believe that a 19 percent flat-rate consumption tax with a $6,800 exemption for a married couple with no children would generate essentially the same revenue as the current system. (Their tax includes a 19 percent capital levy—i.e., all previous savings would be taxed at 19 percent as well.)

Critics of the tax are skeptical. Because the consumption tax base is smaller than that of the flat-rate income tax, the tax rate would have to be higher than with the flat-rate income tax. The magnitude of the required tax rate depends to some extent on the magnitudes of the responses of labor and capital. If labor supply increases significantly in response to the lowering of the marginal tax rate, and if investors are so encouraged that the growth of the economy is significantly affected, it is possible that the 19 percent flat-rate consumption tax would raise the requisite revenue. If labor supply elasticities are low and savings elasticities are low, it is unlikely to raise the requisite revenue.

THE VALUE-ADDED TAX

The value-added tax (V.A.T.) is a tax that is imposed at each stage of production on the difference between the sales of a firm and what it purchases from other firms; that is, on the value added by the firm. Though the V.A.T. has typically not replaced the income tax, it has become a major source of revenue in most European countries, with rates as high as 20 percent.

The tax is equivalent to a national sales tax. The only advantage of this tax over a sales tax is the manner in which it is collected. While there are a large number of retail outlets, the number of producing firms is much smaller. Thus a large portion of the revenues is collected from relatively few sources, and these may be more easily monitored than the myriad small retail establishments. Whether this is a significant advantage in the United States, where the level of tax compliance is relatively high, is a moot question.

Once one recognizes that the tax is really a sales tax, one sees clearly the advantages and disadvantages of such a tax. A uniform tax on output is equivalent to a uniform tax on input (recall our discussion of Chapter 17), since output must equal input. Thus a value-added tax is equivalent to a comprehensive flat-rate income tax with no exemption. The value-added tax, therefore, is neither progressive nor regressive; it does not redistribute income. Only to those who think the government should not redistribute income is this an advantage; most view this as a serious disadvantage.

On the other hand, we noted the serious inequities and inefficiencies that arise from the myriad special provisions of the income tax. There is a belief that compliance with the V.A.T. is more uniform, and in this sense the tax is more equitable and less distortionary than the income tax.

Some degree of progressivity can be added by exempting certain industries. If food is exempted (or taxed at a lower rate), the effective rate on the poor may be lower than on the rich, since they spend a larger fraction of their income on food. Similarly, by imposing a surtax (a tax in addition to the normal tax) on luxuries such as large cars, those with high income will pay a higher than average proportion of their income in taxes. But there is a cost to attempts to increase the degree of progressivity of the tax: one of the virtues of the value-added tax is its uniformity, its simplicity. As soon as there are differential rates on different industries, there are difficult problems of determining the boundaries. How large should a car be to be considered a luxury car? Should the family circumstances of the purchaser be taken into account in determining whether it is a luxury? (For a family with many children, a large car may be a necessity rather than a luxury.) And the pressures of special-interest groups, each trying to make sure that the commodities they sell are classified in the low-tax category, would be enormous.[17]

Another commonly proposed modification in the value-added tax is to exempt investment. Since (ignoring government spending)

$$\text{Investment} + \text{Consumption} = \text{National Output,}$$

a value-added tax that exempts investment goods is equivalent to a proportional consumption tax. The issues we discussed earlier in the context of the consumption tax are relevant here in determining whether total national income or consumption provides a better basis for the value-added tax.

Most proponents of the value-added tax do not advocate that it should replace the income tax. Rather, they believe that it can be used to reduce substantially the revenues to be collected from the income tax, and hence the high marginal tax rates; since much of the tax-avoidance activities are

---

[17] In Chapter 18 we discussed whether different commodities should be taxed at different rates. The results were inconclusive. If there were an optimal consumption tax, if the source of inequality was differences in individuals' productivity, and if individuals' marginal rates of substitution between different commodities did not depend on the amount they worked, a uniform tax should be imposed. In the absence of a consumption tax, while distribution considerations argue for higher rates on luxury goods, concern about deadweight loss argues for lower rates.

related to the level of marginal rates, advocates believe that it will decrease the distortions and increase the equity of the tax system. Critics of this proposal point out that the total distortion of the tax system is related to the sum of the (marginal) tax on income and the value-added tax and that, unless this is reduced, the deadweight loss associated with the tax will not be reduced. Moreover, the gains in compliance costs from the reduction in the marginal tax rate will be more than offset by the additional administrative costs associated with collecting the value-added tax. Finally, there are those who are concerned that because the value-added tax is collected in a piecemeal way, individuals will not be conscious of the full scale of the taxes they pay, and this will lead politicians to increase the overall tax burden: for those who would like to see a larger public sector, this is an advantage; but for those who would like to see a smaller public sector, it is a disadvantage.

REAGAN'S TAX PROPOSALS

We began this chapter by noting that in early 1985 President Reagan had proposed a major reform of the tax system. The proposals themselves were a modification of earlier proposals by the Treasury. The President was criticized by both those who wanted more reform and those who wanted less. Some felt he had not gone far enough, that he had emasculated the original Treasury proposals and given too much to certain pressure groups. Others felt that he had failed to recognize adequately their special needs, that tax incentives were needed for a variety of reasons.

His proposals are best viewed as a modification of two of the reforms we have discussed in this chapter: a modified comprehensive, flat-rate proposal. It was not fully comprehensive, and there were three tax brackets (15 percent, 25 percent, 35 percent) rather than a single, flat rate. Among the major changes were: a) a substantial increase in the individual exemption (to $2,000); b) elimination of the deductibility of state and local taxes; c) limiting interest deductions to mortgages on principle residences; d) limiting deductions for charitable contributions; and e) taxing some fringe benefits. It retained special treatment for capital gains.

It also proposed reforming the corporation tax, lowering the rate, but at the same time eliminating the investment tax credit and the extremely favorable treatment of depreciation that had been introduced in 1981. It had a provision allowing 10 percent of the dividends paid to be deductible from corporate income.

Opposition came from all of the expected sources. State and local communities, particularly those with high tax rates, thought that they would be adversely affected. Teachers' groups and others involved in public education were worried that the increased effective cost of public schools would lead to a reduction in public expenditures. Private schools and other charities were worried that curtailing the charitable deduction would reduce giving, although even if it were left fully in place, the proposed reduction in marginal tax rates would likely lead to a significant reduction. Unions were upset by the taxation of fringe benefits.

Heavy industry was concerned about the change in the depreciation system. High-technology industries were, on the other hand, pleased with the reforms. They had argued (successfully) for the retention of the special treatment of capital gains. For them, the reduction in tax rates more than compensated for the loss of the investment tax credit and the special depreciation provisions.

SUMMARY

1. The four major proposals for the reform of the U.S. tax system have in common several major concerns:
   a) the current tax system imposes high compliance costs on individuals and corporations;
   b) the current tax system is subject to extensive tax-avoidance activities, which erode the tax base and introduce significant inequities; and
   c) there may be large welfare losses resulting from the high marginal tax rates in the current tax system.

2. The thrust of the reforms that we have described is to simplify the tax system, to broaden the tax base, and to reduce the marginal tax rates. The controversies concern what is the best way to do this and at the same time have a tax system that is viewed to be "fair," with the wealthy paying a larger proportion of their income than the poor.

3. The problems we face arise because of our attempt to use the tax system to redistribute income and to impose a proportionately greater share of the tax burden on the wealthy. But there is a concern that, in attempting to do this, we have devised a tax system that allows the very rich to pay less than they would in a tax system with less ambitious redistributive goals.

4. It is clear that most of the proposals for reducing the degree of progressivity reduce the nominal tax rates paid by the very rich. One's view of the reduction in progressivity depends on the resulting gains in efficiency from the flat-rate tax. If these are significant enough, it may be possible that almost all groups will be better off as a result of a flat-rate tax, which is the belief of its ardent advocates.

5. The different reforms should not be viewed as mutually exclusive. If it is possible to broaden the tax base only slightly, as our discussion of the comprehensive tax suggested may well turn out to be the case, then it may be desirable to have a value-added tax, so that the marginal tax rates can be lowered.

6. If past history is any guide to the future, any tax reform that emerges from our political process is likely to be a compromise: a modified flat-rate tax (not a single rate, but two or three), or a modified comprehensive tax (not all of income included: mortgage interest, some fringe benefits, some charitable donations may be exempt), which is a halfway house between a consumption tax and an income tax (with an even larger fraction of interest income exempt from tax than under the current system, but that which is not exempt, such as capital gains, taxed at full rates). Whether such a compromise will exacerbate the inequities and inefficiencies of our present tax system or reduce them remains to be seen.

KEY CONCEPTS

Compliance costs
Comprehensive income tax
Flat-rate tax

Consumption tax
Value-added tax

1. Joe Smith has a family income of $25,000. He gives $2,000 to charity, pays $5,000 interest a year on his mortgage, and pays state and local taxes of $3,000. He has medical bills of $300 and union dues of $100. He has two children. Using the current tax tables, calculate his tax liability. Assume a comprehensive flat-rate income tax were adopted, with an exemption of $1,500 per person. At what marginal tax rate would he be just as well off under the new system as under the old?

2. List the special provisions of the tax code that would be eliminated by a comprehensive income tax. Which of these do you think are justified on grounds of equity? efficiency?

3. There is a widespread view that a consumption tax would hurt the poor. Is this necessarily the case?

4. The adoption of a comprehensive income tax might have a significant effect on the market value of certain assets. Which assets are likely to decrease in value? to increase in value? Should the government do anything to compensate the losers or to tax the gainers? The adoption of a consumption tax would also have a significant effect on the market value of certain assets. Which assets are likely to decrease in value? to increase in value?

5. There is a widespread view that the appropriate basis for taxation is an individual's lifetime consumption (or income). Discuss the inequities and inefficiencies that would arise from a consumption tax with increasing marginal tax rates without any provisions for averaging. How would these be affected by a flat-rate consumption tax?

6. In Chapter 20 we discussed the problems associated with choosing the appropriate unit for taxation (family versus individual). How would these problems be affected by the adoption of a consumption tax? a flat-rate income tax?

PART SIX

STATE AND LOCAL GOVERNMENTS

The United States has a federal system, with some activities being undertaken at the state and local level, others at the national level. Chapter 26 explains the rationale for a federal system and some of the important interactions between the federal government and the state and local governments. We also explore the role of competition among communities in ensuring that the correct levels and kinds of public goods get produced and that they get produced efficiently.

Chapter 27 briefly describes expenditures and taxes at the state and local level. We are particularly concerned with the incidence of taxes and expenditure programs in situations where capital and labor are highly mobile.

26
Fiscal Federalism

In his State of the Union address in January 1982, President Reagan proposed to "alter" the relationship between the states and the federal government in an important way. Certain areas, including education and welfare, in which the federal government had taken an increasingly active role within the past decade or two, would once again be placed more solidly under the purview of the states. At the same time, the federal government would take over responsibility for medicaid (which provides medical assistance to the indigent).[1] His proposals were dubbed "the New Federalism."

The issue of the appropriate division of responsibility and authority between states and the federal government is longstanding. The Constitution stipulated that those powers not expressly delegated to the federal government— such as providing for the national defense, printing money, and running the post office—rested with the states. This seemed to create the presumption that responsibility for the provision of most public services (such as education, police and fire protection, roads and highways) was left with the states; and this was the view that was held for a long time. But the Constitution is a flexible document, and court interpretations of it have essentially freed Congress and the president to provide many services beyond those for which it called.

---

[1] Under the medicaid program, the states take responsibility for determining eligibility standards (within guidelines set by the federal government); the administration of the program is the responsibility of the states, while the funding is shared between the federal government and the states.

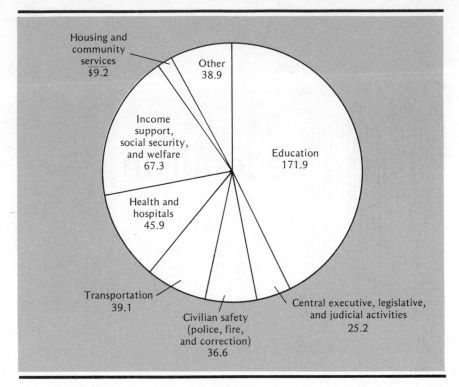

26.1 ALLOCATION OF STATE AND LOCAL EXPENDITURES IN 1983 (BILLIONS OF DOLLARS) Education is the largest state and local expenditure, followed by income-support programs, and health and hospitals. SOURCE: *Survey of Current Business,* July 1984.

THE DIVISION OF RESPONSIBILITIES

The state and local governments have primary responsibility for education (providing 92 percent of the funds), highways and roads (other than the interstate highway system), police and fire protection, and sewage and other sanitation. While the federal government has been responsible for the establishment of the major social welfare programs, public welfare is still the second-largest category of state and local expenditures, accounting for more than one-eighth of total expenditures. Other major portions of state and local budgets are transportation, civilian safety, and health and hospitals; Figure 26.1 gives a breakdown of state and local expenditures, and Figure 26.2 shows the fraction of six major programs financed by the federal government.

Just as there is a division of responsibility between the federal government, on the one hand, and the state and local governments on the other, so there is a division of responsibility between the state governments on the one hand, and the local governments on the other. For instance, while only a quarter of all educational expenditures occur at the state level, almost 60 percent of highway expenditures occur at the state level. Almost all of sewage expenditures and expenditures on firefighting occur at the local level, along with 90 percent of police expenditures.

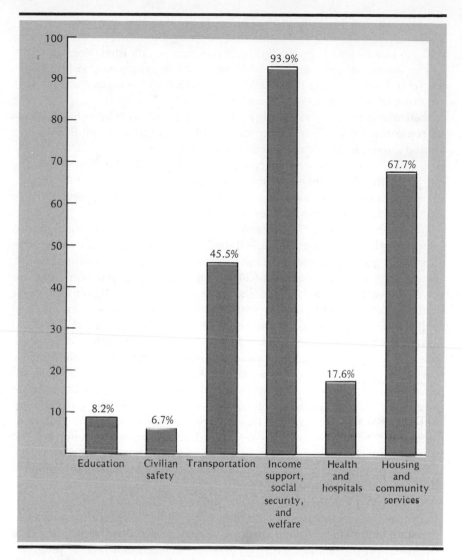

26.2 FRACTION OF EXPENDITURES FOR SELECTED CATEGORIES FINANCED BY FEDERAL GOVERNMENT Of the state and local expenditures, federal financing is strongest for income-support programs, housing programs, and transportation. SOURCE: *Survey of Current Business*, 1984.

The Interaction between the Federal Government and the State and Local Governments

In earlier chapters, we saw the complexity of the interaction between the federal government and individuals and firms: the government regulates, subsidizes, taxes, provides goods and services, and redistributes income. The interaction between the federal government and the state and local governments is equally complex, including federal regulation of and incentives for state and local governments, state and local administration of federal programs, and the sharing of federal revenues with state and local governments.

1. *Regulation.* The Constitution restricts the laws that any state can pass. The states cannot enact legislation that deprives individuals of the right to a trial, no matter how heinous the crime they have committed, nor can states bar an individual from holding a job on racial or religious grounds. Many Supreme Court decisions in recent years have countered state actions that are in violation of the Constitution.

State agencies may also be subject to the same pollution and environmental regulations that affect private firms and individuals. In some cases the federal government has mandated that the state and local governments provide certain services (for instance, access facilities for the handicapped) without providing the requisite funds. The states and local communities have, not surprisingly, complained, arguing that if the federal government attaches such importance to these services, it should also finance them.

2. *Incentives: Categorical Grants and Matching Grants.* Probably more important than direct controls are the efforts of the federal government to alter the actions of state and local governments through financial incentives. It uses both the carrot and the stick: if states develop programs that are consistent with federally set guidelines, they may become eligible for federal funds; if states refuse to comply with certain criteria, they may lose federal funds. Thus federal aid to state universities (as well as to private universities) may be withheld, if the university fails to develop a satisfactory affirmative action program for hiring women and minorities, or if it discriminates in any of its programs.[2] States become eligible to receive federal funds for medicaid or for unemployment compensation provided that they develop appropriate programs. Federal grants to states and localities for specific purposes are called **categorical grants.** The most important categorical grant programs (outside of welfare programs) are for education and urban development. The magnitude of the grants may increase with state and local expenditures; the government may match state expenditures (up to some maximum amount). These are called **matching grants.**

3. *The Administration of Federal Funds.* In some cases, however, virtually all of the funds for some program come from the federal government. The state or local government agency is used to administer the program. For instance, Aid to Families with Dependent Children is a federal program, but it is administered by local government.[3]

4. *General Revenue Sharing: Bloc Grants.* The federal government also transfers income back to the states and localities in **bloc grants,** grants that can be used for any purpose the states and localities desire. These programs are called *general revenue sharing*, as opposed to specific (or categorical) revenue sharing, which are grants designed for specific purposes. There are two reasons for general revenue sharing programs. One is that the federal government may be a more efficient tax collector; the extra administrative costs associated with adding a small increment to the federal tax rate to finance

---

[2]There has been considerable controversy over whether failure to satisfy criteria in one program should entail cutoff of funds for other programs.

[3]The distinction between whether the state is essentially administering a federal program or whether the federal government is supporting a state program is not, of course, a clear one. The difference depends on the extent of discretion given to the state. In the case of the medicaid program, eligibility standards and extent of coverage are both determined by the state, and there is a wide range of variation in practices among the states. Food stamp programs are also administered by the states, but they have far less discretion.

state and local activities is negligible. The second is that the wealth of different states, their potential tax bases, differs markedly, and thus the federal government engages in the redistribution of taxes collected, providing proportionately more to the poor states.

In recent years, the poorest states have had per capita incomes that were 20 percent to 30 percent less than the richest states; there were equally large disparities in per capita state and local taxes. The ratio of state and local taxes to per capita income varies from slightly more than 8 percent in Missouri to over 14 percent in New York.[4]

5. *Tax Expenditures.* This list of mechanisms by which the federal government affects states and localities is not meant to be exhaustive. One of the important ways that the federal government affects state and local expenditures is through the tax expenditures associated with the personal and corporate income taxes. These expenditures were estimated at $33 billion in 1984.

The Size of Financial Transfers

In Chapter 2 we emphasized that the magnitude of governmental expenditures does not provide a complete picture of the role of the government in the economy. Similarly, the magnitude of federal transfers to states and localities does not tell us the extent to which state and local government expenditures are affected by federal activities. Still, it is worth noting several features of these transfers: a) They have grown immensely in the last sixty years, from 1.6 percent of state and local revenues to 19 percent today. This is down slightly from the peak of 21.9 percent reached in 1977.[5] b) Federal aid appears to be more important at the state level than at the local level, accounting for slightly more than one-quarter of state revenues and slightly less than 10 percent of local revenues.

But these figures are somewhat deceptive; much of the money to the states and localities simply passes through them to individuals. Thus 46 percent of the aid to state and local governments in 1982 went for programs such as AFDC, medicaid, and low-income energy assistance. This proportion has been rising; for instance, in 1978 it was only 34 percent of state aid. Similarly, between one-fourth and one-third of federal aid received by state governments is then distributed by them to local governments. Most of the increase in federal aid in the mid-1970s—and the decrease in federal aid since—was in this kind of aid.

THE PRINCIPLES OF FISCAL FEDERALISM

In Chapter 4 we discussed the rationale for government activities. The fundamental theorem of welfare economics—Adam Smith's "invisible hand"—implies that in the absence of a market failure, the economy would be Pareto-efficient. The theorem suggests three reasons for government intervention: the presence of some market failure; dissatisfaction with the distribution

[4] In Alaska, tax revenues amounted to 43 percent of personal income, but this was largely because of taxes on oil.
[5] Source: *Report of the Council of Economic Advisors*, 1984, p. 311.

of income; and the belief that consumers might not take actions that were in their own self-interest (merit goods).

A similar set of arguments can be made for the provision of goods and services by state and local governments, as distinct from the federal government. Competition among communities, it is argued, will result in communities supplying the goods and services individuals want and producing these goods in an efficient manner. This is called the *Tiebout hypothesis*, after Charles Tiebout of the University of Washington, who first formalized the arguments in 1956.[6]

Tiebout was originally concerned with the problem of preference revelation discussed in Chapter 5: while individuals reveal their preferences for private goods simply by buying goods, how are they to reveal their preferences for public goods? When individuals vote, they choose candidates who reflect their overall values, but they cannot express in detail their views about particular categories of expenditures; only limited use of referenda is made in most states. And even were individuals able to vote directly on expenditures for particular programs, the resulting equilibrium is, in general, not Pareto-efficient.

Tiebout argued that individuals could vote with their feet, that their choice of communities revealed their preferences toward locally provided public goods in the same way that individuals' choices of products reveal their preferences for conventional commodities. Moreover, just as there are incentives for firms to find out what commodities individuals prefer and to produce those commodities efficiently, so are there incentives for communities to find out what kinds of locally provided goods individuals prefer and to provide them efficiently. This is seen most strongly in the case of community developers: in recent years these developers have recognized that many individuals would like more security and more communal facilities (swimming pools, tennis courts) than are provided by the typical city. Hence they have formed large developments providing these services. Because these communities better meet the needs of the individuals than the alternatives that are available, individuals are willing to pay higher rents (or spend more to purchase homes in these communities); and it is this that provides the developer a return for his efforts to ascertain what it is that individuals want.

More generally, communities that provide the services individuals like and provide them efficiently will find an influx of individuals; communities that fail to do so will find themselves with an outflux. This migration (with the consequent effect on property values) provides essentially the same kind of signal to the city manager that the market provides to the firm's manager (a firm that fails to provide a commodity individuals like will find its sales declining, a firm that succeeds will find its sales increasing). Politicians (sometimes under pressure from the electorate) respond to these signals in much the same way a firm's managers respond to market signals.

The analogy is an instructive one. Under certain assumptions the separate decisions of each community concerning what public goods to provide and how to provide and finance them lead to a Pareto-efficient allocation, just as

[6] See C. Tiebout, "A Pure Theory of Local Expenditure," *Journal of Political Economy* 64 (1956): 416–24.

the separate decisions of firms and individuals concerning private goods lead to Pareto efficiency.[7]

MARKET FAILURES

The qualifications to the Tiebout hypothesis closely parallel those we discussed in Chapter 4, concerning the circumstances in which market allocations might not be Pareto efficient.

National Public Goods versus Local Public Goods

The benefits of some public goods accrue to those who live in a particular community. This is the case, for instance, with fire protection. The benefits of other public goods accrue to those who live anywhere. National defense is an example.

The same arguments that are used to show that if there is to be an efficient supply of public goods they must be provided publicly implies that if there is to be an efficient supply of national public goods they must be provided at the national level.

Pure public goods (that is, goods for which exclusion is impossible and undesirable) whose benefits are limited to a particular area are called **local pure public goods.** Traffic lights are an example. Just as most goods publicly provided at the national level are not pure public goods, so too most goods provided publicly at the local level are not local pure public goods. For some, such as public libraries, exclusion is easy but undesirable. We use the term **local public goods** to include all of these publicly provided goods.

In Chapter 5 we discussed the advantages and disadvantages of public versus private provision of goods, such as education, which are not pure public goods. If they are provided publicly, they may be provided nationally (education in France) or locally (education in the United States). The advantage of local provision is the greater adaptability to local needs and preferences; the disadvantage is the possibly higher transaction costs (as each community must spend resources choosing, for instance, its own curriculum). In addition, the inevitable inequality in the quality of the services provided in different communities when decisions are made locally may be viewed as a disadvantage, particularly in the case of education.

Externalities

The actions of one community may have marked effects on other communities. If a community constructs a smelly sewage plant or allows the development of an industrial area at its boundary, in a location such that the winds blow the bad odors over the neighboring communities, there is an important

---

[7]Since Tiebout, an extensive literature has developed evaluating the conditions under which the result is valid. See, in particular, J. E. Stiglitz, "Public Goods in Open Economies with Heterogeneous Individuals," in *Locational Analysis of Public Facilities*, J. F. Thisse and H. G. Zoller, eds. (New York: Elsevier–North Holland, 1983), J. E. Stiglitz, "Theory of Local Public Goods," in *The Economics of Public Services*, M. Feldstein and R. Inman, eds. (New York: Macmillan, 1977), pp. 274–333, and T. Bewley, "A Critique of Tiebout's Theory of Local Public Expenditures," *Econometrica* 49 (1981): 713–40.

externality. We sometimes refer to these externalities as **spillovers**. Not all spillovers have negative consequences. Some economists believe that there are important public benefits from having an educated citizenry, and that this provides some justification for public support of education. To the extent that this is true, and to the extent that individuals move away from the community that provided them with a free education, there are spillovers from a local community's public education system.

Migration and Location Inefficiencies. These may be thought of as a particularly important class of externalities. Individuals, in deciding to move into a community, bring both benefits and costs; they may increase the tax base, but they also may lead to increased demands on public services, and increased congestion (for instance, of roads and parks). Since in many cases they neither pay for these costs nor are compensated for the benefits they confer, there are likely to be inefficiencies in location decisions. Many countries have become increasingly concerned about what they view as excessive concentration of population in the major cities (London, Paris, Athens) and have developed decentralization policies to attain what they view as a more efficient pattern of location.

Competition and Profit Maximization

A central assumption in the standard theory is that there are many profit-maximizing firms. The Tiebout hypothesis similarly requires that there be many competing communities.[8] In most areas there are only a limited number of competing communities; there is, in effect, only limited competition. Moreover, communities do not make their decisions on the basis of any simple profit maximization or land value maximization criterion but by a political process along the lines discussed in Chapter 6. The kinds of inefficiencies to which this may give rise will be described in the next chapter; here we simply note that the limited competition provides an explanation for why we should be skeptical about the Tiebout hypothesis.

REDISTRIBUTION

A more important explanation of the role of the federal government is provided by its concern about distribution. There is concern about the distribution of income both among individuals and across communities.

Inequality among Individuals

Should the extent of redistribution—the level of welfare payments—be a local or national decision? Is "redistribution" a local public good? Assume individuals in some community believe strongly that no individual should

---

[8]Indeed, there must be so many that all residents within the community with the same skills have the same tastes for public goods. Another implication is that (provided voters are rational) there would be complete unanimity in voting. Both of these implications are obviously not satisfied. See J. E. Stiglitz, "Public Goods in Open Economies," R. W. Eberts and T. J. Gronberg, "Jurisdictional Homogeneity and the Tiebout Hypothesis," *Journal of Urban Economics* 10 (1981): 227–339, and H. Pack and J. Pack, "Metropolitan Fragmentation and Local Public Expenditure," *National Tax Journal* 31 (1978): 349–62.

live in a slum, and so they provide a good public housing program, while individuals in some other community have different ethical concerns. Is there any reason that individuals in the first community should attempt to impose their ethical beliefs on the second, by attempting to make minimal housing standards a national rather than local issue?

The answer is yes. And the reason is that, with relatively free migration, the extent of redistribution that is feasible at the local level is very limited. Any community that decides to provide better housing for the poor or better medical care might find itself faced with an influx of the poor. Communities have an incentive to try to make their community unattractive to the poor, so that they will move on to the next community. Some communities, for instance, do this by passing zoning laws that require multi-acre lots.[9] Others do it by limiting the provision of certain public services that are particularly valued by the poor and for which the wealthier have good private substitutes, such as bus services.

Indeed, competition among communities to provide local public services at least cost to the taxpayers results in taxpayers paying taxes only commensurate with the benefits they themselves receive. A community that has no welfare program and succeeds in excluding most of the poor would be able to provide public services (education, sewage treatment, libraries, etc.) at lower tax rates than a community that has an ambitious welfare program (public housing, good medical care, etc.) and educational programs aimed at disadvantaged children. The fact that competition is frequently limited and decisions concerning public services are made politically means that there often are local (and state) redistribution programs. But these remain limited.

Inequality across Communities

We have already noted the marked discrepancies among the states in per capita income and per capita public expenditures. For a poor community to provide the same level of services as a rich one requires that it levy much higher taxes.

But why should we be more concerned with the inequality associated with locally provided public goods (and tax rates) than we are with inequality in general? Is there any reason that there should be specific federal programs directed at reducing this particular kind of inequality? If we want more redistribution, why not simply impose a more progressive tax, letting individuals then choose how to spend their money? If they wish to live in communities that spend more or less on local public goods, why not let them? The issues are analogous to those that arose in earlier chapters concerning whether the government should have specific policies directed at increasing the extent of inequality of specific goods, such as medicine, food, and housing. We introduced the concept of *specific egalitarianism*, the view that the consumption of certain commodities should not depend on one's (or one's parents') income or wealth. Education, the most important locally provided public good, is one of those for which the strongest argument for equality of provision can be made.

---

[9]Courts have recently restricted the use of zoning as an exclusionary device.

There are, however, several arguments against programs aimed at reducing inequality in the provision of local public services.

Consumer Sovereignty. The first is the standard "consumer sovereignty" argument: individuals should be allowed to choose the goods they prefer. The government should not force its preferences—for food, housing, or education—on poor communities. Programs aimed at reducing inequality in the provision of local public goods (to the extent that they are effective) distort the consumption pattern of the poor; they result in greater consumption of "local public goods" and less consumption of private goods than a redistributive program providing cash to individuals. Categorical grants (again, to the extent that they are effective) cause a distortion in the mix of locally provided public goods; they may, for instance, result in more education and urban redevelopment and less frequent sewage collection. Whenever there are these distortions there is a deadweight loss.

This consumer sovereignty argument, though relevant, is somewhat less forceful for some locally provided goods than it is for others. For instance, decisions concerning elementary and secondary school education are made not by the individual but by his parents; and the decisions made concerning local public goods are made by a political process, which need not yield efficient outcomes, as we saw in Chapter 6.[10]

The Difficulty of Targeting Communities for Redistribution. A second argument against programs aimed at redistributing income across communities (localities, states) is that such programs are not well-targeted; that is, most communities contain a mix of poor and rich individuals. A program aimed at redistributing resources to a community whose average income is low may simply result in a lowering of the tax rate; the main beneficiary of the program will thus be the rich individuals within the poor communities. On the other hand, certain specific programs, such as the school lunch program, may be more effective in redistributing income to *children* than programs aimed at redistributing income among families.

Location Inefficiencies. A third argument is that programs redistributing income across communities result in location inefficiencies. They distort the decisions of individuals about where to live and the decisions of businesses about where to locate.

The United States is a very mobile society. We move often, and frequently quite far. There have been large migrations from the rural South to the urban North, and in more recent years, from the Snow Belt to the Sun Belt. A variety of reasons induce individuals to move, but economic considerations are among the more important. These include not only an individual's opportunities for employment and the wages he receives but the taxes that are imposed and the public goods that are provided. As demands and technologies change, economic efficiency requires that individuals move to where they can be more productive. This will necessitate that some localities, and indeed even some regions, may face declining populations, while others face rapidly rising populations. Federal aid aimed at redistributing

---

[10] If the restrictive conditions under which the Tiebout hypothesis is valid hold, the supply of locally provided public goods will be efficient. By the same token, however, federal interventions in the local provision of public goods, the nature of which themselves is determined by a political process, need not enhance efficiency.

income from one locality to another may interfere with the efficient alloca-tion of labor and capital. The level of taxes and public services provided by one community will not correctly reflect the economic potential of that com-munity. The inefficiencies to which this gives rise may be small in the short run but become large in the long run. Individuals will be encouraged to stay where they are rather than move to more productive localities. Indeed, it might be better to use the same funds to subsidize emigration out of the unproductive areas.

Similarly, with new highway systems, it may no longer be efficient to have the larger agglomerations of population associated with inner cities. Thus aid to central cities may serve to perpetuate these inefficient patterns of loca-tion.[11]

Note that this inefficiency arises from attempts to redistribute income among communities. If our basic concern is with inequality among individuals, redistribution should be aimed at individuals, not at regions or localities.

In addition, specific redistributive programs, if they are not well designed, may give rise to large distortions. A program, for instance, aimed at meeting measured housing shortages among the very poor, by providing federal sub-sidies, may encourage communities to undertake actions that exacerbate these housing shortages (such as rent control). A program to bail out cities that have borrowed excessively and appear to be in danger of defaulting on their bonds may encourage other communities to borrow more than they other-wise would, knowing that if they get into trouble the federal government is there to rescue them.

PRODUCTION VERSUS FINANCE

In our earlier discussions, we noted an important distinction between public production of some commodity and public financing of the provision of that commodity. A similar distinction needs to be made here: the federal govern-ment can deliver services directly or can use local governmental bodies for the delivery of those services (just as it could in principle use private con-tractors for the delivery of services). We noted earlier that the federal gov-ernment frequently makes use of state and local governments for the administration of programs such as food stamps, job training, etc.

The arguments in favor of what we shall call local production, as opposed to federal production, are parallel to those we discussed in Chapter 7: a) Responsiveness to local preferences and needs. Local communities have the information and the incentives to provide the local public goods in the manner best suited to the needs and preferences of the local constituents. In cases where there are significant variations across communities (say, in education values), this may be an important advantage. b) Incentives for efficiency. Just as competition among firms results in incentives to produce goods efficiently and in the form desired by consumers, so too does compe-tition among communities result in incentives to produce local public goods efficiently and in the form desired by consumers.

We have already noted one limitation to this argument; the limited num-

[11] On the other hand, the aid may compensate for positive externalities produced by the inner cities.

ber of communities may result in limited competition. There is, in addition, an important difference between private goods and locally provided public goods: if a firm succeeds in building a better mousetrap or a mousetrap at less cost, the benefits accrue directly to the purchaser. It pays each individual to look for better and cheaper mousetraps. On the other hand, if voters spend resources to find out who is a better city manager, the benefits that result accrue to all taxpayers and all citizens.[12] Public management is, as we noted in Chapter 6, a public good. Whether these problems are more serious at the local level or the national level remains a matter of debate.

EFFECTIVENESS OF FEDERAL CATEGORICAL AID TO LOCAL COMMUNITIES

The intention of federal categorical aid to local communities is to encourage local spending on particular public services. Aid to bilingual education, aid to vocational education, and aid to school libraries is intended to result in an increase in expenditures in each of these categories. How effective is this aid? Do federal funds just substitute for local funds, or do they actually result in more expenditures for the intended purpose?

From a theoretical perspective, the issue is precisely the same as that which we discussed in Chapter 9. How effective is categorical aid to individuals in encouraging expenditures, say, on food or housing? The answer depends on whether there is a substitution effect or just an income effect.

In Figure 26.3 we have drawn the budget constraint of the community. (We simplify by assuming all individuals within the community are identical, so that we can ignore questions concerning differences in tastes.) The community would choose point E, the tangency between the budget constraint and the indifference curve of the representative individual. Now assume that the federal government provides a bloc grant subsidy to the community. This shifts out the budget constraint, to the line $B'B'$. There is now a new equilibrium, E^*. It entails a higher level of expenditure on local public goods and a higher level of per capita consumption of private goods. That is, the federal aid has in fact resulted in lowering the tax rate imposed on individuals; the federal money has *partially* substituted for local community money. The substitution is only partial. The community, because it now views its budget constraint as being looser, does spend more on public goods.

Assume now, however, that there are two different public goods, garbage collection and education, on which the community can spend funds. We represent the allocation decision of the community between the two public goods by the same kind of diagrammatic devices we have used to represent the allocation between private and public goods.[13] The community has a budget constraint; it needs to divide its total budget between the two public

---

[12] Some have argued that there are incentives for politicians to provide public services more efficiently and to inform the electorate about their abilities.

[13] This kind of analysis assumes that we can separate the allocation decision among public goods from the allocation decision between private and public goods; this kind of separation is possible only under a fairly stringent mathematical condition on preferences known as separability, where we assume that the marginal rate of substitution between public goods 1 and 2 does not depend on the level of consumption of other goods.

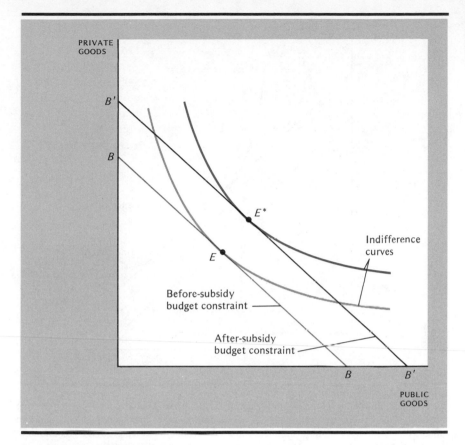

26.3 EFFECT OF BLOCK GRANT A lump sum transfer to a community will result in an increase in public expenditures, but by an amount less than the transfer; local taxes will go down.

goods, as represented by Figure 26.4. The community also has indifference curves between the two public goods. The initial equilibrium is represented in Figure 26.4 by E. Now with the federal aid, the budget constraint has moved out, and the new equilibrium is E^*. Does it make any difference whether the government specifies that the funds be allocated to one public good or the other? Not usually. So long as the total level of expenditure on the public good is less than the amount that the community wishes to spend on it, federal aid will substitute for local support for this particular good, on an almost dollar-for-dollar basis. That is, if the community spends, say, 5 percent of any additional increase in its wealth on education and 5 percent on garbage collection, an appropriation of $1 million will result in $50,000 additional expenditure on education and $50,000 on other public goods. The remaining $900,000 will be used to lower the tax rate. But it makes no difference whether the government stipulates that the money it gives be used for education or not, so long as the community was previously spending more than $1 million on education. If it were not spending this amount, then, of course, there would be a slightly greater effect on the expenditure

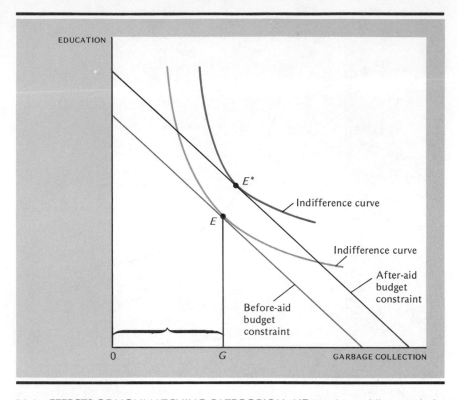

26.4   EFFECTS OF NONMATCHING CATEGORICAL AID It makes no difference whether the federal government stipulates that the funds be used for garbage collection or education, so long as the size of the federal government's grant is less than the total desired expenditure. (If the government stipulates that its funds be used for garbage collection, then, so long as the government gives less than the amount OG, the stipulation has no effect.)

level; expenditure would increase by the amount that the federal aid exceeded the amount previously expended.[14]

These results need to be contrasted with a government program of, for instance, matching local expenditures (e.g., on libraries). This means that if the local community wishes to buy a book that costs $10, it costs the community only $5, with the federal government providing the other $5. This obviously provides a considerable inducement to spend more on these services, as illustrated in Figure 26.5. The new budget constraint, with the subsidy for local expenditures on the public good, is rotated around point B. If the community were to decide to spend nothing on public goods, it would not receive federal aid. For every dollar of private goods that the community gives up, it can obtain twice as many public goods as previously. Thus the budget constraint is much flatter. This outward shift in the budget constraint has an income effect, as before; but now there is, in addition, a substitution effect. Since public goods are less expensive relative to private goods, the community will wish to spend more on public goods.

[14] A full analysis of this problem requires a three-dimensional diagram, with education, garbage collection, and private goods on the three axes.

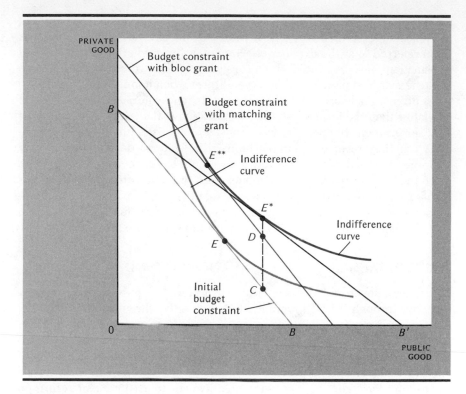

26.5 THE EFFECT OF MATCHING GRANTS Matching grants effectively lower the price of local public goods and result in an increase in the level of consumption of local public goods. With a 50 percent matching grant, to get $1 of public goods, the community need give up only 50 cents' worth of private goods.

If the matching funds are provided for a particular public good, the federal aid will have a marked effect on the budgetary composition; it will encourage those goods whose prices are lowered (perhaps partly at the expense of other public goods, whose relative prices can now be viewed as being higher).

It should be clear that for any given federal budgetary allocation, if the object of the federal government is to encourage the consumption of local public goods, a system of matching grants is far more effective than bloc grants—i.e., a lump sum subsidy.

In Figure 26.5 we have also drawn the community's budget constraint with a bloc grant that results in the community having the same welfare level as the matching grant. (This budget constraint is clearly parallel to the before-subsidy budget constraint.) Two things should be noted: the equilibrium level of expenditure on the public good will be lower than with the matching grant, and the cost to the federal government is lower. There is a deadweight loss associated with the matching grant (of DE^*, in terms of private goods).

Theory and Practice

The prediction that matching grants are more stimulative than bloc grants has been confirmed, but the prediction that nonmatching categorical grants have the same effects as a lump sum increase in private income has not; the evidence suggests that categorical programs do have an effect.[15] This has been referred to as the flypaper effect: money sticks where it hits.[16] Several explanations have been offered. One argument is that voters do not perceive the true marginal price of public expenditures when nonmatching grants are present; marginal costs exceed average costs, and voters are more aware of the latter than the former. Another explanation is that, at least in the short run, government bureaucrats have considerable discretion over their budgets.[17] If they receive additional funds, the "voters" do not immediately know about it; and even if they did, they do not have the means by which to force the bureaucrats to pass the money back to them. A third argument has it that federal administrators can ensure that the money is spent in an incremental manner; they have enough discretion to withdraw funds if they believe that the federal funds are simply being used to substitute for state funds.

THE FEDERAL TAX SYSTEM AND LOCAL EXPENDITURES

The federal government affects local expenditures on public goods not only directly, through its aid programs, but indirectly, through the federal tax system. Two provisions of the income tax code have an important effect on local communities. The first is that interest on state and local bonds is completely exempt from taxation by the federal government. This means that if the individual faces a 50 percent marginal tax rate, a 5 percent return on a tax-exempt local government bond is equivalent to a 10 percent return on any other bond. This obviously lowers the cost to state and local authorities of borrowing funds.

The second provision is that the state and local taxes are deductible from the federal income tax. That is, if an individual has an income of $40,000 and pays $1,000 in property taxes, he can deduct that amount from his income— i.e., he has to pay taxes on only $39,000. This means that if the individual is in the 50 percent tax bracket, his net income (what he can spend to buy cars and other consumption goods) is reduced by only $500. That is, of the $1,000 in property taxes, the federal government is, effectively, paying one-half.

These provisions increase the level of expenditure on local public goods, encourage expenditures on capital projects, and induce some communities to finance their investments by debt.

Consider an idealized community in which all individuals are in the 50 percent tax bracket. If the community increases expenditures per family on education by $1,000 and raises taxes to finance the increased expenditures, the after-federal income tax cost to the individual is only $500. It is as if

---

[15] See E. M. Gramlich, "Intergovernmental Grants: A Review of the Empirical Literature," in *The Political Economy of Fiscal Federalism*, ed. W. E. Oates (Lexington, MA: Lexington Books, 1977).

[16] P. N. Courant, E. M. Gramlich, and D. L. Rubinfeld, "The Stimulative Effect of Intergovernmental Grants: Or Why Money Sticks Where It Hits," in *Fiscal Federalism and Grants-in-Aid*, ed. P. Mieszkowski and W. Oakland (Washington, D.C.: Urban Institute, 1979), pp. 5–21.

[17] For a discussion of this view see, for instance, J. Hannaway, "Administrative Structures: Why Do They Grow?" *Teachers Record*, 1978. The repeated attempts by taxpayers to restrict levels of taxation and expenditure through constitutional amendments suggest that there is a widespread perception that taxpayers have only limited control over the bureaucrats. For a discussion of these attempts, see A. Rabushka and P. Ryan, *The Tax Revolt* (Stanford, CA: Hoover Institution Press, 1982).

there is a federal matching grant for local public goods. The budget constraint facing the individual is identical to that depicted in Figure 26.5.

In most states, communities can only borrow to finance capital projects. If this restriction is binding (as it frequently is), it implies that the effective cost of capital projects is lower than the effective cost of current services (labor and materials); this results in a bias toward capital projects.

Inefficiency of Tax Benefits to Local Communities

There are four reasons why providing aid to local communities through the federal income tax system may be inefficient. The first we have just discussed: aid provides a large incentive for the public provision of goods, regardless of the efficiency with which the local communities are able to deliver these services. It does not result in local communities concentrating their attention on areas in which they should.

The second is that a significant fraction of the benefits of interest exemption accrue not to the communities but to wealthy taxpayers. In the last few years, tax-exempt bonds have yielded higher returns to individuals who face a marginal tax rate of more than 30 percent . (This corresponds to a single individual who had a taxable income of $25,000 in 1983 or an income of $35,000 for a married couple with two dependants.) It also means that the effective subsidy to the borrowing costs of local communities is relatively little.

The third reason that tax exemption may not be an efficient way of subsidizing local communities is that because of competition among communities, a considerable portion of the benefits may accrue to industries within the communities rather than to the communities themselves. Local communities can issue tax-exempt bonds to help finance some of the capital costs required to provide the infrastructure to attract firms to their communities. But if one community does this, other communities respond, either by trying to attract the firms to their community or by trying to prevent the firms from leaving. The net effect is that the level of public goods provided to businesses may be higher than it otherwise would be. If only one community provided the higher level of public goods, it would be reflected in the price firms are willing to pay for land in that community. But when all communities increase the level of public goods they provide, it may leave unaffected the total demand for land and hence the level of rents. The return to capital is thus increased: the benefits do not accrue to the local communities.

The fourth consideration in an evaluation of tax and interest provisions are the inequities it creates for individuals with different tastes and incomes. We have already noted that these provisions represent a considerable subsidy to the public provision of local public goods. Individuals who have a relatively strong preference for the goods that tend to be publicly provided at the local level benefit by such measures, at the expense of those who have a weak preference for these commodities.

Since the magnitude of the reduction in effective costs for public goods depends on the individuals' marginal tax rate, those who face a higher tax rate—usually the more wealthy individuals—receive a larger subsidy, and a larger reduction in their effective price of public goods. To some extent, the "taste" effect and the pure income effect offset each other; wealthier individuals are more likely to send their children to private school and, thus, though they may receive a larger subsidy for each dollar spent on public goods, they may actually spend less on at least certain categories of public goods.

It was partly because of the belief that using the tax system to aid local communities was a particularly inefficient and inequitable way of subsidizing them that President Reagan, in his proposal for tax reform, argued for the elimination of deductibility of state and local taxes. Not surprisingly, this proposal has met with vehement opposition from those states and communities with high tax rates. There has been particular concern because the federal government, at the same time, has reduced direct subsidies. Local government officials are afraid that taxpayers will be unwilling to vote for expenditures as large as they had previously approved, and thus there will have to be major cutbacks in local services. Supporters of the president's proposal are less concerned. Since in all but a few states the median voter does not itemize his deductions, the elimination of tax deductibility may not have a significant effect on the level of expenditures approved by local communities (at least if the majority voting model discussed in chapter 6 is approximately correct). Moreover, supporters of the president's proposal would argue that if there are cutbacks, they only result because voters have decided that, at the previous levels of expenditures, the marginal benefits are less than the marginal costs; and in that case there should be a cutback.

SUMMARY

1. The federal government regulates and subsidizes states and localities. The direct subsidies consist of both categorical grants (grants for specific purposes) and bloc grants. In matching grants, the amount received by the states and localities depends on the amount they spend. Indirect aid is provided by the exemption from taxation of interest on state and local bonds and the tax deductibility of state and local taxes.

2. The Tiebout hypothesis postulates that competition among communities results in an efficient provision of local public goods. The reasons that federal intervention may be required include market failures (national public goods, externalities, particularly those associated with choice of location, and limited competition) and redistribution (the limited ability to redistribute income at the local level).

3. There are marked disparities in income per capita and in the provision of local public services across states and localities. Whether government policy should be directed at reducing inequalities across communities (rather than inequalities across individuals) is debatable.

4. The arguments for local production of public goods are parallel to those for private production: greater responsiveness to needs and preferences and greater incentives to provide services efficiently.

5. Matching grants are more effective in encouraging expenditures in the direction desired, but there is a deadweight loss associated with their use. Though traditional theoretical arguments suggest that nonmatching grants should have just income effects, and thus be equivalent to a transfer of private income, the empirical evidence suggests the presence of a flypaper effect.

6. Tax subsidies lead to excessive expenditures on local public goods and excessive capital investment.

7. Tax subsidies are an inefficient way of subsidizing state and local communities; much of the benefit accrues to wealthy investors rather than to the communities; a considerable portion of the benefits is passed along to businesses (and not to the residents of the communities); and they discriminate in favor of high-income individuals and in favor of individuals who have a strong preference for local public goods.

KEY CONCEPTS

Matching grants	Spillovers
Categorical grants	Specific equalitarianism
Bloc grants	Flypaper effect
Local public goods	

QUESTIONS AND PROBLEMS

1. Discuss the advantages and disadvantages of state versus national determination of eligibility standards and benefits for: food stamps; medicaid; unemployment insurance; Aid to Families with Dependent Children; and old-age and survivors' insurance.

2. In President Reagan's State of the Union message in 1982, he proposed a trade with the states: in return for the states taking over responsibility for the full costs of food stamps and AFDC, the federal government would take over responsibility for medicaid. In addition, he proposed phasing out most categorical grant programs (possibly substituting increases in bloc grants). Evaluate these proposals using the analysis of this chapter.

3. If the income elasticity of demand for education is 1, what will be the effect on expenditures on education of a small bloc grant of $100,000 if presently the community spends 5 percent of its total resources on education?

4. Many matching grant programs specify that the federal government matches on a dollar-for-dollar basis local expenditures up to some particular maximum. Draw the budget constraint between private goods and local public goods facing a community of identical individuals. Discuss the effect of such a matching program on communities that do not go to the maximum. Discuss the effect on communities that go beyond the maximum.

5. What would you expect to be the effects of the elimination of the deductibility of state and local taxes from the federal income tax on expenditures on education? Show diagrammatically why you might expect such a change to increase the relative importance of private education.

6. Consider a community in which everyone is at the 50 percent marginal tax bracket. By how much would educational expenditures be reduced by the elimination of the tax deductibility of state and local taxes, if the price elasticity of demand for education is 1?

7. On the basis of the discussion of Chapters 7, 8, and 9, discuss the relative merits of regulation versus matching grants as devices to elicit desired behavior on the part of state and local governments.

27

State and Local Taxes and Expenditures

In Chapter 2 we discussed the changing pattern of taxation at the state and local levels: the decreased importance of property taxes and the increased importance of sales and income taxes. Does this changing pattern of financing result in a change in who bears the burden of state and local taxes, or only a change in the manner in which they are collected? The first part of this chapter is concerned with answering the question: What is the incidence of state and local taxes? We also address the parallel question: Who benefits from the goods and services provided by local governments? What, in other words, is the incidence of these expenditures? It is necesssary to answer these questions in order to answer our final question: What can we say about how the level and composition of public expenditures are determined locally?

INCIDENCE ANALYSIS APPLIED TO LOCAL PUBLIC FINANCE

In Chapter 17 we developed the basic principles of incidence analysis. There we showed that the incidence of a tax on a commodity or a factor depended on the elasticity of demand and supply for that commodity or factor.

The equilibrium return to a factor is determined by the intersection of the demand and supply schedules. Now assume that a tax is imposed on the use of a factor. That can be represented diagrammatically either as a shift upward in the supply curve (to elicit the given supply, the buyer must pay more, by an amount equal to the tax) or as a shift downward in the demand curve (the amount received by the seller, at each quantity, is smaller). The limiting case is where the supply schedule has an infinite elasticity—i.e., where the supply schedule is completely horizontal. Then the incidence of the tax lies entirely on the buyer. The price he pays goes up by the amount of the tax. The amount received by the seller is unaffected.

The implications of this for local taxes can easily be derived. In the long run most factors are mobile; that is, they can easily move from community to community. This is particularly the case for capital. Investors will invest in a community only if they can obtain the same return that they could obtain elsewhere.

Local Capital Taxes

A community that increases the taxes it imposes on capital will find that investors will not invest in their community; though it may not be possible for those with fixed capital equipment—such as steel mills—to remove their capital, new investments will be reduced until the before-tax return to capital is driven up. The process will continue until the after-tax return is equal to what it is elsewhere.

Thus the burden of the tax on capital is not felt, in the long run, by the owners of capital. It is felt by land and labor. Because there is less capital, the productivity of land and labor and hence their income will be reduced.

If as a result of the tax on capital the productivity of workers is decreased, wages will be lowered. But then, in the long run, workers will emigrate; if labor is perfectly mobile, they will continue to emigrate until their (after-tax) income is the same as it is elsewhere. This leaves land as the only factor that cannot emigrate. With less capital and less labor, the return to land is less: the full burden of the tax is borne by land owners in the long run.

This assumes that labor is perfectly mobile. Of course, in the short run, workers will not instantaneously migrate in response to a small change in the capital tax rate. Indeed, many individuals have strong preferences for living in the community in which they grew up. These laborers are only partially mobile. They will bear some part of the burden of the tax on capital. Their wages will be reduced as a result of the outflow of capital.

Ignoring these considerations may have dramatic consequences. Occasionally states have attempted to impose special taxes on particular industries. Some industries are particularly "footloose." These industries will move out if higher taxes are imposed on them. They will "shop" for states and communities that offer the best deal.

Income, Wage, and Sales Taxes

Similar principles apply to the taxation of labor. If individuals had no particular attachment to their community, a small community would face a perfectly elastic long-run labor supply schedule. A tax on labor would simply increase the before-tax return to labor and leave the after-tax return unchanged. Again, the incidence of a wage tax is borne not by workers but by landlords. It is just an indirect—but inefficient—tax on land.

Uniform sales taxes are, as we noted in Chapter 17, simply equivalent to proportional income taxes. They have effects that are analogous to wage taxes.[1] They are borne by land (and workers with limited labor mobility).

Distortions

The fact that all local taxes are borne by the same, immobile factors does not mean that the taxes all have the same consequences. While a direct tax on land is nondistortionary, all the other ways of raising revenue induce distortions. The property tax (which is partly a tax on land, partly a tax on capital) raises the cost of capital to the community and induces a bias against capital; a wage tax or a sales tax raises the cost of labor and thus induces a bias against the use of labor. In addition, it may induce individuals to do their shopping across state borders. For instance, the higher sales tax in New York City induces many individuals to do their shopping in New Jersey. When Washington, D.C., imposed a higher gasoline tax than neighboring Virginia and Maryland, drivers were induced to buy their gasoline outside the city. State income taxes may induce individuals to live in one state and commute to another to avoid the taxes that might be levied on their income.[2] New Hampshire imposes no income tax; many people find it advantageous to live there and commute to Massachusetts, which has an income tax. The tax is inefficient, both because it raises the cost of using labor in Massachusetts and because it induces unnecessary expenditures on commuting costs.

Limitations on the Ability to Redistribute Income

The fact that taxes are borne by immobile factors means that the extent of redistribution that is feasible at the local level is very limited. Assume, for instance, that some community decides doctors are too wealthy. The local government, accordingly, imposes a licensing tax on doctors in an attempt to redistribute income from this wealthy class of individuals to others. Doctors, in making their decision about where to set up practice, will look at their prospects in different communities. When they discover that after-tax income is lower in this community than elsewhere, they will be discouraged from setting up practice in this community. If the tax is not too high, doctors who are already established will not leave; the costs of moving exceed the losses from the tax. The fact that its doctors do not leave may fool the community into thinking that it has been successful in extracting some additional taxation out of doctors; in the short run, it may be right. But gradually, as fewer doctors move into the community, the scarcity of doctors will become felt, and their wages will be bid up. Wages will continue to bid up until the after-tax wage of the doctor is equal to what he could have earned elsewhere. In the long run doctors do not bear the burden of the tax (although they do in the short run). In the long run, the community as a whole bears the burden of the tax, in the form of less medical services and higher prices for doctors.

---

[1]Income taxes are taxes on wages plus income from capital. These taxes have a particularly distortionary effect on location decisions of wealthy individuals: they may choose not to live and work in a location where their productivity is highest because the net return (taking into account the additional taxes they must pay on their capital income) is lower.

[2]In such situations, they typically still must pay taxes on the wages they receive.

The same principle holds for any factor that is mobile in the long run. A
number of states have suffered under the false impression that they could in fact succeed in taxing capital within their state at higher rates than it is taxed elsewhere. Some states have attempted to include income of international enterprises operating outside the state (or country) in the tax base on which they levy a corporate profits tax. If the above analysis is correct, such attempts cannot, in the long run, be successful. These communities are often misled into believing that they can do this, because capital does not emigrate instantaneously.

Rent Control

A number of communities have similarly been under the impression that they could reduce the return to landlords, who were viewed to be exploiting the poorer renters. They imposed rent control laws, the effect of which was to lower the rents paid by renters below what they otherwise would be. Again, in the short run, such measures may indeed be successful. In the long run, however, landlords will make decisions about the construction of additional apartments and the renovation and maintenance of existing apartments. If the return is lowered below the return they can obtain on capital invested in other sectors of the economy, there is no reason for them to continue to invest in housing.[3] The consequence is that the rental market will "dry up." In the long run, renters will be worse off than they would be if the government had not imposed rent control; some renters cannot obtain a rental apartment at any price. (Not surprisingly, this then results in a demand for the public provision of housing for those dependent on rental markets, necessitating that the community pay the subsidy to the renters through general revenues rather than forcing the owners of rental apartments to bear the burden alone.)

CAPITALIZATION

Consider two communites that are identical in every aspect except that the taxes are higher in one than in the other (say, because of less efficiency in the provision of public services). Clearly, if the price of housing in the two communities were the same, everyone would prefer to live in the community with the lower tax rate. This cannot, of course, be an equilibrium. Individuals care only about the total cost of living in the community; they don't care whether the government or an individual receives the money that they pay. Thus in equilibrium the total cost of living in the two communities must be the same. This means that the community with the higher tax rates will find that the prices of its houses (land) are reduced proportionately. We say that the taxes are **capitalized** in house prices.

The term *capitalized* is used here to refer to the fact that the price will reflect not only current taxes but all future taxes. To calculate the effect of a

---

[3]It may not be the case that, in equilibrium, the after-tax return in all communities will be the same. Notions of loyalty may lead individuals to invest in their own country or community, even when they could obtain a higher return elsewhere.

Differences in information may also lead individuals to prefer investing in their own country and thus reduce the mobility of capital.

constant tax of, say, $1,000 per year on the house price, recall that a dollar next year is worth less than a dollar this year. If we got a dollar this year we could have invested it in a money market fund or bank and obtained a return of, say, 10 percent, so at the end of the year we could have $1.10. Thus getting a dollar today is worth (is equivalent to) $1.10 tomorrow. More generally, a dollar *today* is worth $1 + r$ next year, where r is the rate of interest (i.e., a dollar next year is worth $1/1 + r$ today).[4] Thus, the value of T taxes this year, next year, the year after, and so on is

$$T + \frac{T}{1+r} + \frac{T}{(1+r)^2} + \frac{T}{(1+r)^3} \cdots .$$

This is the present discounted value of the tax liabilities. If the amount by which a house's price is reduced is given by the present discounted value of these tax liabilities, we say that the tax liabilities are fully capitalized in the value of the house. If two houses are identical except for their tax liabilities, but the house prices differ, but by less than this amount, we say taxes are **partially capitalized** in the less expensive house.

Incentives for Pension Schemes

The fact that certain fiscal variables may not be fully capitalized has some important implications itself. There are incentives for communities to take advantage of this. Someone living in a community who thinks there is a reasonable chance that he will move out in ten years or so might vote for a large, unfunded pension scheme for public employees. A generous pension allows the community to attract workers while paying lower current wages. In effect, future house owners in the town are forced to pay for current services. In a sense, the future buyer of a house is being deceived in much the same way that the manufacturer of a product who does not disclose fully some important characteristics of his commodity may attempt to deceive a purchaser. An important characteristic of a house (or any piece of property) is the future tax liabilties that are associated with it, and to know these, one must know the debt and unfunded pension liabilities of the community. Whether the appropriate way to deal with this is through disclosure laws (each community might be required to notify all potential purchasers of a house of the debt obligations of the community prior to the completion of any sale) or through restrictions (not allowing unfunded pension schemes) is a debatable question.

Choice of Debt versus Tax Financing

The extent of capitalization has implications more generally for the decision about whether to finance local public expenditures by debt or taxes. With full capitalization, an increase in the local debt by a dollar would simply decrease the net market value of the community by a dollar. Since house

---

[4]By the same reasoning, a dollar the year after next is equivalent to $1/1 + r = $1/1.10 next year; but this means that, since a dollar next year is worth $1/1 + r = $1/1.10 today, a dollar the year after next is worth $1/(1.10x1.10) this year—i.e., $1/(+r)^2$. See Chapter 10 for a more extensive discussion of present discounted value.

buyers can choose to live in this community, or in some other community, their assumption of the debt of the community is a voluntary action. Therefore they ought to be compensated for it, through a corresponding decrease in the price of a house. This is true no matter how far in the future the debt is to be repaid. It does not have to be repaid during the period in which the next owner owns the house. Assume the debt is to be repaid in forty years, and each individual lives in the house for only ten years. The person who buys the house at the time that the debt is to be repaid clearly will pay less for the house, taking into account the increased tax liability associated with paying off the debt. But the preceding purchaser knows that the person to whom he will sell the house will be willing to pay less for it, and hence he will be willing to pay less for it (by the amount of the tax liability). Similarly, the previous purchaser knows that the price at which he can sell it will be lower by the amount of the increased debt, and so he too will be willing to pay less for it, and so on.

With full capitalization, current owners pay for current services, whether directly, through taxes, or indirectly through the expectation of a lower price on their house resulting from a higher debt used to finance the public services. Which of these two methods is then preferable turns out to depend on the treatment of local taxes and interest on local debt by the federal government, a question we discussed in the previous chapter.[5]

Short-Run versus Long-Run Capitalization

Assume that taxes are increased on apartment buildings. If the amenities the community provides are unchanged, the rents will remain unchanged: renters don't really care about the landlord's costs. In the short run, the market value of the apartment will thus decrease. But this will make investing in apartments in the community less attractive; the supply of apartments will be reduced (as old apartments deteriorate) or in any case will not keep up with population growth. This will result in an increase in rents. Eventually, rents will increase to the point where the after-tax return on the apartment is the same as investors could obtain from investments in any other community. Thus, although the tax is imposed legally on buildings, in the long run it is land and immobile individuals (who must pay higher rents) who bear the tax. The market value of apartment buildings will thus not decrease by the full present discounted value of the taxes their owners pay.

Who Benefits from Local Public Goods: The Capitalization Hypothesis

The same reasoning that leads us to conclude that the incidence of any tax resides with the owners of land (or other partially immobile factors) implies that the incidence of any benefits resides with the owners of land (or partially immobile factors). Any public good that makes it more desirable to live in the community drives up the rents and hence increases the value of property

---

[5]In the presence of credit rationing (limited availability of mortgages), the lower price of a house may increase its salability. The fact that communities may borrow more easily than individuals provides an argument for communities to borrow as much as they can.

in the community. In the short run, some of the benefits may be enjoyed by owners of buildings; but the increased rents on their buildings leads to increased investment in housing (new apartment buildings, replacing small, old apartment buildings with larger ones, etc.), and this drives down their return.[6] Ultimately the value of the public good is reflected in land.

Similarly, some public goods make it more attractive to work in a given community. This will reduce the wage a firm must pay to recruit a worker. But again, the ultimate beneficiaries are the land owners.

To see the link between the wages that individuals receive and the level of public services provided, consider what happens if a city decides to spend more on its symphony orchestra, which provides free concerts in the parks in the summer. This makes the city a more attractive place in which to live and work. A worker who enjoys the symphony, contemplating a job offer in this city, will accept the job at a slightly lower wage than he would accept in a community that is identical in every respect except its level of expenditure on its symphony orchestra. Thus, to the extent that workers in the city (regardless of where they choose to live) value the amenities it provides wages in the city will be lower; firms will find it attractive to locate there. As they move into this city, the price of land will be bid up. Equilibrium is attained when the price of land is bid up just enough to compensate for the lower wages, so that investors receive the same return to their capital that they receive from investing it elsewhere. The ultimate beneficiaries of the provision of better public goods are not the residents in the city but the landowners.

This analysis assumes, of course, that labor is highly mobile, so that when the city provides a more attractive public good, there is sufficient migration to increase rents and decrease wages. If labor is not very mobile (and in the short run it may well not be), wages will not fall to reflect fully the increased amenities, and some of the benefits of the increased provision of local public goods will accrue to the current residents. Note that some current residents may be hurt by the provision of the symphony. Those who do not enjoy symphonies may find that, nonetheless, their rents are increased or wages reduced.

The provision of the symphony orchestra does have important spillovers to other communities. In particular, firms located in the suburbs will find that they too can hire workers at a lower wage than they previously could. This increases the value of their land as well. Bedroom suburbs will also find that the demand for their housing has increased.

Absolute versus Relative Capitalization

We have discussed how, if one community increases its level of expenditure on a public good, the differential expenditure will be reflected in the prices of the land in the community. There is, however, an important difference between the effects of a single community increasing its expenditure in a

---

[6]Current owners of buildings have an incentive to maintain their higher return by restricting further investments, by zoning. The higher returns they enjoy should be viewed not as a return to capital but as a return to the property rights the zoning board has created.

public good and all communities increasing their expenditures on that public good. If all communities increase their expenditures on a public good, the relative attractiveness of living in one community versus another is, of course, unchanged. Thus, in general, rentals will remain unchanged.[7]

This is an example of a phenomenon we noted in earlier chapters. Partial equilibrium effects—the effects of a change in one community (a change in a tax on one commodity)—may be quite different from general equilibrium effects—the effects of a change in all communities (a change in the tax rate on all commodities).

The Use of Changes in Land Rents to Measure Benefits

Changes in rents have often been used to measure the value of certain public services. In studies of the economic effects of American railroads in the nineteenth century, one commonly employed way of measuring the benefits is to measure the change in the land rents after the construction of the railroad. Again, one has to be careful to distinguish partial versus general equilibrium effects. Making one small plot of land more accessible will increase the demand for that plot of land; and the change in the rent will provide an accurate estimate of the reduction of the transportation costs of getting to that piece of land. However, changing the accessibility of a mass of land—as the railroad in fact did—has general equilibrium effects; the change in land rents will not correctly assess the value of such a change.[8]

Land values reflect the valuation of marginal individuals, those who are indifferent when choosing between living in this community and living somewhere else. When there are a sufficiently large number of communities, the valuation of these marginal individuals provides a good measure of the valuation of the entire community, but not otherwise.[9]

Testing the Capitalization Hypothesis

The question of the extent to which the benefits provided by public goods and taxes are reflected in property values has received extensive discussion.

If some communites were more efficient in providing public goods than others, so that they could provide the same level of public goods with lower taxes, property values in the low-tax communities should be higher. If all communities were equally efficient and maximized their property values, differences in taxes would be matched with differences in benefits. There would be no systematic relationship between property values and expendi-

[7]If the communities provide a public good that makes land more desirable, all individuals will attempt to rent or purchase more land, and this will increase the value of land. The opposite will be true if communities provide a public good that makes owning land less desirable. Thus, since public parks are, in part at least, a substitute for back yards, it is conceivable that if all communities spend more on providing public parks, land prices would actually decrease.

[8]There is a second limitation on the use of land rents to measure the value of such changes: they provide a good measure only in the case where there are no inframarginal individuals, no individuals who are enjoying a consumer surplus from living in the community.

[9]R. Arnott and J. E. Stiglitz, "Aggregate Land Rents, Expenditure on Public Goods and Optimal City Size," *Quarterly Journal of Economics* 93 (1972): 472–500; R. Arnott and J. E. Stiglitz, "Aggregate Land Rents and Aggregate Transport Costs," *Economic Journal* 91 (1981): 331–47; D. Starrett, "Principles of Optimal Location in a Large Homogeneous Area," *Journal of Economic Theory* 9 (1974): 418–48.

tures. This is the result obtained by Jan Brueckner of the University of Illinois, in his study based on fifty-four Massachusetts communities.[10]

The proportion of communities providing high levels of public service reflects the proportion of individuals who desire them. If too many communities provided a high level of public services, property values in such communities would be depressed. Thus, the absence of any systematic relationship between property values and expenditures suggests that there is neither an undersupply nor an oversupply of communities providing high or low levels of services.

On the other hand, there is evidence that the value of amenities (such as clean air) for which there are not corresponding taxes are capitalized in property values.

PUBLIC CHOICE AT THE LOCAL LEVEL

In Chapter 6 we described how public choices are made; we showed that, with majority voting, the allocation to public goods reflects the preferences of the median voter.[11] This voter assesses the costs and benefits to him of the expenditure of an extra dollar on public goods. We then assessed the efficiency of the majority voting equilibrium.

The issues at the local level are identical; here, however, our attention is focused on the *incidence* of the benefits and costs associated with any increase in expenditure and taxation. We need to distinguish between the effects on renters and on land owners, under assumptions of perfect and imperfect mobility (with a large or small number of competing communities).

With perfect mobility and a large number of competing communities, any improvement in the amenities provided by a community will be fully reflected in rents; hence marginal renters will be indifferent with respect to the nature of the public services provided. Moreover, since their rents are affected only by the quality of the services that are provided, not by the tax rates, renters will be completely unconcerned about the efficiency with which public services are provided.

Under these same assumptions, land owners as a group will want public services to be increased so long as they lead to increases in rents exceeding the increases in taxes. Thus in a land owner-controlled community, in equilibrium, an extra $1,000 spent on public goods should just increase aggregate rents by $1,000. But the increased rents represent renters' marginal evaluation of the services provided by the community. As a result, a land owner-controlled community will provide an efficient level of public service. Moreover, since if the community can provide the same services at less cost, the after-tax receipts of land owners will be increased, land owner-controlled communities have every incentive to ensure that public services are provided in an efficient manner.

All of this changes if there are relatively few communities competing against each other. Consider a metropolitan region in which there are two towns, A

[10]J.K. Brueckner, "A Test for the Allocative Efficiency in the Local Public Sector," *Journal of Public Economics* 19 (1982): 311–31.
[11]Assuming, of course, that a majority voting equilibrium exists.

and B. A has high taxes and a high level of local public goods; B has low taxes and a low level of public goods. Those who have a strong preference for public goods (relative to private goods) live in A; those who have a strong preference for private goods live in B. The individual who is indifferent with respect to living in the two communities we call the *marginal* individual; the extra public goods he receives in A just compensate him for the extra taxes he has to pay. All other individuals are called **inframarginal.** For those who live in A, for instance, the extra benefits more than offset the extra taxes they have to pay. Were A to increase its taxes slightly, without altering its benefits, they would still not wish to move to B.

Assume that there are houses for half the population in A, and half in B. All housing is rented. If B decides to provide fewer public goods, rents in B will have to adjust so that the *marginal* individual is still indifferent with respect to living in A or living in B. But of all the individuals who live in B, the marginal individual is the one with the *strongest* preference for public goods: the rents will fall in B to just compensate him for the lower level of public goods. If the rents decrease enough to make the marginal individual remain indifferent, the other individuals in B are actually better off. In particular, the median renter in B will have an incentive to vote for a very low level of expenditure on public goods, lower than is Pareto efficient. The same reasoning shows that the median renter in Community A will have an incentive to vote for a very high level of expenditure on public goods, higher than is Pareto efficient.

Land owners have exactly the opposite bias. They are concerned only with the effect of increased expenditure on land values (rents). If the increased rents exceed the increased expenditures, they are worth undertaking. In Community A, the increased rents from an increased expenditure reflect the *marginal* individual's evaluation; this is the individual who has the weakest preference for public goods. Thus the gain to others (the inframarginal renters) exceeds the gain to the marginal renter; but the land owners will pay no attention to this. As a result, they will vote for too little expenditure on public goods. By the same reasoning, in Community B, land owners will vote for too high an expenditure on public goods.

SUMMARY

1. If capital and labor are mobile, the incidence of any tax lies on land, the immobile factor. If labor is only partially mobile, some of the burden may lie upon it.

2. Local taxes that are not imposed on immobile factors—sales taxes (which are equivalent to income taxes), wage taxes, corporation income taxes, property taxes—induce distortions.

3. Improved benefits provided by the government get reflected in rents paid. In a perfectly competitive environment (with a large number of communities with similar individuals), the benefits of improved government services accrue solely to landlords.

4. If the level of expenditures is chosen to maximize property values, and there is effective competition among communities, the resulting allocation of resources is Pareto efficient.

5. If there is limited competition, however, the resulting equilibrium is not Pareto efficient; there is a tendency for too little diversification in the services provided by the different owner-controlled communities.

6. In contrast, when renters control the community, there is a tendency (under the same circumstances) for excessive diversification. Communities that spend a great deal on public goods spend too much; communities that spend little spend too little.

7. Moreover, there is no incentive for renters to be concerned with the efficiency with which the government delivers its services.

KEY CONCEPTS

Rent control   Absolute versus relative capitalization
Capitalization   Inframarginal individual
Partial capitalization

QUESTIONS AND PROBLEMS

1. Explain why the property tax may lead to lower expenditures on capital (buildings) per unit of land.

2. Many firms have employees, plants, and sales in many states. In imposing state corporation income taxes, states use a rule for allocating a fraction of the firms' total profits to their state. Does it make a difference what rule is used? Discuss the consequences of alternative rules.

3. Many of the issues of state and local taxation are similar to issues that arise in international contexts. Many countries have, for instance, imposed taxes on capital owned by foreigners. Discuss the incidence of such taxes. Does it pay to subsidize capital owned by foreigners?

4. Discuss the incidence of a city wage tax.

5. Many cities have passed rent control legislation. Discuss carefully who benefits and loses, in the short run and in the long run, from such legislation. Discuss the political economy of such legislation.
   President Reagan has proposed that no housing aid be given to communities with rent control legislation. Discuss the merits of this proposal.

6. Henry George, a famous nineteenth-century American economist, proposed that only land be taxed (not buildings). Would this be unfair to land owners? Would it distort resource allocations, making land more expensive relative to buildings?

7. Who is the main beneficiary of tax-exempt industrial development bonds (which enable communities to borrow funds to relend to firms constructing new plants within the city): a) workers in the town; b) land owners in the town; or c) the industries that move into the town? Give your assumptions. Does it make a difference whether only one community provides these bonds or whether all communities provide them?

8. Who benefited from the construction of the subway system in Washington: a) owners of land near the subway line at the time the route was announced; b) owners of land near the subway line at the time the subway was completed; c) renters of apartments near the subway line at the time the route was announced; d) renters of apartments near the subway line after the subway was completed; or e) renters of apartments not near the subway line? Give your assumptions.

Further Readings

CHAPTER 1 THE PUBLIC SECTOR IN A MIXED ECONOMY

A. O. Hirschman, *Shifting Involvement: Private Interest and Public Action* (Princeton, NJ: Princeton University Press, 1982).

A. B. Atkinson and J. E. Stiglitz, *Lectures in Public Economics* (New York: McGraw-Hill, 1980), Chapters 1 and 8.

CHAPTER 2 THE PUBLIC SECTOR IN THE UNITED STATES

The question of the sources and explanation of the growth in government has been a question of continuing debate. See, for instance, W. G. Nutter, *Growth of Government in the West* (Washington, D.C.: American Enterprise Institute, 1978) and, in the context of the U.K., R. W. Bacon and W. A. Eltis, *Britain's Economic Problem: Too Few Producers* (London: Macmillan, 1978).

The July issue of the *Survey of Current Business* (U.S. Department of Commerce/Bureau of Economic Analysis) provides statistics on public expenditures at the federal and state and local levels.

J. A. Pechman's *Federal Tax Policy* (Washington, D.C.: Brookings Institution, 4th ed., 1983) provides an excellent brief history of taxation at the federal level, as well as detailed statistics concerning our current tax structure and how it compares with other countries and other times.

Other good sources of current data include the *Annual Report of the Council of Economic Advisors* and the *Budget of the United States Government,* in particular the "Special Analyses." Unfortunately, the budget provides better data on how the government plans (or would like to) spend its funds that it does retrospective data on how the funds were actually spent.

CHAPTER 3 WELFARE ECONOMICS

A basic discussion of welfare economics is provided by E. J. Mishan, *Introduction to Normative Economics* (New York: Oxford University Press, 1981).

The concept of social indifference curves was first developed by A. Bergson in "A Reformulation of Certain Aspects of Welfare Economics," *Quarterly Journal of Economics* 52 (1938).

A general discussion of the issues of welfare economics is provided by W. J. Baumol, *Welfare Economics and the Theory of the State* (Cambridge, MA: Harvard University Press, 2nd. ed., 1965); I. Little, *A Critique of Welfare Economics* (Oxford: Clarendon Press, 2nd. ed., 1957); and J. deV. Graaff, *Theoretical Welfare Economics* (London: Cambridge University Press, 1957).

The controversy over the use of the compensation criterion involves contributions by N. Kaldor, "Welfare Propositions in Economics and Interpersonal Comparisons of Utility," *Economic Journal* 9 (1941): 549–52 and T. Scitovsky, "A Note on Welfare Propositions in Economics," *Review of Economic Studies,* November 1941.

Two philosophers whose ideas have received considerable attention among economists are John Rawls, *A Theory of Justice* (Cambridge, MA: Harvard University Press, 1971) and Robert Nozick, *Anarchy, State and Utopia* (New York: Basic Books, 1974). A concise statement of Rawls's position can be found in J. Rawls, Concepts of Distributional Equity: Some Reasons for the Maximin Criterion," *American Economic Review* 64 (1974): 141–46.

Problems of introducing interpersonal comparisons into social choices are discussed in A. K. Sen, *On Economic Inequality* (Oxford: Clarendon Press, 1973).

CHAPTER 4   THE ROLE OF THE PUBLIC SECTOR

F. Bator, "The Anatomy of Market Failure," *Quarterly Journal of Economics* 72 (1958).

C. Wolf, Jr., "A Theory of Nonmarket Failure: Framework for Implementation Analysis," *Journal of Law and Economics,* October 1980.

F. Bator, "The Simple Analytics of Welfare Maximization," *American Economic Review* 47 (1957).

CHAPTER 5   PUBLIC GOODS AND PUBLICLY PROVIDED GOODS

The classic references for the theory of pure public goods are P. A. Samuelson, "The Pure Theory of Public Expenditure," *Review of Economics and Statistics* 36 (1954): 387–89 and "Diagrammatic Exposition of a Theory of Public Expenditure," *Review of Economics and Statistics* 37 (1955): 350–56.

See also J. Buchanan, *The Demand and Supply of Public Goods* (Chicago: Rand McNally, 1968).

The concept of publicly provided private goods is discussed in J. E. Stiglitz, "The Demand for Education in Public and Private School Systems," *Journal of Public Economics* 3 (1974): 349–85.

For a more advanced treatment of the topics covered in this chapter, see A. Atkinson and J. E. Stiglitz, *Lectures in Public Ecnomics* (New York: McGraw-Hill, 1980), pp. 482–505.

CHAPTER 6   PUBLIC CHOICE

An excellent exposition of many of the topics covered here can be found in D. C. Mueller, *Public Choice* (New York: Cambridge University Press, 1979). A more advanced survey can be found in G. Kramer, "Theories of Political Processes," in *Frontiers of Quantitative Economics III,* ed. M. D. Intrilligator (Amsterdam: North Holland, 1977).

The classic reference on the voting paradox is K. Arrow, *Social Choice and Individual Values* (New York: Wiley, 2nd. ed., 1963). An advanced textbook treatment may be found in A. Sen, *Collective Choice and Social Welfare* (Oakland, CA: Holden Day, 1970).

Two important books exploring the application of economic principles to political behavior are A. Downs, *An Economic Theory of Democracy* (New York: Harper and Row, 1957) and W. Niskanen, Jr., *Bureaucracy and Representative Government* (Chicago: Aldine, 1971).

The problem of revelation of preferences is dealt with by J. Green and J. J. Laffont, *Individual Incentives in Public Decision-Making* (Amsterdam: North Holland, 1979).

For two contrasting views of government production, see E. S. Savas, *Privatizing the Public Sector* (Chatham, NJ: Chatham House Publishers, 1982) and C. T. Goodsell *The Case for Bureaucracy* (Chatham, NJ: Chatham House Publishers, 1983).

See also W. A. Niskanen, Jr., *Bureaucracy and Representative Government* (Chicago: Aldine, 1971).

An early explanation of bureaucratic growth is provided by C. Parkinson, "Parkinson's Law," *Economist*, November 1955, reprinted in E. Mansfield, ed., *Managerial Economics and Operations Research* (New York: W. W. Norton, 4th ed., 1980).

Some of the important consequences of the absence of choice are discussed in A. Hirschman, *Exit, Voice, and Loyalty* (Cambridge, MA: Harvard University Press, 1970).

A popular summary of the Grace Commission report is available in W. R. Kennedy, Jr. and R. W. Lee, *A Taxpayer Survey of the Grace Commission Report* (Ottawa, IL: Jameson Books, 1984).

CHAPTER 8   EXTERNALITIES

For a good general discussion of externalities, see E. J. Mishan, *Introduction to Normative Economics* (New York: Oxford University Press, 1981). For a more technical discussion, see W. J. Baumol and W. E. Oates, *The Theory of Environmental Policy*, (Englewood Cliffs, NJ: Prentice Hall, 1975) or P. Dasgupta, *The Control of Resources* (Oxford: Basil Blackwell, 1982). For a more detailed discussion of particular pollution control programs, see L. G. Hines, *Environmental Issues: Population, Pollution, and Economics* (New York: W. W. Norton, 1973).

The Coase theorem is presented in R. Coase, "The Problem of Social Cost," *Journal of Law and Economics* 3 (1960): 1–44.

For a more advanced discussion of the design of optimal-corrective (Pigovian) taxes, see A. Sandmo, "Optimal Taxation in the Presence of Externalities," *Swedish Journal of Economics* 77 (1975): 86–98 and "Direct versus Indirect Pigovian Taxation," *European Economic Review* 7 (1976): 337–49.

CHAPTER 9   THE ANALYSIS OF EXPENDITURE POLICY

For a discussion of alternative ways of providing public services, and the circumstances under which each may be more desirable, see *Alternatives for Delivering Public Services*, ed. E. S. Savas (Boulder, CO: Westview Press, 1977).

CHAPTER 10   COST-BENEFIT ANALYSIS

There is an extensive literature on the principles and the applications of cost-benefit analysis. An excellent general review is provided by E. M. Gramlich, *Benefit Cost Analysis of Government Programs* (Englewood Cliffs, NJ: Prentice-Hall, 1981).

Cost-benefit analysis has been extensively applied to less developed countries. See, in particular, I. M. D. Little and J. A. Mirrlees, *Project Appraisal and Planning for Developing Countries* (London: Heinemann, 1974) and P. Dasgupta, S. Marglin, and A. Sen, *Guidelines for Project Evaluation* (New York: United Nations, 1972).

For recent discussions of the problems of valuing life, see J. Broome, "Trying to Value a Life," *Journal of Public Economics*, February 1978, pp. 91–200 and E. J. Mishan, "Evaluation of Life and Limb: A Theoretical Approach," *Journal of Political Economy* 79 (1971): 687–705.

For other applications of cost-benefit analysis, see Dorfman, ed., *Measuring Ben-*

efits of Government Investments (Washington, D.C.: Brookings Institution, 1965); J. Hirschleifer, J. C. deHaven, and J. W. Milliman, *Water Supply: Economics, Technology, and Policy* (Chicago: University of Chicago Press, 1969); L. G. Hines, *Environment Issues* (New York: W. W. Norton, 1973); and L. J. White, *Reforming Regulation*, (Englewood Cliffs, NJ: Prentice Hall, 1981).

CHAPTER 11 HEALTH

The questions we have discussed in this chapter are part of what has become an important and growing area of specialization in economics, medical economics. See, for instance, P. Feldstein, *Health Care Economics* (New York: Wiley, 2nd. ed., 1983). For an excellent discussion of the basic issues see V. Fuchs, *Who Shall Live? Health, Economics, and Social Choice* (New York: Basic Books, 1983). Current issues are usually discussed in the annual Brookings Institution volume *Setting National Priorities;* see, for instance, Louise B. Russell, "Medical Care," in *Setting National Priorities: The 1984 Budget*, ed. J. Pechman (Washington, D.C.: Brookings Institution, 1983).

CHAPTER 12 DEFENSE

A number of books were written on the economics of defense in the late 1950s and early 1960s. Among the most notable of these were C. J. Hitch and R. N. McKean, *The Economics of Defense in the Nuclear Age* (Cambridge, MA: Harvard University Press, 1965) and E. S. Quade, ed., *Analysis for Military Decisions* (Chicago: Rand McNally, 1964). See also A. C. Enthoven and K. W. Smith, *How Much Is Enough: Shaping the Defense Program, 1961–1969* (New York: Harper and Row, 1971).

Recent work has been much more limited, at least at a textbook level, though issues of defense contracting continue to receive considerable attention. The Grace Commission (see Chapter 7) in particular has not only uncovered a number of systematic sources of inefficiency but has also prescribed what it views to be some remedies.

A recent study of the organization of defense by Georgetown University's Center for Strategic and International Affairs is summaried in *Toward a More Effective Defense* (Washington, D.C.: Georgetown University, 1985).

The role of the military-industrial complex is discussed in M. Halperin, J. Stockfisch, and M. Weidenbaum, *The Political Economy of the Military-Industrial Complex* (Berkeley: University of California Press, 1973).

The American Enterprise Institute frequently publishes essays on current issues of defense economics. See also W. W. Kaufmann, *Defense in the 1980s* (Washington, D.C.: Brookings Institution, 1981).

CHAPTER 13 SOCIAL INSURANCE

H. J. Aaron and G. Burtless, eds., *Retirement and Economic Behavior* (Washington, D.C.: Brookings Institution, 1984).

M. J. Boskin, *The Social Security System* (New York: Twentieth Century Fund, 1984).

Congressional Budget Office, *Financial Social Security: Issues and Options in the Long Run* (Washington, D.C.: U.S. Government Printing Office, 1982).

L. H. Thompson, "The Social Security Reform Debate," *Journal of Economic Literature,* December 1983, pp. 1425–67.

A. H. Munnell, *The Future of Social Security* (Washington, D.C.: Brookings Institution, 1977).

D. Hamermesh, *Jobless Pay and the Economy* (Baltimore, MD: Johns Hopkins University Press, 1977).

Martin S. Feldstein, "Unemployment Insurance: Time for Reform," *Harvard Business Review,* March/April 1975.

Martin S. Feldstein, "Unemployment Compensation: Adverse Incentives and Distributional Anomalies," *National Tax Journal* 27 (1974): 231–44.

CHAPTER 14   WELFARE PROGRAMS AND THE REDISTRIBUTION OF INCOME

For a survey of the economic effects of income transfer programs, see S. Danziger, R. Haveman, and R. Plotnick, "How Income Transfers Affect Work, Savings, and the Income Distribution," *Journal of Economic Literature* 19 (1981): 975–1028.

For general discussions of the issues involved in designing welfare programs, see A. Okun, *Equality and Efficiency: The Big Trade-Off* (Washington, D.C.: Brookings Institution, 1975); H. Aaron, *Why Is Welfare So Hard to Reform* (Washington, D.C.: Brookings Institution, 1975); and Congressional Budget Office, *Welfare Reform: Issues, Objectives, and Approaches* (Washington, D.C.: U.S. Government Printing Office, 1977).

CHAPTER 15   EDUCATION

For two surveys of the range of economic issues involved in education, see E. Cohn, *The Economics of Education* (Cambridge, MA: Ballinger, 1979) and *Economic Dimensions of Education,* A Report of a Committee of the National Academy of Education.

For two critiques of the role of the government in supporting higher education, see M. Friedman, "The Higher Schooling in America," *Public Interest,* April 1968 and D. M. Windham, "Social Benefits and the Subsidization of Higher Education: A Critique," *Higher Education* 5 (1976): 237–52.

Interest in reforming the financial structure of public schools peaked in the early 1970s. A major contribution to the debate at that time was J. E. Coons, W. H. Clune, and S. D. Sugarman, *Private Wealth and Public Education* (Cambridge, MA: Harvard University Press, 1970). A later survey of the issues can be found in the 1974 Winter-Spring issue of *Law and Contemporary Problems,* entitled "Future Directions for School Finance Reform."

For an example of the controversy raised by the first Coleman report, on *Equality of Opportunity,* see S. Bowles and H. M. Levin, "The Determinants of Scholastic Achievement: An Appraisal of Some Recent Findings," *Journal of Human Resources* 3 (1968): 3–24.

For a general discussion of the relationship between education and inequality, see J. E. Stiglitz, "Education and Inequality," *Annals of the American Academy of Political and Social Sciences* 409 (1973): 135–45.

For a discussion of the implications of the screening hypothesis for educational expenditures, see J. E. Stiglitz, "The Theory of Screening, Education, and the Distribution of Income," *American Economic Review* 65 (1975): 283–300.

A topic we did not discuss in this chapter is the equilibrium level of expenditures on education that emerge from a majority voting political model (as described in Chapter 6). This is analyzed in J. E. Stiglitz, "Demand for Education in Public and Private School Systems," *Journal of Public Economics* 3 (1974): 349–386.

CHAPTER 16   TAXATION: AN INTRODUCTION

For an overview of some of the equity issues, see W. J. Blum and H. Kalven, Jr., *The Uneasy Case for Progressive Taxation* (Chicago: University of Chicago Press, 1953).

For an overview of the United States tax system, see J. A. Pechman, *Federal Tax Policy* (Washington, D.C.: Brookings Institution, 4th ed. 1983).

CHAPTER 17 WHO REALLY PAYS THE TAX: TAX INCIDENCE

A more extensive discussion of the incidence of taxation in the United States is available in J. A. Pechman, *Who Paid the Taxes, 1966–1985* (Washington, D.C.: Brookings Institution, 1985). Somewhat different numbers are presented in E. K. Browning and W. R. Johnson, *The Distribution of the Tax Burden* (Washington, D.C.: American Enterprise Institute, 1979 and D. F. Bradford and the U.S. Treasury Tax Policy Staff, *Blueprints for Basic Tax Reform* (Washington, D.C.: Tax Analysts, 2nd. ed., 1984).

A useful review of the effects of taxation in competitive industries is contained in E. Mansfield, *Microeconomics* (New York: W. W. Norton, 5th ed., 1985); for a review of price and output under pure monopoly, see Chapter 10.

CHAPTER 18 TAXATION AND ECONOMIC EFFICIENCY

E. Mansfield, *Microeconomics* (New York: W. W. Norton, 5th ed., 1985), Chapter 4.

A. Harberger, "Three Basic Postulates for Applied Welfare Economics: An Interpretative Essay," *Journal of Economic Literature* 9 (1971): 785–97.

CHAPTER 19 OPTIMAL TAXATION

For a more advanced treatment of these topics, see A. B. Atkinson and J. E. Stiglitz, *Lectures in Public Economics* (New York: McGraw-Hill, 1980), Chapters 12, 13, 14. For a discussion of the concept of Pareto-efficient taxation, see J. E. Stiglitz, "Self-Selection and Pareto Efficient Taxation," *Journal of Public Economics* 17 (1982): 213–40.

For more recent surveys of what has become a vast literature, see the article by J. E. Stiglitz, "Pareto Efficient and Optimal Taxation and the New New Welfare Economics," in *Handbook of Public Economics,* A. Auerbach and M. Feldstein, eds., (Amsterdam: North Holland, 1985).

See also J. Slemrod, "Do We Know How Progressive the Income Tax System Should Be?" *National Tax Journal* 36 (1983): 361–70.

The classic paper on optimal income taxation is that of J. Mirrlees, "An Exploration in the Theory of Optimum Income Taxation," *Review of Economic Studies* 38 (1971): 175–208.

The classic papers on optimal commodity taxation include those of F. Ramsey, "A Contribution to the Theory of Taxation," *Economic Journal* 37 (1927): 47–61 and P. Diamond and J. Mirrlees, "Optimal Taxation and Public Production, I: Production Efficiency and II: Tax Rules," *American Economic Review* 61 (1971): 8–27 and 261–78.

The synthesis of the theory of optimal income taxation with optimal redistributive commodity taxation is presented in A. B. Atkinson and J. E. Stiglitz, "The Design of Tax Structures: Direct versus Indirect Taxation," *Journal of Public Economics* 6 (1976): 55–75.

CHAPTER 20 THE PERSONAL INCOME TAX

The best comprehensive elementary discussion of the United States income tax system is provided by J. A. Pechman, *Federal Tax Policy* (Washington, D.C.: Brookings Institution, 4th ed., 1983).

A more extended treatment is provided by R. Goode, *The Individual Income Tax*
(Washington, D.C.: Brookings Institution, rev. ed., 1976).

For a discussion of the income tax from a legal perspective, see B. I. Bittker, *Federal Taxation of Income, Estates and Gifts* (New York: Warren, Gorham and Lamont, 1981), 4 vols.

For a survey of the literature of the effects of charitable deductions, see C. T. Clotfelder and C. E. Steuerle, "Charitable Contributions," in *How Taxes Affect Economic Behavior*, H. J. Aaron and J. A. Pechman, eds. (Washington, D.C.: Brookings Institution, 1981) or C. T. Clotfelter, *Federal Tax Policy and Charitable Giving* (Chicago: University of Chicago Press, 1985).

CHAPTER 21 THE CORPORATION INCOME TAX

For an excellent general discussion of the corporation income tax, see J. A. Pechman, *Federal Tax Policy*, Washington, D.C.: Brookings Institution, 4th ed., 1983). For a critical appraisal of the corporation income tax, see Gregory J. Ballentine, *Equity, Efficiency, and the U.S. Corporation Income Tax* (Washington, D.C.: American Enterprise Institute, 1980). For slightly more advanced surveys of the issues discussed in this chapter, see A. B. Atkinson and J. E. Stiglitz, *Lectures in Public Economics* (New York: McGraw-Hill, 1980), Lectures 5–7; P. Mieskowski, "Tax Incidence Theory: The Effects of Taxes on the Distribution of Income," *Journal of Economic Literature* 7 (1969): 1103–1124; Mervyn A. King, *Public Policy and the Corporation* (London: Chapman and Hall, 1977); and A. Auerbach, "Taxation, Corporate Financial Policy and the Cost of Capital, *Journal of Economic Literature* 21 (1983): 905–40.

For a discussion of the problems of integrating the corporation and individual income tax, see C. E. McLure, *Must Corporate Income Be Taxed Twice?* (Washington, D.C.: Brookings Institution, 1979).

C. E. McLure and W. R. Thirsk provide "A Simplified Exposition of the Harberger Model I: Tax Incidence," *National Tax Journal* 28 (1975): 1–27.

The new system of depreciation in 1981 gave rise to a large (almost universally critical) literature. See, for instance, A. Auerbach, "The New Economics of Accelerated Depreciation," *Boston College Law Review*, September 1982, pp. 1327–55.

The issues of leasing are discussed in *Joint Committee on Taxation*, Analysis of Safe Harbor Leasing, (Washington, D.C.: Government Printing Office, 1982).

CHAPTER 22 THE TAXATION OF CAPITAL

Until recently, most studies have analyzed one tax on capital in isolation from others. An important exception is C. E. Steuerle, *Taxes, Loans, and Inflation* (Washington, D.C.: Brookings Institution, 1985). For a discussion of the tax on capital gains, see M. David, *Alternative Approaches to Capital Gains Taxation* (Washington, D.C.: Brookings Institution, 1968).

For a more technical discussion, see J. E. Stiglitz, "Some Aspects of the Taxation on Capital Gains," *Journal of Public Economics* 21 (1983): 257–94.

For a sampling of the more recent controversies over the effects of this tax, see J. A. Minarik, "Capital Gains," in *How Taxes Affect Economic Behavior*, H. J. Aaron and J. A. Pechman, eds. (Washington, D.C.: Brookings Institution, 1981); M. S. Feldstein and S. Yitzhaki, "The Effects of the Capital Gains Tax on the Selling and Switching of Common Stock," *Journal of Public Economics* 9 (1978): 17–36; and M. S. Feldstein, J. Slemrod, and S. Yitzhaki, "The Effects of Taxing on the Selling of Corporate Stock and the Realization of Capital Gains," *Quarterly Journal of Economics* 94 (1980): 777–91.

For a sampling of the controversy over the effect of taxing on savings, see M. J. Boskin, "Taxation, Saving, and the Rate of Interest, *Journal of Political Economy* 86 (1978): 23–27 and E. Phillip Howley and S. H. Hymans, "The Measurement and Determination of Loanable-Funds Savings," in *What Should Be Taxed: Income or Expenditure*, J. Pechman, ed. (Washington, D.C.: Brookings Institution, 1980).

For a recent survey, see L. J. Kotlikoff, "Taxation and Savings—A Neoclassical Perspective," *Journal of Economic Literature*, December 1984.

For a discussion of the property tax, see Henry J. Aaron, *Who Pays the Property Tax?* (Washington, D.C.: Brookings Institution, 1975).

For a discussion of the United States estate and gift tax, see G. Cooper, *A Voluntary Tax? New Perspectives on Sophisticated Estate Tax Avoidance*, (Washington, D.C.: Brookings Institution, 1979).

For a cross-country comparison of capital taxation, see M. King and D. Fullerton, *The Taxation of Income from Capital* (Chicago: University of Chicago Press, 1984).

For a discussion of the effects of inflation, see H. J. Aaron, ed., *Inflation and the Income Tax* (Washington, D.C.: Brookings Institution, 1976). For more recent studies, see M. S. Feldstein, *Inflation, Tax Rules, and Capital Formation* (Chicago: University of Chicago Press, 1983) or A. Auerbach, "Inflation and the Choice of Asset Life," *Journal of Political Economy* 87 (1979): 621–38.

For a discussion of the effects of taxation on risk taking, see E. D. Domar and R. A. Musgrave, "Proportional Income Taxation and Risk-taking," *Quarterly Journal of Economics* 58 (1944): 388–422 and J. E. Stiglitz, "The Effects of Income, Wealth and Capital Gains Taxation on Risk-taking," *Quarterly Journal of Economics* 83 (1969): 262–83.

For a more advanced discussion of some of the topics considered in this chapter, see A. B. Atkinson and J. E. Stiglitz, *Lectures in Public Economics* (New York: McGraw-Hill, 1980), Lecture 5, and A. Sandmo, "The Effects of Taxation on Savings and Risk Taking" in A. J. Auerbach and M. Feldstein, eds., *Handbook of Public Economics* (Amsterdam: North Holland, 1985).

CHAPTER 23   TAXATION AND LABOR SUPPLY

O. Ashenfelter and R. Layard, eds., *Handbook of Labor Economics* (Amsterdam: North Holland, 1985).

J. Hausman, "Labor Supply," in H. J. Aaron and J. A. Pechman, eds., *How Taxes Affect Economic Behavior* (Washington, D.C.: Brookings Institution, 1981).

M. R. Killingsworth, *Labor Supply* (New York: Cambridge University Press, 1983).

J. A. Hausman, "Taxes and Labor Supply," in *Handbook of Public Economics*, ed. A. J. Auerbach and M. Feldstein (Amsterdam: North Holland, 1985).

CHAPTER 24   A STUDENT'S GUIDE TO TAX AVOIDANCE

There is a plethora of books about the specifics of tax avoidance. A good standard, popular book about how to fill in your income tax forms (and avoid paying some unnecessary taxes) is J. K. Lasser, *Your Income Tax* (New York: Simon & Schuster, annual edition). See also R. A. Stanger, *Tax Shelters: The Bottom Line* (Fair Haven, NJ: Robert A. Stanger and Co., 1982). A representative book promising "over 150 ways to reduce your taxes—to nothing" is J. A. Schnepper, *How to Pay Zero Taxes* (Reading, MA: Addison-Wesley, 1986).

For an excellent discussion of the flat-rate consumption tax proposal, see R. E. Hall and A. Rabushka, *Low Tax, Simple Tax, Flat Tax* (New York: McGraw-Hill, 1983).

For an excellent discussion of the consumption tax and how it might be implemented, see the report of the U.S. Treasury, *Blueprints for Basic Tax Reform*, 1977. A study of the British tax system by a special commission, headed by Nobel laureate James Meade, *The Structure and Reform of Direct Taxation* (London: Allen and Unwin, 1978) also argues in favor of a consumption tax. Another excellent exposition of the British tax system, with an analysis of the advantages of the consumption tax, is provided in J. A. Kay and M. A. King, *The British Tax System* (London: Oxford University Press, 1978).

For a discussion of the comprehensive income tax, see J. A. Pechman, ed., *Comprehensive Income Taxation*, (Washington, D.C.: Brookings Institution, 1977) and B. I. Bittker, C. O. Galvin, R. A. Musgrave, and J. A. Pechman, *A Comprehensive Income Tax Base? A Debate* (Branford, CT: Federal Tax Press, 1968).

For a discussion of specific reforms of the tax structure, see J. A. Pechman, *Federal Tax Policy* (Washington, D.C.: Brookings Institution, 4th ed., 1983).

For a discussion of some currently debated issues, see J. A. Pechman, ed., *The Promise of Tax Reform* (Englewood Cliffs, NJ: Prentice-Hall, 1985); J. A. Pechman, ed., *Options for Tax Reform* (Washington, D.C.: Brookings Institutions, 1985).

A brief description of several alternative proposals for tax reform is contained in J. Pechman, *A Citizen's Guide to the New Tax Reforms* (Totowa, NJ: Rowman and Allanheld, 1985). Brief discussions of the president's tax reform proporals are contained in various issues of *Tax Notes*. See, in particular, the February 4, 1985, issue, for discussions of the issues of charitable giving and deductibility of state and local taxes.

Problems with the corporate income tax are discussed in R. S. McIntyre and R. Folen, *Corporate Income Taxes in the Reagan Years: A Study of Three Years of Legalized Corporate Tax Avoidance* (Washington, D.C.: Citizens for Tax Justice, 1984) and *Revising the Corporate Income Tax* (Washington, D.C.: Congressional Budget Office, 1985).

CHAPTER 26   FISCAL FEDERALISM

The classic article is that of C. Tiebout, "A Pure Theory of Local Expenditures," *Journal of Political Economy* 64 (1956): 416–24.

A recent review of the ensuing literature is contained in *Local Provision of Public Services: The Tiebout Model after Twenty-five Years,* ed. George R. Zodrow (New York: Academic Press, 1983).

A general discussion of the issues of fiscal federalism is contained in W. Oates, *Fiscal Federalism* (New York: Harcourt Brace Jovanovich 1978) and G. F. Break, *Financing Government in a Federal System* (Washington, D.C.: Brookings Institution, 1980).

See also G. J. Stigler, "The Tenable Range of Functions of Local Government," in Edmund S. Phelps, ed., *Private Wants and Public Needs* (New York: W. W. Norton, 1965).

The voluntary formation of groups to provide particular services to their members has been extensively studied in the theory of clubs. See, in particular, J. M. Buchanan, "An Economic Theory of Clubs," *Economica* 32 (1965): 1–14 and M. Pauly, "Clubs, Commonality, and the Core," *Economica* 34 (1967): 314–24.

Further Readings

In addition to the readings cited in the previous chapter, the following may be of some use.

For a general discussion of the fiscal problems facing cities, see R. W. Bahl, ed., *The Fiscal Outlook for Cities* (Syracuse, NY: Syracuse University Press, 1978), or P. Mieskowski and M. Straszheim, *Current Issues in Urban Economics* (Baltimore, MD: Johns Hopkins University Press, 1979).

For a general discussion of state and local government, see W. Z. Hirsch, *The Economics of State and Local Government* (New York: McGraw-Hill, 1970).

For a more technical discussion of the theory of local public goods, see J. C. Milleron, "The Theory of Value with Public Goods: A Survey Article," *Journal of Economic Theory* (1968): 419–77.

For a discussion of the incidence of the property tax, see P. Mieszkowski, "The Property Tax: An Excise Tax or a Profits Tax?" *Journal of Public Economics* 00 (1972): 73–96.

See also the readings on the property tax cited for Chapter 22.

Index